OECD *Reviews of Regulatory Reform*

REGULATORY REFORM
IN THE UNITED STATES

ORGANISATION FOR ECONOMIC CO-OPERATION AND DEVELOPMENT

ORGANISATION FOR ECONOMIC CO-OPERATION AND DEVELOPMENT

Pursuant to Article 1 of the Convention signed in Paris on 14th December 1960, and which came into force on 30th September 1961, the Organisation for Economic Co-operation and Development (OECD) shall promote policies designed:

- to achieve the highest sustainable economic growth and employment and a rising standard of living in Member countries, while maintaining financial stability, and thus to contribute to the development of the world economy;
- to contribute to sound economic expansion in Member as well as non-member countries in the process of economic development; and
- to contribute to the expansion of world trade on a multilateral, non-discriminatory basis in accordance with international obligations.

The original Member countries of the OECD are Austria, Belgium, Canada, Denmark, France, Germany, Greece, Iceland, Ireland, Italy, Luxembourg, the Netherlands, Norway, Portugal, Spain, Sweden, Switzerland, Turkey, the United Kingdom and the United States. The following countries became Members subsequently through accession at the dates indicated hereafter: Japan (28th April 1964), Finland (28th January 1969), Australia (7th June 1971), New Zealand (29th May 1973), Mexico (18th May 1994), the Czech Republic (21st December 1995), Hungary (7th May 1996), Poland (22nd November 1996) and Korea (12th December 1996). The Commission of the European Communities takes part in the work of the OECD (Article 13 of the OECD Convention).

Publié également en Français sous le titre :

LA RÉFORME DE LA RÉGLEMENTATION AUX ÉTATS-UNIS

FOREWORD

The OECD Review of Regulatory Reform in the United States is among the first of a series of country reports carried out under the OECD's Regulatory Reform Programme, launched in 1998 in response to a mandate by OECD Ministers.

The Regulatory Reform Programme is aimed at helping governments improve regulatory quality – that is, reforming regulations which raise unnecessary obstacles to competition, innovation and growth, while ensuring that regulations efficiently serve important social objectives.

The Programme is part of a broader effort at the OECD to support sustained economic development, job creation and good governance. It fits with other initiatives such as our annual country economic surveys; the Jobs Strategy; the OECD Principles of Corporate Governance; and the fight against corruption, hard-core cartels and harmful tax competition.

Drawing on the analysis and recommendations of good regulatory practices contained in the 1997 OECD *Report to Ministers on Regulatory Reform*, the Regulatory Reform Programme is a multi-disciplinary process of in-depth country reviews, based on self-assessment and on peer evaluation by several OECD committees and members of the International Energy Agency (IEA).

The country Reviews are not comprehensive, but, rather, targeted at key reform areas. Each Review has the same structure, including three thematic chapters on the quality of regulatory institutions and government processes; competition policy and enforcement; and the enhancement of market openness through regulatory reform. Each Review also contains chapters on sectors such as electricity and telecommunications, and an assessment of the macroeconomic context for reform in the country under review.

The country Reviews benefited from a process of extensive consultations with a wide range of government officials (including elected officials) from the country reviewed, business and trade union representatives, consumer groups, and academic experts from many backgrounds.

These Reviews demonstrate clearly that in many areas, a well-structured and implemented programme of regulatory reform has brought lower prices and more choice for consumers, helped stimulate innovation, investment, and new industries, and thereby aided in boosting economic growth and overall job creation. Comprehensive regulatory reforms have produced results more quickly than piecemeal approaches; and such reforms over the longer-term helped countries to adjust more quickly and easily to changing circumstances and external shocks. At the same time, a balanced reform programme must take into account important social concerns. Adjustment costs in some sectors have been painful, although experience shows that these costs can be reduced if reform is accompanied by supportive policies, including active labour market policies, to cushion adjustment.

While reducing and reforming regulations is a key element of a broad programme of regulatory reform, country experience also shows that in a more competitive and efficient market, new regulations and institutions are sometimes necessary to assure that private anticompetitive behaviour does not delay or block the benefits of reform and that health, environmental and consumer protection is assured. In countries pursuing reform, which is often difficult and opposed by vested interests, sustained and consistent political leadership is an essential element of successful reform efforts, and transparent and informed public dialogue on the benefits and costs of reform is necessary for building and maintaining broad public support for reform.

3

The policy options presented in the Reviews may pose challenges for each country concerned, but they do not ignore wide differences between national cultures, legal and institutional traditions and economic circumstances. The in-depth nature of the Reviews and the efforts made to consult with a wide range of stakeholders reflect the emphasis placed by the OECD on ensuring that the policy options presented are relevant and attainable within the specific context and policy priorities of each country reviewed.

The OECD *Reviews of Regulatory Reform* are published under the responsibility of the Secretary-General of the OECD, but their policy options and accompanying analysis reflect input and commentary provided during peer review by all 29 OECD Member countries and the European Commission and during consultations with other interested parties.

The Secretariat would like to express its gratitude for the support of the Government of the United States for the OECD Regulatory Reform Programme and its consistent co-operation during the review process. It also would like to thank the many OECD committee and country delegates, representatives from the OECD's Trade Union Advisory Committee (TUAC) and Business and Industry Advisory Committee (BIAC), and other experts whose comments and suggestions were essential to this report.

ACKNOWLEDGEMENTS

This series of Reviews of Regulatory Reform in OECD countries was prepared under the direction of Deputy Secretary-General **Joanna R. Shelton**. The Review of the United States reflects contributions from many sources, including the Government of the United States, Committees of the OECD and the IEA, representatives of Member governments, and members of the Business and Industry Advisory Committee (BIAC) and the Trade Union Advisory Committee (TUAC), as well as other groups. This report was peer reviewed in March 1999 in the OECD's Ad Hoc Multidisciplinary Group on Regulatory Reform.

In the OECD Secretariat, the following people contributed substantially to the review of the United States: **Head of Programme and lead drafter:** Scott H. Jacobs; **Document preparation:** Jennifer Stein; **Economics Department:** Chapter 1 was principally prepared by Richard Kohl, and benefited from work by Giuseppe Nicoletti on regulatory indicators; **Public Management Service:** Rex Deighton-Smith; **Trade Directorate:** Vera Nicholas-Gervais, Evdokia Moïsé, Akira Kawamoto, Anthony Kleitz; **Directorate for Financial, Fiscal and Enterprise Affairs:** Darryl Biggar, Patricia Heriard-Dubreuil, Patrick Hughes, Bernard J. Phillips, Sally Van Siclen, Michael Wise; **Directorate for Science, Technology and Industry:** Dimitri Ypsilanti; **General Secretariat:** Pierre Poret. In the **International Energy Agency:** Peter Fraser, Caroline Varley.

TABLE OF CONTENTS

Part 1

Tables

Figures

Annex Figures

Annex Tables

Boxes

Part II

Part I

OECD REVIEW
OF REGULATORY REFORM
IN THE UNITED STATES

EXECUTIVE SUMMARY

Regulatory reforms in the United States helped launch a global reform movement that is still underway. Significant regulatory problems still exist in the United States, but far-reaching economic deregulation combined with efforts to improve the quality of social regulation have contributed to the construction of one of the most innovative, flexible, and open economies in the OECD, while maintaining health, safety, and environmental standards at relatively high levels.

This has not been achieved by indiscriminate deregulation. Measured by the volume and detail of national regulation and the size of the national regulatory administration, the United States does not appear to be *less* regulated than other OECD countries. The United States is, however, often *differently* regulated, even where policy objectives are substantially similar. US regulation tends to be based on two fundamental regulatory styles that support economic dynamism and market adjustment:

- The *pro-competition policy stance* of federal regulatory regimes, supported by strong competition institutions, has meant that regulators tend to prefer policy instruments, such as social regulation and market-driven approaches, that are competition neutral over public ownership and economic regulations that impede competition. In post-war years, regulation has usually been used to establish conditions for competition rather than to replace competition.

- The *openness and contestability of regulatory processes* weakens information monopolies and the powers of special interests, while encouraging entrepreneurialism, market entry, consumer confidence, and the continual search for better regulatory solutions.

Yet regulation that is competition-neutral and transparent can still be inefficient and costly if policies are misguided or outdated, or regulation is badly designed or applied. Enterprises and citizens in the United States suffer from many rigid, complex and highly detailed social regulations and government formalities that impose unnecessarily high costs in many policy areas. The quality of regulations varies widely. Regulators are sometimes hampered by poor and out-dated laws, and mired in lengthy procedures and excessively adversarial approaches that impede good regulatory practices. Overlapping federal/state jurisdictions compound the problem. These difficulties reduce innovation and responsiveness in the federal regulatory system, eroding the benefits of pro-competitive reforms and regulatory transparency.

Chapter 1: *Regulatory reform has produced important static and dynamic benefits, and potential gains from further reform are still large.* An expanding economic deregulation movement has, over 20 years, removed almost all entry and exit restrictions, with some exceptions. These deregulation efforts are still working their way through the economy, but in almost every sector the results for consumers in terms of prices, service quality, and choice are positive. Reform has probably also improved macro-economic performance, with long-term benefits to productivity growth, and the dynamic effects of regulatory reform help position the US to benefit from a global economy. While regulatory reform promoted good job growth and boosted standards of living, there were indirect effects on labour bargaining strength and uncertain effects on distribution of wealth. Concerns that reform would reduce safety and consumer protection are not borne out, though vigilance is needed. These effects illustrate the dualistic and complementary nature of less economic regulation combined with better social regulation.

Chapter 2: A *key challenge for regulatory quality in the* United States *is improving the cost-effectiveness of social regulations and government formalities*, which have rapidly increased in quantity and cost since the 1960s. Many different approaches have been tried, and progress has been made over two decades, in part due to centralised oversight by the Office of Management and Budget (OMB). The use of regulatory impact analysis as an input to decisions is more widespread and rigorous than in other OECD countries, and this has been key to improving regulatory quality. Consultation under notice and comment procedures is open and inclusive, involving a wide range of interests, though there are concerns that the practical ability of various interests to participate is unequal. A new effort to emphasise regulatory performance shows promise in boosting innovation in new regulatory and non-regulatory techniques. Yet there is considerable room for improvement. OMB estimates that the total benefits of new social regulations adopted in 1996-1998 exceed total costs, but the quality of individual regulations varies widely. There is great potential for achieving better social outcomes without increasing regulatory costs. Primary laws in particular are often low quality, and impede efforts to improve regulatory cost-effectiveness. A US regulatory style – adversarial legalism – has produced complexity and rigidity. Co-ordination of reform efforts in the federal-state system is difficult and often unsatisfactory, and layers of regulation and formalities between levels of government add costs that are not monitored and are little understood.

Chapter 3: *Competition principles are integrated into the national regulatory system and provide a consistent policy framework supporting regulatory reform.* Competition policy principles are embedded in regulatory mandates in many policy areas. Effective institutions and strong legal tools implement these broad principles, and have proven to be essential in the aftermath of reform to guard against undue concentration as a result of restructuring. The far-reaching powers of the courts over regulatory policy, competition enforcement, and the unusually important rights of private action have been effective allies in supporting competition principles. Yet common law traditions and pluralistic policy processes have resulted in a large number of special industry rules, sectoral regulators and exemptions, which together constrain application of the basic competition laws. Here, too, the federal system poses difficulties, since the "state action" doctrine can undermine larger-scale pro-competitive reform.

Chapter 4: T*he* US *experience demonstrates the close and supportive relationship between market openness, quality regulation, and competition.* Traditions of openness in the American domestic regulatory system create one of the post-war's most open national markets for global trade and investment. The pro-competition policy stance results in regulation that is, on balance, trade and investment neutral. Moreover, competition and market openness in the US promotes good regulation elsewhere through international competition, example, and persuasion. Despite the general openness of the national regulatory system, however, its complexity, the interplay of federal, state and local regulation, and heavy regulation in some areas have restrictive effects particularly felt by foreign firms. Foreign competitors face a number of sectoral restrictions on foreign investment, and sometimes are affected by *de facto* discrimination arising from regulatory design or implementation. US experience shows that concerns about sovereignty and the effect of international rules on domestic policies can be best resolved by adopting regulations that meet domestic policy objectives cost-effectively and transparently.

Chapter 5: I*n the electricity sector, the* United States *is relying more on markets to attain economic and social policy objectives, but the move has required new institutions and complementary policies that are still in transition.* Reforms aim to encourage competition in power generation by diminishing the threat of discrimination in grid access and by divestiture of some generation assets. Retail-level competition is being promoted at state levels. Since the recovery of costs stranded by introduction of retail competition is a pre-condition for reform, mechanisms for mitigation, measurement, and least-distorting recovery are being established. Environmental goals for the sector are increasingly met through market-based mechanisms, such as trading of SO_2 emissions permits, while efficiency in the generation of "green" electricity is encouraged by using market mechanisms to determine the choice of technology, generator, and price. Expanding the role of markets has required experimentation with new institutions – the independent system operators – to safeguard competition, and other options are being examined, such as transmission companies. The diversity of state structures has promoted faster innovation and learning in regulatory regimes, and has promoted reform by benchmarking good performance. Yet the federal structure also complicates reform, because the scope of efficient regulation, like the scope of many electricity markets, extends beyond state borders. Regional regulatory regimes have been slow to develop. As choice expands, consumer protection is needed. Some states have responded with initiatives to inform consumers about new rights.

Chapter 6: *In telecommunications, rapid evolution of technologies, combined with strong competition policies and regulatory reforms, opened long distance markets to competition. The regulatory challenges in this dynamic field today are to extend competition into local markets and to design regulatory regimes consistent with the convergence of telecommunications and broadcasting.* Regulatory reform and competition law enforcement facilitated an extraordinary level of innovation which has transformed the industry, stimulated new products, and increased consumer choice, with significant positive effects throughout the economy. The recent WTO Agreement builds on these successes in the international context and demonstrates the link between domestic liberalisation and international market openness. But extending competition into local markets has proven difficult. The 1996 Telecommunications Act set out three entry routes for new competitors – resale, unbundling and separate facilities – but litigation delayed implementation, and competition has not developed quickly. The dual federal-state roles produce both costs and benefits: pursuit of different policy initiatives can promote innovation, but jurisdictional overlaps generate costs and uncertainties. Promotion of "universal service", a central US policy goal, appears to be supported by competition, since the number of households with telephones has significantly increased over the reform period.

Chapter 7: *Conclusions and Policy Options.* The major lessons that can be learned from regulatory reform in the United States are:

- If *concrete benefits are to be realised, sustained and consistent reform efforts are needed over many years, supported by strong political leadership and administrative capacities for promoting reform.*

- *The results for consumers of sectoral economic reform in terms of prices, service quality, and choice are solidly positive, but only with sufficient attention to building pro-competitive regulatory regimes and to maintaining consumer protection. Very substantial gains are also possible from efforts to upgrade the cost-effectiveness and flexibility of social regulations.*

- *Therefore, a well-balanced reform programme aims at both economic deregulation and quality regulation.*

- *Dynamic effects were more important than expected. Regulatory reform proved to be a valuable supply-side tool that boosted demand, and improved the efficiency and flexibility of the national economy.*

- *A comprehensive approach produces more benefits, since regulatory reform is more effective when integrated with flexibility in factor markets, when competition is vigorous in upstream and downstream sectors, and when the macroeconomic environment is geared to growth. A policy environment supporting entrepreneurialism and business adjustment multiplies the size of the benefits, and the speed at which changes are felt. Strong competition oversight is needed in reformed sectors (airlines, telecommunications) still adjusting. The US experience supports the OECD recommendation for broad-based reform.*

- *Evaluation of costs and benefits of regulatory reform must be long-term and multi-dimensional to identify the real trade-offs.*

- *Regulatory flexibility and adaptation over time seems to be as valuable as regulatory cost-effectiveness at a single point in time.*

Based on international experience with good regulatory practices, several reforms (further detailed in Chapter 7) are likely to be beneficial to improving regulation in the United States:

- Use *of flexible and market-oriented policy instruments should be expanded.* By failing to use more flexible and market-oriented policy instruments in social policy areas, the United States is missing the opportunity to exploit one of the world's great innovative cultures in the pursuit of important social objectives.

- *The policy responsiveness of the US regulatory system should be improved by streamlining cumbersome and sluggish processes.* Sluggishness, delay, and inefficiencies in regulatory processes will increasingly penalise the United States as the pace of globalisation and innovation steps up. Several concrete steps to this end are suggested in the report.

– *Regulations should be reviewed systematically to ensure that they continue to meet their intended objectives efficiently and effectively.* The current system is very weak with respect to systematic review of the vast body of existing laws and other regulations. The quality of laws merits special attention, since in many areas, poor laws have negative effects on policy implementation and policy outcomes. Regulatory rigidities seem to be durable. Faster updating is important in sectors characterised by fast technological change (telecommunications, electricity).

– *In the electricity sector, further reform of economic regulations would stimulate competition.* Large gains are projected from competition in supply, but they will be maximised only if distortions to competition are reduced.

– *The scope and enforcement of competition policy should be reviewed and weaknesses corrected.* In particular the remaining exemptions and sector-specific jurisdictional provisions should be eliminated.

– *More co-ordination and review are needed to improve the efficiency and coherence of regulations at the federal and state interface.* The role of states as innovators and testing grounds for new ideas is a national asset that can speed up change and regulatory responsiveness. Yet a federal country must work harder to establish efficient regulation and maintain it over time. Losses from uncoordinated state actions can be large and durable.

– *Important gaps in regulatory quality controls should be closed to improve attention to market openness impacts, and to bring economic regulation under benefit-cost requirements.* In particular, assessments of the effects of proposed rules on inward trade and investment should be carried out as part of regulatory impact analysis, and coverage of mandatory quality controls should be expanded to economic regulation, which is now exempted.

– *Continued integration of market openness and regulatory policies will produce benefits both in the United States and in other countries.* Mutual recognition of regulations and conformity assessment procedures, increased use of industry-developed standards in lieu of national regulatory measures, and other approaches to intergovernmental regulatory co-operation offer promising avenues for lowering regulatory barriers to trade and investment. Informal business-driven processes such as TABD have proven valuable catalysts for market-opening regulatory reform across a range of particular sectors and horizontal issues.

Chapter 1

REGULATORY REFORM IN THE UNITED STATES

INTRODUCTION

US *regulatory reforms helped launch a global reform movement that is still underway.*

The United States has been a world leader in regulatory reform for a quarter century. Its reforms and their results helped launch a global reform movement that has brought benefits to many millions of people, and is still underway. Its mistakes have improved understanding of the risks and costs of reform. Significant regulatory problems still exist in the United States, but far-reaching economic deregulation combined with efforts to improve the quality of social regulation have contributed to the construction of one of the most innovative, flexible, and open economies in the OECD, while maintaining health, safety, and environmental standards at relatively high levels.

Contrary to popular belief, the **United States** *does not appear to be, on the whole, less regulated than other* **OECD** *countries.*

This has not been achieved by indiscriminate deregulation. Measured by the volume and detail of national regulation and the size of the national regulatory administration, the United States does not appear to be *less* regulated than other OECD countries. As have other countries, the United States has constructed an enormous and complex regulatory state to provide citizens with a wide range of services and protections ranging from improving the functioning of the market to safer food and cleaner air. More than 140 000 pages of federal rules – many extremely detailed – are now in effect, and credible estimates of their direct costs as well as the value of their benefits for citizens and enterprises range from 4 to 10 per cent of GDP.[1] Regulations at state and local levels must be added to these totals, though their costs are unknown. Today, "federal regulations now affect virtually all individuals, businesses, State, local and tribal governments, and other organisations in virtually every aspect of their lives or operations."[2]

But *the* **United States** *is differently regulated than most countries due to two regulatory styles: the pro-competition policy stance of federal regulatory regimes, and the openness and contestability of regulatory processes.*

The United States is, however, often *differently* regulated than most OECD countries, even where policy objectives are substantially similar. US regulation tends to be based on two fundamental regulatory styles that support economic dynamism and market adjustment:

– The *pro-competition policy stance* of federal regulatory regimes, based on historical values of economic liberty and supported by strong competition institutions, has meant that regulators tend to prefer policy instruments, such as social regulation and market-driven approaches, that are competition neutral over public ownership and economic regulations that impede competition.

In post-war years, regulation has usually been used to establish conditions for competition rather than to replace competition.

– The openness and contestability of regulatory processes weakens information monopolies and the powers of special interests, while encouraging entrepreneurialism, market entry, consumer confidence, and the continual search for better regulatory solutions.

In the United States, competition controls and public ownership are rarely used as instruments of social policy.

More than in other OECD countries, regulations in the United States are based on an implicit but strong policy framework of competition principles. Evidence for this can be seen in the US aversion to competition controls as an instrument of social policy, and the *ad hoc* but almost complete removal of entry controls in most sectors over the past 20 years. Problems, such as the monopoly characteristics of networks, that other countries traditionally addressed through public ownership are addressed in the United States through less interventionist economic regulation. Problems, such as service quality and distributional issues, that other countries address through economic regulation are usually handled in the United States through competition-neutral social regulation, other social policies, or the market, supported by competition and consumer policies.

Box 1.1. What is regulation and regulatory reform?

There is no generally accepted definition of regulation applicable to the very different regulatory systems in OECD countries. In the OECD work, regulation refers to the diverse set of instruments by which governments set requirements on enterprises and citizens. Regulations include laws, formal and informal orders and subordinate rules issued by all levels of government, and rules issued by non-governmental or self-regulatory bodies to whom governments have delegated regulatory powers. Regulations fall into three categories:

- *Economic regulations* intervene directly in market decisions such as pricing, competition, market entry, or exit. Reform aims to increase economic efficiency by reducing barriers to competition and innovation, often through deregulation and use of efficiency-promoting regulation, and by improving regulatory frameworks for market functioning and prudential oversight.

- *Social regulations* protect public interests such as health, safety, the environment, and social cohesion. The economic effects of social regulations may be secondary concerns or even unexpected, but can be substantial. Reform aims to verify that regulation is needed, and to design regulatory and other instruments, such as market incentives and goal-based approaches, that are more flexible, simpler, and more effective at lower cost.

- *Administrative regulations* are paperwork and administrative formalities – so-called "red tape" – through which governments collect information and intervene in individual economic decisions. They can have substantial impacts on private sector performance. Reform aims at eliminating those no longer needed, streamlining and simplifying those that are needed, and improving the transparency of application.

Regulatory reform is used in the OECD work to refer to changes that improve regulatory quality, that is, enhance the performance, cost-effectiveness, or legal quality of regulations and related government formalities. Reform can mean revision of a single regulation, the scrapping and rebuilding of an entire regulatory regime and its institutions, or improvement of processes for making regulations and managing reform. Deregulation is a subset of regulatory reform and refers to complete or partial elimination of regulation in a sector to improve economic performance.

US *regulation illustrates the conclusion that "... public policies [...] are better served by using competition-neutral instruments, such as well-targeted social regulations and market incentives..."*

This pro-competitive regulatory style has proven to be a valuable national asset in a world economy characterised by globalisation, responsiveness, and rapid technological progress. US regulatory practices illustrate well the conclusion in the 1997 OECD Report on Regulatory Reform:

> *... economic regulations have often proven to be extremely costly and ineffective means of achieving public interest goals... In general, public policies... are better served by using competition-neutral instruments, such as well-targeted social regulations and market incentives, to change behaviour in competitive markets.*[3]

Differences between the United States and other countries are narrowing, however, as countries shift policy instruments toward market-based approaches through regulatory reforms.

Regulatory transparency supports market entry and risk-taking.

In transparency, too, US regulatory practices show important differences. The administrative and legal culture shaping regulation in the United States is the converse of that found in corporatist countries, where decisions are often consensual and the administration has wide discretion in application, often sharing powers with organised market interests. Administrative action in the United States is taken within a legalistic and adversarial environment based on open and transparent decision-making, on strict separation between public and private actions, and on competitive neutrality between market actors. These characteristics support market entry and private risk-taking.

Yet, in many policy areas, economic actors in the United States suffer from rigid, complex and highly detailed regulations that impose unnecessarily high costs.

Yet social regulation that is competition-neutral and transparent can still be inefficient and costly if policies are misguided or outdated, or regulation is badly designed or applied. Enterprises and citizens in the United States suffer from rigid, complex and highly detailed social regulations and government formalities that impose unnecessarily high costs in many policy areas. The quality of social regulations varies widely. Regulators are sometimes hampered by poor and out-dated laws, and are mired in lengthy procedures and excessively adversarial approaches that impede good regulatory practices. Overlapping federal/state jurisdictions compound the problem. These tendencies reduce innovation and responsiveness in the federal regulatory system, eroding the benefits of pro-competitive reforms and regulatory transparency. They are the most important challenges to reformers today. As a former head of the President's regulatory reform office says, "The question is not how much regulation, but how good".[4]

The roots of regulatory reform do not lie in any coherent "deregulation" theory in the United States.

Regulatory reform connects many threads in American society, and has not been a product of any coherent "deregulation" theory. Rather, debate ranges widely over *ideological* issues of the role of the state in society; *pragmatic* issues of the quality and cost of public services and protections; *economic* concepts of regulatory and market failures; *federalist* issues of the balance between federal powers and state rights; *institutional* struggles between the powers of the Congress, the President, and the Executive Branch; and *constitutional* issues of individual property rights versus collective rights. In most cases, reforms have been linked to broader

17

changes in policies and institutions. Assessment of regulatory change must be done with caution and appreciation for the complexity of the wider policy environment.

THE MACROECONOMIC CONTEXT
FOR SECTORAL REGULATORY REFORM

Reform of economic regulation in network industries that the United States began in the 1970s is the most visible and studied component of the larger regulatory reform programme. Rather than a comprehensive reform strategy, reform was a case-by-case process that proceeded at different speeds in response to specific problems. Political coalitions and policy consensus varied by sector, though strong and sustained political leadership was essential in every case. Economic deregulation coincided with rapid increases in environmental, health, and safety regulations, and even, in the late 1970s, with direct government intervention in the energy sector and in setting wages and prices.

Two common elements were the search for a response to supply shocks, and awareness of regulatory costs.

In retrospect, two common elements lent an underlying unity to sectoral reforms: the search for an effective policy response to the supply shocks of the 1970s, and increasing doubt among economists about the rationale for economic regulation, both in general and in specific sectors.[5]

Regulatory reform was an *ad hoc* response to stagflation and the productivity slowdown that followed the oil price shocks.

Economic performance seemed to suffer from fundamental structural and macroeconomic problems.

Concerns that US economic performance suffered from fundamental structural and macroeconomic problems were reinforced by the painful aftermath of the oil price shocks of the 1970s. Performance deteriorated both in relation to the "golden" era of the 1960s, and to the performance of the United States' competitors. Higher unemployment and slower growth of per capita GDP (in PPP terms) showed the US economy was already sluggish compared to Japan and Europe.

The low rate of growth in labour productivity was particularly worrying.[6] During the 1960s, US labour productivity grew at half the rate of the war-damaged economies[7] (see Annex Table 1.5). In the 1970s, productivity growth declined OECD-wide but fell even further in the United States, from an average annual rate of 2.9 per cent in the 1960s to less than one per cent.[8] The United States may have lagged in the earlier period because other countries were catching up, but that did not explain why the United States then slowed down even more than others did.

Increasing costs of social and economic regulation were also blamed for poor economic performance.

Along with labour cost pressures and changing demographics,[9] increasing costs of both social and economic regulation were blamed for poor economic performance. Reflecting a growing body of research, the 1979 OECD Economic Survey commented:

Productivity growth has probably been slowed somewhat due to increased government regulations concerning industrial safety, health and environmental protection – the sustained falls in mining productivity appear to be a case in point – as well as government regulation of specific industries (p. 23).[10]

Aggregate demand management had to be supplemented by policies to address the supply side directly.

A view emerged that the US economy faced a problem of aggregate supply for which traditional aggregate demand techniques were inadequate. The "sacrifice ratio" between lower inflation and temporarily higher unemployment was perceived to be too high – contraction would impose heavy costs on the real economy without reducing inflation much.[11] There was debate over whether monetary policy and instruments could be effective.[12] The implication was that demand management had to be supplemented by policies to directly address the supply side.[13]

Interest in regulatory reform was reinforced by increasing concern over budget deficits and sectoral crises.

Interest in regulatory reform was reinforced by concern over budget deficits and grave sectoral crises. The US budget saw substantial deficits in 1975, 1976, and again in 1979 (Annex Figure 1.3). Meanwhile, failure of a major bank (Franklin National) and railroad (Penn Central) and weakness in key manufacturing sectors such as automobiles[14] foreshadowed demands for federal bailouts or, for railroads, nationalisation. Regulation was partly responsible for low profits in banking and railroads, and it was hoped that reform would return them to profitability and avoid the need for direct government assistance.

Empirical research undermined long-standing justifications for economic regulations that block competition.

Replacing regulation by market competition should reduce prices, research suggested.

Economic research cast doubt on traditional justifications for regulation, and suggested that replacing regulation by market competition would in some cases reduce prices. In airlines, comparison between fares on regulated national routes and on unregulated intra-state routes showed that regulated fares were up to 50 per cent higher. In electric power and other sectors operating under rate-of-return regulations, evidence of over-investment and excess capacity suggested that costs were too high. In trucking, entry restrictions were tied to operating inefficiencies, and fragmentation of the network and inability to optimise routing led to higher costs and tariffs.[15] Yet there was little evidence of excess profits, except for the telecommunications giant AT&T. Potential excess profits were either absorbed by competition in service quality (air transport), by inefficiency (electric power), or by rents paid to labour, which were believed to be widespread.

In some regulated sectors, the major problem was that profits were too low. Railroads, barred from abandoning unprofitable routes, were losing market share to road transport. Natural gas producers, facing an increasingly complicated maze of price regulations, channelled investment into supplying less-regulated intra-state markets. The surge in energy prices after 1979, combined with partial deregulation of some gas supplies, led many pipeline buyers to enter long-term contracts, only to suffer losses when market prices fell after liberalisation in 1982-83.

In some sectors there was evidence that lack of competition resulted in rents being earned by labour. In trucking, wages were estimated to be up to 35-40 per cent above those of comparable workers. Communications workers at AT&T were paid premiums of 17-20 per cent above other manufacturing, after adjusting for labour quality.

In financial services, too, the impact of regulations distorted competition and depressed profits. At first, deregulation in this sector was motivated by a desire to "level the playing field"[16] among different kinds of financial institutions. Commercial banks and savings and loan companies were losing market share in the 1970s. As market interest rates rose with inflation, financial institutions that were subject to restrictions on interest rates or to constraints on portfolio choices could not compete against institutions that were free from these restrictions or against foreign banks with access to financing in Eurocurrency markets. Later, declining profitability, evidenced by a rise in bank and savings and loan failures during the 1980-82 recession and subsequent disinflation, reinforced interest in deregulation. Research suggested that Depression-era prohibitions on interstate branching and on combining commercial banking with other financial activities had inhibited diversification of risk across regions and product lines, and thus probably contributed to these failures.

Supply-side strategies were based on reform of economic and social regulations.

Regulatory reform was seen as a more effective anti-inflationary instrument than price controls.

Policies to affect aggregate supply had been tried before[17] but the Carter Administration (1976-80) first made major use of "supply-side" economics.[18] Regulatory reform was part of an overall strategy to restrain inflation by lowering prices and inflationary expectations and by increasing efficiency and overall competitiveness. Price controls in regulated sectors were ineffective and increasingly difficult to administer, particularly for the energy sectors and major energy consumers.[19] The Carter Administration's anti-inflation programme supplemented demand management policies with supply-side measures,[20] including deregulation of road transport, airlines, and oil prices (see Table 1.1 below).[21]

The Reagan Administration came into office facing worsening stagflation, and embraced supply side economics.[22] Its intent was to strengthen the market by reducing the size of government, and to stimulate work effort and investment by cutting tax rates on labour and capital income. Under a theme of "regulatory relief", a programme of deregulation and regulatory reform was launched. The Reagan Administration adopted the first explicit benefit-cost test for new social regulations, created a Task Force on Regulatory Reform in the White House, and strengthened oversight by the Office of Management and Budget (see Chapter 2).

Table 1.1. **Reform of sectoral economic regulations in the United States (status by end-1998)**

Industry	Reasons for deregulation	Key legislative or regulatory changes	Changes in price regulation	Changes in regulation of entry and exit	Remaining regulations on price and entry	Mandated changes in industry structure
Air transport	Evidence of 50% lower fares in unregulated intra-state markets; low load factors; no evidence of scale economies.	Airline Deregulation Act in 1978.	Phased out fare regulation completely as of 1983.	Phased out route regulation completely as of 1981.	None.	None.
Road transport	Research showing constant or decreasing returns to scale; potential for efficiency gains and lower prices.	Regulatory changes culminating in Motor Carrier Act of 1980. Intra-state deregulated in 1994.	Curtailed price collusion by rate bureaux that had been permitted under an anti-trust exemption. Complete price deregulation.	Eliminated restrictions on entry by territory, type of product, backhauls, and intermediate service.	None (except for household goods movers, who may still agree on prices).	None.
Rail freight	Loss of profitable and low rates of return; deteriorating physical plant and low service quality; fear of bankruptcies. Expectations of higher rates, higher profits and greater investment.	Staggers Rail Act of 1980.	Eliminated rate regulation except for maximum tariffs on "captive bulk commodities". Maximum tariffs have not been binding.	Contracts by shippers completely deregulated. Permitted abandonment of low-density routes.	Maximum guidelines on tariffs for certain commodities.	None.
Electric power	Technology change eliminated economies of scale in generating; presence of excess capacity; large price variance across individual states; expectation of lower prices.	Substantial regulation by states. Reforms affecting capital investment in 1980s. 1978 Public Utility Regulatory Policy Act. 1992 Energy Policy Act. FERC order 888, 1996 Deregulation under respective state laws.	Limited inclusion of certain costs in rate base, price caps, demand management. Required non-discriminatory open access tariffs. Market price determination, creation of spot markets, pricing of stranded costs.	Required public utilities to purchase power at avoided cost from certain generators. Required public utilities to provide open wholesale transmission access. Open competition in retail (end user) market.	Individual states may choose to opt in or out of participation in retail wheeling. Requires recovery of stranded capital costs based on revenues lost, imposed as a transmission surcharge.	Required separation of transmission and supply. Establishment of independent system operator of transmission grid. Some forced divestiture of generating capacity.
Telephone	Evidence of monopoly profits by AT&T. Potential savings (60% on long-distance toll charges, large cross-subsidy of local, residential calls.	1982 AT&T divestiture decision, implemented in 1984. Various changes in state regulation. Telecommunications Act of 1996.	Equipment and long-distance prices *de facto* deregulated. Introduction at state level of various alternatives to rate of return regulation: revenue sharing, price caps.	Open entry in long distance and business services and data transmission. Legal barriers to entry into local markets removed. Requires open inter-connection to transmission network, unbundling of access to local loops, resale of any retail services.	Local service remains regulated; Regional Bells (RBOCs) are prohibited from entering long distance unless it can be shown that significant competition has developed in their market.	Divestiture by AT&T of regional telephone operators (Baby Bells) and of equipment manufacture (Western Electric).

Table 1.1. **Reform of sectoral economic regulations in the United States (status by end-1998)** *(continued)*

Industry	Reasons for deregulation	Key legislative or regulatory changes	Changes in price regulation	Changes in regulation of entry and exit	Remaining regulations on price and entry	Mandated changes in industry structure
Natural gas distribution	Existing regulation had created a regionalised and monopolistic industry structure.	FERC ruling.	Change from LT contracts for uninterruptible and interruptible gas to reservation charges on transmission capacity and unit charges for gas shipped.	Created open access to interconnected grid by brokers, distributors and recently end users.		Mandatory separation of pipeline transmission from marketing subsidiaries.
Financial services	Disintermediation of bank deposits caused by high interest rates. Continuing loss of bank market share of financial assets. Possible efficiency gains from creation of financial superstores.	Depository Institutions Deregulation & Monetary Control Act (1980), updated 1982. Interstate branching at state level (1982-1990). Federal regulations permitting some cross-holding in financial services. Riegle-Neil Act (1994). Federal regulations increasing cross-holding in financial services.	Interest payments on deposits were effectively phased-out by 1982.	Permitted interstate bank branching. Permitted commercial bank ownership of separately capitalised subsidiaries in investment banking and securities brokerage. Full interstate branching, limits national and state concentration. Increased financial integration, including in insurance.	Banks are prohibited from ownership or offering of insurance services and ownership of non-banks.	
Other		Bus Regulatory Reform Act of 1982.				

Source: OECD.

ECONOMIC IMPACTS
OF SECTORAL REGULATORY REFORM[23]

Removal of restrictions on pricing, entry, and exit led directly to increased productivity and lower costs.

Benefits from the initial round of reform began to appear once growth resumed after 1982. The removal of most restrictions on pricing, entry, and exit in network industries led directly to increased productivity and lower costs in the reformed sectors. More vigorous competition stimulated industry restructuring and innovation and benefited consumers through better service and lower prices (see Table 1.2).

Box 1.2.   **Estimating the economic impact of regulatory reform**

Regulatory reform can affect both sectoral and macroeconomic performance. Analysis of sectoral impacts draws on the large body of academic research that has developed since the 1970s. Microeconomic effects include benefits to consumers in terms of prices and service, impact on labour markets, changes in industry structure, competition and profits, and changes in costs and productivity, especially from innovations. Where possible, numerical estimates of sectoral effects are based on comparing what actually happened with an estimate of what would have happened without reform; where that is not possible, the observed change is reported. Quantitative measures for features such as service quality and innovation are generally not available, so key changes or anecdotal information are reported. The sectoral impact is summarised in Table 1.2. The impact of regulatory reform on macroeconomic performance is notoriously difficult to measure, and relies on estimates by other authors and previous estimates by the OECD.

The OECD's Regulation, Structure and Performance Database was also used to generate performance benchmarks of relevance to regulation (see Annex Figures 1.4-1.7). Based on information from Member countries and other data sets, macroeconomic and sectoral indicators of economic performance have been developed by the Economics Department. Performance is defined as a multifaceted phenomenon (including static, dynamic and resource mobilisation dimensions). Synthetic indicators were constructed using multivariate data analysis techniques such as factor analysis. The database includes indicators for business sector manufacturing and service industries and for six specific service sectors (electricity, telecommunications, rail transport, air passenger transport, road freight and retail distribution).

Performance across the economy improved as the effects of sectoral reform rippled outward.

Performance across the economy improved as the effects of sectoral deregulation rippled outward. Cheaper, more efficient infrastructure and transportation services let downstream industries reduce prices, while stimulating growth in complementary services.

The economy was able to adapt more quickly to changes in technology and to external shocks.

Dynamic effects were more important than anticipated, though harder to document. An extraordinary surge in innovation and faster introduction of new technologies, services, and business practices multiplied benefits for consumers and produced new high-growth industries. Direct and indirect effects of sectoral reform helped increase flexibility in the labour market and elsewhere. These effects allowed the US economy to adapt more quickly to changes in technology and to external shocks, improved the trade-offs between inflation, growth, and unemployment, and boosted the US lead in productivity.

Sectoral impacts of regulatory reform

Consumers benefited from lower prices and generally better service with no documented deterioration in safety.

Consumer prices in almost all deregulated sectors dropped 30 to 75 per cent.

Consumer prices in almost all deregulated sectors dropped substantially. Declines ranged from 30 to 75 per cent (Winston, 1998). These impacts are reported in Table 1.2.

23

Table 1.2. **Impacts of the reform of sectoral economic regulation in the United States**

Industry	Industry structure and competition	Industry profits	Output and prices: absolute and relative	Service quality and universal service	Sectoral labour: wages, employment	Efficiency: productivity and costs	Innovations and other changes
Air transport	Number of effective competitors declined and concentration increased after some initial entry. Competition per route increased through 1990, then declined slightly. Net increase in effective competition of 70% in long-distance, 2% in short-distance.	Profits have risen slightly on average, but have been highly cyclical and affected by excess investment/capacity and slow adjustment to optimal fleet mix of planes. Large losses and some bankruptcies immediately after deregulation and again in early 1990s.	Pre-reform large cross-subsidies from long to short-haul routes. Total price decline of 33%, 20% from deregulation. Larger declines in prices of long-haul high volume cities; 80% of fares now lower. Sources of declines split 60/40 between greater competition, and efficiency gains. Annual savings of $30 billion (1996).	Safety performance improved after reform, for reasons that are unclear, perhaps because safety regulations were not reduced. Positive changes included increased flight frequency. Negative changes included an increased number of connections, increased connection and travel times, more fare restrictions, more difficulty getting seats on desired flights.	Initial loss of employment of about 7%, larger amongst established carriers. By 1996 total employment had increased by around 40% over initial levels as output soared in response to lower fares. No effect on earnings of mechanics. Flight attendants earnings were lower by 39% or more by 1992. Depending on seniority, pilots' earnings are 22% lower.	Increase in load factors, especially on long-haul routes, from 55% to 70% in 1996. Accelerated network efficiencies through hub and spoke. TFP increases of 15% in early years.	Constant innovation of information technology in pricing and computer reservation systems applied to maximising loads and revenues. Innovation of peak-load pricing, pricing related to embedded option value. Discount fares now available on Internet.
Road transport	Tenfold decline in number of large "less than truck load" (LTL) trucking firms. Increased competition from UPS, Federal Express. 175% increase in number of "truck load" (TL) carriers, but greater concentration in largest firms.	Profitability has been cyclical, many firms with unfunded pensions forced into bankruptcy. Overall profitability has declined, especially in LTL.	TL and LTL prices fell by 25 and 11% through 1982, 75 and 35% by 1995. Large reductions for high volumes and for larger shippers. 30% decline in intrastate rates. Annual savings of $18 billion (1996).	Innovation of negotiated contracts, binding estimates, guaranteed delivery times. Improvements in service time and reliability.	Drop in overall wage level of 1-4.5% (counterfactual), 10% for union workers. Employment declined in LTL and rose in TL, net gain of 16% through 1990. Increase in flexible of work rules.	Initial drop in costs of 2%. By 1996 operating costs fell by 35% (LTL) and 75% (TL). Increased customised service costs partly offset productivity gains in volume service. Evidence of higher capital productivity.	Constant innovation in application of information technology to maximise routing efficiency, track shipments, and analyse shipper distribution patterns; development of third part freight analysts and brokers.
Rail freight	Continued mergers have left four large Class I firms. Substantial entry of small firms creating small systems on abandoned track. Evidence of intense duopoly competition and competition from road freight.	Rate of return on equity rose from under 3% to over 8%. Market share of freight shipments recovered from 33 to 38%. Substantial increase in high volume, container and trailer traffic up 133%.	Initial price declines around 7%, 39% by 1990 and 50% by 1995. Greater price drops for high value, non-bulk than bulk commodities. Permitted railroads to compete in these areas. Relative increase in prices on low-density routes. Annual savings of $12 billion (1996).	Steady improvement in service quality. More frequent departures on high volume routes. Volume discounts and increase in shipper specific rates: tailored to cost, service and demand conditions.	Large additional decline of 41% in employment. Significant initial wage gains above pre-existing rents of 6-40% maintained until late 1980s and then substantially eroded with declining labour demand. Adjustments occurred gradually over a number of years.	Consolidation and abandonment of low density uneconomic routes, decline of about 1/3. Increase in intensity of track usage by 54% by 1990. Annual labour productivity growth doubled and TFP gains tripled in 1980s. Total drop in costs of 60%, about 2/3 due to deregulation.	Same as road transport. Innovation of intermodal, double stacked cars. Pricing more closely based on distance, number of switching.

Table 1.2. **Impacts of the reform of sectoral economic regulation in the United States** (*continued*)

Industry	Industry structure and competition	Industry profits	Output and prices: absolute and relative	Service quality and universal service	Sectoral labour: wages, employment	Efficiency: productivity and costs	Innovations and other changes
Telecommunications	AT&T's market share of long distance fell from 68% in 1984 to under 50% in 1997, with Sprint and MCI accounting for most of the rest of the market. The seven RBOCs, GTE and other local exchange companies control virtually 100% of local services in their regions.		Long distance rates fell, but were partially offset by higher cost of local service. Urban and business customers continue to subsidise residential and rural rates; long distance subsidises shorter distances.	Service has improved: universality of service rose, percentage of calls completed increased.	Loss of jobs in components of AT&T offset by growth in new entrants. Overall sectoral employment fell by nearly 10% through 1992-93 recession, has rebounded to pre-deregulation levels. Evidence of small declines in wages (Hendricks 1994, Winston 1993).	Equipment costs declined by two-thirds after divestiture.	More rapid introduction of fiber optic and digitalised networks. Increase in R&D expenditures and manpower of 50% (Noam, 1992). Automation and computerisation of operator and directory services accelerated.
Natural gas transmission and distribution	Direct market transactions between suppliers and users replaced merchants. 50 gas spot markets. 1 400 distributors hold rights on 21 major pipelines. Nearly complete unification of prices in national market four years after deregulation.		Drop of 31% in transmission and distribution margins between 1984-93. Increase in natural gas demand of 30% (not counterfactual).	Service quality and system reliability have improved.	Decline in employment of 13% by 1994 (not counterfactual).	Drop of 35% real dollars in operating and maintenance. Labour productivity increases of 24% (not counterfactual).	Innovations in automation and information technology in meter-reading, billing, route planning and scheduling. New technologies in boring and extension (not counterfactual).
Financial services	Steady consolidation of industry in 1980-97, net decline of 30-40% in number of firms and increased asset concentration. (top 100 from ½ to ¾ of total assets). 40% foreign-owned.	Rates of return declined in the 1980s with higher costs from paying interest on deposits and higher capital requirements.		Improved service quality, some questions during 1990-94 if decline in lending to small businesses was permanent.			

Source: OECD.

A sector in which the price evidence is not clear is telephony. Per minute rates in domestic and international long-distance have fallen substantially, but local service charges have increased.

Regulatory reform brought about substantial gains in labour and capital productivity.

Gains were seen in all types of productivity: labour, capital and TFP.

Prices declined primarily because real operating costs fell in most sectors by 25 to 75 per cent (Winston, 1998). Gains were seen in all types of productivity: labour, capital and TFP (see Table 1.2). Reform stimulated substantial firm restructuring which improved labour productivity. Entry of non-union competition in traditionally unionised sectors forced concessions on work rules, increasing flexibility and raising labour productivity, although competition with non union labour reduced wage levels and job security in some cases.

Regulatory reform also improved capital productivity. It accelerated the introduction of new technology, such as fibre optic and digitalised networks in telecommunications. It forced firms to eliminate excess capacity, as in electricity generation. It required firms to achieve higher load factors by more appropriate choice of capital stock, such as plane size in air transport. Reform improved efficiency by encouraging:

- *Economies of scope*, as free entry and exit permitted better network systems and more efficient routing. In airlines, freedom of entry and exit accelerated the shift to the hub and spoke system that has been the major source of greater productivity. The trucking industry enjoyed similar gains by centralising maintenance, service, and routing centres. Permitting back hauls and free entry into new routes and different products reduced empty miles.

- *Adoption or innovation of new technologies*, such as information technology, which helped transport firms maximise load factors. Airlines use information technology to continually change the available price and mix of fare categories. Trucking companies applied information technology to track trucks' precise locations and optimise routes, and freight brokers used it to develop systems for finding the least cost intermodal routing. Railroads accelerated adoption of intermodal methods with containers and trailers and innovations such as double-stacked cars. New technologies improved capital productivity in energy and long distance telephony.

- *Creation of deeper and more complete markets*, as a result of more efficient pricing and lower transactions costs. Improved markets have improved the allocation of resources and increased productivity. Deregulation led to unbundling, so each service could be priced at cost.

  • Airlines used computer reservations systems and other technology to offer multiple fare categories based on relative price elasticities and the value of fare restrictions.[24]

This in turn has permitted economies in allocating such resources as airport landing slots.

- Similarly unbundled prices, for such service features as guaranteed delivery times, have appeared in road and rail transport, natural gas, and electric power. Lower transactions costs in these sectors are likely to have reduced long-term costs and increased productivity in their customer industries, by easing industry relocation and expanding supplier networks, which created larger markets. In these larger markets, there are greater opportunities to achieve economies of scale, but also an increased number of competitors and thus increased pressure to contain prices through greater productivity.

- In natural gas, four separate markets have developed: commodity gas (both spot and future), interstate transportation, core distribution, and non-core distribution. Deeper markets permit companies to use the future energy prices revealed in commodity markets to choose the energy intensity of investments in new technology.

Some cost improvements developed over the long-term. The speed of adjustments varies directly with the extent of fixed costs in the industry.

Regulatory reform triggered a long-term process of capacity adjustment that is lowering fixed costs.

Regulatory reform triggered a long-term process of capacity adjustment that is lowering fixed costs. Most reformed sectors are capital intensive, with high fixed costs and low marginal costs. Regulation had burdened firms in these sectors with excess capacity, a mismatch between types of capacity and demand, or both. This was most obvious in air and rail transport, where regulation prevented exit from unprofitable routes. After rapid initial restructuring to improve competitiveness, further adjustments to capacity and the mix of capital stock have been slower, and continue in most sectors, especially those with the highest proportion of fixed costs.

- In air transport, carriers tried at first to compete with more frequent service by buying larger fleets of larger aircraft, but this strategy led to over-investment, fare wars and large losses in the late 1980s.[25] Firms learned from that experience, and in the 1990s slowed the growth of fleet size, while better adapting the mix of aircraft to flight distance and passenger volumes.

- In railroads, with the highest fixed costs of any transportation sector, routes are still being pruned. The slow pace of change is reflected in the slow decline of costs and prices, which fell by 7 per cent in the early 1980s, 39 per cent by 1990, and 50 per cent as of 1995 (Wilson, 1997).

Industry structure is continuously evolving. The trend is toward both greater concentration and greater contestability.

Deregulation attracted substantial entry, followed by consolidation.

In most sectors, deregulation attracted substantial entry, followed by consolidation (Table 1.2). Initial entry of many low cost, non-union air carriers was important in driving down fares, partly through reducing industry wages and liberalising work rules. In railroads and trucking, a dual market developed, combining a few large national firms with many small local ones. In long-distance telephony, AT&T's market share has dropped by almost half since deregulation, but three firms (AT&T, MCI and Sprint) account for 75 per cent of the market.

Vigilance by competition authorities continues to be necessary, but competition has generally increased despite consolidation.

Vigilance by competition authorities continues to be necessary, but consolidation has not prevented competition:

– In transportation, competition in individual sectors was reinforced by intermodal and cross-sectoral competition, a synergy that highlights the importance of reforming all transportation modes simultaneously. In road transport, the emergence and rapid growth of package delivery services such as Federal Express created substantial competition for some forms of trucking.

– The significance of trends in airlines has been hotly debated. Overall, competition has increased under reform, especially on major routes, and prices have dropped dramatically. Morrison and Winston (1998) note that 90 per cent of the realignment of relative prices of different routes reflects differences in underlying costs of serving those routes. But there has been significant retrenchment on smaller routes and around hubs where there is a dominant carrier.[26] In these cases, monopolistic pricing has raised prices by an estimated 2 to 27 per cent (Grimm and Windle, 1998), sometimes substantially reversing the initial price declines.[27]

– Competition in natural gas transmission and the development of commodity markets have all but eliminated arbitrage possibilities from wellhead to final user.

Changes in profits have been mixed across sectors but have been generally small.

The expected impact of reform on profits is uncertain. To the extent that regulated industries face little competition and exploit market power, profits should fall after reform. But if regulation prevented firms from optimising inputs, profits could rise after reform. Cyclical factors make measuring the net effects of reform difficult, but it does not seem that overall profits changed much. Profits rose slightly in airlines and banking and declined slightly in road transport. Profits of natural gas pipelines and railroads rebounded substantially as firms left unprofitable routes and re-negotiated contracts. Rate of return on equity for railroads rose from 3 per cent before reform to over 8 per cent after. Developments in banking are difficult to analyse but interest rate deregulation and interstate branching probably contributed to the decline in profits experienced during the 1980s. Rates of return for AT&T and the regional Bell companies have exceeded those of the S&P 500.

Benefits of sectoral reform are not evenly distributed across society because relative prices of services changed substantially...

For the great majority of consumers, prices declined substantially, but others saw few benefits or even price increases.

Regulatory reform produced mostly winners, but some losers. The distribution of benefits across society varied as the relative prices of different types of service changed. Cross-subsidies between different types of service in many sectors declined or disappeared as rates aligned with costs. For the great majority of consumers, prices declined substantially, but others saw few benefits or even price increases.

These impacts are clear in airlines: 80 per cent of passengers benefit from lower prices, especially on long-haul high volume routes where prices dropped 25 to 50 per cent, but for 20 per cent of passengers real prices have not declined or have increased.[28] In natural gas, prices to industrial users fell substantially, but prices to commercial and residential consumers have been fairly constant as competition in retail delivery is just beginning to emerge (Costello and Graniere, 1997).

... but service quality and safety in sectors under reform have usually been maintained or improved.

Service quality has generally improved. Large customers in particular benefit from more customised services. In road transport and railroads, shippers, especially those transporting high volumes, now enjoy individually negotiated contracts with prices tailored to cost and demand conditions. In addition transporters improved delivery times and reliability and offered innovations such as binding estimates and delivery guarantees. In financial services, interest rate deregulation has resulted not only in higher interest payments on deposits, but also increased customer convenience. Scheduled airline and railroad departures became more frequent except for some smaller cities. Some aspects of airline service have deteriorated: restrictive conditions on some fares have increased (for example, required Saturday overnights), as have connection and travel times.[29] In a competitive market, though, the multiplication of fares (and fare restrictions) has stimulated travel agents and businesses to develop software to find the cheapest fares. Businesses have developed strategies to offset rising business class fares, including direct bargaining with airlines in exchange for exclusive service, and consumers have organised buying clubs to benefit from volume discounts.

Although vigilance is warranted, reform has led to no documented deterioration in safety and reliability.

Although anxiety is still high in some areas and vigilance is warranted as incentives change in more competitive markets, reform has led to no documented deterioration in safety and reliability. This may be because safety regulations were not removed in any sector, but instead were often augmented. Moreover, markets may support rather than erode safety incentives. In trucking and airlines, despite some well-publicised airline crashes, over-all safety records have improved.

Reliability was also maintained after reform.

Reliability was also maintained after reform. Industry observers feared that a competitive environment for natural gas pipelines would undermine system integrity and security from a supplier of last resort. This concern is echoed in current discussions of electric power reform. Yet system reliability in gas pipelines improved. One reason is that development of spot and future markets, a direct result of reform, gave prices a time dimension. Spot and future prices adjust to shortages immediately and, as demand responds, the increased interconnectedness of pipeline networks permit rapid re-routing.[30] Innovations in information technology, metering, route planning, and scheduling contributed.

Sectoral performance after regulatory reform

Performance in sectors that the United States has reformed compares well with that in other OECD countries by measures such as employment, output growth, and labour and total factor productivity, and by a measure of X-efficiency (Annex Figures 1.4-1.7 show US sectoral performance compared to the rest of the OECD).

Sectoral performance improved most when reform was deepest.

US productivity and efficiency performance, relative to other countries, varies substantially across sectors. In telecommunications, US performance is average, but the retail distribution, air and rail transport sectors are productivity leaders, and electricity is in between. This pattern roughly corresponds to the extent of reform.[31]

Restructuring after reform led to high output growth, and low employment growth, and productivity soared in the reformed sectors.

Performance in terms of growth in sectoral output was clearly affected by deregulation. Output growth was relatively high in all sectors in the 1980s, and, combined with relatively low employment growth in labour productivity soared. In the 1990s output growth decelerated in sectors where reform occurred early but accelerated in sectors undergoing reform. Thus in air transport, the US ranking among the G7 in terms of sectoral output growth fell from first to fifth, and electricity and rail transport followed a similar pattern, although the relative movements were smaller. The one sector where US ranking and output rose in the 1990s was telecommunications; as deregulation there became broader and deeper.

Macroeconomic impacts of regulatory reform

Sectoral innovations and productivity gains boosted economy-wide productivity in the 1980s.

Gains in reformed sectors spilled over to other sectors.

Gains in reformed sectors spilled over to other sectors, either through demonstration effects or because reformed sectors supplied important inputs. Improved, unbundled, and customised service permitted customers to improve productivity. Guaranteed delivery times facilitated more efficient supplier-producer relationships such as just-in-time inventories. Development and application of sophisticated pricing, routing and logistical software in formerly regulated sectors had important demonstration effects in other sectors. And their pioneering reduced the costs and improved the quality of new technologies, facilitating their adoption in other industries. Deeper and broader markets, such as the spot and futures markets that developed in natural gas and are emerging in electricity, have allowed energy consumers to set their own output prices with lower risk (see Chapter 5).

Reform also improved the dynamic allocation of resources and investment.

Regulatory reform also improved the dynamic allocation of resources and investment, possibly leading to long-term gains in productivity. While this effect is difficult to measure, deeper markets and more efficient pricing are likely to have generated long-term benefits to productivity growth.

Regulatory reform increased the efficiency of investment, important in the United States where investment levels are low.

Regulatory reform improved the functioning of capital markets, increasing the efficiency of investment. Reforms in banking and other financial markets have been important to facilitating the flow of credit for new investments. Most striking have been reforms that let pension funds invest directly in venture capital. Venture capital is a major source of funding for businesses that generate jobs and new technology.[32] Innovative forms of funding are particularly important in the US economy, where investment levels overall are relatively low. Capital market reform had another benefit for economic growth. Effective overhaul of bank and savings and loan supervision – effective regulatory reform, not deregulation – meant that the US credit crunch was shorter than in other countries that suffered from asset price bubbles.

Spillover effects and efficient application of capital helped maintain high productivity and standards of living, despite lower savings.

Spillover effects, efficient application of capital, efficient use of infrastructure, and better dynamic allocation of investment helped the United States maintain its high productivity and standard of living despite lower rates of savings and investment.[33] While the United States had the slowest capital stock growth in the OECD, it also had the lowest capital-output ratio in the G7, indicating the efficiency with which capital is employed (see Annex Table 1.3).

The combined size of reformed sectors is relatively small – five per cent of GDP – but the benefits of productivity growth in those sectors may have contributed to improvements in productivity performance in the economy as a whole. Correlations must be drawn cautiously, but productivity growth during the 1982-87 recovery, following major reform, was much stronger than during the 1975-79 recovery (see Annex Figure 1.1). Labour productivity growth in the business sector did not decelerate in the 1980s and 1990s as it did in other G7 countries. In the 1990s, labour productivity in manufacturing has risen faster than in other G7 countries, permitting the United States to retain its lead in productivity.[34]

Regulatory reform has helped restore US competitiveness in manufacturing.

Explicit links between regulatory reform in largely non-traded sectors and external performance are difficult to make. Nonetheless, through its effects on productivity growth, regulatory reform has helped restore US competitiveness in manufacturing. Growth in US export volumes has outpaced competitors so that US exporters have gained market share in manufacturing exports relative to the rest of the G7.

The macroeconomic effects of reform include lower inflation and a better tradeoff between price and quantity adjustment.

Lower prices in sectors under reform lowered costs in other sectors, reducing their prices or raising their value added. Price levels in

US manufacturing are the lowest in the OECD by over ten per cent compared to the next best country, and price levels in services are among the five best-performing countries. Studies[35] show that the United States has the highest levels of relative price flexibility of any OECD country.

Lower prices and greater price flexibility helped to reduce inflation while avoiding an increase in unemployment.

Lower prices and greater pricing flexibility have translated into better inflation performance. Despite strong growth and unemployment well below most estimates of the NAIRU, inflation has declined and is now close to the range consistent with price stability. The G7 countries experienced low inflation in the 1990s, and the United States was at the higher end of the range among this group; though probably largely due to more flexible labour markets, regulatory reform helped the United States become one of the few G7 countries to engineer a decline in inflation over the last 20 years while avoiding a secular increase in the unemployment rate.

Regulatory reform worked with flexible labour markets to re-allocate labor to high-growth sectors, especially services, though this may have reduced productivity growth.

The flexibility of the labour market resulted in the rapid absorption in new jobs of workers displaced by restructuring.

The flexibility of the US labour market permitted workers displaced by restructuring to be rapidly absorbed in new jobs, mostly in the service sector. Rapid employment growth within sectors was supported by downward wage flexibility. Reform stimulated employment creation in complementary services such as freight brokers and logistical firms in transport, travel agents and in the travel industry, and financial service jobs in energy commodity markets. Many of these are high wage jobs. A liberal regulatory environment for shop opening hours, zoning and retail store size also stimulated employment in wholesale and retail distribution, restaurants and other services, where many jobs are not highly paid. In occupations like distribution, restaurants and hotels, flexible labour markets permit part-time and temporary employment. Employment of low skill workers is encouraged by low minimum wages and the absence of notification periods for firing and of mandatory vacation, health and pension benefits.

Ironically, reallocation of labour may have lowered total business sector productivity. Many service sector jobs are high-skilled, but on average productivity in services is lower than in manufacturing.[36] As a result, in a full employment economy like the United States, labour released in some sectors may be absorbed in lower productivity sectors, with the net effect of lowering economy wide productivity.

Initial declines in employment were followed by substantial increases. But reform had negative effects on wages in some sectors.

Employment growth was boosted by the rapid expansion of output to meet the higher demand generated by regulatory reform.

In most reformed sectors, long-run employment levels have increased and employment has been reallocated to more efficient firms within the sector. Initial reductions in established, often unionised, companies were largely offset by growth in new, often non-unionised, entrants, and then by growth in pre-existing firms after an adjustment period. Employment growth was spurred by rapid expansion of output to meet the higher demand generated by the results of regulatory reform: lower prices, better customer service and increased product diversity.

– Employment fell in US telecommunications in the 1980s, but grew in the 1990s and was higher than the G7 average. Employment cuts among the original members of AT&T have been offset by substantial growth in other telecommunication companies so that employment in the sector has returned to pre-reform levels.

– In air transport, US employment growth was the highest in the G7 in both decades, and the gap grew in the 1990s as most other G7 countries were restructuring. Initial employment losses were around 7 per cent and were concentrated in large established carriers. New entrants and the explosive growth of demand resulted in a substantial increase in long-run employment of 37-46 per cent (the range depending on whether air freight is included).

Regulatory reform raised unemployment rates briefly, but in the long run contributed to strong employment growth.

Reform increased employment directly by stimulating growth in sectors like airlines and telecommunications, and helped economy-wide employment by boosting demand and by increasing competition, so that firms are more likely to meet higher demand with higher output rather than higher prices. Stronger sectoral employment performance is reflected in labour markets as a whole (see Annex Figure 1.2 and Annex Table 1.3). Employment growth has been much faster than in almost all other OECD countries. The US economy created over 13 million new jobs (net) between 1992 and 1997, equivalent to ten per cent of the labour force. Regulatory reform raised US unemployment rates for brief periods, but in the long run contributed to the overall strength of employment growth. The unemployment rate had fallen by 1999 to just over four per cent, levels not seen since the 1960s, and the largest decline in the OECD. Low unemployment and rising labour force participation have steadily reduced the non-employment rate.

Regulatory reform may have contributed slightly to poor performance of wages and to widening income distribution.

Effects on wages and income distribution must be understood in the context of a general stagnation in real wages.

Effects on wages and income distribution must be understood in the context of the general stagnation in real wages in the US economy since the mid-1970s. Wage growth has been near zero over the last 30 years and compensation growth has only been marginally positive at 0.2-0.3 per cent, in both cases the worst performance among the G7 countries. Growth in per capita compensation was more substantial, in part because of a decline in the savings rate. Poverty measures have improved, but income distribution is likely to have continued the widening which began in the 1970s, as non-wage income grew while wages stagnated.[37]

33

In reformed sectors, wages declined at roughly the same rate as the economy as a whole, except in certain sub-sectors or specific occupations where substantial wage premia had existed.

In reformed sectors, wages declined at roughly the same rate as in the economy as a whole. The exception has been in sub-sectors and specific occupations where substantial wage premia existed under regulation, often as a result of a strong union. These premia were reduced or eliminated. In these sectors and occupations, new entry following reform was often composed largely of non-union firms, putting pressure on unionised firms to reduce wage premiums and relax restrictive work rules. This was particularly true in airlines and road transport. A major sector of road transport found that union wages declined by 10 per cent. In airlines, a study found that wages were 22 to 39 per cent lower than they would have been. By contrast, wages in rail transport rose as the industry recovered, but then declined slightly as employment shrank.

Causes of the poor performance of US wages and widening in income distribution are debated. Reform may have made a minor contribution to both trends.

Causes of the overall poor performance of US wages and the widening in income distribution are extensively debated and the contribution of regulatory reform is difficult to assess. On balance, reform may have made a minor contribution to both trends. This may have occurred directly through downward pressures on wages of relatively well-paid skilled workers in reformed sectors – contributing to the widening between the middle and upper ends of the income distribution – and indirectly by contributing to the overall weakening of the bargaining position of unions and labour in the economy. Balanced against this is the fact that workers overall benefited from lower prices, and potentially higher wages from improvements in labour productivity.

In summary, regulatory reform contributed to improving macro performance in the 1990s.

The United States has moved from stagflation to steady growth with low inflation, falling unemployment and a budget surplus.

The United States has moved from stagflation to steady growth with low inflation, falling unemployment and a budget surplus. All countries have substantially reduced inflation, but the United States is rare in doing this while sustaining high and increasing levels of employment. Real GDP growth has been positive since 1992 and maintained strength even after several years of recovery (see Annex Table 1.4). Poverty measures have fallen since the 1980s. Export performance has been strong, and the United States maintains a productivity advantage in key manufacturing sectors. Price levels, especially in manufacturing, are among the lowest in the OECD, as is the capital-output ratio. This partly compensates for lower levels of savings and investment. At the same time, income distribution has widened and the living standards of a portion of the population may have declined.

Regulatory reform may have increased GDP by two per cent.

Regulatory reform made positive and important contributions to these trends. Attempts have been made to quantify effects on GDP. An attempt by Winston (1993, 1998) to measure first-round effects[38] estimated that the combined sectoral effects of reform in transportation, energy and telecommunications increased US GDP annually and permanently by one percentage point. Previous work by the OECD found that, for the US economy, this can be translated to an overall macroeconomic effect roughly twice the size, suggesting that regulatory reform to date has increased US GDP by two per cent.[39]

Box 1.3. Regulatory lessons from the US savings and loan crisis

The savings and loan (S&L) crisis resulted from the interaction of archaic restrictions on investment with a changing macroeconomic environment.

S&Ls were set up in 1934 to encourage home ownership by channeling funds into residential mortgages. Deposits were insured by the Federal Savings and Loan Insurance Company (FSLIC).

Federal insurance created the potential problem of moral hazard. Owners of S&Ls had incentives to seek as much risk as possible in their investments. They could borrow at a fixed interest rate and then lend at high rates, while passing losses to the FLSIC. To avoid this problem, S&Ls were regularly audited and both the interest rates they could pay on deposits and their eligible investments were tightly regulated. This resulted in investment portfolios composed largely of long-term mortgages financed by short-term deposits.

This arrangement was inherently risky but worked well in the environment of stable inflation and interest rates in the post-war period. Problems emerged in the 1970s when inflation, and market interest rates rose, causing S&Ls to lose deposits to banks and money market funds. Regulators responded by permitting S&Ls to pay higher rates to attract deposits. But as inflation rose, interest rates on short-term deposits exceeded interest earnings from long-term mortgages. Total losses were $8.7 billion in 1980-81, and 118 S&Ls failed between 1980-82 at a cost of $3.5 billion. By 1982, 415 additional institutions with assets of $220 billion were insolvent.

Deregulation made the problem much worse...

The Congress and Administration faced two choices. One was to close down bankrupt institutions and leave the FSLIC to absorb the losses. But the FSLIC had only $6.3 billion in assets, compared with estimated costs of $15-25 billion. A bailout required an injection of taxpayer funds.

The alternative was to hope the industry could grow out of the problem by restoring profitability through easing restrictions on investments. Congress passed new legislation in 1980 and 1982 deregulating interest rates and constraints on investments, and loosening capital requirements and qualifications on S&L owners to encourage new entry. Federal deposit insurance was retained and expanded. The threat of moral hazard thus became a reality. The industry attracted so-called "high-fliers" willing to undertake high-risk investments. Nearly 500 new S&Ls came into existence between 1980 and 1986, and industry assets grew by 56 per cent, twice the rate of commercial banks. The share of residential mortgages in S&L portfolios declined, largely replaced by loans to real estate developers.

Moral hazard problems were exacerbated by other factors. First, lower capital requirements reduced the injection of new capital into the weakened industry. Second, Federal deregulation caused states, which also charter savings and loans, to engage in competitive deregulation. The 1981 Tax Act helped create a boom in real estate which was in large part burst by the 1986 Tax Act. Third, the regulatory system was weak. Examiners assigned to S&Ls had the lowest salaries and poorest training and the industry was allowed greater self-regulation than commercial banks. National chartering and insurance functions were housed in the same agency.

... resulting in even greater losses, an expensive Federal cleanup operation and appropriate reregulation.

Instead of restoring profitability, poorly designed deregulation increased losses as many new loans went sour. The losses were further increased by delays in confronting the problem. Congress, faced with the mounting costs of the crisis, repeatedly delayed legislative changes or injecting needed capital. Serious clean up finally began in 1989 with passage of new legislation (FIRREA) that established the Resolution Trust Corporation (RTC) with initial financing of $50 billion and $55 billion in additional financing. The RTC closed down and liquidated over 700 S&Ls with over $400 billion in assets between 1989 and 1995. The eventual cost was $160 billion, two-thirds borne by the taxpayer.

The 1989 legislation contained several measures to reregulate the industry to avoid future problems. In the new system, safety and soundness regulation is institutionally separated from industry promotion. Higher and risk-based capital requirements are backed up by mandatory corrective action as an institutions' capital deteriorated. The legislation established a new deposit insurance fund with insurance premiums related to differences in risk. Finally, Congress required the insurance fund to maintain a minimum ratio of capital to insured deposits, with powers to increase premia whenever this minimum was breached.

The regulatory lessons from the S&L crisis are clear:

– Problems must be recognised and addressed rapidly. Use of the least cost market-based solution encourages political support, while lowering overall costs.
– Capital and deposit insurance should be risk-based to provide proper incentives.
– Moral hazard problems must be avoided by having powerful independent regulatory agencies with well-trained examiners and strong enforcement powers and clear, transparent and well-defined accounting procedures.
– Safety and soundness regulation needs to be separated from industry promotion.

ANTICIPATED EFFECTS OF FURTHER SECTORAL REFORMS

Additional reforms will increase net benefits to the US economy.

Two decades of regulatory reform in the United States have not completed the reform of sectoral economic controls. Regulations on entry and prices still cost consumers and producers an estimated $70 billion annually, while producing few benefits (OMB, 1998). Hence, these kinds of regulations probably substantially reduce social welfare. Additional reforms are needed to complete reform in some sectors, and new initiatives are needed in areas where more competition or more efficient regulation can yield economic benefits. Reforms in the electricity and telecommunications sectors are assessed in Chapters 5 and 6 of this report. The OECD Report on Regulatory Reform (1997) estimated that the impact of additional sectoral regulatory reforms in transportation, energy and telecommunications would raise labour, capital and total factor productivity in the economy as a whole by one-half percentage point each. This was estimated to increase GDP by an additional one per cent, in addition to the two per cent cited above.

Expansion of market forces in electricity, telecommunications and financial services promise substantial gains for consumers.

As Chapter 5 explains, recent regulatory changes in electric power have moved the industry nearer to full competition. In telephony, the Telecommunications Act of 1996 is designed to introduce competition into local service. Chapter 6 explains that this has not been easy, though the potential benefits are large. Further reforms in these sectors, and to some extent financial services, should have substantial effects.

Potential annual savings in the electricity sector range from 0.25 to 0.50 per cent of GDP.

– Retail competition in electricity generation and distribution will reduce costs and prices. If retail competition is introduced in most states, prices in some could decline by up to 20 per cent over the next five years (OECD 1997) as cost differentials across the country equalise. Estimates of annual savings range from $20 to $40 billion (0.25 to 0.50 per cent of GDP).

Consumer benefits of full competition in the telecommunications industry would range from $4 to $30 billion.

– Until there is competition in local telecommunications markets, cross-subsidies will remain, costing an estimated $6 to $15 billion per year (OECD US 1997). Crandall and Waverman (1995) estimated that consumer benefits of full competition would range from $4 to $30 billion, depending on the distribution of gains between consumers and producers. The FCC estimated potential gains from the 1996 Telecommunications Act at $3.8 to $5.4 billion annually.

– US financial services are relatively efficient, but eliminating remaining barriers can generate small percentage cost reductions. These could be large in absolute terms, because consumers spend $300 billion on financial services annually.

Box 1.4. **Regulatory reform in US health care**

A more carefully constructed regulatory regime for health care could improve service and reduce costs. The major motivations for health care reform in the United States are: 1) rising costs and burdens to private employers and to the Federal government,[1] 2) the perception of widespread inefficiencies in insurance and delivery of services; and 3) concern over the public costs of policy goals such as universal coverage.

Health care expenditures in the United States rose from 8.9 per cent of GDP in 1980 to 13.6 per cent in 1993, and have remained steady since. By a variety of measures, US expenditures are much higher than in any other OECD country, even correcting for differences in per capita income or medical out-comes.[2]

In the past, the predominant form of health insurance was fee-for-service plans, which reimbursed most health expenditures after they were incurred. This market structure led to a large expansion in service and may have generated incentives to develop more costly medical technology (Cutler, 1996). In response to growing price pressures, the private sector has turned to managed care providers such as health maintenance organisations (HMOs). The share of workers covered by such plans rose to about ¾ in 1996 (CBO, 1997a). Because HMOs receive a fixed fee per customer, they have strong incentives to minimise costs. Competition between HMOs, in principle, provides incentives for service quality.[3]

Managed care systems are growing as a share of public health insurance, but the predominant form continues to be fee-for-service. To increase incentives for cost reductions in the Medicare system, Congress implemented several other reforms, principally imposing a fee schedule that reimbursed hospitals and physicians a fixed payment for each type of treatment. In 1997, the Balanced Budget Act mandated that the Health Care Financing Administration extend these systems to other types of health payments, unilaterally lowered reimbursement rates and provided additional incentives for the elderly to choose a Medicare managed care provider. Total cost savings over five years are projected to be about 57 per cent of 1997 expenditures.

The effects of these private and public reforms have been mixed, and the cost savings may be only temporary. The shift to managed care providers clearly produced a one-off reduction in price levels, but effects on long-term trends and quality of service are unclear. Managed care providers are coming under increasing pressure to improve quality, and probably increase costs, as consumers realise that much of the savings come from a reduction in services.[4] The reforms to the federal pricing mechanisms did cut the growth rate of expenditures significantly soon after their introduction, but they have proved to be less effective in limiting the long-run rate of increase.

Health care costs and the trade-offs between cost, quality and coverage will continue to be an issue for the United States. In terms of regulating private insurers, policy makers face a real dilemma. On the one hand, there is the demonstrable case that fee-for-service plans generate wasteful spending on care. On the other hand, managed care providers have strong incentives to limit services, and consumers often have little say in the health services they receive. There is a case for some regulation with a recognition that limiting services can yield efficiency gains.[5]

In terms of reforming public health insurance, the ageing population will increase pressures for cost containment. Few of the modifications to date will lower the long-term growth rate in costs (OECD, 1997c). There are some additional reforms the government can implement without changing the basic nature of the Medicare and Medicaid programmes. Congress could expand competitive bidding in rate setting, and could integrate programmes to make them more cost effective. Others have proposed dramatically increasing the share of managed care providers as a way to control costs. A commission is now studying proposals for long-term reform of Medicare and will report to Congress in 1999.

---

1. For the private sector, rising health insurance premiums were a major source of rising compensation costs for key industries and were perceived as a major source of competitive disadvantage vis-à-vis other countries. For the public sector, which now represents nearly half of all health expenditures, rising prices and an expansion in services led to a surge in the share of total government expenditures. Federal spending on Medicare and Medicaid grew from 2.8 per cent of total outlays in 1967 to 19 per cent in 1997.
2. No other OECD country spent more than 10 per cent of GDP on health care in 1994, and US spending remains several percentage points of GDP higher than can be explained by per capita income and medical out-turns (Oxley and MacFarlan, 1994). Per capita spending on health in the United States measured at purchasing power parity exchange rates is about twice as high as the OECD average and 50 per cent higher than the next highest country (OECD Health Data, 1998).
3. There is evidence that managed care providers generate savings (Cutler and Sheiner, 1997; Newhouse, 1992; CBO, 1997b; Baker and Shankarkumar, 1997), and surveys show that employers view them as an effective means to control costs (CBO, 1997a).
4. Many of these services are of dubious value, but testimony before Congress has demonstrated that in specific cases, HMOs have gone too far. Currently, Congress is developing a number of proposals to regulate the industry to ensure consumer protection, minimum service and quality standards and more transparency regarding service provision. The Administration has developed a "consumers' bill of rights" that encompasses many of these proposals, while it has mandated many of them in the Medicare system.
5. For instance, even though they may be unpopular, requiring a referral from a general practitioner before a patient can see a specialist lowers costs (Oxley and MacFarlan, 1994). One way to balance cost reductions and consumer protection would be to mandate the provision of denial rates and other statistics so that consumers when purchasing a health plan can make an informed choice. Federal and state governments can help by standardising and publishing such information, as the state of Maryland has with its "report cards" on managed care providers (National Governors Association, 1998). This would increase competition on quality of service among providers.

Chapter 2

GOVERNMENT CAPACITY TO ASSURE
HIGH QUALITY REGULATION

A key challenge for regulatory reform in the United States is improving the cost-effectiveness of social regulations.

With the introduction of competition into most previously regulated sectors of the economy, a key challenge for regulatory reform in the United States is improving the cost-effectiveness of social regulations so that they deliver the optimal level of regulatory protections with the best possible use of the country's resources. This requires not only more attention to the quality of regulations and primary laws, but development of flexible and market-oriented instruments in a wide range of policy areas. Reduced economic intervention could, in fact, heighten pressures for more social regulation to protect public interests in new markets, emphasising the importance of this dimension of reform.

The United States places more emphasis on the cost-effectiveness of social regulations than do most countries.

Social regulations impose direct costs 3 to 4 times higher than costs of economic regulations, but may deliver more benefits.

Today, the United States is rare among OECD countries in focusing on improving the quality of social regulations as the main objective of regulatory reform. Estimates of regulatory costs and benefits suggest that social regulations impose direct costs 3 to 4 times higher than costs of economic regulations, and that social regulations, if well designed and targeted, can deliver substantially more benefits to citizens (OMB, 1998).

Improving their quality has proven to be a difficult and long-term task.

Improving the quality of social regulations has proven to be a difficult and long-term task. Attempts to impose quality controls on the use of delegated regulatory powers in social policy areas began in the 1970s "in reaction to the explosive growth of new regulatory programmes" of the 1960s and 1970s.[40] By the mid 1970s, over 100 federal agencies were issuing economic and social regulations in areas such as health, safety, housing, agriculture, labour contracts and working conditions, environment, trade, and consumer protection.

Each President since the early 1970s has attempted to control the costs of the expanding federal regulatory state and to carry out policies more cost-effectively, while at the same time supporting the establishment of major new regulatory programmes. The balance of action has shifted from "regulatory relief" under Reagan to the Clinton philosophy of "regulatory quality".

Social regulations can yield large net benefits, but only if they are high quality, that is, produce net benefits at lowest cost over time.

The net benefits of federal regulation, considered in the aggregate, seem to be increasing.

The ultimate measure of the worth of a country's regulatory system is whether it increases or reduces the quality of life. If net social benefits are positive or increase over time, the regulatory system can be said to be increasing in quality. Measured in that way, the quality of federal regulation, considered in the aggregate, is probably improving.

Direct costs of federal regulation and paperwork appear to be between 4 and 10 per cent of GDP.

Some studies suggest that federal social regulation costs several hundred billion dollars annually, but produces even greater benefits. The total direct costs of regulation and paperwork are credibly estimated at between 4 and 10 per cent of GDP, with considerable uncertainty. The costs and benefits trend upward or downward is also uncertain, though OMB estimated in 1997 that regulatory costs as a percentage of GDP had stayed about the same since 1988[41] and has reported that net benefits of social regulations issued in recent years are increasingly positive, a significant though not a robust finding. Recently, the office of the President reported to Congress that:

– Federal regulations related to the environment, safety, and health and other social policies impose direct costs of between $170 billion to $224 billion per year, and produce between $258 billion to $3.55 trillion in annual benefits (the huge range in benefits estimates is due to considerable uncertainty about the impacts of the 1990 Clean Air Act) (OMB, 1998).

– As noted in Chapter 1, economic controls on entry and prices cost $70 billion each year, produce few benefits, and probably reduce social welfare.

– Other sources estimate the annual costs of federal paperwork for citizens and businesses at around $230 billion (Hopkins, 1996 and 1995), though these figures are contested by OMB, include tax compliance costs, and may overlap with other estimates. OMB data suggest that compliance with federal paperwork requires the full-time equivalent of 3 million private-sector employees and that federal paperwork burdens have increased considerably, from around 20 hours per capita in 1980 to around 25 hours per capita in 1996.

These estimates miss the indirect and dynamic effects of regulation, which are potentially large for both costs and benefits...

Such benefit and cost estimates are uncertain due to what OMB calls "enormous data gaps" and "a variety of estimation problems"[42] (Hahn, 1998a), and more complete data could reverse these conclusions. For example, indirect beneficial effects that result from better health and longer lives are not included, but may be large. Also, estimates of direct costs understate the full costs of regulations, because they miss impacts on productivity and welfare, and dynamic effects such as lost opportunities to create wealth. These effects can be very important for macroeconomic performance. Social regulations appear to have substantial impact on investment levels and innovation in industrial processes,[43] modest adverse impacts on productivity,[44] but little effect on overall economic competitiveness.

... but, overall, the shift from economic to social regulation has improved the potential social benefits of federal regulation.

Despite their weaknesses, these estimates suggest that the shift since the 1970s from economic regulation to social regulation, together with investments in quality control of social regulation, has greatly improved the potential benefits of the regulatory system as a whole, since social regulations are, in aggregate, more likely to produce net benefits.

The United States is the only country to have seriously examined the aggregate costs and benefits of regulations. Though flawed, these aggregate estimates are a large advance in understanding the costs and benefits of regulatory activities, and work is underway in OMB and elsewhere to improve them.

But the quality of individual social regulations varies widely, and many regulations produce more costs than benefits.

These appears to be the potential for very large gains from further reform of social regulation.

The second key question is whether a country's regulatory system produces the highest possible level of benefit from the resources used to reach regulatory objectives. That is, are regulations cost-effective? For most US social regulations, the answer is probably no. Data at the micro-level suggest that there are substantial inefficiencies, and the potential for very large gains from further reform.

Box 2.1. The judiciary in US regulation

No discussion of US regulation would be complete without acknowledging the role that the courts play in regulatory decisions. Issues that in other countries would be resolved through management and dialogue are resolved in the United States by the courts. "The courts have played a profoundly important role in setting the limits of congressional, presidential, and even judicial influence over regulatory policy-making in the agencies [...] the courts are empowered to hear variety of challenges to regulatory decisions, ranging from the delegation of authority to agencies by Congress to the legality and fairness of agency dealings with individual regulated parties" (Kerwin, 1994, p. 40). Legal challenges to major regulations are the norm rather than the exception.

The role of the courts in providing an alternative to regulation is also important. In the US, private legal actions complement the fragmented regulatory system, which can have several advantages. It can deter socially undesirable behaviour without unnecessarily pre-empting private initiative. It probably reduces regulatory costs and the need for direct government oversight. As a system to compensate victims, it may be more precise than broader social safety nets in other OECD countries.*

An assessment of the impact of the courts on regulatory quality is beyond the scope of this review, but it is fiercely debated. Wide opportunities to challenge regulatory decisions before the courts on procedural and substantive grounds in theory enables regulated citizens to challenge and hold accountable the regulatory powers of the government, but also can reduce regulatory innovation and responsiveness, while increasing uncertainty and costs.

As a mediator of social conflict, the US tort system has attracted heavy criticism. The US legal industry is larger than the domestic auto and steel industries. High legal expenses and the risk of potentially large punitive damage awards in liability cases are claimed to increase business costs unnecessarily and discourage innovation and risk taking. The OECD cited evidence that the number of civil cases increased by four-fold between the 1960s and the 1980s and their total cost have risen to 2.7 per cent of GDP, four to five times the levels found in the rest of the OECD (OECD, 1993).

There appears to be the potential for very large gains from further reform of social regulations.

---

* US patent law has been cited as more effective than those of Japan and Germany in enforcing intellectual property rights (Kagan and Axelrad, 1997, p. 162). Similarly bankruptcy law, which is often criticised as being too favourable to debtors, may have helped encourage the entrepreneurialism which has been a hallmark of the US economy.

More than half of federal regulations fail a benefit-cost test.

– Research on 106 federal regulations showed that just two rules (automatic restraints in cars and lead reductions in gasoline) produced over 70 per cent of total net regulatory benefits, and that more than half of federal regulations fail a strict benefit-cost test, using the government's own estimates (Hahn, 1998*b*). The study suggested that net benefits could be increased by $115 billion simply by eliminating those rules that failed the benefit/cost test.

Redirecting regulatory activities away from low-priority to high-priority issues would have enormous payoffs...

– The cost-benefit ratios of different regulations differ greatly. For example, safety and health regulations aimed at reducing fatality risks have saved lives at costs ranging from $10 000 to $72 billion per life saved (Morrall, 1986; Viscusi, 1992 and 1996). Redirecting regulatory activities from low-priority to high-priority issues would have enormous payoffs in terms of delivering benefits at lower cost.

... for example, re-targeting safety and health regulations could avoid 60 000 deaths each year without increasing regulatory costs.

– A recent study found that if existing regulations were re-targeted at those health and safety risks where lives could be saved at lowest cost, some 60 000 more deaths could be avoided each year without increasing regulatory costs[45] (Teng and Graham, 1997, p. 173). Hahn (1996) concluded that "[T]he differences in cost-effectiveness across regulations suggest that there is significant potential for achieving much greater risk reduction at a lower cost to society".

Legalistic and adversarial styles have produced more complex, detailed and inflexible regulations than those in many other countries.

Complex, detailed, and inflexible federal regulations undermine policy results and raise the cost of policies.

One reason why much US regulation is not cost-effective is that legalistic and adversarial administrative styles produce more complex, detailed, and inflexible regulations than those in other OECD countries. This undermines the results and raises the cost of policies.[46] Economists have noted that "many of the laws Congress has passed call for highly prescriptive and often excessively costly regulation".[47] Regulations that mandate specific technologies, rather than set standards and allow industry to develop least cost methods of achieving them, are common. Superfund regulations on cleaning up toxic waste sites and corporate average fuel economy standards for cars are often cited as regulations whose costs vastly exceed benefits. Problems have been identified with coherence and consistency, both horizontally across the US government and vertically in federal/state relations.

A vicious cycle is seen: disappointment with regulatory performance produces demands to "tighten up" standards, which further worsen the problems of complexity and rigidity.

A study of nursing home regulation found that the United States has adopted over 500 federal standards, supplemented by state standards. Australia has adopted 31 broad results-oriented standards. Yet the Australian standards produce the best results and best compliance, and by a very wide margin. Pursuit of reliability in US regulations produced so much complexity and detail that policy performance declined. A vicious cycle appeared: disappointment with regulatory performance produced demands to "tighten up" standards, which further worsened the problem of complexity and rigidity (Braithwaite, 1993).

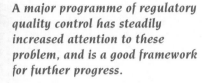
The regulatory process itself has become so encumbered that regulatory problems are difficult to fix.

The regulatory process itself has become so encumbered and adversarial that even commonly-recognised regulatory problems are hard to fix. A presidential inquiry found that a federal agency needed an 18-foot chart, with 373 boxes, to explain the rulemaking process, and "this process was not unusually complex" (Gore, 1993). Producing new regulations or revising old ones often requires several years. Judicial review is routine for important regulations, increasing uncertainties and delays and encouraging risk-avoidance in the administration.

The US government has tackled some of these problems by steadily improving its capacities to produce high quality social regulations.

A major programme of regulatory quality control has steadily increased attention to these problem, and is a good framework for further progress.

Within the constraints of the federal policy process, the capacities of the federal government for improving the quality of social regulation are among the best in OECD countries (see Figure 2.1) and establish a sound framework for further progress. An important measure of success is that, unlike in many countries, regulatory problems are sufficiently transparent and well-defined to support specific remedies. Critical regulatory quality controls in place are summarised in Box 2.2.

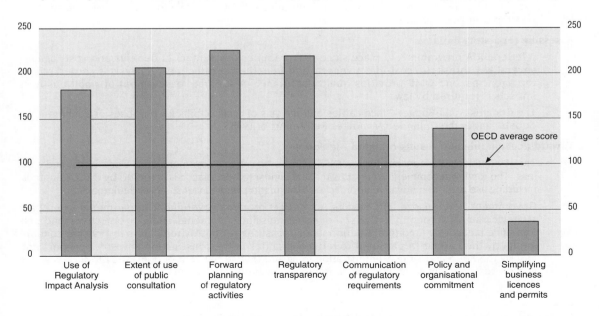

Figure 2.1. **Indicators of strengths and weaknesses in the US regulatory system (These synthetic indicators measure US scores against the OECD average, measured as 100)**

Explanation: These indicators measure the formal aspects of national regulatory reform policies. They do not directly measure the intensity and effectiveness of application of those policies, and hence may not be a good proxy for results.
Source: Public Management Service, OECD, based on information from OECD countries, March 1998.

One lesson to be learned is the value of persistence, policy stability, and political support over the long term.

An impressive element of reform is the steady effort over 20 years to improve analytical capacities and acceptance of the benefit-cost principle within regulatory agencies. The lesson to be learned is the value of persistence, policy stability, and political support over the long term in embedding new ways of thinking into bureaucracies.

Box 2.2. Managing regulatory quality in the United States

Ensuring regulatory transparency:

– A public forward planning system for regulations allows citizens "to be a well-informed participant in the regulatory matters that affect your life", according to Vice-President Gore.* The comprehensive Unified Agenda of Federal Regulatory and Deregulatory Actions is published twice a year, while the Regulatory Plan is published annually as a statement of the Administration's regulatory policies and priorities.

– When draft regulations are proposed, the "notice and comment" process permits open and accessible consultation that allows all interested voices a chance to be heard.

– Once a regulation is adopted, it is easily accessible to affected entities. Final regulations are indexed and published in the consolidated Code of Federal Regulations, which is also available on-line on the Internet.

Promoting regulatory reform and quality within the administration

– Reform policies are established directly by the President on the basis of his executive authority. The Vice-President is identified as the principal advisor to the president on regulatory policy, planning and review.

– Day to day centralised oversight and quality management is conducted by the Office of Management and Budget, located at the very centre of government. The OMB has a strong co-ordination, reviewing, and reporting role for regulatory reform.

Adopting explicit standards for regulatory quality

– President Clinton's 1993 executive order requires regulators to identify the problem to be addressed and assess its significance, identify and assess alternatives to direct regulation, design regulation in the most cost-effective way, regulate only upon a reasoned determination that benefits justify costs, avoid regulations that are inconsistent or duplicative with other regulations, and draft regulations to be simple and easy to understand.

Assessing regulatory impacts

– A federal RIA programme, in place since 1981, requires assessment of benefits and costs against several key threshold, cost-effectiveness, and benefit-cost principles. Analysis is carried out by the agencies, and OMB provides quality assurance. A separate assessment of small business impacts is required by law.

– The Congressional Budget Office carries out analysis of costs of bills for purposes of Congressional debate, under the Unfunded Mandates Reform Act of 1995.

Toward accountable and results-oriented regulation

– The 1993 National Performance Review (NPR) aims to "to create a government that works better and costs less" The Review recommended reforms that are similar to best practices accepted by OECD countries, including use of more innovative approaches to regulation, and consensus-based rulemaking.

– Government Performance and Results Act of 1993 requires government departments to prepare strategic plans that identify, among other issues, mission statements, strategic objectives, and performance measures. Among the performance measures set out by regulators in 1999 are commitments by the Labour Department to reduce fatalities in the construction industry by 3 per cent, and by the Food and Drug Administration to assure that 40 per cent of domestic produce is grown and processed using good practices to minimise dangerous contamination.

---

* Statement by the Vice-President, The Regulatory Plan, 29 October 1997, FR 57003.

A key strength is a high level of transparency. Consultation is open and inclusive, some problems merit attention.

"Notice and comment" procedures increase the quality of policy by reducing the risk that special interests will have undue influence.

Transparency of regulation is essential to an environment that promotes competition, trade, and investment. The primary mechanism for transparency in the United States is a standardised system of public consultation as regulations are developed and revised. The Administrative Procedure Act of 1946 establishes a legal right for citizens to be consulted, and mandates minimum procedures. These "notice and comment" procedures create open channels for public discussion, and increase the quality and legitimacy of policy by reducing the risk that special interests have undue influence. The procedure is simple in theory:

- An agency publishes a proposed rule in the Federal Register (the federal gazette). The regulatory impact analysis is summarised.

- The public is usually given at least 30 days to comment in writing. The agency must consider any comments received. All comments are made public in a formal rulemaking "record".

- When an agency publishes a final rule, it must explain its factual and legal basis, and how it dealt with the public comments.

Yet public consultation tends to be adversarial and procedural, rather than an attempt to communicate and find solutions.

Notice and comment has resulted in a relatively open and accessible regulatory process consistent with international good practices. That said, serious problems with consultation are rooted in the legalistic and adversarial tendencies of the US regulatory system. Notice and comment has tended to develop into a formalistic process that prevents rather than promotes dialogue, co-operation, and communication. It can resemble court proceedings, more focussed on legal procedure than finding efficient solutions. An inquiry by Al Gore noted that, in the past, agencies had sometimes already made their decisions even before the comment period.[48] There have been complaints that interests have unequal capacities to participate in the consultation process.

The key task is to marry a high level of transparency with development of a less adversarial and more efficient system for consultation.

The key task is to marry a high level of transparency with development of a less adversarial and more efficient system for consultation. The National Performance Review recommended that agencies investigate more flexible and more interactive means of consultation, provide assistance to regulated groups to enable them to participate more effectively, increase programme evaluation and make better use of information technologies. Panels of interested citizens have been successfully used in other countries as a supplement to other forms of consultation, though their use in the United States is hampered by inflexible statutes. To support such steps, however, a more thorough reassessment of the notice and comment process and of current administrative procedures is needed. Communication through the Internet has the potential to transform access to decision-making, and even within the current system has already increased participation.

Mechanisms to promote regulatory quality within the public administration are strong.

To promote regulatory reform, both the president and the Congress carry out strong oversight.

Mechanisms to promote reform inside the administration are needed to maintain policy coherence and keep reform on schedule. Both the president and the Congress carry out strong regulatory oversight, the president through a central office accountable directly to him, and the Congress through oversight committees, and investigations by its agencies such as the Congressional Budget Office.

Competition between president and Congress for influence over regulatory decisions has contributed to the emergence of an unusually centralised and hierarchical process for regulatory quality control. The role of the Office of Management and Budget (OMB) within the Executive Office of the President is among the most powerful of the central regulatory oversight bodies in any OECD country. Expert and located at the very centre of government, OMB is responsible for reviewing the cost-effectiveness of major regulations, and for management tasks of government closely linked to regulatory reform, including preparation of the President's budget and legislative review. Direct participation by OMB in these policy processes gives it the capacity to be effective in promoting broad-based reform across the administration. Its dependence on strong presidential support to stop poor regulations supported by the line departments is evidence, however, that administrative processes cannot substitute for strong political leadership.

Regulatory oversight by the Congress is increasing. Recently, it has passed laws requiring that regulations be tabled in the Congress for scrutiny and that costs of new laws on state and local governments and the private sector be assessed. The effect of these new mechanisms on regulatory quality is not yet clear.

The use of regulatory impact analysis as an input to decisions is more widespread and rigorous than in other OECD countries.

The United States was the first country to adopt broad requirements for benefit-cost analysis for regulations.

The OECD Report on Regulatory Reform recommended that governments "integrate regulatory impact analysis (RIA) into the development, review, and reform of regulations". The United States was the first OECD country (in 1981) to adopt broad requirements for regulatory benefit-cost analysis (Jacobs, 1997) and is still one of only a handful of countries to use a benefit-cost test. Such a test is the preferred method for considering regulatory impacts because it aims to produce public policy that meets the criterion of being "socially optimal" (*i.e.*, maximising welfare).

The high priority placed on regulatory analysis reflects a belief that regulators are not truly accountable to the electorate unless the consequences – the social benefits and costs – of their actions are known. Today, quantitative benefit-cost analyses are prepared for over 90 per cent of major social regulations, but only 18 per cent of major economic regulations. (OMB 1998.) OMB provides quality control and guidance for these analyses. RIA has only recently been prepared for primary legislation as part of Congressional processes under the Unfunded Mandates Reform Act of 1995, and its value in improving the quality of primary legislation has yet to be proven.

US experience shows that RIA, when well prepared, helps increase the net social benefit of regulations.

Evidence is building that RIA, when well prepared, helps increase the net social benefit of regulations. In 1987, EPA analysed its experience with RIA in 15 cases and concluded that a $10 million expenditure on RIA had reduced the costs of rules by $10 billion, or a benefit/cost ratio of 1 000 to 1 (EPA, 1987). The General Accounting Office found in 1998 that that, out of 20 RIAs, 12 were used to identify the most cost-effective approaches and that several others helped define the scope and timing of implementation (GAO, 1998).

Yet weaknesses in the quality and completeness of the analysis contribute to wide variance in the quality of federal regulations.

Yet weaknesses in the quality and completeness of the analysis contribute to wide variance in the quality of federal regulations. In 1997, OMB reported that, out of 41 regulations, only in eight cases did agencies provide monetised benefits estimates, while cost estimates were presented in 16 cases. Hahn (1997) found that in fewer than 20 per cent of RIAs were benefits monetised and shown to justify costs. His analysis found important inconsistencies – within and between agencies – in assumptions and methodology. These included the use of different discount rates, the failure to present BCA in net present value terms and wide variations in assumed benefits for reduced death and injury rates. It also seems likely that the multiple assessments now required – benefit-cost analysis, small business analysis, paperwork analysis, and unfunded mandates analysis – are fragmenting efforts and reducing analytical quality overall.

Despite efforts to spur innovation, the federal regulatory system lags behind in flexible and market-oriented regulatory approaches.

Lagging regulatory innovation and sluggish responsiveness in social regulation impose a hidden drag on economic performance.

Many countries are expanding use of innovative policy instruments that are flexible and market-oriented. These approaches spur, rather than block, innovation and adjustment in the economy. One of the anomalies in American regulation is that positive social views toward competition have not led to a greater use of market-based approaches to problem-solving. Market approaches have been recommended for years, most recently by the Vice President's National Performance Review. However, US regulation appears to be less innovative than that in other OECD countries. Only one national system of marketable permits for air emissions exists, though the benefits of the approach are well-documented. Other countries use taxes to restructure incentives to a much greater extent than does the United States, suggesting missed opportunities for cost-effective action. Voluntary approaches, more often used in other countries, have been hampered by inflexible US statutes.

Innovation has been hampered by legalistic styles, risk-avoidance, and cumbersome procedures.

Efforts to expand the use of innovative instruments have struggled with legalistic styles, risk-avoidance, and cumbersome procedures, combined with weak accountability for regulatory results, that discourage experimentation and learning. Positive initiatives include:

– A pioneering law – the Performance Management and Results Act of 1993 – should strengthen incentives to innovate to improve programme results. The Act requires regulators to establish concrete performance measures and annual plans.

– Another good practice is to better use the states as testing grounds. A 1998 agreement[49] gives the states greater scope to implement innovative ideas for achieving better environmental outcomes. More attention to good practices in other countries could also spur regulatory innovation.

– General rules[50] for local air-pollution-permit trading were proposed by the EPA to speed up use of emissions trading by the states.

Innovation will be boosted by increasing attention to policy results, using the states as testing grounds, and learning from other countries.

At the heart of the most severe regulatory problems is the quality of primary legislation.

Poor quality laws limit, and threaten to reverse, the benefits from regulatory reform.

At the heart of the most severe regulatory problems in the United States is the quality of primary legislation. The trend toward higher quality in delegated regulation cannot be seen in the quality of primary legislation in the Congress. This limits, and threatens to reverse, the benefits from regulatory reform. Strikingly, major laws, such as the Clean Air Act, prohibit regulators from using good decision practices. Innovation and the development of more cost-effective policy approaches are often blocked by rigid legislation. Rational priority-setting is difficult. The Environmental Protection Agency "is hobbled by overly prescriptive statutes that pull the agency in too many directions and permit managers too little discretion to make wise decisions", concluded a recent report of the National Academy of Public Administration.

More so than in other OECD countries, the United States has found it extremely difficult to improve legislative quality and coherence. This is partly structural, arising from the constitutional balance of powers between the executive and the legislative. And, unlike parliamentary systems, bills originate from many sources. The result is that there is less attention to quality of laws than to decisions authorised by those laws.

Recent reforms, such as the legal requirement that the Congressional Budget Office estimate the costs of proposed legislation and "unfunded mandates" on state and local governments, are positive. But if it is to have value, the Congress will have to integrate such information in its deliberations. Current proposals to establish a new congressional agency to study the costs and benefits of regulations could improve the attention of the Congress to the downstream consequences of its legislative decisions.

The most important determinant of the scope and pace of further reform is the attitude of the Congress.

In the end, it will be the management of a more results-oriented relationship between the executive and the legislative that will determine the scope and pace of regulatory reform in the United States. Without genuine progress at the legislative level in placing accountability on results and in encouraging risk-taking and policy innovation, it is doubtful that the executive branch can make substantial additional progress in improving the quality of delegated regulations, or can even preserve the progress that has been made. Yet Congressional incentives to relinquish control over how policies are carried out in return for more accountability for policy results are not strong.

OECD 1999

Chapter 3

THE ROLE OF COMPETITION POLICY IN REGULATORY REFORM

A robust competition policy is one of the pillars of regulatory reform, the 1997 OECD Report on Regulatory Reform concluded. Competition principles provide a market-oriented policy framework to guide reform, and competition policy can be a better alternative to economic regulation to protect consumer interests. US experience in sectoral regulation described in Chapter 1 vividly demonstrates the positive interaction between regulatory reform and competition policies.

Competition principles provide a market-oriented framework for regulatory reform in the United States.

Competition principles are woven tightly into the legal framework for regulation, and are backed up by strong watchdog institutions.

Regulatory reform in the United States is market oriented, consistent with the pervasive competition doctrine underlying the Federal use of regulatory powers. Competition principles are woven tightly into the legal framework for regulation, and are backed up by strong watchdog institutions. Where regulation has impaired competition, the legal and policy foundation for reform is already present. This has provided reforms of economic regulation, *ad hoc* though they may be, with a stable long-term policy framework that adds coherence, legitimacy, and credibility to reform. This is one of the key reasons why the United States started earlier and moved faster with regulatory reform than did many countries.

Box 3.1. **The roots of competition policy in the United States**

Government support for competition in the marketplace was formalized in the first national competition laws, the 1887 Interstate Commerce Act and the 1890 Sherman Act, which created federal powers and institutions to apply principles derived largely from common law. The Supreme Court called the Sherman Act "a comprehensive charter of economic liberty aimed at preserving free and unfettered competition as the rule of trade", resting on the premise that "the unrestrained interaction of competitive forces will yield the best allocation of our economic resources, the lowest prices, the highest quality and the greatest material progress, while at the same time providing an environment conducive to the preservation of our democratic political and social institutions".*

---

* Northern Pacific Railway Co. *v.* United States, 356 US 1, 4 (1958).

*US competition policy aims
to promote consumer welfare,
protect the competitive process,
and enhance economic efficiency.*

The US concept of competition policy is basically economic, though there are complexities and occasional contradictions in objectives. Its principal aims are to promote consumer welfare, protect the competitive process, and enhance economic efficiency, aims also pursued through regulatory reform. Its underlying principles assert that:

– Consumer welfare is improved by greater variety, higher quality, and lower prices, and is protected by eliminating restraints that reduce the impact of consumer preference in setting price and output.

– The competitive process is protected by preserving static and dynamic conditions that discourage collusion and permit efficient entry and innovation.

– Efficiency is promoted as competition forces firms to lower costs and respond to market signals.

Laws and enforcement capacities are strong, and provide credible assurance that public interests will remain protected in the absence of economic regulation.

*The United States has strong
competition institutions
and enforcement capacities.*

The United States has strong, well-established enforcement institutions, and so many enforcement methods that maintaining co-ordination and consistency among them is a continual challenge. The two enforcement agencies – the Antitrust Division of the Department of Justice and the Federal Trade Commission – are both staffed by lawyers and economists, both combine policy expertise and prosecutorial duties with political accountability (achieved in different ways), and both implement competition policy by applying general principles case by case. The parallel structure has not historically led to conflict, as the two agencies have managed to avoid duplication and forum shopping. But co-ordination of policies and actions imposes costs.

*Crucially, transparency is high,
and enforcement decisions
do not appear to depend
on political influence.*

Due to institutional independence, a strong tradition of professionalism, and judicial oversight, enforcement decisions do not appear to depend on political influence. Both agencies publicise decisions to initiate actions. Final decisions from the courts or the Commission are almost always accompanied by detailed explanations. But there are concerns that, when the agencies settle a case without a trial, public explanations give little guidance on how doctrines are developing. In some respects, notably concerning the time and expense of their procedures, the agencies' own regulatory process may be improved. Unnecessary delay has long been a concern about competition cases.

*Judicial review provides
a constant process of defining
and balancing the roles
of competition policy institutions
and regulators.*

Competition policy illustrates the important role of the courts in establishing and co-ordinating national regulatory policy. The meaning of the basic competition laws is determined principally by a common-law process in which courts are the highest authorities. The courts also play important roles in interpreting the laws that establish regulatory programmes. The mediating role of the judiciary helps keep US competition policy coherent, despite multiple participants and laws. Judges may be required to acknowledge and accommodate many objectives and effects of different legal aims. The result is a constant process of defining and balancing the roles of competition policy institutions and those responsible for economic and social regulation. The increasing influence of judges with an economic perspective has reinforced the economics-oriented antitrust policy of the last 20 years.

But involvement of many different regulators and other bodies in implementing competition policy may increase uncertainty and inconsistency.

The breadth of support for competition principles has diffused responsibility for implementation. Because so much US economic policy is based on competition, many different regulators and other bodies, in both federal and state governments, implement competition policy. Such wide diffusion risks weakening competition policy by increasing uncertainty. Duplication and second-guessing are virtually inevitable. Resources expended on co-ordination could be better applied to analysis and enforcement.

Competition enforcement policies are stringent, credible and well-designed to deal with potential market abuses in the aftermath of regulatory reform.

Anxiety about reform and deregulation has been to some extent overcome by the credibility of competition law enforcement.

Competition enforcement tools are among the most stringent in OECD countries. Anxiety about reform and deregulation has been to some extent overcome, by the credibility of competition law enforcement. Agreements among competitors about the critical competitive dimensions of price and output can be treated as crimes, subject to felony penalties of high fines and imprisonment. The effect or reasonableness of the prices or market divisions agreed on is not relevant; such agreements are illegal *per se*. Other kinds of horizontal agreement may also be illegal, but their legality depends on the outcome of the "rule of reason" test, that is, on a review of net competitive effects. Sanctions for violation of competition law are unusually harsh, which makes it harder to apply sanctions to conduct that had been previously permitted or even required by other government regulation. High penalties encourage claims for exemption, special treatment, or even regulation as a substitute for competition enforcement. Recognising the risk of disproportion, the agencies have brought most actions against horizontal constraints in regulatory settings as civil, not criminal, cases.

Mergers are handled flexibly so that competition authorities can tailor their actions to the market structures of different sectors.

Mergers are handled flexibly so that competition authorities can tailor their actions to the market structures of different sectors. Mergers and combinations, including joint ventures and open market acquisitions, are covered by the Clayton Act. In part because the statutory test is phrased explicitly in terms of competitive effect, merger law is perhaps the purest expression of the economics-based approach to competition policy. Markets are defined based on data about actual and likely cross-elasticities and substitution responses. Assessment of likely effect depends critically on the long-term significance of entry. Possible entry by a firm that could exit quickly, at no cost, is treated differently than possible entry by a firm that would have to commit sunk resources. Different treatment of entry can be significant in regulatory settings. Hurdles faced

---

Box 3.2.   Competition policy and enforcement support regulatory reform

The law on horizontal agreements has often been used to ensure that deregulated industries become competitive. After airline deregulation, executives attempting to fix prices were indicted.[1] Another suit stopped concerted practices by which airlines tried to establish or maintain price agreements by signaling through computer networks.[2] Tariff bureau agreements about trucking rates were challenged as horizontal price fixing.[3] A non-compete agreement between cable TV firms was challenged as market division.[4]

Self-regulation has been a particular target. Competition law has been used to break down "ethical" constraints that professionals and other service providers have imposed on themselves, typically via their trade associations. The seminal action was the Federal Trade Commission's successful complaint against the American Medical Association for banning price advertising and contracting practices.[5] Scores of other actions followed.

Concerning vertical relationships, state-level regulations mandating exclusive sales territories or protecting dealers and franchisees against contract partners or competitors have been challenged. In health care markets, competition enforcers have sued to eliminate price protection clauses where their net effect may be to discourage entry and price reductions. And agency advocacy has criticized proposals to force medical coverage plans to admit "any willing providers" as contract parties, because the requirement is likely to dampen competition for lower prices.

---

1. United States v. American Airlines, 570 F. Supp. 654 (N.D. Tex. 1983), revÕd, 743 F.2d 1114, 1119 (5th Cir. 1984), cert. dismissed, 474 US 1001 (1985).
2. United States v. Airline Tariff Publishing Co., 1994-2 Trade Cas. (CCH) ¦Ê70,687 (DDC,1994).
3. Southern Motor Carriers Rate Conference, Inc. v. United States, 471 US 48 (1985); New England Motor Rate Bureau v. FTC, 908 F.2d 1064 (1st Cir., 1990).
4. In 1994, the FTC settled charges brought in l988 that Boulder Ridge Cable TV and Weststar Communications, Inc, entered into an agreement not to compete against each other as part of BoulderÕs acquisition of Three Palms, Ltd. The FTC alleged that the agreement was not limited to the area in which the acquisitions occurred.
5. American Medical Association, 94 FTC 701 (1979), affÕd, 638 F.2d 443 (2d Cir., 1980), aff'd *per curiam* by an equally divided Court, 455 US 676 (1982).

---

by a "facilities-based" competitor could be higher than those faced by a reseller of an incumbent's basic service.

Access to essential facilities has been enforced in network industries.

In network industries, law enforcement has ensured access to "essential facilities" in regulatory settings such as telecommunications and electric power (see Box 3.3).

Box 3.3.   Competition enforcement to restructure network monopoly

A Sherman Act monopolisation case, filed in the 1970s, restructured the national telephone system. The consent decree issued in 1982 separated manufacturing, long distance, and local service operations. The basis for the action was the incumbent monopolist's efforts to exclude competitors in equipment and long distance services. The judge considered public comments about how the proposed divestiture would affect other regulatory requirements, including the responsibilities of state-level regulators.* But the consent decree led to prolonged, continued controversy, about the respective competences of the judge, the Antitrust Division, and the sectoral regulator to implement further reforms in telecommunications.

---

*   United States v. AT&T, 552 F. Supp. 131, 150, 153 (DDC, 1982), aff'd *sub nom*. Maryland v. United States, 460 US 1001 (1983).

Private litigation has played a significant role in regulatory reform but this is not a substitute for determined government action.

Private litigation has played a significant role in competition policy and regulatory reform by supplementing government enforcement. Private enforcement, through suits for treble damages or injunctions, has been available since 1890. But the cost and uncertainty of private litigation mean that this is not a substitute for determined government action. Treble damages and attorneys' fees awards were included in the law to compensate for the high cost and risk of taking on a firm that is often the plaintiff's supplier or major competitor. However, now that class actions are available to aggregate many small claims, and criminal fines have greatly increased, it may be worth reconsidering whether awarding exemplary damages in antitrust cases is still a sound policy.

Box 3.4.   Private litigation and regulatory reform

Private litigation played a significant role in deregulating professional services. The landmark case of *Goldfarb* v. *Virginia State Bar* applied the antitrust laws for the first time to the professions. The Supreme Court held that minimum fee schedules for lawyers, adopted by a county bar association and enforced through disciplinary action by the state bar, constituted private, anti-competitive activity. This decision opened the way to private litigation and government enforcement challenging restrictions on professionals' business practices.

Enforcement is complemented by strong advocacy by competition authorities to promote regulatory reform.

US competition agencies have been unusually active in promoting competitive, market methods and outcomes in policy- and regulatory processes. Their advocacy contributed to the first major deregulation successes in airlines and natural gas and continued with trucking, communications, broadcasting, and electric power. Advocacy interventions in recent years have included:

- Price and rate regulations affecting long distance telephone service, liquor distribution, and marine pilotage.

- Entry in such contexts as allocation of airport landing and take-off privileges, certified public accounting, local multi-point telephone and video distribution services, automobile sales, and conveyancing.

- Output regulation such as television's prime time access rules, must-carry rules for television retransmissions by satellite and open video system, and restrictions on collision damage waivers for automobile rentals.

- Limitations on forms of practice, such as rules against commercial relationships by optometrists and veterinarians with non-professionals and against linkages between cemeteries and funeral establishments.

The level of advocacy activity declined in the 1990s, probably because the easier battles at the federal level have been won. Today, the Antitrust Division concentrates advocacy almost entirely on federal agencies and departments, while the FTC addresses about half of its efforts to state and local issues.

Competition policy is closely integrated with consumer policy, reinforcing a virtuous circle of market initiative and openness.

Dealing with both competition and consumer protection in the same organisation allows closer integration of the two complementary policies.

Antitrust and consumer protection policies are complementary tools for achieving the benefits of market competition, and the FTC is responsible for both policies. The general competition law is intended to ensure that markets provide consumers with an appropriate range of options, while the general consumer protection law is intended to ensure that consumers can select freely and effectively from the options offered in the market. Having both responsibilities in the same organisation allows closer integration of the two complementary policies.

Application of competition principles has sometimes been undermined by conflicting regulatory policies exempted from competition law.

Many special industry rules, sectoral regulators and exemptions constrain application of the competition laws.

In the US legal system, competition policy often enjoys priority over regulatory policies. Exercise of authority by another regulatory body will not usually displace competition law. If Congress wants to exempt conduct from competition law or apply special rules, it must say so clearly. It has done so, often. A surprisingly large number of special industry rules, and sectoral regulators and exemptions constrain application of the basic competition laws.

Most national regulation that fixed prices, limited output, reduced quality, divided markets or constrained entry has been eliminated. Many of the remaining sector-specific agencies apply competition policies consistently with the competition agencies. But there is room for more progress. Remaining differences in treatment may not be clearly justified by compelling public interests. The transport sector offers several examples (see Box 3.5). Trucking has been free of nearly all economic regulation since 1995, when Congress pre-empted the remaining state-level regulations. But pockets of regulated immunity remain, the most troublesome being the exemption and economic regulation of household goods removal. There was concern that reform would leave the industry's consumer protection rules unenforceable. But protecting consumers does not require permitting movers to agree not to compete. Industry collusion may mean that individual consumers, lacking the information or bargaining power of larger customers, may receive poorer service or pay too much.

Where regulatory programmes co-exist with general competition laws, introduction of competition principles appears to be proceeding better.

In other sectors, notably energy and telecommunications, regulatory programmes have co-existed with the application of general competition laws. And in those sectors, the introduction of competition principles through the regulatory process appears to be proceeding better. The courts have instructed the regulators to include competition policy in their application of regulatory statutes. Congress has also supported the move toward deregulation, and the competition agencies have encouraged these moves, offering advice and assistance.

Special rules about other sectors show more complex relationships. In banking, overlapping laws and specialised regulators institutionalise the balancing of competition policies against policies on liquidity, solvency, and safety. Consistency in the application of competition principles is accomplished, somewhat inefficiently, by the threat that the competition agency will act independently, and by the fact that decisions are subject to review and correction by general jurisdiction courts. In agricultural sectors, a special competition regime applies to co-operatives, and another to meat-packing, while Depression-era legislation permits the Secretary of Agriculture to issue marketing orders, with the practical effect of enforcing cartels.

Many exemptions and special rules respond to pleading by industry interests.

Many exemptions and special rules obviously respond to pleading by industry interests. Indeed, most of these were enacted after the beneficiaries were found liable for violating the law. The business of insurance is not subject to competition law if it is regulated by state law. A special law substantially immunises the soft drink industry's vertical manufacturing and distribution structures. Some sports leagues are permitted to pool the rights to broadcast their games, in order to sell them as a package to broadcast networks without antitrust liability. And otherwise competing newspapers may enter joint operating arrangements, if all but one is in probable danger of financial failure.

Box 3.5. Sectoral problems with special merger authority

Deregulation of air transportation was a success of competition-based reform. The government-enforced cartel was dismantled in the late 1970's and the regulatory agency was abolished in 1985. But the Department of Transportation (DOT) retained exclusive jurisdiction over mergers among domestic airlines until 1989. DOT approved essentially all of the transactions it reviewed, apparently under the belief that new entry would prevent any exercise of market power. Economic studies have shown that, where these combinations led to eliminating rivals and higher concentration at several hub airports, prices were significantly higher because passengers had fewer choices.

The rail freight system has been substantially deregulated since 1980. But the Surface Transportation Board retains authority over mergers, and it has power to correct complaints about railroads' exercise of market power. In 1996, STB approved the largest merger in US rail history, between two of three major railroads in the western United States. The Antitrust Division urged the STB to reject the merger, because the divestitures required to fix the threats to competition would not be worth the effort. But STB approved the merger with minor conditions. Within a year, severe and persistent operating problems and capacity limitations developed on the merged system. The STB apparently believed that its own regulatory interventions could remedy market power problems. But STB's actions in response to the crisis were tentative, and did not solve the problems.

These failures show the hazards of fragmenting competition policy enforcement among sectoral regulators. As fundamental changes in the deregulated industries attracted new entrants, stimulated reorganisations, forced bankruptcies, and invited new combinations, concerns over the long-term implications of restructurings are heightened. Oversight would probably be better performed by a competition agency with its broader background and perspective.

One protected "special interest" is the government itself. The United States does not submit government entities involved in commercial operations to its competition law. This exemption, unusual in OECD countries, may be significant for government owned power systems, hospitals, and port authorities affected by regulatory reform.

State regulations that impede competition are numerous, and can slow adjustment in key sectors.

The "state action doctrine" exempts private anti-competitive conduct from antitrust law if the conduct is explicitly authorised by state policy.

Another major set of exemptions arises from the US commitment to federalism. The "state action doctrine" exempts private anti-competitive conduct from antitrust law if the conduct is explicitly authorised by state policy. Decisions applying this doctrine have permitted anti-competitive state regulation of transportation, hospitals, health care and other professional services, retail distribution, utilities, residential and commercial rent, and other areas. The doctrine demonstrates that national competition policy, though privileged in relationship to US national regulatory policy, may be less important than some other political values, in this case federalism.

The state action doctrine permits anti-competitive state and local legislation that reduces the benefits of federal regulatory reform. State regulation and special legislation may delay reform, not only in professional services and distribution, but also in telecommunications and electric power. The doctrine and anti-competitive state laws that impair competition affecting interstate commerce are within the power of Congress to correct by federal legislation.

Chapter 4

ENHANCING MARKET OPENNESS THROUGH REGULATORY REFORM

Market openness further increases the benefits of regulatory reform for consumers and national economic performance. Reducing regulatory barriers to trade and investment enables countries in a global economy to benefit more fully from comparative advantage and innovation. With the progressive dismantling of traditional barriers to trade, "behind the border" measures are more relevant to market access, and national regulations are exposed to unprecedented international scrutiny by trade and investment partners. Regulatory quality is no longer (if ever it was) a purely "domestic" affair.

US domestic regulation is largely consistent with market openness principles, which has boosted trade and inward investment.

US domestic regulation contributes to one of the OECD's most open national markets for global trade and investment.

Maintaining an open world trading system requires regulatory styles and content that promote global competition and economic integration, avoid trade disputes, and improve trust and mutual confidence across borders. US domestic regulation is largely based on these principles, and contributes to one of the OECD's most open national markets for global trade and investment. Moreover, competition and market openness in the United States promotes good regulation elsewhere through international competition, demonstration, and persuasion.

The benefits for the United States are considerable. Market-opening regulation promotes the flow of goods, services, investment and technology between the United States and global commercial partners. Expanded trade and investment generate consumer benefits (greater choice and lower prices), raise the standards of performance of domestic firms (through the impetus of greater competition), and boost GDP. Some US regulators have recognised the potential gains to be won from market-opening regulatory reform. In telecommunications services, the FCC expects that "competitive forces will soon result in higher quality, lower priced, more innovative service offerings".[51]

The country's rank as the world's largest host of foreign direct investment underscores the value of US policy to regulate inward investment activity as little as possible.

The country's rank as the world's largest host of foreign direct investment[52] underscores the openness and value of US investment policies. US policy is to regulate inward investment activity as little as possible, and there is no single statute governing foreign investment. While a host of federal, state and local laws governing such matters as anti-trust, mergers and acquisitions, wages and social security, export controls, environmental protection, health and safety have a significant impact on investment decisions, most of these are applied in a non-discriminatory fashion.

The US experience demonstrates the close and supportive relationship between quality regulation, competition, and market openness.

There is a virtuous circle: good regulation at home is good regulation for open markets...

US experience supports the proposition that good regulation at home is also good regulation for open markets. Reform of economic regulation has yielded opportunities for foreign traders and investors, though further progress in major sectors such as telecommunications and electricity is needed, in particular with respect to licensing requirements. Cost-efficient regulation and the search for greater analytical rigour in assessing the costs, benefits, and effects of proposed regulations supports legitimate domestic policies, but can also be market-opening. Likewise, the pro-competition policy stance in domestic markets results in regulation that is, on balance, trade and investment neutral.

... and, in turn, market openness encourages domestic regulatory reform.

The converse is also true: market openness encourages domestic regulatory reform as domestic firms find themselves in need of international rules and efficient regulation to compete with foreign firms.

But expansion of social regulation at federal, state and local levels presents new challenges for trade and investment.

Expansion of social regulation at federal, state and local levels, discussed in Chapter 2, presents new challenges for ensuring that legitimate domestic policies on health, safety and the environment do not unnecessarily restrict trade and investment. A range of initiatives to improve the quality of domestic regulation against benefit-cost, cost-effectiveness, and results tests (Chapter 2) has benefited foreign and domestic firms alike. For example, efforts at federal and state levels to streamline government formalities and "red tape" should benefit foreign traders and investors in the US market.

Concerns that trade liberalisation reduces regulatory protections demonstrate the need for co-ordination between market openness policies and reform aimed at cost-effective domestic regulation.

Concerns are expressed in the United States that, with trade liberalisation, competitiveness pressures could erode government capacities to maintain high regulatory standards. This problem is not discussed in detail in this review, but OECD studies (OECD, 1998, 1995, 1994) suggest that trade liberalisation can in some cases be a positive agent for improvement of social policies. In the absence of effective social policies, however, increased economic activity from trade liberalisation might indeed cause problems. These concerns demonstrate again the need for careful co-ordination between market openness policies and regulatory reform aimed at cost-effective domestic regulation.

The United States is ahead of the OECD average with respect to four out of six efficient regulation principles.

The OECD efficient regulation principles seem to be given ample expression in practice, particularly transparency and openness of decision-making.

The United States is well ahead of the OECD average with respect to all but two of the efficient regulation principles (see Figure 4.1). While not all of the principles are codified in US administrative and regulatory procedures, they seem to be given ample expression in practice. This is most clearly the case for transparency and openness of decision-making, which help to mitigate the complexity and high procedural costs of the US regulatory system (see Chapters 2 and 3).

Market openness could be further enhanced by firmly embedding respect for the principles across all levels of government.

At the same time, US market openness could be further enhanced by finding ways to embed respect for the efficient regulation principles across all levels of government. Further efforts should be made with respect to non-discrimination, avoidance of unnecessary trade restrictiveness, recognition of equivalence of other countries' regulations and conformity assessment systems, and reliance on internationally harmonised standards as the basis of domestic regulations.

Domestic mechanisms for transparency and public consultation set a high standard for openness to foreign parties as well.

Foreign traders and investors are well-positioned to participate actively at various stages of federal rulemaking processes...

The mechanisms on which regulatory transparency is based in the United States are described in Box 2.2 in Chapter 2. The "notice and comment" procedure sets a high standard of transparency and opportunity for comment by interested parties – national or

---

Box 4.1.   **The OECD efficient regulation principles for market openness**

To ensure that regulations do not unnecessarily reduce market openness, "efficient regulation" principles should be built into domestic regulatory processes for social and economic regulations, and for administrative formalities. These principles, described in *The OECD Report on Regulatory Reform* and developed in the OECD's Trade Committee, have been identified by trade policy makers as key to market-oriented, trade and investment-friendly regulation. They are similar to the principles of competition and cost-effectiveness on which current US regulatory reform is based. This review does not judge the extent to which the United States has complied with international commitments, but assesses whether and how domestic regulations and procedures are consistent with these substantive principles.

- *Transparency and openness of decision-making.* Foreign firms, individuals, and investors seeking access to a market must have adequate information on new or revised regulations so they can base decisions on accurate assessments of potential costs, risks, and market opportunities.
- *Non-discrimination.* Non-discrimination means equality of competitive opportunities between like products and services irrespective of country of origin.
- *Avoidance of unnecessary trade restrictiveness.* Governments should use regulations that are not more trade restrictive than necessary to fulfil legitimate objectives. Performance-based rather than design standards should be used as the basis of technical regulation; taxes or tradable permits should be used in lieu of regulations.
- *Use of internationally harmonised measures.* Compliance with different standards and regulations for like products can burden firms engaged in international trade with significant costs. When appropriate and feasible, internationally harmonised measures should be used as the basis of domestic regulations.
- *Recognition of equivalence of other countries' regulatory measures.* When internationally harmonised measures are not possible, necessary or desirable, the negative trade effects of cross-country disparities in regulation and duplicative conformity assessment systems can be reduced by recognising the equivalence of trading partners' regulatory measures or the results of conformity assessment performed in other countries.
- *Application of competition principles.* Market access can be reduced by regulatory action condoning anticompetitive conduct or by failure to correct anticompetitive private actions. Competition institutions should enable domestic and foreign firms affected by anti-competitive practices to present their positions.

Figure 4.1. **The trade-friendly index of the US regulatory system**

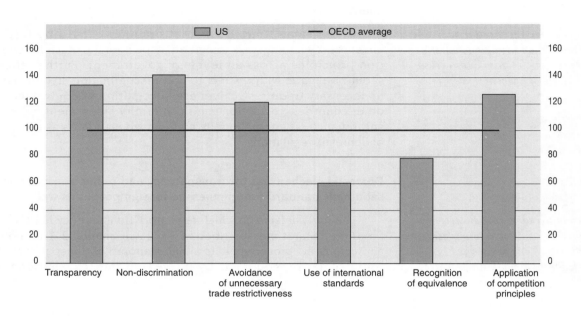

Explanation: These indicators measure the formal aspects of national regulatory reform policies. They do not directly measure the intensity and effectiveness of application of those policies, and hence may not be a good proxy for results.
Source: Trade Directorate, OECD, based on information from OECD countries, March 1998.

non-national. Foreign traders and investors are well-positioned to participate actively at various stages of rulemaking processes. Other procedures to improve the quality of domestic regulations – such as forward planning for future regulations, and publication of regulatory impact analyses – give foreign competitors opportunities to act as informed and potentially influential participants in the regulatory process. Extensive use by the US government of the Internet across a wide range of agencies and departments could prove a powerful tool in further enhancing regulatory transparency worldwide.

... but respect for transparency at state and local levels should be encouraged.

Nonetheless, federal procedures are only part of the story. The complexity and reach of subfederal regulation underscores the need to encourage respect for transparency at state and local levels. Co-ordination of federal regulatory reform with efforts at state and local levels will be increasingly relevant to international market openness.

Discriminatory regulatory content is rare, however, there are enduring exceptions.

The United States makes effective efforts to share information about preferential agreements to those interested.

Preferential agreements give favourable treatment to specified countries and are thus inherent departures from two core principles of the multilateral trading system – Most-Favoured-Nation (MFN) and National Treatment (NT). To reduce discriminatory impacts, third countries need access to information about their content and operation to make informed assessments of impacts on commercial interests. The United States, party to two free trade agreements[53] and a network of bilateral investment agreements, makes effective and good faith efforts to share this information as widely as possible. Information is readily available through many avenues. Generally, information on actions to be taken by the United States and requests for comments on proposed actions are published in the *Federal Register* and made available by US agencies through press statements, fact sheets, or the Internet. Submission of information to the WTO and both FTAs improve transparency through public notice.

Overtly discriminatory regulation is rare, but discriminatory elements in regulation for maritime transport, domestic air services, and trucking cabotage block foreign participation.

Overtly discriminatory regulation is rare. Regulatory reform has eliminated many opportunities for discrimination. However, there are enduring exceptions. Discriminatory (nationality-based) elements in regulatory structures for maritime transport services, domestic air services, trucking cabotage, and operation of power facilities preclude foreign participation. US commitments in the WTO Financial Services Agreement grandfather deviations from the non-discrimination principle. Nationality-based restrictions in important sectors have been in place for long periods, suggesting the need for a comprehensive review of prevailing measures and their economic rationales. As seen in Box 4.2, subfederal regulation also risks generating discriminatory effects.

There are gaps in the measures taken to avoid unnecessary trade restrictiveness of regulations.

To avoid unnecessary trade restrictiveness, regulators should assess the impact of regulations on international trade and investment; consult trade policy bodies, foreign traders and investors in the regulatory process; and ensure access by foreigners to dispute settlement.

The regulatory impact analysis programme does not assess regulatory impacts on inward trade and investment.

In the United States, the principal tool for measuring the effects of proposed federal regulations is regulatory impact analysis, or RIA (see Chapter 2), based on benefit-cost and cost-effectiveness principles. The RIA programme does not, however, require assessment of regulatory impacts on inward trade and investment. Hence, information on potential impacts on trade and investment is most likely to surface during the public comment phase, which is open to foreign and domestic parties. The onus is on foreign firms to make their concerns known. Their capacity to do so is thus closely linked to regulatory transparency. Too, the RIA mechanism does not cover the rulemaking activities of the independent federal commissions.

A second line of defence is also weak. OMB and USTR consult informally when questions arise with respect to regulatory compliance with WTO commitments. Proposed regulations with no obvious impacts on international obligations would normally escape scrutiny. OMB staff are not trained to assess the trade effects of proposed regulations. USTR is neither mandated nor staffed to review the 4 000 federal regulations proposed each year for adverse effects on inward trade and trade-related investment. Under this system, there is a risk that the trade-restrictive effects of a regulation will be identified only after damage has occurred, and trade frictions have arisen.

Differing standards and duplicative certification procedures between the United States and trading partners reduce trade flows.

A relatively low use of international standards in the United States is a cause of trade frictions.

The United States has produced many standards widely used in the global market, but trading partners point to a relatively low use of international standards in the United States as a cause of trade frictions. The European Commission contends that "the relatively low use, or even awareness, of standards set by international standardising bodies" is a problem in the United States, and that although a "significant number of US standards are claimed to be 'technically equivalent' to international ones, and some are indeed widely used internationally, very few international standards are directly adopted". In some cases, "US standards are in direct contradiction to them."[54] Trading partners also complain about what is perceived to be an extremely complex system for public and private, federal and sub-federal standards.[55] They criticise the latitude of private quality

---

Box 4.2.   **Sub-federal regulation and market openness**

Chapters 2 and 3 describe how US regulation is a complex mix of federal, state and local rules and enforcement procedures. Regulation at sub-federal levels violates the principles of efficient regulation more often than does federal regulation. Sustaining and increasing market openness in the United States will require additional efforts to embed the principles into these levels of government.

- In a 1992 case involving federal and state measures for alcoholic and malt beverages, a GATT panel found that Canadian producers were discriminated against by state regulatory requirements on listing and delisting, beer alcohol content, distribution to points of sale, transport into states by common carriers (as opposed to transportation of a product by a producer or wholesaler in its own vehicle), and licensing fees.*

- Some states require direct branches or agencies of foreign banks, but not bank subsidiaries of foreign banks, to register or obtain licenses in order to engage in some banking activities. Some states restrict various commodities transactions by foreign bank branches and agencies, but not by other depository financial institutions.

- Government procurement laws at the state and local level contain "Buy American" and "Buy Local" provisions similar to those contained in the federal Buy American Act which give preferential treatment to domestically and locally produced goods. These provisions are superseded by non-discrimination commitments under the WTO GPA, when applicable. In addition, some states (California) have amended their laws to prevent preferential treatment. However, since state governments account for roughly half of US public purchases, considerable scope remains for discriminatory purchasing practices.

- State procurement laws can also take on an extraterritorial dimension in support of broader policies. In 1996, Massachusetts enacted a law regulating state contracts with companies doing business with or in Myanmar. According to a trading partner, the state government created a "restricted purchase list" of companies that meet a set of "negative criteria" stipulated in the law. In principle, companies so identified would be barred from bidding on state contracts or, when allowed to bid, subject to less favourable terms. In November 1998, the US District Court found the law to be unconstitutional as it impinged on the exclusive authority of the federal government to regulate foreign affairs.

---

* See United States: Measures Affecting Alcoholic and Malt Beverages, Report by the Panel adopted on June 1992 in Basic Instruments and Selected Documents (39S/206).

Source: GATT Basic Instruments and Selected Documents; 1998 Report on the WTO Consistency of Trade Policies by Major Trading Partners, Industrial Structure Council, Japan.

assurance organisations, such as the Underwriters Laboratories, to impose – and modify frequently and unpredictably – the use of non harmonised standards.[56]

Increased US reliance on third party certification and on international standards as the basis of domestic regulations is promising.

The poor performance of the United States on the OECD trade friendly index with respect to the use of international standards (see Figure 1) is, however, somewhat misleading, since many US standards have a *de facto* international application. Recent moves to increase US reliance on third party certification and on international standards as the basis of domestic regulations are promising.[57] Better US participation in international standards development is also needed. International standards are often developed without adequate US input or representation, and the US administration is concerned about effects on competitiveness.[58] Complex standardisation and conformity assessment procedures should be streamlined to improve market openness.

In recognising the equivalence of regulatory measures in other countries, US policy is moving in the right direction.

Progress has been made in recognising the equivalence of regulatory measures and conformity assessment.

The United States has made progress in recognising the equivalence of trading partners' regulatory measures and results of conformity assessment:

- Unilateral approaches are used in some cases, such as the Department of Transportation's self-declaration of conformity with safety standards for the automotive sector.

- The US-EC MRA signed in May 1998 provides a framework for recognition of conformity assessment procedures for several products (telecommunications equipment; electromagnetic compatibility; electrical safety; recreational craft; pharmaceutical good manufacturing practice; and medical devices).

- Regional trade agreements have been a useful mechanism. Chapter 9 of NAFTA requires partner countries to "accredit, approve, license or otherwise recognise conformity assessment bodies in the territory of another Party" on a national treatment basis without requiring further negotiation.

- The 1998 EU-US Transatlantic Economic Partnership aims to improve regulatory co-operation in manufactured goods; agriculture; services; electronic commerce; and intellectual property rights.

Application of competition principles from an international perspective are broadly satisfactory.

Foreign firms generally enjoy non-discriminatory treatment to pursue competition cases.

US procedures for initiating and advancing complaints about alleged anti-competitive regulatory or private actions are satisfactory from the perspective of market openness. Though different procedures may introduce uncertainties into the handling of particular complaints, foreign firms generally enjoy non-discriminatory treatment to pursue cases along the track they see fit.

Closer co-ordination between OMB and USTR oversight of regulatory quality could enhance complementarity between trade and domestic policies.

Closer working relations between OMB and USTR processes could avoid regulatory problems before they surface in the market.

One reason that domestic regulations sometimes surface as trade irritants is the failure to identify problematic regulations early in the process. The quality management process for regulation described in Chapter 2 – based on quality principles and oversight by the Office of Management and Budget – does not require explicit consideration of trade impacts. The Office of the US Trade Representative (USTR) oversees implementation of transparency provisions relating to US obligations, and those on non-discrimination; national treatment; prohibition of unnecessary obstacles to trade;

Box 4.3. US social regulation and trade

Social regulations aim to protect public interests such as health, safety, and the environment, the interests of consumers and vulnerable social groups. These policies fall within the realm of national sovereignty. While social regulations may not be expressly discriminatory or trade-restrictive, their design or implementation may introduce *de facto* barriers to trade. In most cases, measures can be taken to regulate effectively while not unnecessarily affecting market openness. The following examples illustrate the trade implications of some US social regulations as seen by some trading partners.

- **Environmental Regulations:** A WTO case involving reformulated gasoline shows how some environmental regulations can have trade impacts. Under a law requiring that only "reformulated gasoline" be sold in highly polluted areas, the Environmental Protection Agency issued regulations on the composition and emissions effects of gasoline to improve air quality. In the regulations for reformulated gasoline, EPA methodology for determining domestic refiners' baselines was based on quality data and volume records for 1990, while most importers (also foreign refiners) were required to use a different baseline set by the EPA. Levels required of foreign refiners were seen as more difficult than those required of US refiners. Venezuela and Brazil successfully argued in the WTO that these regulations violated the principle of national treatment. In 1997, EPA removed the discriminatory element of the regulation.

- **Health regulations:** The 1990 Nutrition Labelling and Education Act requires certain products to be labelled with respect to content, but some trading partners have alleged that the rules differ from international labelling standards established by the Codex Alimentarius. Additional state-level requirements may apply to agriculture and food imports.

- **Plant health regulations:** Phytosanitary regulations for fruits and vegetables set by the Department of Agriculture (USDA) are viewed by some foreign producers as unnecessarily burdensome. Exporters seeking entry to the US market for commodities that may carry pests or diseases must pay for all USDA expenses to research and approve quarantine treatments for products. Shipments of the fruit or vegetable may be subject to an inspection process in both the country of origin and the US port of entry.

- **Consumer protection regulations:** The American Automobile Labelling Act requires passenger vehicles and light trucks to bear labels indicating the percentage of value added in the United States and Canada. The intent is to help consumers make informed decisions. But some foreign competitors see the law as a *de facto* "Buy American" provision. Other features of the law, such as methodology for calculating US content of cars produced by foreign automakers within the United States, are viewed by some trading partners as expressly discriminatory.

Principal sources: 1998 Report on the WTO Consistency of Trade Policies by Major Trading Partners (Industrial Structure Council, Japan); EU Sectoral and Trade Barriers Database; US Trade Barriers to Latin American Exports in 1996 (UN Economic Commission for Latin America and the Caribbean); Opening Doors to the World: Canada's International Market Access Priorities, 1998.

use of international standards, recommendations and guidelines; and considerations of equivalence. USTR is not directly concerned with the making of domestic regulations on a day-to-day basis, but closer working relations between OMB and USTR processes could promote the efficient regulation principles, enhance complementarity between trade and domestic policies, and avoid regulatory problems long before they surface in the market.

Trade and investment friendly regulation can be compatible with strong regulatory protections. High-quality regulation can be trade-neutral or market-opening, coupling consumer gains from enhanced market openness with more efficient domestic policies in areas such as the environment, health and safety. But it is doubtful that this can be achieved in the absence of purposeful, government-wide adherence to the principles of efficient regulation. Avoiding the potentially restrictive effects of domestic regulation through more focused attention to these principles would benefit US consumers and economic performance.

Chapter 5
REGULATORY REFORM IN THE ELECTRICITY INDUSTRY

In the United States, as in most OECD countries, regulatory reform in the power sector lagged behind that of other sectors, but is beginning to catch up. The complexity of regulatory reform in the federal structure in the United States, the benefits and risks of further competition and consumer choice, and the need to balance multiple economic and social policy goals within a comprehensive programme of reform are illustrated in dramatic reforms now underway in the sector.

Reform must balance the diversity of interests and powers among many different actors.

The principal aim of electricity reform is to stimulate competition in power generation and deliver the benefits to consumers. But other aims are pursued in the regulatory regime.

The principal aim of reform in the electricity sector is to stimulate competition in power generation and supply and deliver the benefits of competition to consumers. But many other aims are pursued in the regulatory regime. The federal government desires lower government spending and increased reliability. Its social goals include cleaner generation, increased energy efficiency, and reduced greenhouse gas emissions, along with protection of consumers and adequate service to the poor. State-level environmental goals include reducing emissions in fossil-fuel based states and maintaining wildlife populations in hydropower-based states.

Structural and legal constraints also determine the reform path: the federal structure of the country, the diversity of starting points among different states, the emphasis on individual rights and private property even in this sector which in other countries is often government-owned.

A complex institutional setting increases the difficulty and risk of comprehensive reform...

The complex institutional setting increases the difficulty and risk of comprehensive reform. The industry is dominated by several hundred vertically-integrated, investor-owned companies, which typically operate local franchise monopolies. These are regulated by the Federal Energy Regulatory Commission (FERC) and by utility commissions in every state. Several large federal power projects sell power wholesale. Many government-owned state and local utilities deal directly with end-users. Private, independent producers sell power to distribution systems. Voluntary organisations of private and public utilities ensure system co-ordination and reliability. Specialised regulators oversee nuclear power, financial markets, and environmental protection.

... but open public discussion stimulated arguments over regulatory design, reduced the threat of capture by special interests, and improved the outcome.

The openness of US regulatory processes led to a characteristically high level of public debate about reform. Federal and state reforms have been discussed by utilities, academics, regulators and other officials, at conferences and public meetings and in the newspapers, trade press and academic literature. Public discussion has stimulated arguments over the design of mechanisms and institutions, reducing the threat of capture by special interests and in principle improving the outcome generally. The open process helped to co-ordinate the interests of diverse jurisdictions and interests.

A central challenge of reform is to encourage competition in power generation and supply by ensuring fair access to the grid...

To ensure "fair" access to the grid, utilities are required to offer competing firms the same information and services available to their own generators. But competition authorities recommend deeper "operational" separation.

Effective competition among generators requires that competing generators have non-discriminatory access to the transmission grid. Vertically integrated utilities are increasingly required to separate power generation from transmission and distribution. FERC rules limit discrimination by requiring utilities that own transmission facilities to offer competing generators the same information and services that they give to their own generators. But US competition authorities

---

Box 5.1.   Diversity of electricity generation among states

The type of generation varies greatly among areas of the United States. The Pacific Northwest has overwhelmingly hydropower, the Midwest overwhelmingly coal, the mid-Atlantic coal and nuclear, and the Northeast a mix of coal, oil, and nuclear. This heterogeneity results in a range of average state prices,* hence of stranded costs, and the pattern of public ownership (since, in the United States, large water control projects are, historically, publicly owned).

Geographic distribution of generation by energy source

Census division	Terawatt-hours	1997 net generation by energy source (percentage)					
		Coal	Petroleum	Gas	Hydro	Nuclear	Other
New England	73.0	26.2	30.8	14.1	6.4	22.5	
Middle Atlantic	308.4	43.4	3.5	7.6	9.4	36.0	
East North Central	520.0	79.9	0.4	1.2	0.8	17.7	
West North Central	253.4	74.9	0.5	1.5	6.7	16.4	
South Atlantic	633.4	60.3	4.7	6.0	2.0	27.0	
East South Central	331.5	70.1	0.9	2.0	7.3	19.7	
West South Central	429.9	49.4	0.2	33.4	1.9	15.1	
Mountain	282.1	69.0	0.1	3.9	16.6	10.4	
Pacific Contiguous	273.7	3.1	0.1	13.9	69.3	13.6	
Pacific Noncontiguous	12.7	1.9	66.1	23.8	8.2	0	
US Total	3 125.5	57.2	2.5	9.1	10.8	20.1	0.2

---

*   Average state prices for industrial users varied from 2.7 cents per kilowatt-hour to 10.0 cents per kilowatt-hour in 1996 (EIA, 1998a). In California, the price of electric power was 30 to 50% higher than the United States average. Much of the five-fold difference in average cost among 136 vertically integrated IOUs is attributed to the degree of participation in nuclear power. Smaller factors are the degree of exposure to independent power purchase agreements under the 1978 Public Utilities Regulatory Policy Act, and exposure to exogenous regional differences in factor prices and resource endowments (White, p. 218).

Source: US Department of Energy, Energy Information Administration 1998d, Tables 7 to 13.

recommend "operational" separation or "structural" separation (divestiture) over "functional" separation. They argue that functional separation leaves in place both incentives and opportunity for utilities to discriminate against competitors, and that regulatory oversight to detect problems, such as subtle reductions in quality of service to competitors, is difficult.

... preferably through divestiture of some generation assets...

Divestiture is constrained by private property rights, so some states provide powerful financial incentives for firms to sell off their generation capacity.

Divestiture of generation from transmission eliminates both the incentive and the opportunity to discriminate. It also reduces concentration in power generation. Yet divestiture is constrained by the rights of private property, and the legal tools to mandate divestiture are not yet in place. Many regulators are not empowered to order divestiture. To avoid these limitations, some states, such as California and Arizona, provide powerful financial incentives for firms to sell off some or all of their generation capacity. Already, a significant amount of the fossil-fuel generating capacity in California and in New England has been divested to new owners from outside these areas.

... and by creating trading institutions such as spot and future markets to improve price transparency and deepen markets.

Spot markets both facilitate competition and dampen volatility...

Spot markets have been established in more liberalised jurisdictions such as California. As Chapter 1 noted, spot markets can facilitate competition by improving liquidity and price transparency, and reducing transactions costs. Buyers can more easily compare and switch among competing generators. As spot markets develop, they will help dampen volatility. A well-publicised episode of price spikes in the Midwest in 1998 prompted establishment of a centralised, deep spot market to reduce the risk of a repetition. In addition, an open market for electricity futures has operated for several years. Initially based on two nominal locations in the West, futures contracts are now spreading across the country. Options contracts have been introduced, too. Buyers can turn to these other instruments, as well as financial instruments based on natural gas, to reduce their exposure to electricity spot market risk.

... but pricing for transmission services does not provide incentives for efficient investments in transmission and generation capacity.

Pricing for transmission services still does not reflect market incentives well. Some regions have already experimented with alternatives to traditional methods, such as varying prices in different delivery zones or even at particular locations (termed "nodal" pricing), corresponding to differences in costs and demand. These experiments may help discover a workable pricing method that better reflects transmission costs, and thus provides incentives for efficient investments in transmission and generation capacity.

Expanding the role of markets has required new institutions to safeguard competition.

The independent systems operator is the new watchdog to ensure fair access to the grid, and safe and reliable operation.

An important means to prevent anti-competitive discrimination in new electricity markets is the "independent system operator" (ISO). ISOs are a new institution designed to reduce the ability to discriminate in access to the transmission grid – even while it is owned by vertically integrated utilities – and to ensure system reliability. Four ISOs were approved, as of July 1998, in various states and regions. ISOs are managerially and operationally independent of the vertically integrated utilities. FERC rules require only "functional" separation, but FERC encourages formation of regional ISOs to achieve deeper "operational" separation.

The effectiveness of this form of separation will depend on assuring the ISO's real independence, from generators, transmission owners, and users, while maintaining access to the vertically integrated firms' technical competence in order to ensure safe and reliable operation. Different systems have adopted different governance structures to deal with these concerns. In California, a board of political appointees oversees both the ISO and the spot market operator; in New England, the ISO is monitored by the state regulators.

The effectiveness of this new institution is not yet proven, and experimentation continues.

States are experimenting with different approaches. Some ISOs perform many functions, such as managing transmission tariffs and the spot market. Others limit their function to managing the transmission grid. The institutional structure of ISOs is evolving with experience. No ISO has operated long enough to show whether this new institution will deliver on its promise, to maintain reliable and efficient operation while preventing anti-competitive discrimination. Meanwhile, other options are being examined, such as transmission companies that combine the ownership of the grid with the responsibilities of an ISO, that could ultimately be a better institutional solution.

The second major reform with potential for substantial consumer gains is introduction of retail-level competition at state levels.

Several states already permit end-users to choose their electric power supplier, and Federal reforms, if adopted, would permit all end-users to choose their electric power supplier by 2003.

The second major reform is promoting competition to supply all end-users. This "retail" competition (or "full end-user choice") is allowed, but not required, under federal law, and is a matter of state regulatory policy. Several states already permit end-users to choose their electric power supplier. End-user choice provides generators with greater incentives to compete. As of July 1998, Massachusetts, California, and Rhode Island (partially) had introduced retail competition, nine other states had enacted laws leading to retail competition (by dates ranging from 2000 to 2004), and several others were advancing. A federal reform proposal would permit all end-users to choose their electric power supplier by 1 January 2003; however, it would permit individual states (and certain non-regulated utilities) to opt out if, after a public proceeding, they find that another policy would better serve consumers. This reform is projected to result in US$20 billion or more in annual consumer benefits by raising the productivity of the average utility.

The prices end-users pay have been regulated, for the most part, by the state public utility commissions. Most states provide a transitional price-cap for residential consumers. In California and Massachusetts, for example, for several years after open access the maximum residential price is to be ten per cent below the former regulated price.

The third major reform element is to resolve disputes about private property rights through policies on "stranded costs".

Mitigation, measurement, and compensation of stranded costs was an essential condition for launching market reforms.

Mitigation, measurement, and compensation of stranded costs was an essential condition in the United States for launching market reforms. Stranded costs are unamortised costs, prudently incurred under the prior regulatory regime, that will not be recovered in a market environment. They are due mostly to investments in nuclear generation and in long-term power purchase agreements. Compensation for stranded costs reduces the incumbent firms' incentive to resist competition.

The distribution of stranded costs and benefits has important wealth effects, so the decision about who pays for stranded costs is important for political and consumer support for reform. Estimates of their magnitude vary widely, but a likely mid-range is US$135 billion to US$200 billion. These figures are sensitive to assumptions about future market prices and the date when open, direct access becomes effective. But by any measure, stranded costs are large enough, in comparison to book value and revenues, that the design of the cost recovery system will significantly affect the sector's future development.

Putting stranded cost charges in a tariff that does not vary with use will reduce distortions of market behaviour.

In the United States, decisions about how to measure and recover stranded costs are the responsibility of the regulators for assets and operations under their jurisdictions. The key regulatory challenges are to provide incentives for incumbents to reduce stranded costs, to measure them accurately, and to design a means for recouping them that is fair but that does not impede efficient entry or pricing. Putting stranded cost charges in a tariff that does not vary with use will reduce distortions of market behaviour. Preventing users from by-passing the costs will avoid impeding efficient entry.

Environmental goals for the sector are increasingly met through market-based mechanisms...

Traditional measures such as subsidies and command and control regulation are increasingly supplemented by market-based measures.

Other policy goals are sometimes pursued by a combination of markets and direct government intervention. For environmental goals, traditional measures such as subsidies – cash, tax advantages, or surcharges on end-users – and command and control regulation are increasingly supplemented by market-based measures. A programme of tradable permits for sulphur dioxide emissions has significantly reduced SO_2 emissions from generating plants, as is discussed in Box 5.2. There is ample opportunity to expand the use of market instruments.

... and efficiency in generation of "green" electricity is encouraged by market-based choices of technology, generator, and price.

A market-based mechanism, is proposed to promote use of renewable fuels and increase the national share of green electricity to 5.5 per cent in 2010-2015.

Among other initiatives, the Clinton Administration proposes to use "renewable portfolio standards", a market-based mechanism, to promote use of renewable fuels. A specified percentage of electricity would be generated from renewable energy sources, subject to a price ceiling. Similar requirements already apply in some states.

This device encourages efficiency in the generation of "green" electricity. It creates two separate markets, one for electricity generated by renewable fuels and another for all other electricity. "Green" electricity is then traded in the competitive market at market prices. The state of Maine has imposed the largest required share of "green" generation, at 30 per cent (including hydropower). The Administration's proposal would increase the national share to 5.5 per cent in 2010-2015.

Diversity of state structures promotes faster innovation and learning in regulation, and benchmarking good performance.

State reforms are acting as "test beds" for reform in other states and at the federal level, promoting faster innovation and vigorous competition in reform.

State reforms act as "test beds" for reform in other states and at the federal level, promoting faster innovation and vigorous competition in reform. There are common themes in what reform-minded states are doing. Most, for example, are opening choice to all end-users at the same time, rather than phasing in choice for different classes of customers. In some states, reform efforts are limited. Idaho, with virtually the lowest electricity prices in the country, is not liberalising and is working to retain preferential access to low-cost federally owned hydropower. Michigan, with a local duopoly and constrained imports, allows some end-users to switch suppliers but has made few other changes. But Virginia, with an industry similar to Michigan's, will begin full retail competition in 2004.

Yet the federal structure also complicates reform, because the scope of efficient regulation extends beyond state borders.

Pacts about regulatory principles and decisions, within regions that coincide with electricity markets, could reduce the costs fragmented and inconsistent state regulation.

Costs of the federal structure arise from the need to build interfaces between different regulatory regimes, the efficiencies lost as regional markets operate under several sets of rules, and the need for individual firms to operate under multiple regimes. The largest cost is that regulatory jurisdictions do not match the most efficient

---

Box 5.2. Marketing pollution permits – cleaner air at lower cost

Marketable permit or obligation programmes provide an alternative to traditional regulatory techniques. If developed and applied appropriately, they can reduce the cost of regulation, increase compliance flexibility, and support economic-growth, while achieving regulatory goals.

Perhaps the best known example of such trading is the acid rain programme operated by the US Environmental Protection Agency that is designed to reduce US sulphur dioxide emissions by 10 million tons annually from 1980 levels. In the programme, emitters of SO_2, a precursor to acid rain, have been issued a finite number of allowances (permits) that can be used over the next 50 years. SO_2 allowances are denominated in tons of SO_2, but not by year. This is because acid rain is a cumulative problem, so the absolute amount deposited matters more than the timing.

Strict enforcement measures are built into the federal legislation for failure to demonstrate ownership of sufficient allowances. For intentional non-compliance, heavy fines and jail terms are possible.

The programme has produced significant unexpected cost savings, and reductions in emissions are ahead of schedule. Annual costs of meeting the full reductions are expected to be between $2 and $2.5 billion per year, about half the cost estimated originally. Costs are 25 per cent lower than achieving the targets through traditional regulation.

electricity market, which is probably regional. Some states are actively harmonising regulatory reforms to enlarge the market and reduce the costs of operating across state lines. Pacts about regulatory principles and decisions, within regions that coincide with efficient electricity markets, could reduce costs, while retaining flexibility to allow regulatory innovation.

Environmental policy provides an example of the potential for conflict. Electricity markets are generally larger than states, so generators competing in the same market are subject to different state environmental rules with different costs of compliance. Liberalisation implies that there are limits to differences in compliance costs between states in the same electricity market. If a state imposes rules that increase generating costs too much, more power might be generated in, and imported from, an adjacent state. To prevent this, Massachusetts requires that all power sold there must meet its environmental rules, no matter where it was generated. Rather than handle this issue state-by-state, it would be more efficient to broker these state policies at the federal level, or form regional pacts, to be sure that environmental externalities are fully internalised.

Regional regulatory regimes have been slow to develop, but should be the next major push for reform...

Under market conditions, voluntary compliance with reliability standards is expected to decline, and institutional changes may foreshadow the emergence of regional regulatory structures.

The reliability regime, which has worked well over the past three decades, will necessarily change as economic regulation of the electricity sector changes. Voluntary compliance with reliability standards is expected to decline. The system will probably move toward mandatory self-regulation, overseen by the independent regulators of the three North American countries. These institutional changes may foreshadow regional regulatory structures.

It is not clear whether efficient long distance transmission investments will be made under a system of state-by-state as well as federal regulation. It is not clear how the introduction of ISOs will transform the reliability regime, still based primarily on utilities. Some ISOs are limited to a single state, while others control multi-state areas. The reliability regime now divides the country into ten regions for co-ordination and control. Some predict eventual consolidation into perhaps three ISO-controlled systems for the entire country. Adapting state and federal regulatory regimes to these new functions and structures will take time and experimentation.

As choice expands, more consumer protection is needed.

The shift from regulated monopoly to market supply means consumers face new rights and risks. Some states have responded with initiatives to inform consumers about new rights.

Consumer protection issues and remedies are similar to those for other goods and services, and, as in other newly liberalised sectors, there is a transition role for enhanced consumer education. The shift from regulated monopoly to market supply means consumers face new rights and risks. In some reforming states, utilities have sent consumers brochures to tell them about the reform and its implications. California spent $89 million, mandated by the public utility commission, to inform consumers about their new right to switch electric energy suppliers. Confusion about the costs and

75

Controlling unfair marketing practices will require new regulations in some cases.

benefits of the new system can be met by requiring disclosure of separate charges, terms, and characteristics such as fuel mix and emissions, to help consumers make comparisons and evaluate the benefits of switching suppliers.

Experience from telecommunications deregulation has been applied in electric power to control an unfair marketing practice. "Slamming" is switching a consumer's account to a new supplier without the consumer's consent. California law requires third party verification that the consumer wants to switch, and provides a three day period for a small consumer to cancel a change without cost. California also requires sellers, marketers and aggregators to register, providing some protection that consumers will not be cheated by "fly-by-night" operators. Another concern is false advertising about "green" generation. The Federal Trade Commission has guides about environmental marketing claims, which explain legal requirements that such claims be truthful and substantiated.

Potential effects of reform on universal service are unclear, but some states are acting to protect low-income consumers in new markets.

Reforms in some states are designed not to endanger existing social protections to retail customers, which in the US regulatory

---

Box 5.3.   Experiment and conflict: variations among state and federal reform programmes

Since circumstances and powers vary among fifty jurisdictions, reform proposals and programmes also differ. Some differences are beneficial demonstration projects and experiments from which others can learn. But other differences represent conflicts over fundamental issues. California has moved to open access, while other states in the region are unsure, concerned about prices increasing as California bids supplies away.

Priorities about environmental goals: some states want to reduce their own emissions to reduce local pollution, some want emissions reduced in other states to reduce the effects of acid rain, and still others, with large hydro-power establishments, are concerned about protecting or restoring wildlife habitats.

Environmental issues: maine requires 30 per cent "green" power, but includes hydro-power in that total (because Maine has many dams); Massachusetts, in the same region, requires less, but excludes hydro-power – and also requires that imported power meet its own environmental standards.

ISO organisation and governance: in New England and the mid-Atlantic – Pennsylvania, New Jersey, Maryland, Delaware and Washington DC – the ISOs are under a two-tiered system, with independent governing boards (whose members are not affiliated with market participants) advised by committees of stakeholders. In California, the ISO and the operator of the spot market are both overseen by a board of political appointees.

ISO responsibilities: the mid-Atlantic ISO has the broadest responsibilities, for centralised dispatching, maintaining system stability and reliability, managing the open access transmission tariff, facilitating the spot market, and accounting for energy and ancillary services. The New England ISO has similar responsibilities, except for accounting functions. By contrast, in California, the ISO controls the transmission grid, but does not centrally dispatch, although it can revise the merit order in the spot market to manage the transmission grid efficiently.

Transmission pricing: zonal pricing is used in California, and nodal pricing in the mid-Atlantic (after a disappointing experiment with zonal pricing).

system are primarily issues of state, not federal, concern. In California and Massachusetts subsidies to low-income consumers will continue to be paid, out of a fee assessed on all end-users. Most systems incorporating retail supply competition provide for a "retail supplier of last resort," so that consumers are not cut-off from electricity supply. "Red-lining", or refusal to supply areas where service is less lucrative, is being countered in California with the requirement that utilities continue to supply areas they were assigned before open access became effective.

Chapter 6

REGULATORY REFORM IN THE TELECOMMUNICATIONS INDUSTRY

The telecommunications industry is extraordinarily dynamic. Rapid evolution of technologies has shaken up industries and regulatory regimes long based on older technologies and market theories. Twenty-three OECD countries now have unrestricted market access to all forms of telecommunications, including voice telephony, infrastructure investment and investment by foreign enterprises, compared to only a handful a few years ago. The industry's boundaries are blurring and merging with other industries such as broadcasting and information services.

Regulatory regimes must simultaneously promote competition and protect other social policies in dynamic markets.

Strong competition policies and efficiency-promoting regulatory regimes are crucial to the performance and future development of the industry.

While the role of regulatory reform in launching and shaping the rapid evolution of the industry has been described by some as pivotal, and by others as at best supportive, strong competition policies and efficiency-promoting regulatory regimes that work well in dynamic and global markets are crucial to the performance and future development of the industry.

The central regulatory task is to enable the development of competition in all telecommunications markets, while protecting other public interests such as reliability, universal service and consumer interests. Entry must be actively promoted in markets where formerly regulated monopolists remain dominant, and consideration must be given to convergence of separate regulatory frameworks applicable to telecommunications and broadcasting infrastructures and services.

The United States is a world leader in the reform of telecommunications regulation.

The 1984 antitrust action breaking up AT&T provides a striking example of the central role of competition policy in regulatory reform.

The United States pioneered the reform of telecommunications regulation. The famous 1984 divestiture which split AT&T into a long-distance company and seven local operating companies was a pivotal step that directly addressed underlying anticompetitive incentives, and provided a sound foundation for pro-competitive regulatory reform. It also helped to open network equipment markets and contributed, among many factors, to a dramatic decline in telecommunications switching and transmission costs. The 1984 antitrust action provides a striking example of the central role of competition policy in regulatory reform.

The structure of the US telecommunications industry is unique in OECD countries, and, consequently, so are the regulatory challenges.

By any measure, the telecommunications market in the United States is large. Nine of the world's twenty largest carriers are American. The total revenue of the US market at a little over $257 billion is equivalent to 42 per cent of the OECD total.

Regional monopolists are not permitted to compete in long distance markets in order to eliminate the incentive to discriminate.

The 1984 divestiture generated a market structure that is unique. Under the decree, AT&T was required to divest its local operating subsidiaries, creating seven Regional Bell Operating companies (the RBOCs) which, subject to some exceptions, were not allowed to provide "long-distance" service. The divestiture separated long-distance services and local exchange services. It defined 164 different Local Access and Transport Areas ("LATAs"), generally smaller than states, and stipulated that the RBOCs were not allowed to provide any services that crossed these lines.[59] RBOCs were not allowed to provide information services, either.

This structure was based on the view that local exchanges have natural monopoly properties, though developments have eroded those properties.

These restraints, by assuring that regulated monopolists could not compete in long distance or other competitive markets, eliminated the risk of discrimination between competing long-distance carriers and the monopolist's own long-distance service.[60] This structure was based on the view that local exchanges had natural monopoly properties, though technological developments since 1984 have eroded those properties.

Tendencies toward concentration can be seen as the market structure evolves, which may presage a stronger role for competition authorities.

Within these constraints, market structure continues to evolve.

Within these constraints, market structure continues to evolve. The number of important carriers in long distance markets has increased, though a recent merger between MCI and WorldCom, the second and fourth largest providers of domestic long-distance services, suggests that a period of concentration may be starting. Concentration has recently increased at the level of local exchange carriers. From the mid-1990s, US long-distance carriers entered into international alliances with carriers from other countries. To promote international competition, the alliances were permitted on the condition that safeguards are in place to assure that other US carriers have equal access to foreign local markets.

Consumers of long distance and mobile services have been the main winners from regulatory reform...

Regulatory reform facilitated a level of innovation that has transformed the industry and had positive effects throughout the economy.

The most important impact of regulatory reform is its contribution to facilitating a level of innovation that has transformed the industry and had positive effects throughout the economy. Regulatory decisions by the FCC played an important role in facilitating the development of markets for value added network services (*i.e.*, data processing) and for the rapid diffusion of the Internet in an unregulated environment. Estimates suggest that over thirty million people

Net economy-wide gains are estimated at between $4 and $30 billion per year, and consumers gained considerably more.

in the US use the Internet. Further diffusion of innovation is likely in future years as new initiatives, such as Internet II,[61] are considered.

The benefits of regulatory reform in the United States have been concentrated in long-distance, international and mobile communications markets. It is difficult to quantify these benefits, because they include dynamic elements such as new products and increased consumer choice. Crandall and Waverman (1995) provide an estimate of net economy-wide gains of between $4 and $30 billion per year. Consumers gained considerably more because firms have largely transferred efficiency gains to consumers, and have seen lower profits.

Overall costs to subscribers of long distance toll and international services (as well as mobile) have fallen significantly (see Box 6.1). Total revenue earned by domestic long distance and international carriers is currently well over $100 billion per year, therefore reductions in average price levels (30 per cent and higher) are saving US business and residential subscribers billions of dollars each year. Reductions in expenditures on telecommunications services also benefit consumers indirectly, since reductions in the costs of doing business generally translate into lower prices for goods and services throughout the economy.

... but distribution of direct benefits has been uneven with respect to both quality and price gains.

Customers who consume primarily local services have not seen significant benefits from price reductions, and may have seen price increases.

As Box 6.1 shows, distribution of consumer benefits due to price reductions has been uneven across users of telecommunications services. Large business customers enjoyed the most gains while the savings for individual residential subscribers varied, depending on calling patterns. Customers who consume primarily

---

Box 6.1. **Indicators of the effects of regulatory reform**

	Price changes (nominal)		Incumbent market share	
	1984-1992	1992-1996	1984	1996
Local Residential:	Up 45%	Up 5%	Near 100%	Near 100%
Intra-state Toll:	Down 10%*	Up 3%*	Near 100%	75%
Inter-state Toll:	Down 50%**	Down 17%	85%	55%
International:	N/A.	Down 33%	100%	55%
Mobile:	N/A.	Down 37%	Competitive	Competitive

* Based on Bureau of Labour Statistics data that does not include discount plans. Thus the data may understate price reductions.
** Includes both long-distance and international and composed only of AT&T information.

Source: FCC (1998), *Trends in Telephone Service*, CCB, July. Local price is the average monthly rate including taxes and the subscriber line charge, long-distance (interstate) and international is average revenue per minute. Mobile is average monthly bill and includes both cellular and broadband Personal Communications Service. Incumbent market share is according to total revenue.

Figure 6.1.   **OECD residential tariff basket, August 1998**[1, 2]

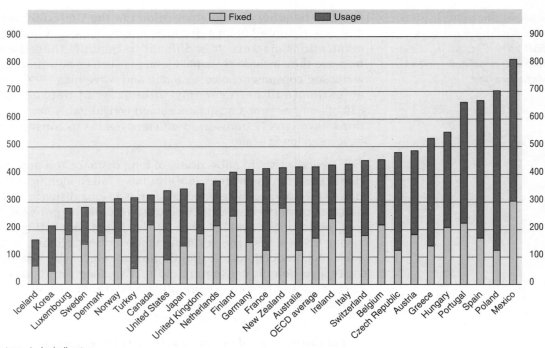

Notes: 1. Including tax.
        2. Calculation is based on PPP expressed in US$.
Source: OECD, Eurodata.

local services have not experienced significant benefits from price reductions, and may have seen price increases. Yet the overall price level of local services continues to be low in the United States, compared to other OECD countries (see Figure 6.1).

Similarly, the quality of telecommunications service has improved particularly for large business customers.

The quality of telecommunications service in the US has improved, particularly for large business customers, because of technological improvements and also because telecommunication operators compete on the basis for service quality. Moreover, the number of households with telephones increased over the reform period.

Despite considerable "downsizing" by carriers, since 1990 employment in the telecommunications industry as a whole has in fact grown modestly. Most of the growth in employment is the result of rapid growth in the radiotelephone (cellular, beepers, paging) industry.

The key policy challenge today is introducing competition into local markets.

The divestiture did not facilitate competition into local markets.

Divestiture did not facilitate competition into local markets. Conditions of entry into local markets varied, and still vary, significantly across states. In the early 1990s, some state regulators developed initiatives to extend the beneficial effects of regulatory reform

High expectations surrounding the prospects for cable companies and others to compete in local markets have been disappointed.

into their local markets. By 1995, at least 23 states had certified one or more local competitors.

There were high expectations surrounding the prospects for cable companies and Competitive Access Providers as possible entrants into local markets in the early 1990s. They possess potential alternative technologies since they "pass-by" more than 95 per cent of residences in the United States.[62] Yet potential new entrants have not been a significant competitive influence to date. Cable companies remain strong potential competitors as they develop the ability to provide broadband Internet access on a widespread commercial basis.

The approach to promoting local competition differs from the strategy for long-distance markets. The Telecommunications Act of 1996 attempts to strengthen earlier initiatives by making approval to enter in-region inter-LATA toll markets contingent on a demonstration that local markets are open to competition. This was meant to establish incentives for the RBOCs to open local monopolies in return for competing in long distance markets.

Local competition has not developed as quickly as hoped.

The US government has acknowledged that local competition has not developed as quickly as hoped.[63] The current share of nation-wide local service revenues of new entrants is about 1.4 per cent.[64] Applications from RBOCs in several states to enter long distance markets were rejected when the government concluded that the local markets were not sufficiently open to competition.

Box 6.2.   **Key features of the 1996 Telecommunications Act**

Interconnection: incumbent local exchange carriers (the incumbent "LECs") are required to provide interconnection to any requesting carrier at any technically feasible point. The FCC concluded that prices should be based on Total Element Long-Run Incremental Cost (TELRIC) plus a reasonable share of forward-looking joint and common costs.

Unbundling: incumbent LECs are required to provide requesting telecommunications carriers non-discriminatory access to network elements on an unbundled basis at any technically feasible point. The FCC concludes that prices should be based on TELRIC plus a reasonable share of forward looking joint and common costs.

Resale: incumbent LECs are required to offer for resale, any telecommunications service that the carrier provides at retail to subscribers. The FCC concludes that the price of resale services should be set at a discount off retail based on the costs that the incumbent LEC can avoid by selling at wholesale rather than retail.

Universal Service: an explicit mechanism to maintain local rates at affordable rates is mandated.

Access Charge Reform: to facilitate the development of an explicit mechanism for universal service, the FCC reformed the access charge rate structure.

Entry into long-distance: RBOCs are allowed to provide out-of-region inter-LATA service. A procedure is provided for under which the RBOCs are permitted to enter in-region inter-LATA when their local markets are found to be sufficiently open to competition. In assessing whether the local markets are open, the FCC is directed to give "substantial weight" to the DOJ's assessment of a "competitive checklist". Once an RBOC gains approval to offer inter-LATA service, they are required to do so subject to an accounting separation for a three-year period.

Forbearance: the FCC is directed to forbear from aspects of regulation that are deemed to be unnecessary.

Removal of State Barriers to Entry: state regulation that raises barriers to entry into local markets is pre-empted.

83

Yet local competition is promising due to technological advances in alternative delivery systems. Further regulatory changes can speed up competition.

Cable systems, mobile services and wireless local loop can provide local access that is superior to traditional networks in terms of bandwidth and speed.

There remains considerable promise for local competition to develop. Technological advances such as digitalisation, compression, fiber optics have paved the way for a variety of alternative delivery systems. Technological trials and small scale new entry[65] suggest that alternative networks – cable systems, mobile services and wireless in the local loop – can provide local access that is superior to traditional networks in terms of bandwidth and speed.

The speed with which these alternative delivery systems develop depends in part on regulatory developments.

The speed with which these alternative delivery systems are likely to develop depends in part on regulatory developments such as local rate rebalancing. Current geographic rate averaging requirements mean that some high-cost (*e.g.*, rural) subscribers are served at prices below true cost. These are the customers for which wireless technologies are likely to be most well suited. The speed with which these alternative delivery systems develop also depends on the speed with which new information services are introduced. There is an increased incentive to enter if a new network can expect to earn revenue from both voice telephony and other new information services.

Restrictions on RBOCs may be increasingly costly to the economy as the potential for competition grows.

Restrictions on RBOCs arising from the divestiture may become increasingly burdensome and costly to the economy.

The restrictions on RBOCs arising from the divestiture may become increasingly burdensome and costly to the economy (through loss of scope economies). These restrictions have had beneficial effects as a competitive safeguard and as an incentive to

---

Box 6.3. **Why has local competition not developed as quickly as anticipated?**

Local Rate Distortions? Are continuing subsidies that hold the price of local service below competitive levels impeding entry?

Technical Impediments? Many states do not provide intra-LATA equal access and number portability will not be fully implemented until 1999. Unlike traditional telecommunications carriers, cable networks' voice telephony service cannot operate in the case of a power outage. Have these technical barriers made entry unattractive?

Restraints on Competition? RBOCs have been prevented from providing one-stop-shopping – *i.e.*, providing local and long-distance service on a single bill. Prior to the 1996, AT&T and other interexchange carriers were faced with legal barriers to intra-LATA entry in some states. Are these barriers to providing one-stop-shopping inhibiting competition?

Judicial Uncertainty? Central aspects of regulatory policy are currently the subject of judicial challenge. Has uncertainty surrounding regulatory rules created a disincentive for investments by new entrants?

No Clear Strategy to Promote Facilities-Based Competition? Local competition initiatives in the US encouraged resale entry as well as some facilities-based entry. Would a focused effort to promote local interconnection at a small number of points of the network, and selected unbundling of elements (if any are necessary) be more successful?

Technical Problems Faced by Cable Operators? Efforts to provide telephony on cable networks have demonstrated technical problems. Were claims in the early 1990s that cable systems were capable of providing two-way communications excessively optimistic?

Incumbent LEC Anticompetitive Conduct? An objective of the 1996 Act was to give incumbent LECs an incentive to co-operate in facilitating competition. Was the promise of inter-LATA toll entry a sufficient incentive?

open local markets. However, as technological developments erode the case that local exchanges have natural monopoly characteristics and increase the importance of being able to provide "one-stop-shopping", the burden imposed by these restraints will become greater over time.

The dual federal-state roles can promote innovation, but also produces complexity and uncertainty in the regulatory regime.

Jurisdictional overlaps generate costs and uncertainties for market players.

Regulatory structures in the United States are complex webs that involve the states and the federal government, the relationship between sector-specific regulation and antitrust law, as well as between these agencies and the courts. In OECD countries such as Canada and Australia, the regulatory structure is simpler because there is exclusive federal jurisdiction. The dual federal-state role can give rise to both costs and benefits. The scope for states to pursue different policy initiatives can promote regulatory innovations. But jurisdictional overlaps generate costs and uncertainties for market players. In the highly litigious and adversarial regulatory environment (see Chapter 2) in the United States, uncertainties have bred legal challenges and costs.

Federal pre-emption in areas where states have been slow to act could be a step in the right direction.

Successes in reducing barriers to entry, promoting cost-based interconnection, rate rebalancing and equal access have been most pronounced at the federal level. The 1996 Telecommunications Act provides for the pre-emption of state legislation that raises barriers to entry. While it is too early to assess the implementation of this provision, it is a positive step in the right direction.

Implementation of universal service policies is generally efficient and non-distorting.

Promotion of "universal service" has been central to US telecommunications policy.[66] For many years, regulatory bodies at the state level maintained low prices for local telecommunication service facilitated by long-distance prices well above competitive levels.

Policies aimed at promoting universal service through distorting prices impede regulatory reform efforts to rebalance rates and thus giving rise to reductions in economic efficiency.[67] Introduction of competition erodes the ability to maintain price distortions thus causing proponents of other policy goals to oppose regulatory reform initiatives so as to protect implicit subsidies.[68] Cross-subsidies are coming under increased pressure to be eliminated or reduced. A growing number of countries are putting in place other funding mechanisms that are competitively neutral such as general tax revenues (Chile), contributions from carriers (United States) or contributions from spectrum auctions (Guatemala).

The three principal universal service programmes in the United States are generally consistent with these principles. Box 6.4 provides highlights of the reforms to universal service.[69]

85

Box 6.4. Reforms to universal service

1. Introduction of transparent and explicit support for universal service. All carriers satisfying specific conditions can obtain support from the federal Universal Service Fund regardless of the technology used. All carriers, including wireless carriers, are required to make contributions to the universal service fund based on end-user revenues. To qualify for access to the fund, a carrier must be able to offer (and advertise) service throughout a geographic region known as a "service area". The size of these service areas is left to the discretion of state regulators.

2. Revision and extension of subsidies for hook-up costs and the cost of monthly phone bills to qualifying low income customers (Lifeline and Link-Up America).

3. Introduction of a specific fund for the needs of schools, libraries and rural health care centers. Discounts to assist schools, libraries and rural health care centers to connect to the "Information Superhighway" were designed to cut between 20 and 90 per cent off the monthly charges of connecting to the network, and in some cases, some of the internal wiring costs. The discounts attracted applications from more than 40 000 schools and libraries.

4. Restructuring of the Subscriber Line Charge and the Common Carrier Line Charge, to partially transfer Universal Service Fund support costs to subscribers and interexchange carriers; increased subscriber line charges for second residential lines and multiline business customers; gradual phasing out of the existing traffic sensitive Common Carrier Line charge with a flat-rate Presubscribed Interexchange Carrier charge.

Application of benefit-cost analysis to telecommunications regulation should be strengthened.

Telecommunications regulations are not subject to the quality controls applicable to federal social regulations.

As an independent commission the FCC is, in general, not covered by presidential orders on regulatory quality (see Chapter 2). This is rooted in historical relations between the independent commissions and the President, but means that telecommunications regulations are not subject to the quality controls applicable to federal social regulations.

The 1996 Act provides two mechanisms for systematic review of FCC regulations. First, the Act provides for a "Biennial Regulatory Review". The FCC is required to review all regulations applicable to providers of telecommunications service in every even numbered year beginning in 1998, to determine whether the regulations are no longer in the public interest due to meaningful economic competition between providers of the service and whether regulations should be appealed or modified.

The 1996 Act also provides "forbearance" procedures to eliminate regulations that are no longer necessary given current market conditions.[70] Carriers can request initiation of the review procedure. While enactment of these provisions is an important step, they do not include an explicit recognition of the costs that regulation imposes, and important provisions of the 1996 Act are exempted.[71] Additional benefits are possible from a more systematic review process.

Regulatory reform is far from finished. Innovation in the sector will require continual review and adjustment.

Continued review and reform of the regulatory regime in this sector will be critical to encourage and permit new technologies to be brought into the market as quickly as possible.

Continued review and reform of the regulatory regime will be critical to encourage and permit new technologies to be brought into the market as quickly as possible. For example, despite the lack of local competition, technological change will continue to improve the prospects for entry in the next few years. As effective competitive safeguards are implemented in telecommunications industries and market forces introduced, the need for sector-specific economic regulation declines. As dominant positions of formerly regulated monopolists erode, reliance on market forces subject to economy-wide competition policy rules becomes a more effective means of promoting economic efficiency in the industry.

Chapter 7

CONCLUSIONS AND POLICY OPTIONS FOR REGULATORY REFORM IN THE UNITED STATES

The balance between economic deregulation and attention to better social and pro-competitive regulation is a valuable aspect of the US reform programme.

Starting earlier and from a lower level of economic intervention, the United States has gone further than most OECD countries in eliminating the most harmful types of economic regulations, but within the context of strong competition policies and more efficient forms of regulatory protection. It has also done more to build quality controls into the public administration to ensure that social regulations make the best use of national resources. The balance between economic deregulation and attention to building better social and pro-competitive regulatory regimes is among the most valuable aspects of the US reform programme. These difficult reforms were aided by a culture of market competition, market openness, and administrative transparency. It was helpful that these institutions were already in place and did not have to be built.

Other countries are catching up. Continuing attention to regulatory quality is needed if the United States is to enjoy competitive advantages from good regulatory practices.

The United States was in the forefront of regulatory reform ten years ago and still sets the benchmark in many areas, but the performance gap has narrowed. By being among the first to move to efficiency-enhancing regulation, the United States faced higher risks, but reaped more benefits in global markets. Today, other countries are catching up and in some areas, such as use of flexible regulatory alternatives, surpassing the United States. Continuing attention to regulatory quality is needed if the United States is to enjoy its traditional competitive advantages from good regulatory practices.

The results for consumers of sectoral economic reform in terms of prices, service quality, and choice are solidly positive, but only with sufficient attention to building pro-competitive regulatory regimes and to maintaining consumer and other protections. This demonstrates the complementary nature of less economic regulation combined with better social regulation.

Concerns that reform would reduce safety and consumer protection are not borne out, probably because these regulatory protections were not reduced in any of the reformed sectors.

The effects of sectoral reforms are still working their way through the economy, but the medium-term results are clear: *in almost every sector the results for consumers in terms of prices, service quality, and choice are solidly positive.* Concerns that reform would reduce safety and consumer protection are not borne out, probably because regulatory protections in these areas were not reduced in any of the reformed sectors. Distributional effects of price changes are not clear in sectors previously characterised by cross-subsidies, such as telephony and electricity, where some consumers may benefit little or pay more for some services. A trend toward both greater concentration and greater contestability in reformed sectors must be carefully watched to ensure that the first does not erode the second.

Attention to consumer protection is important in parallel with economic deregulation.

Debate on the right level of regulatory protection in markets, such as consumer rights in health care, continues to be intense, demonstrating that attention to consumer protection is important in parallel with economic deregulation. As US consumers have struggled with expanding choice in areas such as health care, telecommunications, and financial services, regulators and competitive markets have tried to respond with better information, new standards for quality, and new definitions of consumer rights. The balance is still evolving, but earlier attention to consumer issues in new markets at federal and state levels would have been beneficial in maximising the consumer benefits of reform.

**Dynamic effects were more important than expected.
Regulatory reform proved to be a valuable supply-side tool
that boosted demand, and improved the efficiency and flexibility
of the national economy.**

In most sectors, gains from innovation were more important than static efficiency gains.

In most sectors, gains from innovation were more important than static efficiency gains. Reform unleashed a level of innovation in products, services, production methods, and corporate organisation that is responsible for most of the economic gains. The ripple effects across sectors as new technologies and business practices had upstream or downstream impacts were unexpected, but accounted for many of the most important gains. The innovation effects of regulatory reform are long-term and are still evolving with the industries themselves.

Reforms helped the US economy to adapt more quickly to changes in technology and external shocks.

Sectoral reforms boosted demand in many sectors. They helped increase flexibility in the labour market and elsewhere. These effects amplified consumers gains, and produced new high-growth industries. They also allowed the US economy to adapt more quickly to changes in technology and to external shocks, improved trade-offs between inflation, growth, and unemployment, and boosted the US lead in productivity.

A well-balanced reform programme includes both deregulation and quality regulation.

These reforms show that there is a close and supportive relationship between quality regulation, competition, and market openness.

These reforms show that there is a close and supportive relationship between quality regulation, competition, and market openness that amplifies their value as a common framework for regulatory action. Regulatory reform will be more sustainable and will produce greater benefits in terms of economic and policy performance if these three dimensions are integrated. In particular, US experience shows that market performance and protection of social values can be pursued simultaneously by combining economic deregulation and market openness with application of quality and efficiency standards to effective social regulation.

A comprehensive approach produces more benefits, since regulatory reform is more effective when integrated with flexibility in factor markets, when competition is vigorous in upstream and downstream sectors, and when the macroeconomic environment is geared to growth.

A comprehensive approach to regulatory reform across related policy areas created positive synergies:

A comprehensive approach to regulatory reform across related policy areas created positive synergies:

- Stable macroeconomic policy, flexible labour markets, and complementary structural reforms provided a stable environment, and often a context of strong growth, which facilitated adjustments that followed from regulatory reform. Where macroeconomic policy was poor, such as when monetary expansion contributed to the asset bubble of the mid-1980s, it exacerbated regulatory problems in the financial sector and helped fuel the overexpansion in air transport.

- Strong competition authorities helped prevent consolidation in new markets from going too far and undermining the benefits of reform.

- The positive effects of regulatory reform on employment were amplified and the negative effects minimised in part because of the flexibility of US labour markets.

- Positive effects on competition of new entrants and the ability to innovate new products were stimulated by the efficiency of US capital markets.

- Pro-competitive regulation allows entrepreneurship to flourish in combination with other institutions such as private financing and well developed stock markets, corporate governance such as bankruptcy laws, patent laws, and, again, flexible labour markets. With this policy mix, the United States has created one of the most favourable regulatory regimes for entrepreneurs (OECD, 1997c).

These linkages suggest that the impacts of reform are sensitive to local conditions, and hence lessons learned in the United States must be carefully considered for relevance to other countries.

A multi-sectoral approach can also boost gains.

A multi-sectoral approach can also boost gains. The benefits of sectoral reform are amplified when competition is vigorous in upstream and downstream sectors. In the United States, innovations in information technology and networking in transportation sectors reinforced each other. Nearly simultaneous reform allowed the development of intermodal transport and increased competition across sectors, further stimulating productivity increases and a more rational allocation in the transportation market as a whole. Simultaneous reform prevented efficient consolidation from increasing monopoly power.

A sustained macroeconomic policy environment within which the market forces released by regulatory reform can operate is important to gain the full benefits of reform. This was achieved in the United States through fiscal consolidation and stable inflation.

Evaluation of costs and benefits of regulatory reform must be long-term and multi-dimensional to identify the real trade-offs.

Often, reform had far-reaching, long-term, and multi-sectoral effects on economic behaviour that were not predictable in advance.

US experience shows that many benefits of reform are long term and require sustained commitment to reform. In network industries characterised by high levels of capital intensity, readjustment of capital stock and producing efficiency benefits takes time. Often, reform had far-reaching, long-term, and multi-sectoral effects on economic behaviour that were not predictable in advance. Some effects were positive – such as innovation – while others were negative – such as consumer abuses and weakening of labour bargaining strength that contributed to an unknown degree to income inequity. More systematic monitoring and evaluation in the aftermath of reform would probably have helped the United States adjust to unexpected impacts more quickly, though in any case responsiveness would be hampered by sluggish regulatory process.

Reform promoted good job growth and boosted standards of living, but there were indirect effects on labour bargaining strength and uncertain effects on distribution of wealth.

Evaluation of the costs and benefits of regulatory reform must also be multi-dimensional to identify the real trade-offs. Reform promoted good job growth and boosted standards of living, but there were indirect effects on labour bargaining strength and uncertain effects on distribution of wealth. In the United States, slower productivity growth and widening of income distribution are related to high employment growth: high levels of human and physical capital imply lower growth of total factor productivity.

Regulatory flexibility and adaptation over time seems to be as valuable as regulatory cost-effectiveness.

Technological change and globalisation will increasingly reward dynamic regulatory efficiency.

The US experience suggests that regulation that adapts over time to changing conditions contributes more to economic and policy performance than does regulation that is optimally efficient at a point in time. Technological change and globalisation will increasingly reward dynamic regulatory efficiency. Hence, flexibility and capacity for regulatory adaptation are important in today's regulatory regimes.

The implications are far-reaching, since regulatory rigidities are common. A question often asked in OECD countries is how regulatory reform can be initiated and sustained against powerful special interests who benefit from existing regulatory practices. US experience suggests that one element of the capacity for change is contestability of regulatory policies. In the United States, contestability is driven by open processes, multiple actors in the federal system, and administrative, political, and judicial channels for challenge. These characteristics are key assets for the American regulatory system, even though they might lead to static regulatory costs and inefficiencies. A frequent element of economic reform of network industries in the United States was that some firms in each sector believed reform would benefit them, but this produced change only because they had channels to pursue their interests.

Transparency in regulatory decisions and application helps to cure many reasons for regulatory failures.

The high level of regulatory transparency in the United States has been particularly valuable. Transparency in regulatory decisions and application helps to cure many reasons for regulatory failures: capture and bias toward concentrated benefits, inadequate information in the public sector, policy rigidity, uncertainty, and lack of accountability. Moreover, transparency helps create a virtuous circle – consumers trust competition more because special interests have less power to manipulate governments and markets.

POLICY OPTIONS FOR REGULATORY REFORM

Yet there are recurring patterns in US regulatory regimes that reduce consumer welfare and policy effectiveness.

This report is not a comprehensive review of regulation in the United States, but the areas reviewed show recurring patterns in regulatory regimes that reduce consumer welfare and policy effectiveness. Problems with complexity, coherence and consistency, both horizontally across the US government and vertically in federal/state relations, have been identified in many policy areas. Regulatory quality controls are fragmented, and have important gaps in the areas of primary legislation, economic regulation, and state-level regulation. US regulatory habits of detail, legalism, and rigidity are still dominant, reducing innovation and responsiveness, and undermining market openness. Consistent application of the benefit-cost principle requires more years of effort, and better data reveals substantial inefficiencies in net benefits and cost-effectiveness of social regulations. New regulatory challenges have emerged with new technologies in network industries.

This section identifies actions that, based on international consensus on good regulatory practices and on concrete experiences in OECD countries, are likely to be particularly beneficial to improving regulation in the United States. The summary recommendations presented here are discussed in more detail in the background reports to Chapters 2-6, published in this volume. They are based on the recommendations and policy framework in The OECD Report to Ministers on Regulatory Reform.

Use of flexible and market-oriented policy instruments should be expanded.

The United States is missing the opportunity to exploit one of the world's great innovative cultures in the pursuit of important social objectives.

There are outstanding examples of regulatory innovations in the United States – such as the marketable permit system used for SO_2 – but these are rare. By failing to use more flexible and market-oriented policy instruments in social policy areas, the United States is missing the opportunity to exploit one of the world's great innovative cultures in the pursuit of important social objectives. Although the private sector is innovative, public sector regulators are typically not. The hidden costs of the rigid and legalistic regulatory style typical in the United States are even higher in an innovative and entrepreneurial economy.

– *Operational guidance should be developed for ministries and support experimentation on a wider range of co-operative methods.* A good practice that should be considered government-wide, and by other countries, is to build responsibility for innovation into the bureaucracy through processes such as the 1998 ECOS-EPA Agreement, which creates a transparent channel for new ideas from states and regions to be considered at the federal level.

- *Use the Government Performance and Results Act to focus on the performance of regulators in delivering net benefits.* Innovation has been discouraged by traditionally weak accountability mechanisms for the performance of regulatory programmes, which have emphasised inputs such as inspections and rules, rather than outcomes in terms of results and costs. Increased attention to results-oriented management in public sector can help break through legalistic and procedural bottlenecks to regulatory innovation.

- *In the electricity industry, subsidies for public purposes should be supported by non-bypassable and transparent fees.* The regulatory system to promote "green" generation should provide incentives for such generation to be provided at least-cost. *Provision should be made for consumers to be allowed voluntarily to buy "green" generated electricity beyond that required.*

The policy responsiveness of the US regulatory system should be further improved by streamlining cumbersome and sluggish processes.

Sluggishness, delay, and inefficiencies in regulatory processes will increasingly penalise the United States as the pace of globalisation and innovation steps up.

Sluggishness, delay, and inefficiencies in regulatory processes will increasingly penalise the United States as the pace of globalisation and innovation steps up. New regulations that are socially beneficial should be issued faster, and existing regulations should be updated regularly. The cost and length of time needed for regulatory change has imposed large hidden costs on the quality of the regulations. Regulators are less willing to implement new regulatory quality procedures when it already takes so long to get regulations through the pipeline. Beneficial modifications to old regulations are less likely to be carried out. Regulators are less likely to innovate and take risks, since a setback can cost several years of effort.

- *Continue to seek means to streamline regulatory processes through the National Performance Review process.* The 1993 NPR noted that a layering of procedural requirements has "made the rulemaking process increasingly burdensome and rigid".[72] Since 1993, the situation has worsened.

- *Strengthen quality management in executive and legislative branches as a substitute for some aspects of judicial review.* There is little doubt that litigation rights, whatever their benefits, increase costs and slow innovation in regulation. The 1996 Small Business Regulatory Enforcement Fairness Act, for example, allows judicial review of agency studies of small business impacts; several cases have been filed. A less costly approach would have been to establish a stronger watchdog in the administration to resolve problems before regulations are issued. At the same time, stronger internal controls and filters will help to increase the percentage of regulations that meet the benefit-cost test and increase regulatory net benefits.

- *Review current administrative law practices for regulatory development and consultation.* A thorough review of administrative practices would be an important contribution to identifying where regulatory procedures can be simplified, while maintaining transparency and full consultation. Supplements to "notice and comment" procedures that enrich dialogue and draw in a wider range of interests should be considered as part of the review of the Administrative Procedure Act. The National Performance Review recommended several potential innovations, including providing assistance to underrepresented interests, that merit serious attention.

– *Better integrate numerous regulatory quality procedures such as impact analyses, review processes, and performance measurement.* The current system of regulatory quality control is the sum of various piecemeal procedures that have accumulated over years. In this case, the whole is less than the sum of its parts, because scarce resources are scattered through many steps rather than targeted on the most important issues. Rationalisation of benefit-cost analysis, unfunded mandates analysis, paperwork estimates, small business analysis, environmental assessments, and others into a single integrated assessment will produce better results at lower cost, better target real problems, improve consistency of treatment, and avoid duplication of effort.

Regulations should be reviewed systematically to ensure that they continue to meet their intended objectives efficiently and effectively.

The incremental and piecemeal nature of legislative change in the United States compares unfavorably to the greater capacity for fundamental reform often enjoyed by parliamentary governments.

A strong point of the US system is the central review mechanisms within OMB and elsewhere to test the quality of new regulations. Yet the current system is very weak with respect to systematic review of the vast body of existing laws and other regulations. It looks forward, but not back, though in many areas poor laws have substantial negative downstream effects on the quality of policy implementation and policy outcomes. Other OECD countries have unfavorably compared the incremental and piecemeal nature of legislative change in the United States to the greater capacity for fundamental reform often enjoyed by parliamentary governments. The job is not done, for example, in important sectors characterised by fast technological change (telecommunications, electricity) and strong competition oversight is needed in reformed sectors (airlines, telecommunications) still adjusting. Here, the sluggishness of US regulation can erode competitiveness.

Current regulatory review processes seem focused on pruning each tree rather than improving the health of the forest. The reinvention principle should guide future regulatory policy reviews.

– *Expand the value, speed and scope of review of primary legislation and other regulations by launching a structured process of rolling reviews, reviewing policy areas rather than individual rules, and experimenting with use of advisory bodies for the reviews.* High priority should be placed on systematic review and upgrading of laws and major regulatory policies through a rolling review process based on prioritisation of policy areas. Areas subject to a fast technological change or where regulatory failure is most costly should have highest priority. The reinvention principle should guide the reviews to improve understanding of interactions between regulations having a cumulative and overlapping impact, originating from different agencies or even different levels of government. Such linkages are often not analysed. In every law reviewed, emphasis should be given to encouraging innovation in approaches, with clear accountability for results, and to identifying the most efficient federal/state relationship in the policy area. Comprehensive regulatory review could be improved by involvement of panels of users or advisory boards.

Market openness considerations should be incorporated into regulatory reviews.

– *Include a market openness perspective in the reviews of existing legislation and sectoral regulation.* The six efficient regulation principles (see Chapter 4) should be incorporated into regulatory reviews. FCC biennial regulatory reviews provide a useful model for such an exercise in other sectors.

– *Review existing sectoral restrictions on foreign investment with a view to preparing the ground for their early removal.*

– *Increase the use of sunsetting to ensure that regulations are kept on the books only if they are still necessary.* Due to its high cost, sunsetting is probably not a comprehensive solution, but when technologies are changing quickly or uncertainty is high, it can reduce the risk of damaging regulatory rigidities.

The universal service funding mechanism in the telecommunications sector should be reviewed.

– *In the telecommunications industry, the US universal service funding mechanism should be reviewed to minimise the economic distortion in the telecommunications market.*

– *In the telecommunications industry, barriers to entry by alternative communications networks should be reduced by eliminating asymmetries in the treatment of communications services. In particular, the regulatory regime for broadcasting should be reviewed, in the light of convergence, as soon as possible.*

In the electricity sector, further reform of economic regulations would stimulate competition.

Distortions to competition between public and private electricity utilities should be eliminated.

– *In the electricity industry, distortions to competition should be reduced by making appropriate changes in the tax and subsidy systems, the jurisdiction of FERC and the antitrust authorities, and other different treatment of public and private utilities.* Consideration should also be given to privatisation of the electricity-generating businesses of publicly owned utilities, or at minimum corporatisation with market-like returns to debt and equity-holders for their commercial activities. Distortions of energy choices through subsidies, taxes, and other support policies should not unnecessarily distort competition.

Where mandatory divestiture is not feasible, "operational separation" should be required and divestiture encouraged.

– *In the electricity industry, to achieve effective competition in generation and non-discriminatory access to the transmission grid and system operation, divestiture of generation from transmission should be required. Where mandatory divestiture is not feasible, "operational separation" should be required and divestiture encouraged. Connections for new generation to the existing transmission grid should be provided on non-discriminatory terms. To achieve effective competition in supply, entry into supply should not be economically restricted and non-discriminatory access to distribution should be ensured. To provide greater incentives for efficiency in the sector, direct access by all end-users to electricity markets ("retail competition") should be granted as soon as possible and within technical feasibility. The governance of entities such as independent system operators, power exchanges and reliability councils should be structured in such a way as to avoid discrimination.*

Locational pricing could improve efficiency in the power sector.

– *Also in the electricity sector, further experimentation in locational pricing of electric power should be undertaken.* Decisions about grid pricing schemes should take into account not only the economic efficiency losses from imposing the price constraints implicit in those schemes, but also implementation costs. Based on these results, consideration should be given to the widespread application of locational pricing. Multi-part transmission tariffs might provide appropriate incentives for grid investment.

Likewise, the scope and enforcement of competition policy should be reviewed and some weaknesses corrected.

The risk of inconsistency and gaps in competition law coverage should be corrected.

– *Eliminate from the competition law the remaining exemptions and sector-specific jurisdictional provisions.* The risk of inconsistency and gaps in coverage should be corrected by eliminating unnecessary exemptions and clearly assigning responsibility to the general competition law rather than a sectoral regulator. Sector-specific authority concerning mergers and other competition issues in energy and telecommunications should also be eliminated in the course of deregulation.

Competition authorities should intensify their oversight of the electricity sector as reform proceeds.

– *In the electricity industry, the antitrust authorities should continue their advocacy of competition at both federal and state levels.* In order to ensure adequate enforcement of the competition law, competition authorities should refine the methodology for reviewing mergers in this sector, should closely oversee the spot market surveillance by the independent system operators, and be responsible for investigating and remedying anticompetitive behaviour detected through this surveillance.

More co-ordination and review are needed to improve the efficiency and coherence of regulations at the federal and state interface.

The role of states as innovators and testing grounds for new ideas is a national asset that can speed up change and regulatory responsiveness.

The quality of US regulation is both boosted and hindered by the federal state structure. The role of the states as innovators and testing grounds for new ideas is a national asset that can speed up change and regulatory responsiveness. States can better adapt regulation and reform to local conditions. This asset is under-utilised by federal regulators, who tend to prefer standardised federal solutions to problems.

Yet a federal country must work harder to establish quality regulation and maintain it over time.

Yet the value of experimentation and learning in the federal system should not discourage efforts to find efficient regulatory solutions through co-ordination and, if justified, pre-emption. More attention to the coherence of the regulatory framework through comprehensive reviews and more co-ordination between federal and state actions would reduce the costs of overlaps and inconsistencies, speed up reforms of sectoral regulatory regimes, and improve the cost-effectiveness of social regulation. A federal country must work harder to establish quality regulation and maintain it over time. Static losses from uncoordinated state actions can be large and durable. This review has identified several areas where co-ordinated regulatory reform would produce gains.

State regulation and special legislation impairs competition and may delay reform.

- In *competition policy, undertake a comprehensive study of the extent and effect of the state action doctrine, in preparation for legislation to reduce its scope or eliminate it.* The impact of the state action doctrine, and of anti-competitive state and local legislation, is a matter of concern. State regulation and special legislation impairs competition and may delay reform in many areas, such as professional services, distribution, telecommunications and electric power. Congress has already corrected this in some sectors, such as trucking, where anti-competitive effects of continued state regulation were clear. A comprehensive study should be undertaken to assess the competitive effects of state laws and regulations and to identify sectors where reform is most needed. A model for such a study is the review of state constraints on competition now underway in Australia.

- In *competition policy enforcement, develop clearer assignments of responsibility among enforcement officials between the federal and state levels to avoid overlap and duplication.* Adoption of rules to permit greater informal staff-level consultation in enforcement matters among sectoral agencies with competition policy responsibilities would improve co-ordination.

Transparency and non-discrimination in state and local regulation needs work.

- *Heighten awareness of and encourage respect for the* OECD *efficient regulation principles in state and local regulatory activities affecting international trade and investment.* Ensuring transparency of subfederal regulation is crucial to international market openness. Experience shows that rigorous attention to ensuring non-discriminatory subfederal regulation is also needed.

New ideas for permits and licenses used in other countries could be useful in the United States.

- *Encourage entrepreneurialism by streamlining permits and licenses at the federal level, by co-ordinating with the states on review and streamlining of permits and licenses, and by building more complete information systems for enterprises.* Ex ante permits and licenses can inhibit business start-ups and are costly to administer. Efforts in the United States place too little focus on ensuring that such requirements are the minimum necessary to achieve policy objectives, probably due to the fact that most such requirements are state and local. New ideas – such as the move to a "supply model" in Germany that offers choices to investors depending on the degree of risk they wish to accept – are being developed and implemented in OECD countries, and could be useful in the United States.

More attention is needed to creating efficient regional electricity markets.

- In *the electricity sector, to reduce overlapping or duplicative regulatory responsibilities, and to promote clearer, simpler and more practical regulation, a framework for the establishment of regional pacts among states for electricity regulation should be established, and the respective roles of federal and state regulators should be clarified.* Lost efficiencies stem from regional markets having to operate under multiple regulatory regimes, and there are increased compliance costs from utilities operating in multiple regimes. Regional pacts regarding the regulation of the sector, where the regions are coincident with electricity markets, could reduce some of these costs, while retaining the flexibility and heterogeneity to allow regulatory innovation.

– *In the electricity industry, consideration should be given to granting to the Federal Energy Regulatory Commission siting authority for transmission.*

Larger independent system operators would, for example, reduce reliability costs.

– *To reduce the cost of reliability in electricity grids, larger independent system operators should be promoted; where independent system operators are sufficiently large, they should be given some responsibility for reliability. To adapt the reliability regime to the development of markets for electricity, the Federal Energy Regulatory Commission should be given oversight of reliability councils, and their recommendations should become mandatory.*

If states continue to erect barriers to entry in telecommunications, Federal authority to regulate the sector should be expanded.

– *Successes in reducing barriers to entry, promoting cost-based interconnection, rate rebalancing and equal access have been most pronounced at the federal level. If current initiatives fail to eliminate state actions that have the effect of raising barriers to entry, consideration should be given to vesting exclusive authority in the federal government as is done in Australia and Canada.*

Important gaps in regulatory quality controls should be closed to improve attention to market openness impacts, and to bring economic regulation under benefit-cost requirements.

Trade and investment impacts are neglected when assessing regulatory benefits and costs...

– *Require assessments of the effects of proposed rules on inward trade and investment as part of the Regulatory Impact Analysis (RIA).* Requirements for benefit-cost analysis do not include specific reference to assessing impacts on trade and investment. Weaknesses in oversight by OMB and USTR suggest that this aspect is neglected in the quality control process, increasing the risk that such impacts will be discovered only through trade frictions. The six efficient regulation principles provide a good guide to incorporating market openness impacts into benefit-cost analysis.

... and the independent commissions responsible for most economic regulations are not required to base their decisions on benefit-cost analysis.

– *Expand coverage of mandatory quality controls to economic regulation.* Economic regulation is less likely to produce net benefits than is social regulation. An ideal regulatory reform programme would put stricter controls on the use of economic regulations than on social regulations. The US programme does the opposite. The independent commissions responsible for most economic regulations are not required to base their decisions on benefit-cost analysis. This gap is rooted in historical and legal relations between the independent commissions and the president, but the result is that these commissions provide relatively little information on the benefits and costs of their actions. Streamlining of regulations in the US telecommunications industry, for example, would be supported by extending mandatory regulatory quality controls to regulatory activities of the Federal Communications Commission.

Continued integration of market openness and regulatory policies will produce benefits both in the United States and in other countries.

Regulatory barriers to trade can be lowered through regulatory co-operation with trading partners.

- *Seek to ensure that bilateral or regional approaches to regulatory co-operation are designed and implemented in ways which will encourage broader multilateral application.* Mutual recognition of regulations and conformity assessment procedures, increased use of industry-developed standards in lieu of national regulatory measures, and other approaches to intergovernmental regulatory co-operation offer promising avenues for the lowering of regulatory barriers to trade and investment.

Business initiatives to lay the groundwork for regulatory co-ordination could drive market-opening reforms.

- *Build on the* TABD *model to encourage the continued involvement of the* US *and international business communities in domestic regulatory reform efforts.* Informal business-driven processes such as this have proven valuable catalysts for market-opening regulatory reform across a range of particular sectors and horizontal issues. Wider government-to-business partnering on regulatory issues holds strong potential for pragmatic, result-oriented reform attuned to evolving business realities.

- *Intensify efforts to use existing international standards and to participate more actively in the development of internationally harmonised standards as the basis of domestic regulations.* A useful step would be to systematically assess the extent to which regulators currently rely on international standards and to explore rationales for departures from this practice.

- *In the electricity industry, the United States should consider whether the objectives of the reciprocity requirement in the federal open access regulation could be met in a less trade restrictive manner.*

MANAGING REGULATORY REFORM

Continued reform will proceed faster and more deeply if reformers take concrete steps to demonstrate that protection has been maintained and good regulations are well enforced.

While the US public debate over regulatory reform is among the most well-informed and transparent in OECD countries, there is still too little information on the results of reform strategies, including their effects on programme effectiveness, costs, economic performance, and distribution of gains and losses. Such information is critical if reform is to enjoy support from citizens who place high value on safety, health, environmental quality, and other values promoted by regulation. At this juncture, it seems that fears about the effects of reform on levels of protection have not been borne out, but continued reform will proceed faster and more deeply if reformers take concrete steps to demonstrate that protection has been maintained and good regulations are well enforced. Evaluation of the economic and social impacts of reform, communication with the public and major stakeholders, and faster capacities for mid-course corrections will be increasingly important to further progress.

NOTES

1. A summary of these estimates is given in US Office of Information and Regulatory Affairs, Office of Management and Budget (1998), Draft Report to Congress on the Costs and Benefits of Federal Regulations, 17 August.

2. US Office of Information and Regulatory Affairs, OMB (1994), Report to the President on Executive Order No. 12866, 1 May.

3. US Office of Information and Regulatory Affairs, Office of Management and Budget (1997) Report to Congress on the Costs and Benefits of Federal Regulations, 30 September, p. 44.

4. Katzen (1999).

5. Many of the economists who were responsible for reform moved from agency to agency, leading to continuity of personnel as well as of ideas.

6. This was reinforced by the decline of the dollar after the collapse of the Smithsonian Agreements which tried to re-establish a new stable fixed exchange rate system.

7. Labour productivity for France, Germany, Japan and the United Kingdom grew at an annual rate of 5.3 per cent between 1961 and 1973, *versus* 2.4 per cent in the United States. The UK growth rate was 3.6 per cent.

8. In the non-US G7, it fell 5.4 per cent to 3.2 per cent. The decline in percentage points of 1.9 per cent was lower than that of Japan and Italy, which fell from very high levels, but it was as large or larger than the other G7 countries. Cross-country comparisons of labour productivity growth must be done with caution; productivity growth in many countries may be considered as "too high" if it results from labour shedding and closing productive capacity rather than improvement in underlying productive performance.

9. See the OECD Survey (1977), pp. 23-24 and the references cited therein; and the OECD Survey (1979), p. 47.

10. Demographics and regulation were estimated as accounting for about 0.3 percentage point each of the 1.1 per cent decline in productivity growth. Other factors listed in the Survey included a decline in R&D expenditures, slower rates of investment leading to a decline in the growth of the capital/labour ratio, and the smaller share of high productivity sectors in the economy, such as agriculture (p. 22-23).

11. The OECD Economic Survey (1980) noted on p. 44, "[I]t is uncertain how much economic slack must be created in order to reduce inflation to acceptable levels, and how long any given degree of slack must be maintained. [...] Another serious shortcoming in relying mainly on prolonged demand restraint is that price shocks can overwhelm any gradual policy-induced deceleration".

12. See OECD *Economic Survey* (1980), pp. 31-35.

13. "[...] there is no reason why [...] demand restraint should not be complemented by other measures [...] capable of exerting an independent influence on inflationary expectations and pressures."

14. This eventually led to the Federal bailout of the Chrysler Motor Corporation in 1981.

15. See the discussions in Friedlander (1969) and MacAvoy and Snow (1977), among others.

16. Policy makers were concerned about the declining share of financial assets intermediated by banks for several reasons, among which were the implications for effective monetary control. Political pressure from banks also played an important role.

17. Wage and price guidelines under the Kennedy Administration (1962-66) and Nixon-era wage-price controls.

18. The administration also considered using tax-based incomes policies (TIP's) which are tax incentives for individuals and businesses to pursue smaller wage and price increases.

19. In retrospect, policy appears somewhat incoherent here, as the Administration, through the Council on Wage and Price Stability, was increasing the use of wage and price guidelines in some respects while simultaneously supporting price deregulation in others.

20. Summarised in OECD (1979), p. 70. These were: monitoring the impact of proposed social regulations on inflation, which included Inflation Impact Statements drafted by the Council on Wage and Price Stability and the threat of vetoes of proposed legislation which would raise prices, such as farm price supports; use of Federal procurement policies to reduce inflation; deregulation of road transport and airlines; voluntary guidelines on the setting of wages, benefits and prices and ongoing consultation with interest groups involved in wage and price setting; and decontrol of oil prices (after the initial price shock, this was expected to induce a reduction in demand).

21. The budget package was initially stimulating, but nominal spending targets were not altered as inflation accelerated and in the event the high employment deficit ended up in balance. In regards to monetary policy, during the last years of the decade the Fed moved away from its traditional policy of targeting interest rates to targeting monetary and credit aggregates as an anti-inflationary weapon. In 1979 monetary growth repeatedly exceeded targets. Monetary growth was reduced and as a result short-term interest rates quickly climbed to high double-digit levels with an accompanying increase in their variance.

22. Irrespective of their ideological orientation, the two Reagan Administrations were characterised by substantial fiscal stimulus leading to growing structural budget deficits.

23. This section covers reforms of economic regulations only.

24. Air carriers can engage in peak load pricing by changing the number of low cost versus full fare seats available on flights depending on the hour of departure, so that seats at peak times (early morning and evening weekday flights) effectively cost more. While consumers often complain of the multiplication of airfares and restrictions on low fares, the value of being able to change reservations has now been priced and peak load pricing has been adopted.

25. This was compounded by the fact that airlines misforecast demand growth in the face of the business cycle swings.

26. Winston (1994, 1996) argues that competition per route is the relevant measure of contestability. This measure increased substantially through the late 1980s and has remained roughly at those levels, though the net increase in route competition was concentrated almost entirely on high density long haul routes, where the greatest price drops have been. However competition on routes from hubs where a dominant carrier has emerged may have declined from levels reached in the mid-1980s, and increasing consolidation within the industry has also been a countervailing force, though the impact of the new system of alliance between major carriers is too recent to be measured. Concern over declining competition in air transport was stimulated not just by the emergence of dominant carriers at certain hubs but also the effects of frequent flyer programmes, ownership of computer reservation systems, and special arrangements with travel agents. A national commission which studied the problem in 1993 concluded the impact at that time was small.

27. Borenstein, S. (1990), pp. 400-404.

28. Historically long-haul high volume routes, which benefit from higher load factors, subsidised short-haul and low volume routes. After deregulation prices on high volume long distance routes such as New York-Los Angeles dropped substantially in real terms, whereas prices on short-haul low volume flights (*i.e.*, regional flights to or from small cities) have been flat or even increased.

29. This can only be indirectly attributed to deregulation, as the primary causes have been safety-inspired slower airspeeds and greater airport congestion. By contrast, deregulation has helped reduce connection times and lost baggage problems as most passengers fly the entire trip on the same airline.

30. Prohibitions on re-routing in the mid and late 1970s actually created and exacerbated gas shortages.

31. Comparable figures for labour and total factor productivity are available for telecommunications, where the United States ranked fourth among the G7, and electricity, where it ranked first (labour) and second (total factor). X-efficiency measures show the US ranked first in air and rail transport, fifth in electricity and seventh in telecommunications. Efficiency in retail distribution is more difficult to measure, but US performance indicated high levels of productivity per employee and per establishment.

32. OECD Survey (1997), see the special chapter on entrepreneurialism.

33. US private savings rates have been historically less than half the G7 average, and they have remained low in the 1990s despite substantial capital market liberalisation and innovations. Investment in the US during the

1990s expansion has been unusually strong compared to previous cycles. Leading the OECD countries, real US annual investment growth rates have been close to nine per cent since 1992.

34. Productivity growth in the business sector remained the slowest of all comparable countries, though this is largely attributable to the rapid growth of employment in the lower productivity service sector, though measurement problems may understate productivity gains in services. The US has the largest service sector as a share of employment of any OECD country. As was noted in the 1993 OECD Survey (p. 56 and footnotes 43 and 44) the Commerce Department arbitrarily sets productivity growth in government and financial services to zero. Financial services and community, social and personal services (largely government) accounted for 11.2 and 34.6 per cent of total employment in 1996, respectively, about two-thirds of total service sector employment. The Performance Indicators database shows negative LP and TFP growth in both sectors throughout the 1982-95 period, and productivity growth in construction as near zero.

35. For a summary of the literature on relative price flexibility, see Van Bergeijk, Peter A.G. and Robert C.G. Haffner (1996), *Privatisation, Deregulation and the Macroeconomy*. Cheltenham, UK; Edward Elgar.

36. Slifman and Corrado (1996), however, provide some evidence suggesting that the level of output and hence productivity in the non-farm non-corporate sector is understated. Nearly half of this sector's income is counted as services, suggesting measured productivity in the service sector may be too low. See, Slifman, L. and C. Corrado (1996), "Decomposition of Productivity and Unit Costs", Occasional Staff Studies, Board of Governors of the Federal Reserve System.

37. Indicators of household or family income distribution and poverty widened over the decade from the mid-1970s to the mid-1980s. There was probably some further widening in the income distribution from the mid-1980s to the mid-1990s as well, although changes in data definitions make it more difficult to gauge the degree of this increase.

38. The economy-wide effects of economy reform can be separated into direct or "first-round" effects in the specific sector under reform, "second-round" effects on other sectors, and macroeconomic effects, including intangible effects like spill-overs or changes in the structure and functioning of labour markets.

39. See OECD (1977), Vol. II, Chapter 1: "The Economy-wide Effects of Regulatory Reform" and "The Economy-wide Effects of Regulatory Reform: Country Notes".

40. Much of this discussion is adapted from US Office of Management and Budget (1988), Introduction to The Regulatory Program of the United States Government, 1 April 1987-31 March 1988.

41. Office of Management and Budget (1997), Report to Congress on the Costs and Benefits of Federal Regulations, September 30, p. 27.

42. Moreover, there are significant methodological problems. For example, the estimates mix different data sources.

43. See the reference to Jaffe *et al.*, cited by Landy and Cass (1997).

44. In the case of productivity, a study by Robinson found that US manufacturing productivity levels in 1986 were 11 percentage points lower than otherwise because of environmental and occupational health regulations and the impact on specific sectors such as chemicals, petrochemicals, paper products, mining and primary metals was much greater. Robinson's study covered 445 manufacturing industries for the period 1975-86. He found much higher effects in specific sectors of paper products, chemicals, coal and petroleum products and primary metals: these averaged around 30 per cent. See James C. Robinson, (1995) "The Impact of Environmental and Occupational Health Regulation on Productivity Growth in US Manufacturing", Yale Journal of Regulation.

45. Tengs and Graham noted: "[...] We find no apparent relationship between the cost-effectiveness of the 185 life-saving interventions and their implementation". They note that fire-retardance regulations on children's' clothing cost $1.5 million per lives saved yet smoke alarms are not mandatory in homes, which are estimated to cost $200 000 per year per life saved.

46. For comparisons of US regulatory styles with other countries, see, *inter alia*, Vogel, David (1986) National Styles of Regulation, Cornell University Press: Ithaca; Badaracco, Joseph (1985) Loading the Dice: A Five-Country Study of Vinyl Chloride Regulation, Harvard Business School Press, Boston; Kelman, Steven (1981) Regulating America, Regulating Sweden (MIT Press: Cambridge); Heidenheimer, Arnold; Heclo, Hugh; Adams, Carolyn (1983) Comparative Public Policy: The Politics of Social Choice in Europe and America (St. Martin's Press: New York).

47. Crandall *et al.*, 1997, p. 5.

48. More Benefits, Fewer Burdens, p. 18.

49. The ECOS-EPA Regulatory Innovations Agreement.

50. Called the Open Market Trading Program.

51. See FCC 97-398, Report and Order on Reconsideration adopted on 25 November 1997.

52. US FDI inflows increased in 1995 by more than 21 per cent over the previous year, reaching $60 billion, twice the size of inflows to the United Kingdom, the second most important FDI recipient amongst developed countries. See World Investment Report 1996 (UNCTAD 1996).

53. NAFTA and the US-Israel Free Trade Agreement. The United States also grants unilateral preferences to a number of developing countries under the Andean Trade Preferences Act, the Caribbean Basin Initiative and more generally under the Generalised System of Preferences.

54. See EC Sectoral and Trade Barriers Database.

55. According to the UN Trade Barriers to Latin American Exports in 1996 [Washington Office of the UN Economic Commission for Latin America and the Caribbean (ECLAC)] "a vast maze of standards and regulations makes exporting to the United States a daunting task. The complexity of the system can be partly attributed to the three separate tiers of regulations that exist: federal, state and local. These regulations are often inconsistent between jurisdictions, or needlessly overlap. It is estimated that more than 44 000 federal, state and local authorities enforce 89 000 standards for products within their jurisdictions. These structural barriers, although unintentional, still create major hurdles for foreign firms attempting to enter the US market".

56. See EC Sectoral and Trade Barriers Database.

57. Some US trading partners have objected to US reliance on third-party conformity assessments when less onerous means (such as reliance on manufacturers' or purchasers' declarations of conformity) could be employed. However, concerns about the safety, health, or environmental impact of some products may be too important to be left to self-assessments. This would be true of products whose failure could lead to injury, illness, property damage or loss of life. Drug safety certification provided by the FDA, for example, requires third-party assessment to verify product safety. See Standards, Conformity Assessment, and Trade into the 21st century, National Research Council (National Academy Press, Washington DC, 1995).

58. See Speech of Belinda Collins, Acting Director, OSS, NIST before the Committee on Science, Space and Technology on "International Standards and US Exports: Keys to Competitiveness or Barriers to Trade".

59. Soon after the divestiture, the FCC mandated equal access in regard to inter-LATA long-distance, allowing subscribers to choose among long-distance carrier as the default carrier on an equal basis.

60. For a more detailed explanation of the theory, see Timothy J. Brennan, "Is the Theory Behind US *v.* AT&T Applicable Today?" *Antitrust Bulletin*, Vol. 40, No. 3, pp. 455-482.

61. For discussion see, for example, President William J. Clinton and Vice-President Albert Gore Jr., "A Framework for Global Electronic Commerce", posted July, 1997 at "www.iift.nist.gov/telecom/ecomm.htm#background".

62. See FCC, In the Matter of the Annual Assessment of the Status of CS Docket No. 97-141, Competition in Markets for Video Programming. In June 1997, the number of homes capable of receiving cable programming was 94.2 million, which accounts for 97.1 per cent of television homes.

63. See Joel Klein, "The Race For Local Competition: A Long Distance Run, Not a Sprint", Speech before the American Enterprise Institute, 5 Nov. 1997 and William E. Kennard, "Section 271 of the Telecommunications Act of 1996", Statement Before the Subcommittee on Communications of the Committee on Commerce, Science, and Transportation, United States Senate, March 25, 1998. In particular, Chairman Kennard stated: "I do not come here, however, to announce my satisfaction with the pace of competition. We can and must do better".

64. FCC, "Local Competition Factsheet", *supra*, note 1.

65. For detailed discussion of the impact of these technological advances see, for example, the FCC's En Banc hearing dated 9 July 1998 posted at: "www.fcc.gov/enbanc/070998/tr070998.txt" and the FCC's Bandwidth Forum dated 23 January 1997 posted at "www.fcc.gov/Reports/970123.txt". The UK provides an additional example of the capacity of cable to provide telephony service. See, for example, Affidavit of Oliver E. Williamson, at p. 14 (31 May 1994), submitted on behalf of Motion by Bell Atlantic Corporation, Bell South Corporation, Nynex Corporation and Southwestern Bell Corporation to vacate the Decree, United States *v.* Western Electric Co., No. 82-0192 (D.DC. filed 6 July 1994) cited in Robert W. Crandall and J. Gregory Sidak, "Competition and Regulatory Policies for interactive Broadband Networks", Southern California Law Review, July, 1995.

66. For example, the Communications Act of 1934 specifies as a policy objective in communications to: "make available, so far as possible, to all people of the United States a rapid, efficient, nation-wide, and world-wide wire and radio communication service with adequate facilities at reasonable charges".

67. As former FCC Chief Economist Michael Riordan commented: "The tension between universal service and competition is the great drama in the Telecom Act. These are like two horseshoe magnets, that, when held face-to-face, repel each other. Yet there is an abiding belief that, if one could just turn one of the magnets upside down, and look at it differently, everything would be all right". Michael Riordan, "Conundrums for Telecommunications Policy", *Mimeo.*, 28 May 1998.

68. As Lawrence White put it, "cross-subsidies are the enemy of competition because competition is the enemy of cross-subsidies". See Joseph Farrell, 1996.

69. Until the end of 1997, universal service programmes were financed by per line monthly charges imposed on long distance carriers. Under the new rules which took effect in January 1998, the per-line charges previously paid by large long distance carriers have been discontinued. Instead, all providers of interstate telecommunications, including local exchange carriers, long-distance providers and wireless carriers, now contribute to the provision of universal service based on the amount of their telecommunications revenues.

70. Sections 401 and 402 of the 1996 Telecommunications Act provide procedures to forbear from regulation in response to specific petitions and to review its own regulations to check if they are no longer in the public interest. Importantly, these streamlining provisions do not include an explicit recognition of the costs imposed by continued regulation

71. Section 401(*d*) exempts sections 251(*c*) (*i.e.*, interconnection and unbundling requirements) and 271 (the in-region inter-LATA restraints on BOCs) from consideration under a forbearance petition.

72. "Improving Regulatory Systems", *op cit.*

Annex

OTHER FIGURES AND TABLES

Figure 1.1. **United States labour productivity growth, business sector**
Actual 3-year moving average *vs* trend[1]

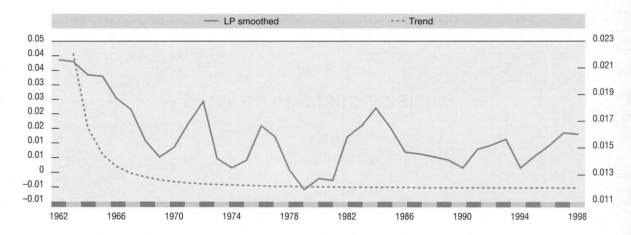

Figure 1.2. **United States labour market performance**[2]

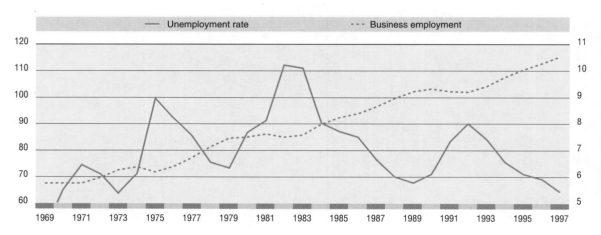

Figure 1.3. **United States budget balance**
As a percentage of GDP

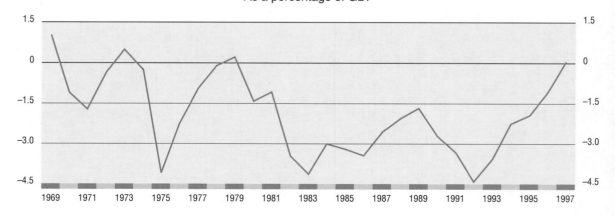

1. Data for trend refers to the right scale.
2. Business employment in millions (left scale).
Source: OECD, ADB database.

Figure 1.4*a*. **United States growth performance in telecommunications**
vs OECD countries

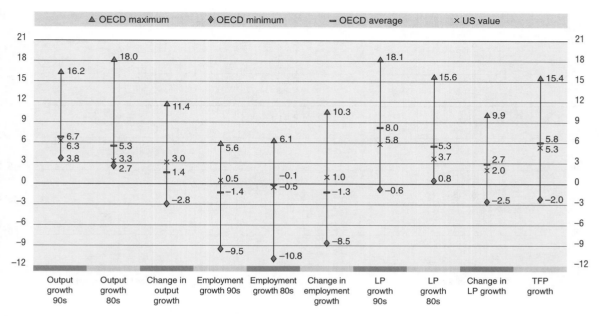

Figure 1.4*b*. **United States performance in levels in telecommunications**
vs OECD countries

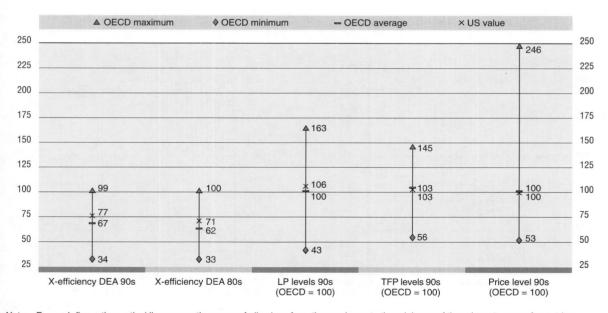

Note: For each figure the vertical line covers the range of all values from the maximum to the minimum of the relevant group of countries.
Output = mainlines + cellular subscribers
Employment = total employment
Labour productivity (LP) = mainlines + cellular subscribers/employment
Total factor productivity (TFP) = capital is calculated using the perpetual inventory method and the investment PPP (the labour share is set to 0.54 which the OECD average for communications)
DEA = results of data envelope analysis with revenue (converted with sectoral PPP), mainlines + cellular subscribers and numbers of pay phone as output concepts and employment and capital (as in TFP) as inputs.
Price level = simple average of a basket of services (including business and residential prices of local, trunk and international fixed voice telephony; mobile telephony, leased lines and Internet).
Source: OECD Telecommunications database 1997, *OECD Communications Outlook* 1997.

Figure 1.5*a*. **United States growth performance in electric power
vs OECD countries**

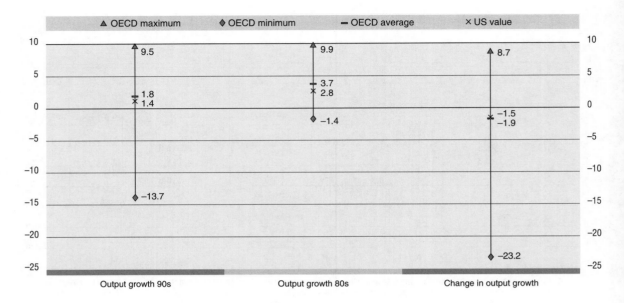

Figure 1.5*b*. **United States performance in levels in electric power
vs OECD countries**

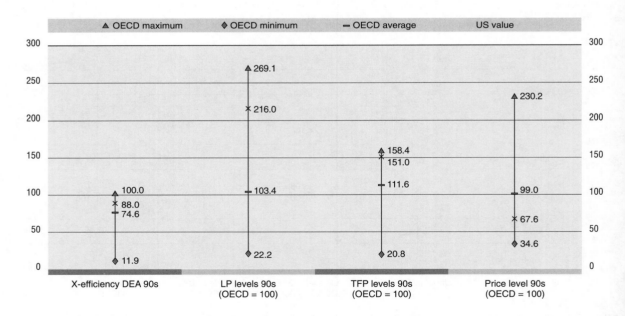

Note: For each figure the vertical line covers the range of all values from the maximum to the minimum of the relevant group of countries.
Output = net electricity production
Employment = total employment
Labour productivity (LP) = net electricity production/employment
Total factor productivity (TFP) = output is net electricity production, inputs are employees and total installed capacity (the labour share is set 0.25 which is the OECD average for electricity, gas and water).
DEA = data envelope analysis with net electricity production as output and labour and installed capacity as inputs
Price level = business electricity price, converted with GDP-PPP
Source: International Energy Agency.

Figure 1.6. **United States growth performance in rail transport
vs OECD countries**

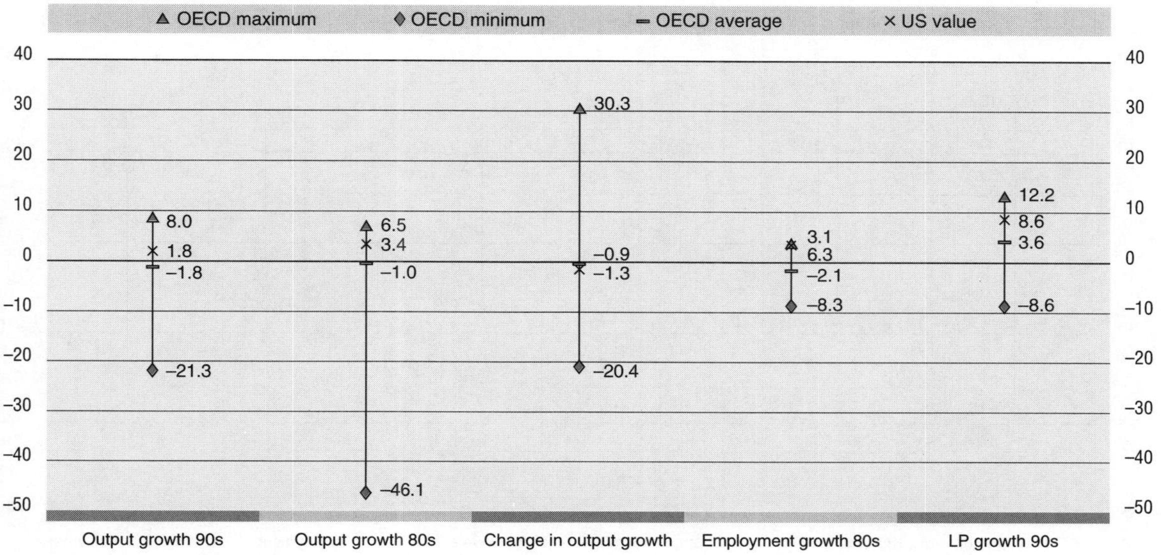

| ▲ OECD maximum | ◆ OECD minimum | — OECD average | × US value |

Note: For each figure the vertical line covers the range of all values from the maximum to the minimum of the relevant group of countries.
    Output = passengers-km
    Employment = total employment
    Labour productivity (LP) = passengers-km/employment
    Total factor productivity (TFP) = passengers-km as output, employment and number of locomotives as inputs (the labour share is set to 0.6, which is the OECD average for transport)
Source: European Conference of Ministers of Transportation (ECMT), United Nations.

Figure 1.7. **United States growth performance in air transport**
***vs* OECD countries**

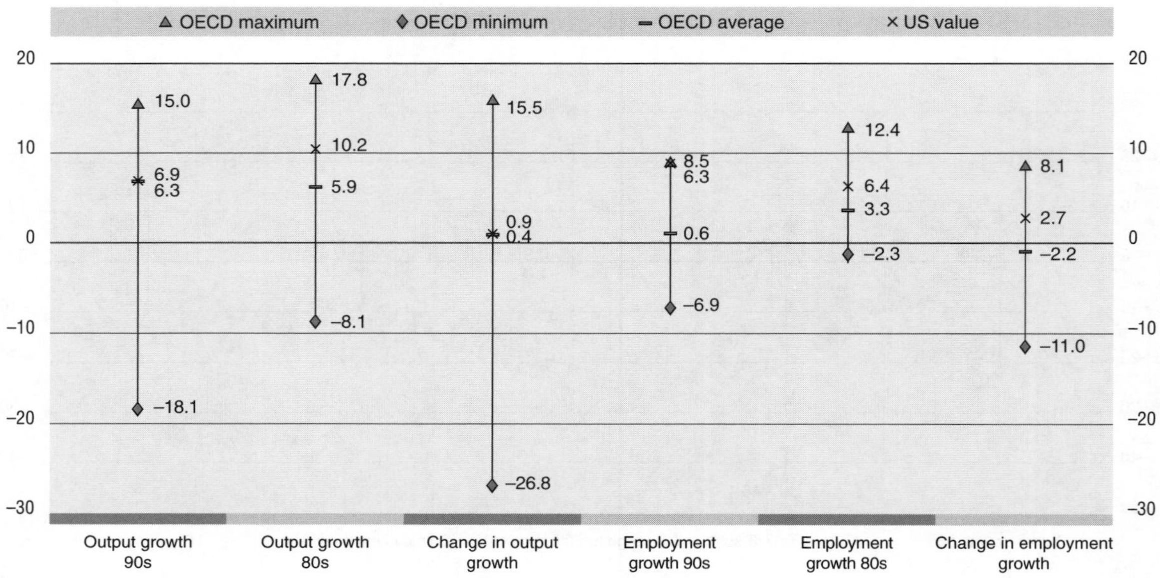

| ▲ OECD maximum | ◆ OECD minimum | — OECD average | × US value |

Output growth 90s · Output growth 80s · Change in output growth · Employment growth 90s · Employment growth 80s · Change in employment growth

Note: For each figure the vertical line covers the range of all values from the maximum to the minimum of the relevant group of countries.
Output = transported passenger-km (TPK)
Employment = total employment
Labour productivity (LP) = TPK/employment
Total factor productivity (TFP) = output is TPK and capital is total seating capacity (the labour share is set to 0.6, which is the OECD average for transport)
Source: European Conference of Ministries of Transportation (ECMT), United Nations.

Table 1.3. **Primary strengths in United States macroeconomic performance**

	Total employment growth (per cent)				Unemployment rate (per cent)				Non-employment rate to working age population (per cent)				Capital output ratio				Growth rate of exports of goods and services, volume (per cent)			
	1969-79	1979-89	1989-96	1990s less 1970s	1969-79	1979-89	1989-96	1990s less 1970s	Avg. 1969-79	Avg. 1979-89	Avg. 1989-96	1990s less 1970s	1969-79	1979-89	1989-96	1990s less 1970s	Avg. 1969-79	Avg. 1979-89	Avg. 1989-96	1990s less 1970s
USA	2.4	1.7	1.1	-1.3	6.0	7.1	6.2	0.2	36.8	32.5	28.2	-8.6	1.3	1.4	1.4	0.0	7.7	5.7	7.4	-0.3
Japan	0.8	1.1	0.8	0.0	1.6	2.5	2.6	0.9	29.8	29.3	26.5	-3.3	1.6	2.1	2.5	0.8	9.5	6.2	4.5	-4.9
Germany	0.1	0.4	3.2	3.0	2.2	6.4	8.2	6.0	32.9	36.4	35.8	2.9	2.5	2.8	2.8	0.3	5.4	4.6	2.3	-3.1
France	0.6	0.2	0.0	-0.6	3.7	8.7	10.7	7.1	34.5	38.7	40.4	5.9	2.6	2.8	2.9	0.3	8.4	3.7	4.5	-3.9
Italy	0.6	0.2	-0.5	-1.1	4.6	8.2	10.3	5.7	44.2	45.6	46.8	2.7	2.6	2.6	2.7	0.1	7.6	3.2	6.1	-1.5
UK	0.2	0.6	-0.3	-0.5	3.5	9.1	8.3	4.9	29.3	32.4	30.5	1.2	3.3	3.4	3.4	0.1	5.1	2.9	5.1	0.0
Canada	2.9	2.0	0.6	-2.3	6.5	9.2	9.8	3.3	36.0	32.1	30.8	-5.2	1.0	1.5	2.0	1.0	5.6	5.3	7.6	2.0
Non-US G7 median	0.6	0.5	0.3	-0.6	3.6	8.4	9.1	5.3	33.7	34.4	33.3	1.9	2.5	2.7	2.8	0.3	6.6	4.1	4.8	-2.3
Non-US G7 average	0.9	0.7	0.6	-0.2	3.7	7.4	8.3	4.6	34.5	35.7	35.2	0.7	2.3	2.5	2.7	0.4	6.9	4.3	5.0	-1.9
USA less Non-US G7																				
Average	1.5	1.0	0.5	-1.1	2.3	-0.2	-2.2	-4.4	2.3	-3.3	-7.0	-9.3	-0.9	-1.1	-1.4	-0.4	0.8	1.4	2.4	1.6
Median	1.8	1.2	0.8	-0.7	2.4	-1.3	-2.9	-5.1	3.0	-1.9	-5.2	-10.6	-1.2	-1.3	-1.4	-0.3	1.1	1.6	2.6	2.0
Rank	2	2	2	6	2	5	6	7	2	4	6	7	6	7	7	7	3	2	2	3

Source: OECD Secretariat.

Table 1.4. **Secondary strengths of United States macroeconomic performance**

	Government budget balance to GDP				Growth rate of private non-residential investment				Growth of real consumption per capita				Growth of real GDP per capita				Consumer inflation			
	Avg. 1969-79	Avg. 1979-89	Avg. 1989-96	1990s less 1970s	1969-79	1979-89	1989-96	1990s less 1970s	1969-79	1979-89	1989-96	1990s less 1970s	Avg. 1969-79	Avg. 1979-89	Avg. 1989-96	1990s less 1970s	Avg. 1969-79	Avg. 1979-89	Avg. 1989-96	1990s less 1970s
USA	-1.0	-2.4	-2.4	-1.3	5.0	2.4	5.4	0.4	2.4	2.0	1.1	-1.3	3.2	2.7	1.9	-1.2	6.5	5.3	3.2	-3.3
Japan	-2.4	-1.0	-0.9	1.5	2.6	8.0	-0.3	-2.9	4.0	2.8	2.0	-2.0	5.2	3.8	2.3	-2.9	8.8	2.5	1.2	-7.6
Germany	-1.9	-1.6	-3.2	-1.3	1.5	3.1	2.2	0.7	3.8	1.5	0.3	-3.4	3.1	1.8	3.6	0.5	4.8	2.9	3.1	-1.7
France	-1.0	-1.7	-3.4	-2.3	2.4	3.0	-0.9	-3.3	3.2	1.9	1.0	-2.1	3.7	2.3	1.4	-2.4	9.0	7.2	2.3	-6.7
Italy	-8.1	-11.0	-8.1	0.0	2.5	2.1	-0.5	-3.0	3.9	2.7	1.1	-2.8	3.7	2.4	1.2	-2.5	13.0	11.4	5.5	-7.5
UK	-4.7	-2.3	-4.3	0.4	1.9	6.4	-0.1	-2.0	2.4	3.2	0.9	-1.5	2.4	2.4	1.3	-1.1	12.2	7.0	4.1	-8.1
Canada	-2.1	-4.5	-3.7	-1.5	8.8	3.9	1.3	-7.6	3.0	1.7	0.2	-2.8	4.4	2.9	1.3	-3.1	7.3	6.2	2.3	-5.0
Non-US G7 median	-2.3	-2.0	-3.5	-0.7	2.5	3.5	-0.2	-3.0	3.5	2.3	1.0	-2.5	3.7	2.4	1.3	-2.4	8.9	6.6	2.7	-7.1
Non-US G7 average	-3.4	-3.7	-3.9	-0.6	3.3	4.4	0.3	-3.0	3.4	2.3	0.9	-2.4	3.8	2.6	1.8	-1.9	9.2	6.2	3.1	-6.1
USA less Non-US G7																				
Average	2.3	1.3	1.5	-0.8	1.7	-2.0	5.2	3.5	-1.0	-0.3	0.2	1.2	-0.6	0.1	0.1	0.7	-2.7	-0.9	0.1	2.8
Median	1.2	-0.4	1.1	-0.7	2.6	-1.1	5.7	3.4	-1.1	-0.3	0.1	1.2	-0.6	0.3	0.6	1.2	-2.4	-1.3	0.5	3.8
Rank	2	5	2	5	2	6	1	2	7	4	3	1	5	3	3	3	6	5	3	2

Source: OECD Secretariat.

Table 1.5. **Weaknesses in United States macroeconomic performance**

Percentages

	Growth rate of real wages				Growth of labour productivity in the total business sector				Private sector savings ratio				Growth rate of the capital stock				Current account balance to GDP			
	1969-79	1979-89	1989-96	1990s less 1970s	1969-79	1979-89	1989-96	1990s less 1970s	Avg. 1969-79	Avg. 1979-89	Avg. 1989-96	1990s less 1970s	1969-79	1979-89	1989-96	1990s less 1970s	Avg. 1969-79	Avg. 1979-89	Avg. 1989-96	1990s less 1970s
USA	0.1	0.1	0.2	0.1	1.0	1.0	0.6	-0.4	23.7	22.8	20.3	-3.3	3.6	3.0	2.3	-1.4	0.0	-1.7	-1.4	-1.5
Japan	4.4	0.8	0.8	-3.5	4.5	2.7	1.6	-2.9	36.0	31.4	30.5	-5.5	9.3	5.9	4.5	-4.8	0.8	1.8	2.3	1.5
Germany	3.7	1.0	-0.4	-4.0	3.4	1.6	0.8	-2.6	28.9	28.7	29.3	0.4	4.2	2.7	4.1	0.0	0.9	1.9	0.4	-0.6
France	3.2	0.8	1.0	-2.2	3.7	2.5	1.8	-1.9	27.9	24.4	26.3	-1.6	4.6	2.6	2.3	-2.3	0.2	-0.5	0.3	0.1
Italy	5.1	0.4	-0.4	-5.6	3.4	2.0	2.0	-1.4	32.3	30.5	28.4	-3.8	3.8	2.7	2.6	-1.2	0.3	-0.8	0.0	-0.2
UK	2.2	2.5	0.6	-1.6	2.7	2.2	1.1	-1.6	20.8	21.5	21.0	0.3	3.1	2.4	2.5	-0.7	-0.2	-0.1	-1.7	-1.5
Canada	1.4	0.7	0.1	-1.3	1.8	1.1	0.7	-1.1	31.3	34.4	31.0	-0.3	6.7	7.1	5.1	-1.6	-2.6	-2.3	-2.7	-0.1
Non-US G7 median	3.4	0.8	0.3	-2.9	3.4	2.1	1.3	-1.7	30.1	29.6	28.9	-1.0	4.4	2.7	3.4	-1.4	0.2	-0.3	0.1	-0.2
Non-US G7 average	3.3	1.0	0.3	-3.1	3.2	2.0	1.3	-1.9	29.5	28.5	27.8	-1.8	5.3	3.9	3.5	-1.8	-0.1	0.0	-0.2	-0.1
USA less Non-US G7																				
Average	-3.2	-1.0	-0.1	3.2	-2.3	-1.0	-0.7	1.5	-5.8	-5.7	-7.4	-1.6	-1.7	-0.9	-1.3	0.4	0.1	-1.7	-1.2	-1.3
Median	-3.3	-0.7	-0.1	3.0	-2.4	-1.1	-0.8	1.3	-6.4	-6.8	-8.5	-2.4	-0.8	0.3	-1.1	0.0	-0.2	-1.4	-1.6	-1.3
Rank	7	7	4	1	7	7	7	1	6	6	7	5	6	6	7	4	5	6	5	6

Source: OECD Secretariat.

REFERENCES

Baker, Laurence C. and Sharmila Shankarkumar (1997),
  "Managed Care and Health Expenditures: Evidence from Medicare, 1990-1994", NBER Working Paper No. 6187, September.

Baltagi, Badi H., James M. Griffin and Daniel Rich (1995),
  "Airline Deregulation: The Cost Pieces of the Puzzle", International Economic Review, Vol. 36, No. 1, February, pp. 245-258.

Berger, Allen N., Anil Kashyap and Joseph Scalise (1995),
  "The Transformation of the US Banking Industry: What a Long, Strange Trip It's Been", Brookings Papers on Economic Activity, No. 2, pp. 55-201.

Bernekov, C.C., and A.N. Kleit (1996),
  "The Efficiency Effects of Railroad Deregulation in the United States", International Journal of Transport Economics, Vol. XVII No. 1, February, pp. 21-36.

Borenstein, Severin and Nancy Rose (1994),
  "Competition and Price Dispersion in the US Airline Industry", Journal of Political Economy, Vol. 102, August, pp. 653-83.

Borenstein, Severin (1990),
  "Airline Mergers, Airport Dominance and Market Power", American Economic Review, Vol. 80, May.

Borenstein, Severin (1992),
  "The Evolution of US Airline Competition", Journal of Economic Perspective, Spring.

Boyer, Kenneth D. (1993),
  "Deregulation of the Trucking Sector: Specialisation, Concentration, Entry and Financial Distress", Southern Economic Journal, Vol. 59(3), pp. 481-95.

Braeutigam, Ronald. R. and John C. Panzar (1993),
  "Effects of the Change from Rate of Return to Price Cap Regulation", AEA Papers and Proceedings, Vol. 83, 20 May 1993, pp. 191-98.

Braithwaite, John (1993),
  "Improving Regulatory Compliance: Strategies and Practical Applications in OECD Countries", PUMA Occasional Papers in Public Management, OECD, Paris.

Brown Johnson, Nancy (1991),
  "Airline Workers' Earnings and Union Expenditures under Deregulation", Industrial and Labour Relations Review, Vol. 45(1), October.

Card, David (1986),
  "The Impact of Deregulation on the Employment and Wages of Airline Mechanics", Industrial and Labour Relations Review, Vol. 39, July, pp. 527-38.

Card, David (1998),
  "Deregulation and Labor Earnings in the Airline Industry," Chapter 5 in Peoples, ed. (1998).

Clinton, Bill (1993),
  Executive Order No. 12866, Regulatory Planning and Review, 30 September.

Crandall, Robert, et al. (1997),
  An Agenda for Federal Regulatory Reform, AEI and The Brookings Institution.

Crandall, Robert (1991),
  After the Break-Up: US Telecommunications in a More Competitive Environment, The Brookings Institution, Washington DC.

Crandall, Robert W. and L. Waverman (1995),
    Talk is Cheap, The Brookings Institution, Washington DC.

Crémieux, Pierre-Yves (1996),
    "The Effect of Deregulation on Employee Earnings: Pilots, Flight Attendants, and Mechanics, 1959-92", Industrial and Labor Relations, No. 49:2, pp. 223-42.

Congressional Budget Office (1997*a*),
    "Trends in Health Care Spending by the Private Sector", April.

Congressional Budget Office (1997*b*),
    "Predicting How Changes in Medicare's Payment Rates Would Affect Risk-sector Enrolment and Costs", March.

Cutler, David (1996),
    "Public Policy for Health Care", NBER Working Paper No. 5991, May.

Cutler, David M. and Louise Sheiner (1997),
    "Managed Care and the Growth of Medical Expenditures", NBER Working Paper No. 6140, August.

De Vany, Arthur, and W. David Walls (1994),
    "Natural Gas Industry Transformation, Competitive Institutions and the Role of Regulation", Energy Policy, No. 22:9, pp. 755-63.

Evans, William and Ioannis Kessides (1993),
    "Structure, Conduct and Performance in the Deregulated Airline Industry", *Southern Economic Journal*, Vol. 59(3), pp. 450-67.

Farrell, Joseph (1996),
    "Creating Local Competition," *Federal Communications Law Journal*, Vol. 49; 1 November.

Formby, John P., Paul D. Thistle and James Keeler (1990),
    "Costs under Regulation and Deregulation: The Case of US Passenger Airlines", The Economic Record, Vol. 66(195), pp. 308-21.

Friedlander, Ann. F. (1969),
    The Dilemma of Freight Transport Regulation, The Brookings Institution, Washington DC.

GAO (1998),
    "Regulatory Reform: Agencies Could Improve Development, Documentation, and Clarity of Regulatory Analysis", May.

Gaynor, Martin and John Trapani (1994),
    "Quantity, Quality and Welfare Effects of US Airline Deregulation", Applied Economics, Vol. 26(5), May, pp. 543-50.

Gegax, Douglas and Kenneth Nowotny (1993),
    "Competition and the Electric Utility Industry: An Evaluation", *Yale Journal on Regulation*, Vol. 10(1) (Winter), pp. 63-87.

Good, David H., Lars-Hendrix Roller and Robin Sickles (1993),
    "US Airline Deregulation: Implications for European Transport", *Economic Journal*, Vol. 103 419, July, pp. 1028-41.

Gore, Al (1993),
    "Creating a Government That Works Better and Costs Less: Improving Regulatory Systems" Accompanying Report of the National Performance Review, September.

Graham, John D. (1995),
    "The Future of Risk Regulation", Strategies for Improving Environmental Quality and Increasing Economic Growth, Charles E. Walker, Mark Bloomfield, and Margo Thorning (eds.), American Council for Capital Formation.

Grimm, Curtis and Robert J. Windle (1998),
    "Regulation and Deregulation in Surface Freight, Airlines and Telecommunications", Chapter 2 in Peoples, ed. (1998).

Hahn, Robert W. (1998*a*),
    "An Analysis of the First Government Report on the Benefits and Costs of Regulation," Belfour Center for Science and International Affairs, John F. Kennedy School of Government, Harvard University, May.

Hahn, Robert W. (1998*b*),
    Reviving Regulatory Reform: A *Global Perspective*, Cambridge University Press and AEI Press, forthcoming.

Hahn, Robert W. (1997),
"Regulatory Reform: Assessing the Government's Numbers", AEI Working Paper, January 1997, Revised: April 1998.

Hahn, Robert W. (1996),
"Regulatory Reform: What Do the Government's Numbers Tell Us?", Chapter 10, *Risks, Costs, and Lives Saved: Getting Better Results from Legislation*, Oxford University Press, New York and Oxford, and The AEI Press, Washington DC.

Hahn, Robert W., and John A. Hird (1991),
"The Costs and Benefits of Regulation: Review and Synthesis," *Yale Journal on Regulation*, Vol. 8, No. 1, Winter.

Hausman, Jerry, Timothy Tardiff and Alexander Belitante (1993),
"The Effects of the Break-up of AT&T on Telephone Penetration in the United States", *American Economic Review 83*, pp. 178-98.

Hawk, B.E. (1989),
"Airline Deregulation After Ten Years: The Need for Vigorous Antitrust Enforcement and Intergovernmental Agreements", Antitrust Bulletin, Vol. 34, No. 2, pp. 267-306.

Hendricks, Wallace (1977),
"Regulation and Labor Earnings", *Bell Journal of Economics*, Vol. 8(2), Autumn.

Hendricks, Wallace (1994),
"Deregulation and Labor Earnings", *Journal of Labor Research*, Vol. 15(3), Summer.

Henning, Bruce, Lee Tucker and Cindy Liu (1995),
"Productivity Improvements in the Natural Gas Distribution and Transmission Industry", *Gas Energy Review*, February, pp. 17-20.

Henny, Alex (1996),
"The Power Exchange: California Goes Competitive?" Public Utilities Fortnightly, March, pp. 22-25.

Hirsch, Barry T. and David A. Macpherson (1998),
"Earnings and Employment in Trucking: Deregulating a Naturally Competitive Industry". Chapter 3 in Peoples, ed. (1998).

Høj, Jens, Toshi Kato and Dirk Pilat (1996),
"Deregulation and Privatisation in the Service Sector", OECD Economic Studies No. 25, 1995/II, pp. 37-73.

Hopkins, Thomas D. (1995),
"Profiles of Regulatory Costs", Report to US Small Business Administration.

Hopkins, Thomas D. (1996),
"Regulatory Costs in Profile", Policy Study No. 132, Center for the Study of American Business (August).

Hopkins, Thomas D. and Arthur J. Gosnell (1991),
"Cost of Regulation", RIT Public Policy Working Paper, Rochester Institute of Technology, November.

Hsing, Yu (1994),
"Estimating the Impact of Deregulation on Returns to Scale and the Marginal Product of Labour in Trucking: Further Evidence", *International Journal of Transport Economics*, Vol. 21(1), February, pp. 47-56.

Isaac, R. Mark (1991),
"Price Cap Regulation: A Case Study of Some Pitfalls of Implementation", *Journal of Regulatory Economics*, Vol. 3(2), June, pp. 193-210.

Jacobs, Scott H. (1997),
"An Overview of Regulatory Impact Analysis in OECD Countries," in *Regulatory Impact Analysis: Best Practices in OECD Countries*, OECD, Paris.

Jacobs, Scott H., *et al.*, (1997),
"Regulatory Quality and Public Sector Reform", (1997), *The OECD Report on Regulatory Reform: Sectoral and Thematic Studies*, OECD (Paris).

Joskow, A., G. Werden and R. Johnson (1994),
"Entry, Exit and Performance in Airline Markets", *International Journal of Industrial Organisation*, Vol. 12, No. 4, pp. 457-471.

Joskow, Paul and Nancy L. Rose (1989),
"The Effects of Economic Regulation" in *Handbook of Industrial Organisation*, Vol. 2, Richard Schmalensee and Robert Willig (eds.).

Joskow, Paul L. (1989),
"Regulatory Failure, Regulatory Reform and Structural Change in the Electrical Power Industry", *Brookings Papers on Economic Activity: Microeconomics*.

Joskow, Paul L. and Richard Schmalensee (1986),
"Incentive Regulation for Electric Utilities", *Yale Journal on Regulation*, Vol. 4, Fall.

Joskow, Paul (1991),
"The Evolution of an Independent Power Sector and Competitive Procurement of New Generating Capacity", *Research in Law and Economics*, Vol. 13, pp. 63-100.

Kahn, Alfred (1991),
"The Changing Focus of Electric Utility Regulation", *Research in Law and Economics*, Vol. 13, pp. 221-31.

Katzen, Sally (1999),
Statement made at the Global Forum on Reinventing Government, 14-15 January, Washington DC. (unpublished)

Keeler, Theodore (1972),
"Airline Regulation and Market Performance", *Bell Journal of Economics*, Vol. 3, Autumn, pp. 399-424.

Keeler, Theodore (1978),
"Domestic Trunk Airline Regulation: An Economic Evaluation", Studies in Federal Regulation, US Senate Committee on Governmental Affairs, December, pp. 75-160.

Keeler, Theodore (1989),
"Deregulation and Scale Economies in the US Trucking Industry: An Econometric Evaluation of the Survivor Principle", University of California at Berkeley Working Paper in Economics, No. 89-100, January.

Kerwin, Cornelius (1994),
Introduction to the Congressional Quarterly's Federal Regulatory Directory, Washington DC.

Kim, E. Han and V. Singal (1993),
"Mergers and Market Power: Evidence from the Airline Industry", *American Economic Review*, Vol. 83, June, pp. 549-569.

Krueger, A.B. and L.H. Summers (1988),
"Efficiency Wages and the Inter-Industry Wage Structure", *Econometrica*, Vol. 56, No. 2, pp. 259-293.

Kwoka, John, Jr. (1995),
"Privatisation, Deregulation, and Competition: A Survey of Effects on Economic Performance", Paper prepared for the World Bank, September. Unpublished.

Landy, Marc and Loren Cass (1997),
"US Environmental Regulation in a More Competitive World", Chapter 5, NIVOLA, Pietro (ed.) Comparative Disadvantages, cited below.

Litan, Robert E. with Jonathan Rauch (1998),
American Finance for the 21st century, The Brookings Institution, Washington DC.

Macavoy, Paul W., and John W. Snow (1977),
Regulation of Entry and Pricing in Truck Transportation. Washington DC., The American Enterprise Institute for Public Policy Research.

MacDonald, James M. and Linda C. Cavalluzzo (1996),
"Railroad Deregulation: Pricing Reforms, Shipper Responses, and the Effects on Labour", Industrial and Labour Relations Review, No. 50:1, pp. 80-91.

Meyer, Laurence (1998),
Testimony before the House Committee on Banking and Financial Services, April 29, Federal Reserve Board, Washington DC.

Moore, Thomas Gale (1975),
"Deregulating Surface Freight Transportation", *Promoting Competition in Regulated Markets*, Almirin Phillips (ed.), The Brookings Institution, Washington DC.

Moore, Thomas Gale (1978),
"The Beneficiaries of Trucking Regulation", *Journal of Law and Economics*, Vol. 21, October, pp. 327-44.

Morrall, John, III (1986),
"A Review of the Record", Regulation, 10:2.

Morrison, Steven A. and Clifford Winston (1995),
The Evolution of the Airline Industry, The Brookings Institution, Washington DC.

Morrison, Steven A. and Clifford Winston (1996),
The Economic Effects of Airline Deregulation, The Brookings Institution, Washington DC.

Morrison, Steven A. and Clifford Winston (1998),
"Regulatory Reforms of US Intercity Transportation", unpublished working paper, The Brookings Institution, Washington DC.

Moyer, R. Charles (1993),
"The Impending Restructuring of the Electric Utility Industry: Causes and Consequences", Business Economics, Vol. 28(4), pp. 40-44.

National Governors Association (1998),
"Strategies to Improve Managed Care Quality and Oversight in a Competitive Market", Policy Issue Brief No. 9802, 20 February.

Nelson, Randy (1989),
"The Effects of Regulation on Capacity Utilisation: Evidence from the Electric Power Industry", Quarterly Review of Economics and Business, Vol. 29(4) (Winter) pp. 37-48.

Newhouse, Joseph P. (1992),
"Medical Care Costs: How much welfare loss?", *Journal of Economic Perspectives*, 6(3) Summer, pp. 3-21.

Nivola, Pietro (1998),
Comparative Disadvantages? Social Regulations and the Global Economy, Brookings Institute Press, Washington DC.

OECD (1998),
"Open Markets Matter. The Benefits of Trade and Investment Liberalisation", Paris.

OECD (1997),
The Future of International Air Transport Policy, OECD, Paris.

OECD (1997),
"The Economic Effects of Regulatory Reform: Country Notes", in *The OECD Report on Regulatory Reform*, Vol. II, Paris.

OECD (1997),
OECD *Economic Surveys 1996-1997: United States*, OECD, Paris.

OECD (1983-1997),
OECD *Economic Surveys: United States*, OECD, Paris.

OECD (1995),
"Report on Trade and Environment to the OECD Council at Ministerial Level", Paris.

OECD (1994),
"The Environmental effect of Trade", Paris.

Office of Management and Budget (1998),
"Draft Report to Congress on the Costs and Benefits of Federal Regulations", US Office of Information and Regulatory Affairs, 17 August.

Oum, Tae Hoon and Yimin Zhang (1995),
"Competition and Allocative Efficiency: The Case of the US Telephone Industry", Review of Economics and Statistics, pp. 82-95.

Oxley, Howard and Maitland MacFarlan (1994),
"Health Care Reform: Controlling spending and increasing efficiency", OECD Economics Department Working Paper No. 149.

Peoples, James, ed. (1998),
Regulatory Reform and Labour Markets, Kluwer Academic Publishers, London.

Robinson, James (1995),
"The Impact of Environmental and Occupational Health Regulation on Productivity in US Manufacturing", *Yale Journal of Regulation*, No. 12, Summer.

Rose, Nancy L. (1987),
"Labour Rent-Sharing and Regulation: Evidence from the Trucking Industry", *Journal of Political Economy*, December, Vol. 95(6).

Rose, Nancy L. (1992),
"Fear of Flying? Economic Analyses of Airline Safety", *Journal of Economic Perspectives*, Vol. 6(2), Spring, pp. 75-94.

Shin Richard T. and John S. Ying (1992),
"Unnatural Monopolies in Local Telephones", RAND Journal, Vol. 23, pp. 171-83.

Shin Richard T. and John S. Ying (1993),
   "Costly Gains to Breaking Up: LECs and the Baby Bells", Review of Economics and Statistics 75, pp. 357-61.

Talley, Wayne K. and Ann V. Schwarz-Miller (1998),
   "Railroad Deregulation and Union Labour Earnings". Chapter 4 in Peoples, ed. (1998).

Taylor, William E. and Lester D. Taylor (1993),
   "Postdivestiture in Long-Distance Competition in the United States", AEA Papers and Proceedings, Vol. 83(2), May, pp. 185-190.

Teng, Tammy and John Graham (1997),
   "The Opportunity Costs of Haphazard Social Investments in Life-Saving", published in Hahn, Robert, Risks, Costs and Lives Saved – Getting Better Results from Regulation (Oxford University Press, New York and Oxford), Chapter 8.

Teng, Tammy, et al. (1995),
   "Five Hundred Life Saving Interventions and their Cost-Effectiveness", Risk Analysis, No. 15, June, pp. 369-89.

United States Government, Environmental Protection Agency (1987),
   EPA's Use of Benefit Cost Analysis 1981-1986, Washington DC.

United States Government, Office of Management and Budget (1997),
   "Report to Congress on the Costs and Benefits of Federal Regulations", Washington DC., 30 September.

United States Government, Office of Management and Budget (1998),
   "Draft Report to Congress on the Costs and Benefits of Federal Regulations", Washington DC., 17 August.

United States Government, Office of Technology Assessment (1989),
   Electric Power Wheeling and Dealing, 101st Congress of the United States, May.

United States Government, Federal Energy Regulatory Commission (1996a),
   "Promoting Wholesale Competition Through Open Access Non-Discriminatory Transmission Services by Public Utilities: Recovery of Stranded Costs by Public Utilities and Transmitting Utilities", Order No. 888, Final Rule, April.

United States Government, President's Council of Economic Advisors (1996b),
   Economic Report of the President, Ch. 6, GPO, Washington DC.

Viscui, W. Kip (1996),
   "Economic Foundations of the Current Regulatory Reform Efforts", Journal of Economic Perspectives, Vol. 10, No. 3.

Viscusi, W. Kip (1992),
   Fatal Tradeoffs: Public and Private Responsibilities for Risk, Oxford University Press.

Watkiss, Jeffrey D. and Douglas W. Smith (1993),
   "The Energy Policy Act of 1992: A Watershed for Competition in the Wholesale Power Market", Yale Journal on Regulation, Vol. 10(2) (Summer), pp. 447-92.

Wenders, John T. and Bruce L. Egan (1986),
   "The Implications of Economic Efficiency for US Telecommunications Policy", Telecommunications Policy, Vol. 10, March.

Wilson, Wesley (1997),
   "Cost Savings and Productivity in the Railroad Industry", Journal of Regulatory Economics, No. 11, pp. 21-40.

Winston, Clifford (1998),
   "US Industry Adjustment to Economic Deregulation", Journal of Economic Perspectives, forthcoming.

Winston, Clifford, et al. (1990),
   The Economic Effects of Surface Freight Deregulation, The Brookings Institution, Washington DC.

Wolak, Frank A. (1996),
   "The Welfare Impacts of Competitive Telecommunications Supply: A Household level Analysis", Brookings Papers on Economic Activity, No. Microeconomics, pp. 269-350.

Ying, John S. (1990),
   "The Inefficiency of Regulating a Competitive Industry: Productivity Gains in Trucking Following Reform", The Review of Economics and Statistics, May.

Ying, John S. and Theodore E. Keeler (1991),
   "Pricing in a Deregulated Environment: the Motor Carrier Experience", Rand Journal of Economics, Summer.

Part II
BACKGROUND REPORTS

BACKGROUND REPORT
ON GOVERNMENT CAPACITY TO ASSURE
HIGH QUALITY REGULATION*

* This report was principally prepared by **Scott H. Jacobs,** Head of Programme on Regulatory Reform, and **Rex Deighton-Smith**, Administrator for Regulatory Management and Reform in the Public Management Service. It has benefited from extensive comments provided by colleagues throughout the OECD Secretariat, by the Government of the United States, by Member countries as part of the peer review process, and by the Trade Union Advisory Committee and the Business Industry Advisory Committee. This report was peer reviewed in June 1998 in the OECD's Working Party on Regulatory Management and Reform of the Public Management Committee.

TABLE OF CONTENTS

OECD 1999

Executive Summary

Background Report on Government Capacity to Assure High Quality Regulation

Can the national administration ensure that social and economic regulations are based on core principles of good regulation? Regulatory reform requires clear policies and the administrative machinery to carry them out, backed up by concrete political support. Good regulatory practices must be built into the administration itself if the public sector is to use regulation to carry out public policies efficiently and effectively. Such practices include administrative capacities to judge when and how to regulate in a highly complex world, transparency, flexibility, policy co-ordination, understanding of markets, and responsiveness to changing conditions.

Regulatory reform was pioneered in the United States and initiatives to improve the quality of national regulation have been underway for 25 years. They have been promoted mainly by the President, though recently the Congress has been more active. The most important general trend is the enormous shift since the 1970s away from anti-competitive economic regulation toward social regulation, which has greatly improved the benefits of the regulatory system as a whole, since social regulations are much more likely to produce net benefits than do economic regulations.

By many measures, the capacities of the US federal government for assuring the quality of federal regulation are among the best in OECD countries. Considerable investments in the institutional, policy, and legal infrastructure for quality regulation has produced well-functioning systems in the critical areas of forward planning, regulatory impact analysis, centralised quality control, and consultation with affected entities. The public debate is intensive and well-informed, and includes input from academia and think-tanks which provide innovative ideas and critical analysis of efforts and progress. Annual reports from the Executive Office of the President reporting on the costs and benefits of federal regulation are a valuable contribution to reform efforts, and are unique among OECD countries.

But the US regulatory system continues to have problems with both cost and policy effectiveness. Studies from different sources suggest that net social benefits for social regulations issued in recent years are positive, a significant though not a robust finding, but that many individual regulations impose costs higher than benefits. This means that aggregate costs of regulations – credibly estimated at between 4 and 10 per cent of GDP – could be substantially reduced without reducing social welfare. US regulatory habits of excessive detail, legalism, and rigidity are still dominant. At the heart of the most severe federal regulatory problems is the poor quality of primary legislation, which limits, and threatens to reverse, the benefits to be gained from regulatory reform. These problems are exacerbated by the inconsistencies, uncertainties, and complexities arising from the state/federal interface, which sometimes reduces accountability for regulatory decisions.

A series of improvements relating to performance measures, more intensive impact analysis, and congressional oversight has been launched in recent years, but there is as yet no assessment of their effects on regulatory quality and no comprehensive view of how these reforms fit together.

A more structured process of rolling reviews of primary legislation could contribute to correcting some of these problems. Continuing efforts are needed to improve the responsiveness of the regulatory system. Substantial gains could be won by rationalising the proliferation of regulatory quality controls; reviewing policy areas rather than individual rules; and experimenting with use of advisory bodies for the reviews. Mandatory regulatory quality controls should be expanded to cover economic regulation. Operational guidance on use of alternative policy instruments could encourage regulators to be more innovative. Finally, co-ordination with the states on regulatory reform could preserve and extend the benefits of regulatory reform at the national level.

1. THE INSTITUTIONAL FRAMEWORK FOR REGULATORY REFORM IN THE UNITED STATES

1.1. The administrative and legal environment in the United States

Like other OECD countries, the United States has over the course of a century constructed an enormous and complex regulatory state to provide citizens a wide range of vital services and protections, ranging from accessible buildings to safe food to a cleaner environment. In addition to new laws, over 60 executive agencies in the federal government are authorised to issue subordinate regulations. Each year, they issue between 4 000 and 5 000 new regulations. More than 200 volumes of federal rules are now on the shelves, and credible estimates of their direct costs as well as the value of their benefits for citizens and enterprises range from 4 to 10 per cent of GDP.[1] The result is that "federal regulations now affect virtually all individuals, businesses, State, local and tribal governments, and other organisations in virtually every aspect of their lives or operations".[2]

The role of regulation in American governance is at the centre of an intensive decades-long debate involving *ideological* issues of the role of the State in society; *economic* issues of the role of regulation in a dynamic and innovative economy integrating into world markets; *social* issues of the services and protections that should be provided by the State to its citizens; *federalist* issues of the balance between federal powers and state rights; *institutional* issues rooted in the constant struggle between the powers of the Congress, the President and the Executive Branch and the judiciary; and *constitutional* issues such as individual property rights versus collective rights.

Each President since Nixon has vowed to control the costs of the expanding federal regulatory state and to carry out policies more cost-effectively, while at the same time supporting the establishment of major new regulatory programmes. The balance of federal action has shifted from "regulatory relief" under Reagan to the Clinton philosophy of "regulatory quality" based on the idea that "The American people deserve a regulatory system that works for them, not against them".[3] Fuelling the debate is a veritable industry of regulatory reform analysis produced by think tanks and academia, by well-funded

---

Box 1. **Good practices for improving the capacities of national administrations to assure high-quality regulation**

The OECD Report on Regulatory Reform, which was welcomed by ministers in May 1997, includes a co-ordinated set of strategies for improving regulatory quality, many of which were based on the 1995 Recommendation of the OECD Council on Improving the Quality of Government Regulation. These form the basis of the analysis undertaken in this report, and are reproduced below:

A. **BUILDING A REGULATORY MANAGEMENT SYSTEM**
1. Adopt regulatory reform policy at the highest political levels.
2. Establish explicit standards for regulatory quality and principles of regulatory decision-making.
3. Build regulatory management capacities.

B. **IMPROVING THE QUALITY OF NEW REGULATIONS**
1. Assess regulatory impacts.
2. Consult systematically with affected interests.
3. Use alternatives to regulation.
4. Improve regulatory co-ordination.

C. **UPGRADING THE QUALITY OF EXISTING REGULATIONS** (In addition to the strategies listed above)
1. Review and update existing regulations.
2. Reduce red tape and government formalities.

and energetic interest groups, and by Congressional, Presidential, and state offices. As in other OECD countries, much of the debate in the United States has centred about the economic costs of providing social benefits, and the difficulty of balancing the two.

The intensity and visibility of the debate on regulation is characteristic of policy-making in the United States. As in any country, the legal and administrative culture reflects the values implicit in the organisation of state, market, and society. In the United States, the nature and concept of regulation have been shaped by many values, key among them being traditional concerns for property rights and the rights of the individual (increasingly including rights to be free of externalities imposed by others); positive views of competition as consistent with individual self-reliance and risk-taking;[4] and a preference for universal and specific processes and rules that bind everyone "fairly" (including the government). The tensions among these values explain much of the current debate on regulatory reform.

In many ways, the administrative and legal culture shaping regulation in the United States is the converse of that found in corporatist countries, where decisions are traditionally consensual and the administration has wide discretion in application, often sharing powers with organised market interests. Administrative action in the United States is taken within a strongly legalistic and adversarial environment based on open and transparent decision-making, on strict separation between public and private action, and on competitive neutrality between market actors. There are opportunities for anyone with an interest to challenge regulatory decisions before the courts on procedural and substantive grounds, which in theory enables regulated citizens to challenge and hold accountable the regulatory powers of the government, but also can reduce regulatory innovation and responsiveness.

These styles of the US regulatory system, in particular its aversion to competition controls as an instrument of social policy, have helped create the regulatory framework for one of the most entrepreneurial and dynamic economies in the world, while establishing high levels of protection for consumers, workers, and the environment. The highly open, pluralist, and participative rulemaking process – in which multiple interest groups compete at every stage to have their concerns heard and reflected in the outcome – is seen as essential to legitimacy (by avoiding "capture" by special interests) and to informed decision-making.[5]

Yet legalistic and adversarial styles have also produced what comparative studies of the American system find are more complex, detailed and inflexible regulations than those in other OECD countries. This undermines the results and raises the cost of policies.[6] Experts have noted that "many of the laws Congress has passed call for highly prescriptive and often excessively costly regulation".[7] Superfund regulations on cleaning up toxic waste sites and corporate average fuel economy standards for cars are often cited as examples of regulations where costs vastly exceed benefits. A recent book warning against US regulatory complexity noted that "modern regulatory law resembles central planning", and identified the cause as an extreme result of the American distrust of government discretion.[8] Calling for a return to "common sense", the book became a national best seller. A study of nursing home regulation reported that the United States had adopted over 500 federal nursing home standards, supplemented by state standards that doubled or tripled the volume of regulation. Australia had adopted only 31 broad results-oriented standards. Yet it was the Australian standards that produced the best results and best compliance, and by a very wide margin. The pursuit of reliability in US regulations produced so much complexity and detail that they reduced the performance of the whole. A vicious cycle was seen: disappointment with regulatory performance produced demands to "tighten up" standards, which further worsened the problem of complexity and rigidity.[9]

The regulatory process has become so encumbered that the term "ossification" has been used.[10] Procedures and relations with regulated entities tend to be highly formalised. One inquiry found a federal agency that needed an 18-foot chart, with 373 boxes, to explain its rulemaking process, and "this process was not unusually complex".[11] Producing new regulations or revising old ones often requires several years. A regulation to reduce worker exposures to methylene chloride, a toxic chemical, required 12 years from beginning to finish. Such procedural complexity extends through the entire regulatory system, from development to judicial review to application.

There is considerable interest in the costs and benefits of federal regulation in the United States, though as in other OECD countries the costs of regulation continue to receive less attention than the costs of direct government spending. Several studies carried out in recent years suggest that federal regulation costs several hundred billion dollars annually, and may produce even greater benefits. Most recently, the Office of Management and Budget (OMB) in the Executive Office of the President reported to Congress that federal regulations related to the environment, safety, and health cost between $170 billion to $230 billion per year, and produce between $260 billion to $3.5 trillion in annual benefits (the huge range in benefits estimates is largely due to uncertainties about the impacts of the Clean Air Act).[12] Economic controls on entry and prices cost around $70 billion per year, while producing few benefits. Hence, these kinds of regulations probably reduce social welfare. In addition, the annual costs of federal paperwork for citizens and businesses have been estimated by Hopkins at around $230 billion, though these figures are contested by OMB, include tax compliance costs, and may overlap with other estimates.[13] As noted, the total direct costs of regulation and paperwork appear to be between 4 and 10 per cent of GDP, while the total benefits are uncertain. The costs and benefits trend upward or downward is also uncertain, though OMB estimated in 1997 that regulatory costs as a percentage of GDP had stayed about the same since 1988.[14]

These studies recognise that such benefit and cost estimates are very uncertain due to what OMB calls "enormous data gaps" and "a variety of estimation problems". The direct costs are significant understatements of the full costs of regulations, because they miss impacts on productivity, welfare, and dynamic effects such as lost opportunities to create wealth.[15] Indirect beneficial effects that result from better health and longer lives are not included either. There are significant methodological problems; for example, the estimates mix different data sources.[16] Yet these estimates are a large advance in understanding the costs and benefits of regulatory activities, and work is underway in OMB and elsewhere to improve them. Unfortunately, these aggregate cost estimates cannot be compared with those of other OECD countries due to an almost total lack of such data outside of the United States.

These kinds of global estimates are not very useful, however, in assessing whether particular regulations are beneficial, nor whether the regulatory costs maximise net benefits. In both cases, data at the micro-level suggest that the opportunities for improving the cost-effectiveness of federal regulation are very large. Research on 106 regulations suggests that just two federal rules (automatic restraints in cars and lead reductions in gasoline) produced over 70 per cent of total net regulatory benefits, and that more than half of the federal government's regulations fail a strict benefit-cost test, using the government's own estimates.[17] Studies have repeatedly shown that redirecting regulatory activities away from low-priority to high-priority issues would have enormous payoffs in terms of delivering benefits to citizens at lower cost. For example, safety and health regulations aimed at reducing fatality risks have saved lives at costs ranging from $10 000 to $72 billion per life saved.[18] A recent study found that if existing regulations were re-targeted at those health and safety risks where lives could be saved at lowest cost, some 60 000 more deaths could be avoided each year without increasing regulatory costs.[19]

Legislative branch. All regulation starts in an act of Congress that defines the goals of regulatory programmes, identifies the agency responsible for achieving them, and contains substantive and procedural requirements as to how the agency will work.[20] Hence, the quality of law is a crucial issue for regulatory quality at all levels. Delegations of regulatory authority to the public administration vary widely. In some cases, laws are so specific that they require no subordinate regulations. In other cases, laws are so broad and general that subordinate regulations determine their impacts. In these cases, federal regulatory agencies have wide substantive discretion on when, what and how to regulate. A trend is underway, however, toward more detailed laws that circumscribe administrative discretion. This trend is rooted in Congressional frustrations about the performance of regulatory agencies and the continual tussle between the Congress and the President for control over policy. It has given rise to concerns that the Congress is "micro-managing" regulatory decisions, particularly in environmental protection, in ways inconsistent with good regulatory decisions and innovation. Congressional oversight after regulations are developed is also quickly increasing. Since 1996, final regulations are sent to the Congress for review (though the Congress has not yet exercised its authority to block any of these regulations), and since 1998 regulators are required to set performance standards for their actions.

Executive Branch. The President has constitutional authority to oversee the activities of the executive branch, but the wide range of designs in regulatory bodies varies the extent to which he can control their actions. In general, federal regulatory bodies are organised in two ways: as executive departments and agencies directly accountable to the president (which include most of the social regulatory agencies) or as independent commissions (a model begun in 1887 with the Interstate Commerce Commission) whose officers are appointed by the president, with the consent of the Senate, but whose terms are fixed by law (which include most of the economic regulatory agencies). The heads of some regulatory agencies are Cabinet officers; others are not.

Judiciary. No discussion of US regulation would be complete without acknowledging the role that the courts play in regulatory decisions. Issues that other countries would resolve through management and dialogue are resolved in the United States by the courts. "The courts have played a profoundly important role in setting the limits of congressional, presidential, and even judicial influence over regulatory policy-making in the agencies [...] the courts are empowered to hear variety of challenges to regulatory decisions, ranging from the delegation of authority to agencies by Congress to the legality and fairness of agency dealings with individual regulated parties."[21] Legal challenges are the norm rather than the exception. In the environmental area, almost every major regulation is challenged in court. The workings of the common law system led to the emergence of a single judge as the *de facto* regulator of the huge telecommunications industry. An assessment of the impact of the courts on regulatory quality is beyond the scope of this review, but it is fiercely debated. For example, since successful legal challenges can be based on the poor quality of information and analysis, judicial review may have promoted the use of empirical analysis by regulators. But since judicial review increases uncertainties and delay in regulatory policies, it may also have undermined the responsiveness and transparency of the regulatory system.

The States. Finally, regulation in the United States is a complex mixture of federal, state, and local rules and enforcement responsibilities. The 50 state governments have legal and regulatory authority in their areas of competence, including all areas not expressly pre-empted by federal legislation, and may delegate legal and regulatory authority to regional, local, or municipal governments. Interactions between federal and state regulatory powers are in constant flux, with concentration in some policy areas and decentralisation in others. The states are often seen as laboratories for regulatory innovation and experimentation, but, as in other federal governments, however, the United States has experienced a dramatic and increasing centralisation of regulatory power toward the federal level.[22] Many of the concerns heard about regulation in the United States focus on the complexity, coherence, and lack of accountability resulting from the interaction of federal and state regulations.

The effect of this complex environment on the quality of the national regulatory system is one of the key questions facing the United States. The great challenge of regulatory management and reform in the federal government has been construction of government-wide quality principles and processes of regulatory quality control. This requires both "discipline and flexibility" in the reform programme to accommodate such variety.[23] Even this goal has been contested. Development of regulatory quality controls in the federal government has been characterised, to a degree unusual among OECD countries, by tension between, on one hand, the need for clearer political accountability and strong management of a large and fragmented regulatory system, and, on the other hand, the desire that individual regulatory decisions should be free from political influence (which dates from the anti-corruption "good government" movement of the 1920s).

1.2. Recent regulatory reform initiatives to improve public administration capacities

The focus of reform shifted in the 1980s from economic deregulation to fast-growing social regulation. Today, the United States is rare among OECD countries in focusing on improving the quality of social regulations (defined as meeting benefit-cost and cost-effectiveness tests, while reaching defined policy goals) and reducing paperwork burdens as the main objectives of regulatory reform. This is consistent with the fact that estimates of the costs of federal regulation suggest that social regulations impose costs 3 to 4 times higher than do economic regulations, though this report concludes that economic regulations have been neglected in the current reform programme.[24]

Box 2.   **Milestones in improving the quality of social regulation in the United States**

1971   Quality of Life Review is undertaken as a means of improving regulatory co-ordination.

1974   Inflation Impact Statements are prepared for major regulations by the Council on Wage and Price Stability.

1978   Economic Impact Analysis is conducted by regulatory agencies and CWPS.

1980   Office of Information and Regulatory Affairs (OIRA) is established by the Paperwork Reduction Act to provide centralised paperwork review and information management.

   Regulatory Flexibility Act requires agencies to assess the impact of regulations on small entities and publish regulatory activities in annual Agenda of Federal Regulations.

1981   Presidential Taskforce on Regulatory Relief is established (a Cabinet level regulatory policy group, chaired by the Vice-President). OIRA is charged with responsibility for formal regulatory review (policy and analytical oversight) by executive order of most federal regulations at proposed and final stages.

   Regulatory Impact Analysis (including mandatory benefit-cost analysis) is mandated by executive order.

1985   Regulatory planning process is established, including publication of annual Regulatory Program of the US Government, containing descriptions of about 500 "significant" regulations under development.

1989   Council on Competitiveness (Cabinet level regulatory policy group chaired by Vice-President) is established.

1993   Regulatory review by OIRA (with new time limits) and benefit-cost analysis are reaffirmed by President Clinton; the Regulatory Working Group is established to advise the Vice-President. Council on Competitiveness is disbanded.

   National Performance Review is established under the Vice-President to "reinvent" government on results-oriented principles. Regulators are ordered to work co-operatively with the regulated community to find the best regulatory solutions.

   Government Performance and Results Act requires government departments to prepare for Congress strategic plans that identify, among other issues, a mission statement, strategic goals and objectives, strategies to achieve goals, programme evaluations, major management problems, and data capacity.

1995   Executive order requires all regulators to conduct a comprehensive review of regulations, with the aim of eliminating 16 000 pages of regulations from the 140 000 pages in the Code of Federal regulations.

   Unfunded Mandates Reform Act provides the first statutory basis for government-wide RIA; regulators are required to assess expected costs and benefits for most important regulations (but the benefit-cost principle is not included); the federal government must find financing if costs fall on state, local, or tribal governments.

   Amended Paperwork Reduction Act widens OMB authority and requires OIRA to establish government wide and agency specific paperwork reduction goals.

1996   *Small Business Regulatory Enforcement Fairness Act* toughens requirements to consider small business impacts of regulations.

   Congressional Review Act requires regulators to send all regulations to the Congress for review; most important rules have a delay of 60 days before becoming effective. Congress may nullify all rules within 60 days.

1997-98 *Treasury and Government Appropriations Act* requires OMB to submit to Congress estimates of total annual costs and benefits of federal regulations, and recommendations for improvements.

133

For the Congress and the Executive, the 1990s have been an active period for regulatory reform (see Box 2 for milestones). A series of important improvements to performance measures, impact analysis, and congressional oversight has been launched and is in the implementation stage. These reforms hold considerable promise for improving regulatory quality, but they have been piecemeal in nature, and there is no comprehensive view of how they fit together. Indeed, in some cases, they are narrow in objective, and not entirely consistent. Although these reforms have not yet worked their way through the system, a series of additional reforms are being debated in the Congress. While useful additional steps can be taken, it should also be recognised that a multi-year period of policy stability and determined implementation, combined with a thorough re-assessment of the long-term objectives of reform and how these various reform strategies support those objectives, is needed to allow the reforms to take hold.

In 1993, President Clinton issued an executive order (an instruction to the executive branch that in most cases does not establish legal rights) on "Regulatory Planning and Review" that aimed at "building the foundation for a regulatory system that will improve the lives of Americans without imposing undue costs and burdens". Based on earlier orders issued by President Reagan, it mandates for regulators a programme of regulatory quality standards, rational decision procedures, development of consensual rather than adversarial approaches, promotion of innovative policy instruments, and centralised oversight by the Office of Management and Budget of the most important regulations.

In 1993, Vice-President Al Gore launched a systemic view of institutional reform and the "culture" of the public administration under the National Performance Review (NPR). The NPR aims to "move from red tape to results to create a government that works better and costs less". Under the goal of "eliminating regulatory overkill", the Review recommended 10 regulatory reforms that are similar to best practices accepted by OECD countries, including:

– Encourage more innovative approaches to regulation.

– Encourage consensus-based rulemaking.

– Streamline agency rulemaking procedures.

– Rank risks and engage in "anticipatory" planning.

– Provide better training and incentives for regulators.

Although subject to considerable criticism, the NPR has promoted review activity, and six years on remains a potentially important reform mechanism in the administration.

Another tool with potentially profound impacts on regulation is the Government Performance and Results Act of 1993. This law requires government departments to prepare and submit to Congress strategic plans that identify, among other issues, a mission statement, strategic goals and objectives, strategies to achieve goals, programme evaluations, major management problems, and data capacity. The strategic plans are supplemented by government-wide and agency-specific annual performance plans, the first of which were required in February 1998. If it works as intended, the Results Act should stimulate regulatory reform by making regulatory failures more transparent and increasing accountability to the Congress. Its own performance in this respect is not yet demonstrated. Identifying results-oriented performance measures has been difficult, but in the 1999 budget requests, regulators have generated a series of quantitative measures of real importance (see Box 3).

The 104th Congress (1995-1996) debated a raft of legislation on regulatory reform. Significant laws emerging from the debates include the Unfunded Mandates Reform Act of 1995, the Paperwork Reduction Act of 1995 and the Small Business Regulatory Enforcement Fairness Act of 1996. These are discussed below.

Historical background. The current programme builds on 25 years of earlier efforts that saw the development of two very different reform trends: deregulation of economic controls, and establishment of quality standards and processes for new social regulations and federal paperwork.

Box 3.   **Selected 1999 performance measures proposed by regulatory agencies under the Government Performance and Results Act**

Department of Labour
- Decrease fatalities in the construction industry by 3% by focusing on the four leading causes of fatalities (falls, struck-by, crushed-by, and electrocutions and electrical injuries).
- Increase compliance with fair labour standards laws and regulations by 5% in the San Francisco and New York City garment industries and poultry processing.

Food and Drug Administration
- Achieve adoption of the Food Code by 25 per cent of states.
- Assure that 40 per cent of domestic produce is grown and processed using good agricultural and manufacturing practice guidance for minimising microbial contamination.

Transportation Department
- Reduce the number of transportation-related fatalities to fewer than 44 407, even with a projected increase in the miles travelled.

Economic objectives with respect to price stability, competition, job creation, and trade have provided strong and consistent support for regulatory reform efforts. The economic recession and surge of inflation that began in 1974 made regulatory costs for the first time "a national preoccupation",[25] and President Nixon directed that major regulations be assessed for inflationary impact. In 1980, the Congress resolved that the president should implement a "Zero Net Inflation Impact" policy that would require existing regulations to be eliminated as new regulations were added.[26] This unrealistic resolution was soon forgotten.

Deregulation became central to economic policy in the mid-1970s as evidence grew that government intervention was needlessly restricting competition and harming the performance of many sectors. This led to deregulation in many areas: financial deregulation (abolition of fixed brokers' fees) began in 1975, followed by deregulation of the railroads (1976), air cargo (1977), airlines and natural gas (1978), satellite communications (1979), trucking, railroads again, financial institutions, cable television (1980), petroleum, radio (1981) and buses and communications equipment (1982). Replacement of price and entry controls with pro-competitive regulatory regimes, backed up by strong competition policies, continues today in many sectors (see Chapters 1, 3, 5, and 6 in Part I).

Attempts to impose quality controls on the use of delegated regulatory powers in social policy areas began in the 1970s "in reaction to the explosive growth of new regulatory programs" of the 1960s and 1970s.[27] By the mid 1970s, over 100 federal agencies were issuing economic and social regulations in areas such as health, safety, housing, agriculture, labour contracts and working conditions, environment, trade, and consumer protection. Their output was voluminous: the Code of Federal Regulations (the comprehensive collection of federal regulations) grew from 9 745 pages in 1950 to more than 100 000 pages by 1980 to almost 140 000 pages by 1995.

The new social regulations affected a far broader cross-section of economic, production and consumption activities than had older-style economic regulation, and hence they were far more visible and interactive. The administrative and economic side-effects of rapid regulatory expansion began, in the late 1960s, to command political attention. Conflict and duplication, for example, between various regulatory agencies occurred more and more frequently. Regulatory costs, both on and off-budget, escalated. The administrative on-budget costs of federal regulatory activities rose from $4 billion in 1970 to over $11 billion by 1994, while staffing of regulatory agencies rose from 70 000 to over 128 000 in the same period.[28]

Through the 1980s, new data on aggregate direct and indirect regulatory costs drew increasing attention to the cumulative economic burden of social regulations. Other studies suggested that workplace and environmental regulation had had significant negative effects on productivity.[29] As information about such regulatory costs improved, regulation began to be viewed as a form of government spending that should be controlled as systematically as fiscal expenditures (regulatory budgeting is discussed in Box 8).

Criticism grew of the failure of detailed regulations to keep up with changing social, economic and technological conditions. By the 1980s, a political backlash against regulation had emerged, fuelled by the economic crisis of the time. The message was simple: "American life is burdened by too much regulation".[30] To federal officials, the problem was that existing control and oversight processes were not suited to regulations. "The response from the vast array of entities subject to the new forms of regulation created an urgent demand for greater co-ordination, rationality, and executive accountability in the regulatory process", wrote the Office of Management and Budget. New means were needed to manage the enlarged federal regulatory structure.

In 1981, President Reagan made "regulatory relief a top priority [...] one of the cornerstones of my economic recovery program". Agencies were directed to "weed out and eliminate wasteful, unnecessary, intrusive regulatory standards". Late in the 1980s, competitiveness in opening global markets became key to the regulatory reform program. "Domestic policies, including regulation, have to be considered in the much larger context of our ability to compete in an international economy", OMB stated in 1987. In 1989, regulatory reform was linked directly to US trade policy when President Bush established the cabinet-level Council on Competitiveness, chaired by the Vice-President, to review major regulatory issues. The Council was abolished by President Clinton in 1993 due to concerns about lack of transparency and bias toward business concerns.

2. DRIVERS OF REGULATORY REFORM: NATIONAL POLICIES AND INSTITUTIONS

2.1. Regulatory reform policies and core principles

The 1997 OECD *Report on Regulatory Reform* recommends that countries "adopt at the political level broad programmes of regulatory reform that establish clear objectives and frameworks for implementation".[31] The 1995 OECD *Council Recommendation on Improving the Quality of Government Regulation* contains a set of best practice principles against which reform policies can be measured.[32] The content of, and formal political commitment for, US regulatory reform policies demonstrates a high level of consistency with these recommendations.

The current reform policy for the executive branch establishes clear political accountability at the highest political levels. The framework reform policies are established directly by the President on the basis of his executive authority. In the Clinton executive order, the Vice-President is identified as the principal advisor to the president on regulatory policy, planning and review, OMB (part of the White House office) as the "repository of expertise" on regulatory issues, and the head of the Office of Information and Regulatory Affairs (appointed by the president) as the co-ordinator of the policies. These administrative policies are backed up in some respects by laws supporting central review and impact analysis.

During the Clinton Administration, the National Performance Review has constituted another mechanism for regulatory reform. The NPR is conducted under the responsibility of the Vice-President, strengthening political commitment to reform and accountability at the highest levels.

Consistent with the OECD recommendation that governments "establish principles of 'good regulation' to guide reform", explicit standards for regulatory quality have been adopted, as have principles of regulatory decision-making. Clinton's 1993 executive order is the primary reference for regulatory quality standards. The order requires that agencies take a "minimalist" approach to regulation, by promulgating "... only such regulations as are required by law, are necessary to interpret the law or are made necessary by compelling public need, such as material failures of private markets..."[33] It requires regulators to:

- Identify the problem to be addressed and assess its significance.
- Identify and assess alternatives to direct regulation, including economic incentives and information, and use performance standards to the extent possible if regulation is chosen.
- Set priorities by considering the degree and nature of risks from different sources.
- If regulation is the best method, design it in the most cost-effective way.
- Regulate only upon a reasoned determination that benefits justify costs.
- Base decisions on best, reasonably obtainable information on the need for and consequences of regulation.
- Avoid regulations that are inconsistent or duplicative with other regulations.
- Draft regulations to be simple and easy to understand.

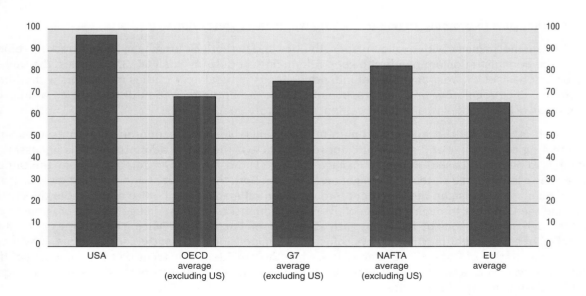

Box 4.   **Indicators of policy commitment to regulatory reform in selected OECD countries***

In this synthetic indicator of the formal commitment to and comprehensiveness of regulatory reform policies (based on self-assessment), the United States receives a very high score. This indicator looks at several broad aspects of reform policy, and ranks more highly those that cover all policy areas of regulation, that establish explicit standards for regulatory quality, and that are accountable to the highest political levels. The United States ranks among the highest among OECD countries on this indicator, indicating that much of the machinery of reform is in place. It must be noted, however, that the US regulatory quality policy does not cover independent regulatory commissions, a gap in the programme that is not picked up in this indicator.

*   The indicators used here are part of a dataset under construction as a contribution to the OECD Secretariat's horizontal work programme on regulatory reform. They are based in part on a survey of all OECD countries carried out in March-April 1998.
Source: OECD Public Management Service.

These and similar principles in place since 1981 represent a critical shift in US regulatory culture: they reversed the burden of proof for regulation (by, for example, ordering that regulations not be issued unless regulators showed that benefits justified costs). Under this programme, regulators themselves must show why they should regulate, and demonstrate that regulation is the most beneficial feasible approach. In principle, uncertainty and lack of information work against rather than for regulation.

It is notable that the United States is one of only a handful of OECD countries to adopt a strict benefit-cost test for regulations. The OECD has recommended as a key principle that regulations should "produce benefits that justify costs, considering the distribution of effects across society". Such a test is the preferred method for considering regulatory impacts because it aims to produce public policy that meets the criterion of being "socially optimal" (i.e., maximising welfare).[34]

Maximisation of social welfare, perhaps the broadest conceivable aim of reform, was placed alongside regulatory relief in 1981 as a major objective of regulatory reform. The 1981 executive order was the first to explicitly require that new regulations pass a social benefit-cost test and that regulatory objectives, not just individual rules, "be chosen to maximise the net benefits to society". The president, OMB said in 1991, seeks "a regulatory structure that appropriately balances the benefits and costs of Federal regulations for the country's long-term well-being…"

Although the economic concept of social welfare as articulated by OMB has always been quite broad, including both quantifiable and non-quantifiable benefits and costs, the benefit-cost test has drawn heavy criticism from those who believe that, in practice, quantified costs to businesses are given more weight than non-tangible social benefits. The Reagan Administration continued through the 1980s to emphasise regulatory "relief", a goal not always consistent with the principle of maximising social welfare. This had the effect of confusing the purpose of benefit-cost analysis and reducing its credibility.

In his 1993 order, President Clinton reaffirmed the importance of the benefit-cost test and stated that maximising social welfare is the aim of the regulation, but took care to recognise that "some costs and benefits are difficult to quantify" and that net benefits can include "potential economic, environmental, public health and safety, and other advantages, distributive impacts, and equity".[35]

2.2. Mechanisms to promote regulatory reform within the public administration

Reform mechanisms with explicit responsibilities and authorities for managing and tracking reform inside the administration are needed to keep reform on schedule. As in all OECD countries, the United States emphasises the responsibility of individual heads of regulatory bodies for matters within their portfolios. Each regulatory body has responsibility for the implementation of its policies within the constraints of applicable law and the president's regulatory quality policy.

But it is often difficult for regulators to reform themselves, given countervailing pressures, and maintaining consistency and systematic approaches across the entire administration is necessary if reform is to be broad-based. Hence, to manage the large and complex US regulatory system, the United States has established a series of oversight mechanisms. Both the president and the Congress carry out strong regulatory oversight, the president through a central management office accountable directly to him, and the Congress through a system of oversight committees organised largely along program lines, and through investigations by its organs such as the General Accounting Office. The concerns of the two branches of government may not always coincide; a congressional committee, for example, may focus on implementation of a specific regulatory law, while the president may focus on the functioning of the regulatory system as a whole, consistency with empirical tests of benefit-cost and cost-effectiveness, and its consistency with his policies.

A long running theme of central management has been enhancing accountability for regulatory decision-making in a sprawling and fragmented regulatory system. Centralisation of review authority in the Office of the President is a means of exercising oversight on broad discretionary powers delegated to unelected officials. Semi-legislative delegation has been described as "counter to the basic democratic tenets" of the US system of government, requiring new forms of political oversight.[36] On practical grounds, the regulatory system seemed increasingly distant from elected officials: "... costly regulations [...] germinating and percolating through several Administrations, became creatures seemingly immune to political or policy influence, gaining and retaining a life of their own", complained OMB. Oversight of the regulatory system was placed in the Office of the President to enable the president to carry out his constitutional responsibilities as Chief Executive: "... because the President is accountable to the public – the voter – for how his appointees execute the law, he is obligated to oversee and manage what they do".[37] The high priority placed on better regulatory analysis reflected a belief that regulators would not truly be accountable to the electorate unless the consequences – the social benefits and costs – of their actions were known.

Co-ordination between overlapping and inconsistent regulatory programs was an early objective of regulatory reform, and has continued to be an important stimulus, under both major political parties, for stronger central management. The first presidential initiative to improve regulatory management, a "Quality of Life Review" – established in 1971 – was intended to improve interagency co-ordination in expansive areas of regulation. In 1978, interagency consultation and co-ordination were further strengthened, and executive orders on regulatory reform in 1981, 1985, and 1993 setting up and refining centralised regulatory oversight in OMB were intended in part to "minimise duplication and conflict" between regulations.

Co-ordination expanded over time from a focus on "consistent rules" to a wider focus on how to better balance competing values through the regulatory and political system. In 1986, the director of the White House Office of Management and Budget declared that "regulatory disarray" had resulted because "regulatory agencies, individually and collectively, did not appreciate the impact or the burden of what they were doing" and that "the regulatory system is desperately in need of a mechanism for balancing the demands of competing and conflicting regulatory agencies and programs".[38] Regulations, according to OMB, must fit into the larger legal, social, and economic context. The institution responsible for ensuring this was OMB itself.

In the executive branch, competition between president and Congress for influence over regulatory decisions had contributed to the emergence of an unusually centralised and hierarchical regulatory oversight process. The Office of Management and Budget within the Executive Office of the President has evolved to become among the most powerful of the central oversight bodies in any OECD country. This reflects the strong constitutional powers of the President in overseeing the executive branch.

The OMB has had a strong co-ordination, reviewing, and reporting role on regulatory reform since the earliest days of the policy. Located at the very centre of government, OMB is responsible for many central management tasks of government that have been very helpful to regulatory reform. These include preparation of the President's budget, legislative review, information policy, financial management, and procurement policy. The current staff of OMB in the responsible Office of Information and Regulatory Affairs (OIRA) number around 22, about half of its size 10 years ago.[39] The traditional government-wide authority of OMB and its control of many levers of influence in the public administration has given it the potential for enormous authority in promoting broad-based reform. This is an important lesson from the US experience.

A distinguishing characteristic of the Office of Information and Regulatory Affairs (OIRA) in OMB is its intimacy with every stage of regulatory decision-making in the agencies. President Reagan's 1981 order and subsequent orders have placed OMB firmly and unavoidably within the normal process of regulatory development. OIRA reviews the most important regulations three times: 1) at the planning stage during preparation of the annual Regulatory Plan; 2) at the proposed stage before they are published for comment in the Federal Register (the national gazette); and 3) at the final stage before publication as a finished rule. OIRA's role is to review the regulations and the impact analyses in order to identify decisions and policies that are not consistent with the president's policies, principles, and priorities; to co-ordinate among agencies; to discuss any inconsistencies with the regulators, and to suggest alternatives that would be consistent. OIRA is, in effect, the President's trusted intermediary in overseeing the regulatory apparatus of the federal government.

In addition, OIRA has legal authority under the Paperwork Reduction Act to review and nullify any "information collection" requirement imposed on citizens, businesses, or state and local governments. This far-reaching authority is described in more detail in Section 4.

Closeness to Presidential power is a two-edged sword. When OMB has the support of the President, it ranks among the most effective of regulatory reformers in the OECD area. Yet the President has other policy priorities as well as regulatory reform priorities, and OIRA has not always enjoyed consistent support. Criticisms of OIRA are often rooted in the ambiguous position of a body that claims to simultaneously represent a set of quality principles based on empirical decision-making, *and* the position of the President who must deal with political priorities and other possibly conflicting claims.

The growing role of OMB in the 1980s also raised concerns about fairness and accountability. During the Reagan administration, OMB regulatory review attracted considerable opposition on the grounds that the presidential supervisory program had "the potential to transgress substantive or procedural substantive limits"[40] and that it intruded on the decision-making authority of the regulatory agencies. Critics charged that the review program was a "pervasive and persistent" effort "to shift the locus of discretionary decision-making authority from the agencies designated by the Congress to OMB".[41] Efforts to make the OMB review more transparent have laid to rest many of these concerns, and centralised presidential oversight of regulation has today become a permanent and routine element of the Washington policy-making apparatus.

The Small Business Administration has an increasing role, too, in reviewing assessments of small business impacts. The regulatory difficulties of small and medium-scale enterprises (SMEs) has been prominent since the early days of reform. The 1997 OECD Report on Regulatory Reform suggests that a priority reform issue in most OECD countries is reducing regulatory burdens on small and medium-scale businesses, which are disproportionately hit by administrative and other regulatory burdens to the extent that there are fixed compliance costs. The degree to which these are particular problems in the United States is not clear. Reports have found that SMEs in the United States are disproportionately affected by regulatory costs,[42] while a recent OECD report highlights the positive institutional framework existing in the United States, where a vibrant and diversified SME sector operates.[43] It is entirely possible, however, that both of these are true, and that a vibrant SME sector would perform even better if regulatory burdens were reduced. For these reasons, an important feature of the regulatory and paperwork reduction programmes in the United States has been the focus on SMEs.

The Congress enacted the Regulatory Flexibility Act (RFA) in 1980, and sixteen years later, the Small Business Regulatory Enforcement Fairness Act of 1996 (SBREFA) to correct flaws in the RFA that had undermined its effectiveness. The Small Business Administration's (SBA) Office of Advocacy has been the main institution to monitor compliance with these laws. Both acts increased SBA powers in the federal regulatory process.

The most significant mechanism concerns the RFA review process which requires federal agencies to analyse the anticipated effects of proposed rules on small entities unless they certify that the rules will not have a "significant economic impact on a substantial number of small entities".[44] Agencies are also required to identify alternative regulatory approaches. This review is done through a "Regulatory Flexibility Analysis" and notification in the *Federal Register*.[45] SBREFA reinforced these requirements by permitting judicial review of agency compliance with the RFA and enhanced the authority of the SBA Office of Advocacy to file *amicus* briefs in court involving agency violations. In practice, this provides to the aggrieved SME court awards, attorney's fees, and costs when an agency has been found to be excessive in its enforcement of federal regulations.

A second innovation introduced by SBREFA concerns the establishment of EPA and OSHA Regulatory Review Panels to review the initial Regulatory Flexibility Analysis for each draft rule. The panel process supplements the public comment requirements established by law. Each panel consists of employees from OIRA and SBA's Office of Advocacy, the regulatory agency responsible for the draft rule and representatives of affected small entities. Since the biggest problem for SMEs seems to be tax-related burdens, as is true in most countries, it is unfortunate that a Review Panel was not established for tax compliance issues.

Although the emphasis on SME impacts is understandable, an issue that should be closely watched is the tension between treating SMEs fairly and treating them preferentially. Too much tailoring of rules could result in a "positive" discrimination mechanism that distorts competition. Undue attention to the particular interests of a very diverse set of SMEs may create a more complex regulatory system. Exception and loopholes may reduce the transparency of the system. SME concerns may also hinder important global reforms, affecting consumers as well as other firms. For instance, the SBA Office of Advocacy persuaded the Federal Communication Commission to adopt a plan that telephone carriers receive full funding to support universal service to high-cost and rural areas. This cross-subsidy from consumers to some producers to a particular class of SMEs may be imposing costs on new or high tech SMEs, among other consumers. The SBA review could, in these cases, produce contradictory results to the more complete benefit-cost analysis required by executive order.

2.3. Co-ordination within and between levels of government

The 1997 OECD Report advises governments to "encourage reform at all levels of government". This difficult task is increasingly important as problems and regulatory responsibilities are shared among many levels of government, including supranational, international, national, and subnational levels. High quality regulation at one level can be undermined or reversed by poor regulatory policies and practices at other levels, while, conversely, co-ordination can vastly expand the benefits of reform. Given the structure of the United States as a federation of fifty states, co-ordination of regulatory management and its reform between levels of government is of major importance.

The States have constitutional authority to issue laws and regulations in areas not pre-empted by Federal law, while the federal government also delegates authority to the states to implement many federal regulatory programmes, often on a cost sharing basis. Municipalities and local governments, such as counties, are creations of the states, and typically have regulatory and legal authorities of their own. A substantial volume of regulation is issued by the states, and, like the federal government, state governments are regulating more. "This increased rulemaking activity threatens to rival, or even replace, state legislatures as the principal source of new laws emanating from state government", an observer wrote in 1990.[46] Federal regulatory reform does not necessarily affect state regulations, and OMB has not done very much to promote reform at the state level. Many of the states, however, have employed some form of review to oversee their own regulatory agencies, and 27 states require economic impact analysis for their proposed rules.[47] This suggests that co-ordination and exchange of good practices could have significant benefits.

Expansion of federal regulation over many decades has centralised more and more regulatory authority in the federal government. The federal government has also increasingly regulated the activities of the states themselves, by mandating large new burdens and costs that have often proved difficult for state and local governments to finance. In the 1960s and 1970s "federal mandates and regulations began to rival grants and subsidies in importance as federal tools for influencing the behaviour of state and local governments".[48]

A more "structural" critique also developed. In 1986, the Working Group on Federalism established by the White House concluded that "expansive, intrusive and virtually omnipotent national government" had transformed state governments from being "the hub of political activity [...] into administrative units of the national government". Federalism was soon after officially established as a regulatory principle, with President Reagan ordering in 1987 that regulations should pre-empt state authority only if required by Congress or if necessary to address a problem of national scope.

The continued importance of this issue was demonstrated by the adoption in 1995 of the Unfunded Mandates Reform Act. This Act is important in a number of areas and is discussed below. However, from the point of view of federalist relations the key requirement is for a cost analysis of any bill that would impose costs on state, local or tribal governments. If a mandate exceeds $50 million, or if the cost analysis is not attached, a procedural point of order can be raised in either chamber of the Congress (by end 1998, no bill had been blocked through this procedure, although points of order had been raised several times in the House). The Congressional Budget Office, which scrutinises compliance, has testified that this analytical requirement seemed to have a preventive effect in reducing regulatory costs.

The Federal government has recently begun to pay more attention to co-ordination of Federal regulatory actions with those at state and other levels. The Clinton executive order states that "respect" for other levels of government is fundamental, and instructs regulators to consult earlier with state, local, and tribal authorities. In some cases, progress has been seen in developing new consultation capacities to harmonise regulations among many jurisdictions. The Great Lakes Water Quality Initiative is a comprehensive plan to restore and maintain water quality in the Great Lakes Basin. It was the result of a collaborative effort by EPA, eight state governments, environmentalists, and local representatives. The flexibility for states to adapt standards to their own needs is expected to reduce the costs of protection. Such examples are not, however, very common, and there is enormous scope for further progress in co-ordinating regulatory approaches among levels of government.

3. ADMINISTRATIVE CAPACITIES FOR MAKING NEW REGULATION OF HIGH QUALITY

3.1. Administrative transparency and predictability

Transparency of the regulatory system is essential to establishing a stable and accessible regulatory environment that promotes competition, trade, and investment, and helps ensure against undue influence by special interests. Just as important is the role of transparency in reinforcing the legitimacy and fairness of regulatory processes. Transparency is a multi-faceted concept that is not easy to change in practice. It involves a wide range of practices, including standardised processes for making and changing regulations; consultation with interested parties; plain language in drafting; publication, codification, and other ways of making rules easy to find and understand; and implementation and appeals processes that are predictable and consistent. The US regulatory system is one of the most transparent among OECD Members, but some problems merit attention.

Transparency of procedures: administrative procedure laws

With some exceptions, the 1946 Administrative Procedure Act (APA) established a legal right for citizens to participate in rulemaking activities of the federal government on the principle of open access to all. The APA sets out specific requirements for administrative procedures to be followed in promulgating subordinate regulation, and hence meets the OECD benchmark in this area. The key mechanism through which participation occurs is known as "notice and comment" (described in more detail in the section on consultation, below).

Transparency for affected groups: forward planning of regulatory actions

The United States has had for many years an extensive planning system for regulations under development that ranks among the most developed in OECD countries. There are two major planning documents:

- The Unified Agenda of Federal Regulatory and Deregulatory Actions is published twice a year. It provides information in a common format to help the public identify which new regulations will affect them. All entries include information about the regulation's priority, its affect on SMEs and other levels of government, whether it is part of the NPR programme, an abstract and timetable for action.

- The Regulatory Plan is published annually as a defining statement of the Administration's regulatory and deregulatory policies and priorities. Entries are restricted to only the most important regulations, and contain a statement of need, a description of the alternatives considered, and description of the magnitude of risks and risk reduction expected.

The April 1999 document that combined both the *Agenda* and the *Plan* is 1 602 pages long, and contains over 4 500 entries from 63 federal departments and regulatory agencies. A subject index is included. The documents are produced through a computer regulatory tracking system maintained by the Regulatory Information Service Center, which also provides information about federal regulatory activities to the president, his Executive Office, the Congress, regulatory agencies, and the public.

The forward planning process has been a core element of the regulatory quality control system. In 1985, President Reagan ordered that federal agencies conduct, under the oversight of OIRA, an annual process of regulatory planning that would produce the *Regulatory Program of the United States Government*, to be issued under the president's signature. The planning process was intended to improve interagency co-ordination, establish the president's regulatory priorities, increase the accountability of agency heads for the regulatory actions of their agencies, and improve public and Congressional understanding of the president's regulatory objectives.[49] Regulatory planning was needed because regulation was "one of the most important and costly activities of government", yet, despite the regulatory review process set up in 1981, it was "managed far less systematically than direct government spending".[50]

According to OMB, regulatory planning also put into place a more rigorous and careful priority-setting process:

> *Scarce government resources must be allocated according to some set of priorities. Given his Constitutional responsibilities, the President decided that regulatory priorities should not be determined unilaterally by each agency. Rather, these priorities should be selected by the President's Administration as a whole, through a process that takes into account a wide spectrum of agency demands and Presidential polices.[51]*

The 1993 Clinton executive order retained forward planning, and put more emphasis on its value for communication and consultation. The regulatory plan made it possible for the citizen "to be a well-informed participant in the regulatory matters that affect your life", Vice-President Gore wrote to the readers of the 1997 Regulatory Plan.[52]

Transparency for affected groups: use of public consultation

Public consultation is highly developed in the United States. Almost all federal regulations are developed through mandatory administrative procedures intended to ensure public consultation and openness. These "notice and comment" procedures dominate the rulemaking process in Washington by establishing the channels through which multiple interest groups strive to influence the regulatory decision by developing empirical or legal arguments supporting their positions.

The Administrative Procedure Act, enacted in 1946, establishes minimum procedural requirements for rulemaking. While it leaves agencies great flexibility to develop procedures, the Act requires that an agency publish a proposed rule in the Federal Register. Except for some widely used exceptions,[53] the public must be given at least 30 days to comment in writing and the agency must consider any comments received. The comments themselves are made public via the establishment of a legal rulemaking "record", which contains all factual material received and potentially relied upon in the regulatory decision. When an agency publishes a final rule, it must explain the factual and logical basis for its decision, how it reached its conclusion, and how it dealt with the public comments received. Where important new material is received, there may be a need for more than one round of comments. Rules must be published not less than 30 days before becoming effective.

Written comments may be supplemented by a public hearing. Hearings tend to be formal in character, with limited opportunity for dialogue or debate among participants. Experimentation with "on-line" hearings has also commenced. A separate consultation process on paperwork requirements is established by the Paperwork Reduction Act, which is described below.

The American system of notice and comment has resulted in an extremely open and accessible regulatory process at the federal level that is consistent with international good practices for transparency. The theory of this process is that it is open to all citizens, rather than being based on representative groups. This distinguishes the method from those used in more corporatist models of consultation, and also from informal methods that leave regulators considerable discretion in who to consult. Its effect is to increase the quality and legitimacy of policy by ensuring that special interests do not have undue influence.

That said, there are serious problems with consultation that are rooted in the legalistic and adversarial tendencies of the American regulatory system. Notice and comment has tended to develop into a legalistic, formalistic process that can prevent rather than promote dialogue, co-operation, and communication. The role of the formal record in subsequent court challenges has too often meant that interest groups use it as the first stage of litigation, rather than as an honest inquiry. This has helped to discredit consultation. The Clinton Administration noted that, in the past, the agencies had already made up their minds even during the comment period and were unlikely to make changes based on public comment.[54]

Too, effective ability to participate is often limited by the complexity of the rules in question, particularly where scientific or technical matters dominate. The failure of regulators to clearly state the implications of regulatory decisions leaves the field to well-funded experts representing highly organised interests. Rather than organising information and communication, regulators have a passive role, in most cases simply waiting for the public to respond.

The key task is to marry a high level of transparency with development of a less adversarial system for consultation. The National Performance Review considered the performance of existing consultation processes. It concluded that, notwithstanding the extensive consultation processes already in place, "without exception", all groups wanted earlier and more frequent consultation opportunities. Moreover, while these were potentially costly, there were significant potential benefits in terms of greater regulatory quality and compliance. NPR recommended that agencies investigate more flexible and more interactive means of consultation, provide assistance to regulated groups to enable them to participate more effectively, increase programme evaluation, and make better use of information technologies.

The 1993 Clinton executive order, too, dealt with a number of these concerns. Consultation periods for proposed regulations have increased from an average of 30 to an average of 60 days. Agencies were ordered to involve affected parties earlier in the regulatory development process and to use consensual mechanisms such as negotiated rulemaking. There has been progress, as noted above in the section on state co-ordination and below in the discussion on negotiated rulemaking (though assessments indicate that this approach has been unsuccessful to date). Another important reform with the potential to transform access to the US consultation system is that public comments are now solicited through the Internet, which has noticeably increased participation. The United States probably conducts more communication with the public on regulatory matters through the Internet than any other country. The limitations of this method in providing equal access in practice have not, however, been adequately assessed.

Transparency in implementation of regulation: communication, compliance and enforcement

Once a regulation is adopted, it is easily accessible to affected entities. To become effective, final regulations must be published in the *Federal Register*, which is also available on-line. Final regulations are indexed and published in the consolidated *Code of Federal Regulations*, which is also available on-line. The *Code* provides a comprehensive view of the regulation in force at a given time.

A "simplicity and clarity" policy was adopted in June 1998 when President Clinton instructed civil servants to write all documents "in plain language". This is the latest effort in a long series of battles dating from the Carter Administration that seem to have had little success. One notable effort to improve communication of regulatory text has been the publication by some regulators of plain language "Small Business Compliance Guides" distributed by "outreach" programmes.

Improving enforcement strategies became a national priority only recently, though concerns about a possible decline in the capacities of the regulatory agencies to adequately enforce regulations have been prominent for many years. Budget cuts were, it was feared, disproportionately focused on enforcement capacities, indiscriminately reducing the performance of good and bad regulations alike. Comparative analysis sheds no light on whether the United States suffers lower levels of compliance

Box 5.   Transparency of regulatory systems in selected OECD countries

Based on self-assessment, this broad synthetic indicator is a relative measure of the openness of the reg-ulation-making and regulatory review system. It ranks more highly national regulatory systems that provide for unrestricted public access to consultation processes, access to regulation through electronic and other publica-tion requirements, access to RIAs, and participation in reviews of existing regulation. It also ranks more highly those programmes with easy access to licence information, which tends to favour unitary over federal states. The United States scores very highly on these criteria relative to other OECD countries. It loses points due to the absence of single contact points for obtaining information on business licence and permit requirements.

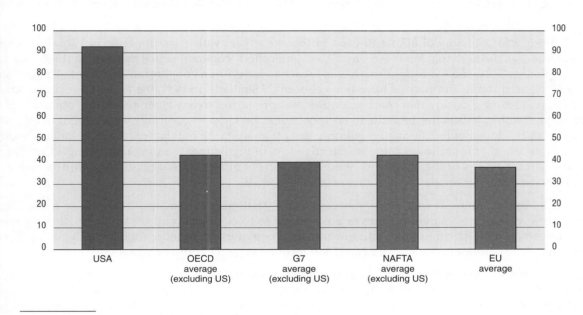

Source: OECD Public Management Service.

than do other countries, or whether the compliance trends are moving in the right direction. Almost nothing is known on this topic in any OECD country.[55]

The Vice-President, through the National Performance Review, instructed agencies to shift the focus of enforcement activities away from "paperwork violations" to an emphasis on performance results and to move away from adversarial relations with regulated parties toward a more co-operative approach. Several specific innovations are discussed below in Section 3.2. Compliance assistance and enforcement issues for SMEs were also targeted in the 1996 SBREFA. The Act obliges agencies to pub-lish compliance guides for all rules with a significant small business impact. SBREFA also establishes a complaint process whereby any SME can complain about enforcement actions to the new SBA Ombudsman or one of the 20 small business regulatory fairness boards established across the country.

3.2. Choice of policy instruments: regulation and alternatives

A core administrative capacity for good regulation is the ability to choose the most efficient and effective policy tool, whether regulatory or non-regulatory. In the OECD area, the range of policy tools and their uses is expanding as experimentation occurs, learning is diffused, and understanding of mar-kets increases. At the same time, administrators face risks in using relatively untried tools. Bureaucra-cies are highly conservative, and there are typically strong disincentives for public servants to be innovative. This is particularly the case in a litigious environment such as the United States. A clear leading role – supportive of innovation and policy learning – must be taken by reform authorities if alternatives to traditional regulation are to make serious headway into the policy system.

Here, the US system presents both strengths and weaknesses. Legal liability for actions that harm others is itself a strong alternative to government regulation in many social areas. Because liability is outcome oriented and based on economic incentives, it is likely to be in many cases more cost-effective than regulation at reducing risks, but the cost-effectiveness of some aspects of the US tort system has been questioned. High legal expenses and the risk of potentially large punitive damage awards in liability are claimed to increase business costs unnecessarily and reduce innovation and risk-taking. The number of civil cases has risen to 2.7 per cent of GDP, four to five times the levels found in other OECD countries.[56]

There is a long history of efforts to expand the use of innovative instruments. In 1978, President Carter issued an order to regulators – to install what he called "common-sense management for the regulatory process" – to show that "alternative approaches have been considered and the least burdensome of the acceptable alternatives have been chosen".[57] Similarly, in 1981, the Reagan executive order required regulators to ensure that "Among alternative approaches to any given regulatory objective, the alternative that maximises net benefits to society should be chosen". Crucially, assessment of alternatives was to be documented through regulatory impact analysis. "If regulatory reform is judged useful according to whether it improves the cost-effectiveness of regulation, then regulatory impact analyses that contain estimates of the costs and benefits to society of alternative regulatory approaches is a necessary condition for regulatory improvement", OMB wrote.

The current Clinton executive order as well as the National Performance Review also make clear that alternatives such as market incentives are preferable to command and control regulations. A considerable amount of effort has gone into encouraging regulators to be more innovative by using three main approaches: performance standards, market incentives, and information strategies.

Anecdotes suggest that innovative approaches are beginning to pose genuine competition to old styles of regulation. Expectations are higher that alternatives will be seriously considered, and several approaches now underway are useful experiments that should, if successful, help persuade a public administration that is extremely risk-adverse of the benefits of innovation.

Yet progress continues to be very slow. Despite two decades of effort, the US regulatory system still relies mainly on command and control rules. Progress is most evident in the environmental area, but overall there is little sign that the diversity and scope of alternative instruments has increased very much in recent years, and in fact the US system seems less innovative than some other OECD countries, such as the Netherlands. The 1993 NPR found that regulators continued to over-rely on command and control regulations, and blamed several factors, including:

– Congressional and agency lack of know-how about innovative approaches and how to design them.

– Congressional distrust of agencies, which means that Congress does not give agencies the flexibility to try new approaches.

– Agency and congressional distrust of the regulated public.

In addition, the legalistic culture and procedural complexities that inhibit innovation in the US public sector are probably major reasons for the cautious approach to regulatory innovations. The NPR recommended creation of a regulatory working group to consider new, creative and more effective alternatives and approaches to regulating (the interdepartmental Regulatory Working Group has made some effort to carry this out), and development of guidance on alternative instruments for regulators (not yet implemented).

A source of innovative and experimentation in the US regulatory system is the 50 states, although the states have not been as innovative in the regulatory area as in other areas of public policy. One reason may be that the federal government, by creating a rigid national regulatory regime, stifles innovation at lower levels. A key problem, according to the Environmental Council of the States (ECOS), was that federal agencies have no procedures for dealing with new ideas. That is, innovations do not fit into standard operating procedures, and hence cannot be pursued effectively by civil servants. A solution was to create new procedures through which civil servants could legitimately deal with experimentation and innovation. The 1998 ECOS-EPA Agreement to Pursue Regulatory Innovation "creates a path and a process that is clear to everyone" for how EPA will deal with state innovations.[58] The agreement contains operating principles giving states greater scope to implement innovative ideas to achieve better environmental outcomes and giving states and regional EPA offices the freedom to test different projects, as well as providing monitoring and information-sharing of the results.

Market incentives. Properly structured, economic incentives offer two great advantages over traditional "command and control" regulation. First, they allow business and others to achieve regulatory goals in the least costly manner. Second, market incentives reward the use of innovation and technical change to achieve these goals. There is some experience with the use of market-based instruments in the United States. The most innovative policy field is environmental protection, where a wide range of instruments is employed. The most celebrated is lead phasedown in gasoline (1982-1987), which persuasively demonstrated the potential effectiveness of credit trading: lead emissions in 1997 were 2 per cent of 1970 emissions. While the United States has played a pioneering role in the use of tradable permits (and is among the small number of countries where these are used to any significant extent), it is striking to see that the tax instrument is hardly used, especially in energy and transport-related issues. This is exactly the reverse of the situation in most OECD countries.

In the last decade, marketable permits are slowly increasing their reach, due in part to the increased complexity of pollution controls. The EPA views tradable permits as offering both the possibility of stricter standards and better environmental protection, due to the lower unit costs of pollutant reduction, as well as holding "promise for addressing problems, such as polluted runoff, that have not been brought under control through traditional regulatory means". Standardised regulatory approaches to control of emissions from factories, for example, do not work well with non-point sources of pollution that require flexible and source-specific solutions.

In particular, the EPA states that emissions trading "has become a standard environmental management tool, with the number of national programs offering this compliance option increasing markedly in recent years".[59] Recently, the Clinton administration has promoted the use of an international permit trading system as the most cost-effective to reduce greenhouse gases. There are several examples of emissions permits trading at local and regional levels. For example, CFC production allowance trading (1990) was quite successful. Southern California's Regional Clean Air Incentives Market (RECLAIM) aims to reduce industrial emissions by 80 per cent by 2010. A general set of rules for local air-pollution-permit trading has been proposed by EPA. This set of rules, called the Open Market Trading Programme, allows any state whose air quality problems and planning for compliance with federal air-pollution-laws are consistent with emissions trading to adopt a trading programme without a lengthy EPA review process.

Examples of trading arrangements in other policy areas include:

- Marketable permit programmes for water rights in the western United States have been active for many decades. In contrast to the active water market in Colorado, years of efforts to create a state-wide market for water in California – to move water from agricultural to urban uses – have been unsuccessful, partly because of complex property rights rules and numerous oversight bodies.[60]

- Major US airlines are trading landing slots at busy airports at prices in the range of US$1 million per slot.

- The New Jersey programme of tradable Regional Contribution Agreements allows a town to meet its legal obligation to provide low- and moderate-income housing by transferring the housing requirement to another willing municipality through a regional contribution agreement (RCA). An RCA is a cash payment from one municipality (usually suburban) to another municipality for the purpose of building or refurbishing low- and moderate-income housing in the receiving municipality. These obligations have been recently traded at a cost of $27 000 per unit.[61]

Other economic incentives used in the environmental area include tax incentives, including a federal incentive that encourages commuting, and pricing reforms that ensure that environmental costs are better reflected in consumer choices for services such as household garbage collection and disposal. Proposed policies for the year 2000 on climate change technologies would establish tax credits for energy-efficient purchases and renewable energy.

Information approaches. One of the most powerful alternative approaches to regulation is the use of information to empower citizens and consumers to take actions in their own interests. Typically for the United States, information has been approached in many policy areas from the perspective of a legal "right to know" rather than a flexible programme response to problems. There are many interesting examples of the use of information in the United States as a substitute or complement to other forms of regulation.

– Drinking water information for consumers. Stating that "an informed and involved public is necessary to keep [a high] level of safety" in water quality,[62] the EPA proposed in February 1998 to provide consumers with better information about the quality of water in the community. Water suppliers would, for the first time, be required to report to their customers at least once a year on the quality and sources of local drinking water, its compliance with health standards, likely sources of any contaminants, and the risks of any contaminants. This "consumer confidence reporting" would apply to all of the nation's 56 000 community water systems.

– Toxic release inventory. The 1986 Emergency Planning and Community Right to Know Act mandated that plants communicate information about toxic releases to local communities. Some 66 000 firms are covered nation-wide. Together with recent changes in 1997, the information is intended to provide a picture of how toxic chemicals are being managed within communities, and thereby improve the accountability of the private sector to those who may be affected by its activities.

– Consumer labelling. In 1996, EPA launched an initiative to improve consumer labelling information on pesticides, cleaning supplies, and other household products. Labels are being made more user friendly, with phone numbers for more information, and efforts are being made to standardise environmental information and storage and disposal instructions. A consumer education programme is planned to improve consumption of the information provided.

Voluntary, market-driven, and other co-operative approaches. Voluntary, market-driven, and co-operative approaches are interesting because they offer the advantages of speed, consensus, and flexibility, as opposed to arduous, adversarial, and formal rulemaking. Costs of compliance can be lowered, while incentives to comply can be strengthened compared to traditional sanctioning approaches. There is a broad spectrum of experimentation underway in OECD countries to expand use of these policy instruments. The use of market-driven standards has a long history in the United States, but the United States lags behind in the use of other voluntary and co-operative approaches. This is largely because relations between the public and private sector are legalistic and rule-driven rather than results-oriented, and co-operation between firms is highly constrained due to strict competition policy regimes.

Market-driven standards are used frequently in the United States relative to other OECD countries (see background report in this volume on Enhancing Market Openness through Regulatory Reform for a detailed discussion). The US standards development process is mostly industry-led, operating on a private, voluntary basis through more than 600 private standards-setting bodies. Government policy with respect to standardisation directs Federal agencies to participate in voluntary standards development activities and to use voluntary consensus standards in lieu of purely government standards except where inconsistent with law or otherwise impractical. This recognises that many voluntary consensus standards are appropriate or adaptable for the Government's procurement and regulatory purposes. Recently, the US preference for market-driven regulations has been seen in the government's approach to Internet and electronic commerce: "In our view, the voluntary, open, market-driven and consensus-paced standards development process has proven effective in balancing diverse and often competing interests in the computer and telecommunications market".[63]

Environmental programmes experimented with a variety of voluntary programmes in the 1990s, under names such as the Pesticide Environmental Stewardship Program, Encouraging Environmental Excellence, and Common Sense Initiative. A recent study[64] found that voluntary programmes in the United

States combine the features of the unilateral, negotiated, and public voluntary approaches employed in the European Union. In the United States, Voluntary Agreements (VAs) are primarily employed to address legislative shortcomings. Most US voluntary efforts are co-operative, non-mandatory strategies.

Box 6.   Marketing pollution permits – clean air at lower cost

Marketable permit or obligation programmes provide administrators with an alternative to traditional regulatory techniques. If developed and applied appropriately, they can reduce the cost of regulation, increase compliance flexibility, support economic-growth goals, and reduce the adversarial nature of regulation while still achieving regulatory goals.

Perhaps the best known example of such trading is the acid rain programme operated by EPA that is designed to reduce US sulfur dioxide emissions by 10 million tons annually from 1980 levels. In the programme, emitters of SO_2, a precursor to acid rain, have been issued a finite number of allowances (permits) that can be used over the next 50 years. SO_2 allowances are denominated in tons of SO_2, but not by year. This is because acid rain is a cumulative problem, so the absolute amount deposited matters more than the timing of the deposition.

There are two deadlines for individual plants to reduce emissions: at the end of 1995, SO_2 emitters had to achieve a first level of emissions reductions. A second round of reductions must be achieved by 2000. The number of allowances issued to individual plants reflects these reduction targets. Plants that over-comply and have excess allowances may sell them.

SO_2 trading regulations were developed from 1991 to 1992, and the programme was launched in 1992. Strict enforcement measures are built into the federal legislation, including automatic fines (indexed to inflation), plus a requirement to purchase the missing allowances in the next period, for failure to demonstrate ownership of sufficient allowances. For intentional (criminal) non-compliance, heavy fines and jail terms are possible consequences. As of March 1996, there have been no violations (Kruger, 1996). CEMS technology enables EPA to match output with allowances. When allowances are traded, the buying and selling entities must register the trade with EPA. The traders' computerised inventories are updated so that compliance in terms of the new levels of allowances can be monitored.

An important design feature of the SO_2 programme that was debated in Congress concerned how much electric utilities should have to spend to reduce SO_2 emissions. To estimate cost, an estimate of the value and volume of tradable allowances was needed. Utilities predicted that a one-ton allowance would cost roughly US$1 000; USEPA thought between US$500 and US$600. In fact, allowance prices originally (in 1992) traded for $250, and as of June 1995 were trading for $140, well below any prediction (Wald, 1995).

The original over-estimation of allowance prices had important public policy implications. Part of Congress's decision on how much acid rain reduction to require was based on predictions of how much the clean-up would cost. That is, Congress not only considered the health, ecological, and other impacts of acid rain when choosing a target for reductions, but it also had in mind a reasonable spending target for electric utilities. Because the cost of allowances was over-estimated, the overall SO_2 reduction goal is lower than it might have been. While some criticism has been levelled at the programme for this reason, it overall has been viewed as a success, since compliance costs have fallen dramatically.

There is a great deal of speculation as to why the cost of SO_2 allowances fell so far below predicted levels. Among the possible explanations are that utilities purposely overestimated allowance cost, aware of the link between allowance cost and total obligation to reduce SO_2 emissions (Wald, 1995), that the cost of natural gas, a low-sulphur substitute for coal, has fallen more than expected, that costs of low-sulphur-coal mining and transport by rail are lower than predicted, making low-sulphur coal a more attractive substitute for high-sulphur coal, and that the price of technologies that reduce sulphur emissions, such as scrubbers, has fallen (Palmisano, 1995). The unexpected but key link between SO_2 reductions and railroad deregulation is another example of the synergies between regulatory reforms in a broad-based reform programme.

The programme has produced significant, additional, unexpected cost savings, and reductions in emissions are ahead of schedule. Estimates of cost-savings just from allowing trading range from 25 to 43 per cent, and other factors, such as the cheaper transport of coal, further reduced costs. For example, the EPA forecast in 1990 that the cost of SO_2 reductions in 2010 would be between $2.6 billion and $6.1 billion (in 1995 dollars). But a 1998 study projected that these costs would be just over $1 billion (in 1995 dollars).*

---

*   Economic Report of the President, February 1999, p. 198.

Implementation problems have led to lower-than-expected environmental results for all VA categories. Among the different types of VAs employed in the United States, programs designed to reduce greenhouse gas emissions and a subset of toxic chemicals have contributed to emissions declines. However, weak evaluation methods likely caused EPA to overstate the environmental effectiveness of both climate change and prevention programs. In all cases, VA assessment is hampered by program novelty, lack of data, and weak monitoring and evaluation methods. In most cases, it is difficult to attribute environmental changes exclusively to voluntary programs. Due in part to the lack of environmental data, virtually no studies have been developed to demonstrate whether voluntary approaches are efficient.

The data that do exist identify a number of "soft effects". Participants in most VAs cite public opinion and/or regulatory goodwill as significant benefits. In some cases, VAs may confer competitive advantages to participants as well. Improved goodwill may indirectly lower costs associated with permitting and reporting, as well as minimise the threat of more stringent regulation. Soft factors may indirectly reduce administrative and abatement costs. At a minimum, VAs have the potential to promote interaction among groups who normally interact through the regulatory process as adversaries. Such VAs provide more opportunities for stakeholder participation than the status quo. However, implementation is hampered by the lack of clearly-defined administrative, monitoring, and participatory procedures. Thus, VAs – particularly unilateral and negotiated approaches – lack credibility among environmental groups and some industries. To promote trust, VAs must be made more transparent.

As with other innovative approaches, federal laws often impede VA implementation, particularly industry-led efforts and public projects that employ negotiation.[65] As a result, voluntary approaches remain largely "marginal" to federally-mandated air, water, waste, and toxics programs. Implementation may be strengthened by taking legal factors into consideration. However, in the United States, it is likely that the effectiveness of VAs will remain limited until the existing legislative framework is changed.

Co-operative approaches are more promising in the area of occupational safety and health. The design of rules and monitoring and enforcement regimes can encourage compliance by providing incentives or rewards for high voluntary compliance and compliance innovation. A recent survey of research concluded that, although empirical results are sketchy, where enforcement style were "more co-operative, it was more effective at reducing injury rates than where enforcement had been more adversarial".[66] One example is an Occupational Safety and Health Administration (OSHA) experiment initiated in 1993 in Maine. The Maine OSHA office used its databases to identify 200 employers with the highest number of injuries. Each was given work site specific injury and illness profiles and then asked to 'choose their OSHA': either they could use OSHA's help to survey hazards, and correct and implement worksite safety systems or they would be targeted for more frequent traditional comprehensive inspections because of their risk prioritisation. All but 2 firms chose partnership with OSHA.

The results were encouraging. Total workers compensation claims dropped by 35 per cent in those worksites during the program; employers identified 95 800 hazards and abated 55 200 (in comparison with the 36 780 that OSHA inspectors had discovered and cited in the previous eight years at those sites); at least 320 worksite health and safety committees were established; and nearly 60 per cent of employers reduced their injury and illness rates even as fines and inspections diminished.[67] OSHA hoped to expand the most successful features of this program nation-wide, although a recent court case has stopped expansion. Ironically, the innovative OSHA programme was overturned in federal court because it did not go through the rulemaking process, with notice and comment procedures.

The OSHA Voluntary Protection Program recognises achievement by companies that successfully integrate a comprehensive safety and health program into their total management system. Employers with exceptional programs receive special recognition including: the lowest priority for enforcement inspections, the highest priority for assistance, regulatory relief, and penalty reductions of up to 100%. For firms who are well intentioned but have room for improvement, a sliding scale of incentives is offered. The results: Overall injury incidence rates were 55 per cent below expected average for similar industries. Overall, participating companies were 51 per cent below expected lost workday injuries in

Box 7.   Regulatory innovation through HAACP

The US Food and Drug Administration was an early advocate of an alternative form of regulation known as "process regulation". This approach requires producers to document and analyse the different stages of the production process, identifying key points at which hazards arise and putting into place site-specific strategies to manage them. The idea is that producers are better at identifying hazards and developing lowest-cost solutions than is a central regulatory authority. This approach is particularly useful where there are multiple and complex sources of risk, and *ex post* testing of the product is either relatively ineffective or prohibitively expensive.

The FDA's Hazard Analysis Critical Control Points (HACCP) programme to regulate seafood safety shifts the basis of regulation to one consistent with quality assurance principles, rather than the older approach focused on verifying "end of pipe" compliance. The seven key HACCP components are:

- Hazard analysis: identification of likely hazards that could occur in specific products as a result of specific processes.
- Critical control points (CCPs): the key elements of the production process in terms of potential for health hazards to arise in the absence of adequate control measures.
- Critical limits: measuring levels of control performance at CCPs.
- Monitoring: keeping watch over CCPs to assess if controls are within critical limits.
- Corrective action: steps to be taken when monitoring indicates that critical limits are exceeded.
- Record-keeping: recording and maintaining information about results of monitoring, corrective actions and verification.
- Verification: reviewing all HACCP components periodically or when a production element changes.

FDA's economic analysis concluded that the present value of benefits of HACCP, compared with existing regulatory approaches, would be in the range of $1.4 billion to $2.6 billion, with up to 58 000 illnesses due to contaminated seafood being avoided annually.

HACCP approaches have now been recommended by the UN based Codex Alimentarius Commission and a number of other countries (*e.g.* Canada in relation to seafood) have also moved toward HACCP.

Source: This discussion is adapted from Chenok, Daniel J. (1997), "Flexibility Through Public-Private Partnerships: Prevention and Harmonization in FDA's Seafood HAACP Regulatory Alternative", in OECD Public Management Occasional Papers No. 18, *Co-operative Approaches to Regulation.*

similar industries, saving $94 500 000 for 3 500 lost work-days avoided. Many sites had production improvements, reduced absenteeism and lower workers' compensation costs.[68]

N*egotiated rulemaking.* Negotiated rulemaking, new to the United States, is familiar in most OECD countries where consensus-based approaches to regulation are used. Involvement of affected parties in decisions seeks to improve regulatory performance in several ways: by drawing on the expertise of the regulated to improve the technical quality of regulation; by fostering "ownership" of the outcome and, hopefully, the level of consent and voluntary compliance; by increasing the legitimacy of regulations; by diminishing the risk of hostile litigation by achieving a high degree of consensus; and by reducing the time to develop and implement new rules.

The legalistic environment for rulemaking in the United States has discouraged consensus-based approaches. The Negotiated Rulemaking Act of 1990 formalised a legal process to bring stakeholders into the process of developing rules at an early stage. It sets out a range of process requirements that establish a framework for attempts by regulators to reach consensus among major regulated groups on new regulations. It is carried out via an iterative, committee-based approach to rule development, with safeguards to ensure that all significant interest groups have an opportunity to request involvement. The negotiation is an additional element in the rulemaking process. The agreed text is published as a proposed rule and undergoes subsequent consultation in the normal way.

While there were some experiments with negotiated rulemaking in the 1970s and 1980s, the passage of the Negotiated Rulemaking Act in 1990 gave it a higher profile in the regulatory system. This innovation received significant political support. A 1993 executive order asked agency heads to identify potential areas for negotiated rulemaking. By the end of 1996 – or almost six years after the introduction of the Act – 17 agencies had initiated at least one negotiated rulemaking. The total number of negotiated rule-makings was 67, although approximately one quarter of these predated the introduction of the 1990 Act which formalised the process. Agencies had abandoned the process without any consensus in at least 13 of these cases.

As these figure suggest, negotiated rulemaking carries risks. The process can be resource intensive and yield little if agreement is not reached. The parties may use the process as a rent seeking opportunity by trying to insert particular advantages for their constituents into the regulation. The low rate of use suggests that regulators are unconvinced as to the benefits of using the process or, alternatively, that the situations where negotiated rulemaking can be useful are rare.

Early assessments[69] suggested that significant time savings had been achieved by negotiated rule-making, but a subsequent comprehensive study[70] disputes this finding and adds that not only has the process failed to save time, it has also required a more intensive use of agency resources. This observation has intuitive merit since the negotiated rulemaking process is conceived formally as an addition to processes already mandated in the Administrative Procedure Act. The notice and comment procedures still apply at the conclusion of negotiations. This design of negotiated rulemaking reflects a desire to maintain an "open" process of consultation in all cases and avoid charges of "corporatism" and lack of transparency, but results in a process still mired in formalistic and time-consuming steps.

Similarly, evidence suggests that negotiated rulemaking has failed to reduce the incidence of legal challenge to regulations. Analysis of EPA's experience (EPA is the largest user of negotiated rulemaking) indicates that the incidence of litigation is no lower than for conventionally made rules, despite the fact that the criteria for use imposed by the Act would tend to favour the selection of rules which were likely to be less prone to litigation. Possible explanations for this observation include the exclusion of affected interests from the negotiations, the extent to which the final rule reflects the agreed consensus and conflict over matters not dealt with in the agreements. It has also been suggested that, by raising expectations of accommodation of private interests in the rulemaking process, regulatory negotiation may make parties more sensitive to outcomes adverse to their interests and so more inclined to litigate.

Despite these concerns, it remains possible that negotiated rulemaking has improved the technical quality of regulations. It seems to work best when there is a defined number of players, and the issue is concrete and well-defined. As noted above, attempts to reform consultation procedures in general have pointed toward the need for more intensive, iterative procedures which commence far earlier in the development of regulatory proposals. Negotiated rulemaking appears to respond to all of these requirements. Moreover, the theoretical potential for it to compromise regulatory quality via the insertion of self-serving elements in proposed rules by the parties must be much attenuated by the very open "notice and comment" process which must be undertaken after the negotiations and by the real threat of subsequent litigations.

There is also the possibility that a number of the shortcomings of negotiated rulemaking result at least partly from relative inexperience with its use by all parties. If so, this may be a self-sustaining problem, as agencies may be reluctant to extend their use of the process precisely because early experiences are not favourable.

3.3. Understanding regulatory effects: the use of Regulatory Impact Analysis (RIA)

The 1995 *Recommendation of the Council of the* OECD *on Improving the Quality of Government Regulation* emphasised the role of RIA in systematically ensuring that the most efficient and effective policy options were chosen. The 1997 OECD *Report on Regulatory Reform* recommended that governments "integrate regulatory impact analysis into the development, review, and reform of regulations". A list of RIA best practices is discussed in detail in the OECD 1997 report, *Regulatory Impact Analysis: Best Practices in OECD Countries.*[71] This report provides a framework for the following description and assessment of RIA practice in the United States.

Regulatory impact analysis was pioneered in the United States, beginning in 1974 with inclusion of benefit-cost analysis in Inflation Impact Assessments. In fact, a review of OECD countries found that the United States was the first country to adopt broad requirements for benefit-cost analysis for regulation.[72] Full RIA has been required by executive order for all major social regulations from 1981, with the OMB responsible for quality control. The value of RIA has been considerably enhanced by its full integration into public consultation process. Today, quantitative benefit-cost analyses are prepared for over 90 per cent of major social regulations, but only 18 per cent of major economic regulations.[73] RIA is not typically prepared for primary legislation.

Under the current executive order, the design of the federal RIA programme is based on several key threshold, cost-effectiveness, and benefit-cost principles (noted in Section 2):

- The government should not regulate unless there is adequate information concerning the need for and consequences of regulatory action.
- Regulatory action should not be undertaken unless potential benefits to society justify potential costs.
- Regulatory objectives should be chosen to maximise the net benefits to society.
- Among alternative approaches to a given objective, the one chosen should be that which maximises the net benefits.

The trend today is to further standardise and upgrade RIA methods by establishing binding legal requirements, rather than relying on executive orders. A 1995 law (UMRA) requires cost-effectiveness analysis of a "reasonable number" of alternatives for any regulation that would require expenditures of more than $100 million by state and local governments, and $100 million by the private sector in any one year. This is an important step, though the UMRA cost-effectiveness test is weaker than the benefit-cost test contained in the executive order, and the "expenditures" threshold is less analytically sound than the broader "effects" test, including both costs and benefits, in the executive order. Proposals to strengthen the legal framework for regulatory analysis by legislating the benefit-cost principle, by establishing independent peer review outside of OMB, and by subjecting RIA to judicial review were unsuccessfully pursued in the Congress through 1998.

At the same time, independent review by OMB has become more selective. While an average of over 2 000 agency rules and 75 RIAs per year were reviewed by OMB during the 1980s and early 1990s, this fell to fewer than 500 rules by 1996, although the number of RIAs remained roughly the same. This is the result of a policy of focusing resources on more important rules to maximise the expected benefits of the review process. In addition, OMB has attempted to become more closely involved with agencies during the drafting of major rules. Input at an earlier stage of development potentially maximises OMB's ability to achieve change, and indeed some 60 per cent of regulations are changed during OMB review. It is also argued that this targeted approach allows routine regulations to be completed more quickly, speeding up the clogged regulatory process.[74]

This change in policy has coincided with a sharp reduction in the percentage of rules that OMB returned to the agencies to be revised – from an average of 1.2 per cent of those reviewed in the period to 1993 to 0.2 per cent from 1994-1996. The implications of this with respect to OMB oversight of regulatory quality are unclear. Absent other factors, the drop seems counter-intuitive, given the focus on more important regulation, as potential gains from improvements are greater for these regulations. Moreover, if reviews have become more thorough and intensive, discovery of cost-effective improvements seems more likely. On the other hand, as OMB argues, earlier involvement with regulators during the development phase may have reduced the likelihood that regulations containing major problems are sent to OMB for formal review, and problems are more easily worked out during OMB review.

Evidence on the results of RIA. Evidence on the value-added of RIA indicates that it has significantly improved the quality of some regulations, but that implementation is uneven across policy areas. In part due quality problems and in part to legal mandates that prohibit its use in some areas, RIA has not been successful at preventing the adoption of many low-quality regulations.

The evidence is building that RIA, when well prepared, helps increase the net social benefit of regulations. As long ago as 1981, an analysis of regulatory proposals critiqued by a Carter-era regulatory analysis review group showed that about one third were significantly improved. In 1987, the EPA analysed its experience with the use of RIA in 15 cases and concluded that its $10 million expenditure on RIA had reduced the costs of proposed rules by $10 billion, or a benefit/cost ratio of 1 000 to 1. The GAO found in 1998 that that, out of 20 RIAs, 12 were used to identify the most cost-effective approaches, and that seven of the other RIAs were used to define the scope and timing of implementation.[75] The suggestion that RIA is apparently genuinely integrated into policy processes is very positive, since many OECD countries are encountering difficulties on this point. Responding to concerns that RIA systematically overstate likely costs, a recent study of the limited number of cases where both pre- and post-implementation cost estimates exist found that, prior to 1981, compliance costs for new regulations were usually over-estimated, but that since 1981 the accuracy of estimates has improved and "the balance has been more equal".[76]

There is also evidence of a profound cultural change among regulatory agencies, insofar as the need to take economic impacts into account is much more widely accepted than in the 1970s. Viscusi presents data on the cost effectiveness of regulations from several agencies and argues that there is a clear correlation between internal agency attitudes and the efficiency of the regulations.[77] For example, a Department of Transportation policy to issue only regulations that are estimated to save statistical lives at a cost of less than $3 million is consistently applied in practice.

Yet there are substantial weaknesses in the quality and completeness of the analysis. In its 1997 report to Congress, OMB was unable to present aggregate cost and benefit numbers for 41 major regulations reviewed, due to lack of data. Of the 41 regulations, 21 required substantial additional private expenditures, but only in eight cases did agencies provide monetized benefits estimates, while cost estimates were presented in 16 cases. Hahn[78] finds that, of 92 health, safety and environment rules, in fewer than 20 per cent of the RIAs were benefits quantified in monetary units and shown to justify costs. His analysis found considerable inconsistency – within and between agencies – in assumptions and methodology. These included the use of different discount rates, the failure to present BCA in net present value terms and wide variations in assumed benefits for reduced death and injury rates. These findings of inconsistencies and incompleteness in RIAs were again corroborated by GAO's 1998 review of RIAs. Another dimension of quality is accuracy. The infrequency of efforts to "look back" and assess the real impacts of regulations against the *ex ante* projections in the RIAs means that there is very little information about how accurate RIAs have been in presenting the consequences of decisions.

While full quantification of the benefits of regulation is perhaps unachievable, Hahn suggests that significant benefits would be expected (both directly and indirectly) by "making key assumptions explicit, using best estimates and appropriate ranges to reflect uncertainty, providing estimates of the NPV of benefits and costs and summarising sensitivity analyses and base case results". In addition, "Agencies should also do more peer review to improve quality of analysis, but the nature of this peer review needs to be carefully designed".[79] Use of independent peer review panels have been advocated by some Members of Congress and by OMB.

Uneven application of RIA has contributed to wide variance in the quality of federal regulations. As previously noted, OMB's 1998 report to Congress on the costs and benefits of economic and social regulations[80] concludes that the annual benefits of regulations in force exceeds their costs (though there is considerable uncertainty in the estimates, since net benefits could range from $34 billion to $3.3 trillion). But the benefit/cost ratios for regulations differ markedly. As noted, more than half of the federal government's regulations fail a strict benefit-cost test, using the government's own estimates.[81] Hahn's analysis of agency RIAs showed a net benefit for 92 health, safety and environment regulations of $280 billion, but suggested that net benefits could be increased by $115 billion by eliminating those rules that failed the benefit/cost test. While regulatory quality appears high in many areas, it appears that RIA has had limited success in preventing poor quality regulation, notwithstanding the considerable experience with the tool in the United States and the significant amount of resources devoted to it.

Box 8. Regulatory budgeting: a new way to control regulatory costs?

An innovative policy tool that has been examined in the United States is regulatory budgeting, which uses traditional budgeting concepts to better manage aggregate regulatory costs. The regulatory budget concept is modelled on the fiscal budget approach, in which an agency or programme head is given a budget ceiling, within which funds are allocated among competing needs. In the regulatory budget, however, the ceiling would be measured by the economic costs of regulatory compliance borne by the private sector. That is, the regulatory body would be given a ceiling on new regulatory compliance costs.

While this tool has had limited practical implementation to date, it has the potential to transform the transparency, accountability, and incentives of regulatory decisions. Recent estimates of the annual cost of federal regulation are in the range of $280-$700 billion. and projections show the costs of regulation continuing to climb. These costs can be seen as a form of indirect taxation because the economic effects of taxes and regulatory costs are similar. From this perspective, regulation is a mechanism for government spending and regulatory costs are a form of government expenditure. Regulatory expenditures are the major government expenditure still "off-budget", that is, not included in the accounting and control system called the fiscal budget.

Budgeting would produce four major benefits when applied to regulatory costs. First, a budgeting approach would require explicit consideration of the aggregate economic cost of regulation. Second, placing a fixed limit on the amount of resources available to an agency or programme head with a defined mission should result in more cost-effective allocation of those goods, because priorities would have to be set among possible actions. Third, the regulatory budget, like the fiscal budget, would rely more on decentralised decision-making by the programme office than on centralised regulatory reviewers, and hence place decisions closer to the real expertise in allocating scarce resources. Fourth, it would increase legislative accountability for regulatory costs.

The key problem with development of a regulatory budget is the lack of information on regulatory costs. Budgeting will require a consistent and comprehensive set of estimates on the costs of new regulation. After almost two decades of effort, the United States has established a process of regulatory analysis that could form the basis for aggregate estimates of regulatory expenditures. Several accounting problems, mostly arising from difficulties in measuring indirect regulatory costs, are still troubling and will need to be answered. The regulatory budget has been under discussion in the United States for the past decade and continues to command significant interest. However, it is clear that its adoption, should it come about at all, is still some way off.

Experimentation with regulatory budgeting concepts is already underway. In an informal way, a cost ceiling was used as a benchmark for negotiation between the President and the Congress on the content of the Clean Air Act Amendments of 1990. The agreed ceiling, about $25 billion in annual costs, served to focus the negotiations on the most highly valued alternatives and may have been responsible for some of the most innovative provisions of the Act.

A possible use of the regulatory budget is the inclusion of a "regulatory cost ceiling" in new legislation that delegates regulatory authority. Each new law would place a ceiling on the total private sector costs that agencies could impose in writing implementing regulations. Once the ceiling was reached, new regulations would require either additional legislation to raise the ceiling or offsetting changes in other regulations to stay within the ceiling. This system would increase the accountability of the legislature and provide agencies with incentives to produce regulations that produce benefits at the least possible cost. The long-term goal is to develop a management or budgeting system that treats fiscal and regulatory expenditures in an equal manner, since both ultimately are diverted from private use. Integrating the fiscal budget with the regulatory budget – creating a "superbudget" that measures the full cost of government action – appears to be the logical final step.

Source: This discussion is adapted from John F. Morrall III (1993), *Controlling Regulatory Costs: The Use of Regulatory Budgeting*, OECD Occasional Papers in Public Management and from the *Budget of the United States Government*, Fiscal Year 1993, "Reforming Regulation and Managing Risk Reduction", Chapter 17.

Assessment against best practices

Maximise political commitment to RIA. The United States scores well here. Political commitment to RIA has come from the highest political level in the United States. The obligation to carry out RIA has, since its inception in 1981, been through executive orders. Moreover, each president since 1981 has issued his own revision of RIA, ensuring that the commitment to RIA has been reaffirmed by the current presidency. The support of Congress in promoting RIA has been tentative. Some laws prohibit the use of benefit-cost analysis to make policy decisions. It was only with the passage of the Unfunded Mandates Reform Act in 1995 that there was a government-wide legal requirement for RIA, albeit one that is weaker than the executive order.

Allocate responsibilities for RIA *carefully.* Experiences in OECD countries show no exception to the rule that RIA will fail if left entirely to regulators, but will also fail if it is too centralised.[82] To ensure "ownership" by the regulators while at the same time establishing quality control and consistency, responsibilities should be shared between regulators and a central quality control unit. The US approach is an international benchmark in this regard. The United States has established clear responsibility for regulators to conduct RIA in the first instance and a strong role for a central review authority and quality control. Moreover, the authority (OMB) is located within the Executive Office of the President and is functionally close to the budgeting authority. The clarity of its mission, its specialised and expert staff, and its location within central management bodies provides OMB with considerable ability to exercise quality control over RIA.

Train the regulators. OMB has published detailed guidance on conducting RIA.[83] The document sets out the objectives of RIA under executive order 12 866 as well as methodological guidance on issues such as discount rates and valuation of human life. However, written guidance is not supported by training for regulators in using RIA, or in related topics such as assessing regulatory alternatives. This is an area where US RIA policy could learn from other countries such as Canada. OMB in 1998 recognised the need to expand training and technical assistance for agencies in improving RIA quality.[84]

Use a consistent but flexible analytical method. In mandating benefit-cost analysis as the preferred method for RIA, the United States government carries out the most rigorous and far-reaching regulatory analysis of any OECD country. Yet it has proceeded pragmatically in expanding its use across the government. In practice, regulators need flexibility in conducting useful and feasible analyses. OMB's 1996 RIA guidance document states:

> *This document is not in the form of a mechanistic blueprint, for a good economic analysis cannot be written according to a formula. Competent professional judgement is indispensable for the preparation of a high-quality analysis. Different regulations may call for very different emphases in analysis. For one proposed regulation, the crucial issue may be the question of whether a market failure exists, and much of the analysis may need to be devoted to that key question. In another case, the existence of a market failure may be obvious from the outset, but extensive analysis might be necessary to estimate the magnitude of benefits to be expected from proposed regulatory alternatives.*

Flexibility does not mean, however, that regulators should be able to escape rigorous analysis. Emerging inconsistencies in the methodologies required for RIA are a matter for concern. While the executive order imposes the benefit-cost principle, the Unfunded Mandates Reform Act requires cost effectiveness analysis, and SBREFA requires a partial analysis of effects on one group of economic actors. The existence of parallel and different requirements is not necessarily a danger, since several methods are complementary to good decision-making, but the potential for conflict between implicit principles will have to be carefully managed to ensure that the core benefit-cost principle is not undermined.

Develop and implement data collection strategies. Lack of information is a key reason for quality problems in RIA. Development of innovative and more cost-effective data collection strategies could play an important role in improving analytical quality. Like other OECD countries, the United States ranks low in this RIA element. OMB has not provided guidance to agencies on the development and implementation of data collection strategies. This seems to be an area worthy of consideration as a "next step" in refining RIA processes.

Target RIA efforts. RIA resources should be targeted to regulations where impacts are largest, and where prospects are best for altering outcomes. The amount of time and effort spent on regulatory analysis should be commensurate with the improvement in the regulation that the analysis is expected to provide.[85] US RIA efforts rate relatively well according to this criterion, although the scope of coverage is still patchy. Formal RIA is targeted toward "major" or "significant" regulations. "Major" regulations were defined in 1981 as those imposing annual costs exceeding US$100 million, likely to impose major increases in costs for a specific sector or region, or have significant adverse effects on competition, employment, investment, productivity or innovation. The executive order distinguishes between "economically significant" regulations and "significant" regulations, and requires a full cost/benefit analysis for the former.

The degree of targeting has varied over time. During the Bush Administration, two changes significantly increased the number of rules subject to RIA. In 1991, OMB extended the impact assessment requirement by ordering that analyses be conducted on all "significant" rules, while in 1992, President Bush further extended the requirement by directing agencies to estimate the likely costs and benefits of all proposed legislation within their jurisdictions. The approach to RIA became more selective under the Clinton Administration and, as noted above, the number of rules reviewed by OMB in 1996 was less than one quarter of the average for the years 1984-1993. Although OMB reviewed several hundred final regulations, only 41 final rules met the definition of economically significant regulations in the year to 31 March 1997, and only 33 in the year to March 1998, thereby qualifying for a full benefit/cost analysis. This was less than one per cent of the final regulations published in 1998, but OMB stated that the 33 regulations accounted for the "vast majority of the costs and benefits" of new regulations.[86]

While these changes presumably represent differing views over time on the desirable degree of targeting, three significant concerns exist regarding the limited "reach" of RIA requirements. First, some major statutes specifically exclude the consideration of economic costs by rulemaking agencies in particular areas. Either RIA will not be conducted in these cases or, when conducted, regulators are effectively prohibited from using their conclusions in determining policy. Passage of the Unfunded Mandates Reform Act will not alter this situation. The second concern is that RIA is not usually done for proposed legislation. This is at variance with international practice, since at least 15 OECD countries focus RIA on legislation, and allows many important regulatory decisions to escape entirely from the discipline of impact analysis. Third, the executive orders requiring RIA do not apply to a large group of independent regulatory agencies. Thus, a class of important regulations are effectively exempt from RIA requirements because of the legal status of their sponsoring agencies, rather than their intrinsic importance.

Integrate RIA with the policy-making process, beginning as early as possible. Integration of RIA into the policy process is a strong element in the United States, compared to many countries where RIA is prepared too late, after decisions are taken. US RIA procedures require that RIA for both proposed and final rules be released for public consultation, ensuring that agencies are accountable for the quality and relevance of RIA throughout the decision process. OMB has recently attempted to become involved with agencies at an earlier stage in rulemaking to improve RIA quality and reduce conflict at the formal review stage. It can also be argued that the considerable exposure of US rules to legal challenge in the courts favours the effective integration of RIA with the policy process. While the standard of RIA itself is not justiciable, RIA can be used as evidence. This creates incentives for agencies to ensure that decisions taken on rules are supported by the results of RIA.

Involve the public extensively. The assumptions and data used in RIA can be improved if they are tested through public disclosure and consultation. Only a minority of OECD countries do this. RIA in the United States, by contrast, is fully integrated into the public consultation process, and provides a good benchmark for other countries. RIA are required to be released to the public at both proposed and final stages as part of the "notice and comment" process that allows all interested members of the public to comment on the assumptions and results of the impact analysis.

Use of risk assessment. A discussion of RIA in the United States would be incomplete without noting the key role of quantitative risk assessment. The United States is rare among OECD countries in making extensive use of various forms of risk analysis (including risk-risk analysis – see Box 10) as an input into benefits assessment. Fewer than 10 OECD countries use risk assessment systematically, and of these the US federal government is the most systematic consumer of risk information in setting health and safety standards.

Box 9. **The Formal Scope and Breadth of the RIA System**

This indicator looks at several aspects of the use of RIA, and ranks more highly those programmes where RIA is applied both to legislation and lower-level regulations, where independent controls on the quality of analysis are in place, and where competition and trade impacts are identified. The United States receives the highest ranking among the OECD countries on this criterion, although some elements of the RIA process, such as its applicability to legislation, are new and the quality of application shows continuing problems.

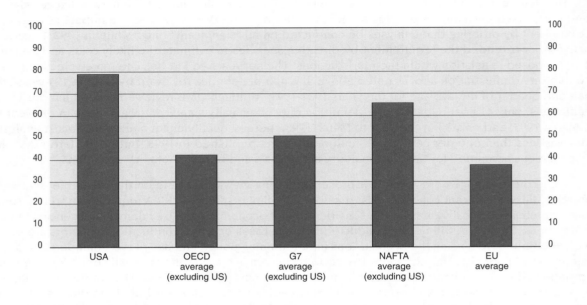

Source: OECD Public Management Service.

Quantitative Risk Assessment (QRA) typically forms the basis for regulation in the health, safety and environment areas – among the most important and fastest growing areas of regulatory activity. The first formal use of QRA occurred in the early 1970s, when the Food and Drug Administration used QRA to determine the need for regulation of various drug residues with carcinogenic potential in food producing animals. Since 1981, OMB has encouraged the use of QRA to calculate the benefits of all risk reducing regulations. OMB stated that, "For government to carry out its risk-management responsibilities, there must be extensive investment in the careful assessment and quantification of risks".[87] The courts have also supported the use of risk assessment as a way of defining and limiting the discretion of agencies in regulating risk.

However, laws are highly inconsistent about how risks are to be regulated and hence agency practices vary considerably. One fundamental problem is that, as with benefit-cost analysis, a number of important statutes prohibit the use of risk assessment. In some cases this is due to the statutes dating from periods in which detection techniques were much less advanced than today: The recently repealed "Delaney Clause" for pesticides, which prohibited any trace of a potentially carcinogenic pesticide in food items, had become widely recognised by regulators as an impediment to the competent management of such risks as the threshold of detection of such substances fell precipitously over past decades. It must be noted, however, that similar Delaney clauses for food additives, and cosmetics remain on the books.

Even in the absence of legislative limitations, agencies may adopt very different benchmarks as to what constitutes an "acceptable" risk or an acceptable mandated cost of risk reduction. For example,

---

Box 10.   Using risk-risk analysis: when does a regulation really save lives?

Risk-risk analysis is a variant of risk analysis which looks beyond the direct impacts of a regulation on risk. Its starting point is the question of whether a regulation designed to reduce one risk would also have identifiable effects on other risks. Risk-risk analysis has arisen from concerns that some regulation has actually increased, rather than reduced, total risks due to perverse indirect effects outweighing the direct risk reductions which initially motivated the regulation.

Two major mechanisms by which other risks can be increased exist. Firstly, the regulation may lead to a risk trade off in terms of a behavioural response. Regulations which restrict or discourage the consumption of one risky substance may lead to consumers substituting another which has its own, possibly greater risks. For example, regulation of artificial sweeteners may lead to increased consumption of sugar, which may have greater risks in terms of heart disease than the risks associated with the artificial sweeteners.

Secondly, actions taken to reduce one risk can simultaneously increase another, even without behavioural change. For example, chlorinating drinking water reduces the risk of bacteria borne illnesses but may slightly increase cancer risks. Similarly, switching to lead-free petrol reduces the developmental problems of high blood lead levels in children but may also increase cancer risk due to increased exposures to benzene.

A variant of risk-risk analysis considers the impact of income on health. Studies show that as income declines, mortality rates increase, with one widely cited study indicating that each $12 million (1991 prices) reduction in aggregate income costs a statistical life. Thus, every regulatory expenditure of this amount may cost a statistical life. This form of analysis has received some prominence in the United States.

Source: Viscusi, W.K., "Improving the Analytical Basis for Decision-making" in *Regulatory Impact Analysis: Best Practices in OECD Countries*, Paris, OECD, 1997, pp. 200-204.

---

regulators often use worst-case assumptions so as to build a safety margin into the regulatory decision. Done systematically, this practice can severely distort regulatory activities. OMB has summarised the problem thus: "The continued reliance on conservative (worst case) assumptions distorts risk assessment, yielding estimates that may overstate likely risks by several orders of magnitude... Conservatism in risk assessment distorts the regulatory priorities of the Federal Government, directing societal resources to reduce what are often trivial carcinogenic risks while failing to address more substantial threats to life and health".[88]

A detailed analysis of the inclusion of several mutually reinforcing "safety margins" in risk assessment was contained in a report commissioned by the Department of Energy in 1993.[89] It identified ten key policy assumptions, each widely used in risk assessment, each of which introduced a conservative bias into the results. The accumulation of these biases can lead to policy outcomes that are inconsistent with each other and with cost-effective approaches to risk management. A frequently cited example is the pursuit of clean-ups of toxic sites under the 1980 "Superfund" legislation, where critics argue that the high cost of conducting clean-ups to reduce risks to unnecessarily low levels has meant that only a small minority of identified sites have received any remedial action at all.

An additional issue is the often large degree of uncertainty attached to risk calculations, in terms of both the calculation of the initial risk and the productivity of measures that can be taken to ameliorate it. Again, different approaches are likely to be taken in dealing with this uncertainty in the absence of clear guidance.

For these and other reasons, there is huge inconsistency in risk management across the federal government. As noted earlier, federal health and safety regulations show an extremely wide variability in the costs per life saved – from thousands to billions of dollars. The highest costs are associated with regulations aimed at low-probability cancer risks resulting from occupational and environmental exposure. This enormous variance in the cost-effectiveness of various regulations has suggested to OMB that "aggregate risk mortality would be substantially reduced at considerably lower cost by shifting the Federal government's regulatory focus away from relatively small [...] cancer threats toward other health risks and causes of injury".

Initiatives have been taken in recent years to improve and standardise risk assessment techniques. In 1991, the White House Office of Science and Technology Policy convened a number of interagency groups to develop guidelines for agencies to use in conducting risk assessments. The National Academy of Sciences has also conducted a review of risk assessment. While risk assessment remains a highly imperfect tool, and one whose utility in policy-making continues to be questioned in some quarters, the United States is in the forefront in its adoption and refinement as a policy tool.

4. DYNAMIC CHANGE: KEEPING REGULATIONS UP TO DATE

The OECD Report on Regulatory Reform recommends that governments "review regulations systematically to ensure that they continue to meet their intended objectives efficiently and effectively". In the United States, three key mechanisms are currently employed to review existing regulations, each authorised by executive order 12 866.

The first mechanism is adoption of a general principle of review. Section 5 of the current executive order directs agencies to undertake periodic reviews of their existing "significant" regulations in order to identify modifications or repeals that would better contribute to achieving regulatory objectives, reduce burdens or better align regulation with the President's principles and priorities as reflected in the order. No specific mechanisms are set out to ensure compliance with this requirement. However, the Performance Management and Results Act may have an impact in holding agencies accountable for compliance with this general obligation.

The second review mechanism is based in OMB. The administrator of OIRA is required to work with a regulatory working group, drawn from regulatory agency personnel, to identify regulations that require modification. The design of this mechanism scores highly in terms of consistency with OECD best practice recommendations which emphasise the need to balance regulatory agency responsibility for reform with centralised co-ordination and management by an expert reform body.

Third, the Vice-President leads a programme of regulatory review. The National Performance Review set an ambitious target of a 50 per cent reduction in the number of existing regulations within five years. OMB reported in 1996[90] that NPR efforts had lead to the removal of 16 000 pages from the Code of Federal Regulations and that another 31 000 pages were modified out of a total of 86 000 pages reviewed to that point. That is, a total of about 40 per cent of the total number of pages of the Code were either removed or modified. Nonetheless, it is unclear that this review activity produced significant benefits, since cost-savings were not documented. Experiences in other countries show that it is not difficult to produce impressive results if non-monetary units such as page numbers or numbers of regulations revised are used instead of more relevant measures. For example, the General Accounting Office looked more closely at four agencies and found that these reported page reductions were almost entirely offset by new regulatory requirements in the same period.[91]

Sunsetting and automatic review requirements are not drivers of significant review activity in the United States, except in the case of three-year sunsets on all government formalities and paperwork requirements (see below). A new requirement in the small business act requires periodic reviews every ten years for small business impacts.

4.1. Cutting red tape

The US federal government has an enormous appetite for information that must be fed by enterprises and citizens. This seems to be a natural result of the information age, of pressures on public

Figure 1. **Aggregate number of hours spent filling out federal government forms**

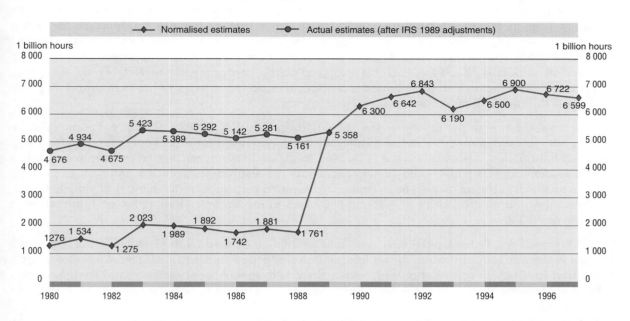

Note: The upper estimates, designated by the higher line, are more accurate. The sharp increase in FY 1989 is due to a comprehensive reassessment of the tax-related compliance burdens, which found that the burdens had been substantially undercounted in earlier years. The normalised estimates (the upper line) adjust the previous burden estimates to incorporate the revised tax estimates.
Source: Antonelli, A., and OIRA (1997).

administrations to target and assess programmes, and of budget cuts that have shifted costs from public to private sectors. The demand is also driven by the trend toward the use of information as a supplement or alternative to traditional forms of regulation. Indeed the magnitude of the problem is impressive. In 1996, businesses and citizens spent 6.7 billion hours filling out Federal government forms, responding to surveys, keeping records, collecting information, and dealing with other kinds of government paperwork (see Figure 1). This is equivalent to the private sector employing 3 million fulltime employees to respond to Federal information needs. Tax formalities accounted for roughly 80 per cent of the total burden

Since 1980, the United States has developed an intensive system (characteristically highly legalistic) for controlling paperwork burdens. The Paperwork Reduction Act establishes an independent reviewing agency (OIRA) and a centralised approval procedure, and offers legal protection to citizens if agencies attempt to enforce paperwork requirements that are not OIRA-approved. Granting legal authority to a central review agency to disapprove decisions by regulators – an authority that seems to be the only one of its kind in OECD countries – indicates the depth of public frustration over mandated paperwork.

Yet the success of Federal efforts in managing the paperwork burden is mixed. OMB made significant progress in improving awareness of the costs and consequences of information collection activities, and has succeeded in slowing the growth of paperwork. Yet OIRA's efforts are overwhelmed by major new regulatory programmes that require information from the public. Hence, the programme has not been successful in reducing the burden on the public, though this was a major goal of the PRA. Between 1980 and 1996 total paperwork burden grew from 4.6 billion hours per year to 6.7 billion hours per year. This is an increase from 20 hours per citizen in 1980 to 25 hours per citizen in 1996.

The Paperwork Reduction Act. Under the Act, each federal requirement that the public or businesses collect, keep, or submit information to the government must be approved by OIRA at least once every three years. The Act gives OIRA broad authority to disapprove a paperwork requirement or order its revision if OIRA finds that 1) it does not have practical utility; 2) is not the least burdensome necessary; or 3) duplicates information otherwise available. Requests for OIRA approval are published in the Federal Register, and the public is given 30 days to provide comments. If OIRA approves a requirement, an approval number is issued that must be displayed on the form or regulation. Notably, the three year "reapproval" cycle means that consultation is conducted on an *ex post* basis, rather than simply an *ex ante* basis, as is the case with most consultation requirements.

A crucial element of the process is the self-enforcing aspect of the PRA. If a current approval number is not displayed, a member of the public cannot be penalised for refusing to keep or submit the required information. Agencies are not supposed to expend resources carrying out unproved collections of information. OMB follows up any violations with the responsible agencies, and notifies the Congress annually of such violations. There appear, however, to be a substantial number of violations. The US General Accounting Office in 1999 found 800 cases where agencies had collected information in violation of the PRA.[92]

The Information Collection Budget (ICB). A second instrument created by the PRA to control paperwork burden is the annual publication of the Information Collection Budget (ICB). The ICB is the vehicle through which OIRA, in consultation with each agency, sets annual agency goals to reduce information collection burdens. At the end of the fiscal year, OIRA reports to Congress the results for the whole government and each agency and the achievement of the goals. Since 1980, the reduction targets have varied. In 1996 the PRA set an annual government-wide goal for the reduction of the total information collection burden of 10% during each of fiscal years 1996 and 1997 and 5% during each of fiscal years 1998 through 2001.

The ICB is built around fiscal budgeting concepts. Each agency calculates its total information collection "budget" by totalling the time required to complete all its information requests. This budgeting exercise is then used to measure progress toward reduction goals. The ICB is also an important mechanism in developing a comprehensive strategy to manage Federal information resources. The budgeting process has been considered useful because it assists agencies to evaluate broad categories of information as they relate to programme objectives, rather than as isolated collections of information. It encourages trade-offs between low and high priority information.

Recent reports have revealed some weaknesses in the ICB process. First, reduction targets have important measurement limitations. Estimating the time for an individual to collect and provide information is not simple. OIRA has not issued guidance on how to measure such burdens. Consequently, the ICB is undermined by a lack of quality and comparability of targets among agencies. For example, in 1989, IRS re-estimated the tax-related burden, tripling the government-wide burden. In 1997, the same agency concluded that tax compliance burdens may have been overstated by a factor between 3.8 and 5 and should be re-adjusted downward.[93] Second, the reduction targets lack binding force.[94]

New uses for information technologies. These responsibilities are closely tied to OMB's responsibility for management and co-ordination of federal information policies. An important advance in the PRA was the placement of paperwork reduction objectives squarely within a comprehensive framework for managing information resources. Paper is viewed merely as a means of handling information, and is not different in kind from other means such as electronic media. Reducing paperwork makes sense only within the broader context of information management. In a recent report, Vice-President Gore stated his intent to use information technologies to create a government that works better and costs less.[95] This has been accelerated by the increasing use of the Internet which provides not only linkages and research capacities but the possibility to build user-friendly electronic one-stop shops.

Two approaches have been used by Federal agencies: use of IT to collect information more efficiently and rapidly, and use of IT to better inform the public of its rights and obligations. An example of the former concerns new ways to complete forms by "taking the paper out of paperwork". A recent initiative by the Internal Revenue Service (IRS) to offer Telefile to most single filers allows over 4 million taxpayers who used to file a paper form to file tax returns using a touch-tone phone. An example of the use of IT to provide better information and open new channels for consultation is the electronic one-stop link Business.Gov (http:/www.business.gov). This service provides practical assistance to businesses through answers to frequently asked questions, search capacities for Federal information, browsers for Government documents, and viewing of business-related items from Federal agencies.

Simplifying permits and licenses. One of the more damaging forms of regulation is the *ex ante* licensing or permitting requirement. These kinds of regulations increase investment delays and uncertainties, have disproportionate effects on SME start-up, and are very costly for public administrations to apply. Yet they are pervasive in OECD countries. The United States has made some reforms in this area, although the potential for further gains remains substantial.

Permitting and licensing activities are split between levels of government in the United States. States use licences and permits to control the proficiency and quality of professional services (*e.g.* lawyers, doctors, accountants) and the impacts of activities at the local level (*e.g.* zoning permits). At the federal level, licences and permits are used mainly to control environmental hazards, such as

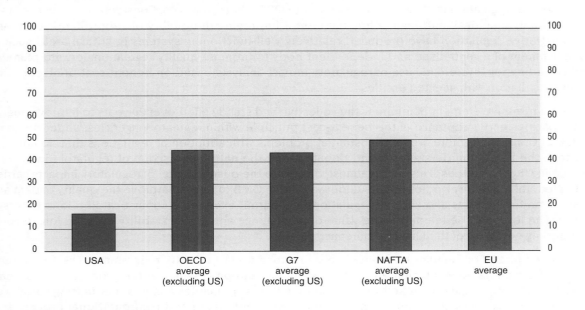

Box 11. **Simplifying business licences and permits**

This synthetic indicator of efforts to simplify and eliminate permits and licences ranks more highly those programmes where countries use the "silence is consent" rule to speed up decision or have set up one-stop shops for businesses, where there is a complete inventory of permits and licences; and where there is a specific programme, co-ordinated with lower levels of government, to review and reduce burdens of permits and licences. Despite efforts related to the PRA, the United States ranks low on these scores relative to other OECD countries. The lack of attention to the costs of licences and permits may reflect the relatively prominent role of the states in this area, given the US federal structure. Yet other federal states, such as Australia, have nonetheless acted at federal level to reduce the burdens of licences and permits at all levels of government.

Source: OECD Public Management Service.

from new chemicals or municipal sewerage systems, or risks arising from activities in interstate commerce, like medicines, or that involve special concerns, such as nuclear reactors. Such Federal procedures can be very complex and time consuming. They often require overview by different agencies, previous notification in the Federal Register or third party approvals.[96] After issuance, the licence or permit can be challenged in court.

The use of licenses and permits at the federal level has evolved very slowly in the past decade. Alternatives to this "command and control" measure are still scarce. Despite the opportunity offered by the PRA, no federal programme has concentrated on simplifying or reducing them government-wide. There may be a perception that the United States simply has fewer permits and licensing requirements, although the lack of any inventory at federal or state levels means this is difficult to assess. Some isolated steps are underway.

- In the environment area, the need for new air emission permits whenever there is a change in operations has inhibited companies from rapidly responding to changes in market demand and burdened the federal administration. A system piloted by the Environment Protection Agency will pre-approve certain operational changes over the five-year life of an air permit, which will reduce regulatory delay and permit the EPA to focus on higher priority pollution issues.[97]

- There are also indications that some large cities are taking steps to streamline licensing to attract investment, and this is a positive dynamic.

However, if the extensive experiences of other OECD countries are a guide, this is an area where more attention in the United States could yield substantial efficiencies.

5. CONCLUSIONS AND POLICY OPTIONS FOR REFORM

5.1. General assessment of strengths and weaknesses

The US government faces formidable legislative, institutional, judicial and structural constraints on good regulatory practices. Yet, by most measures, the capacities of the US federal government for assuring the quality of federal regulation are among the best in OECD countries. The synthetic qualitative indicators presented here generally place the United States in the first rank of countries. The policy framework for regulation is clear and consistent with OECD best practices. Considerable investments in institutional, analytical, and legal infrastructure for improving the quality of subordinate social and administrative regulation have produced relatively well-functioning systems in critical areas such as establishment of a centralised and independent body to promote quality regulation, forward planning and co-ordination, systematic use of regulatory impact analysis based on benefit-cost principles, and open consultation with affected entities.

An impressive element of reform is the collective and steady effort over 20 years to improve analytical capacities and acceptance of the benefit-cost principle within regulatory agencies, under the leadership of OMB. While there are still substantial problems with adoption of regulations that do not pass the test, the level of understanding and debate about the nature and scope of regulatory impacts is unique in OECD countries. This is due almost entirely to the quantification of regulatory impacts carried out in federal regulatory bodies. Efforts underway within OMB to further improve the quality of data and analysis on the benefits and costs of regulations will permit even more sophisticated reform efforts in future. The lesson to be learned is the value of persistence and policy stability over the long term in embedding new ways of thinking into bureaucracies.

The emphasis on regulatory quality is also a strong point in the US programme. The 1980s was a period of considerable investment in reform institutions and processes, but the programme was weakened by stressing "regulatory relief" rather than benefit-cost principles aimed at maximising social welfare. The programme also relied too much on an over-centralised and confrontational process that improved the quality of individual regulations, but did little to change incentives and administrative cultures within the regulatory agencies. For example, the role of the central oversight body (OMB) was oriented toward reacting to transactions, and not to general systemic and institutional change. This lesson was learned, and a retuning of the reform programme took place in the 1990s, with a targeting of OMB's efforts and a focus on government reinvention and on results-oriented policy-making.

This review of regulatory reform in the United States should help dispel the myth that the United States is, on the whole, less regulated than other OECD countries. The United States appears to be different from many countries, not in the amount or detail of regulation, but in its nature and style. American regulatory culture incorporates competition principles to a greater extent than in most countries, which stems more from deep-seated habits and values than from any organised vigilance. As a result, there is less of the most damaging forms of economic regulation, but as much or more social regulation and paperwork that do not present direct barriers to competition. This pro-competitive doctrine is an asset of increasing value in a world economy characterised by globalisation, responsiveness, and rapid technological progress. The US regulatory system illustrates well the conclusion in the 1997 OECD Report on Regulatory Reform:

> ... economic regulations have often proven to be extremely costly and ineffective means of achieving public interest goals [...] In general, public policies such as protection of health, safety, and the environment are better served by using competition-neutral instruments, such as well-targeted social regulations and market incentives, to change behaviour in competitive markets.[98]

The American public is well-served by this characteristic. Yet, the key question today deals with the direction of change: are federal regulations of higher quality than 25 years ago, that, is, do they, in the aggregate, produce higher net social benefits for the American people? While no answer can be definitive, the answer is probably yes, for two reasons:

1. The enormous shift since the 1970s from anti-competitive economic regulation toward more neutral styles of social regulation has greatly improved the benefits of the regulatory system as a whole, since social regulations are much more likely to produce net benefits than do economic regulations. OMB has calculated that the total benefits of social regulation in 1998 greatly exceeded costs, while the costs of economic regulations greatly exceeded their benefits.[99]

2. Controls on quality of social regulations and paperwork have steadily developed and government capacities to assure high-quality decisions are relatively strong.

This improvement is a longer-term trend, since application of quality controls can obviously vary over time. The overall quality of new federal regulations probably varies significantly, depending on political commitment and support for quality management. Yet the trend is in the right direction.

This positive trend should not induce complacence. US regulatory habits of detail, legalism, and rigidity are still dominant. There continue to be severe problems with costs and policy effectiveness in the US regulatory system. Much legislation and regulation is seriously outdated. Quality control processes are not co-ordinated, and have important gaps in the areas of primary legislation, economic regulation, and state-level regulation. Studies from different sources suggest that net social benefits for social regulations issued in recent years are positive, a significant though not a robust finding, but that many individual regulations impose costs higher than benefits. This means that aggregate costs of regulations can be substantially reduced without reducing social welfare.

Coherence and consistency, both horizontally across the US government and vertically in federal/state relations, still pose problems. The United States faces enormous difficulties in establishing consistent regulatory quality standards and controls on the sprawling regulatory apparatus of the federal government, and even more difficulty in managing coherence and complexity in federal/state interactions. There are tensions in the system between due process and flexibility, between legal clarity and innovation, and between empirical and legal/adversarial methods. An analysis of governance in the United States found difficulties with coherence to be inherent in the constitutional set-up of the American government:

> The problem of governance in the United States is mainly one of creating institutions or governing arrangements that can pursue policies of sufficient coherence, consistency, foresight, and stability that the national welfare is not sacrificed for narrow

or temporary gains. The United States has difficulty in arriving at such arrangements because it must fashion them out of three substantially autonomous political institutions: Congress, the presidency, and the bureaucracy.[100]

This suggests that imperfections in the American regulatory system are rooted in the American way of governance. But reformers still have an important role: there is considerable distance to travel before these structural constraints are binding.

At the heart of the most severe regulatory problems is the quality of primary legislation. The trend toward higher quality in delegated regulation cannot be seen in the quality of primary legislation, and this limits, and threatens to reverse, the benefits to be gained from regulatory reform. More so than in other OECD countries, the United States has found it extremely difficult to develop controls on legislative quality. This is partly structural, arising from the constitutional balance of powers between the executive and the legislative. And, unlike parliamentary systems, bills originate from many sources. The result is that, perversely, there is less attention to quality of laws than to decisions authorised by the laws.

In the past, the Congress has ignored even those slight controls that it adopted for itself, though recent reforms, such as the UMRA requirement that the Congressional Budget Office estimate the costs of proposed legislation and "unfunded mandates" on state and local governments, are positive. If this is to have value, members of Congress will have to become consumers of such information. It remains to be seen how such estimates will be considered in Congressional processes, but anecdotes suggest that it has helped raise the level of debate on such costs.[101] Current proposals to establish a new congressional agency to study the costs and benefits of regulations could improve matters if the agency were to focus on bills and existing legislation as its top priority. Strikingly, some recent laws, such as the Clean Air Act of 1990, expressly prohibit good decision practices by regulatory agencies.

Innovation and the development of cost-effective policy approaches are often blocked by rigid legislation. "EPA is hobbled by overly prescriptive statutes that pull the agency in too many directions and permit managers too little discretion to make wise decisions. Congress should stop micro-managing EPA." concluded a recent report of the National Academy of Public Administration. A deeper problem, noted a former head of the US Environmental Agency (and as noted earlier for nursing home regulation), is that frustration with regulatory performance, perhaps justified or perhaps stemming from unrealistic expectations, can lead to a vicious cycle of controls and increased barriers to good performance:

When traced to their source, many of the more vexing problems [...] have their roots in the underlying statutes. Besides being prescriptive, these statutes tend to over-promise setting up expectations of absolute safety within extremely tight time frames. While this is well-intentioned, it has an undermining effect on the Agency and those who rely on it. As EPA misses one deadline after another, the courts intervene, as requested by an aggrieved party, and Congress turns the screws even tighter, further limiting the Agency's ability to respond creatively and responsibly to problems far more complex than lawmakers could have possibly envisioned.[102]

OMB has similarly warned that, "It is our view that highly prescriptive legislation [...] has contributed to a regulatory system that is sometimes unmanageable or is driven by plaintiffs rather than by a rational planning process that directs the nation's resources to the most important problems and the most cost-effective solutions".[103]

Without genuine progress at the legislative level in placing accountability on results and in encouraging risk-taking and policy innovation, it is doubtful that the executive branch can make substantial additional progress in the quality of subordinate regulations, or even preserve the progress that has been made. It is clear that there is no quick fix. The two most positive steps in recent years are the Performance Management and Results Act, which builds a foundation for results-oriented policies and more accountability to Congress, and the trend toward improving dialogue and consensus on innovative regulatory approaches, which experience in other countries shows is a necessary condition for building the trust that is needed if administrators are to have the flexibility to innovate and take risks.

The importance of a vigorous academic community in producing policy-relevant data to support regulatory reform should not be over-looked. The continuing efforts of researchers in American think tanks and universities have mapped the evidence of benefits from reform and posed strong challenges to the status quo. Such scholarship is, in fact, one of the most influential exports of the United States to the rest of the world.

5.2. Policy options for consideration

There is a large and growing volume of recommendations from many sources on ways to improve regulatory reform in the United States. Most of these consist of fine-tuning existing structures; some, such as those in the NPR, are more profound, aimed at changing the incentives and culture of regulators. This section identifies actions that, based on international consensus on good regulatory practices and on concrete experiences in other OECD countries, are likely to be particularly beneficial to improving regulatory management and reform capacities in the United States. Future reforms should seek to:

- *Improve the responsiveness and quality of the national regulatory system by*:

  - *Continuing to seek means to streamline regulatory processes through the NPR process.*

  - *Strengthening quality management in the executive and legislative branches as a better substitute for some aspects of judicial review.*

  - *Reviewing current administrative law practices pertaining to regulatory development and consultation.*

  - *Better integrating numerous regulatory quality procedures such as impact analyses, review processes, and performance measurement.*

  - *Increasing the use of sunsetting to ensure that regulations are kept on the books only if they are still necessary.*

Sluggishness, delay, and inefficiencies in regulatory processes will increasingly penalise the United States as the pace of globalisation and innovation steps up. New regulations that are socially beneficial should be issued faster, and existing regulations should be updated more regularly. The lack of policy responsiveness and flexibility implied by the long and cumbersome regulatory process has long been recognised. The 1993 NPR noted, for example, that a layering of procedural requirements has, cumulatively, "made the rulemaking process increasingly burdensome and rigid".[104] Since 1993, the situation has worsened.

At the same time, better data is revealing substantial shortfalls in meeting benefit-cost and cost-effectiveness tests, and persistent problems with the quality of economic analysis. Although regulations that fail these tests may be adopted for good reasons such as equity or justice, there is widespread agreement that substantial gains to public welfare are possible by boosting regulatory quality as measured by those empirical methods. The answer to both problems lies in rationalising the current system rather than in adding new procedures and expanding judicial review.

The cost and length of time needed for regulatory change has imposed large hidden costs on the quality of the national regulatory system. Regulators are less willing to implement new regulatory quality procedures when it already takes so long to get regulations through the pipeline. Beneficial modifications to old regulations are less likely to be carried out. Given the enormous investment needed, regulators are less likely to innovate and take risks, since a setback can cost several years of effort. Of concern is the tendency by regulators to use policy statements, guidance, and memos to agency personal that side-step procedural requirements. While such methods can be efficient, incentives to use them as time-saving measures are likely to be perverse, and can undermine the transparency of the regulatory system.

Further, the adversarial and legalistic process for producing new regulations produces an incentive for "all or nothing" solutions that drive regulators away from the rule of reason, and limit the sensible application of rules in the field. The NPR found that "Lack of information is [a] serious problem. To some extent, this stems from the adversarial nature of the rulemaking process; in many rule-makings, regulated entities, public interest groups, and other parties are more interested in protecting their own positions than in providing useful information to the agency or finding a solution to the problem".

Improving regulatory responsiveness while at the same time strengthening quality management will be difficult, since procedural and legal formalism is so heavily embedded in the US policy system, but this review suggests that a series of concrete steps should be considered:

– A thorough review of the Administrative Procedure Act (APA) and its current application by regulators and the courts would be an important contribution to identifying where regulatory procedures can be simplified, while maintaining transparency and full consultation. Supplements to "notice and comment" procedures that enrich dialogue and draw in a wider range of interests should be considered as part of the review of the APA, and IT approaches should be critically assessed. The UK has eased procedures to revise existing rules if the revisions improve cost-effectiveness, and perhaps similar streamlining could be considered in the United States.

– In parallel with a review of the APA, a review of all existing regulatory procedures such as impact analyses and review processes should be carried out. The current system of regulatory quality control is the sum of various piecemeal procedures that have accumulated over years. In this case, the whole is less than the sum of its parts, because scarce resources are scattered through many steps rather than targeted on the most important issues. Rationalisation of benefit-cost analysis, unfunded mandates analysis, paperwork estimates, small business analysis, environmental assessments, and other into a single integrated assessment will produce better results at lower cost, better target real problems, improve consistency of treatment, and avoid duplication of effort. Compliance with these quality processes should also be linked to the Performance Management and Results Act. One performance measure, for example, could be the increase in the net social benefits produced by the agency each year, as estimated in *ex ante* impact analysis, though this will necessitate strong quality control to offset incentives to overstate net benefits. Targeting of OMB review to only major reviews eliminated a step for many regulations, but probably has had only minor effects on the overall speed of rulemaking.

– Strengthening management and quality disciplines in the administration or in the Congress – in OMB, CBO, or a new congressional agency – should be considered as a lower-cost substitute to judicial review of some aspects of regulatory quality. There is little doubt that litigation rights, whatever their benefits, slow change and innovation in the regulatory system. Proposals to subject regulatory analysis to judicial review could worsen regulatory responsiveness by increasing the scope for legal uncertainties and delays. The 1996 Small Business Regulatory Enforcement Fairness Act allows judicial review of agency studies of small business impacts; several cases have been filed. A less costly approach would have been to establish a stronger watchdog in the administration to resolve problems before regulations are issued. At the same time, stronger internal controls and filters will help to increase the percentage of regulations that meet the benefit-cost test and increase regulatory net benefits. For this reason, Hahn and Breyer have also recommended that the role and capacities of OMB and CBO be upgraded, but they did not link this to reduced judicial review.[105] Too, with the Results Act, the role of OMB should focus more on the performance of regulators rather than the quality of individual rules.

– The role of sunsetting and systematic evaluation of regulations, rarely used in the United States, could be important in keeping regulations up to date, but will have real value only if procedures to revise existing rules are streamlined at the same time. Evaluation and sunsetting in other countries have often become rubber-stamping exercises, and this is a higher risk in the United States, given the procedural costs of making even minor changes.

– Regulatory negotiations and consensus-building processes such as those promoted by the NPR offer the best chance for real change. They will require cultural shifts in the administration, and a more supportive legal environment for dialogue and innovation.

– Regulatory benefits should be increased by developing methods to improve government-wide priority-setting.

The single regulatory reform measure likely to produce the most substantial gains in social welfare is improvement of priority-setting mechanisms across the government. The importance of allocative efficiency across the range of regulatory activities has been neglected in attempts to increase the static efficiency of individual rules. The finding by Hahn that just two federal rules out of 106 produced over 70 per cent of net regulatory benefits suggests the magnitude of the potential gains from better priority setting. No OECD country has solved this problem. To the extent that it can develop methods for comprehensive regulatory priority-setting, the United States has an opportunity to lead the way for other OECD countries in the next major phase of regulatory reform.

Several attempts have been made to improve priority-setting within legislative constraints. Forward planning through the Regulatory Plan has been useful for other reasons, but has been ineffective in forcing trade-offs between regulatory agencies, though this was one of its original purposes. The regulatory budget concept is attractive from a theoretic view, but its methodological and political difficulties have prevented its implementation. Current efforts by OMB, required by law, to improve global estimates of costs and benefits of federal regulation could establish a firmer methodological basis for regulatory budgeting. Others have recommended that the regulatory budget be applied only to new regulatory costs,[106] a partial solution that may be more practical than a global budget constraint. The NPR recommended that similar risks be ranked and that priorities be set across agencies, but nothing has come of the recommendation. It is possible that the Performance Management and Results Act is a step toward a priority-setting mechanism through which fiscal budgeting decisions are linked to the ability of regulatory programs to deliver more per dollar expended. Certainly, this is the expectation of some members of Congress.[107]

- *Expand the value, speed and scope of review of primary legislation and major regulations by launching a structured process of rolling reviews, reviewing policy areas rather than individual rules, and experimenting with use of advisory bodies for the reviews.*

A strong point of the US system is the central review mechanism within OMB for new regulations and formalities. Quality procedures have been integrated into the regulatory culture of the public service. Yet the current system is very weak with respect to systematic review of the vast body of existing laws and other regulations. It looks forward, but not back. For example, while reviews by the regulators themselves in 1993-1994 eliminated many pages of regulations, the actual benefits in terms of cost-savings or policy effectiveness were not well documented, and are unlikely to be significant since most changes were marginal.

A high priority should be placed on developing better evaluation and review procedures for major regulations, and for legislation in particular. As noted, American laws are likely to be lower quality than subordinate regulations, due to the imbalance in quality controls between the two instruments and the lack of any consistent evaluation of the performance of existing laws. This has substantial negative downstream effects on the quality of policy implementation and policy outcomes. This review has documented in particular the negative effects of current styles of law on innovation and experimentation by the administration.

More attention should be placed on systematic review and upgrading of laws with their subordinate regulations through a rolling review process based on a prioritisation of manageable policy areas. Policy areas subject to a high level of technological change or where regulatory failure is most costly should have highest priority. Structuring of an effective review process will be key to its results, and may require strengthening the capacities of the OMB and congressional offices such as CBO. Two approaches should be considered. First, efforts in other OECD countries show that achieving consensus in advance on a transparent and measurable set of principles for review is essential. This was seen in the current Australian regulatory review against competition principles, which includes both federal and state governments and is unprecedented in its scope. The requirement in UMRA for a cost-effectiveness test for new legislation is a good step toward consensus on results-oriented principles, but a benefit-cost test and an emphasis on innovation and experimentation will produce the best results in increasing social welfare. One purpose of the reviews should be to progressively close legislative gaps in the use of benefit-cost analysis.

Second, the reinvention principle should guide the reviews. In their peer review of this report in June 1998, other OECD countries unfavourably compared the incremental and piecemeal nature of legislative change in the United States to the greater capacity for fundamental reform often enjoyed by parliamentary governments. Similarly, current regulatory review processes in the United States are transactions-oriented rather than results-oriented. They work better in analysing individual regulations than in understanding interactions between a group of regulations affecting an economic or social sector, having a cumulative and overlapping impact, originating from different agencies or even different levels of government. Such linkages are often not analysed. US regulatory reviews seem focused on pruning each tree rather than improving the health of the forest.

The effectiveness of US regulatory review could be improved by comprehensive assessments by a high-level advisory board, commission or task force of how the regulatory framework affects an economic sector, emphasising policy effectiveness and impacts on consumer welfare as performance measures. Recommendations would include groups of reforms affecting different instruments or policies, packaged together to permit quicker regulatory improvement. In every law reviewed, emphasis should be given to encouraging innovation in approaches, with clear accountability for results, and to identifying the most efficient federal/state relationship in the policy area.

Panels of affected interests are used in the United States to comment on proposed regulations, but the United States is missing an opportunity to use such panels to evaluate and reinvent existing regulations. Setting up of advisory groups representing a good cross-section of stakeholders can gain from the experience of various OECD countries where *ad hoc* or standing task forces, often formed by senior business and trade union representatives, have proposed reform measures. Australia set up in 1996 the Small Business Deregulation Task Force to propose changes to reduce "the burden of paperwork and red tape on small business by 50 per cent".[108] In the United Kingdom, a Better Regulation Task Force was recently established, with members drawn from big and small businesses, consumer and citizen groups, charity and voluntary sectors, trade unions and enforcers, to comprehensively review nine regulatory areas (principles of good regulation, consumer law, employment law, social services, charities and the voluntary sector, company law and corporate governance, environmental regulation, food, and licensing). The Danish regulatory programme has gained coherence and speed from the establishment of high-level commissions and task forces. Using this approach effectively may require review and revision of the restrictive procedures in the Federal Advisory Committee Act.

An area where such an approach has been shown to be useful is in the simplification of tax-related paperwork, the largest single source of paperwork burden on enterprises in any OECD country. In the United States, tax-related paperwork burdens represent 80 per cent of the total burdens. The "Van Lunteren Commission" in the Netherlands is a model for an effective ad hoc commission in this area.

– *Expand coverage of mandatory quality controls to economic regulation.*

As noted, economic regulation is less likely to produce net benefits than is social regulation. An ideal regulatory reform programme therefore would put stricter controls on the use of economic regulations than on social regulations. The US programme does the opposite. The independent commissions responsible for most of the economic regulations are not covered by the executive order on regulatory quality. This gap is rooted in historical and legal relations between the independent commissions and the president. The result is that these commissions provide relatively little quantitative information on the benefits and costs of their actions, and reviews by the GAO and the OMB have found that they produce no information useful for estimating aggregate costs and benefits.[109] Similar to the coverage of the Paperwork Reduction Act, regulatory quality controls applicable to social regulation, particularly benefit-cost analysis and consideration of alternatives, should be extended to the independent regulatory commissions, which may require law rather than executive order.

– *Further encourage the use of cost-effective alternative policy instruments by developing operational guidance for ministries and by developing a wider range of co-operative methods.*

One of the anomalies in the American regulatory system is that positive social views toward competition have not led to a greater use of market-based approaches to problem-solving. Market approaches have been recommended for years, most recently by the Vice-President's National

Performance Review. However, the US regulatory system is relatively less innovative than those in some other OECD countries. For example, ten years later there is still only one nation-wide system of marketable permits for air emissions, though the benefits of such an approach have been well-documented in other areas. Other OECD countries use taxes to restructure incentives to a much greater extent than does the United States, suggesting missed opportunities for cost-effective action. Voluntary approaches have been hampered by inflexible statutes.

The current Clinton executive order requires that analysis of alternatives be documented and subjected to public scrutiny through the RIA process to stimulate genuine comparisons of the benefits and costs of various approaches. UMRA requires agencies to certify that they are choosing the most cost-effective approach. These are good practices of value to other OECD countries. However, they do not seem sufficient in themselves to stimulate innovation, since there are powerful countervailing pressures to risk-taking and co-operation.

One of these pressures is the legalistic habits that, while intended to promote fairness and transparency, lead almost always to traditional command-and-control means. This is reinforced by traditionally weak accountability mechanisms for the performance of regulatory programmes, which have emphasised inputs such as inspections and rules, rather than outcomes in terms of results and costs. Incentives within the bureaucracy have been deeply conservative and risk-avoiding. Finally, the traditional adversarialism of decision-making emphasises an all or nothing approach.

There has been progress in recent years. The Performance Management and Results Act should weaken incentives to avoid risk-taking at any cost to programme results, and measures of the use of innovative approaches could be built into the performance measures for each regulatory agency. The focus on consensus-building is another positive step, though current approaches seem to be hampered by legal constraints and formalistic habits. A good practice that should be considered government-wide, and by other OECD countries, is to build responsibility for innovation into the bureaucracy through processes such as the 1998 ECOS-EPA Agreement, in which there is a legitimate and transparent channel for new ideas to be considered.

As recognised by the NPR in 1993, policy makers are likely to require assistance in the identification and development of suitable alternative policy tools. Operational guidance on the characteristics and use of alternative approaches should be developed for use by the line ministries. Such guidance has been useful in several countries such as Australia and Canada. General rules, called the Open Market Trading Programme, for local air-pollution-permit trading that were proposed by the EPA to speed up use of trading by the states is a good step that should be considered for other innovative approaches.

An important lesson for the United States from other countries is the value in terms of flexibility, cost-effectiveness, and responsiveness of more co-operative approaches to problem solving. Already, agencies in the United States are experimenting with such approaches. Negotiated rulemaking is one such effort, but the current approach still relies very heavily on traditional regulatory processes, and its value is not yet proven. It may be that covenants as used in many European countries are an example of a different approach. Continued leadership from the centre to encourage risk-taking and experimentation, and evaluation will be needed to promote efforts to inject a degree of co-operation into adversarial systems.

> — *Develop a stronger role for the central reform authority in benchmarking analytical quality, and in facilitating and providing practical guidance to regulatory agencies.*

As noted above, stronger internal controls on regulatory quality, perhaps in OMB, could boost the rate of compliance with the benefit-cost principle, and is highly preferable to judicial review as a method of quality management. Increased attention in OMB to improving the methods and comparability of analysis, now underway in response to a legal mandate, could assist in establishing clearer benchmarks of acceptable analysis that would be useful in filtering out poor regulations. In particular, more investment in evaluation of regulatory impacts after implementation would provide useful feedback in gauging the accuracy of ex ante RIAs, and could support the refining of the RIA programme to reduce any systematic biases.

OMB has recently moved to develop more co-operative relationships with regulatory agencies and to become involved at earlier stages in rule-making processes. It proposed in 1998 to raise the quality of RIA by promoting better use of Best Practices guidelines, and by offering technical outreach and training sessions.[110] This is consistent with changes in a number of countries with extensive experience with reform, including the Netherlands, Canada and Australia, where central reform bodies have moved from adversarial toward more supportive approaches to regulators. However, OMB has not emphasised the provision of tools to assist agencies to regulate better. Such tools include practical guidance on issues such as regulatory alternatives, principles of good regulation and regulatory impact assessment, backed by extensive training programmes to ensure skills acquisition by regulators. Initiatives of this sort could help build on the cultural changes among regulators that previous OMB reform efforts have produced, by giving regulators better tools for reinventing regulation. It is also useful in the context of a more results-oriented environment in which regulators become problem-solvers rather than production lines for legal texts.

- *Encourage entrepreneurialism by streamlining permits and licenses at the federal level, by co-ordinating with the states on review and streamlining of permits and licenses, and by building more complete information systems for enterprises.*

Though *ex ante* permits and licenses can be among the most damaging of government formalities with respect to business start-ups and among the most costly regulations to administer, current efforts in the United States place too little focus on ensuring that such requirements are the minimum necessary to achieve policy objectives. This is probably due to the fact that most such requirements take place at state and local levels. Yet new ideas – such as the move to a "supply model" in Germany that offers various choices to investors, depending on the degree of risk they wish to accept[111] – are being developed and implemented in many OECD countries, and could be useful in the United States.

One problem is that there is no general overview of the use of licensing. At the federal level, the Administration should consider having OIRA lead an interagency programme to "re-engineer" important licences and permits. The thrust of this programme could be to reduce the most frequently used and costly licences and permits, and co-ordinate between federal and state authorities. An important criterion would be to minimise costs collectively as well as individually (*i.e.* reducing overlaps, increasing information collection synergies between agencies).

The federal government should consider means of promoting the streamlining of permits, licenses, and other government formalities carried out at state and local levels. For example, it may wish to encourage adoption of paperwork reduction acts at state levels. A programme of regulatory benchmarking across states may help stimulate political interest in improving the business environment, as it has in Australia and Mexico. Also, Australian State governments have agreed to adopt parallel regulation in many areas where divergent regulations would impose extra costs. The federal government has been a key facilitator of this process in Australia.

Finally, information technology has been under-used in this area in the United States. Development of a user-friendly public registry and inventory of formalities on the Internet could provide useful information on approved information collections, such as a plain language list of the items would be available: all the information elements required, the statutory time responses of the authorities, if the 'consent is silence' rule applies, the means or procedure to present (or maintain) it an electronic copy of the forms, etc. This central data base could evolve progressively into becoming an electronic one-stop shop where the formalities could be directly inputted and sent to the agencies.

5.3. Managing regulatory reform

The most important determinant of the scope and pace of further reform is the attitude of the Congress. Congressional incentives to relinquish control over *how* policies are carried out in return for more accountability for policy results are not strong, though they are improving. In the end, it will be the management of a more results-oriented relationship between the executive and the legislative that will determine the scope and pace of regulatory reform in the United States.

While the US public debate over regulatory reform is among the most well-informed and transparent in OECD countries, there is still too little information on the results of reform strategies, including their effects on programme effectiveness, costs, economic performance, and distribution of gains and losses. Yet this information is critical if reform is to enjoy support from citizens who place high value on safety, health, environmental quality, and other values promoted by regulation. At this juncture, it seems that fears about the effects of reform on levels of protection have not been borne out, but continued reform will proceed faster and more deeply if reformers take concrete steps to demonstrate that protection has been maintained. Evaluation of the impacts of reform and communication with the public and all major stakeholders with respect to the short and long-term effects of action and non-action, and on the distribution of costs and benefits, will be increasingly important to further progress.

NOTES

1. A summary of these estimates is given in US Office of Information and Regulatory Affairs, Office of Management and Budget (1997), Report to Congress on the Costs and Benefits of Federal Regulations, September 30.

2. US Office of Information and Regulatory Affairs, OMB (1994), Report to the President on Executive Order No. 12 866, 1 May.

3. President Bill Clinton (1993), Executive Order No. 12 866, Regulatory Planning and Review, 30 September.

4. This characteristic has deep roots in American history. Perhaps the most important condition for the economic development of the United States over the past 150 years "was the social creed of untrammelled freedom for the producer, which was used to legitimise the physical exploitation of the continental domain after 1865", remarked a noted historian. Greenleaf, William (ed) (1968), American Economic Development Since 1860 (University of South Carolina Press), p. 1.

5. Noll, Roger and Bruce Owen (1983), The Political Economy of Deregulation: Interest Groups in the Regulatory Process, American Enterprise Institute, Washington DC, pp. 26-27.

6. For comparisons of US regulatory styles with other countries, see, inter alia, Vogel, David (1986), National Styles of Regulation, Cornell University Press, Ithaca; Badaracco, Joseph (1985), Loading the Dice: A Five-Country Study of Vinyl Chloride Regulation, Harvard Business School Press, Boston; Kelman, Steven (1981), Regulating America, Regulating Sweden, MIT Press, Cambridge; Heidenheimer, Arnold; Hugh Heclo; Carolyn Adams (1983), Comparative Public Policy: The Politics of Social Choice in Europe and America, St. Martin's Press, New York.

7. Crandall, Robert, et al. (1997), An Agenda for Federal Regulatory Reform, AEI and The Brookings Institution, p. 5. See also US General Accounting Office (1999), Regulatory Burden: Some Agencies' Claims Regarding Lack of Rulemaking Discretion Have Merit (GAO/GGD-99-20), 8 January.

8. Howard, Philip K. (1994), The Death of Common Sense: How Law is Suffocating America, Random House: New York.

9. Reported in Braithwaite, John (1993), "Improving Regulatory Compliance: Strategies and Practical Applications in OECD Countries", PUMA Occasional Papers in Public Management, OECD, Paris.

10. McGarity, Thomas, cited in Kerwin, Cornelius (1994), Introduction to the Congressional Quarterly's Federal Regulatory Directory, Washington DC.

11. Vice-President Al Gore (1993), "Creating a Government That Works Better and Costs Less: Improving Regulatory Systems" in Accompanying Report of the National Performance Review, September.

12. Office of Information and Regulatory Affairs, Office of Management and Budget (1999), "Report to Congress on the Costs and Benefits of Federal Regulations", 4 February.

13. Hopkins, Thomas D. (1996), "Regulatory Costs in Profile", Policy Study No. 132, Center for the Study of American Business, August; see also Hopkins, Thomas D. (1995), "Profiles of Regulatory Costs", Report to US Small Business Administration.

14. US Office of Information and Regulatory Affairs, Office of Management and Budget (1997), Report to Congress on the Costs and Benefits of Federal Regulations, September 30, p. 27.

15. See, among others, Hazilla, Michael and Raymond Kopp (1990), "Social Cost of Environmental Quality Regulations: A General Equilibrium Analysis", Journal of Political Economy, Vol. 98, No. 4; and Jorgensen, W. Dale and Peter J. Wilcoxen (1990), "Environmental Regulation and US Economic Growth", Rand Journal of Economics, Vol. 21, No. 2.

16. Hahn, Robert W. (1998), An Analysis of the First Government Report on the Benefits and Costs of Regulation, Belfour Center for Science and International Affairs, John F. Kennedy School of Government, Harvard University, May.

17. Hahn, Robert W. (1998), Reviving Regulatory Reform: A Global Perspective, Cambridge University Press and AEI Press, forthcoming.

18. Morrall, John, III (1986), "A Review of the Record", Regulation, 10:2; Viscusi, W. Kip (1992), *Fatal Tradeoffs: Public and Private Responsibilities for Risk*, Oxford University Press; Viscui, W. Kip (1996), "Economic Foundations of the Current Regulatory Reform Efforts", *Journal of Economic Perspectives*, Vol. 10, No. 3.

19. Teng, Tammy and John Graham (1997), "The Opportunity Costs of Haphazard Social Investments in Life-Saving," published in Hahn, Robert, *Risks, Costs and Lives Saved – Getting Better Results from Regulation*, Oxford University Press, New York and Oxford, p. 173.

20. Kerwin, Cornelius (1994), *Introduction to the Congressional Quarterly's Federal Regulatory Directory*, Washington DC, p. 16.

21. Kerwin, p. 40.

22. Beam, David, *et al.* (1992), "Federal Regulation of State and Local Governments: Regulatory Federalism a Decade Later" draft report prepared for the US Advisory Commission on Intergovernmental Relations.

23. US Office of Information and Regulatory Affairs, Office of Management and Budget (1994), Report to the President on Executive Order No. 12 866, Regulatory Planning and Review, May 1.

24. US Office of Information and Regulatory Affairs, Office of Management and Budget (1997), "Report to Congress on the Costs and Benefits of Federal Regulations", September 30.

25. McCraw, Thomas K. (1984), *Prophets of Regulation*, Belknap Press, p. 259.

26. House Concurrent Resolution 448, 94 Stat. 3 680, November 20, 1980.

27. Much of this discussion is adapted from US Office of Management and Budget (1988), *Introduction to The Regulatory Program of the United States Government*, April 1, 1987-March 31, 1988.

28. Data from the Washington University Center for the Study of American Business.

29. One study found that 0.44 per cent, or 31 per cent, of the decline in US manufacturing productivity in the 1970s was due to these kinds of regulation. See Gray, W. (1987), "The Cost of Regulation: OSHA, EPA and the Productivity Slowdown", *American Economic Review*, December, 77(5), pp. 998-1006. See also Gray, W. (1991), "The Impact of OSHA and EPA Regulation on Productivity Growth", *Journal of Regulation and Social Costs*, June, 1(3), pp. 25-47.

30. President Ronald Reagan, "The Regulatory Message of the President", Regulatory Program, April 1, 1988-March 31, 1989, p. vii.

31. OECD (1997), *The OECD Report on Regulatory Reform: Synthesis*, Paris, p. 37.

32. OECD (1995), "Recommendation of the Council of the OECD on Improving the Quality of Government Regulation", Paris.

33. Presidential Executive Order 12 866, Regulatory Planning and Review, September 30, 1993.

34. Deighton-Smith, Rex (1997), *Regulatory Impact Analysis: Best Practices in OECD Countries*, OECD, Paris, p. 221.

35. President Bill Clinton (1993), Executive Order No. 12 866, September 30.

36. See Rosenberg, Morton (1986).

37. Testimony of James C. Miller III, Director of the Office of Management and Budget, in hearings before the Subcommittee on Intergovernmental Relations, Committee on Governmental Affairs, US Senate, January 28, 1986 (S. Hrg. 99-839), p. 104.

38. Testimony of James C. Miller III, Director of the Office of Management and Budget, in hearings before the Subcommittee on Intergovernmental Relations, Committee on Governmental Affairs, US Senate, January 28, 1986, S. Hrg. 99-839, p. 104.

39. Communication to the OECD from US General Accounting Office, May 1999.

40. Bruff (1989), "Presidential Management of Agency Rulemaking", Geo. W.L. Rev., p. 562, as cited in A *Guide to Agency Rulemaking*.

41. Rosenberg, Morton (1986), "Regulatory Management at OMB", Congressional Research Service, Library of Congress, published in Office of Management and Budget, *Evolving Roles and Future Issues, the Committee on Governmental Affairs*, US Senate, Feb., (S. Prt. 99-134), p. 213.

42. Hopkins, Thomas (1995), A Survey of Regulatory Burdens, Report to the Small Business Administration, June, Washington DC.

43. OECD (1997), Economic Surveys, United States.

44. The RFA is aimed at "small entities": small businesses, small organisations, small governmental jurisdictions, GAO March 1998, p. 2.

45. Although the RFA does not require agencies to use the Unified Agenda to publish the statutory notices, the Agenda has been increasingly used by the agencies.

46. Bowers, James. R. (1990), *Regulating the Regulators: An Introduction to the Legislative Oversight of Administrative Rulemaking*, Praeger Publishers, New York, p. xi.

47. Reported in Hahn (1998).

48. Beam (1992).

49. President Ronald Reagan (1985), Executive Order No. 12 498, "Regulatory Planning Process", January 4.

50. White House (1985), Memorandum for the Heads of Executive Departments and Agencies, "Development of Administration's Regulatory Program", January 4.

51. Regulatory Program, April 1, 1988-March 31, 1989, p. 15.

52. Statement by the Vice-President, The Regulatory Plan, 29 October 1997, FR 57003.

53. The exemptions from the requirement to publish a proposed rule are widely used, however. Over 50 per cent of final regulations are not preceded by a proposed rule, and as a result escape many of the regulatory quality standards and processes. See US General Accounting Office (1998), *Federal Rulemaking: Agencies Often Published Final Actions Without Proposed Rules* (GAO/GGD-98-126), 31 August.

54. More Benefits, Fewer Burdens, p. 18.

55. The Public Management Service of the OECD launched in 1998 a continuing project to assess compliance trends and challenges in OECD countries, and to assess innovative approaches to improving compliance.

56. OECD (1993), OECD *Economic Surveys: United States*, OECD, Paris.

57. Executive Order No. 12 044 of March 23, 1978, "Improving Government Regulations".

58. Environmental Council of the States, Press release of 30 April 1998.

59. US Environmental Protection Agency (1998), *The Changing Nature of Environmental and Public Health Protection: An Annual Report on Reinvention*, March.

60. Haddad, Brent M. (1997), "Putting Markets to Work: The Design and Use of Marketable Permits and Obligations", OECD Public Management Occasional Papers, Paris.

61. Haddad (1997).

62. Environmental Protection Agency (1998), p. 28.

63. Magaziner, Ira (1997), "Opening Remarks at Global Standards Conference", Brussels, 1 October.

64. Mazurek, Janice (1998), *The Use of Voluntary Agreements in the United States: An Initial Survey. Resources for the Future*, at <http://www.oecd.org/env/lists4>.

65. Davies *et al.* (1996), *Pollution control in the United States: Evaluating the System*, Resources for the Future/Johns Hopkins Press; Kappas, Peter (1997), *The Politics, Practice, and Performance of Chemical Industry Self-regulation*. Doctoral dissertation in political science, University of California Los Angeles; Boyd, Krupnick and Mazurek (1998), Intel's XL Permit: A framework for evaluation. Discussion Paper 98-11 Resources for the Future, Washington DC.

66. Lyons, Max R. (1996), "The Economics of Workplace Safety", Employment Policy Foundation Policy Paper, Washington DC.

67. Sparrow, M. (1996), *Regulatory Reform: Lessons from the Innovations Awards Program*, Mimeo, John F. Kennedy School of Government, Harvard University & OSHA website (http://www.osha.gov/oshinfo/reinvent/reinvent.html).

68. Feitshans, Ilise with Oliver, Cathy (1997), "More than just a pretty program: OSHA Voluntary Protection Programs improve compliance by facing problems head on" 5 Corporate Conduct Quarterly 69-73, 79; Gunningham, N. & Rees, J. (1998), "Industry self-regulation" forthcoming Law & Policy.

69. See, *e.g.*, Kerwin, C.M. & Furlong, S.R. "Time and Rulemaking: An Empirical Test of Theory" cited in Coglianese, G. "Assessing Consensus: The Promise and Performance of Negotiated Rulemaking", *Duke Law Journal*, Vol. 46, No. 6 (April 1997).

70. Coglianese, G. *op. cit.*, from which much of the following discussion is adapted.

71. OECD (1997), Paris.

72. Jacobs, Scott H. (1997), "An Overview of Regulatory Impact Analysis in OECD Countries", in *Regulatory Impact Analysis: Best Practices in OECD Countries*, OECD, Paris.

73. OMB (1998), p. 44 049.

74. Katzen, Sally (1997), Administrator, OIRA, cited in *Business Daily*, Los Angeles, March 18.

75. GAO (1998), "Regulatory Reform: Agencies Could Improve Development, Documentation, and Clarity of Regulatory Analysis", May.

76. Reported in Economic Report of the President, February 1999, p. 199.

77. Viscusi (1996).

78. Hahn (1997).

79. Hahn (1998).

80. US Office of Information and Regulatory Affairs, Office of Management and Budget (1998).

81. Hahn, Robert W. (1998), *Reviving Regulatory Reform*: A *Global* Perspective, Cambridge University Press and AEI Press, forthcoming.

82. Jacobs (1997), p. 19.

83. "Economic Analysis of Federal Regulations Under Executive Order 12 866", 1996.

84. OMB, 1998.

85. Morrall, John and Ivy Broder (1997), "Collecting and Using Data for Regulatory Decision-making", published in *Regulatory Impact Analysis: Best Practices in* OECD *Countries*, OECD, Paris, p. 245.

86. OMB (1998), p. 44 048.

87. Regulatory Programme, 1990-1991, p. 13.

88. Regulatory Program 1990-91, *op. cit.*, p. 14.

89. Choices in Risk Assessment: The Role of Science Policy in Risk Management Choices. Cited in "Risk Assessment: The US Experience" paper delivered by Steven Milloy to the conference "Managing Risk: A Balancing Act", European Policy Centre, London, April 29, 1998.

90. Office of Management and Budget (1996), "More Benefits, Fewer Burdens".

91. General Accounting Office (1997), "Agencies' efforts to eliminate and revise rules yield mixed results", p. 2.

92. US General Accounting Office (1999) *Paperwork Reduction Act: Burden Increases and Unauthorised Information Collections* (GAO/GGD-99-59), 20 April.

93. GAO, Paperwork Reduction. Government-wide Goals Unlikely to be Met. 4 June, 1997 (GAO/T-GGD-97 114), p. 19.

94. Antonnelli, A., p. 15.

95. Gore, Al (1997), *Access America: Reengineering Through Information Technology.*

96. Kerwin, Cornelius (1994), *Introduction to the Congressional Quarterly's Federal Regulatory Director*, Washington DC, p. 18.

97. Environmental Protection Agency (1998), "The Changing Nature of Environmental and Public Health Protection: An Annual Report on Reinvention", Washington DC, March, p. 38.

98. US Office of Information and Regulatory Affairs, Office of Management and Budget (1997), Report to Congress on the Costs and Benefits of Federal Regulations, September 30, p. 44.

99. US Office of Information and Regulatory Affairs, Office of Management and Budget (1998), Draft Report to Congress on the Costs and Benefits of Federal Regulations, 17 August.

100. Chubb, John E. and Paul E. Peterson (1989), *Can the Government Govern?*, Brookings Institution, Washington DC, p. 4.

101. Congressional Quarterly Weekly (1998), "Unfunded Mandates Reform Act: A Partial 'Contract' Success", 5 September, p. 2318.

102. "Enterprise for the Environment", statement by William D. Ruckelshaus, Chairman, Browning-Ferris Industries, Inc. before the Senate Appropriations Committee Subcommittee on VA-HUD Independent Agencies, February 29, 1996.

103. OMB (1994), "Report to the President on Executive Order No. 12 866 Regulatory Planning and Review", May 1.

104. "Improving Regulatory Systems", *op. cit.*

105. Hahn, Robert (1997), *Achieving Real Regulatory Reform*, The University of Chicago Legal Forum, Vol. 1997; Breyer, Stephen (1993), *Breaking the Vicious Circle: Toward Effective Risk* Regulation, Harvard.

106. Crandall, Robert, *et al.* (1997), An Agenda for Federal Regulatory Reform, AEI and The Brookings Institution.

107. Armey (1997).

108. Howard, John (Prime Minister) (1997), "Statement: More time for business", 14 March.

109. OMB (1998), p. 44050.

110. OMB (1998), p. 44056.

111. See Jacobs, Scott H., Deighton-Smith, Rex, Huigen, Hans, and Buchwitz, Rebecca (1997), "Regulatory Quality and Public Sector Reform", Chapter 2 in *The* OECD *Report on Regulatory Reform: Thematic Studies*, OECD, Paris.

BACKGROUND REPORT
ON THE ROLE OF COMPETITION POLICY
IN REGULATORY REFORM[*]

[*] This report was principally prepared by **Michael Wise** in the Directorate for Financial and Fiscal Affairs of the OECD. It has benefited from extensive comments provided by colleagues throughout the OECD Secretariat, by the Government of the United States, and by Member countries as part of the peer review process. This report was peer reviewed in June 1998 in the OECD's Competition Law and Policy Committee.

TABLE OF CONTENTS

Executive Summary

Background Report on the Role of Competition Policy in Regulatory Reform

Is competition policy sufficiently integrated into the general policy framework for regulation? Competition policy is central to regulatory reform, because (as the background report on Government Capacity to Produce High Quality Regulations shows) its principles and analysis provide a benchmark for assessing the quality of economic and social regulations, as well as motivate the application of the laws that protect competition. Moreover, as regulatory reform stimulates structural change, vigorous enforcement of competition policy is needed to prevent private market abuses from reversing the benefits of reform. A complement to competition law enforcement is competition advocacy, the promotion of competitive, market principles in other policy and regulatory processes. This report addresses two basic questions: First, is the US conception of competition policy, rooted in its history and culture, adequate to support pro-competitive reform? Second, do national institutions have the right tools to effectively promote competition policy? That is, are the competition laws and enforcement structures sufficient to prevent or correct collusion, monopoly, and unfair practices, now and after reform? And can its competition law and policy institutions encourage reform?

US competition policy is grounded in principles of economics and has been a powerful tool in regulatory reform. Competition law enforcement and policy advice have played central roles in successful efforts over the last 20 years to reform and often eliminate anti-competitive economic regulation of transport, energy, telecommunications, and services. The belief that market competition should underlie the US economy is broadly supported, so national sectoral regulators also operate under mandates to promote competition. To be sure, the ostensible commitment to competition has faltered in particular settings, and it has led to anomalies where regulators' mandates for competition have been vague, ambiguous, or arguably inconsistent with others. But connecting regulation to competition has made it easier to reform in many cases where sectoral regulation has led to anti-competitive results. Advocacy by the competition authorities was often important in pushing other regulators to focus on competition issues and to apply competition policy concepts consistently, and in clarifying the positive role competition policy could play in achieving regulatory objectives.

The basic legal enforcement tools are quite strong, so competition enforcement is a credible assurance that public interests remain protected in the absence of economic regulation. Paradoxically, the breadth of commitment to competition policy, and the strength of the US competition law and sanctions for violating it, may impede the direct application of competition law in some potential reform settings. Responsibility for competition policy is diffused widely and subject to myriad potentially competing interests. The number of special industry rules, jurisdictional oddities, and sectoral regulators and exemptions, which together constrain the application of the basic competition laws, is surprisingly large. Some of the sectoral regulatory programmes harmonise reasonably well with the general competition laws, but some have fallen short. One major source of exemption, the "state action" doctrine that permits individual states to impose non-competitive local regulatory programmes, can undermine larger-scale pro-competitive reform. Responding in part to these jurisdictional limitations and exemptions, the enforcement agencies have been vigorous public advocates of pro-competitive reform, to introduce competition by changes in regulation where they cannot do so by enforcement of competition law.

1. THE CONCEPTS OF COMPETITION POLICY IN THE UNITED STATES: FOUNDATIONS AND CONTEXT

The US's conception of competition policy as a principal component of its economic "constitution", and the central role competition policy plays in the design of economic legislation and regulation, constitute a powerful basis for fundamental reform. Basing regulation on a presumption of competition is not a radical idea in the United States, as it is in some OECD countries. Instead, reforms that emphasise competition can be represented, accurately, as a return to political and policy roots. That basic political support probably explains why the United States has done so much to remove price and entry controls over industries that are structurally competitive.

In the last 20 years, the two US competition policy agencies, the Antitrust Division of the Department of Justice and the Federal Trade Commission, as well as the courts, which are the ultimate authorities, have embraced a basically economic conception of competition policy. In truth, US competition policy has been based on economic principles for at least the last 50 years. A principal reason for establishing the Federal Trade Commission in 1914 was to bring economic and commercial expertise to the application of general competition law. As different economic principles have gained ascendancy, anti-trust law has generally followed.

Competition law prevents private constraints on the achievement of economic goals, principally the more efficient use of resources. This basically economic purpose for the law about competition is consistent with the directions and foundations of regulatory policy generally. The annual economic report of the President in 1996 introduced its discussion of regulatory policy by highlighting the importance of market competition to drive down costs and prices, induce firms to produce the goods consumers want, and spur innovation and the expansion of new markets from abroad.[1] Policies pursued by other federal regulatory agencies are typically conceived as intended to promote competition, rather than substitute for it, as much as possible. For example, the mission statement for the federal agency that regulates energy requires it "to foster and assure competition among parties engaged in the supply of energy and fuels".[2]

Despite the strong support for the idea of competition in US political culture, there is no single, generally accepted, authoritative statement of purpose for national competition policy. The first national competition laws, the 1887 Interstate Commerce Act and the 1890 Sherman Act, made federal powers and institutions available to apply substantive principles that were derived largely from common law. Just exactly what purpose those laws were to accomplish by challenging cartels and abusive monopolistic practices debated then and has been debated since. Later laws, such as the 1936 Robinson-Patman Act about price discrimination and the 1950 Celler-Kefauver Act about mergers, seem to respond to different purposes at the time they were enacted, namely to protect firms against unfair practices by their competitors and suppliers and to control industrial concentration. No doubt the lack of a single authoritative statement in the basic legislation reflects how purposes can be multiple, changing, and sometimes conflicting. The most often-quoted description of the motivation for US competition law does not come from the legislature, but from the Supreme Court, which has called the Sherman Act "a comprehensive charter of economic liberty aimed at preserving free and unfettered competition as the rule of trade", resting on the premise that "the unrestrained interaction of competitive forces will yield the best allocation of our economic resources, the lowest prices, the highest quality and the greatest material progress, while at the same time providing an environment conducive to the preservation of our democratic political and social institutions".[3]

In such statements about purpose, different elements of competition policy often appear together, as policy makers are reluctant to admit priorities. The recent US statement about competition policy to the WTO exemplifies this eloquent indecision. It concludes that the three "principal touchstones" of US competition policy are "promoting consumer welfare, protecting the competitive process and enhancing economic efficiency". Here "consumer welfare" is understood quite broadly. It means that the ultimate question is always the effect on consumers; effects on other producers are considered only to the extent they ultimately affect consumers. It holds that consumers' welfare is improved by greater

---

Box 1. Competition policy's roles in regulatory reform

In addition to the threshold, general issue, whether regulatory policy is consistent with the conception and purpose of competition policy, there are four particular ways in which competition policy and regulatory problems interact:

- Regulation can **contradict** competition policy. Regulations may have encouraged, or even required, conduct or conditions that would otherwise be in violation of the competition law. For example, regulations may have permitted price co-ordination, prevented advertising or other avenues of competition, or required territorial market division. Other examples include laws banning sales below costs, which purport to promote competition but are often interpreted in anti-competitive ways, and the very broad category of regulations that restrict competition more than is necessary to achieve the regulatory goals. When such regulations are changed or removed, firms affected must change their habits and expectations.

- Regulation can **replace** competition policy. Especially where monopoly has appeared inevitable, regulation may try to control market power directly, by setting prices and controlling entry and access. Changes in technology and other institutions may lead to reconsideration of the basic premise in support of regulation, that competition policy and institutions would be inadequate to the task of preventing monopoly and the exercise of market power.

- Regulation can **reproduce** competition policy. Rules and regulators may have tried to prevent co-ordination or abuse in an industry, just as competition policy does. For example, regulations may set standards of fair competition or tendering rules to ensure competitive bidding. Different regulators may apply different standards, though, and changes in regulatory institutions may reveal that seemingly duplicate policies may have led to different practical outcomes.

- Regulation can **use** competition policy methods. Instruments to achieve regulatory objectives can be designed to take advantage of market incentives and competitive dynamics. Co-ordination may be necessary, to ensure that these instruments work as intended in the context of competition law requirements.

---

variety, higher quality, and lower prices. This state is "efficient" in the sense that consumers "pay no more and no less than it costs society as a whole – in real terms – to produce those goods and services". This formulation echoes conventional static equilibrium analysis, which values competition to the extent it leads to a price-output combination that maximises output at a given cost. The focus on consumers receiving the benefit of that low cost is notable. But the consumer's welfare is not determined just by an area on an economic diagram. Rather, "the test" for identifying what the competition law considers undesirable is whether the restraint "reduc[es] the importance of consumer preference in setting price and output". The second element, the competitive process, is protected by preserving static and dynamic conditions that discourage collusion and permit efficient entry and innovation. And the third, efficiency, is promoted as competition forces firms to lower costs and respond to the market's signals.

The benchmark for US competition law is effect on competitive outcomes, more than process alone. To some extent, process issues underlie the increasing attention to strategic, exclusionary behaviour. Sensitivity to dynamic efficiency may revive some old competition law rules, adapted to new settings. But US competition law rarely intervenes simply to preserve the possibility of greater rivalry, except to redress an unfair practice by a firm with market power or to prevent a merger that threatens such a result. Nor is the law or policy particularly concerned about structure, at least not at the present time. Some years ago, when economic theory considered concentration to be significant or even determinative regardless of entry conditions or other factors, so did US competition policy.

The use of fairness as a competition policy value is controversial. The entire corpus of US competition law is included in the FTC Act, which prohibits "unfair method of competition". But the statute's sense of "unfair" has been transformed since the law was passed in 1914. Now, it is taken to mean "unfair to consumers". That is, it is unfair to deprive consumers of the benefits of an open, competitive marketplace. Some other, sector-specific competition laws are still concerned about preserving fair competition among business rivals, and it is not always clear that the other enforcers have adopted the same understanding as the competition agencies themselves.[4] And one US antitrust law, the Robinson-Patman Act, is based on traditional principles of unfair competition among competitors. US competition policy does not admit any special purpose for growth, although its policy presumes that competition promotes growth, and experience seems to bear this out. And it does not include any specific solicitude for small or medium sized businesses, although at one time it did, and the protection of small business was one of its political foundations.

Assigning a primary role to competition policy is consistent with the long-standing US cultural emphasis on individualism and entrepreneurial initiative. When national-scale regulatory institutions, such as the Interstate Commerce Commission and the Federal Trade Commission, were first created, they were conceived as necessary to protect and promote market competition, not as means of directly controlling business behaviour and investment. In those early years, farmers and local businesses complaining about abuses by railroads and national-scale firms called for these laws to stop discriminations and other abuses that, they said, unfairly prevented them from competing themselves. During the period from the Depression to the 1970's, when most of the other national regulatory institutions were created, there appeared to be a presumption in favour of federal economic regulation in many sectors. But even then, laws such as the Federal Power Act and Federal Radio Act (later the Federal Communications Act) often explained or justified regulation as a means of perfecting or correcting competitive markets.

One reason the notion of "competition" enjoys wide support, of course, is that the term can mean different things to different observers or in different contexts. In the first half-century of US competition policy, promoting competition was often understood to mean protecting opportunities for smaller competitors against putative monopolists. Sector regulators, who also claim to be promoting, rather than displacing, competition, have sometimes interpreted and applied the terms differently than the enforcement agencies would have. To some extent, those conflicts persist and have delayed achieving all the benefits of reform. But the basic cultural acceptance of a competition norm may explain why it has been politically feasible for the US to reform so many of its non-competitive regulatory policies. When dissatisfaction with the cartel-like results of economic regulation led to formal deregulation projects under the Ford and Carter administrations in the 1970's, those efforts drew support from the competition policy tradition. And competition law enforcement was applied directly as a reform tool, to break up the national telecommunications monopoly and to eliminate price-fixing through "private" regulation of professional services.

The multitude of institutions responsible for "competition" underscores that in the US, as elsewhere, competition policy must be understood as broader than just the basic laws about restrictive business practices and corporate combinations. Competition policy results from the combined effects of all the laws, policies, and institutions that protect, prevent, promote, or employ market competition. The basic competition laws are federal statutes, but their content and meaning is determined principally by a common-law process in which the courts are the highest authorities. Most other regulatory programmes are specified by detailed laws and statutes, but for those too the courts play important roles in interpretation and application. The power and role of the independent judiciary in the US legal system helps keep US competition policy coherent, despite the multiplicity of participants. Judges deciding particular cases may often be required to acknowledge and try to accommodate the many objectives and effects of these different legal commands. The result is a constant process of defining and balancing the roles of competition policy institutions and those responsible for economic and social regulation.

The strength and pervasiveness of competition policy concepts may explain some other features of US regulation. US competition law enforcement does not balance other policy goals against the goal of protecting competition. Thus a reduction in competition cannot usually be justified on the grounds that some other purpose is being served. And efforts to achieve other goals by means that appear to reduce competition run a serious risk of antitrust liability. Because the goals cannot be achieved by restricting competition, the US relies mostly on other methods, including direct regulation, to achieve them. It is a separate, and important, question whether the benefits of the direct regulation or other methods are justified by the costs they incur, including perhaps indirect effects on competition too.

2. THE SUBSTANTIVE TOOLKIT: CONTENT OF THE COMPETITION LAW

US competition law appears vigorous and strong. Its substantive provisions can reach all the kinds of possible competition problems that might arise after regulations are changed to permit greater market competition. The law has already been used, directly, to accomplish reform objectives. But one aspect of its strength disguises a potential handicap when applied to regulatory settings. Sanctions for violation are unusually harsh. High fines, trebled damages, and imprisonment can appear disproportionate, as punishment for conduct that had only recently been permitted, or even required, by other government regulation. The high penalties for violation encourage claims for exemption, special treatment, or even regulation as a substitute for competition enforcement.

2.1. Horizontal agreements: rules to prevent anti-competition co-ordination, including that fostered by regulation

Under US antitrust law, agreements among competitors about the critical competitive dimensions of price and output can be treated as crimes, subject to felony penalties of high fines and imprisonment. The actual effect or the reasonableness of the prices or market divisions agreed on is not relevant. Such agreements are illegal *per se*. Less severe penalties can also be applied, such as cease and desist orders. Other kinds of horizontal agreement may also be illegal, but their legality depends on the outcome of the "rule of reason" test, that is, on a review of the net competitive effects in the particular factual setting.

The law prohibiting horizontal agreements has often been used to ensure that deregulated industries do not continue their previous habits. After airline deregulation, executives attempting to fix prices were indicted.[5] Another suit stopped concerted practices by which airlines tried to establish or maintain price agreements by signalling through computer networks.[6] Tariff bureau agreements about trucking rates were challenged as horizontal price fixing.[7] A non-compete agreement between cable TV firms was challenged as market division.[8]

Self-regulation has been a particular target. Competition law has been used to break down "ethical" constraints that professionals and other service providers have imposed on themselves, typically via their trade associations. The seminal action was the Federal Trade Commission's successful complaint against the American Medical Association for banning price advertising and contracting practices.[9] Scores of other actions followed, most of them resolved by consent orders. In 1996, the FTC prohibited the California Dental Association from restricting truthful, non-deceptive advertising and solicitation practices. The Commission found that broad, categorical bans on advertising of low prices and discounts are as anti-competitive as outright price fixing.[10] And in 1997, the Commission ordered a voluntary professional association, the International Association of Conference Interpreters and its US affiliate members, to stop using rules that effectively fixed prices for interpreter services. Similar cases have been brought in industries outside the learned professions, such as automobile dealer associations and associations of insurers. Firms in industries subject to regulatory change can obtain some assurance against antitrust action, by asking for the agencies' advice in advance. Thus, in 1995, the Antitrust Division approved a proposal by the Intermodal Council of the American Trucking Associations, Inc. to begin a series of discussions about improved efficiencies in intermodal operations. This approval took the form of a "business review letter", an informal but binding assurance that the proposed actions would not be challenged.[11]

The strength of the law about price fixing follows naturally from the economic basis of US competition policy. There is a moral element as well: some have justified the harsh treatment by analogising the law against price fixing to the law against theft, reasoning that both take money out of the consumers' pockets without their knowledge and against their will. But harshness is less appropriate in regulatory contexts, and thus most actions against horizontal constraints in regulatory settings have been civil cases. (The exceptions are naked attempts to fix prices long after the regulatory price-setting methods have been formally repealed.)

Box 2. **The competition policy toolkit**

General competition laws usually address the problems of monopoly power in three formal settings: relationships and agreements among otherwise independent firms, actions by a single firm, and structural combinations of independent firms. The first category, **agreements**, is often subdivided for analytic purposes into two groups: "horizontal" agreements among firms that do the same things, and "vertical" agreements among firms at different stages of production or distribution. The second category is termed "**monopolisation**" in some laws, and "**abuse of dominant position**" in others; the legal systems that use different labels have developed somewhat different approaches to the problem of single-firm economic power. The third category, often called "**mergers**" or "concentrations", usually includes other kinds of structural combination, such as share or asset acquisitions, joint ventures, cross-shareholdings and interlocking directorates.

Agreements may permit the group of firms acting together to achieve some of the attributes of monopoly, of raising prices, limiting output, and preventing entry or innovation. The most troublesome **horizontal** agreements are those that prevent rivalry about the fundamental dynamics of market competition, price and output. Most contemporary competition laws treat naked agreements to fix prices, limit output, rig bids, or divide markets very harshly. To enforce such agreements, competitors may also agree on tactics to prevent new competition or to discipline firms that do not go along; thus, the laws also try to prevent and punish boycotts. Horizontal co-operation on other issues, such as product standards, research, and quality, may also affect competition, but whether the effect is positive or negative can depend on market conditions. Thus, most laws deal with these other kinds of agreement by assessing a larger range of possible benefits and harms, or by trying to design more detailed rules to identify and exempt beneficial conduct.

Vertical agreements try to control aspects of distribution. The reasons for concern are the same – that the agreements might lead to increased prices, lower quantity (or poorer quality), or prevention of entry and innovation. Because the competitive effects of vertical agreements can be more complex than those of horizontal agreements, the legal treatment of different kinds of vertical agreements varies even more than for horizontal agreements. One basic type of agreement is resale price maintenance: vertical agreements can control minimum, or maximum, prices. In some settings, the result can be to curb market abuses by distributors. In others, though, it can be to duplicate or enforce a horizontal cartel. Agreements granting exclusive dealing rights or territories can encourage greater effort to sell the supplier's product, or they can protect distributors from competition or prevent entry by other suppliers. Depending on the circumstances, agreements about product combinations, such as requiring distributors to carry full lines or tying different products together, can either facilitate or discourage introduction of new products. Franchising often involves a complex of vertical agreements with potential competitive significance: a franchise agreement may contain provisions about competition within geographic territories, about exclusive dealing for supplies, and about rights to intellectual property such as trademarks.

Abuse of dominance or **monopolisation** are categories that are concerned principally with the conduct and circumstances of individual firms. A true monopoly, which faces no competition or threat of competition, will charge higher prices and produce less or lower quality output; it may also be less likely to introduce more efficient methods or innovative products. Laws against monopolisation are typically aimed at exclusionary tactics by which firms might try to obtain or protect monopoly positions. Laws against abuse of dominance address the same issues, and may also try to address the actual exercise of market power. For example under some abuse of dominance systems, charging unreasonably high prices can be a violation of the law.

Merger control tries to prevent the creation, through acquisitions or other structural combinations, of undertakings that will have the incentive and ability to exercise market power. In some cases, the test of legality is derived from the laws about dominance or restraints; in others, there is a separate test phrased in terms of likely effect on competition generally. The analytic process applied typically calls for characterising the products that compete, the firms that might offer competition, and the relative shares and strategic importance of those firms with respect to the product markets. An important factor is the likelihood of new entry and the existence of effective barriers to new entry. Most systems apply some form of market share test, either to guide further investigation or as a presumption about legality. Mergers in unusually concentrated markets, or that create firms with unusually high market shares, are thought more likely to affect competition. And most systems specify procedures for pre-notification to enforcement authorities in advance of larger, more important transactions, and special processes for expedited investigation, so problems can be identified and resolved before the restructuring is actually undertaken.

Where regulation has been in place, there may often be at least a colourable argument that the restraint accomplishes a proper purpose or even promotes competition. The agencies and the courts have tried several approaches to acknowledging and weighing the potential efficiencies of horizontal restraints, while minimising costly, time-consuming evidentiary analysis, if possible. The FTC adopted a protocol of shifting burdens and escalating standards of proof in its *Massachusetts Board of Optometry* decision in the 1980s and then used the test extensively in striking down private regulation among professional and trade associations. While the FTC has now evidently abandoned the *Massachusetts Board* method,[12] the Antitrust Division has announced that it is applying a three-step process that looks very much like it. The first step is determining whether an agreement among competing firms restrains competition that would otherwise have occurred. If the answer is yes, but the agreement does not fall into a usual *per se* category, the next step is to challenge the parties to the agreement to explain why, despite the evident risk to competition, their agreement nonetheless produced pro-competitive effects. If they fail to do so, the Antitrust Division claims it should then win the case, even though it has not demonstrated actual net anti-competitive effects in the particular factual setting. If the parties do come forward with evidence of significant efficiencies or pro-competitive effects, though, then it is necessary to undertake the third step, the balancing test of the rule of reason, applied to the particular setting.[13] There is Supreme Court precedent for some such middle-range decision method.[14] An approach limited to only the traditional full rule of reason and the traditional *per se* rule could affect enforcement costs and priorities, and make challenges to horizontal restraints less effective.[15]

Regardless of the particular test, other social policies and effects cannot be weighed in the balance in a competition law enforcement matter. The Supreme Court itself has held[16] that any argument to the effect that some other public interest, even safety, outweighs the law's interest in free competition must be addressed to the legislature, not to the courts or the enforcement agencies. This doctrine, that constraints on economic competition cannot be legally justified on the grounds of protecting other interests, has not necessarily undermined the protection of those interests. But it may explain, in part, why there is so much direct regulation in the US to promote or protect social values. Examples include rules applied by the Environmental Protection Agency, the Food and Drug Administration, the Department of Agriculture, and the Consumer Product Safety Commission. Some of this is regulation to correct market failures, especially those due to consumers' lack of accurate information. Direct regulation avoids the inefficiency that would result from preventing competition; however, it remains to be determined in particular cases, whether the benefits of direct regulation justify the costs. The refusal of competition law to admit defences based on protecting other values does not prevent competitors from acting together to improve safety or to correct information failures. Rather, it prevents them from agreeing to eliminate economic competition. Where another regulatory programme also applies to the conduct at issue, a balance between policies may be achieved by limiting or channelling the application of competition law. Balancing with other policy interests is accomplished through doctrines of exemption or assignments of jurisdiction, rather than through decisions about the application of the competition law.

US law about horizontal agreements could be less useful in regulatory situations because of long-standing difficulties in dealing with "tacit" conspiracy and co-ordinated action, even under the more flexible Federal Trade Commission Act. But careful economic analysis and presentation of evidence have supported successful application of the Sherman Act to tacit conspiracy in the post-deregulation airline industry, showing that this weakness can probably be overcome in appropriate cases.

A more important concern is the perception that penalties are disproportionate. Allegations about draconian penalties (including risks of treble damages in litigation outside the government's control) may lend credence to claims that previously regulated conduct ought not to be subject to the entire range of antitrust law. Many of the dozens of statutory special provisions, discussed in Section 4 below, appear designed to prevent the application of criminal penalties and treble damages for just this reason.

2.2. Vertical agreements: rules to prevent anti-competitive arrangements in supply and distribution, including those fostered by regulation

The text of US law, like the texts of most other competition laws, does not distinguish between horizontal and vertical agreements. But the doctrine developed by US courts and enforcement agencies draws a sharp distinction. Only one kind of vertical agreement, to fix minimum resale prices, is clearly illegal *per se*. Despite the *per se* label, resale price maintenance is not treated like horizontal price fixing, in terms of remedy and enforcement. The agencies bring very few cases, and virtually never bring criminal charges against this violation. Certain tying agreements are sometimes described as illegal *per se*, but the accuracy of that classification is doubtful, for the courts have also required that the party imposing the agreement have economic power over the tying good or service. Thus, illegality depends on more than just the form of the agreement. Most vertical relationships are thus assessed under the rule of reason and are considered illegal only if net anti-competitive effects are demonstrated. The usual remedy is an injunction or cease and desist order, or damages in private cases.

Competition law principles have been applied to vertical relationships imposed by regulation or adopted in order to thwart the goals of regulatory reform. State-level regulations mandating exclusive sales territories or protecting dealers and franchisees against contract partners or competitors have been criticised and challenged. In health care markets, some parties have responded to greater competition by adopted "most favoured customer" pricing clauses, assuring their customers or suppliers that their competitors will not get better treatment. These have been the target of several enforcement actions, because in some circumstances the clauses' net effect may actually be to discourage entry and price reductions. And some providers have sought regulations imposing "any willing provider" guarantees, to force medical coverage plans to admit them as contract parties. Agency advocacy has criticised these regulations as likely to dampen competition for lower prices.

The "rule of reason" approach to nearly all vertical relationships exemplifies how US law follows economic principles. The agencies and courts are sensitive to the difficulty of determining the net competitive effect of most vertical restraints and to the likelihood that they serve some useful, efficient purpose. And the approach is consistent with the US libertarian streak. Presuming that parties to business contracts entered them freely, competition law does not usually intervene to redress a perceived imbalance in negotiating power.

Nevertheless, there are some curiosities in US vertical restraint law, mostly related to the effort to maintain *per se* treatment for resale price maintenance. US law appears less regulatory than, for example, the elaborate structure of prescribed and prohibited contract terms under EC block exemptions. But in US law, there is a complex and obscure interplay of case law doctrines about how a vertical agreement can be inferred or avoided.

2.3. Monopolisation (abuse of dominance): rules to prevent or remedy market power, especially arising from reform-related restructuring

The Sherman Act does not prohibit being a monopolist, or even acting like one by charging high prices or reducing output. Rather, what is forbidden is conduct that, by unfair means, achieves or maintains a monopoly, principally by excluding other efficient competitors. The available sanctions are substantial, reaching all the way to mandated divestiture and restructuring, to undo the monopoly structure and create competing firms in its place. But monopolisation cases can be enormously complex, so few are brought.

The monopolisation law has been used to restructure regulated network monopolies. The principal illustration is the use of a Sherman Act monopolisation case, filed in the 1970s, to restructure the national telephone system. The consent decree issued in 1982 separated manufacturing, long distance, and local service operations. The basis for the action was the incumbent monopolist's efforts to exclude competitors in equipment and long distance services. The consent decree led to prolonged, continued controversy, though, about the relative competences of the federal judge overseeing it, the Antitrust Division, and the sectoral regulator, the Federal Communications Commission, to implement further reforms in telecommunications. These are discussed further in the background report on Regulatory Reform in the Electricity Industry.

In determining liability for monopolisation, only competition policies are taken into account. But in designing a remedy, courts may consider other public policies, because the remedy must be in the public interest and thus must not unnecessarily impair other important policies. Thus, in the AT&T divestiture, the judge who entered the consent decree considered public comments about how the proposed divestiture would affect other regulatory requirements, including the responsibilities of state-level regulators.[17]

Monopolisation law is not used as a direct remedy for the exercise of market power through high prices. Because the policy is implemented through judicial law enforcement, this would require that judges or prosecutors become price regulators. Those roles are not suitable in the US administrative system, because those officials lack the technical support or political accountability necessary to those tasks. Monopolisation law enforcement may, however, be employed to counter actions that deny access to "essential facilities", and it has been employed in many regulatory settings, such as telecommunications and electric power, for that purpose. The inability of competition law to address the pricing aspects of market power, but only underlying conditions that make market power possible, may encourage retaining regulatory programmes that control prices directly.

2.4. Mergers: rules to prevent competition problems arising from corporate restructuring, including responses to regulatory change

Combinations of all kinds, including joint ventures and open market acquisitions, are covered by the general merger statute, the Clayton Act. The legal test is whether the transaction is likely to harm competition or tend to create a monopoly. The law is prospective; mergers can be prevented on a showing of likely future effects, and showing of actual, historic effect or non-competitive conditions is not necessary. The law can also be applied to undo a merger that has already happened, but because of pre-merger notification that is rarely necessary any more. The premerger filing obligation depends only on the size of the parties and the transaction. The process thus sweeps in many deals that have no competitive effect. The process of filing will impose some delay, even if the agencies exercise their power to terminate an investigation early, and the filing can cost over $100 000 even if there is no likely problem. The filing fee alone is nearly $50 000 per party per transaction. This figure may be significant for firms or transactions that just barely meet the reporting requirement, of sales or assets of about $15 million. The enforcement process is disciplined by deadlines and the fact that the agencies cannot act solely on their own, but must obtain an order from a federal judge to block a transaction.

In part because the statutory test is phrased explicitly in terms of competitive effect, merger law is perhaps the purest expression of the economics-based approach to competition policy. The agencies' guidelines outline a market definition protocol (based on demand substitution incentives and behaviour as proxies for cross-elasticity of demand), specify how to identify and characterise market participants (as "in" the market or committed entrants), state presumptions about structural measures, and set standards for evaluating likely competitive effects of entry. The guidelines and applicable law contain market share tests. These tests appear highly precise, seeming to declare that a combination of two firms with market shares of about seven per cent in a five-firm industry is illegal, and that one among such firms in a ten firm industry is suspect. But the precision is only apparent, and transactions of that low magnitude are rarely challenged. Decisions to challenge are based on detailed assessment of likely effect in the particular circumstances. Markets are defined based on data about actual and likely cross-elasticities and substitution responses. Assessment of likely effect depends critically on the long-term significance of entry. Possible entry by a firm that could exit quickly, at no cost, is treated differently than possible entry by a firm that would have to commit sunk resources. This difference in treatment of entry could be quite significant in regulatory settings. The hurdle faced by a "facilities-based" competitor could be much higher than that faced by a reseller of the incumbent's basic service.

The law speaks only of competitive effects. Other values, including industrial development, employment, and the values and purposes promoted by other regulatory programmes are not considered, at least explicitly. In practical fact, the agencies may be aware of the possible impact of other policy considerations when deciding whether to act. And applications in market-based health care are instructive about how the courts view the balance with other policies. Health care reform has led to a great deal of restructuring, such as mergers and acquisitions of hospitals and drug firms. The enforcement agencies have lost several hospital merger cases, as courts resisted the precept that competition cannot be balanced against other social goals.

The merger law has often been used to maintain and protect gains from reform and restructuring. The natural gas industry was essentially deregulated a decade ago; recently, the FTC stopped an acquisition that would have protected a local market gas pipeline against the threat of competition.[18] Other examples come from television and radio, where special sectoral rules about competition have been relaxed or discarded. In September, 1996 the FTC challenged Time-Warner's acquisition of Turner Broadcasting because it would restrict distributors' access to video programming and programme producers' access to distribution outlets, increase concentration by combining two leading producers, and increase vertical integration.[19] After sector-specific ownership constraints were relaxed, the Antitrust Division has challenged mergers of radio stations.[20] In telecommunications, an Antitrust Division challenge led to restructuring of the Nextel-Motorola acquisition to preserve competitive opportunities among entrants into wireless communication that might challenge the regulated landline telecommunications monopolies. In 1995, the Division insisted on modifications to the proposed alliance among Sprint, France Telecom, and Deutsche Telekom to preserve competitive opportunities for US firms in newly developing world telecommunications markets.

Jurisdiction over mergers in regulated industries has been scattered, though. Some sectoral regulators have shared or even exclusive jurisdiction over mergers in their industries. Most sectoral regulation is being dismantled, but separate merger control authority has proven difficult to uproot. As a consequence, application in regulation settings has sometimes been problematic. Because of their limited experience, and in some cases their responsibility to promote industry well-being, sector regulators may have systematic bias in favour of seeing the world the same way the regulated industry has, and may fail to appreciate the scope of possible competitive effects from novel industry combinations. The particular jurisdictional exemption are discussed below, under the relevant sectoral exemptions. Eliminating this bureaucratic balkanisation of analysis and enforcement could make the merger law a more effective reform tool, by ensuring that general competition law methods and principles are applied consistently.

2.5. Competitor protection: relationship to rules of "unfair competition"

The US federal law about unfair competition has developed from a law to remedy harm to competitors into the basis for a competition policy that is concerned fundamentally about harm to consumers. The basic law is the Federal Trade Commission Act, whose substantive section includes "unfairness" in two senses, both of which depart in some respects from usual doctrines of unfair competition. On the competition side, it prohibits "unfair methods of competition", and it is taken to mean the acts prohibited by the other antitrust laws. On the consumer protection side, it prohibits "unfair or deceptive" acts or practices. The implied distinction between "unfair" acts and "deceptive" ones seems to treat one of the basic, traditional kinds of unfair competition, namely deceptive advertising, as something different from "unfairness". These oddities are explained by how the purpose of US law has evolved. The traditional law of unfair competition is about unfairness among competitors. The US law now treats these terms as referring to unfairness to consumers, including harms to the competitive process on which consumers have a right to rely. In fact, federal competition law is increasingly interpreted to ignore claims of unfairness among competitors, except as the actions complained of might harm consumers. The US antitrust laws no longer include much of the traditional doctrine about unfair competition. That doctrine is now sometimes called "business torts" in the US. Since the interests being protected are usually private, business torts are pursued primarily through private actions. An exception to this trend, though, is the Robinson-Patman Act, a part of the federal antitrust laws which regulates discriminations in price and marketing services. This law has long been considered as an act to promote fairness, although that word does not appear in its text. Even though the law's basic prohibition includes a competitive-effects requirement, it is a technically complex statute that can sometimes be applied to protect competitors. The federal agencies do little to enforce this law themselves, and 20 years ago the Antitrust Division even called for its repeal. Despite the lack of public enforcement, it is still important in private lawsuits.

Often, competition law and policy have been invoked to undermine or remove rules ostensibly preventing unfair competition. A chief example is rules or even state laws prohibiting sales "below cost". The FTC has expressed concern about these laws, because the sales they prohibit often benefit consumers through low prices. Yet it is unlikely that competition is impaired, either in the short run or the long run, because it is rarely possible to recoup losses from "predation" in the settings where these claims are often made, such as retail trade. Another example is professional codes of ethics that try to prevent price competition or advertising, which have been frequent targets of competition law enforcement.

2.6. Consumer protection: consistency with competition law and policy

US policy treats antitrust and consumer protection law enforcement as complementary tools for achieving the benefits of market competition. The general competition law is intended to ensure that markets provide consumers with an appropriate range of options. These laws therefore prohibit conduct that would substantially and artificially limit choices in the marketplace. The general consumer protection law (principally Section 5 of the FTC Act, but also including other special-purpose consumer protection laws) is intended to ensure that consumers can select freely and effectively from the options offered in the market.[21] These laws prohibit conduct that can impair consumer choice even if carried out only by a single firm. Because these two bodies of law advance the public purpose of supporting a market economy, they are appropriately enforced by public agencies and boards. The FTC, responsible for both bodies of law, is a valuable integrator. Having both responsibilities in the same organisation can provide opportunities to test the two sets of policies' relationship to each other. These possibilities for cross-fertilisation often appear in regulatory contexts. US consumer groups generally favour strong competition law enforcement, sometimes even criticising the enforcement agencies for not being active enough. In general, though, anxiety about some aspects of reform and deregulation has been met, and to some extent overcome, by the knowledge that backup of competition law enforcement is credible.

3. INSTITUTIONAL TOOLS: ENFORCEMENT IN SUPPORT OF REGULATORY REFORM

Reform of economic regulation can be less beneficial or even harmful if the competition authority does not act vigorously to prevent abuses in developing markets. The US has strong, well-established basic enforcement institutions. In fact, it has so many different enforcement methods that maintaining co-ordination and consistency among them is a continuing challenge. To a large extent, the constant potential for appeal to the court system encourages a degree of consistency. But the proportion of cases decided by actual contests in the courts remains small. Application of US competition law has come to look more like regulation over the last decade, as the agencies have turned to issuing guidelines about important policy issues, such as health care and intellectual property, and to negotiating detailed behaviour requirements in consent decrees in complex merger cases. Thus it becomes a matter of interest whether the processes meet desirable standards of regulatory quality.

3.1. Competition policy institutions

With two national-level competition agencies, the US presents two different models of institutional design. One agency, the Antitrust Division of the Department of Justice, is part of the executive branch of the government. Its location in the Department of Justice, rather than in a department more specifically charged with economic policy, follows from the Sherman Act's origins as a criminal statute. It suggests a tradition of prosecution, as much as of policy analysis. The other agency, the Federal Trade Commission, is an independent body, located politically and geographically between the legislature and the executive. One reason for its creation was to bring greater technical expertise to competition policy; however, the FTC's basic law was built on the common law of unfair competition, and the FTC was also charged with a law enforcement role and process. Proposals to create a competition agency with the powers of direct economic regulation were rejected at the outset in 1914. Thus, the US has two law-enforcement agencies, both staffed by a combination of lawyers and economists, both combining policy expertise and prosecutorial skill with political accountability (achieved in different ways), and both implementing policy about competition mostly by applying general principles case by case to particular situations. The redundancy has not historically led to conflict, as the two agencies have strictly divided their responsibilities to avoid duplicating effort or inviting forum shopping. But it does impose some costs on each agency, to co-ordinate policies and actions with the other one.

Independence and transparency are ensured by roughly comparable methods at the two agencies. The Antitrust Division has a tradition of separate decision, without influence from or consultation with higher political authorities. It is required by law to publish and solicit public comment about proposed consent decrees. And it cannot issue binding orders on its own authority, but must make its cases to independent, tenured federal judges. At the FTC, independence is established by the Commissioners' tenure for fixed terms, not subject to removal over disagreements about policy. The political check on each agency is the fact that the top officials (the Commissioners and the head of the Antitrust Division) are appointed by the President, subject to Senate confirmation. In addition, the President designates which FTC Commissioner will be the chair. At the Commission, no more than a bare majority (three out of five) can be from the same political party. At both agencies, there is a strong tradition of professionalism, and enforcement decisions do not appear to depend on political influence. Both agencies publicise their decisions to initiate actions. Final decisions, from the courts or the Commission, are almost always accompanied by detailed opinions and explanations. But neither agency routinely explains its reasons for not taking action, although they may do so where there is unusual interest in a matter. (Decisions not to take action are not appealable; the disappointed complainant's recourse is to bring suit itself.) And there have been concerns that the consent order process sometimes obscures the agencies' reasoning, because public explanations are often phrased in conclusory terms that give little guidance to how doctrines are developing.

The competition agencies' relationships with regulatory bodies and policy makers differ some, as might expected from the difference in their institutional design. Because the heads of other agencies and regulators are also Presidential appointees, in principle all should be responsive to the same broad political themes. The Antitrust Division, as part of the executive branch, deals as one ministry to another, and thus has a stronger connection to the setting of economic policy within the executive branch of government. The FTC, as an independent agency, is more of an outsider with respect to other departments. Both competition agencies are outsiders with respect to the other independent agencies that have been responsible for major infrastructure industries such as telecommunications, energy, and transportation. Especially in their relations with these other independent agencies, the competition policy interactions with other policies can become formalistic. The competition agencies' efforts to promote competitive approaches at these other agencies have tended to be more successful when they have been built on long-standing staff-level contacts and consultations. For example, telecommunications reform has involved many years of interaction between the Antitrust Division and FCC staffs, and many of the competition agencies' statements about FCC regulatory proposals have been developed co-operatively, to support the direction of FCC efforts. This co-operative direction was crucial to the design of the antitrust divestiture which built on the FCC's separation rules between competitive and monopoly parts of AT&T's network, but was less effective in its implementation. To date, co-operation in regard to provisions in the new Telecommunications Act relevant to this issue has been effective, though it remains a source of possible future friction.

3.2. Competition law enforcement

Both competition agencies have adequate powers to take action independently, to gather the information they need to reach reasoned decisions, and to ensure that their decisions are effective. And despite the law-enforcement culture in which each operates, and the fact that policies other than competition are not formally taken into account in determining liability, both agencies have proven sensitive to regulatory contexts. They have tried to ensure that their enforcement programmes are consistent with regulatory reform initiatives. In some respects, notably concerning the time and expense of their procedures, the agencies' own regulatory process might be improved; for the most part, though, the agencies are taking steps to meet appropriate standards.

Both agencies implement their enforcement programmes independently and can take initiatives without necessarily obtaining formal authorisation from other parts of the government. The two agencies may consult informally, though, with other parts of the government that are known to have regulatory or law enforcement interests in particular companies or industries. Both agencies have broad powers to demand documents and testimony. The enforcement processes differ slightly, although both contemplate adversarial evidentiary hearings. The Antitrust Division appears in federal court as a party plaintiff or prosecutor, filing a conventional complaint or indictment. The process may lead to a trial before a judge or a jury and an opinion by the independent federal judge. The FTC issues complaints in its own internal process, which may lead to a hearing that is similar to a judicial trial, but is held before an Administrative Law Judge, a Commission employee with somewhat protected tenure and status. The decision and opinion by the Commission itself is usually on appeal from the initial decision by the Administrative Law Judge. It was originally hoped that the FTC's administrative process would be a more efficient way to find facts and apply expert analysis to them, but that hope has been disappointed. The Commission's internal processes have proven to be no speedier or less expensive than federal court litigation.

Some kinds of matters, especially mergers and criminal prosecutions, are subject to strict statutory deadlines. Others are not, though, and in the absence of that discipline, matters can languish. Taking a long time for some matters may not imply inattention. Rather, because easy cases settle fast, while hard ones take much longer, the long ones may show that the agency is taking on difficult issues. But unnecessary delay has long been a concern about competition litigation. The FTC adopted new rules in 1997 intended to set new, shorter deadlines for administrative litigation.[22] An initial decision must be filed within 12 months after the Commission issues its administrative complaint, barring extraordinary circumstances. In some circumstances, "fast track" procedures can require a final Commission decision (if the initial decision is appealed) within 13 months after issuance of a complaint. Experience so far has been promising, as the Commission has met this deadline when it has set it for itself.

The sanction in most non-criminal matters is an injunction or cease-and-desist order, to prevent future violations. Auxiliary measures to ensure compliance are often included also. Fines are available only in criminal cases, but settlements of civil cases may include pecuniary elements, and the government can sue to recover its own damages. An individual convicted of violating the Sherman Act may be imprisoned for up to three years and fined up to $350 000 for each count. For corporations, basic fines can be up to $10 million for each count, but in addition the fine may be increased to twice the gain from the illegal conduct or twice the loss to the victims. More recent violations are governed by general sentencing regulations, which tend to increase the potential incarceration for individual antitrust convictions, while reducing their fines; the net result of the new formulae for calculating fines against corporate violators leads to generally greater penalties.

The ultimate check on the agencies' enforcement policies and processes is the availability of judicial review. An initial substantive decision finding liability, either by a trial judge or jury or by the FTC in adjudicative matters, can always be appealed to a federal Court of Appeals. These independent appellate judges, who also hear appeals from private cases and decisions about other regulatory programmes, can control for consistency in the interpretation and application of the competition law, and have a great influence on how competition principles relate to other regulatory programmes. Judicial review also tends to ensure continuity of policy. The increasing influence of judges with an economic perspective has reinforced the economics-oriented antitrust policy of the last 20 years.

Box 3.   Enforcement powers

Does the agency have the power to take action on its own initiative? The FTC, like most Member country agencies (19), has power to issue prohibitory orders on its own initiative. The Antitrust Division does not, though; it must make its cases in court. Neither is required to wait for a complaint. Unlike the agencies in about half of Member countries, neither agency can usually assess financial penalties directly, but instead must obtain a court order.

Does the agency publish its decisions and the reasons for them? Like virtually all Member country enforcement agencies, the FTC publishes its decisions, and courts publish opinions in many of the Anti-trust Division's cases. (Trial-level opinions do not appear in criminal cases decided by juries.)

Are the agency's decisions subject to substantive review and correction by a court? All Member country competition agencies must defend their actions in court if necessary.

Can private parties also bring their own suits about competition issues? Some kind of privately initiated suit about competition issues is possible in nearly all Member countries, but provisions for private relief in US law are probably the most substantial, and the greatest use is made of the option, too. Unlike most Member countries, the US agencies do not typically explain the reasons why they do not take action in a particular case, though. But this does not seem to inhibit plaintiffs from going to court.

3.3. Other enforcement methods

The competition agencies are not the only entities with the power to apply national competition law. Private enforcement, through suits for treble damages or injunctions, was provided in the original Sherman Act and continues to be important. Private suits can supplement government enforcement, but the litigants' priorities and motivations may not always be consistent with the government agencies' views on competition policy. A common type of private antitrust case is an auxiliary claim in a contract dispute, added because the threat of treble damages can be a powerful negotiating tool. But some private cases have been important on their own merits. Moreover, having the outlet available can be valuable check on government policies. If the government agency refuses to investigate a complaint, the complainant has the legal right to bring the case itself. Thus, the courts still hear cases about price discrimination and types of vertical restraints that are not high priorities in the agencies' enforcement programmes. Treble damages and attorneys' fees awards were included in the law to encourage private enforcement, by compensating for the high cost and risk of taking on a firm that is often the plaintiff's supplier or major competitor. But now that class actions are available to aggregate many small claims, and criminal fines have greatly increased, it may be worth reconsidering whether awarding exemplary damages in antitrust cases is still a sound policy.

Private litigation has played a significant role in regulatory reform, particularly in the professional services sector. The landmark case of *Goldfarb* v. *Virginia State Bar*, 421 US 773 (1975), applied the antitrust laws for the first time to the professions. In *Goldfarb* the Supreme Court held that minimum fee schedules for lawyers, adopted by a county bar association and enforced through disciplinary action by the state bar, constituted essentially private, anti-competitive activity. This decision opened the way to considerable private litigation and government enforcement challenging restrictions on professionals' business practices.

In addition to actions by purely private parties, there are two possible kinds of competition law enforcement actions by state and local officials. First, they can appear in a role similar to that of a private party, in suits under the general federal competition law. In addition, state-level officials can enforce their own competition laws. Forty-eight of the 50 American states have antitrust statutes of general application. These statutes generally mirror the federal antitrust laws. By statute or judicial interpretation, the majority of the states refer to and generally follow federal case law in construing comparable provisions under their state antitrust laws. However, many states have specific antitrust statutes aimed at particular industries, such as insurance, petroleum, or dairy, or at specific practices, such as below-cost pricing, bid rigging or price discrimination between areas within the state. Statutory exemptions provided for in state antitrust laws are numerous and vary widely from state to state.

State-level action is another supplement to federal enforcement and provides yet another check on the federal agencies' policies and priorities. There is some history of conflict between federal and state enforcers about how the federal laws should be applied. Local officials tended to be more aggressive in the 1980s. This additional tier of potential enforcement power can complicate business planning. The state enforcers have developed their own shared guidelines about mergers and vertical restraints, which differ in significant details from those of the federal agencies. The process by which these rule-like pronouncements have issued is irregular, and the scope of their authority is unclear. Direct conflicts about enforcement actions have declined, as the agencies and state enforcers have developed better means of co-operation in the 1990s. But state enforcers have tried to block some mergers that the federal government did not challenge, and they have brought actions against vertical restraints that the federal enforcers probably would not have challenged.

3.4. International trade issues in competition policy and enforcement

Foreign firms have the same rights as US firms and individuals, to make complaints to the enforcement agencies and to bring their own suits for treble damages or other relief. Even foreign governments may also sue, if they have standing to complain of injury covered by US antitrust law; however, a foreign government can only recover single damages. Foreign firms can, and do, bring complaints about exclusionary conduct of US firms to the attention of the two competition agencies. Indeed, they have sometimes brought complaints about actions by other agencies of US government, such as anti-dumping orders, that they claimed impaired access to the US market. The competition agencies do not have the power to bring enforcement actions against other parts of the government. But where there was cause for concern that US consumers could be harmed by an unnecessary reduction in competition, those situations sometimes prompted advocacy efforts at other agencies.

In general, the content and application of US competition policy does not depend on the nationality of the parties or even the location of the conduct. Anti-competitive conduct that affects US domestic or foreign commerce may violate the US antitrust laws regardless of where the conduct occurs or the nationality of the parties involved. An important set of recent price-fixing cases resulted in large fines against Japanese paper firms. Firms from Germany and Brazil paid a record fine for violating the pre-merger reporting requirement. In general, the proportion of agency matters involving foreign firms or individuals has greatly increased in the last decade.[23] In defining markets and assessing the likelihood of market entry, the methods used make no presumptions about national boundaries or origins, but instead treat the issue simply as one of fact.[24] In the US premerger notification programme, there are no special procedures for obtaining information, or for notification or reporting with respect to foreign firms and products. There are, however, exemptions from the premerger notification requirements for certain international transactions that typically have little nexUS to US commerce but otherwise meet the statutory thresholds.[25]

Dealing with foreign firms and products can raise some specific practical problems. To obtain evidence, the US agencies are increasingly turning to co-operation agreements with other countries. The US has entered four, with Germany, Australia, Canada, and the EC. In 1997, the US agencies made over 70 notifications to other countries' competition agencies under the OECD Recommendation about antitrust co-operation. The agreements with Canada and the EC have adopted the OECD Recommendation's principle of "positive comity", calling on each party to weigh the impact of anti-competitive conduct on the other party as an additional reason to challenge conduct that also violates the country's own laws. The genesis of the US-Canada agreement was in avoiding conflict over sensitive cases, but it now emphasises law enforcement co-operation. The two countries' enforcers have brought several joint price-fixing investigations, leading to convictions on both sides of the border. The positive comity provision in the EC agreement was recently invoked in an investigation concerning computer reservation

---

Box 4.   International co-operation agreements

Eight Member countries have entered one or more formal agreements to co-operate in competition enforcement matters: Australia, Canada, Czech Republic, Hungary, Korea, New Zealand, Poland and the US. And the EC has done so as well.

---

systems. Co-ordination under the agreement led to US agencies deferring to European enforcement in several other matters, too. It is difficult to generalise about the degree of agreement among the various national enforcement policies, when they have been concerned about the same conduct or transaction. In some well-known cases, such as Boeing-McDonnell Douglas, it appeared that the European enforcers took a harder line than the US enforcers did. But in others, US enforcers insisted on divestitures after the European agencies had cleared the mergers.

3.5. Agency resources, actions, and implied priorities

The US backs its commitment to competition policy with substantial resources. Staffing at the two competition agencies has increased about 15 per cent over the last five years and now stands at about 1 300 (plus about 500 at the FTC who concentrate on the "consumer protection" part of that agency's jurisdiction). In addition, hundreds of staff at other agencies enforce other laws and regulations with significant competition policy aspects, and hundreds more in state governments are involved in applying national and state-level competition law. This commitment evidences more than just ceremonial seriousness. US firms can expect that competition laws will actually be applied to them and tend to behave accordingly.

Both agencies assign the highest enforcement priority to horizontal restraints and horizontal mergers. The FTC has recently begun paying more attention than in the past to vertical issues. Half of its new non-merger matters in 1997 involved vertical relationships. This is about double the proportion of five years ago. A large share of resources goes to merger investigations. The agencies have received about 2 200 filings per year. The rate has increased recently; in 1997, there were over 3 700. In 1997, about 15 per cent of the transactions notified to the government received some further investigation, although only about two per cent of the total ended up the subject of enforcement action.

Both agencies have been active in sectors affected by reform. In 1997, the Commission took four law enforcement actions against efforts to fix prices or otherwise prevent competition in professional services, including health care services provided under government-regulated programmes. And two other enforcement actions were aimed to preserve competition in the now-deregulated natural gas industry. These two sets of issues, "private" regulation of professional services and preserving competition in deregulating markets such as energy and broadcast, have been subject to continuing enforcement attention. It is difficult, though, to estimate what proportion of enforcement resources the agencies have applied to cases where regulation has a significant competitive effect. Both competition agencies have been active advocates for competition policy solutions; those efforts are described in more detail below, in Section 5. The resources devoted to advocacy efforts have declined significantly in the 1990s.

4.   THE LIMITS OF COMPETITION POLICY FOR REGULATORY REFORM

Whether competition policy can provide a suitable framework for broad-based regulatory reform is partly determined by the extent and justification for exemptions, exclusions, or special treatment for sectors, types of enterprises or actions. In the US legal system, competition policy enjoys some priority over regulatory policies; however, a host of exemptions and special jurisdictional provisions have developed over the past century, and the actual relationships between competition policy and regulation are highly complex.

4.1. Economy-wide exemptions or special treatments

Government authorisation

Exercise of authority by another regulatory body will not usually displace competition law, unless a statute makes the exclusion explicit. At the federal level, the general rule applied by the courts is that "repeal by implication" from another regulatory statute is disfavoured and will be found only "in cases of plain repugnancy between the antitrust and regulatory provisions".[26] This doctrine evidences the primacy of competition principles, and it means that, if Congress wants to exclude conduct from competition law or apply special rules to it, it must say so clearly. Courts have found implied exclusions only in a few circumstances, the chief examples being securities regulation supervised by the *Securities and Exchange Commission*[27] and common carrier tariffs filed with regulatory agencies.[28] Where regulatory and antitrust requirements conflict, the courts' usual practice is to exempt only to the minimum extent necessary to make the regulatory statute work. Conflicts are sometimes avoided by postponing them. If both the competition law and a regulatory programme might cover a situation, courts may assign "primary jurisdiction" to the regulator to deal with the situation first. But competition law enforcement remains as a backstop in the event that the competition problem remains after the regulator has acted. In general, federal officials have no independent authority to exempt conduct from the antitrust laws. Thus, at the federal level, the issue of regulatory authorisation or compulsion arises principally under the plethora of (mostly) statutory special provisions, discussed below.[29]

For regulations imposed by one of the fifty states, the relationship with national competition policy is different, and the result of the difference may be significant. The "state action doctrine" immunises private anti-competitive conduct from antitrust liability if the conduct is undertaken pursuant to a state policy to replace competition. The state may not simply announce that private, anti-competitive conduct is permitted. Rather, the regulatory policy to displace competition must be both clearly articulated and affirmatively expressed, and the policy's implementation must be subject to active supervision by the state.[30] The state must have exercised sufficient independent judgement and control that the conduct is the product of deliberate state intervention, and not merely acquiescence in the anti-competitive conduct of the private parties.[31] It is not necessary, though, that the text of the state law explicitly declare that the conduct is to be covered and thus excluded by the doctrine. The doctrine also shields actions taken by the states themselves and by cities, counties, and other political subdivisions to which the state has delegated authority to adopt competition-suppressing regulatory measures. (A corollary to the doctrine, enacted when the Supreme Court was still developing some of its details, is a statutory immunity from liability for damages in private actions, for conduct engaged in or directed by a local government official or employee acting in an official capacity.)[32]

The state action doctrine embodies the US commitment to federalism. Its source is a late Depression-era Supreme Court case that permitted a state to sponsor a cartel, despite claims of harm to consumers both in the state and nationally.[33] Decisions applying this doctrine have permitted anti-competitive state regulation of transportation, hospitals, health care and other professional services, retail distribution, utilities, residential and commercial rent, and other subjects. Federal competition agencies have tried to keep the doctrine under control, by bringing enforcement actions to define its elements and boundaries. But the doctrine looks well entrenched.

The state action doctrine risks holding US national competition policy hostage to local legislative relief. The doctrine is based on the courts' interpretation of the competition statutes and of Congress's intent in passing them. The exclusion resulting from the doctrine could, in principle, be revised or even eliminated by Congressional action. Congress has in effect done so in particular cases. An example is Congress's termination of state regulation of local trucking, which courts had excluded under the state action doctrine. But it does not appear likely that the general doctrine will be modified soon, either by the courts or the legislature. The doctrine demonstrates that national competition policy, though privileged in relationship to US national regulatory policy, is treated as less important than some other political values, in this case federalism.

Another privileged value, the Constitutional protection of the right to petition the government, has led to another kind of general antitrust exemption. Joint or individual efforts to persuade a government body or official to take an action, even an action that excludes a competitor or authorises the elimination of competition, are immune from attack by the antitrust laws. This exemption, like the state action doctrine, was created by court decisions. Further decisions have refined the principle. For example, there is no protection for a purported petition that is actually a sham, intended not to influence the government but to intimidate a competitor. The basic exemption (labelled the *Noerr-Pennington* doctrine, after the two decisions that first announced it[34]) is commonly invoked in regulatory settings, as the government action sought is often the imposition or revision of a regulation or a regulatory action. The exemption is supposed to cover only joint action to influence the government, and not other anti-competitive agreements that might be reached at the same time or under the same circumstances. But it may be difficult to detect and isolate side agreements or understandings reached in the course of joint lobbying or petitioning efforts. Even if there is no anti-competitive side agreement, the anti-competitive effect of a successful petition undermines competition policy goals. An arena where both concerns often arise is anti-dumping proceedings, in which the preparation of a petition asking to discourage or exclude foreign competition may provide occasions for reaching other kinds of agreements too.

Government entities

Government entities, even those that are involved in commercial operations, are beyond the reach of competition law enforcement or private litigation. Entities that are owned and operated by the US government are immune from antitrust liability. Those that are owned and operated by state and local governments may be shielded from antitrust liability under the state action doctrine. The immunity may be particularly significant for government owned electric power systems, hospitals, and port authorities, all of which are being affected by regulatory reforms. Private competitors in these fields have occasionally complained that the government-related entities enjoy unfair competitive advantages, especially in access to financing.

Small and medium sized enterprises

There is no general exemption from the federal antitrust laws for small and medium sized enterprises. And there is no *de minimis* rule for conduct covered by the *per se* standard of liability. Of course, a firm that is too small to affect competition is unlikely to be subject to any enforcement attention concerning conduct subject to the rule of reason. The one statutory immunity for small business is not really an exemption, for the conduct it covers would probably not violate the law. Certain narrowly defined agreements (joint research and development and those that the President determines contribute to the national defence) among small "independently owned and operated businesses" that are "not dominant" in their "field of operation" are immune from antitrust attack.[35] (The enforcement agencies are unaware of any instances in which this protection has been invoked). Small and medium sized enterprises enjoy no particular protection against liability as defendants,[36] but there are some provisions that were intended to benefit them as plaintiffs. One of the justifications offered for awarding treble damages plus attorney's fees, and of permitting parties to join together in class actions, is to encourage smaller firms, with fewer resources, to initiate private lawsuits.

Joint research and production

Special legislation ensures that joint ventures for research, development, and production (even between horizontal competitors) will not be judged by the harsh *per se* standard, but instead by the multi-factor rule of reason.[37] This protection was first enacted in 1984, applicable only to research and development, and was expanded in 1993 to cover production joint ventures as well. The protection does not extend to agreements about marketing and distribution, exchanges of information on costs, sales, profitability, and prices, or allocating markets with a competitor. It is an example of a response to

---

Box 5.   Scope of competition policy

Is there an exemption from liability under the general competition law for conduct that is required or authorised by other government authority? Like most Member countries (15 out of the 27 reporting), the US provides exemptions from the general competition law for conduct required by other regulation or government authority. The US's federal structure has led to different levels of exemption doctrine for national regulatory action and for state law or regulation.

Does the general competition law apply to public enterprises? The US is one of only two Member countries that do not apply general competition laws to the commercial actions of public enterprises (the other one is Portugal).

Is there an exemption, in law or enforcement policy, for small and medium sized enterprises? Like the majority of Member countries, US law contains no special exemption based on the size of the enterprise.

---

concern that stringency of the basic competition law was inappropriate for these activities, and indeed was likely to have discouraged them unnecessarily. In addition to ensuring rule of reason treatment, the law also provides for a reduction in potential liability in private lawsuits, to single damages, if parties file their joint venture plans with the enforcement agencies. The concerns about chilling may have been overstated, for filings are infrequent, averaging about 60 per year. There may be some differential impact on foreign firms, for the limit to single-damages exposure for production activities only applies if there are production facilities in the US.

4.2. Sector-specific exclusions, exemptions and special rules or enforcers

There are few sectors in the US economy from which competition policy and law are completely excluded. But in many sectors, the policy is implemented through special rules or enforcement structures. Many of the differences in law and structure are practically insignificant, because the exception or special treatment applies to conduct that probably would not have been considered in violation of law in any event, or that may have been undertaken pursuant to an order or instruction of a government regulatory programme. These exemptions may have been thought necessary to avoid any risk that private antitrust litigation would interfere with accomplishing other regulatory objectives. And they seem plausible in some cases, where they may moderate the strictness and severity of competition law standards and penalties. Most of the national regulation that fixed prices, limited output, reduced quality, divided markets or constrained entry has been eliminated. Many of the remaining sector-specific agencies apply competition policies reasonably consistently with those of the competition agencies themselves. But for some, remaining differences in treatment may not be clearly justified by compelling public interests that cannot be served in other ways. The following discussion focuses on the remaining exemptions and on cases where there have been apparent inconsistencies between the sectoral agency's conception of competition policy and that of the competition agencies. Some of these have arisen in what were intended to be transition settings, as old agencies retained powers over mergers or other conduct and applied them in ways that probably increased, rather than reduced, long-term competitive risks. The experience counsels in favour of clear, firm deadlines for changing regulatory standards, and for reducing to a minimum any period of overlap between regulatory and competition regimes.

Transportation: air

Removal of economic regulation from air transportation must be counted as a principal success of competition-directed reform. The government-enforced cartel controlling entry, service, and rates was dismantled in the late 1970's and the enforcement agency, the Civil Aeronautics Board, was abolished in 1985. But a sectoral regulator, the Department of Transportation (DOT), retained some jurisdiction to handle competition policy in the industry.

Mergers and acquisitions among domestic airlines were the exclusive responsibility of DOT, rather than the antitrust agencies, until 1989. The legislature's choice to keep this function with a sectoral agency, even though economic regulation of entry and rates was eliminated, probably represented a political bargain as part of deregulation. Making decision-making more efficient would not have been a compelling factor, because the historic regulator, which would have been familiar with the industry's structures, disappeared. DOT had authority to invoke other policy goals in order to approve an other-wise anti-competitive transaction, but never did so; rather, it claimed to have based its merger decisions on its interpretation and application of competition policy. DOT approved essentially all of the transactions it reviewed. DOT evidently believed that city-pair markets were highly contestable and so tended to assume that new entry would prevent any exercise of market power. The Antitrust Division noted its objections to some of the transactions that DOT nevertheless approved. Economic studies have shown that, where these combinations led to eliminating rivals and higher concentration at several hub airports, prices were significantly higher because passengers going to or from those locations had fewer choices. DOT's special jurisdiction over domestic mergers was terminated in 1989 and the Anti-trust Division took over responsibility. The Division announced that its analysis would not assume con-testability, but instead would be concerned about national market positions. The Division also took action against other kinds of transactions that threatened to limit competition, such as acquisitions of rights to use airport gates.

Although the special merger jurisdiction did not formally lead to a gap in coverage, it did leave a gap as a practical matter. The agency responsible for applying competition policy restraints did not find any occasions to do so. It is doubtful that the *de facto* repeal of merger law in this sector for a decade was supported by a compelling public interest. On the contrary, as fundamental changes in the industry's basic competitive dynamics attracted new entrants, stimulated reorganisations, forced bankruptcies, and invited new combinations, concern over the long-term implications of these restructurings should have been heightened. Especially because the sectoral regulator had no experience with market condi-tions other than those it had regulated, it would have been particularly important for this function to be performed by an agency with a broader background and perspective.

"Unfair competition" among airlines remains a DOT responsibility, under a statute whose operative language is identical to the Federal Trade Commission Act. There was some debate about giving these competition and consumer protection responsibilities to the general purpose agencies, but here too it appears that a bargain was reached in the legislature to maintain a sectoral agency. The scope of DOT's "unfair competition" authority overlaps substantially with the antitrust laws. DOT has applied it to claims about monopolisation through control of computer reservation systems and to claims about pre-dation. In both cases, DOT is asserting jurisdiction over conduct that has also been the subject of active investigation by the Antitrust Division. On these issues, DOT has worked with the competition agencies to develop enforcement tools that complement and extend competition policy.

DOT's 1998 rulemaking concerning predation is an interesting case study. The perceived problem is hub airlines' strategic, targeted responses to threatened entry. As DOT describes the problem,

> Following Congress' deregulation of the air transportation industry in 1978, all of the major air carriers restructured their route systems into "hub-and-spoke" networks. Major carriers have long charged con-siderably higher fares in most of their "spoke" city-pairs, or the "local hub markets", than in other city-pairs of comparable distance and density. In recent years, when small, new-entrant carriers have insti-tuted new low-fare service in major carriers' local hub markets, the major carriers have increasingly responded with strategies of price reductions and capacity increases designed not to maximise their own profits but rather to deprive the new entrants of vital traffic and revenues. Once a new entrant has ceased its service, the major carrier will typically retrench its capacity in the market or raise its fares to at least their pre-entry levels, or both. The major carrier thus accepts lower profits in the short run in order to secure higher profits in the long run. This strategy can benefit the major carrier prospectively

as well, in that it dissuades other carriers from attempting low-fare entry. It can hurt consumers in the long run by depriving them of the benefits of competition.[38]

DOT's proposed rules to deal with this behaviour differ in two important respects from the rules that courts have imposed in competition law cases. First, it would not be necessary to show that the predator had priced below variable cost (or some other cost measure). Rather, predation would be found from a combination of fare cuts and capacity increases that result in the predator making less profit than it would have if it had accommodated the entrant's impact on its operations. And there would be no formal requirement to show likelihood of recoupment after the entrant was driven out. However, DOT believes that the conduct it is targeting is economically rational only if, after the new entrant is forced to exit, the major carrier can readily recoup the revenues it has sacrificed. DOT consulted with the competition agencies in developing this rule, but DOT maintains that the rule, under its "unfair competition" standard, is not to be considered an antitrust rule.

The predation rule demonstrates how a sector-specific regulatory regime might be used as an experimental test-bed for competition policy. The "opportunity cost" concept at the heart of DOT's proposed rule has been endorsed by two economists who have held top positions at the Antitrust Division. But it could be difficult to implement in court proceedings. Standard US antitrust law rules about predatory pricing are wary of discouraging vigorous price competition, and thus they impose a stringent cost-based test, as well as require showing the likelihood of recoupment, in order to avoid "false positives". It remains to be seen whether a sectoral regulator, familiar with its industry's strategic methods, might be able to apply the economically more sensitive, but more difficult, test based on opportunity costs, without discouraging more competition than it protects. If the test succeeds, the demonstration might be a basis for extending it to other areas, and potentially for changing the rules that apply under the competition law generally.

On the other hand, a special airline-industry rule might not have been necessary to counter this conduct, had the industry not been permitted to consolidate into "fortress" hubs in the decade after deregulation. Preventing any single airline from dominating a significant potential hub would have made predation less likely, for a predatory strategy is more difficult to execute if it must be co-ordinated with other firms.

Agreements concerning foreign air transportation are also under DOT jurisdiction, subject again to a competition-based substantive test, and they are exempted from antitrust liability if DOT approves them.[39] This power has been used, in conjunction with bilateral diplomatic efforts, to authorise co-operative arrangements with national airlines of other countries. Some of these, such as the KLM-Northwest agreement, seem to have clearly opened up markets to new competition. The Antitrust Division has objected to some other grants, though, on the grounds that immunity is not needed for conduct that does not violate the law, and should not be granted to conduct that does. DOT and the Antitrust Division may find themselves concerned with different aspects of the same relationship. DOT may be responsible for approving international aspects of airline co-operation, while the Antitrust Division is concerned about domestic consequences. An example of this dual consideration is the two agencies' concurrent review of proposed co-operation between American Airlines and British Airways. Coherent competition policy requires that, in such situations, the sectoral regulator and the competition agency strike a consistent balance between competition standards and other policies.

These are particular issues where the scheme of regulation in air transport has not coincided with generally applicable competition policy principles. These subjects are not necessarily excluded from the competition laws. Indeed, the Antitrust Division is looking at some of the same issues that DOT is concerned about, and will be examining other developments such as proposed code-sharing and other alliances among US domestic carriers. Thus, the issue is not so much exemption or exclusion from competition law, as of potential regulatory conflict over the content and application of similar, if not identical, substantive standards.

Transportation: rail

The rail freight system has been substantially deregulated since 1980, but in a different way than airlines. The historic economic regulatory body, the Interstate Commerce Commission, was eliminated, but many of its functions were transferred to a new entity, the Surface Transportation Board (STB). And much of the deregulation is accomplished by expanding STB's powers to authorise exemptions from regulatory requirements. The major deregulatory steps were removing most of the constraints on rates and services and limiting how much railroads could discuss and agree about rates, although they can still do so to some degree, subject to STB approval.[40] But STB retains authority over mergers, which are exempt from antitrust liability if STB approves them,[41] and STB has power to hear and correct complaints about railroads' exercise of market power over "captive" shippers. In these respects, STB's authority displaces the competition laws, and in the latter, it may act much like a traditional rate regulator, although its authority is exercised only in conditions that in other legal systems would be called "abuse of dominant position".[42]

Creating the STB, rather than completely eliminating sectoral regulation for surface transport, was a legislative decision, again probably reflecting a bargain and expectation of sympathetic treatment, compared to the likely results if general purpose competition law were applied. And as in airlines, the STB's exercise of its merger powers has been problematic. In 1996, STB approved the largest merger in US rail history, between the Union Pacific and Southern Pacific railroads. These were two of only three major railroads in the western United States. The Antitrust Division made a formal appearance in the STB proceeding, contending that the merger would significantly reduce competition in many markets where the number of competing railroads would decline from two to one or from three to two. The parties proposed an agreement to make track rights available to competitors, but the Antitrust Division argued that these rights would be inadequate, in part because they would often apply in a non-competitive duopoly situation. The Antitrust Division ultimately urged the STB to reject the merger outright, because the extensive divestitures required to fix it would not be worth the effort. But in August 1996, STB approved the merger with only minor additional conditions. Within a year, severe and persistent operating problems and capacity limitations developed on the merged system, many of them where the Antitrust Division had pointed out the problems that would result if parallel operations were no longer available to shippers as competitive alternatives. The breakdown in rail service has persisted and has become a major controversy, with shippers' groups calling for regulatory intervention. One reason STB approved the merger was evidently its faith that its own regulatory interventions would be sufficient to remedy market power problems that might result. But STB's actions to date seem to hope that the problem will solve itself. It has called for railroads and shippers to develop a dialogue about service problems, to discuss possible standards for sharing track and facilities, and to nominate experts to recommend ways to identify market power problems that STB ought to correct. That is, STB does not appear capable of solving the problems it helped create by approving a merger that led to substantial market power.

Here too, there is not necessarily a gap in the coverage of some form of competition law or policy, so much as a significant difference in how a sectoral regulator conceives and applies it. The first explicit policy set out in the statute governing rail regulation is "to allow, to the maximum extent possible, competition and the demand for services to establish reasonable rates for transportation by rail".[43] Other aspects of the explicit statutory policies are also consistent with generally applicable competition policy. Although creating a merged corporation with a larger asset base may have been consistent with another statutory policy, "to foster sound economic conditions in transportation", it is not clear that this purpose was so compelling that it justified creating market power, nor that there was not a less anti-competitive alternative. As in airlines, it appears that the sectoral regulator, unfamiliar with the dynamics of unregulated markets, was not sensitive enough to the problems that this combination might lead to, nor to the great difficulty of solving them after the merger was an accomplished fact.

Transportation: ocean shipping and terminal operators

Cartels in ocean shipping have been subject to a special regulatory system since 1916. The relationship between that system and the antitrust laws was a long-standing source of controversy, with a chief source of friction being foreign trading partners' concerns to protect their national firms against US antitrust liability. In 1984, Congress revised the Shipping Act in several ways, including making the antitrust immunity more explicit. The Act was revised again in 1998, to reduce the impact of some of its anti-competitive features. A separate body, the *Federal Maritime Commission* (FMC), regulates common carriers in this sector. The regulatory scheme is neither full economic regulation of rates and entry, nor government supervision and enforcement of the cartel, nor open competition, but a combination of all these elements. The mixture of elements probably reflects the mixture of contradictory reasons for oversight. On the one hand, US law has to recognise the fact that international liner shipping has long been dominated by cartels that have enjoyed some legal protection elsewhere. On the other hand, the US antitrust tradition is uncomfortable with such thorough-going price-fixing. The result is a regulatory system that permits considerable cartel conduct that would be *per se* illegal, indeed criminal, if attempted in other sectors. Conference agreements fixing rates, dividing markets, pooling revenues, limiting output, and otherwise preventing competition, as well as conduct pursuant to them, are immune from antitrust liability if they are filed with the FMC. But, at least, conferences in US trades must be open and they must not discriminate among shippers or ports. Moreover, they must permit members to take independent action, in effect to cheat on the cartel agreement. Until 1998, tariffs had to be filed with the FMC, although the FMC does not regulate rate levels. Enforcement oversight is limited to complaints of discrimination or failure to adhere to terms of tariffs. The FMC may go to court to seek an injunction to prevent the operation of an agreement that it determines is likely, by a reduction in competition, to produce an unreasonable reduction in transportation service or an unreasonable increase in transportation cost. The FMC has not actually had to obtain any court orders on this basis. On the few occasions when the FMC has raised concerns about competitive effects, the matters were settled. The general competition law has some residual application, to anti-competitive conduct that is not covered by a filed agreement and to mergers and acquisitions in the industry.

Some of the original rationale for separate regulation was based on the international dimension. It appeared unfair and impracticable to apply US competition rules to US firms trying to compete against foreign firms that were colluding, or to attempt to apply US law to foreign firms that had minimal ties in the US. Other rationales sometimes offered are relatively weak. First, the industry's cost structure and the movable nature of its assets are said to make it unique in a way that makes application of general competition law inappropriate. But the liner shipping industry shares with the airline industry a high ratio of fixed to variable costs and highly movable assets. Yet in airlines, experience with deregulation shows that open competition does not lead to asset-wasting, output-reducing "destructive competition". Second, the industry is said to be highly competitive despite the constraints. But industry performance suggests that the current conference system does reduce competition. The cartels are not perfectly effective, but economic analysis shows that rates are lower where the conferences' competition-restraining rules are weaker.[44]

The FMC has taken only a few, tentative actions under its mandate to protect competition. Its practice seems to be to accept settlements in terms of temporary rate reductions, rather than require basic structural corrections. Congress's clear purpose in establishing this system was to prevent the application of standard competition policy principles and remedies. Thus, it is unsurprising that the sectoral regulator would rely on regulatory remedies for competition concerns. But the effect is to leave a substantial and unjustified gap in the coverage of consistent competition policy.

Congress has recently revised the system substantially. Eliminating the requirement of filing tariffs at the FMC has ended the FMC's residual role as cartel enforcer. The scope of independent action has been expanded to include individual service contracts. And Congress has tried to instruct the sectoral agency to enforce this law's competition rules more strictly, voicing a concern that the industry has moved toward greater concentration and less competition since the 1984 statute. But the new legislation stops well short of assigning competition enforcement responsibility to the competition agencies themselves. Instead, it calls for consolidating the FMC's enforcement function with that of STB.

The long history of special treatment for this sector offers little support for continuing the exemption from general antitrust jurisdiction. From a competition policy perspective, the best that can be said for the situation is that conditions could be worse. As other nations are reconsidering how much to tolerate cartels in this sector, it may be that difficulties of transnational application and fears of diplomatic friction are less important factors now. In the absence of competition law immunity, conflicts about the scope of competition policy in this sector could be dealt with as they are increasingly in other sectors, by consultations among national competition enforcement authorities to ensure consistent treatment.

Transportation: *trucking*

Nearly all economic regulation of trucking has been eliminated, now that Congress in 1995 pre-empted the remaining state economic regulations.[45] But Congress has left pockets of regulated immunity at the national level. Rate bureaux continue to enjoy antitrust immunity for agreements about some subjects: commodity classifications, documentation, packaging, tariff structures, mileage guides, through routes and joint rates, rules and divisions, non-price activities, and pooling agreements between carriers.[46] But there is no longer any antitrust immunity for agreements on single-line rates, with one glaring exception. Motor carriers of household goods are permitted to agree on rates, subject to regulation by the STB, and this joint rate-making is immune from antitrust liability.[47] The reason for retaining this exemption is unclear. There was some concern that eliminating the Interstate Commerce Commission would leave the industry's consumer protection rules unenforceable. But protecting consumers does not require permitting movers to agree not to compete. The exemption's net impact on competitive conditions is unknown. Many larger interstate movers, which deal repeatedly with corporate clients, probably have had to offer competitive rates and services to maintain those relationships. But industry collusion may mean that individual consumers, lacking the information or bargaining power of larger customers, may be receiving poorer service or paying too much for it. In the absence of any plausible justification, this last significant exemption for trucking should be removed. The residual exemption and immunity for agreements about joint and through rates probably should be removed, too, as it seems unnecessary in the current, competitive industry environment. It is unlikely that efficient collaborations along this vertical dimension would be found illegal under normal antitrust principles today.

Transportation: *motor carrier, passenger*

In 1982 the FTC argued forcefully for complete deregulation of intercity bus service, including pre-emption of any state regulations that inhibited competition. The FTC noted then that the weakest firms in the industry were the two major national lines and attributed their weakness to lack of competition between them. Subsequent reforms opened the industry to new entry, but left some economic regulation in place. STB has authority to review and approve, and thus immunise from antitrust liability, mergers, transfers of control, pooling agreements, and certain other transactions involving intercity bus companies.[48] Passenger bus tariffs must be filed at STB, and STB has authority to hear complaints about their reasonableness. STB also has authority to grant or deny applications to enter the industry, but the legal standard of "fitness" does not consider competitive or market effects and applications are rarely rejected. Entry is thus essentially unrestricted. Nearly all of the many new bus companies are charter operators, though, and the two national regular-route carriers were permitted to combine into one because the smaller one was evidently failing. The necessity and effect of the remaining regulatory oversight should be examined. Lower air fares have diverted many of the bus lines' traditional riders to the airlines. It may be that costs of alternatives are so low that the remaining demand for intercity bus service is too small to support more than one system. But the population that still uses the bus system is probably highly dependent on it, as it includes principally those who are too poor, too young, or too old to drive or fly. Perhaps regulation could be justified, to protect those consumers who may be considered particularly vulnerable. But if there are aspects of the regulatory structure that unnecessarily reinforce the *de facto* monopoly, more competitive alternative approaches should be explored.

Energy

Special sectoral regulation of the natural gas and electricity industries at the federal level has moved steadily toward increasing consistency with generally applicable competition policy. This contrast with the more uncertain course of transportation regulation is due to several factors. The regulatory structure did not displace the competition law completely, but coexisted with it. The courts have instructed the regulator to include competition policy in its understanding and application of broader "public interest" criteria, and the regulator has followed that instruction. Congress has clearly supported the move toward deregulation, taking actions in the late 1970s that began to eliminate price controls for gas and to introduce competitive alternatives for electric power generation. And the competition agencies have encouraged these moves at every stage, offering informal and formal advice and assistance.

The sectoral regulator, the *Federal Energy Regulatory Commission* (FERC), shares responsibility over mergers with the antitrust agencies. In natural gas, FERC has jurisdiction to approve acquisitions of physical assets, and the antitrust agencies have jurisdiction over combinations through merger or acquisition of securities. In electric power, FERC is responsible for combinations involving firms subject to its regulatory jurisdiction, applying a "public interest" standard; however, this power is shared with the competition agencies' application of the Clayton Act. FERC has imposed conditions on approval of mergers that have had the effect of extending its efforts to promote competition into areas where it probably lacks authority to order change directly. FERC's basic regulatory authority is over pricing and access issues for the network operations of natural gas transmission and electric power transmission. Here too, FERC authority overlaps with the coverage of the competition law. A government monopolisation suit first applied the Sherman Act to the problem of access to electric power transmission,[49] and private parties have continued to bring antitrust cases on this issue. FERC also has some authority over pricing of wholesale electric power (retail prices and service are regulated by the states), but this authority is being exercised less now, as FERC decisions have led to *de facto* market pricing in much of that part of the industry. FERC regulatory action does not generally confer absolute antitrust immunity. That lack of immunity may explain why FERC's policies and decisions have converged on the coverage of the competition laws. Convergence is increasingly explicit. FERC's recently-amended rules about mergers have embraced the methodology of the competition agencies' *Merger Guidelines*. Its rules about when gas pipeline rates will be set by the market rather than by regulation also track the analysis used in the *Merger Guidelines*. And its decisions about regulating oil pipelines apply somewhat similar antitrust-based principles. There, regulation typically amounts to a hands-off decision to allow market forces to work, as long as the market is not too concentrated.

The complex of special energy industry rules has several sources. The original regulatory legislation did not carve out a separate regulatory domain, immunised and isolated from antitrust coverage, but instead asserted that competition was one of the elements of regulation. Court decisions admonished the regulator to interpret the "public interest" as consistently as possible with general antitrust principles. Later legislation, by initiating deregulation of wellhead prices and electric power, signalled continued support for moves toward competition. The regulator generally followed that course, in decisions about prices, access, structural separation of monopoly and competitive parts of the businesses, and relations with state regulatory responsibilities over local service. And the competition agencies themselves have encouraged and advised the regulator, while backing the deregulation moves with merger enforcement. FERC adoption of antitrust agencies' merger analysis under its own "public interest" standard may be a fruitful compromise between sector regulation and generally applicable law. On the other hand, industry changes might have been accomplished more swiftly under a general authority. FERC has been tentative in its application of the *Merger Guidelines* so far, evidently because of the complex jurisdictional problem it faces. Because it has no regulatory authority over retail-level operations, it is unclear whether it can take action concerning a merger whose principal competitive effects appear at the retail level. FERC has deferred to state regulators on those issues, yet those regulators are likely to try to deal with those issues through direct control over rates and service, rather than structural, competition-based solutions. Application of the general merger law under generally applicable standards and analysis would be more straightforward.

There are two minor exemptions to remove the threat of antitrust litigation inhibiting industry co-operation with certain energy security efforts. Voluntary international agreements and plans of action about energy industry responses to supply crises are exempted from antitrust liability, if approved by the Attorney General after consultation with the FTC.[50] This "exemption" appears much like a business review or advisory opinion, but it goes further, by conferring immunity from private lawsuits as well as an assurance against prosecution. And certain meetings and related actions by natural gas producers enjoy a limited exemption from antitrust liability, where undertaken pursuant to a presidential order and monitored by the Department of Justice and the FTC.[51]

Banks and financial institutions

Financial institutions are not exempt from the antitrust laws.[52] But there are some special competition rules, particularly about mergers, and enforcement responsibility is shared between the Antitrust Division and banking regulators, of which there are four, each with jurisdiction over a particular type of financial institution, each applying the same basic laws. The bank merger laws[53] include competition standards like those of the Sherman Act and Clayton Act. They also permit a "public interest" defence that would be inadmissible in pure competition cases. A banking agency may approve a transaction, even if it is anti-competitive, if it finds that the anti-competitive effects are clearly outweighed in the public interest by the probable effect of the transaction in meeting the convenience and needs of the community to be served. The bank regulators must consult with the Department of Justice (except for transactions involving bank holding companies), and the Attorney General may seek an injunction against a merger that the bank regulator has approved. In such a challenge, though, the "public interest" defence is still available before the court. The banking agencies and the Antitrust Division apply different substantive standards, even concerning the competition analysis. Both are based on the competition agencies' *Merger Guidelines*, but the bank regulators and the antitrust enforcers make different presumptions about the likely contours of product and geographic markets. Special anti-tying laws also apply to banks, preventing them from conditioning their services on acceptance of any other service except four traditional banking functions: loans, discounts, deposits, and trust services.[54] This special provision is not an exemption, but rather an intensification, of otherwise applicable competition law. Finally, the recent federal law that enabled greater inter-state expansion also set statutory limits on resulting concentration (measured in terms of deposits): no more than 10 per cent on a national basis, or 30 per cent in a single state.[55]

These various forms of special treatment represent conscious legislative decisions, motivated in part by concerns over the special role of financial institutions in the economy. Assigning specialised regulators institutionalises some balancing of concerns about competition against concerns about liquidity, solvency, and safety. Consistency in the application of competition principles is accomplished, somewhat inefficiently, by the threat that the competition agency will act independently, and by the fact that decisions are subject to review and correction by general jurisdiction courts.

Securities and futures

The courts have fashioned a limited immunity for the securities industry, inferred from the extensive system of regulation and oversight by the SEC. The statute providing for securities industry regulation calls on the SEC to consider the competitive impact of its actions. The course of deregulation in this sector demonstrates the potential value of private antitrust litigation for that purpose. A court decision in a private lawsuit extended antitrust immunity to agreements to fix commissions.[56] Congress responded by revising the basic securities law to forbid such price-fixing. Similar rules and results apply to commodity futures, which are subject to a different regulatory body. For commodity futures, there is also a limited, implied immunity and a "competitive effects test" in the basic law, and there too antitrust litigation led to the abandonment of fixed commissions. As legislative and regulatory actions have moved these industries strongly toward competitive market methods, the judicially created implied immunities may no longer be very important.

Insurance

The business of insurance is not subject to the Sherman or Clayton Acts, nor to the Federal Trade Commission Act, to the extent it is regulated by state law. This statutory exemption, the McCarran-

Ferguson Act,[57] was a direct Congressional response to a government prosecution for price-fixing. The law was said to protect the states' traditional powers to tax insurance companies and regulate the content of insurance contracts, after the Supreme Court's finding that insurance was interstate commerce subject to oversight by Congress.[58] The exemption does not apply to actions that amount to boycott, coercion, or intimidation. And mergers in the insurance industry are still covered by the general merger law. But Congress has generally kept the antitrust enforcers away from the insurance industry where possible. In the late 1970s, the FTC staff studied and reported on consumer protection and competition problems in the insurance industry. Even though these were only studies, and did not call for law enforcement action, Congress responded by preventing the FTC from using any of its funds to study or report on any aspect of the business of insurance, unless specifically requested by Congress. Promoting competition in this sector is the responsibility of state law and state insurance regulators. The funding limitation prevents the FTC from advocacy action here, and the Antitrust Division has historically done little advocacy at the state level. The institutional basis for applying national competition policies consistently in this industry is therefore weak.

Communications

In general, the competition laws are fully applicable to telecommunications, broadcasting, and cable. There are no general exemptions; indeed, the basic laws underlying broadcast and telecommunications regulation state explicitly that the antitrust laws also apply.[59] There are two, limited exemptions. The television industry enjoys a limited exemption for joint actions to develop and disseminate voluntary guidelines to reduce the negative impact of TV violence.[60] And local officials involved in granting cable franchises are immunised from treble damage liability in lawsuits over their decisions.[61] The sectoral regulator, the *Federal Communications Commission* (FCC), has promoted competitive methods where regulatory authority remains, although promotion of pro-competitive methods has been tempered by pursuit of the goal of diversity. For example, the FCC has been changing rules about broadcast licensing and operation that have had significant competition policy dimensions. These rules included limits on the number of broadcast licenses that could be held in common and constraints on vertical relationships between networks and programme sources. When they were adopted, these rules were probably reasonably consistent with standard competition law doctrine; indeed, they were supplemented by Antitrust Division law enforcement actions on the same issues, notably network control over programming. But as antitrust doctrine has changed, so have the FCC's rules, albeit with some delay.

The competition agencies have played an effective role in promoting competition in telecommunications. The most visible role, of course, was the Sherman Act monopolisation case that led to the break-up of the national telephone monopoly and court-ordered line-of-business restrictions. Co-operation between the FCC and Antitrust Division was central in establishing an effective divestiture framework, although questions have been raised in regard to its implementation. In particular, while the administration of the consent decree strayed into questions better suited to an industry-specific regulator, the FCC abandoned its role in separating competitive and monopoly elements soon after the divestiture. The recent Telecommunications Act supersedes the antitrust restrictions of the monopolisation case and provides for a role for the competition agency to advise the FCC in the FCC's application of Section 271 of that Act (the "competitive checklist" for RBOC entry into inter-LATA services). These restrictions are becoming increasingly burdensome to the economy (for example, through the loss of scope economies). These issues are discussed further in the background report on Regulatory Reform in the Electricity Industry.

Agriculture

Several statutes accord special treatment to agriculture and related activities. The existence and normal operations of producer co-operatives do not violate the antitrust laws.[62] A special competition regime, the Capper-Volstead Act, applies to them.[63] This regime is administered by the Department of Agriculture, not the competition agencies. (Protections like those of the Capper-Volstead Act also apply to fisheries; that exemption is administered by the Secretary of Commerce.)[64] The Secretary of

Agriculture may take action against co-operative associations that have monopolized or restrained trade to the extent "that the price of any agricultural product is unduly enhanced". Depending on how much price increase is "undue", this standard may leave room for these entities to exert market power. These special statutes were enacted in response to early enforcement efforts by the Federal Trade Commission against monopolisation by these organisations. Other exemptions permit these groups to exchange price, production, and marketing information[65] and to make internal payments without liability under the Robinson-Patman Act.[66] Most of these provisions according special treatment to co-operatives do not apply to agreements between a co-operative and others, nor do they immunise monopolising conduct aimed at other businesses. Depression-era legislation permits the Secretary of Agriculture to issue marketing orders, with the practical effect of enforcing cartels for some agricultural products. The agreements among the producers and the Secretary leading to these orders are exempt from antitrust liability.[67] (After the FTC staff had undertaken studies of the anti-competitive effects of some of these orders in the 1970s, Congress cut off FTC funding for that purpose. The Antitrust Division has continued its advocacy efforts here, though.) Some other agreements or actions approved by the Secretary are exempt from antitrust liability; these include arbitration meetings and awards concerning dairy co-operatives,[68] and marketing agreements for serum against hog cholera.[69]

In meat-packing, competition issues are subject to a special law, the Packers and Stockyards Act,[70] and to the joint supervision of the Secretary of Agriculture and the Department of Justice. This law was enacted in 1922 after a vigorous FTC investigation of competitive abuses in the industry. Congress responded by removing the FTC's jurisdiction and assigning enforcement oversight to a sympathetic sectoral regulator. The law deals with deceptive practices and monopolisation, but not mergers, which are subject to the Clayton and Sherman Acts. The Packers and Stockyards Act does not create an exemption, but rather a parallel competition regime, with some priority over the general law.

Newspaper combinations

The Newspaper Preservation Act of 1970 permits joint operating arrangements among otherwise competing newspapers.[71] The asserted goal is to protect editorial diversity. The joint operation must maintain separate editorial functions for the two papers, but may merge business functions such as sale of papers and of advertising. The agreement is not subject to Section 1 of the Sherman Act; however, the joint operation may not engage in conduct that would be considered monopolising in violation of Section 2 of the Sherman Act. Proposed agreements are subject to review and approval by the Attorney General. For the joint operation to receive the exemption, all but one of the papers must be in probable danger of financial failure. The exemption represents a legislative expansion of a general principle of merger law, the "failing firm" doctrine. The statutory standard is more forgiving than the failing firm doctrine, however. The wide diversity of other sources of information and opinion that are now available suggests that this relaxation of the law is not the least anti-competitive way to serve a compelling public interest.

Sports

Some sports leagues are permitted to pool the rights to broadcast their games, in order to sell them as a package to broadcast networks without antitrust liability.[72] The Sports Broadcasting Act effectively reversed a court finding that pooling violated the Sherman Act. The exemption is fine-tuned to protect a home team's interest in full attendance and to discourage broadcasts of professional games in competition with school and college contests. In addition, a one-time special-interest exemption in the 1960's permitted the merger of two professional football leagues, on the condition that the total number of teams would not decline. No similar protection has been afforded to later sports league mergers. And the Supreme Court is responsible for a long-standing anomaly, the complete exemption of major league baseball. In 1922, the Court decided that baseball was not interstate commerce and hence not covered by the antitrust laws. It has stuck to that decision ever since, acknowledging that it is inconsistent with the modern treatment of all other sports and similar activities.

Soft drinks

In response to government and private actions against the soft drink industry's vertical manufacturing and distribution structures, Congress enacted a special rule that substantially immunises them from liability.[73] The justification offered for this extraordinary special interest exemption, and the applicable legal test, is the existence of sufficient competition among products with different brands. The exemption applies only to vertical agreements about distribution of trademarked products, and is intended principally to permit a system of tight exclusive distribution territories. The exemption does not extend to horizontal agreements. Congress evidently believed that the competition law enforcement agency and the judges who decided these cases did not adequately understand the practices and their actual competitive effects. But the apparent statutory immunity has hampered efforts to investigate whether these vertical arrangements could prevent entry of new brands or permit the industry to monitor and police tacit, horizontal collusion. The exemption serves no necessary purpose that would not also be served by judicious application of the general competition law.

Health care peer review

Private antitrust lawsuits against joint actions in "peer review" processes, by which health care professionals evaluate the quality of their colleagues' work, can only recover single damages.[74] Competition law violations could still be subject to government enforcement action. This is an example of a concern that the antitrust law's *per se* rule and treble damage threat inappropriately inhibit legitimate co-operation.

Copyright royalties

The copyright law contains several provisions requiring compulsory licensing, to facilitate media transmission of recordings and similar material. Several provisions grant limited antitrust immunity to parties negotiating agreements about dividing the resulting fees and royalties.[75] Similar immunities apply to certain royalties in connection with public broadcasting,[76] and to royalties collected in connection with digital audio recording technology.[77] The statutory programme requires some intra-industry joint action, and the exemption ensures against opportunistic antitrust litigation disrupting that process.

Charities and non-profit institutions

Several statutes accord some degree of special treatment to non-profit institutions. Non-profit, charitable enterprises enjoy a statutory exemption from Section 5 of the FTC Act.[78] Competition (and consumer protection) violations by those entities must be handled by the Department of Justice or private plaintiffs, under the Sherman and Clayton Acts. The Robinson-Patman Act's prohibition of various kinds of price discrimination and related practices does not apply to purchases by non-profit schools, colleges, universities, public libraries, churches, hospitals, and charitable institutions of supplies for their own use.[79] The Robinson-Patman exemption is particularly significant in health care, where there have been disputes over how non-profit hospitals or managed care organizations use pharmaceuticals purchased at discount prices. And in response to a government lawsuit that successfully challenged an agreement among major universities about the calculation of financial aid awards,[80] Congress enacted an exemption from the Sherman Act for the use of common standards and agreements on this subject.[81] That temporary exemption expired in 1997.[82]

The exemption from FTC Act jurisdiction is a historical oddity and an unjustifiable and costly obstacle to Commission action against violations by non-profit firms. The exemption dates from the agency's creation as the successor to the *Bureau of Corporations*, with a mission to rein in the excesses of business corporations. It serves no valid purpose (as illustrated, perhaps, by the fact that there is no such exemption applicable to competition enforcement by the Department of Justice), it complicates the FTC's enforcement efforts against non-profit professional and trade associations, and it prevents FTC action against non-profit firms even when they compete directly against for-profit firms. At a minimum, the exemption concerning competition matters should be narrowed to cover only charitable organisations that do not compete with for-profit firms.

Labour

To the consternation of those who saw the Sherman Act as a tool to control business, it was used first to stop efforts to prevent competition in labour. Congress responded with a statutory exemption from the antitrust laws for the existence and usual operations of organised labour groups.[83] The exemption does not apply to agreements or concerted actions between labour groups and business or other non-labour parties. However, courts have devised a "non-statutory" exemption that shields some, but not all, concerted conduct that involves non-labour parties. Generally, this applies to activities and agreements arising in a collective bargaining setting that do not have "a potential for restraining competition in the business market in ways that would not follow naturally from elimination of competition over wages and working conditions".[84]

Export trade

The antitrust laws do not apply to associations whose joint actions restrict competition in export trade, under certain conditions.[85] There must be no effect on US prices of the commodities being exported, nor any other substantial lessening of US competition. The association must be for the sole purpose of export trade and not in restraint of the export trade of the association's competitors. These associations must register and file annual reports with the FTC. The FTC recommended the exemption, very shortly after the Commission was established, in order to permit US companies to compete more effectively against foreign cartels. Association activities outside the boundary of the exemption, such as agreements that involve foreign firms or non-members, are subject to public or private antitrust action.

A somewhat similar, but more limited, immunity is available through a procedure at the Department of Commerce.[86] On application, that Department may issue a "certificate of review" of export trade activities, with substantive standards parallel to the Webb-Pomerene Act. This certification requires the concurrence of the Attorney General. Certification does not provide total immunity, but only immunity from criminal prosecution, and a limitation of possible recoveries in private lawsuits to single damages. Its scope may be slightly broader than Webb-Pomerene, in that it can cover exports of services as well as goods.

Import trade

The *International Trade Commission* (ITC) enforces a law prohibiting "unfair methods of competition and unfair acts in the importation of articles into the United States", if the effect is to destroy or substantially injure a US industry, or if the acts relate to importation of articles infringing intellectual property rights granted under US law.[87] The principal remedies are an order excluding the offending goods from entry into the US and a cease and desist order against offending US firms and individuals. The law's substantive standard is essentially identical to the basic standard of Section 5 of the Federal Trade Commission Act. But the ITC has rejected suggestions that this "unfair competition" law be applied with the same consumer-oriented analysis and purpose as the FTC Act. The import "unfair practices" law is now applied almost entirely to patent disputes, though, so inconsistency with the interpretation and application of other competition principles is less important than it might have been. The ITC is required to give the competition enforcement agencies an opportunity to comment before making a final determination. In practice, this consultation opportunity is rarely significant, because the ITC's processes allow insufficient time for the competition agencies to respond. The Department of Justice has a later opportunity for input, because it participates in the interagency group that recommends whether the President should approve the import relief proposed by the ITC.

An implied immunity covers certain actions under other US trade laws. If specified procedures are followed in settling trade disputes through agreements with foreign competitors about price and quantity,[88] those agreements are immune from antitrust liability. The immunity fails if the agreements do not comply with these procedures or go beyond the measures authorised.[89]

National defence

Agreements initiated by the President, authorised and actively supervised by the president or designee, and subject to a presidential finding that "conditions exist which may pose a direct threat to the national defence or its preparedness programmes", are given a partial exemption.[90] The exemption does not apply if the actions are taken for the purpose of violating the antitrust laws. The competition agencies monitor these agreements.

5.   COMPETITION ADVOCACY FOR REGULATORY REFORM

The US competition agencies have been unusually active in promoting competitive, market methods and outcomes in the policy-making and regulatory processes. Their advocacy contributed to the first major deregulation successes, in airlines and natural gas, and continued with trucking, communications, broadcasting, and electric power. The rate of their advocacy activity has declined substantially in the last few years, though. Since the 1970s, they have made over 2 000 comments or other formal public appearances in proceedings at other agencies or government bodies. In the late 1980s, these appearances came at a rate of over a hundred a year. By 1997, though, the annual total was less than 20. This decline probably reflects the fact that, at the federal level at least, the easier and more obvious battles have been fought and won. The Antitrust Division concentrates its advocacy almost entirely at other federal agencies and departments, while the FTC has addressed about half of its efforts to state and local issues.

The analytic principles motivating competition advocacy are summarised in the Antitrust Division's operating manual. The foundation assumption is that exceptions to the general rule of free market competition (subject to antitrust law oversight) can be justified only by compelling evidence that competition is unworkable or that it prevents achieving another, overriding social objective. Advocacy's goals are to eliminate existing regulation that is unnecessary or too costly, to discourage unnecessary new regulation, to minimise distortions where regulations are necessary by encouraging use of the least anticompetitive regulatory methods, and to ensure that regulation is properly designed to meet legitimate objectives. Some basic issues to address include: identifying the costs or disadvantages of competition in the setting at issue; determining whether regulation, if already in place, has actually fulfilled its purpose, and whether the conditions that were said to have justified it still obtain; and identifying the necessary elements of a transition from a regulated market to a competitive one. Ultimately, the question is the balance of costs and benefits. The agencies typically argue that the burden of proof is on those who would establish or maintain the regulatory system.

Competition issues in industries undergoing restructuring remain a focus of advocacy efforts. Several recent comments from both agencies have dealt with the electric power industry. They have pointed out the advantages of structural remedies over regulatory, behavioural solutions in safeguarding non-discriminatory access to the transmission grid and in dealing with market power in electricity generation. Comments have also discussed the appropriate framework of analysis for review of electric utility mergers, supporting the regulator's eventual decision to apply standard competition analysis in making its "public interest" determinations. In the last few years, comments have concentrated on the changes in the regulation of broadcasting and telecommunications. Many of these comments are related to the FCC's implementation of the Telecommunications Act of 1996. The competition agencies have successfully advocated, for example, cost-based pricing and forbearance where appropriate.

Some comments are in support of other agencies' efforts to apply competition principles under their own laws. Recent examples include the comments to FERC about electric power merger policy and comments to the Department of Transportation supporting proposed DOT rules under its unfair competition jurisdiction to address anti-competitive practices by airlines' computer reservation systems.

Some comments have assessed the likely effects of proposed exclusions and exemptions from competition law. A recent FTC staff report to Congress analysed a proposed settlement of litigation against cigarette manufacturers, which would include an antitrust exemption for certain joint practices to implement the settlement. The report concluded that the exemption could enable cigarette companies to co-ordinate price increases and raise profits. Another FTC staff comment objected to proposed state legislation to authorise "certificates of public advantage" conferring state-action antitrust immunity on co-operative agreements among healthcare providers. The comment pointed out that the exemption could lead to reduction of consumer choices and increase in consumer prices. If the state nonetheless proceeded with the programme, staff recommended that the anti-competitive risk be reduced by setting fixed, limited terms and terminating certificates that are found to harm consumers.

Privatisation issues arise infrequently. A recent FTC staff comment about introducing competition into the system for assigning Internet domain names assessed the likely consequences of using a not-for-profit corporation organised to include diverse stakeholders. The comment concluded that diversifying the board of directors would alleviate concerns about anti-competitive joint actions.

Many comments have addressed particular regulatory constraints on competition. Price and rate regulations subject to recent comments include those affecting long distance telephone service, liquor distribution, and marine pilotage. Entry has been addressed in such contexts as the allocation of airport landing and take-off privileges, certified public accounting, local multipoint telephone and video distribution services, and automobile sales. The two competition agencies filed a joint opposition to a rule preventing non-lawyers and title company attorneys from handling real estate closings, arguing that it would increase costs for consumers who would not otherwise hire an attorney and would increase prices by eliminating competition. Output regulation was the subject of comments on television's prime time access rules, must-carry rules for television retransmissions by satellite and open video system, allocation systems governing airport landing and take-off privileges, and restrictions on collision damage waivers for automobile rentals. Limitations on forms of practice are addressed in comments on optometrists' and veterinarians' commercial relationships with non-professionals and on linkages between cemeteries and funeral establishments.[91]

Fewer comments have addressed competition problems with social or environmental regulation. At one time, the FTC staff commented on such issues as economic impacts of auto fuel economy requirements and market-based methods for reducing CFC production. But since the 1980s, the only FTC comments on environmental issues have been about advertising claims. In comments on health care regulation, the agencies generally deal only with economic impacts and suggestions of market-based alternative methods. They typically decline to engage in debate about the priority and weight of other policy considerations.

Recent advocacy efforts represent the continuation, now on a somewhat smaller scale, of long-established themes. At the FTC, the programme is co-ordinated by one individual, now assigned to the Office of Policy Planning. At the Antitrust Division, the programme is generally monitored by a Deputy Assistant Attorney General. At both agencies, staff lawyers and economists with enforcement-based experience in the industries involved are more directly responsible for identifying problems and preparing responses. The exact resource commitment to advocacy is not clear, but is obviously very small. The FTC estimates that advocacy now consumes about one per cent of its staff and financial resources. That proportion has probably never been as high as five per cent, even in the late 1980s when the FTC staff alone was issuing about a hundred comments per year.

Advocacy should be backed by enforcement. The need for reform can be demonstrated by law enforcement actions. Because regulation is often accompanied by exemption or exclusion from the competition law, this effect is indirect, and appear in two ways. Sometimes, as in the Commission's actions against "ethical practice" agreements among professionals, enforcement succeeds and shows that conduct required by regulation has anti-competitive effects. And sometimes enforcement succeeds by failure. If an action brought against clearly anti-competitive behaviour must be dismissed because of a regulatory exclusion, the failure can support a call to eliminate the exclusion. Unsuccessful suits against tariff bureaux which were found to enjoy protection under the state action doctrine may have helped set the stage for trucking deregulation.

213

It can be difficult, perhaps impossible, to assess accurately whether advocacy is effective. There are too many other factors that may influence a regulator's or legislator's decision. A few generalisations about methods may be drawn from the two agencies' long experience, though. Advocacy is probably more effective when it is one part of a larger strategy that includes enforcement. And formal, public advocacy is more effective when it is combined with informal co-operation with other regulators. The relative success of deregulation in energy and communications might be traced to a long tradition of staff-level consultations and exchanges between the antitrust agencies, FERC, and the FCC, as well as shared ideas among political-level appointees. At the FCC, staff-level contacts have been facilitated by changes to the FCC's rules which now allow off-the-record, *ex parte* communications between its staff and other agencies. By contrast, at the Department of Transportation informal staff consultation is not permitted in contested matters. Thus, the Antitrust Division's participation in the recent rail merger matter had to be formal, public, and adversarial, rather than consultative. Competition policies could be integrated into other regulatory programmes more effectively if remaining barriers to informal staff-level consultations could be lowered.

6. CONCLUSIONS AND POLICY OPTIONS FOR REFORM

6.1. General assessment of current strengths and weaknesses

Competition policy and institutions have been employed very effectively in the process of reforming economic regulations to stimulate competition. At the federal level, commitment to competition is a part of general regulatory policy, so regulatory programmes are generally subject to statutory instructions to promote and protect competition. Where regulation has instead impaired competition, the legal and policy foundation for reform was already present. US competition policy is also strongly linked to consumer interests. Maintaining that linkage, embodied in the broad jurisdiction of the Federal Trade Commission, may justify the otherwise peculiar redundancy of federal law enforcement structures.

Competition policy institutions have used their enforcement and advocacy powers widely, and sometimes quite systematically, to promote reform. Their efforts have helped eliminate economic regulations that restricted entry into airlines and other transport industries, that prevented exit from the rail industry, that controlled pricing for natural gas, electric power, and telecommunications, that limited output of airlines, and that prevented normal commercial practices and forms of business organisation in health care and other professional services.

Commitment to reform extends well beyond the national competition agencies. Since the 1970s, Congress and the federal courts have generally backed reform efforts, too. Major reforms in trucking, railroads, natural gas, and electric power were stimulated or enabled by legislation. Judicial oversight encouraged regulators to adopt policies that were consistent with antitrust principles.

But the breadth of support for competitive reform means responsibility for implementing it is diffused. Because so much of US economic policy is based on competition, many different regulators and other bodies profess to be implementing competition policy. Their conceptions have differed, sometimes significantly. For the general competition law, there are two essentially equivalent national enforcement agencies, fifty state officials with similar and overlapping responsibilities, and an unlimited number of private "enforcers", all subject to several hundred independent federal judges who are ultimately responsible for ensuring policy coherence, but who are not, for the most part, experts in competition policy. Special sectoral regulators are charged with following competition-like policies, but their relationship to general competition policy principles is not always well conceived. The Congress has created dozens of special requirements and exemptions, often simply reversing or forestalling particular law enforcement decisions, that do not all appear consistent with an integrated competition policy. This diffusion of power, both within the federal government and between the federal and state governments, which is a general characteristic of

US government, may weaken the focus of competition policy. With so many entities claiming some competence over competition policy, the two national government enforcement agencies enjoy less authority and policies are necessarily more uncertain. Duplication and second-guessing are virtually inevitable. Resources expended on co-ordination could be better applied to analysis and enforcement.

Not all reform efforts have succeeded. Some of the legislated exemptions are obviously responses to organised special interests. Some assignments of regulatory responsibility appear designed to preserve non-competitive conditions or permit potentially non-competitive mergers. Efforts to introduce market methods in health care may be encountering a backlash of opposition, motivated both by concerns over the appearance of new forms of market power and by efforts to retain old ones. Competition agency participation in reform of non-economic regulations has been much less systematic. And any broad reform effort is complicated by the potential for "state action" immunity, permitting local regulatory programmes to contradict national competition policy.

6.2. The dynamic view: the pace and direction of change

The process of reforming economic regulation has slowed, largely because most of the work has been done. What remains are mostly isolated issues and subsectors. In two large sectors, electric power and telecommunications, reform is being delayed by firms' jockeying for advantageous positions, but these projects will proceed. Congress has recently passed legislation intended to make telecommunications more competitive, and it is considering national legislation to stimulate electric power reform. These actions evidence a political commitment to the principle of pro-competitive reform. Retrenchment is unlikely, for competition policy is an integral element of the national regulatory system.

Although some anomalies remain at the federal level, the principal opportunities for further reform of economic regulation probably lie at the state and local level, where the integration of competition policy is less well established. Some state laws protect retailers and distributors against competition in motor vehicles, liquor, and other products. Some states have general laws against sales "below cost" which do not adequately consider real competitive effects. Some states law grant protection against antitrust oversight to health care providers and facilities. Many states still support anti-competitive regulation of professional practices. Situations vary widely from state to state, so it is very difficult to generalise or even estimate the size of the potential problems. While some states have reformed or eliminated these laws, others have moved in the opposite direction.

The competition authorities' role in the reform process has become less visible. That trend may continue. The agencies are still involved in the major, national efforts about telecommunications and electric power. They will face significant political challenges dealing with state level issues, with international trade and ocean shipping, and with social regulation. On those subjects, promoting competition policy principles in reform may depend on other institutions.

6.3. Potential benefits and costs of further regulatory reform

At the national level, completing the task of eliminating regulatory constraints on economic competition will not generate nearly the benefits of the major reforms already accomplished. But the costs should not be as great, either. First, the difference between the current state and the fully competitive market is smaller. Second, experience with previous deregulation should suggest likely restructuring strategies that will minimise transition costs.

At the state level, the balance is less clear, because there is no complete, systematic estimate of the net effects of anti-competitive state-level regulations. But it is likely that potential gains from eliminating them are substantial.

6.4. Policy options for consideration[92]

Further reform in the United States should:

- **Undertake a comprehensive study of the extent and effect of the state action doctrine, in preparation for legislation to reduce its scope or even eliminate it.**

The impact of the state action doctrine, and of anti-competitive state and local legislation, is a matter of concern. State regulation and special legislation impairs competition and may delay reform, not only in professional services and distribution, but also in telecommunications and electric power. The state action exemption, and anti-competitive state laws that impair competition affecting interstate commerce, are within the power of Congress to correct, either in particular applications or by general legislation. Congress has already done so in some sectors, such as trucking, where the anti-competitive effects of continued state regulation were patent. A comprehensive study should be undertaken to assess the competitive effects of state laws and regulations and to identify sectors where reform is most needed. A model for such a study in a federal context is the review of state-level constraints on competition that is underway now in Australia. Prime targets for action would be state and local laws that continue to permit business and professional associations to restrict price and other forms of competition among their members and laws that protect dealers against new competition or prohibit aggressive pricing and other marketing methods.

- **Develop clearer assignments of responsibility among different enforcement officials, particularly between the federal and state levels, to avoid overlap and duplication.**

At the federal level, the two competition agencies co-ordinate well, but the quality of co-ordination with other regulators that share competition policy authority varies. In general, that relationship is worked out through consultation, advocacy, and the intervention of the courts. Adoption of rules to permit greater informal staff-level consultation in enforcement matters among sectoral agencies with competition policy responsibilities would improve co-ordination even more.

The co-ordination problems are more difficult between the federal and state levels. State-level enforcement capacity adds resources, but the risk of multiple and inconsistent enforcement priorities is a significant cost. Some state-level officials have shown a greater interest than the federal agencies have in cases about vertical relationships. It has been said that, at one time, that concern filled a gap left by lax federal-level enforcement. But that interest is also consistent with the state laws protecting competitors against aggressive competition. A logical division of responsibility would have local officials deal with local problems, while national officials dealt with national ones. But US law does not now require that division of labour. At best, clarity and predictability are undermined when a major federal-level enforcement effort, such as the monopolisation case now pending against Microsoft, is second-guessed by a group of local enforcement officials bringing a separate, similar, and simultaneous lawsuit. Co-ordination with the states is being managed more amicably now than ten years ago, but the duplication of effort remains problematic. And the difference in likely priorities can undermine policy coherence.

- **Eliminate remaining exemptions and sector-specific jurisdictional provisions.**

Despite the general move toward deregulation, areas remain where competition policy is applied uncertainly. The risk of inconsistency and gaps in coverage should be corrected by eliminating unnecessary exemptions and clearly assigning responsibility to the general competition law rather than a sectoral regulator. Significant exceptions from normal antitrust jurisdiction that remain in transport include sector-specific merger authority for railroads, immunity in trucking for collective ratemaking on joint and through rates and for household goods, immunity and resulting cartelisation of ocean shipping, and sector-specific authority about unfair competition for airlines. The special enforcement body, the Surface Transportation Board, has illustrated the problems with sector-specific competition enforcement. Its powers should not be expanded, by assigning it responsibility for monitoring the cartels in ocean shipping too. Rather, it should be eliminated and competition enforcement authority consolidated in the general competition agencies.

Sector-specific authority concerning mergers and other competition issues in energy and telecommunications should also be eliminated in the course of deregulation. In those sectors, potential conflicts are being managed more successfully than they have been in transport, and it appears more likely that reform will end naturally in the termination of overlapping sectoral competition responsibilities.

Anomalous exemptions and special provisions should be eliminated. Some are simply clutter in the statutes, with little practical significance. But the exemption for non-profit firms from the FTC Act should be repealed, or at a minimum narrowed to apply only to organisations that do not compete with for-profit firms. The special protections for vertical agreements in the soft drink industry are not defensible. The exemption for newspaper joint operations does not seem necessary any more, in the modern media era, nor does the immunity for pooling sports broadcasts. Alone among OECD Member counties, the US does not apply its general competition law to the commercial operations of publicly owned enterprises. Although there are few such enterprises, the exemption probably has significant effects in some markets, and the special treatment should be reconsidered. The special treatment of insurance under the McCarran-Ferguson Act leaves a major national industry subject only to local-level competition oversight; that imbalance in jurisdiction should be re-examined and probably corrected.

6.5. Managing regulatory reform

Experience in the US suggests that the "transition" from economic regulation to a competitive market can rarely be managed or controlled, so it is more effective for it to happen quickly.[93] In airlines, a phased transition was planned, but once the airlines realised change was inevitable, they insisted on speeding it up. Deregulation was achieved *de facto* years before the end of the projected timetable. In natural gas, a somewhat longer-term transition seems to have worked reasonably well, but that may have been because competition law had coexisted with regulation and thus was already familiar. There too, once the industry realised the change was inevitable, it came rapidly. Litigation slowed the process some. A principal complication was sorting out liability for contract commitments entered when the rules and expectations were different. Eventually, deals were reached, mostly through private litigation. The threat of similar complications is delaying change in electric power, though similar deals will no doubt be reached eventually.

A lengthy, planned transition process may be an invitation to resist the final step, or at least to postpone it. Setting a date certain does announce that the issue is no longer debatable. But the farther that date is in the future, the less credible is the commitment to change. The regulated industry may continue to stall in the interim, lobbying for a change of political will. Or it may use the intervening time and the transition tools themselves to build up resources and develop strategies for fending off new entry after regulated protection ends. Thus, a firm date is necessary, and it must not be too far off. Once the industry understands that it cannot stop the process, the industry itself is likely to adapt quickly in anticipation.

The incumbent firms may well still have some monopoly advantages during and after this process of anticipated change. Abuse can be prevented by shifting to the application of general competition law as promptly as possible. The incumbents' use of unfair or abusive methods to perpetuate the monopoly or cartel could then be challenged under generally applicable standards. General competition law should of course be applied with due regard for an appropriate choice of sanctions, while the industry is becoming familiar with the new expectations. But in the US, antitrust law has already applied to most of the sectors where remaining economic regulation is being removed. The "grace period" could be quite short.

NOTES

1. Council of Economic Advisors (1996), *Economic Report of the President*, p. 155.

2. 42 USC. § 7112(12) (Department of Energy).

3. Northern Pacific Railway Co. *v.* United States, 356 US 1, 4 (1958).

4. A little-known example is the Federal Alcohol Administration Act, 27 USC. § 203, which sets rules about marketing practices in distribution of alcoholic beverages. Although Congress stated that its purpose was to ensure a competitive market, the rules that the Bureau of Alcohol, Tobacco, and Firearms has adopted to implement the law prohibit many practices that current competition policy would not object to.

5. United States *v.* American Airlines, 570 F. Supp. 654 (N.D. Tex. 1983), *rev'd*, 743 F.2d 1114, 1119 (5th Cir. 1984), *cert. dismissed*, 474 US 1001 (1985).

6. United States *v.* Airline Tariff Publishing Co., 1994-2 Trade Cas. (CCH) ¶ 70,687 (DDC 1994).

7. Southern Motor Carriers Rate Conference, Inc. *v.* United States, 471 US 48 (1985); New England Motor Rate Bureau *v.* FTC, 908 F.2d 1064 (1st Cir. 1990).

8. In 1994, the FTC settled charges brought in 1988 that Boulder Ridge Cable TV and Weststar Communications, Inc, entered into an agreement not to compete against each other as part of Boulder's acquisition of Three Palms, Ltd. The FTC alleged that the agreement was not limited to the area in which the acquisitions occurred.

9. American Medical Association, 94 FTC 701 (1979), *aff'd*, 638 F.2d 443 (2d Cir. 1980), *aff'd per curiam by an equally divided Court*, 455 US 676 (1982).

10. California Dental Ass'n, Docket No. 9 259, 5 Trade Reg. Rep. (CCH) ¶ 24,007. That order has since been affirmed on appeal, although the court used different reasoning.

11. Text at 6 Trade Reg. Rep. (CCH) ¶ 44,095 (letter 95-2).

12. In the recent *California Dentists* decision, the Commission tried to base its decision on a plain *per se* standard, arguing that there had been enough experience with the practices to justify placing them in that category. The court disagreed, though, and affirmed on the basis of a more standard rule of reason analysis.

13. See Klein, Joel, "A Stepwise Approach to Antitrust Review of Horizontal Agreements", Address to the ABA Antitrust Section (Nov. 7, 1996), discussed in A*ntitrust*, spring 1998, p. 41.

14. FTC *v.* Indiana Federation of Dentists, 476 US 447 (1986).

15. Kattan, J. (1996), "The role of efficiency considerations in the Federal Trade Commission's Antitrust Analysis", A*nti-trust* L.J., Vol. 64, p. 613.

16. National Society of Professional Engineers *v.* United States, 435 US 679 (1978).

17. United States *v.* AT&T, 552 F. Supp. 131, 150, 153 (DDC 1982), *aff'd sub nom.* Maryland *v.* United States, 460 US 1001 (1983).

18. Questar Corp., File No. 961-0001, 5 Trade Reg. Rep. (CCH) ¶ 23,949.

19. Time Warner Inc., File No. 961-0004, 5 Trade Reg. Rep. (CCH) ¶24,104. For a more detailed discussion, *see* PITOFSKY, Robert (1997), remarks before the Fordham Corporate Law Institute on "Vertical Restraints and Vertical Aspects of Mergers – A US Perspective", October 16-17, 1997, at 8-10.

20. On August 5, 1996, the Division sued to block the proposed merger of two of the nation's largest radio station owners, alleging that they would control more than 50 per cent of sales of radio advertising time in Cincinnati, and could enable the companies to increase prices to advertisers and substantially lessen competition. The parties agreed to divest a leading Cincinnati contemporary music station to an independent buyer. *See* 7 Trade Rep. Reg. (CCH) ¶ 50,807, Case No. 4225.

21. See Averitt, N. & Lande, R. (1997), "Consumer Sovereignty: A Unified Theory of Antitrust and Consumer Protection Law", *Antitrust L. J.* Vol. 65, p. 713.

22. FTC Rule 3.51 and 61 Fed. Reg. 50,640 (1996).

23. See Swanson, Daniel G. and Diethelm, U. Markus (1998), "Ignore US Antitrust Rules at Your Own Peril", *Wall Street Journal Europe*, 9 February.

24. Sections 1.2, 1.3, and 3 of the *Horizontal Merger Guidelines*. The analysis in these sections about market definition, identification of market participants, and entry is similar to the analysis that is applied to foreign trade aspects of these issues in non-merger cases as well.

25. *See* section 4.22 of the *Antitrust Enforcement Guidelines for International Operations* and 16 C.F.R. §§ 801-803 (1994). In contrast to those exemptions that offer foreign firms some degree of relief from otherwise applicable requirements, a geographic requirement in the special program for joint research or production, discussed below in Section 4, might work to their disadvantage.

26. United States *v.* Philadelphia Nat'l Bank, 374 US 321, 350-51 (1963).

27. Gordon *v.* New York Stock Exchange, 422 US 659 (1975).

28. Keogh *v.* Chicago & North-western Railway, 260 US 156 (1922). The "filed rate" doctrine only protects against suits for damages based on the rate levels.

29. A relic in the statute book is an exemption for discussions held by subcouncils of the Council on Competitiveness, each of which included a representative of the government; that Council no longer exists.

30. California Retail Dealers Ass'n *v.* Midcal Aluminium, Inc., 445 US 97 (1980).

31. FTC *v.* Ticor Title Insurance Co., 504 US 621 (1992).

32. Local Government Antitrust Act of 1984, 15 USC. §§ 34-36.

33. Parker *v.* Brown, 317 US 341 (1943).

34. Eastern Railroad Presidents Conference *v.* Noerr Motor Freight, Inc., 365 US 127 (1961); United Mine Workers *v.* Pennington, 381 US 657 (1965).

35. 15 USC. §§ 638(d)(2), 640.

36. Although small businesses do enjoy the possibility of compensation for some of their legal bills, if they prevail in a government enforcement action against them. This applies to all kinds of government enforcement action, not just those under the antitrust laws.

37. National Co-operative Research and Production Act of 1993 (NCRPA) 15 USC. § 4301-06 (1994).

38. Department of Transportation (1998), Statement of Enforcement Policy Regarding Unfair Exclusionary Conduct (April 6, 1998).

39. 49 USC. § 41308(b), (c).

40. 49 USC. §§ 10706(a)(2)(A), (a)(3)(B)(ii), (a)(4), (a)(5)(A), (d).

41. 49 USC. § 11321(a).

42. There is also an exemption from antitrust liability for agreements between rail carriers about co-ordination and unification of operations, if the agreement is reached at a conference held by the Secretary of Transportation and it is approved by the Secretary. The statutes also contain a relic of earlier reforms, an exemption for actions taken to formulate or implement the final plan under the Regional Rail Reorganisation Act of 1973. 45 USC. § 791(a). And there is an exemption for certain agreements with the national rail passenger service, AMTRAK, about joint use or operation of facilities and equipment. 49 USC. § 24301(j).

43. 49 USC.A. § 10101.

44. Clyde, P.S. and Reitzes, J.D. (1995), *The Effectiveness of Collusion under Antitrust Immunity: the Case of Liner Shipping Conferences*.

45. *See* 49 USC. § 11501(c), § 14501(c)(3).

46. 49 USC. §§ 13703(a)(1), (a)(6), (c). The Surface Transportation Board also has some power to approve, and thus immunise, agreements about pooling or dividing traffic and services. 49 USC. § 14302(f).

47. 49 USC. § 13703(a)(1)(B). See also 49 USC. § 13097(d), exempting discussions between a carrier and its agent or another carrier about shipping rates for household goods.

48. 49 USC. § 14303(f).

49. Otter Tail Power Co. *v.* United States, 410 US 366 (1973).

50. 42 USC § 6272.

51. 15 USC. § 3364(3).

52. They are, however, free from the jurisdiction of the Federal Trade Commission. 15 USC. § 5(a)(2).

53. 12 USC. §§ 1828(c), 1849.

54. 12 USC. §§ 1971-1978.

55. Riegle-Neal Interstate Banking and Branching Efficiency Act of 1994, 12 USC. §§ 1849.

56. Gordon v. New York Stock Exchange, 422 US 659 (1975).

57. 15 USC. §§ 1011-15.

58. United States v. South-Eastern Underwriters Ass'n, 322 US 533 (1944).

59. 47 USC. § 313(a), Telecommunications Act of 1996 § 601(b)(1). The 1996 Act also made telephone company mergers subject to generally applicable antitrust procedures and standards under the Clayton Act.

60. 47 USC. § 303c(c).

61. 47 USC. § 555a. This immunity essentially duplicates that which is also available to local officials generally, discussed above.

62. Clayton Act, § 6.

63. 7 USC. § 291.

64. 15 USC. § 521.

65. 7 USC. § 455.

66. 15 USC. § 13b (1994); 7 USC. § 207(f).

67. 7 USC. § 608(b).

68. 7 USC. § 671(d).

69. 7 USC. § 852.

70. 7 USC. §§ 181, 192.

71. 15 USC. §§ 1801-1804.

72. 15 USC. §§ 1291-1295.

73. Soft Drink Interbrand Competition Act of 1980, 15 USC. §§ 3501-03.

74. 42 USC. §§ 11101, 11111-11115.

75. 17 USC. §§ 111, 114, 115, 116.

76. 17 USC. §§ 118(b), (e)(1).

77. 17 USC. §§ 1007(a)(2).

78. 15 USC. §§ 44, defining "corporation" subject to FTC jurisdiction to exclude those not for profit.

79. 15 USC. §§ 13c.

80. United States v. Brown University, 5 F.3d 658 (3d Cir. 1993).

81. Pub.L. 103-382, Title V, §§ 568(a) – (d), Oct. 20, 1994, 108 Stat. 4 060.

82. There is also a curious immunity against treble damages for certain charitable gift annuities and charitable remainder trusts. Charitable Gift Annuity Antitrust Relief Act of 1995, Pub. L. 104-63. 15 USC. § 37. This appears to be a response to a particular threat of a private lawsuit.

83. Clayton Act, §§ 6, 20; Norris-La Guardia Act, 29 USC. §§ 104, 105, 113(b).

84. Connell Construction Co. v. Plumbers & Steamfitters Local Union No. 100, 421 US 616, 635 (1975).

85. Webb-Pomerene Act, 15 USC. §§ 61-66.

86. Export Trading Company Act of 1982, 15 USC. §§ 4011-4021.

87. 19 USC. § 1337, amended by the Uruguay Round Agreements Act, Pub. L. No. 103-465, 108 Stat. 4 809 (1994).

88. These are set out in 19 USC. § 1673c.

89. A limited exemption was also enacted to cover certain actions taken before 1 January, 1975 in connection with steel import quotas. 19 USC. § 2485.

90. Defence Production Act of 1950, § 708(j).

91. Some of the FTC staff comments have addressed regulations to prevent or redress fraud and deception. Examples include comments concerning telemarketing fraud, 900-number rules, licensing fraud, pharmaceutical marketing, and environmental marketing claims.

92. These options correspond to the relevant recommendations of OECD (1997), *Report on Regulatory Reform*.

93. Kahn, A.E. (1986), "The Theory and Application of Regulation," *Antitrust* L.J., Vol. 55, p. 177.

BACKGROUND REPORT
ON ENHANCING MARKET OPENNESS THROUGH
REGULATORY REFORM*

---

* This report was principally prepared by **Vera Nicholas-Gervais**, consultant, **Evdokia Moïsé**, Administrator and **Akira Kawamoto**, Principal Administrator, of the Trade Directorate. It has benefited from extensive comments provided by colleagues throughout the OECD Secretariat, by the Government of the United States, and by Member countries as part of the peer review process. This report was peer reviewed in September 1998 in the Working Party of the OECD's Trade Committee.

223

TABLE OF CONTENTS

OECD 1999

Executive Summary

Background Report on Enhancing Market Openness through Regulatory Reform

Does the national regulatory system allow foreign enterprises to take full advantage of competitive global markets? Reducing regulatory barriers to trade and investment enables countries in an expanding global economy to benefit more fully from comparative advantage and innovation. This means that more market openness increases the benefits that consumers can draw from regulatory reform. Maintaining an open world trading system requires regulatory styles and content that promote global competition and economic integration, avoid trade disputes, and improve trust and mutual confidence across borders. This report offers an assessment of the US performance from these perspectives. However, it does not consider the equally important debate as to whether and how trade and investment affect the pursuit and attainment of legitimate policy objectives.

The generally liberal nature of US trade and investment policies is broadly reflected in the national regulatory system. Active US participation in the multilateral trading system and in a range of other regional and bilateral instruments has largely complemented domestic efforts to achieve higher quality regulation that fulfils legitimate policy objectives without unnecessarily compromising foreign competition in the market. International regulatory co-operation through the US-EU New Transatlantic Agenda and the Trans-Atlantic Business Dialogue (TABD) signal a new sophistication in dealing with the increasingly complex dimensions of effective market access. At the same time, a long US history of pathbreaking deregulation has steadily moved the country towards a highly participatory regulatory style and pro-competitive regulatory content. These trends have reinforced the development and maintenance of open markets for international trade and investment, and market openness has been broadly sustained despite the competitive pressures and social tensions wrought by globalisation.

Nonetheless, further efforts are needed if the US regulatory system is to promote optimal market openness. Although not unique to the US case, particular features of the US regulatory environment continue to cause frictions with trade and investment partners. The complexity of the national regulatory system, the interplay of federal, state and local regulatory activities, and the fact that certain areas of the economy remain heavily regulated present both domestic and foreign firms with formidable challenges regarding regulatory coherence, cost of regulatory compliance, and transparency. Beyond this, subtleties in the ways regulations are designed or implemented sometimes result in de facto discrimination against foreign competitors. Extensive social regulations – rules to protect legitimate public interests and societal preferences spanning such areas as the environment, public health, consumer protection, and product and workplace safety – introduce the greatest potential for this result. This may signal a need for enhanced vetting and scrutiny of proposed rules from a market openness perspective, in addition to the existing system of public review. Such an improvement would ensure that legitimate domestic objectives are successfully achieved without unnecessarily compromising open market policies. Other broad policy areas such as product standards and conformity assessment systems would benefit from exploration of alternatives to third party certification and increased reliance on international standards as the basis of domestic regulation. Finally, particular aspects of substantive sectoral regulation merit renewed assessments of their effects on inward trade and investment.

Improvement of a national regulatory system cannot be successfully undertaken without the broad support of civil society and regulators themselves. Furthermore, legitimate policy objectives cannot be compromised. On this, efforts must be made to effectively communicate the complementary relationship between sound domestic regulation (be it deregulation or more efficient regulation) and international market openness. Efficient regulation successfully supports legitimate domestic objectives but can also be market-opening, accelerating progress towards a more efficient and innovative economy, encouraging greater competitiveness on the part of domestic firms, and yielding greater benefits for US consumers.

1.   MARKET OPENNESS AND REGULATION: THE POLICY ENVIRONMENT IN THE UNITED STATES

The general US policy environment toward international market openness and its evolution in recent years has been primarily shaped by developments at the multilateral, regional and bilateral levels. Active US participation in the GATT and successor WTO and in regional agreements and arrangements such as NAFTA and APEC have together established one of the most open national markets for global trade and investment in the post-war world. Multilateral trade liberalisation has led to historically low tariffs for a broad spectrum of goods in the United States and elsewhere, trade in services has been set on the path of progressive multilateral liberalisation, and US participation in sector-specific initiatives, such as the Information Technology Agreement, has further contributed to a widening and deepening of the liberalisation agenda. Despite what may be a backlash against globalisation in some domestic quarters, this basic policy stance seems set to prevail. The US role in promoting incipient free trade areas such as the Free Trade Area of the Americas and in innovative approaches to deepening existing trade ties through mechanisms such as the Transatlantic Economic Partnership[1] and the Trans-Atlantic Business Dialogue (TABD) appears to reflect an enduring commitment to liberal trade and regulatory policies. While international opinion is strong in its opposition to certain features of US trade policy (notably extraterritorial application of domestic legislation and occasionally aggressive use of domestic trade law provisions to achieve expanded market access in foreign markets), few dispute the leading role that an open US market has played in fostering the steady expansion of world trade.

The country's rank as the world's largest host of foreign direct investment[2] underscores the openness of the US investment regime. Stated US policy is to regulate inward investment activity as little as possible, and there is no single statute governing foreign investment. While a host of federal, state and local laws governing such matters as anti-trust, mergers and acquisitions, wages and social security, export controls, environmental protection, health and safety have a significant impact on investment decisions, most of these are applied in a non-discriminatory fashion. Exceptions to this principle are generally for reasons of national security or prudential considerations.

In part due to the sheer volume of trade and investment activities involving the United States, frictions inevitably arise with global commercial partners. Domestic regulatory issues have often surfaced in this context. On occasion, US trading partners have challenged certain features of US social regulations applied in support of legitimate policy objectives relating to environment, health and safety as unnecessarily trade-restrictive (Box 1), and economic regulations continue to bar meaningful foreign participation in some sectors. However, disputes and prevailing barriers to international market openness should be viewed from the perspective of a largely trade and investment-friendly regulatory environment, and prospects for enhanced market openness through regulatory reform seen in the dynamic setting of achievements to date.

Four main features of the US regulatory system account for its generally positive performance. First, consistent with a strong political tradition of transparency and public accountability, US regulatory procedures are very open. Nothing prevents active foreign participation in regulatory decision-making. In practice, both domestic and foreign firms are afforded ample and non-discriminatory opportunities to shape the regulatory process from proposed to final rule. Foreign firms can and do make active use of these procedures.

Second, in accordance with executive orders and statutorily-driven procedural requirements, most US agencies take a relatively rigorous (if complex) approach to rule-making. Explicit assessments of the effects of proposed rules on international market openness are not formally required in this context. In practice, however, both domestic and foreign firms benefit from an overall adherence to efficient regulation principles and scrutiny of rationales underlying proposed regulations.

Third, while many economic activities are heavily regulated at federal, state, and local levels, existing regulation is on balance trade and investment neutral. In cases where the design and implementation of regulations has raised questions about discriminatory effects on foreign competitors (as has been argued in respect of clean fuel (reformulated gasoline) standards, which was challenged by foreign

Box 1. US social regulation and trade

Social regulations play a key role in the promotion and protection of public interests such as health, safety, and the environment, as well as safeguarding the interests of consumers and vulnerable social groups. Their objectives are legitimate and clearly fall within the realm of national sovereignty. Social regulations do not generally aim at discriminating against particular parties. However, depending on the means chosen to achieve their stated aims, they may vary in efficacy and give rise to unintended side effects. Thus, while certain social regulations may not be expressly discriminatory or trade-restrictive on their face, their design or implementation may introduce *de facto* barriers to trade. As traditional barriers to market openness continue to fall, "behind the border" measures such as these are falling under increased international scrutiny by trading partners. The range of measures which may be taken in connection with standards, conformity assessment, or sanitary and phytosanitary systems in support of domestic objectives relating to product quality, safety, health and environmental protection is a virtually infinite universe, underscoring the importance of ensuring that social regulation does not unnecessarily compromise market openness. The following examples illustrate the trade implications of some US social regulations as seen by selected trading partners.

Environmental Regulations: GATT and WTO cases involving US corporate average fuel economy (CAFE) standards and reformulated gasoline provide examples of the trade impacts of environmental regulations. The latter case involved EPA regulations on the composition and emissions effects of gasoline to improve air quality introduced pursuant to the 1990 Amendment to the Clean Air Act (CAA). The CAA required that only "reformulated gasoline" could be sold to consumers in highly polluted areas of the country. In establishing regulations for reformulated gasoline, EPA methodology for determining domestic refiners' baseline was based on quality data and volume records for 1990, while most importers (also foreign refiners) were required to use the statutory baseline set by the EPA. Levels required of foreign refiners were seen as more difficult to achieve than those required of US refiners. Venezuela and Brazil successfully argued in the WTO that these regulations violated the principle of national treatment. In 1997, the EPA issued a final regulation removing the discriminatory element of the regulation.

Application of US environmental laws has also led to direct import restrictions on products such as yellowfin tuna and shrimp.

Health regulations: Health regulations apply to a broad range of products, for example foodstuffs and pharmaceuticals. The 1990 Nutrition Labelling and Education Act requires certain products to be labelled with respect to content, but some trading partners have alleged that the rules differ from international labelling standards established by the Codex Alimentarius. Additional state-level requirements may apply to agriculture and food imports.

Safety regulations: One US trading partner has alleged onerous compliance costs associated with the 1990 Fastener Quality Act (legislation which seeks to deter the introduction of sub-standard industrial fasteners in the United States). While according to the US, neither the law nor its implementing regulations discriminate against non-NAFTA suppliers with respect to laboratory testing, that trading partner alleges that the compliance mechanism of FQA regulations imposes a heavier burden on foreign manufacturers without good reason. The United States maintains that concerns about possible trade disruption were taken into account to the extent possible in drafting implementing regulations for the FQA. However, in August 1998, the President signed into law legislation further delaying implementation of the FQA regulations until 1 June 1999, pending submission to Congress by the Department of Commerce by 1 February 1999 a report on 1) changes in fastener manufacturing practices that have occurred since the enactment of the FQA; 2) a comparison of the FQA to other regulatory programmes that regulate the various categories of fasteners, and an analysis of any duplication that exists among programmes; and 3) any changes in the FQA that may be warranted because of changes reported under 1) and 2). Bilateral mutual recognition negotiations on fasteners have also been launched. Thus, US handling of this case may yet provide a positive example of how trade and regulatory interests can be favourably reconciled.

Plant health regulations: Phytosanitary regulations for fruits and vegetables set by the US Department of Agriculture are viewed by some foreign producers as unnecessarily burdensome. Exporters seeking entry to the US market for commodities with the potential to carry pests or diseases of quarantine significance must cover all USDA expenses in researching and approving quarantine treatments for products and, if market access is gained, shipments of the fruit or vegetable may be subject to an inspection process in both the country of origin and the US port of entry. A stringent USDA import plan contains nine specific safeguards specific to avocados from Mexico to prevent exotic pests from entering the United States, including packing house and port of arrival inspections and limited distribution to certain US states.

Box 1. US social regulation and trade (*cont.*)

Under the Agricultural Marketing Agreement Act, the Secretary of Agriculture can issue grade, size, quality or maturity regulations for certain commodities through domestic marketing orders. These orders are also applicable to comparable import commodities. However, comparable commodities harvested under different growing conditions may not be able to meet these regulations as easily as domestic produce. Imported avocados, dates, grapefruit, limes, tomatoes and oranges are amongst a range of products which have been subject to such regulations in the past. Inspections requirements associated with meat import regulation are also viewed by some exporters as excessively lengthy and costly.

In light of a strong rise in US imports of foreign foodstuffs over the last decade, a recent GAO study recommended that Congress authorise the Food and Drug Administration (FDA) to require that other countries adopt safe practices for fruit, vegetables, fish, and processed foods shipped to the United States, mirroring the authority already exercised by the Department of Agriculture with respect to imported meat and poultry (which has already attracted the attention of some trading partners). President Clinton has called the study "further confirmation" of the need for an earlier Administration proposal to extend this authority to the FDA.

Consumer interest regulations: The American Automobile Labelling Act requires all passenger vehicles and light trucks to bear labels indicating their domestic content per centage of value added in the United States and Canada. The stated aim of the Act is to help consumers make informed purchasing decisions. But some foreign competitors see the law as a *de facto* "Buy American" provision. Other features of the law, such as methodology for calculating US content of cars produced by foreign automakers within the United States, are perceived by some trading partners as expressly discriminatory.

Sources: 1998 Report on the WTO Consistency of Trade Policies by Major Trading Partners (Industrial Structure Council, Japan); EU Sectoral and Trade Barriers Database; US Trade Barriers to Latin American Exports in 1996 (UN Economic Commission for Latin America and the Caribbean); Opening Doors to the World: Canada's International Market Access Priorities, 1998.

---

trading partners under GATT/WTO dispute settlement procedures),[3] US regulators have shown some flexibility in moving to resolve the causes of trade tensions. Domestic avenues exist for foreign firms wishing to challenge adverse trade or investment effects of existing regulations.

Fourth and finally, a long US history of regulatory reform efforts has already yielded considerable benefits for domestic and foreign firms. Economic regulation – rules that intervene directly in market decisions such as pricing, competition, and market entry or exit – has been largely dismantled, though significant barriers to trade and investment still apply in some areas. A range of initiatives aimed at improving the quality of domestic regulation has the potential to yield important dividends for foreign and domestic firms alike (see background report on Government Capacity to Assure High Quality Regulation). In addition, ongoing efforts to streamline administrative regulation at both federal and state levels – "red tape" or government paperwork and administrative formalities faced by individuals and firms – should benefit foreign traders and investors entering or expanding activities in the US market.

2. THE POLICY FRAMEWORK FOR MARKET OPENNESS: THE SIX "EFFICIENT REGULATION" PRINCIPLES

An important step in ensuring that regulations do not unnecessarily reduce market openness is to build the "efficient regulation" principles into the domestic regulatory process for social and economic regulations, as well as for administrative practices. "Market openness" here refers to the ability of foreign suppliers to compete in a national market without encountering discriminatory or excessively burdensome or restrictive conditions. These principles, which have been described in the 1997 OECD *Report on Regulatory Reform* and developed further in the Trade Committee, are:

- *transparency and openness of decision making;*

- *non-discrimination;*

- *avoidance of unnecessary trade restrictiveness;*

- *use of internationally harmonised measures;*

- *recognition of equivalence of other countries' regulatory measures; and*

- *application of competition principles.*

They have been identified by trade policy makers as key to market-oriented, trade and investment-friendly regulation. They reflect the basic principles underpinning the multilateral trading system, concerning which many countries have undertaken certain obligations in the WTO and other contexts. The intention in the OECD country reviews of regulatory reform is not to judge the extent to which any country may have undertaken and lived up to international commitments relating directly or indirectly to these principles; but rather to assess whether and how domestic instruments, procedures and practices give effect to the principles and successfully contribute to market openness. Similarly, the OECD country reviews are not concerned with an assessment of trade policies and practices in Member countries.

In sum, this report considers whether and how US regulatory procedures and content affect the quality of market access and presence in the United States. An important reverse scenario – whether and how inward trade and investment affect the fulfilment of legitimate policy objectives reflected in social regulation – is beyond the scope of the present discussion. This latter issue has been extensively debated within and beyond the OECD from a range of policy perspectives. To date, however, OECD deliberations have found no evidence to suggest that trade and investment *per se* impact negatively on the pursuit and attainment of domestic policy goals through regulation or other means.[4]

2.1. Transparency, openness of decision making and of appeal procedures

To ensure international market openness, foreign firms and individuals seeking access to a market (or expanding activities in a given market) must have adequate information on new or revised regulations so that they can base their decisions on an accurate assessment of potential costs, risks, and market opportunities. Regulations need to be transparent to foreign traders and investors. Regulatory transparency at both domestic and international levels can be achieved through a variety of means, including systematic publication of proposed rules prior to entry into force, use of electronic means to share information (such as the Internet), well-timed opportunities for public comment, and rigorous mechanisms for ensuring that such comments are given due consideration prior to the adoption of a final regulation.[5] Market participants wishing to voice concerns about the application of existing regulations should have appropriate access to appeal procedures. This sub-Section discusses the extent to which such objectives are met in the United States and how.

The basic rulemaking process to be followed by all agencies of the US Government is set out in the Administrative Procedures Act (APA). The APA sets a high standard of transparency and opportunity for comment by any interested parties – national or non-national. Foreign traders and investors are thus well positioned to participate actively at various stages of the rulemaking processes.

The path from proposed to final rule affords ample opportunity for such participation. At a minimum, the APA requires that in issuing a substantive rule (as distinguished from a procedural rule or statement of policy), an agency must:

- Publish a *notice of proposed rulemaking* in the *Federal Register*. This notice must set forth the text or the substance of the proposed rule, the legal authority for the rulemaking proceeding, and applicable times and places for public participation. Published proposals also routinely include information on appropriate contacts within regulatory agencies.

– Provide all interested persons – nationals and non-nationals alike – an opportunity to participate in the rulemaking by providing written data, views, or arguments on a proposed rule. This *public comment process* serves a number of purposes, including giving interested persons an opportunity to provide the agency with information that will enhance the agency's knowledge of the subject matter of the rulemaking. The public comment process also provides interested persons with the opportunity to challenge the factual assumptions on which the agency is proceeding, and to show in what respect such assumptions may be in error.

– Publish a *notice of final rulemaking* at least 30 days before the effective date of the rule. This notice must include a statement of the basis and purpose of the rule and respond to all substantive comments received. Exceptions to the thirty-day rule are provided for in the APA if the rule makes an exemption or relieves a restriction, or if the agency concerned makes and publishes a finding that an earlier effective date is required "for good cause". In general, however, exceptions to the APA are limited and must be justified.

Other APA provisions further enhance transparency and openness of decision-making. For example, each federal agency is required to afford interested persons (again, without regard to nationality) the *right to petition for the issuance, amendment, or repeal of a rule*. Though they retain ultimate discretion in determining whether a request is "meritorious", agencies must by law respond to all such requests. In cases where a request is deemed meritorious, work would commence on developing a proposed rule. The APA also provides for *advance notice of proposed rulemaking*, which allow agencies to seek general comments on issues prior to the development of specific regulatory proposals. This offers important benefits to domestic and foreign firms alike in terms of sequencing: a public comment period available only late in the process (when a proposed rule may have already undergone considerable development) may reduce it to little more than a pro forma step in respect of a virtual *fait accompli* (a concern that has arisen in respect of some other national regulatory regimes).

Beyond the APA, other statutes require additional rulemaking procedures either for specific regulatory areas or in general (see the background report on Government Capacity to Assure High Quality Regulation). The President requires additional procedures. Executive Order (EO) 12 866 on Regulatory Planning and Review issued in September 1993 requires all but the independent regulatory agencies to send "significant rules" to the *Office of Management and Budget* (OMB) for review prior to publication in the *Federal Register* as either proposed or final rules (see related discussion in Section 2.3). OMB's Office of Information and Regulatory Affairs (OIRA) reviews all agency proposals to implement or revise Federal regulations and information requirements consistent with the overarching regulatory philosophy set out in EO 12 866.

One of the many stated objectives of EO 12 866 is to make the regulatory process more accessible and open to the public. Numerous principles embodied in EO 12 866 relate to this objective. Although these principles are not inspired from an international perspective, in practice there is no operative distinction in their application as between domestic and foreign firms. Thus, foreign interests enjoy equal standing with domestic interests with respect to key EO transparency procedures including the annual publication of agency Regulatory Plans (including those of independent regulatory agencies) in the biennial *Unified Regulatory Agenda* (see the background report on Government Capacity to Assure High Quality Regulation); submission of views on any aspect of any agency Plan; participation in OIRA conferences convening representatives of businesses, non-governmental organisations, and the public to discuss regulatory issues of common concern; and maintenance by OIRA of a publicly available log containing detailed information pertinent to regulatory actions under review. Foreign competitors interested in US regulatory developments thus have many opportunities to act as informed and potentially influential participants in the regulatory process.

The established vehicle for communication of proposed regulations is the *Federal Register*. An official publication of the US Government, the *Federal Register* is designed to make available to the public all regulations and legal notices issued by Federal agencies and the President. This may include Presidential proclamations and Executive Orders and Federal agency documents having general applicability and legal effect; documents required to be published by act of Congress; and other Federal agency documents

231

of public interest. In addition, entries routinely include information on appropriate contacts within regulatory agencies. The *Federal Register* is published on working days and is available online without charge.

Other electronic means of accessing information on regulations also exist: indeed, the United States makes active use of leading edge technology to communicate information to the public. Dissemination of information in this way typically knows no borders and access to online information is unrestricted and free of charge. Extensive US use of the Internet across a wide range of government agencies and departments – many of which maintain highly informative, user-friendly websites – could prove a powerful tool in enhancing the transparency of regulatory processes and regulations world-wide. Clearly, however, ultimate responsibility for exploiting this possibility lies with users and their ability to effectively navigate such systems. In some cases, "information overload" may inadvertently cloud transparency if key data is not readily accessible.

Information on regulations is also available in the context of implementation of US WTO obligations. Title IV of the Trade Agreements Act of 1979, as amended by the Uruguay Round Agreements Act, or URAA, provides the legal basis on which the WTO Agreement on Technical Barriers to Trade (TBT Agreement) and the WTO Agreement on the Application of Sanitary and Phytosanitary Measures (SPS Agreement) were implemented in the United States. The US Administration's Statement of Administrative Action sets forth a detailed plan to guide the Executive Branch in implementing the obligations under these agreements. This includes the establishment of "enquiry points" to respond to requests for information as foreseen in the WTO Agreements. Contact information has been provided to the respective WTO Committees and is publicly available. Enquiry points also provide interested parties with more specific regulatory contacts in response to requests received.

Apart from regulatory authorities directly involved, one other government body is directly involved with transparency issues. The Office of the US Trade Representative (or USTR, part of the Executive Office of the President) oversees implementation of transparency provisions relating to US obligations contained in the WTO and other trade agreements. This oversight concerns not only obligations regarding transparency, but also those concerning non-discrimination; national treatment; prohibition of unnecessary obstacles to trade; the use of international standards, recommendations and guidelines; and considerations of equivalence.

USTR plays the lead role in the development of US policy on trade and trade-related investment. An interagency trade policy mechanism was established under the Trade Expansion Act of 1962 to assist USTR with its implementation of these responsibilities.

USTR is not directly concerned with the making of domestic regulations on a day-to-day basis. However, the interagency mechanism it leads is intended to play a co-ordinating role in encouraging government-wide awareness of and respect for international obligations relating to domestic regulatory matters, such as GATT Article III (National Treatment on Internal Taxation and Regulation) and regulatory commitments arising from other WTO Agreements, such as the Technical Barriers to Trade (TBT), Sanitary and Phytosanitary Measures (SPS), and Basic Telecommunications Agreements.

For all its strengths, this essentially legalistic approach to trade policy making may be detracting from a wider opportunity to ensure greater complementarity between trade and domestic policies. In this sense, the broad reach of the interagency trade policy mechanism across different layers of decision-making may present an informal (though perhaps under-utilised) opportunity to infuse domestic regulatory activities with greater attention to market openness considerations. In particular, more active promotion of the efficient regulation principles through the mechanism could help shape a new regulatory culture responsive to the needs of international trade and investment. As currently structured (and with the notable exception of independent regulatory agencies), the mechanism involves a wide range of agencies and policymakers:

– Three tiers of committees develop US Government positions on international trade and trade-related investment issues. The Trade Policy Review Group (TPRG) and the Trade Policy Staff Committee (TPSC), administered and chaired by USTR, are the subcabinet interagency trade policy co-ordination groups central to this process. The TPSC, the first line operating group, is represented by senior civil servants. Supporting the TPSC are more than 60 subcommittees responsible for specialised areas and several task forces charged with particular issues.

– Member agencies of the TPRG and the TPSC include the Departments of Commerce, Agriculture, State, Treasury, Labor, Justice, Defence, Interior, Transportation, Energy, and Health and Human Services, the Environmental Protection Agency, Office of Management and Budget, the Council of Economic Advisers, the International Development Co-operation Agency, the National Economic Council, and the National Security Council. The US International Trade Commission is a non-voting member of the TPSC and an observer at TPRG meetings. Representatives of other agencies may also be invited to attend meetings depending on the specific issues discussed.

– The final, third tier of the interagency trade policy mechanism is the National Economic Council (NEC) chaired by the President. NEC representation includes the Vice President, the Secretaries of State, the Treasury, Agriculture, Commerce, Labor, Housing and Urban Development, Transportation, Energy, the Administrator of the Environmental Protection Agency, the Chair of the Council of Economic Advisers, the Director of OMB, USTR, the National Security Advisor, and the Assistants to the President for Economic Policy, Domestic Policy, and Science and Technology Policy. All executive departments and agencies, whether or not represented on the NEC, co-ordinate economic policy through the NEC.

During interagency review of US trade and trade-related investment policies, advice is generally sought from private sector advisory committees and from Congress. Virtually all issues are developed and formulated through the interagency process, though in some cases USTR advice may differ from that of the interagency committees. While USTR ultimately assumes responsibility for directing the implementation of policy decisions as they are made, it may delegate this responsibility to other agencies where desirable or appropriate.

A *reverse* interagency mechanism – one which would formalise consultation among the trade policy agencies (including USTR) and other government agencies during the development and formulation of domestic regulations – does not exist. This point is revisited under Section 2.3 on measures to avoid unnecessary trade restrictiveness.

In sum, federal regulatory procedures are highly transparent and open. The United States ranks among top OECD performers in terms of opportunities for public (including foreign) consultation and comment, publication of regulatory measures and notification to international organisations, and use of the Internet (see Figure 1). These strengths, evident in most OECD countries, are closely linked to observance of international trade obligations and strong political traditions for open decision-making processes.

Nonetheless, federal regulatory procedures tell only part of the story. The complexity and reach of subfederal regulation underscores the need to encourage respect for transparency and other efficient regulation principles at state and local levels as well. While GATT Article XXIV:12 requires each WTO Member to "take such reasonable measures as may be available to it to ensure observance of the provisions of this Agreement by the regional and local governments and authorities within its territory" (an approach reflected also in the WTO TBT Agreement), ultimate responsibility for adherence to transparency and other principles of efficient regulation lies with the subfederal authorities concerned. In practice, the US government has not found it necessary to interpret GATT Article XXIV:12 language. Its self-described approach is to use all reasonable measures, including legal means, to encourage compliance by subfederal authorities. For regulatory matters, the United States interprets existing GATT language to mean it will actively educate and promote such compliance, and it has accepted responsibility at the Federal level on behalf of the states. However, the US position on whether or not existing GATT language requires affirmative action to force subfederal authorities into compliance or to eliminate inconsistent state regulation is less clear.[6] Box 2 in Section 2.2 illustrates the kinds of (discriminatory) subfederal regulatory measures which have created trade and investment frictions in the past.

2.2. Measures to ensure non-discrimination

Application of non-discrimination principles aims to provide effective equality of competitive opportunities between like products and services irrespective of country of origin. Thus, the extent to which respect for two core principles of the multilateral trading system – Most-Favoured-Nation (MFN) and National Treatment (NT) – is actively promoted when developing and applying regulations is a helpful gauge of a country's overall efforts to promote trade and investment-friendly regulation.

On the other hand, preferential agreements give more favourable treatment to specified countries and are thus inherent departures from the MFN and NT principles. The extent of a country's participation in preferential agreements (which overall can be trade-creating or trade-diverting) is not in itself indicative of a lack of commitment to the principle of non-discrimination. However, in assessing such commitment it is relevant to consider the attitudes of participating countries towards non-members in

---

Box 2. **Subfederal regulation and market openness**

As discussed in the background report on Government Capacity to Assure High Quality Regulation, US regulation is a complex mix of federal, state and local rules and enforcement procedures. The 50 state governments have legal and regulatory authority in their areas of competence, including all areas not expressly pre-empted by federal legislation, and may delegate this authority to regional, local or municipal governments.

While there has been a marked concentration of regulatory powers at the federal level in recent years, state and local regulation has maintained a significant profile on the international trade and investment agenda. Ensuring transparency of subfederal regulation in the first instance is crucial to international market openness. However, as the following cases illustrate, rigorous attention to ensuring non-discriminatory subfederal regulation is also necessary:

- In a June 1992 case involving both federal and state measures affecting alcoholic and malt beverages, a GATT panel found that foreign (in this case Canadian) producers were effectively discriminated against by certain state regulatory requirements in respect of such issues as listing and delisting policies; beer alcohol content; distribution to points of sale, transport into states by common carriers (as opposed to transportation of a product by a producer or wholesaler in its own vehicle), and licensing fees.*

- Government procurement laws at the state and local level contain "Buy American" and "Buy Local" provisions similar to those contained in the federal Buy American Act which accord preferential treatment to domestically and locally produced goods. These provisions are superseded by non-discrimination commitments under the WTO GPA, when applicable (this to the credit of the United States, which was under no obligation to subject its state entities to the GPA). In addition, some states (*e.g.*, California) have recently amended their laws to prevent preferential treatment. However, with state governments accounting for roughly half of all US government purchases, considerable scope remains for discriminatory purchasing practices at the subfederal level.

- State procurement laws can also take on an extraterritorial dimension in support of broader political objectives. In 1996, Massachusetts enacted a law regulating state contracts with companies doing business with or in Burma (Myanmar). According to one trading partner, the state government created a "restricted purchase list" of companies that met a set of "negative criteria" stipulated in the law. In principle, countries so identified would be barred from bidding on state contracts or, when allowed to bid, subject to less favourable terms than those available to non-listed companies. On 4 November 1998, the US District Court found the Law to be unconstitutional as it impinged on the exclusive authority of the federal government to regulate foreign affairs.

---

* See United States: Measures Affecting Alcoholic and Malt Beverages, Report by the Panel adopted on June 1992 in Basic Instruments and Selected Documents (39S/206).

Sources: GATT Basic Instruments and Selected Documents; 1998 Report on the WTO Consistency of Trade Policies by Major Trading Partners (Industrial Structure Council, Japan).

respect of transparency and the potential for discriminatory effects. Third countries need access to information about the content and operation of preferential agreements in order to make informed assessments of any impact on their own commercial interests. In addition, substantive approaches to regulatory issues such as standards and conformity assessment can introduce potential for discriminatory treatment of third countries (if, for example, standards recognised by partners in a preferential agreement would be difficult to meet by third countries).

Preferential agreements to which the United States is party, including two free trade agreements[7] and a network of bilateral investment agreements (essentially investment protection instruments with partners from the developing countries and transition economies),[8] are managed in a highly transparent manner. Information on such arrangements is readily available to interested non-parties through a variety of avenues. Generally, information on actions to be taken by the United States and requests for comments on proposed actions are published in the *Federal Register*. In addition, information on preferential agreements is typically made available by US government agencies concerned through a variety of means, including press statements, fact sheets, and the Internet. Submission of information to relevant WTO bodies in accordance with WTO obligations establishes another avenue for information, and both of the FTAs to which the United States is party encourage and require transparency through public notice. Collection and publication of relevant data by other international organisations (such as UNCTAD's *Compendium of International Investment Instruments*) further contributes to ensuring the transparency of preferential arrangements. In sum, available evidence points to well-orchestrated and good faith efforts in the United States to share this kind of information as widely as possible.

Importantly, comments by third parties on US preferential agreements are welcomed, either in response to a public request for comment published in the *Federal Register*, in the appropriate forum of the WTO, or on an *ad hoc* basis to the relevant US government agency. At the same time, with the notable exception of relevant international obligations, third countries or foreign firms which consider themselves prejudiced by these agreements enjoy no specific rights of recourse under US law.

There is no overarching requirement in US law or in Presidential policy to incorporate MFN and NT principles into domestic regulations. Here again, USTR is responsible for the implementation of non-discrimination provisions *insofar as obligations stemming from the* WTO *and other international trade and trade-related investment are concerned*. However, USTR seems too far removed from day-to-day regulatory activities to exert a systematic effect on individual decisions.

Overtly discriminatory regulatory content is fairly exceptional when viewed in a broad, economy-wide context. Existing measures which discriminate against foreign ownership tend to be fairly limited in scope (see discussion in Section 3) and complete or partial deregulation across many sectors of the economy has already generated attendant pro-competitive effects for international market openness. However, enduring exceptions to this general trend remain. Expressly discriminatory (nationality-based) elements in regulatory structures for maritime transport services, domestic air services or trucking cabotage, for example, effectively preclude foreign participation in these sectors.[9]

Other examples may be found of regulations that are inconsistent with the non-discrimination principle. US commitments in the WTO Financial Services Agreement grandfather certain deviations from the non-discrimination principle more generally. For instance, foreign banks are required to register under the Investment Advisers Act of 1940 to engage in securities advisory and investment management services in the United States, while domestic banks are exempt from registration. The registration requirement involves record maintenance, inspections, submission of reports and payment of a fee. Foreign banks cannot be members of the Federal Reserve System, and thus may not vote for directors of a Federal Reserve Bank. Foreign-owned bank subsidiaries are not subject to this measure.[10] Some states require direct branches or agencies of foreign banks to register under securities broker-dealer or investment adviser measures, while bank subsidiaries of foreign banks are exempt from such registration to the same extent as domestic banks incorporated in the state. These limitations do not apply to federally licensed branches or agencies. Some states require direct branches or agencies of foreign banks, but not bank subsidiaries of foreign banks, to register or obtain licenses in order to engage in some banking activities. Some states restrict various commodities transactions by foreign bank branches and agencies, but not by other depository financial institutions. Offers and sales of securities to foreign bank branches and agencies in the some states are subject to registration/disclosure require-ments that do not apply if the transaction involves other financial institutions. Federal and state law do not permit a credit union, savings bank, home loan or thrift business in the United States to be pro-vided through branches of corporations organised under a foreign country's law. In order to accept or maintain domestic retail deposits of less than $100 000, a foreign bank must establish an insured bank-ing subsidiary. This requirement does not apply to a foreign bank branch that was engaged in insured deposit-taking activities on 19 December 1991.

There may also be certain deviations from the principle of non-discrimination which arise from inconsistencies between the US GATS commitments and its preferential commitments made in bilateral or regional trade arrangements such as NAFTA. For instance, with respect to banking and other financial services (excluding insurance), in the US Schedule to the GATS Financial Services Agreement, there is an MFN exception made for broker-dealers registered under US law that have their principal place of business in Canada. Such broker dealers may maintain their required reserves in a bank in Canada sub-ject to the supervision of Canada.[11] Also, for purposes of the Glass-Steagall Act – which provides for cer-tain separation of ownership of banks, trusts, insurance companies and industrial companies – Canadian government securities fall within an exempt category so that Canadian banks may underwrite and trade in such securities without prohibition which would otherwise be the case.

In some cases, social regulations may be designed and implemented in ways which may give rise to discriminatory *effects*. A useful illustration of how this has occurred in the United States was the EPA's CAFE regulation noted earlier in Box 1. CAFE regulations enacted in support of the Energy Policy and Conservation Act of 1975 required automobile manufacturers and importers to achieve specified aver-age fuel economy standards for their entire fleets, but stipulated that these be calculated separately for domestic and imported vehicles. In 1994, a GATT panel established at the request of the European Commission found, *inter alia*, that the separate fleet accounting methodology used for imported vehicles effectively placed large foreign cars at a competitive disadvantage *vis-à-vis* like domestic products.[12] Explicit attention to the principle of non-discrimination during the design of the CAFE regime may have averted this dispute.

The discriminatory effects of subfederal regulation continue to attract the attention of foreign trad-ers and investors, suggesting a need for more focused efforts at the federal level to ensure respect for non-discrimination and other efficient regulation principles by state and local regulators. Recent illus-trative examples of state-level regulation (Box 2) show that discriminatory regulation has been developed in some cases in support of domestic producers or broader social objectives.

Discriminatory elements of the US regulatory regime therefore range from overt (nationality-based) to more subtle regulatory schemes in other policy areas (such as the environment) with the potential to introduce discriminatory effects. Nationality-based restrictions still operative in a number of important sectors (see also discussion in Section 3) have in some cases been in place for long periods, suggesting the need for a comprehensive review of prevailing measures and their economic rationales. As seen in Box 2, subfederal regulation also risks generating discriminatory effects.

2.3. Measures to avoid unnecessary trade restrictiveness

To attain a particular regulatory objective, policy makers should seek regulations that are not more trade restrictive than necessary to fulfil a legitimate objective, taking account of the risks non-fulfilment would create. Examples of this approach would be to use performance-based rather than design stan-dards as the basis of a technical regulation, or to consider taxes or tradable permits in lieu of regula-tions to achieve the same legitimate policy goal. At the procedural level, effective adherence to this principle entails consideration of the extent to which specific provisions require or encourage regulators to avoid unnecessary trade restrictiveness (and the rationale for any exceptions), how the impact of new regulations on international trade and investment is assessed, the extent to which trade policy bodies as well as foreign traders and investors are consulted in the regulatory process, and means for ensuring access by foreign parties to dispute settlement.

In the United States, the principal tool for measuring the effects of proposed federal regulations is the regulatory impact analysis, or RIA (see related discussion in the background report on Government Capacity to Assure High Quality Regulation). For "significant" regulatory actions (defined as having an annual effect on the economy of $100 million or more or adversely affecting in a material way the economy, a sector of the economy, productivity, competition, jobs, the environment, public health or safety, or State, local or tribal governments or communities), agencies must generally provide to OIRA the following additional information:

- an assessment, including the underlying analysis, of benefits anticipated from the regulatory action (such as, but not limited to, the promotion of the efficient functioning of the economy and private markets, the enhancement of health and safety, environmental protection, and the elimination or reduction of discrimination or bias) together with, to the extent feasible, a quantification of those benefits;

- an assessment, including the underlying analysis, of costs anticipated from the regulatory action (such as, but not limited to, the direct cost both to the government in administering the regulation and to businesses and others in complying with the regulation, and any adverse effects on the efficient functioning of the economy, private markets (including productivity, employment and competitiveness) health, safety, and the natural environment, together with, to the extent feasible, a quantification of those costs; and

- an assessment of costs and benefits of potentially effective and reasonably feasible alternatives to the planned regulation, identified by the agencies or the public (including improving the current regulation and reasonably viable nonregulatory actions), and an explanation why the planned regulatory action is preferable to the identified potential alternatives.

Thus, there is no specific provision requiring an assessment of the impact of proposed regulatory measures on inward trade and investment. In principle, nothing would bar a discussion of effects on market openness in the context of broad economic effects outlined above with respect to covered "significant" rules. However, were they to occur at all and in the absence of any other guidance, it seems reasonable to expect that such discussions would more likely relate to effects on outward trade and investment (as US firms often charge that regulatory burdens detract from their global competitiveness) than on market openness concerns.

In practice, therefore, information concerning the potential impact of a proposed rule on inward trade and investment is most likely to surface during the public comment phase. As seen earlier, this comment period is open to both foreign and domestic parties. Still, in the absence of a formalised requirement to assess the impact of a proposed regulation on inward trade and investment, the onus is on foreign firms to make their concerns known. Their capacity to do so effectively is thus closely linked to the transparency issue.

It should be recalled here that the RIA mechanism does not cover the rulemaking activities of the independent federal regulators. As seen earlier, the APA sets out detailed rulemaking procedures to be followed by all federal government agencies – including the independent regulators. But only Executive Branch agencies are subject to additional rule-making provisions like the RIA required by the President.

The APA does not formally require or encourage an assessment of the impact of proposed rules on international trade and investment and lacks the broad "economic effects" language present in the RIA under which such an analysis could theoretically occur. While this incongruity might be perceived as a procedural shortcoming, it does not necessarily imply that the independent federal regulators are less attuned to the possible impact of proposed rules on trade and investment than might be otherwise be the case in an RIA setting. In practice, APA-governed rulemaking in sectors characterised by international trade and investment activity (such as the telecommunications sector) may reflect a greater sensitivity to trade and investment impacts than might be the case through a broader regulatory oversight function, if only due to the active role played by foreign parties in shaping the process.

OMB and USTR consult informally when questions arise with respect to the WTO legality of proposed regulations, and may also do so before a regulation goes forward for publication in draft in the Federal Register. In such instances, OMB, USTR and the regulatory authority concerned seek to ensure that proposed regulatory measures are in line with US obligations under the WTO and other trade agreements. In addition, Title IV of the Trade Agreements Act of 1979 (19 USC 2532) (as amended by the URAA) specifically prohibits US agencies from using standards, technical regulations or conformity assessment procedures, including sanitary and phytosanitary measures, as unnecessary obstacles to trade. Under US law, unnecessary obstacles to trade are not created if the demonstrable purpose of the standards-related activity is to achieve a legitimate domestic objective (*e.g.*, protection of health or safety) and if such activity does not operate to exclude imported products which fully meet those legitimate objectives. Section 402 specifically obliges agencies to ensure that imported products are treated no less favourably than like domestic or other imported products.

However, proposed regulatory measures with no immediately obvious implications for international obligations would normally escape such scrutiny. OMB staff members are not trained to assess the trade effects of proposed regulations. USTR is neither mandated nor adequately staffed to review the possible adverse effects on inward trade and trade-related investment of proposed regulations which, while they may be WTO-consistent on their face, may carry potential to introduce *de facto* discriminatory effects on some other level. Thus, responsibility for drawing out the possible impact of proposed rules on inward trade and investment ultimately lies with the regulators themselves and is overseen by foreign competitors, who may only be in a position to identify the trade-restrictive effects of a given regulation once the damage has occurred and trade frictions have arisen. In such cases, an ounce of prevention may well be worth more than a pound of cure.

Recalling the nature of some well-known trade frictions involving US regulations, it becomes clear that what was called into question was not a given domestic policy or its underlying objectives, but the fact that these policies or objectives could have been achieved just as or even more efficiently by using less trade-restrictive means. For example, CAFE standards were challenged on the grounds of the method for calculating fuel efficiency of foreign manufacturers; similarly, concerns with respect to the regulation of tuna harvesting related *inter alia* to the method for calculating the average incidental taking rate of foreign fleets.

In sum, the collective foreign experience with US domestic regulation and trade suggests that more could be done to ensure that the impact of proposed regulations on international market openness is systematically assessed in accordance with transparent, uniform criteria. Under the current system, USTR may only be consulted on an *ad hoc* basis, if at all, during regulatory decision-making on issues which may appear to have no direct implications for international trade obligations. Some government agencies may also take a "do-it-yourself" approach, conducting their own assessments of the trade effects of proposed regulations without soliciting input from USTR. At the same time, the magnitude of the problem – and the resources that would be required to redress it – need to be seen in perspective. Many domestic regulations that reflect societal values and preferences (*e.g.*, speed limits and drinking age) have no implications for international trade in goods or services and are therefore of no interest here. Nonetheless, the range of policy areas that *do* carry this potential seems sufficiently broad to warrant a more formalised vetting of proposed rules from a market openness perspective.

2.4. Measures to encourage use of internationally harmonised measures

Compliance with different standards and regulations for like products often presents firms wishing to engage in international trade with significant and sometimes prohibitive costs. Thus, when appropriate and feasible, reliance on internationally harmonised measures (such as global standards) as the basis of domestic regulations can readily facilitate expanded trade flows. National efforts to encourage the adoption of regulations based on harmonised measures, procedures for monitoring progress in the development and adoption of international standards, and incentives for regulatory authorities to seek out and apply appropriate international standards are thus important indicators of a country's commitment to efficient regulation.

In the United States standardisation and conformity assessment activities are decentralised with a mixture of public and private responsibilities and participants. The standards development process is mostly industry-led, operating on a private, voluntary basis, but including government participation. The Federal government on the other hand develops regulations, sets some standards, procures products and provides technical expertise to a host of standards committees. Technical experts from industry and government come together to support the activities of more than 600 private standards-setting bodies. The American National Standards Institute (ANSI), a federation of industry, standard setting bodies and government agencies, serves as an "umbrella" organisation. ANSI has adhered to the TBT Code of Good Practice on behalf of its Member organisations and is the recognised US member body to ISO, IEC, the Pacific Area Standards Congress (PASC) and the Pan American Standards Commission (COPANT).

US government policy with respect to standardisation, as expressed in the National Technology Transfer and Advancement Act (NTTA) of 1995 and guidance issued by OMB pursuant to that Law directs Federal agencies to participate in voluntary standards development activities and to use voluntary consensus standards in lieu of purely government standards except where inconsistent with law or otherwise impractical. This is in recognition that many voluntary consensus standards are appropriate or adaptable for the Government's procurement and regulatory purposes.

Standardisation activities under the NTTA are co-ordinated by the National Institute of Standards and Technology (NIST). NIST is an agency of the US Department of Commerce's Technology Administration and its primary mission is to develop and apply technology, measurements and standards in co-operation with industry. The NTTA Act requires NIST to co-ordinate activities with other federal agencies to achieve greater reliance on voluntary standards and conformity assessment bodies with lessened dependence on in-house standards. Co-ordination takes place through the Interagency Committee on Standards Policy (ICSP).

NIST prerogatives are exercised through a host of services, including : the Office of Standards Services (OSS), which formulates and implements standards-related policies and procedures and provides representation to domestic and international organisations and federal agencies concerned with standardisation, product testing, certification, laboratory accreditation, and other forms of conformity assessment; the National Voluntary Laboratory Accreditation Programme (NVLAP), which provides third-party accreditation of testing and calibration laboratories; or the National Center for Standards and Certification Information (NCSCI), which is a central repository for standards-related information in the United States. NCSCI provides access to standards, technical regulations, and related documents published by US and foreign governments as well as by domestic, foreign, and international private-sector standards organisations. It also serves as the US enquiry point under the TBT Agreement and NAFTA. All proposed US government rules (mandatory technical requirements or conformity assessment systems), including proposed revisions, are published in the Federal Register by the responsible Federal agency. NCSCI staff regularly review the Register to identify those proposed regulations that might potentially affect trade and notify them to the WTO.

For WTO Members, a broad requirement to use international standards as the basis of domestic regulations stems only from adherence to multilaterally-agreed trade rules. However, departures from this basic obligation are permitted. Article 2.4 of the WTO TBT Agreement requires Members to use relevant international standards (or relevant parts of them) as a basis for their technical regulations "except when they would be an ineffective or inappropriate means for the fulfilment of legitimate objectives pursued". A parallel orientation in Article 3 of the Agreement on the Application of Sanitary and Phytosanitary Measures (SPS Agreement) requires Members to base their sanitary or phytosanitary measures on international standards, guidelines, or recommendations, where they exist, although Members may introduce or maintain measures based on more stringent standards under certain narrowly-defined conditions.

Accordingly, Title IV of the Trade Agreements Act of 1979, as amended by the URAA, calls upon agencies to take into consideration international standards and, when appropriate, to base their standards on international ones. In co-operation and co-ordination with relevant agencies, USTR is responsible for monitoring US compliance with WTO and any other international obligations relating to the use of internationally harmonised standards and certification procedures, and for responding to complaints by foreign governments on perceived violations of all obligations flowing from such agreements.

National defence, human health and safety, environmental protection, or technological consider-ations, and other rationales such as protection of animal or plant life or health or worker safety are amongst recognised exceptions which may justify departures from international standards and certifica-tion procedures as the basis of domestic regulations. The extent of US invocation of such exceptions in practice – or conversely, the extent of US reliance on international standards as the basis of domestic regulations – is difficult to discern in the absence of systematic efforts to monitor the adoption of internationally harmonised standards and certification procedures.

The United States has fostered the emergence of a host of significant leading standards widely used in the global market. In such settings, US standards tend to serve as *de facto* international stan-dards. However, the extent of US adherence to existing international standards is less clear. Some trad-ing partners allege a relatively low use of international standards in the United States as a cause of trade frictions. The European Commission, for example, points to "the relatively low use, or even aware-ness, of standards set by international standardising bodies" in the United States and further alleges that although a "significant number of US standards are claimed to be 'technically equivalent' to inter-national ones, and some are indeed widely used internationally, very few international standards are directly adopted" and that in some cases, "US standards are in direct contradiction to them".[13] The United States rejects such charges as based on an excessively narrow definition of international stan-dards and international standards bodies, a problem compounded in its view by the scarcity of factual data on adoption and use of international standards (see previous paragraph).

US trading partners are also concerned by what is perceived as an extremely complex combination of public and private, federal and sub-federal responsibilities, lacking a single co-ordination agent[14] (see also Section 3 below). They further criticise the considerable latitude available to private organisa-tions providing quality assurance, such as the Underwriters Laboratories, to impose – and modify frequently and unpredictably – the use of non-harmonised standards.[15]

World-wide acceptance of pioneer US product technology, standards and technical specifications may also have induced a disinterest on the part of certain US industry groups and standards setting bodies in international standardisation activities. As a result, some international standards have been developed without adequate US input or representation, creating concerns within the US administration about the consequences of this situation for US competitiveness.[16] In other cases, however, US industry has been actively engaged in global standardisation work, including in a leadership capacity.[17]

Fears that reliance on internationally harmonised measures may somehow lead to a lowering of domestic regulatory standards – or impatience with the generally slow pace of international standard-setting activities – may also be contributing to the situation. As provided for in WTO rules, there may also be legitimate reasons for departures from given international standards. Nonetheless, a lack of understanding on US policies and practices in this area suggests that much would be gained from a clar-ification of the extent to which international standards are in fact reflected in domestic regulations and a systematic assessment of the reasons for departures from this general principle.

2.5. Recognition of equivalence of other countries' regulatory measures

The pursuit of internationally harmonised measures may not always be possible, necessary or even desirable. In such cases, efforts should be made in order to ensure that cross-country disparities in reg-ulatory measures and duplicative conformity assessment systems do not act as barriers to trade. Recog-nising the equivalence of trading partners' regulatory measures or the results of conformity assessment performed in other countries are two promising avenues for achieving this result. In practice, both ave-nues are being pursued in the United States in various ways. Recognising certification given to foreign products by foreign laboratories is one example. Such recognition can be accorded unilaterally, but also through the mechanism of a Mutual Recognition Agreement (MRA) between trading partners. Another example arises when certification operates through self-declaration of conformity by manufacturers; in this case, recognition of equivalence means that declarations of conformity by foreign manufacturers are also accepted: foreign (as well as domestic) producers can assess the conformity of their product with requirements set in a given market as they deem appropriate and will be treated the same way by regulatory authorities. The latter may then test products on the market under established procedures and take necessary measures as warranted, regardless of the origin of products.

US WTO obligations again provide the chief context for the recognition of equivalence of other countries' regulatory measures and conformity assessment results. Title IV of the Trade Agreements Act of 1979, as amended by the URAA, is the legal basis for US implementation of the WTO TBT and SPS Agreements. Both Agreements expressly encourage Members to recognise other countries' technical regulations, SPS measures and results of conformity assessment procedures as equivalent, though in all cases Members retain ultimate discretion in deciding whether a satisfactory basis exists for doing so.[18] Section 492 of Subtitle F of the URAA (on International Standard-Setting Activities) contains specific provisions concerning equivalence determinations for sanitary and phytosanitary measures. USTR has overall responsibility for monitoring US compliance with these and other obligations under its trade agreements, in co-operation and co-ordination with relevant agencies, and for responding to complaints received from foreign governments concerning perceived violations of such obligations.

Determinations of equivalence of other countries' regulatory measures rest with the US regulatory authority concerned. In general, however, regulatory authorities would only recognise as equivalent those regulatory measures which afford the same level of regulatory protection as that established by US law. Individual regulators have wide discretion in deciding this issue and are not held to any broad-based criteria on how such determinations should be made. Irrespective of this shortcoming, however, US efforts to recognise trading partners regulatory measures as equivalent appear to be highly sporadic and generally reactive (in the face of related trade frictions) in nature. This may be attributable in part to the technical complexities of the task itself: establishing credible grounds for determinations of equivalence may itself be a resource-intensive, time-consuming and politically sensitive process. However, there may also be untapped potential for a more concerted, government-wide effort on this front, perhaps involving the business community. For example, TABD calls for the development of functionally equivalent standards in the automotive sector (see Box 4) may help foster greater adherence to this efficient regulation principle.

A number of US agencies permit the recognition of the results of conformity assessment regardless of the geographic location of the conformity assessment body (*e.g.*, via accreditation and/or recognition programmes which accept applications on a non-discriminatory basis).

A comprehensive list of regulatory measures and results of conformity assessment performed in other countries which are partially or fully recognised as equivalent by US regulatory bodies is not available. However, two concrete examples illustrate how the approach is applied in practice:

– The US Department of Transportation (DOT) recognises a declaration of conformity by manufacturers (or importers) of motor vehicles and motor vehicle equipment. Under US law, manufacturers are required to certify that their products comply with all applicable Federal Motor Vehicle Safety Standards (FMVSS). This certification is in the form of a permanent label affixed to the product. This label is required for all vehicles and equipment covered by the FMVSS, and must be present if a vehicle or equipment covered by the FMVSS is to enter the United States. For purposes of enforcement, DOT's National Highway Traffic Safety Administration (NHTSA) may test the vehicle or equipment for compliance with one or more of the FMVSS after the product is on the market. If the product fails the test, and either the manufacturer or NHTSA determines that the product, in fact, does not comply, the manufacturer must notify the product's owner and remedy the non-compliance at no cost to the owner. Additional penalties may also apply. A manufacturer outside the United States who offers its product for importation into the United States must submit itself to the jurisdiction of US Federal courts by designating an agent in the United States to receive legal papers on behalf of the manufacturer.

– The US Department of Labor Occupational Safety and Health Administration (OSHA) maintains a programme to ensure the safety of products used in the workplace. Under this programme, certain products (including electrical equipment) need to be certified by a "nationally recognised testing laboratory" (NRTL). Such a facility need not be geographically located in the United States to qualify as an NRTL. To obtain this status, a candidate facility must apply to OSHA and provide information on the relevant test standards for which it wishes to be recognised. OSHA then makes a determination as to whether these test standards are appropriate under its regulations (Part 1910 of Title 29 of the Code of Federal Regulations).

The United States also pursues recognition of other countries' regulations and conformity assessment procedures through negotiated MRAs at bilateral and regional levels. The US-EC MRA signed on 18 May 1998, for example, provides a broad framework for recognition of conformity assessment procedures and specific procedures to be followed in six areas (telecommunications equipment; electromagnetic compatibility; electrical safety; recreational craft; pharmaceutical good manufacturing practice; and medical devices). Similar initiatives are being pursued with Canada (for example, on fish inspection systems).

A basis for achieving greater compatibility of conformity assessment procedures and moving towards mutual recognition of test results has also been established in some regional trade agreements. Chapter 9 of NAFTA requires partner countries to "accredit, approve, license or otherwise recognise conformity assessment bodies in the territory of another Party" on a national treatment basis without requiring the negotiation of an additional agreement.[19] In addition, Parties are to give "sympathetic consideration" to requests by another to negotiate agreements for the mutual recognition of the results of another Party's conformity assessment procedures.[20] Sector-specific advances in the area of conformity assessment have also been made. For telecommunications equipment, Parties agreed to adopt as part of their conformity assessment procedures "provisions necessary to accept the test results from laboratories or testing facilities in the territory of another Party for tests performed in accordance with the accepting Party's standards-related measures and procedures".[21] Such provisions still leave scope for differing interpretations and resulting trade frictions. But they are promising steps in the right direction in an area fraught with potential for dispute.

Possible approaches to recognition of results of conformity assessment procedures are under consideration in APEC. Current discussions are addressing potential arrangements in such areas as electrical safety, electronic equipment, and telecommunications equipment. If and when agreed, such arrangements would be open to participation by individual APEC economies. Recognition of standards and conformity assessment issues are also on the agenda of other incipient regional economic integration agreements in which the United States is involved, notably the FTAA. Existing and incipient trade agreements thus continue to foster regulatory reform efforts in the United States and partner countries.

Beyond MRAs, the United States is also engaged in efforts to enhance market openness through other approaches to international co-operation on regulatory issues. Among the stated objectives of the EU-US Transatlantic Economic Partnership announced in May 1998 are the improvement of regulatory co-operation in such areas as manufactured goods; agriculture, including biotechnology; services; industrial tariffs; global electronic commerce; intellectual property rights; investment; government procurement; and competition and improvement of the efficiency and effectiveness of regulatory procedures such as standards, testing and certification.

The US business community has played an important role in prompting regulatory reform in this area. Working in tandem through the TABD, the US and European business communities have helped move their respective governments to act on regulatory barriers to trade, particular those posed by standards and conformity assessment issues. Based on its performance to date, the organisation of the TABD along sectoral and thematic lines (Box 3) seems to offer a useful formula for rapid and highly focused progress on regulatory issues. Identification of barriers encountered on the front lines of industry followed by pragmatic, business-developed approaches to reducing or eliminating such barriers has

---

Box 3.   **The Trans-Atlantic Business Dialogue: a business-driven approach
to regulatory reform**

The TABD was launched in Seville, Spain in November 1995 as part of the EU-US New Transatlantic Agenda. Its principal aim was to boost transatlantic trade and investment opportunities through the removal of costly inefficiencies caused by excessive regulation, duplicative product testing, redundant standards certification, and heterogeneous standards. The TABD is a unique, informal process for enhanced co-operation between the business community and governments of the United States and the European Union. CEOs and business associations work closely with government officials to develop joint policy recommendations for consideration by the European Commission and the US Administration. The TABD is co-chaired by two senior business executives from the EU and US, with about thirty working groups addressing a range of sectoral and horizontal issues. By mid-1998 the US and EU administrations had taken concrete action towards the implementation of one-third of the TABD recommendations, supported, *inter alia*, by the creation of a US Government interagency group on the implementation of TABD recommendations (a similar group having been created by the European Commission). The TABD expects as much as half of its recommendations to be implemented by December 1998.

More specifically, in the field of standards and conformity assessment, TABD's Transatlantic Advisory Committee on Standards, Certification, and Regulatory Policy (TACS) addresses issues in an open-ended set of goods and services sectors. Sixteen different sectors (among them aerospace, agri-biotech, automobiles, chemicals, and telecommunications services) are currently on the agenda, though new issues may be introduced on the basis of EU-US industry consensus. The TACS advocates a new transatlantic regulatory model for products based on the principle "approved once, accepted everywhere". Among instruments recommended by TACS to achieve this principle are MRAs for standards testing (to eliminate duplicative procedural requirements); greater acceptance in specific sectors of Manufacturer's Declarations of Conformity to standards and technical regulations; harmonisation of certain technical standards and regulations; increased transparency and regulatory co-operation between EU and US governments; and the use of performance-based standards rather than design specifications.

Source: TABD Website; TABD 1998 Mid-Year Report presented at the May 1998 EU-US Summit.

---

already yielded tangible results for traders and investors (such as the EU-US MRA). The challenge is to further extend and embrace this new paradigm for regulatory reform while ensuring that results achieved promote wider reduction of barriers at the multilateral level.

In sum, the United States has made limited progress towards broader recognition of equivalence of trading partners' regulatory measures and results of conformity assessment procedures. Taken together, unilateral approaches such as DOT's self-declaration of conformity with safety standards (for the automotive sector), occasional negotiation of bilateral MRAs in specific sectors, and pursuit of possible mechanisms for recognition of the results of conformity assessment procedures within the context of regional agreements suggest that US policy is moving in the right direction on this issue. Nonetheless, efforts in this area need to be intensified and accelerated. Heterogeneous or redundant standards and duplicative conformity assessment requirements continue to burden US trading relationships with extra and sometimes prohibitive costs. These issues, more acute in some sectors than others, are revisited in Section III.

2.6. Application of competition principles from an international perspective

The benefits of market access may be reduced by regulatory action condoning anticompetitive conduct or by failure to correct anticompetitive private actions that have the same effect. It is therefore important that regulatory institutions make it possible for both domestic and foreign firms affected by anti-competitive practices to present their positions effectively. The existence of procedures for hearing and deciding complaints about regulatory or private actions that impair market access and effective competition by foreign firms, the nature of the institutions that hear such complaints, and adherence to deadlines (if they exist) are thus key issues from an international market openness perspective.

Three main procedural avenues are open to foreign firms wishing to advance complaints against alleged anticompetitive regulatory or private actions: 1) judicial review of regulatory action; 2) the filing of a private lawsuit under the Clayton Act and any other relevant laws, such as state antitrust or "business torts" laws; and 3) provision of information and request for assistance from US antitrust authorities (the Department of Justice and the Federal Trade Commission). In some cases, federal regulatory agencies may also entertain complaints about the behaviour of regulated entities in accordance with other statutory administrative procedures.

At the federal level, most final agency decisions are subject to judicial review under the APA (5 USC. Sections 701 et seq.) and/or the specific terms of the agency's Congressional mandate. Courts may overturn agency action over matters of both law and fact, although the court review is not typically a de novo decision, and the agency's action does receive a degree of deference which may vary in different regulatory settings. For the most part, aggrieved foreign persons generally enjoy rights similar to aggrieved domestic persons to obtain such judicial review, though in practice foreign persons may find it more difficult to assert standing to complain due to the more indirect or remote effect that agency actions may have on their business or property. Agency rules may contain deadlines for decisions and time limits for filing appeals tend to be fairly short. The Courts, however, are usually not subject to any particular time limits, introducing a potential for protracted proceedings. A four-year statute of limitations for commencement of private antitrust complaints applies, and federal court rules contain certain time limits as well.

Under US law, persons injured in their business or property are entitled to obtain trebled money damages and/or injunctive relief for antitrust violations. These rights are very well established and frequently used. Neither the antitrust laws nor federal court rules contain discriminatory provisions against foreign plaintiffs seeking to conduct, or actually conducting, business in the United States.[22] Similarly, the Department of Justice and the FTC do not discriminate on the basis of nationality in their enforcement activities.

An exception, however, is the special legislation that ensures that joint ventures for research, development, and production (even between horizontal competitors) will not be judged by the *per se* standard, but instead by the multi-factor rule of reason.[23] The law also provides for a reduction in potential liability in private law suits to single damages, if parties file their joint venture plans with the enforcement agencies. This legislation may have different impacts on foreign parties and ventures than it does on US ones while the US authority has not been aware of any complaint from firms or of cases where the legislation had actual impact on joint venture parties. The guarantee of single-damages exposure for production activities only apply if: 1) the principal facilities are located in the United States; *and* 2) each person who controls any party to the joint venture is a US person, or comes from a country whose antitrust laws relating to production joint ventures provide national treatment for US persons.[24]

Often, domestic or foreign persons adversely affected by the behaviour of regulated enterprises may be able to obtain redress from the relevant regulatory body. Judicial remedies under state competition laws or state laws on breaches of contract or business torts may also be available. US authorities are unaware of any significant exceptions to these procedures, or significant market access complaints advanced by foreign persons in the last three years.

A particular setting for concern is the exertion or extension of market power by a regulated or protected monopolist into another market. The substantive problem, sometimes called "regulatory abuse", is addressed by US antitrust laws about monopolisation, as well as by US regulatory laws applied to particular markets. Foreign firms and trade could be implicated in two ways. First, an incumbent domestic regulated monopolist might gain an unfair advantage over foreign products or firms in an unregulated domestic market. Or, an incumbent foreign regulated monopolist might use the resources afforded by its protection at home to gain an unfair advantage in another country.

In the first case, the US regulated monopolist might use resources that its protection affords it to achieve unfair advantages over its suppliers and its potential competitors in markets where it lacks formal protection. Where the concern is with the effects in the United States arising from the extension or exertion of market power from one regulated market to another non-regulated market, the US antitrust and other regulatory laws might apply to sanction that conduct. Particular applications would depend on the scope of regulatory authority, or of any antitrust immunity (for further discussion, see background report on The Role of Competition Policy in Regulatory Reform). However, there may well be disputes about whether a particular conduct falls within a regulatory agency's authority to grant immunity from antitrust liability. These "regulatory abuse" scenarios are arising frequently in domestic US energy and telecommunications regulation. It may be that foreign firms and trade are also involved, but the United States indicated that it did not have comprehensive data about significant complaints by foreign firms during the past three years concerning the situations described above.

In the second case, the regulated monopolist is a foreign firm, and its regulated market is a foreign market. In principle, US substantive antitrust law about "regulatory abuse" would apply if there were effects in the US market. But in this setting, some technical exemptions could apply. For example, US courts might not apply the law to the actions of foreign state owned enterprises that are not engaging in a commercial activity; or to actions that are compelled (rather than merely sanctioned or encouraged) by a foreign government. In general though, if the foreign monopolist is exerting or extending its market power into the US market, it would not be insulated from US legal sanction. The United States indicated that it did not have comprehensive data about significant complaints during the past three years concerning regulatory or antitrust treatment of foreign firms with monopoly power in the situations described above. It is worth noting, however, that in the telecommunications sector several major US service suppliers have been very supportive of the provisions in the GATS and the Reference Paper to the WTO Basic Telecommunications Agreement relating to the abuse by a monopoly service supplier of its monopoly position outside the scope of its monopoly rights.

Whether the concern with the exertion or extension of market power from a regulated market to a non-regulated market is with respect to a foreign or domestic firm, the procedures available for hearing and deciding complaints would be as described above. However, because foreign persons, even when they have a significant US commercial nexus, often have the location of the pertinent conduct abroad, a variety of additional considerations may militate against taking action. There may be questions of jurisdiction, international comity, appropriate choice of forum or the practical effectiveness of efforts to obtain evidence or order relief.

On balance, US regulatory procedures for initiating and advancing complaints about alleged anti-competitive regulatory or private actions are broadly satisfactory from the perspective of international market openness. However, the issues raised in the preceding paragraphs may benefit from further consideration.

3. ASSESSING RESULTS IN SELECTED SECTORS

This Section examines the implications for international market openness arising from US regulations currently in place for four sectors (two manufacturing and two service sectors): telecommunications equipment; telecommunications services; automobiles and components; and electricity (generation and access to transmission grid). For each sector, an attempt has been made to draw out the effects of sector-specific regulations on international trade and investment and the extent to which the six efficient regulation principles are explicitly or implicitly applied. Particular attention is paid to product standards and conformity assessment procedures, where relevant. Other issues addressed here include efforts to adopt internationally harmonised product standards, use of voluntary product standards by regulatory authorities, and openness and flexibility of conformity assessment systems. In many respects, multilateral disciplines, notably the WTO TBT Agreement, provide a sound basis for reducing trade tensions by encouraging respect for fundamental principles of efficient regulation such as transparency, non-discrimination, and avoidance of unnecessary trade restrictiveness.

3.1. Telecommunications equipment

The US market for telecommunications equipment is the largest in the world and, since the AT&T divestiture, one of the most open. Competition between domestic and foreign suppliers is intense, with imports accounting for over 20 per cent of the market in recent years. Current industry trends such as liberalisation of telecommunications services markets, consolidation through mergers, acquisitions, and strategic alliances, and the convergence of digital and communications technologies are driving a further globalisation of the sector, presenting foreign suppliers with opportunities for expanded trade in the US and other markets.

The 1984 break-up of AT&T fostered a number of pro-competitive developments in the market for telecommunications equipment. First, the Department of Justice broke off equipment manufacturing from the Regional Bell Operating Companies (RBOCs) on the grounds that if monopoly local exchange carriers had equipment-producing subsidiaries, rate-of-return regulation would give them an artificially large incentive to meet their needs in-house rather than looking to other (possible foreign) suppliers. Second, the 1984 divestiture gave rise to a competitive long-distance services market. This in turn promoted a more open equipment market with several purchasers seeking to realise lower costs, greater market share, and deeper profits through competitive procurement.

The positive performance of US telecommunications equipment markets, including from the market openness perspective, has been most readily apparent in the area of terminal equipment (also called customer premise equipment – *e.g.*, phone sets, fax machines and modems). This is largely attributable to specific FCC decisions (the First Order and Second Order Registration Programmes) which have granted customers freedom to connect their own terminal equipment. These decisions essentially precluded incumbent carriers from arbitrarily deciding which equipment could be connected to their networks, thus loosening their hold on exclusive purchasing patterns. A surge in imports resulted as many US firms globalised their manufacturing bases.

The performance of the network equipment market (*e.g.*, switches and transmission equipment) from the perspective of market openness has been less clear-cut. One trading partner, for example, has claimed that its prospective exporters are burdened by heavy costs of compliance with US equipment standards (including environmental and safety standards); significant delays in obtaining required certification by US-based bodies; and difficulties in getting listed as potential suppliers by large network equipment users, notably AT&T and the RBOCs.[25] However, the FCC maintains that US carriers have procured significant amounts of equipment, including network switches, from foreign firms.

The focal point for US regulatory activities in the sector is the FCC's Office of Engineering and Technology (OET). As for all other independent federal agencies, administrative procedures are governed by the APA, and OMB's regulatory oversight activities do not extend to proposed rules for the sector. Mirroring the APA's principal strengths, regulatory procedures for telecommunications equipment are broadly trade-friendly, scoring high in terms of key principles such as transparency and openness of decision-making. Like other Commission bureaux, OET has made exemplary use of the Internet in support of such goals. For example, all FCC Rules and Regulations under OET responsibility are available on-line; an on-line Equipment Authorisation Database allows applicants to electronically file applications for equipment authorisation and to check their status; and a "Frequently Asked Questions" site clearly outlines procedures for importation of electronic equipment and radio transmitters, linking users to relevant provisions in the Code of Federal Regulations.

The regulatory framework for telecommunication equipment is broadly trade and investment-friendly. Measures stemming from international trade obligations, notably those under WTO TBT Agreement, require or encourage explicit recognition of non-discrimination (MFN and NT) principles; the avoidance of unnecessary trade restrictiveness; and encourage the use of internationally harmonised standards and certification procedures wherever possible and appropriate[26] (though a broad range of exceptions relating to issues such as national defence, technological considerations, or "other legitimate domestic objectives" may result in a departure from this general stance in this as in other sectors). Efforts have been made towards recognition of the "functional equivalence" of regulatory measures in other countries as well as recognition of the results of conformity assessment procedures carried out in other countries. The signature in May 1998 of an MRA with the European Union on conformity assessment covering telecommunications equipment and electromagnetic compatibility is one illustration of this trend. In addition, recent efforts by the FCC to move a growing number of products to suppliers' self-declarations of compliance and consequent reductions in the number of products still requiring explicit FCC authorisations prior to marketing or importation should go a considerable distance to improving market openness.

Regulatory content for the sector is by nature complex, reflecting the technical sophistication of telecommunications networks and the radio spectrum. However, a wide range of technical standards applicable to individual types of equipment and additional requirements for FCC-issued equipment authorisations for certain products are neither discriminatory nor excessively burdensome in comparison with most other countries' regulatory frameworks.

Standards-setting for the sector is an essentially industry-driven process which is open and transparent in nature. Compliance with FCC-defined product standards relating to issues such as safety and technical compatibility with US systems are also of central importance in gaining entry to the US market.[27] Here, differences between US and other national regulations on telecommunications equipment and the related need for conformity assessment continue to introduce scope for trade friction.

Concerns of this nature appear to be largely borne out by some US trading partners. Prevailing cross-country divergence in product standards, costs of certification procedures relating to certain US Federal and State standards applicable to the sector (including environmental and safety standards)[28] and delays in approval processes are recurrent themes in this context. Moreover, rapid technological progress in the sector has fostered a surge in industry-driven standards development here as elsewhere in the world. In light of the potential for increasing trade tension, this argues for more attention to the use of existing international standards as the basis of domestic regulations as well as more vigorous participation in the development of new, flexible international standards capable of embracing improvements in US as well as foreign technology. At the same time, this approach may not always be workable, as when the industry-driven process leads to multiple standards rather than a unique single standard. In such cases, US practice is to enable the market to decide what standards to implement and allow industry to determine support for equipment based on particular standards.

Much of this points to the fundamental issue, from a market openness perspective, of a pro-competitive, open and transparent setting for standard-making activities. As earlier noted, sectoral regulation is a mix of industry and government-defined standards. However, recent steps taken in response to the Telecommunications Act of 1996 suggest that the US regulator may be moving away from its role as standard-setter towards an enhanced advisory role to industry. For example, the United States is seeking to propose a framework intended to encourage competition for manufactured products through the increased availability of network and planning information and fair and open forums for establishing equipment standards and for certifying equipment in the industry setting.

Procurement of telecommunications equipment is another area which has been prone to trade friction, with at least one trading partner alleging that opportunities for foreign suppliers are restricted by historical purchasing patterns between US telecommunications companies and domestic suppliers and by adherence of rural telephone co-operatives to "Buy America" requirements for purchases of telecommunications equipment.[29]

Regulatory barriers to trade in telecommunications (terminal) equipment have been or are currently being addressed in a number of regional trade fora involving the United States and may provide useful models for enhanced market openness. NAFTA, for example, sets clearly-defined parameters on standards-related measures relating to attachment of terminal or other equipment to public telecommunications transport networks, including those measures relating to the use of testing and measuring equipment for conformity assessment procedures.[30] In APEC, guidelines have been adopted for a regional harmonisation of telecommunications equipment certification procedures, and sector-specific standards and regulatory policy issues are being explored in both the TABD and FTAA settings. Concrete progress towards enhanced US market openness for the trading partners concerned and its possible impact on third countries in still difficult to discern. However, the transparency of these efforts, the global reach of the key issues, and continued dynamism of telecommunications equipment markets around the world suggest that initiatives such as these are likely to yield a wider model for market-opening regulatory reform. The successful negotiation (at US instigation) of the Information Technology Agreement has led on to negotiations on ITA II and seems likely to yield important dividends in improving regulatory style and content for the sector.

In sum, the regulatory style in this sector is fairly well-adapted to the requirements of international market openness. Regulatory decision-making procedures are highly transparent and open and inroads have been made towards recognising the equivalence of trading partners' regulatory measures and conformity assessment systems at bilateral and regional levels. Other initiatives, notably recent FCC moves to "graduate" more products to self-declarations of compliance, are particularly encouraging in light of significant costs and delays sometimes associated with third-party certification procedures. More systematic consultation between the regulator and trade policy bodies could help ensure that new regulations, when required, are modelled after the efficient regulation principles. Where possible, greater reliance on international equipment standards as the basis of domestic regulation and deeper commitment to the development of global standards may alleviate trade friction (though as noted in the Section on the use of internationally harmonised measures definitional and interpretative differences cloud this issue). In the longer term, however, a more promising avenue may lie in broader support for transparent industry-driven standards-making processes open to all interested players, domestic or foreign.

3.2. Telecommunications services

Progressive liberalisation of the US market for telecommunications services over time has earned this sector a strong historical record of international market openness. Certain US service sectors such as domestic long distance, international value added network services, and the IMTS switched resale (basic telephony) market have been open to foreign participation for years. More recently, important policy developments at national and international levels have dramatically altered the competitive landscape for telecommunications services and further improved prospects for enhanced market openness in the sector. At the national level, the *Foreign Carrier Entry Order* issued by the FCC in November 1995 ushered in a new regulatory philosophy on foreign participation in the US telecommunications market. But the defining event in shaping the current US regulatory regime for foreign participation in the telecommunications services market was the successful conclusion in February 1997 of the WTO agreement on basic telecommunications. With its entry into force on 5 February 1998, the agreement set telecommunications services on the path of progressive liberalisation and pro-competitive regulatory reform in 72 signatory countries, including the United States and most of the world's major trading nations. The United States made significant market-opening commitments in the agreement and joined 64 other WTO Members in subscribing to a Reference Paper on Pro-Competitive Regulatory Principles.[31] The FCC acted quickly to give concrete effect to the agreement through the creation of a new regulatory framework for international telecommunications.

Substantive regulation and market openness in the sector are thus best understood from pre and post-WTO agreement perspectives. Pre-WTO, foreign participation in the market was regulated on the basis of the *Foreign Carrier Entry Order*. The Order had three main objectives: *a)* to promote effective competition in the US telecommunications services market, particularly the market for international telecommunications services; *b)* to prevent anticompetitive conduct in the provision of international service facilities; and *c)* to encourage foreign governments to open their own communications markets. This latter objective was pursued through application of a reciprocity-based "effective competitive opportunities" (ECO) test[32] as part of an overall public interest analysis for authorisations relating to the provision of international telecommunications services under Section 214 of the Communications Act, indirect foreign ownership of common carrier radio licenses under Section 310(b)(4) of the Act, and cable landing licenses. Foreign companies could pass the ECO test by showing with respect to a given service that the foreign market had no legal or practical barriers to entry. The ECO policy ordinarily required several months to process each application by a foreign carrier to provide service in the US market.

New FCC rules introduced in anticipation of the entry into force of the WTO agreement took effect on 9 February 1998. The *Foreign Participation Order* significantly liberalised treatment of foreign telecommunications carriers and investors from countries that are signatories to the WTO agreement. A key outcome of this process was the removal of the ECO test in favour of an open entry standard for carriers from WTO Member countries. Open entry standard means that these carriers benefit from a rebuttable presumption that applications for Section 214 authority do not introduce concerns that would justify denial of an application on competitive grounds. The same presumption is now made in respect of applications for cable landing licenses and applications to exceed the 25 per cent foreign ownership benchmark in a common carrier radio licensee.

However, the revised rules retain certain safeguards designed to prevent foreign carriers with market power from distorting competition in the US market and maintain the Commission's authority to deny or condition such entry if required by the public interest. How might such a determination be made? First, while benefiting from the presumption in favour of entry on a "streamlined" basis (see discussion of streamlined procedures below), carriers from WTO countries may still be restricted from providing facilities-based service to their affiliated markets if this would result in a very high risk to competition on that route. Second, a US-licensed carrier may not provide facilities-based service to a country in which it has an affiliate unless its foreign affiliate offers US carriers settlement rates at a certain level (see discussion on benchmark settlement rates below). Finally, a license may still be denied if there are national security, law enforcement, and foreign policy and/or trade concerns raised by the Executive Branch.[33] The FCC therefore retains discretionary power to decline licenses for reasons which may be unrelated to anticompetitive conduct in the international telecommunications services market.[34] Some foreign carriers interviewed for this project expressed concern that this leveraging of licenses in support of US objectives in other policy areas may have a chilling effect on license applications by other prospective competitors, eroding prospects for enhanced foreign participation in the sector.

On the procedural side, concerns about market openness have related primarily to the length of time required to process license applications by prospective international service providers. Improvements in US processing procedures, notably the FCC's undertaking to act within a set timeframe on Section 214 applications, should contribute to enhanced market openness. With its adoption of the new foreign participation rules, the FCC stated that it would act within 90 days on all Section 214 applications except those that raise issues of "extraordinary complexity".[35] US authorities expect that "almost all" applications will be granted within this 90-day period.[36] In addition, the Commission expanded its streamlined processing rules under which, absent any objections, a license may be presumed granted after 35 days. According to the FCC, practically all Section 214 applications qualify under streamlining procedures,[37] with over 200 Section 214 and 310(*b*)4 authorisations processed under the rules in the period 1 January-15 May 1998.[38] Foreign and domestic carriers alike have benefited from streamlined treatment: recent examples of foreign beneficiaries include an application by Japan's NTTA Communications to operate as facilities-based and resale carrier to Japan and an application by Canada's Teleglobe Inc. for the transfer of control of Excel Communications to Teleglobe. Still, US authorities note that some applications will generate significant public comment or raise issues of first impression, in which cases 90 days may be insufficient to render a decision.[39] The degree to which such applications may languish at the hands of the regulatory authorities thus remains of considerable concern to affected carriers.

More specific concerns sometimes arise regarding regulatory treatment of foreign-affiliated carriers. Licenses granted under Section 214 enable a foreign carrier to use its own facilities (*e.g.*, its own cable circuits) or engage in resale of existing US carrier facilities in order to provide a service. On facilities use, many telecommunications regulators around the world grant global licenses. The FCC's rules provide that applicants from WTO countries may file an application to provide global facilities-based and/or switched resale services and receive "streamlined processing". Applications for global facilities-based service by applicants that are affiliated with a foreign telecommunications carrier that possesses market power in such countries will receive streamlined processing only if the application includes certification that the applicant will comply with the FCC's dominant carrier safeguards on routes where it has such affiliations.[40]

Applications for global switched resale service by carriers from WTO countries are eligible for streamlined processing without restriction. Applicants for facilities-based and switched resale service with affiliates with market power in non-WTO countries will receive authorisation to provide service on the affiliated route only to the extent that the foreign market satisfies the FCC's ECO test. In the experience of one foreign-affiliated carrier with geographically far-flung operations around the world (many of which are located in non-WTO countries where "monopoly" models prevail), such licensing criteria have proven particularly onerous. In one illustrative case, the same carrier processing a Section 214 application for a global calling card service based in the United Kingdom dropped a number of desired destination countries from its application in order to meet licensing criteria, with attendant consequences *vis-à-vis* competing calling card schemes.

International settlement rates (per-minute rates paid by carriers to terminate international traffic at its domestic destination) have also emerged as a market access issue from the perspective of foreign carriers seeking to serve the US market. The United States has been a world leader in seeking reform of the existing system of international settlement rates and continues to work with other countries in the ITU towards a multilateral consensus on lowering accounting rates. However, in the continuing absence of such a consensus, US handling of the issue has fostered tension with foreign competitors. Much of this turns on the FCC *Benchmark Order*, which would require US carriers to reduce the settlement rates they pay to foreign carriers and impose certain conditions on participation in the US market aimed at "reducing the incentives and ability of a foreign carrier to act anticompetitively to the detriment of US consumers".[41] Thus, facilities-based licenses to serve markets in which a licensee's affiliate possesses market power would not be activated until the affiliated foreign carrier agrees with US carriers to *benchmark settlement rates* linked to the level of economic development in a terminating country. Under the proposed matrix, target benchmark rates of 15, 19 and 23 cents per minute would apply to high, medium and low-income countries respectively.

Moreover, foreign-affiliated carriers with Section 214 authorisations granted prior to 1 January 1998 are effectively exempted from the benchmark settlement rate condition insofar as the Order applies only to *new* market entrants. A later adjustment to the Order requiring US carriers to adopt the benchmark rates by a date certain has been extended indefinitely. Thus, depending on their particular circumstances, foreign-affiliated carriers seeking to launch new facilities-based services may find themselves at a competitive disadvantage *vis-à-vis* established foreign and domestic entities. Leasing existing services in accordance with the international simple resale rule is one alternative for carriers so affected, but a much more costly one. And additional conditions would apply in such a scenario: no carrier may lease a private line circuit and provide international switched services until 50 per cent of all traffic on the route is based on benchmark settlement rates or the foreign country offers resale opportunities equivalent to those available in the United States. As discussed above, however, all carriers from WTO countries are eligible for streamlined global authorisation to provide switched resale service.

Sectoral regulatory procedures reflect a high-level commitment to openness and transparency.[42] Based on APA requirements, FCC administrative procedures are very open and regulations highly transparent. In addition, certain sector-specific procedures aimed at regulatory streamlining mentioned above may ultimately yield benefits for both domestic and foreign carriers. For example, Section 11 of the Communications Act, as amended, requires the FCC to review all of its regulations applicable to providers of telecommunications service in every even-numbered year, beginning in 1998, to determine whether the regulations are no longer in the public interest due to meaningful economic competition between providers of the service and whether such regulations should be repealed or modified. As part of this process, the FCC has proposed to grant blanket authority to provide international services and to reform its international settlements policy. Section 202(h) of the Telecommunications Act of 1996 also requires the Commission to review its broadcast ownership rules biennially as part of the review conducted pursuant to Section 11. The FCC has determined that the first biennial regulatory review "presents an excellent opportunity for a serious top-to-bottom examination of all the Commission's regulations, not just those statutorily required to be reviewed".[43] Domestic and foreign carriers alike should benefit from this exercise.

The picture that emerges is largely positive, but some issues continue to require attention. Regulatory style and content for the sector is highly pro-competitive in tone and intent, and pivotal developments in domestic and international policies for the sector are making a decisive and irreversible contribution to enhanced market openness in the US as in other markets. National policies for the sector reflect clear leadership qualities in moving national and global telecommunications markets towards greater competition. FCC regulatory procedures are exemplary in terms of transparency and openness of decision-making. Nonetheless, several types of regulatory barriers that may be undermining optimal market openness in the United States have been identified. To recall some earlier examples, specific regulatory practices such as current US international settlements policy may be overly burdensome or generate discriminatory effects for some foreign carriers; and the preservation of regulatory discretion to deny licenses on the basis of anticompetitive safeguards, public interest factors, or (for non-WTO Members) the ECO test may be contributing to an air of uncertainty about prospects for enhanced foreign participation in the US market. The extent to which these various powers will be exercised in practice, however, remains to be seen.

3.3. Automobiles and components

Concerns about market openness and domestic regulation of automotive industries around the world are not new. Due to the historic dynamism of global economic activity in the sector and traditionally interventionist policies of some governments aimed at protecting domestic automotive industries, trade tensions related to domestic regulatory issues in general and standards and certification procedures in particular have long figured on bilateral and regional trade agendas. This reflects the fact that automobiles remain among the most highly regulated products in the world primarily for reasons relating to safety, energy conservation, and the environment. Divergent national approaches to the achievement of legitimate domestic objectives in these key policy areas are therefore likely to remain a significant source of trade tension as global demand for automobiles continues to rise. This is true with respect to many countries, including the United States.

US regulatory content for the sector is a hybrid of safety and environmental requirements. A motor vehicle destined for the US market must meet an array of US regulatory requirements stemming from two different Executive agencies. The Department of Transportation's National Highway Traffic and Safety Administration (NHTSA) promulgates and enforces federal safety standards, while the formulation and enforcement of motor vehicle emission standards fall under the jurisdiction of the Environmental Protection Agency (EPA).

NHTSA issues safety standards for new motor vehicles and new motor vehicle equipment. Vehicles and components manufactured or imported for sale in the United States must comply with all applicable safety standards.

As seen earlier, conformity with NHTSA safety standards is based on self-certification by vehicle manufacturers. Under this approach, automobile manufacturers must certify compliance of their products with all applicable standards. Though NHTSA seeks to ensure the integrity of the system by conducting annual compliance investigations to verify the compliance of motor vehicle equipment with safety performance requirements of relevant regulations. However, this would normally only occur in the case of a suspected product failure, and the primary onus to report alleged safety problems rests with consumers. This system contrasts with the type-approval system[44] used elsewhere in the world, notably in the European Union, Japan, Australia and Korea. Self-certification is widely viewed as less burdensome than formal inspection by third parties, and may be a model for possible application in other sectors (*e.g.*, telecommunications equipment).

Conformity with motor vehicle emission standards is based on certification granted by the EPA (Office of Mobile Source Regulations). The central statutory authority for EPA regulatory action is the Clean Air Act of 1970, legislation which established the first specific responsibilities for government and private industry to reduce emissions from vehicles and other pollution sources. Amendments to the Act introduced in 1990 strengthened components of the earlier law (for example, exhaust standards for cars, buses, and trucks were tightened, and Inspection and Maintenance programmes expanded to include more areas and allow for more stringent testing) and introduced new concepts for reducing motor vehicle-related air pollution. And for the first time, fuel, along with vehicle technology, was treated as a potential source of emission reductions. Many of the 1990 amendments have already been phased in. Others, designed to encourage production of clean fuels and vehicles (including clean-fuel fleet programmes to be introduced in certain in certain "non-attainment" cities and the California Pilot Programme) are still to be fully implemented.

US environmental regulation specific to the automotive sector has not always proven trade-friendly. As earlier noted in this report, GATT/WTO cases brought in respect of reformulated gasoline and corporate average fuel economy standards revealed that certain elements of both regimes effectively discriminated against foreign manufacturers. Similarly, the European Commission maintains that aspects of the operation of other measures applicable to the sector, such as the luxury and gas guzzler taxes, discriminate against foreign manufacturers, especially where they have an effect equivalent to technical rules. The policy objectives underlying such regimes were never in question. In such cases, the trade-restrictive impact of the rules in question may have been averted through wider advance consultation with the trade policy community without compromising the achievement of environmental objectives.

Trade frictions arising from heterogeneous or redundant standards and conformity assessment procedures have sparked less international profile. But it is precisely this kind of low-level, pervasive irritant that continues to penalise foreign suppliers active in the US market (though this is not a problem unique to the US regulatory scheme) To its credit, the United States has actively participated in activities aimed at ensuring greater uniformity of automotive standards, notably the UN-ECE and TABD processes (Box 4). However, standards applied at the state level, such as the Californian Low Emission Vehicles regulation, still retain the potential to generate trade friction.

Box 4.   **Towards greater regulatory harmonisation in the automotive sector**

The United Nations Economic Commission for Europe (UN-ECE) has played a central role in moving the automotive sector towards international harmonisation of motor vehicle safety and environmental regulations and co-ordination of vehicle safety and environmental research. A specialised ECE body, the Working Party on the Construction of Vehicles (commonly referred to as WP 29) has become a *de facto* global forum for the international harmonisation of technical standards for motor vehicle regulations. WP 29 brings together regulators and non-governmental organisations representing manufacturers of vehicles and parts, consumers and other stakeholders from a wide range of countries, including the United States.

It was the United States which proposed the opening of WP 29 to worldwide membership. The effective transition from a regional to a global forum has created the only intergovernmental venue for development and harmonisation of environmental and safety requirements applicable to vehicles, engines, and engine-powered equipment.

Related initiatives underway in the TABD provide useful insights into possible future directions in pro-competitive regulatory reform in the sector. TABD partners have identified four priorities in this context: *a*) commitment by the European Union and the United States to engage in one common process of international harmonisation (represented by the June 1988 agreement on a mechanism for established Global Technical Regulations); *b*) expeditious response to US automaker petitions before the NHTSA for the development of functionally equivalent standards (with the EU to take corresponding action); *c*) commitment by EU and US governments not to introduce future automotive regulations without prior consultation, with a view to harmonising such regulations; and *d*) pursuance of multilateral discussions beyond TABD (*e.g.*, a trilateral working group comprising experts from the European Automobile Manufacturers Association (ACEA), the American Automobile Manufacturers Association (AAMA) and the Japan Automobile Manufacturer Association (JAMA) has since been established and is developing a joint industry workplan for advancing global standards).

Sector-specific labelling requirements may also compromise market openness by implicitly encouraging consumers to "buy American". The American Automobile Labelling Act (discussed earlier in Box 1) requires all new passenger cars and light trucks sold in the United States to bear a label indicating the per centage of US or Canadian content. Though not formally discriminatory, the law has attracted the attention of foreign trading partners who see it as an effective prompt to US consumers to act on their local content preferences.

Organisation of distribution in the sector is broadly consistent with an open market philosophy. In contrast to some other markets where exclusive dealerships are the norm, multiple franchise sites are common in the United States, with the Big Three domestic producers (GM, Ford and Chrysler) and some Japanese manufacturers marketing several vehicle makes on the same premises. Much of the regulation of motor vehicle franchising in the United States takes place at the State, rather than the Federal, level. In contrast to Europe and Japan, all sales in the United States must pass through dealers and manufacturers are not permitted to undertake direct selling. As in many OECD countries, the automobile distribution system responds to local market demands and probably does not represent one of the major barriers to market openness.

In contrast to the other three sectors examined in this section, regulatory processes for automobiles and components are subject to OMB oversight. Thus, in addition to meeting APA requirements, proposed rules for the sector are subject to additional vetting in accordance with OMB procedures. Sector-specific regulatory practices also apply. For example, 49 CFR sets out detailed procedural rules (Part 551), rules regarding petitions for rule-making, defect and non-compliance orders (Part 552) and rulemaking procedures (Part 553). Many NHTSA and EPA rulemaking activities are conducted on-line.

On balance, US automotive regulation has the potential for greater trade and investment friendliness. Important progress has been made to this end on both domestic and international levels. Traditional US reliance on self-certification by vehicle manufacturers with respect to safety standards, complemented by active US participation in moves towards global harmonisation of environmental and safety requirements, are positive factors in favour of market openness (though the latter initiative is not likely to yield speedy results). Still, particularly for so heavily regulated a sector, more could be done in the short to medium term to foster greater market openness. For example, in the absence of global standards, there may be a case for greater recognition of other countries' technical standards as functionally equivalent. The design and implementation of environmental regulation affecting the sector could be improved through more formal advance consultation with the trade policy community. And finally, continued commitment to the TABD process could spur important progress on "front-line" issues, allowing an incremental approach to lasting regulatory reform in this sector.

3.4. Electricity

Progressive deregulation of the US electricity sector aimed at promoting further wholesale competition and introducing retail competition has had important implications for foreign firms seeking to enter or expand access in the US market. Regulatory reform efforts (see background report on Regulatory Reform in the Telecommunications Industry) have involved both federal and state regulators, with wholesale and retail power markets falling under federal and state jurisdiction respectively.

At the wholesale level, industry restructuring has been implemented by the independent federal regulator, the Federal Energy Regulatory Commission (FERC). Sweeping changes for the industry were introduced in 1996. On April 24 of that year, FERC issued two orders which fundamentally altered the competitive landscape for the wholesale industry. The first was *Order* 888 on "Promoting Wholesale Competition Through Open Access Non-discriminatory Transmission Services by Public Utilities; Recovery of Stranded Costs by Public Utilities and Transmitting Utilities". Entry into force of this rule (on 9 July 1996), *inter alia*, effectively required all FERC-jurisdictional utilities that own, control, or operate transmission facilities to provide non-discriminatory open access transmission services. The second of the two rules, *Order* 889, entitled Open Access SameTime Information Systems and Standards of Conduct (OASIS), required utilities to develop an Internet-based bulletin board system to provide information on the availability of transportation capacity on transmission lines. FERC views implementation of these two open access rules as the single greatest transformation of the industry since the passage of the Federal Power Act in 1935. The Commission has estimated that these initiatives will save consumers between US$3.8 and $5.4 billion annually and will also pave the way for state retail access or customer choice initiatives (approximately three quarters of the states have either implemented or are actively considering retail competition).

This emerging competitive market for wholesale power service has in principle created important new opportunities for existing and potential foreign entrants to the US electricity market. In practice, however, the manner of implementation of *Order* 888 has led to trade friction.

The Canadian experience is particularly instructive in illustrating why such tensions have arisen. While ordering all FERC-jurisdictional utilities (essentially investor-owned utilities, or IOUs) to provide open wholesale access, *Order* 888 also empowered individual utilities to deny such access where reciprocity was not available.[45] Such reciprocity may be required as a condition of access to the open US wholesale market both of certain *domestic* utilities beyond FERC jurisdiction and of Canadian utilities seeking access to the US wholesale market. In practice, some utilities have exercised this authority while others have not, thus creating an uneven and unpredictable situation. The US regulator however views the requirement to be inherently non-discriminatory as between domestic and foreign utilities and therefore consistent with the national treatment obligation contained in Chapter 6 of NAFTA.

Implementation of the *Order* 888 reciprocity test has impacted Canadian utilities in different ways. For provincial utilities in Manitoba, Quebec, and British Colombia, where energy exports represent a core business, domestically-generated power is highly competitive, and wholesale loads are negligible (so that providing open access to transmission lines was not viewed as exerting much, if any, competitive pressure on existing market share), compliance with the FERC reciprocity requirement proved the chosen course for accessing the US wholesale market.

For another provincial utility, however – Ontario Hydro – the reciprocity issue has played out very differently. Due to fundamental differences in the Ontario industry structure, the province was not in a position to comply with the reciprocity requirement,[46] resulting in denial of its bid for open access to the US wholesale market. Ontario Hydro has subsequently challenged FERC's authority to order open access as a condition of Canadian participation in the US market, an issue which is before US courts. In the meantime, Ontario Hydro has claimed that US border utilities have been able to exert market power over it by refusing to sell transmission services.

Given a prevailing divergence of views on the issue, State legislative proposals that would feature similarly-applied reciprocity requirements for the retail market are also of concern to Canada. A number of US states are currently studying or have already implemented retail competition (*e.g.*, California and Massachusetts). Policy directions taken by US states on this matter would also have potential implications for federal regulatory action. FERC cannot order retail access; however, once mandated by a state, the "unbundled" transmission tariff used to supply retail load falls within FERC jurisdiction.

Speculation about the future direction of FERC's authority has also fostered international concerns about regulatory sovereignty. Initiatives that could give FERC oversight of transmission reliability standards currently set by the North American Electric Reliability Council (a voluntary organisation of transmission-owning utilities utility) and assessment of penalties for non-compliance with reliability rules;[47] involvement in merger conditions and formation of mandatory independent system operators (ISOs, or entities independent of market participants that control operations of a transmission system in a non-discriminatory manner) have all been cited in this context.[48]

Thus, the regulatory path chosen to implement a pro-competitive vision for the US wholesale market appears to be significantly undermining international market openness in the sector. In principle, *Order* 888 set the scene for enhanced foreign competition in the sector. In practice, however, the means may be thwarting the end. In particular, FERC's delegation of authority to IOUs to require reciprocity of certain domestic (and foreign) utilities as a condition of access to the open US wholesale market has effectively negated prospects for predictable, consistent access by the latter (except those who opted, at little or no competitive cost to themselves, to comply with the reciprocity requirement). Viewed from this perspective, claims that the reciprocity requirement is non-discriminatory (however framed) are likely to meet with further objections by some trading partners. Revoking or redesigning this feature of the regulatory framework to remove its discriminatory element and avoiding its emulation at the state (retail) level may prove essential steps towards smoother trade relations.

Certain sector-specific restrictions on *foreign investment* continue to apply. Such restrictions typically turn on nationality requirements and are thus expressly discriminatory. The Federal Power Act, for example, limits licenses for any construction, operation, or maintenance of facilities for the development, transmission, and use of power on Federal land to US citizens and US companies. The Geothermal Steam Act limits leases to US citizens and companies for the development of geothermal steam and associated resources on Federal lands. The Atomic Energy Act of 1954 (42 USC. Sections 2 011 et seq.) stipulates that a license is required for any person in the United States to transfer, manufacture, produce, use or import any facilities that produce or use nuclear materials. Such licenses may not be issued to any entity known or believed to be owned, controlled, or dominated by an alien, a foreign corporation, or a foreign government. Grant of a license is also prohibited in respect of production or utilisation facilities for such uses as medical therapy or research and development activities to any corporation or other entity owned, controlled, or dominated by one of the foreign persons described earlier. Under corporate organisation requirements of the Ocean Thermal Energy Conversion Act of 1980, only US citizens may obtain a license to own, construct or operate an ocean thermal energy conversion (OTEC) facility located in US territorial waters or connected to the United States by pipeline or cable; or a moving OTEC plant ship wherever located. Among other nationality requirements regarding corporate organisation, the law contains a reciprocity provision for plant ships. Finally, an additional foreign utilities are subject to ownership restrictions under the Public Utility Holding Companies Act (PUCHA) of 1935.[49] Various legislative initiatives on electric power legislation and PUCHA reform do not appear to contemplate any changes to this.

These types of sector-specific restrictions may be based on legitimate public policy objectives relating to such issues as security of supply and national security rather than on overtly discriminatory trade or investment rationales. Whether or not such legitimate domestic objectives can be met through less restrictive means, however, seems a fair question.

4. CONCLUSIONS AND POLICY OPTIONS FOR REFORM

4.1. General assessment of current strengths and weaknesses

US regulatory procedures meet a high standard from the perspective of international market openness. An analysis of the OECD indicators questionnaire on market openness undertaken as part of the OECD Project on Regulatory Reform found the United States to be well ahead of the OECD average with respect to all but two of the efficient regulation principles (see Figure 1 below).

While not all of the six efficient regulation principles examined in this report are expressly codified in US administrative and regulatory oversight procedures to the same degree, the weight of available evidence suggests that they are given ample expression in practice. This is most clearly the case for transparency and openness of decision-making. Continued impetus behind pro-competitive reform in given sectors, regulatory streamlining efforts, and the search for greater analytical rigour in assessing the costs, benefits, and effects of proposed regulations are all contributing to the steady, progressive enhancement of US market openness. At the same time, US market openness might be further enhanced by finding ways to ensure that awareness of and respect for the efficient regulation principles is firmly embedded across all levels of regulatory activity. Further efforts should particularly be made with respect to non-discrimination, avoidance of unnecessary trade restrictiveness, recognition of equivalence of other countries' regulations and conformity assessment systems, and reliance on internationally harmonised standards as the basis of domestic regulations. As the six principles reflect fundamental tenets of the multilateral

Figure 1. **US's trade friendly index by principle
(OECD averages = 100)**

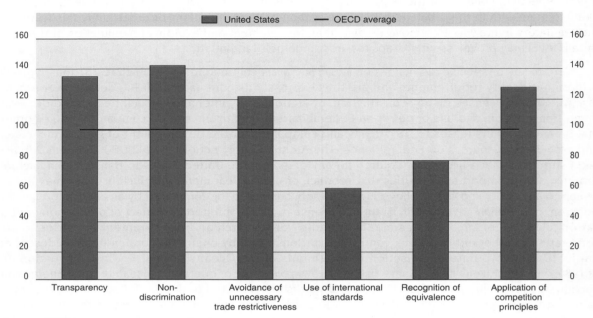

Source: OECD.

trading system, it is clear that there is a strong mutual relationship between progress in multilateral liberalisation and domestic efforts to achieve quality regulation.

In general, US regulatory reform initiatives have been highly receptive to concerns voiced by both domestic and foreign business communities. The potential for this result seems highest in situations where there are formalised mechanisms for business-to-government and business-to-business dialogue, such as the TABD. Working through this latter mechanism, EU and US firms have been instrumental in shaping the bilateral agenda for regulatory co-operation – drawing out particular difficulties encountered with incompatible or duplicative regulatory policies, developing agreed approaches for resolving underlying problems, and presenting them for consideration to their governments.

Substantive regulation in the US is on balance trade and investment-friendly. However, the nature of some trade frictions suggests that the design of certain regulations may introduce potential for unnecessarily restrictive trade effects. In the case of a GATT complaint brought by the European Union in respect of US CAFE standards, for example, environmental protection objectives underlying the regime might have been met using less trade-restrictive means (such as a tax on motor fuel) while at the same time ensuring superior fulfilment of domestic policy objectives.[50]

Why do domestic regulations often surface as trade irritants? Failure to arrest potentially problematic regulations before they become *faits accomplis* appears to be more a result of benign neglect than passive tolerance of potentially restrictive domestic regulation. One explanation is that consultative and institutional links between trade and regulatory agencies may not be completely adequate. With the necessary resources, trade and trade-related agencies (notably USTR) would play a positive role in vetting proposed regulations from the perspective of market openness. In practice, however, many regulatory bodies harbour suspicion towards the trade policy community, fearing that the latter cannot be an effective advocate for the country's regulatory interests and that trade involvement in domestic regulatory activities may somehow lead to a lowering of standards. A resulting reticence across regulatory agencies to openly share information with the trade policy community on domestic regulations in-the-making clearly creates broad potential for regulatory jeopardy from a market openness perspective.

This suspicion largely reflects widely shared concerns in American society that, in the context of trade liberalisation, competitiveness factors could inhibit the ability of the US to maintain high standards over the longer term. However, several studies conducted in the OECD[51] suggest that trade liberalisation can be viewed as a positive agent for improvement in the context of social policies, except where, in the absence of effective social policies, increased economic activity generated from trade liberalisation might exacerbate existing problems. It may thus be useful to undertake efforts in order to share more widely this evidence among regulators and public opinion alike.

In some cases, complexity or opacity of regulatory content may adversely affect both domestic and foreign firms. The experiences of some US firms are illuminating in this regard. In response to a GAO study on federal regulatory burden, selected US companies cited a number of concerns including adverse effects on competitiveness; high costs of compliance; the unreasonableness or inflexibility of certain regulations; excessive paperwork; the unclear nature of certain regulatory requirements; overly severe regulatory penalties; a "gotcha" enforcement approach; and duplicative or poorly co-ordinated regulations.[52] Company experiences with the US regulatory regime undoubtedly vary by firm and industry, and such concerns should not be interpreted as representative of the collective experience of the US business community. Nonetheless, it seems plausible that foreign traders and investors may be encountering some or all of these types of difficulties when seeking to enter or expand activities in the US market.

As the discussion under Section 3 revealed, certain features of extant regulatory regimes in given sectors are also problematic. While foreign traders and investors generally enjoy high-standard, non-discriminatory treatment in terms of access to and participation in regulatory administrative procedures, the experience of some foreign firms suggests that certain substantive regulations either expressly or inadvertently place them at a competitive disadvantage *vis-à-vis* domestic competitors. This is true to varying degrees in each of the sectors examined in this report. Relatedly, while continued efforts in support of pro-competitive regulatory reform in some of these same sectors are to be encouraged, other candidates for sectoral deregulation (such as domestic air services) remain unaddressed to date.

Generic issues related to *product standards and conformity assessment procedures* also warrant further attention, although notable progress has already been achieved at bilateral, regional and multilateral levels. Heterogeneous manufacturing standards and duplicative certification procedures between the United States and some trading partners continue to dampen potential for trade flows. Moves towards regulatory harmonisation or mutual recognition of standards or conformity assessment procedures are promising steps, though the substantial commitments of time and resources required for such initiatives risk eroding institutional and political support for their continued pursuit. Increased US reliance on alternatives to third party certification and on the use of international standards as the basis of domestic regulations may provide additional opportunities for lowering regulatory barriers to trade, though such approaches may not always be appropriate.[53] More focused participation in the further development of international standards where appropriate and feasible may also reduce regulatory conflict and help find wider multilateral solutions. On another level, the complexity of US standardisation and conformity assessment activities presents difficulties for *both* domestic and foreign firms, so that measures to streamline the US system generally would yield important improvements from a market openness perspective as well.

The issue of subfederal (state and local) regulation will require careful monitoring to ensure optimal market openness. In accordance with WTO obligations, the federal government must take "reasonable measures" to ensure compliance by regional and local governments with international obligations.[54] However, this approach is not airtight in ensuring optimal regulatory coherence and respect for principles of efficient regulation. Transparency and openness of decision-making at the subfederal level is critical in this regard.

4.2. The dynamic view: the pace and direction of change

Globalisation has dramatically altered the world paradigm for the conduct of international trade and investment, creating new competitive pressures in the United States and elsewhere. At the same time, the progressive dismantling or lowering of traditional barriers to trade and increased relevance of "behind the border" measures to effective market access and presence has exposed national regulatory regimes to a degree of unprecedented international scrutiny by trade and investment partners, with the result that regulation is no longer (if ever it was) a purely "domestic" affair. Trade and investment policy communities have generally kept pace with these twin phenomena. However, a degree of regulatory catch-up is required. Concrete steps to increase awareness of and effective adherence to the efficient regulation principles and deepen international co-operation on regulatory issues are encouraging trends in this context. Overcoming systemic intransigence and fostering a new regulatory culture will be pivotal to these efforts.

The progressive dismantling of economic regulation in the United States has already yielded significant opportunities for foreign traders and investors, though further progress in major sectors such as telecommunications and electricity remains to be achieved. At the same time, the shift in focus to social regulation and the extent of its current reach at federal, state and local levels present new challenges for ensuring that the pursuit of legitimate domestic objectives relating to health, safety and the environment do not unnecessarily restrict trade and investment flows.

In terms of transparency and overall regulatory coherence, the co-ordination of federal regulatory reform with efforts at the state and local levels is also likely to become increasingly relevant from the perspective of international market openness. Enhancing market openness at one but not other levels, particularly in areas of overlapping jurisdiction, risks mitigating the effectiveness of continued reform efforts.

Increased reliance on input from domestic and foreign business communities, as already occurs in the TABD context, is an encouraging trend. A business-driven approach to market-opening regulatory reform has allowed early identification of issues of material concern to industry and joint development of possible solutions to sectoral and cross-cutting issues. TABD successes to date suggest that for certain types of regulatory barriers, this kind of business-government dialogue may be a more effective driver of regulatory reform than traditional government-to-government negotiations.

As prior experience has shown, continued multilateral liberalisation of trade and investment should bolster future regulatory reform efforts. Conversely, any backsliding in the face of protectionist pressures could wreak havoc on regulatory achievements to date.

4.3. Potential benefits and costs of further regulatory reform

Market-opening regulation promises to promote the flow of goods, services, investment and technology between the United States and global commercial partners. And expanded trade and investment flows generate important consumer benefits (greater choice and lower prices), raise the standards of performance of domestic firms (through the impetus of greater competition), and boost GDP.

The need for all governments to address market failures through sound regulatory action is an undisputed sovereign prerogative. Nonetheless, ill-conceived, excessively restrictive or burdensome regulation exacts a heavy price on commercial activity, domestic or foreign, and places a disproportionately heavy burden on small and medium-sized enterprises. Foreign firms established in the US market face the same regulatory burden as domestic firms. Heavy compliance costs may also adversely affect the competitiveness of domestic firms, including those which use foreign inputs. In either scenario, opportunities for expanded trade and investment (and US consumer gains) which might have otherwise occurred in the absence of regulatory handicap are simply foregone.

US regulators have themselves recognised the potential gains to be won from market-opening regulatory reform in some sectors. In telecommunications services, for example, the FCC has openly stated its expectation that "competitive forces will soon result in higher quality, lower priced, more innovative service offerings".[55]

Trade and investment friendly regulation need not undermine the promotion and achievement of legitimate US policy objectives. High-quality regulation can be trade-neutral or market-opening, coupling consumer gains from enhanced market openness with more efficient realisation of domestic objectives in key areas such as the environment, health and safety. But it is doubtful that this can be achieved in the absence of purposeful, government-wide adherence to the principles of efficient regulation. Avoiding the potentially restrictive effects of domestic regulation through more focused, systematic attention to these principles – as might be achieved through the creation of an interagency consultative mechanism involving USTR and other trade policy bodies – would therefore generate important efficiency benefits for US consumers and the broader economy.

4.4. Policy options for consideration

Future reforms should:

– *Continue to foster good regulatory practices already instituted in areas such as transparency and openness of decision-making.* The United States sets an enviable standard in providing scope for participation by foreign governments and firms in regulatory processes through strict adherence to codified procedures and innovative use of the Internet.

– *Increase the responsiveness of the US regulatory system to the needs of international trade and investment.* Adjustments in regulatory procedures are required to formalise consideration of international market openness considerations in the regulatory decision-making process and minimise the potential for trade friction. At a minimum, this should include systematic reviews of proposed regulations with a view to identifying and minimising their potentially restrictive effects on international market openness. This could be achieved, for example, through the creation of an interagency mechanism to review proposed economic, social, and administrative regulations with input from USTR and/or other agencies involved in the trade policy process. Alternatively, it may be possible to adjust the mandate and operation of the *existing* interagency trade policy mechanism to meet this objective. Such a mechanism should address rulemaking by both executive agencies and independent regulators. Closer consultation with foreign trade and investment partners as well as the international business community might also be contemplated in this context.

– *Require explicit assessments of the effects of proposed rules on inward trade and investment as part of the Regulatory Impact Analysis (RIA) and rule-making activities of the independent regulators.* The criteria for such assessments should be based on the six efficient regulation principles.

– *Heighten awareness of and encourage respect for the OECD efficient regulation principles in subfederal (state and local) regulatory activities affecting international trade and investment.* The creation of new institutional bridges or adjustment of existing consultative mechanisms could be foreseen in this context.

– *Seek to ensure that bilateral or regional approaches to regulatory co-operation are designed and implemented in ways which will encourage broader multilateral application.* Mutual recognition of regulations or of conformity assessment procedures, increased use of industry-developed standards in lieu of national regulatory measures, and other approaches to intergovernmental regulatory co-operation offer promising avenues for the lowering of regulatory barriers to trade and investment. At the same time, consideration should be given to ways which will enhance prospects for adherence by third country competitors. As a counterpart to this:

– *Continue to promote pro-competitive regulatory reform in the WTO context.* The WTO TBT, SPS and Basic Telecommunications Agreements are prime examples of how trade agreements can complement domestic regulatory reform efforts. Concerted efforts should be made to advance liberal regulatory philosophies and practices in all WTO countries.

259

- *Build on the TABD model to encourage the continued involvement of the US and international business communities in domestic regulatory reform efforts.* Informal business-driven processes such as this have proven valuable catalysts for market-opening regulatory reform across a range of particular sectors and horizontal issues. Wider government-to-business partnering on regulatory issues holds strong potential for pragmatic, result-oriented reform attuned to evolving business realities.

- *Intensify efforts to use existing international standards and to participate more actively in the development of internationally harmonised standards as the basis of domestic regulations.* A useful point of departure would be to systematically assess the extent to which regulators currently rely on international standards and to explore rationales for departures from this practice.

- *Review existing sectoral restrictions on foreign investment with a view to preparing the ground for their early removal.*

- *Conduct periodic reviews of existing sectoral regulation from a market openness perspective with reference to the six efficient regulation principles.* FCC biennial regulatory reviews might provide a useful model for such an exercise.

4.5. Managing regulatory reform

The steady pursuit and successful implementation of international trade and investment agreements can be a catalyst for domestic regulatory reform. Once achieved, such agreements lock in policy commitments to regulatory reform regarding both generic and sector-specific themes and provide transparent benchmarks by which to gauge progress towards reform objectives.

At the same time, lag times between fast-changing competitive conditions and government-negotiated outcomes can be significant, pointing to the need to supplement these activities with domestically-driven efforts to achieve and maintain optimal market openness. In some cases, identifying and addressing recurrent patterns of trade friction through more focused, systematic application of the efficient regulation principles may dramatically reduce the scope for trade conflicts in the first instance. This alone should generate important gains to government in terms of encouraging optimal allocation of time and (limited) resources to pursue given policy objectives, be it at the multilateral, regional or bilateral level. And when regulatory styles and content succeed in averting trade disputes altogether, net gains accrue to both US consumers and global economic welfare.

In order for this undertaking to be successful, however, a public relations campaign may be necessary to educate regulators, legislators, the public, and consumer and special interest groups about the ultimate costs to American consumers and firms of regulatory barriers to international market openness. At a minimum, such a campaign should convey three main messages: first, that regulatory reform does not necessarily mean deregulation. Like all other governments, the United States will continue to establish levels of protection for health, safety and the environment it deems to be appropriate. The challenge is to eliminate inefficient regulation that fuels higher prices without offering any additional protection to the public it is designed to protect. A second major message should be that regulatory reform can be market-opening, with no adverse effects on the fulfilment of legitimate policy objectives. Domestic and foreign firms alike will be required to adhere to the level of regulatory protection deemed appropriate by US authorities. Third and finally, domestic constituencies should understand that market-opening, pro-competitive regulatory reform ultimately serves US interests. By removing obstacles to greater efficiency and innovation, easing the regulatory burden on domestic and foreign firms alike will contribute to the enhanced competitiveness of US firms abroad while stimulating greater global competition. American consumers will thus be well-positioned to draw optimal benefits from regulatory reform.

NOTES

1. Among the stated objectives of the (EU-US) Transatlantic Economic Partnership announced in May 1998 are the improvement of *regulatory co-operation* in such areas as manufactured goods; agriculture, including biotechnology; services; industrial tariffs; global electronic commerce; intellectual property rights; investment; government procurement; and competition and improvement of the *efficiency and effectiveness of regulatory procedures* such as standards, testing and certification.

2. US FDI inflows increased in 1995 by more than 21 per cent over the previous year, reaching $60 billion, twice the size of inflows to the United Kingdom, the second most important FDI recipient amongst developed countries. See World Investment Report 1996 (UNCTAD 1996).

3. See "Trouble for Us and Trouble for Them: Social Regulations as Trade Barriers" by David Vogel in Comparative Disadvantages? Social Regulations and the Global Economy, edited by Pietro S. Nivola, Brookings Institution Press, Washington DC (1997).

4. See, in particular OECD (1998), "Open Markets Matter. The benefits of Trade and Investment Liberalisation", Paris; OECD (1994), "The Environmental Effects of Trade", Paris and the OECD (1995), Report on Trade and Environment to the OECD Council at Ministerial level.

5. See related discussion in OECD (1997), "Regulatory Quality and Public Sector Reform", *The* OECD *Report on Regulatory Reform*, Volume II: *Thematic Studies*, Chapter 2, Paris.

6. It should be noted however that on occasion, inconsistency with GATT provisions has been used by US courts to invalidate state laws on the basis of the supremacy clause.

7. NAFTA and the US-Israel Free Trade Agreement. The United States also grants unilateral preferences to a number of developing countries under the Andean Trade Preferences Act, the Caribbean Basin Initiative and more generally under the Generalised System of Preferences.

8. US bilateral investment agreements take three basic forms: treaties of Friendship, Commerce and Navigation (FCNs); Bilateral Investment Treaties (BITs); and Overseas Private Investment Corporation (OPIC) agreements. Both the FCNs and BITs establish rights and obligations of the signing parties concerning the treatment of investment. 47 FCNs are currently in force. Since the inception of the BIT programme in the early 1980s, the United States has signed BITs with nearly 40 countries. US activity on BITs remains high, with twelve agreements concluded in the period January 1994-June 1996. See description of US Foreign Investment Regime prepared by the APEC Committee on Trade and Investment and World Investment Report: Investment, Trade and International Policy Arrangements (UNCTAD 1996).

9. Significant and expressly discriminatory barriers to market entry continue to characterise the US regulatory structure for both sectors. The regulatory structure for US maritime transport activities features well-known trade irritants such as Section 19 of the Merchant Marine Act of 1920 (the "Jones Act") which mandates retaliatory measures against actions by foreign governments deemed to violate the interests of US shipping. The Public Law Lifting the Ban on the Export of Alaskan Oil of 1995 provides that Alaskan crude oil shall only be transported by a vessel under the laws of the United States and owned by a US citizen with a US crew on board. In the domestic aviation sector, the Federal Aviation Act of 1958, as amended and recodified in 49 USC. Subtitle VII, Part A, stipulates that only air carriers that are citizens of the United States may operate aircraft in domestic air service (cabotage) and may provide international scheduled and non-scheduled air service as US air carriers. US citizens enjoy blanket authority to engage in indirect air transportation activities such as air freight forwarding and charter activities. Non-US citizens seeking to conduct such activities must, however, obtain authority from the Department of Transportation (DOT). Applications for such authority may be rejected on grounds related to the failure of effective reciprocity or if the Department determines that it is in the "public interest" to do so. In the absence of any other visible criteria to encourage pro-competitive treatment of such applications, the degree of discretionary power underlying reliance on either test appears distinctly at odds with an open market philosophy. Finally, "foreign civil aircraft" – defined as aircraft of foreign registry or aircraft of US registry that are

owned, controlled, or operated by persons who are not citizens or permanent residents of the United States – also require DOT authority to conduct speciality air services in US territory.

10. United States of America Schedule of Specific Commitments Supplement 3, GATS/SC/90/Suppl. 3.

11. United States of America List of Article II (MFN) Exemptions Supplement 3, GATS/EL/90/Suppl. 3.

12. See article by David Vogel, *op. cit.*

13. See EC Sectoral and Trade Barriers Database.

14. According to the UN Trade Barriers to Latin American Exports in 1996 [Washington Office of the UN Economic Commission for Latin America and the Caribbean (ECLAC)] "a vast maze of standards and regulations makes exporting to the United States a daunting task". The complexity of the system can be partly attributed to the three separate tiers of regulations that exist: federal, state and local. These regulations are often inconsistent between jurisdictions, or needlessly overlap. It is estimated that more than 44 000 federal, state and local authorities enforce 89 000 standards for products within their jurisdictions. These structural barriers, although unintentional, still create major hurdles for foreign firms attempting to enter the US market.

15. See EC Sectoral and Trade Barriers Database.

16. See Speech of Belinda Collins, Acting Director, OSS, NIST before the Committee on Science, Space and Technology on "International Standards and US Exports: Keys to Competitiveness or Barriers to Trade".

17. Examples are the US computer and telecommunications equipment industries, which have actively participated in international standardisation work at the ISO, IEC, and their joint technical committee (JTC 1) on information technology.

18. See TBT Articles 2.7 and 6.1 and SPS Article 4.

19. NAFTA Article 908(2).

20. NAFTA Article 908(6).

21. NAFTA Article 1304(6).

22. See Laker Airways *v.* Sabena Belgian World Airways, 731 F.2d 909 (DC Cir. 1984).

23. See National Co-operative Research and Production Act of 1993 (NCRPA) 15 USC. § 4301-06 (1994).

24. The legislative history of the NCRPA provides that a venture can utilise or place significant production and production support facilities outside the United States as long as they are "ancillary in nature". The legislative history further provides that all international agreements and other binding obligations between the United States and another country that provide national treatment satisfy the national treatment requirements of the law.

25. See Annex to Section 6, Recent Examples of Product Standards Related Barriers to Market Access of Telecommunications Equipment in OECD (1997), "Product Standards, Conformity Assessment, and Regulatory Reform" in T*he* OECD *Report on Regulatory Reform: Volume* 1: *Sectoral Studies*, Chapter 6, Paris.

26. The main intergovernmental standardisation body for telecommunications is the International Telecommunications Union (ITU). ITU develops standards covering safety, network security, interoperability of services, interconnectivity of networks, and performance issues.

27. A brief overview of FCC rules governing importation of telecommunications equipment underscores the central importance of technical regulations and conformity assessment procedures in gaining entry to the US market. Foreign providers of telecommunications equipment destined for the United States must typically satisfy a range of federal regulatory requirements. The FCC requires exporters of terminal equipment destined for the US market to obtain documentary evidence based on laboratory testing that their product conforms to FCC-defined standards. Typically, such evidence must establish that the product is safe to use; that it will not cause radio frequency interference; that it will not disrupt interconnection networks; and that it can be used by disabled consumers. In sum, a three-step process is in place, requiring that: 1) importers have a product tested by a laboratory for compliance with FCC product standards; 2) the product be registered as meeting FCC standards (usually involving submission to the FCC of laboratory test results, general product description, and photographs) and a certificate issued to this effect; and 3) individual batches of the product must be accompanied by a copy of the FCC registration certificate for border checks by customs officials. See Measuring the Costs of Regulations on International Trade: Progress Report in TD/TC/WP(98)37.

28. For example, the FCC is required by the National Environmental Policy Act of 1969 to evaluate the effect of emissions from FCC-regulated transmitters on the "quality of the human environment". In the current absence of a federally-mandated radio frequency (RF) exposure standard, the Commission has adopted recommended maximum limits developed by the National Council on Radiation Protection and Measurements (NCRP). In addition,

certain applicants may be required to routinely perform an environmental evaluation to determine compliance with FCC exposure limits, and submission of an Environmental Analysis is required in the event of non-compliance. See RF Safety Programme, FCC Office of Engineering and Technology at FCC website.

29. See discussion in OECD (1997), "Product Standards, Conformity Assessment and Regulatory Reform", in *The OECD Report on Regulatory Reform: Volume I: Sectoral Studies*, Chapter 6, Paris.

30. NAFTA Article 1304 embodies the principle of least-trade restrictiveness by requiring Parties to ensure that standards-related measures are adopted or maintained only to the extent necessary to *a*) prevent technical damage to public telecommunications transport networks; *b*) prevent technical interference with, or degradation of, public telecommunications transport services; *c*) prevent electromagnetic interference, and ensure compatibility, with other uses of the electromagnetic spectrum; *d*) prevent billing equipment malfunction; or *e*) ensure users' safety and access to public telecommunications transport networks or services.

31. The Reference Paper contains a binding, enforceable set of competition rules, including guarantees of fair and economical interconnection between competing carriers; prohibitions on anticompetitive conduct; and independent regulation of the telecommunications industry.

32. The ECO test – still in place for carriers from non-WTO Member countries – looks at such issues as legal barriers to entry; interconnection factors (reasonable and non-discriminatory charges, terms or conditions and whether adequate means exist to monitor and enforce these charges); competitive safeguards to protect against anticompetitive practices (cost-allocation rules, protection of carrier and customer proprietary information); and regulatory framework (separation between regulator and operator, transparent regulatory procedures).

33. Section 66 of the Foreign Participation Order states that the Commission will make an independent decision on applications and evaluate concerns raised by the Executive Branch in light of all the issues raised (and comments in response) in the context of a particular application. The US authorities expect trade policy concerns to be raised "only in very rare circumstances" and that any Executive Branch concerns communicated to the FCC in respect of a given application would be fully consistent with US law and international obligations. Comments by US Delegation at the Trade Committee Working Party, 16 September 1998.

34. In the past, Japan has claimed that when US subsidiaries of NTT and KDD applied to the FCC for licenses to provide international telecommunications services between the US and Europe, USTR, the Department of Commerce, and the Department of State required that the applications be suspended because of "trade concerns" (specifically, the extension of the NTT procurement agreement). The suspensions were later lifted and the applications ultimately approved after agreement was reached on NTT procurement. See 1998 Report on the WTO Consistency of Trade Policies by Major Trading Partners (Industrial Structure Council, Japan). FCC has noted that USTR, after co-ordination with other Executive Branch agencies, asked the Commission on four occasions during a recent two-year period not to act on certain applications because of trade concerns. However, all these requests occurred before the effective date of the WTO BT Agreement. See FCC Report and Order on Reconsideration 97-398 in the Matter of Rules and Policies on Foreign Participation in the US Telecommunications Market.

35. The regulator may take an additional 90 day period for review of applications which raise issues of extraordinary complexity, and each successive 90 day period may be so extended. See 47 C.F.R., Section 63.12.

36. Comments by the US Delegation at the Trade Committee Working Party, 16 September 1998.

37. Applications by carriers affiliated with foreign carriers that possess market power in non-WTO markets are not eligible for streamlined processing.

38. See FCC Public Notice (1998), "FCC Grants over 200 International Service Applications in First 90 Days of New Foreign Participation Rules" released 14 May.

39. Comments by the US Delegation at the Trade Committee Working Party, 16 September 1998.

40. US dominant carrier regulation does not discriminate between US and foreign carriers, its objective being to discipline monopoly power wherever it may have domestic effects on US consumers of telecommunications services. The Foreign Participation Order clarifies that dominant carrier regulation will be applied to all US licensed carriers affiliated with foreign carriers regardless of their ownership. Criteria applied to identify "dominant" carriers are also set out in the Order. In general: any US international carrier, irrespective of ownership, would be classified as dominant on a route where it is affiliated with a foreign carrier that has sufficient market power in a relevant market on the foreign end to affect competition adversely in the US market. Relevant markets on the foreign end of a US international route generally include: international transport facilities or services, including cable landing station access and backhaul facilities; inter-city facilities or services; and local access facilities or services on the foreign end. The FCC also adopted a rebuttable presumption to identify a category of foreign carriers that do not possess market power in any relevant market on the foreign end of an international route and therefore lack the

ability to affect competition adversely in the US market. This presumption of non-dominance applies to carriers with less than 50 per cent market share in each of the relevant markets on the foreign end; accordingly, such carriers are not normally subject to dominant carrier safeguards on the affiliated route. Parties may also make a showing that a foreign carrier with a market share of 50 per cent or more in a relevant market does not have sufficient market power to harm competition and consumers in the US market, so that its US affiliate should be classified as non-dominant. Comments by the US Delegation at the Trade Committee Working Party, 16 September 1998.

41. International Settlement Rates, IB Docket 96-261, Report and Order, FCC 97-280 (released 18 August 1997). The US approach has met with pointed criticism by trading partners. Japan, for example, views the system as constituting barriers to potential new entrants to the US market; sees it as a unilateral imposition of settlement rates linked to market entry regulation (instead of being determined primarily on a commercial basis); and questions its WTO consistency. From comments by the Japanese Delegation in the Trade Committee Working Party on 16 September 1998.

42. The FCC has publicly stated its commitment to transparency, noting that "to implement the telecommunications law fairly, the decision making must be transparent, which means that public input form all interested parties should be welcome and the final decision must explain why parties' views were or were not adopted. Not only must the system be transparent, but its decisions must be made in a timely fashion".

43. See the FCC 1998 Biennial Review Home Page at FCC website.

44. Under this system, a national regulatory body certifies that a type of vehicle or separate technical unit satisfies technical requirements set out in relevant regulations. This involves bringing each vehicle model (domestic or imported) to the regulatory body's testing facility where it must be tested and certified as meeting relevant technical regulations. See "Standards and Certification Procedures in the Automobile Sector" by Denis Audet (1997), in *Market Access Issues in the Automobile Sector*, OECD Proceedings.

45. FERC has traditionally regulated US investor-owned (*i.e.*, privately-owned) utilities but not federal power utilities such as the Tennessee Valley Authority and the Bonneville Power Administration or other government owned entities, such as the New York Power Authority and municipal utilities (some of which own a significant amount of transmission). As noted in Chapter 6, about 350 IOUs account for 73 per cent of electricity generated in the United States.

46. In contrast to most US utilities that have less than 10 per cent wholesale load (and FERC-guaranteed recovery of stranded assets in the move to greater competition), Ontario Hydro has a 70 per cent wholesale load and no analogous mechanism for stranded asset recovery. Ontario Hydro maintains that it cannot offer open access until provincial industry restructuring is complete – expected in the year 2000. As it restructures, the province is addressing many of the same issues faced by US States as they move to retail access.

47. See Chapter 6 for a fuller discussion of NERC.

48. See, for example, "Impact of Industry Restructuring in the US on Canada: Ontario Hydro Perspective", speech by Barry Green, Senior Advisor-Regulatory Affairs (External Markets).

49. USC. Title 15, Chapter 2C, Sections 79z-5b.

50. For a development of this argument, see article by David Vogel, *op. cit.*

51. OECD (1998), "Open Markets Matter. The Benefits of Trade and Investment Liberalisation", Paris; OECD (1995), "Report on Trade and Environment to the OECD Council at Ministerial Level", Paris; OECD (1994), "The Environmental effect of Trade", Paris.

52. See GAO (1996), *Regulatory Burden: Measurement Challenges and Concerns Raised by Selected Companies*, November.

53. Some US trading partners have objected to US reliance on third-party conformity assessments when less onerous means (such as reliance on manufacturers' or purchasers' declarations of conformity) could be employed. However, concerns about the safety, health, or environmental impact of some products may be too important to be left to self-assessments. This would be true of products whose failure could lead to injury, illness, property damage or loss of life. Drug safety certification provided by the FDA, for example, requires third-party assessment to verify product safety. See Standards, Conformity Assessment, and Trade into the 21st Century, National Research Council, *National Academy Press*, Washington DC, 1995.

54. GATT jurisprudence sheds light on how this obligation has been interpreted in practice with respect to US state measures. A 1992 GATT panel report on US measures affecting alcoholic and malt beverages examined the application of Article XXIV in relation to various measures of US state and local governments relating to imported beer, wine and cider. The panel ruled, *inter alia*, that some state measures were discriminatory and that the United States had not demonstrated to the panel that conditions for the application of Article XXIV:12 had been met. See DS23/R, adopted on 19 June 1992, in Basic Instruments and Selected Documents, 39S/206.

55. See FCC 97-398, Report and Order on Reconsideration adopted on 25 November 1997.

BACKGROUND REPORT
ON REGULATORY REFORM
IN THE ELECTRICITY INDUSTRY*

*   This report was principally prepared by **Sally Van Siclen** of the OECD's Division for Competition Law and Policy in consultation with **Peter Fraser** of the International Energy Agency, **Bernard J. Phillips**, Head of Division for the OECD's Division for Competition Law and Policy, and **Caroline Varley**, Head of Division, Office of Long Term Co-operation and Policy Analysis of the IEA. It has benefited from extensive comments provided by colleagues throughout the IEA and OECD Secretariats, by the Government of the United States, and by Member countries as part of the peer review process. This report was peer reviewed in October 1998 by the Standing Group on Long-Term Co-operation of the IEA and the Competition Law and Policy Committee of the OECD.

TABLE OF CONTENTS

Executive Summary

Background Report on Regulatory Reform in the Electricity Industry

Regulation of the electricity supply industry in the United States has been undergoing a major reform for several years. While inter-utility trading of electricity and generation by independent power producers have become substantial over the past few years, the present reform promotes an intensification of competition in generation by further diminishing the scope for discrimination in grid access, by divestiture of some generation assets, and by the creation of trading institutions such as spot markets. The introduction of independent system operators, which operate transmission facilities in a region, independently of their owners, are designed to further dampen the ability of vertically integrated owners to discriminate against competitors in generation. Some states are introducing further reform whereby all end-users may buy electricity directly from generators. Other states are reforming only to the extent required by changes at the federal level. That is, in the less reforming states, utilities are subject to *inter alia* "functional separation" and the requirements to file open-access transmission tariffs, to provide real-time information about transmission availability, and non-discriminatory transmission access.

Another key element of the reform is the transitional arrangements, which include mitigating, measuring, and compensating sunk costs that the reforms make unrecoverable by traditional regulatory means. New pricing schemes are also being introduced, so that *inter alia* reliability for large end-users is being transformed from an engineering concept into an economic good. In one area of the United States, a system of spot market nodal pricing, in which transmission congestion costs are reflected in the price of electricity, along with a system of tradable fixed transmission rights, has been adopted. Environmental goals for the sector are increasingly being met through market-based mechanisms, such as through the trading of SO_2 emissions permits, and the introduction of technology-neutral requirements that a pre-determined percentage of electricity be generated from non-hydropower renewable fuels.

The reform in the United States is being driven by the potential for lower prices and by technological change. A comparison of average prices charged industrial and residential users in each state shows that the highest statewide average was almost four times higher than the lowest in 1996. California and the states of the Northeast – all high-priced states – have leading positions in the reform wave. Technological change enables more time-of-use metering, which enables more demand shifting by end-users of electricity.

The first state reforms were implemented in March 1998 and the most recent set of major federal reforms are not much older, so it is too early to assess fully their effectiveness. Nevertheless, it is already clear that further reform will be necessary to reduce current policy inconsistencies. States' reforms differ markedly but the geographic scope of electricity markets generally extend beyond individual states, though are much smaller than the country. The geographic scope of independent system operators do not always extend beyond state boundaries, thus potentially subjecting different parts of individual markets to differing rules. Both of these imply efficiency-reducing distortions. Further, traditional transmission pricing methods hamper the development of markets for power, both because of their effect on short-term transactions and because of their effect on grid investment.

1. THE ELECTRICITY SECTOR IN THE UNITED STATES

1.1. Key features

The United States' electricity supply industry and its reform are distinct from those of other countries. There are a large number of economic entities of diverse types active in the sector and a large number and diversity of regulations and regulators. There is extensive trade in electricity for re-sale among utilities. The sector is vast, with annual sales exceeding US$200 billion, about ten per cent of physical capital investment in the country, and large sunk costs. The reform is shaped by the federal nature of the country, the diversity of states' starting points, the traditional emphasis on individual rights and "open government", and the predominance of private property in the sector.

Economic actors in the sector can be grouped into five broad types. The predominant type is the vertically integrated, privately owned utility ("investor-owned utility" or "IOU"). These several hundred companies are subject to pervasive economic, safety, and environmental regulation by independent federal and state regulators. The size distribution is very skewed, with the largest ten IOUs accounting for almost 30 per cent of total electric operating revenue for IOUs (Table 33, EIA, 1997g). Traditionally, in most states they have franchise areas where they are the state-designated monopolist with an obligation to serve any customer within that area. They have interconnection agreements with neighbouring utilities and long-term requirements contracts[1] with municipal, co-operative, and other investor-owned utilities. The second type of economic entity is the federally owned utility, some of which are very large. Usually, they generate and transmit electricity but do not sell it directly to end-users. The third type of economic entity is a variety of state and municipal utilities, public utility districts, irrigation districts, state authorities and other state organisations, and rural co-operatives. While a few members of this group are large vertically integrated municipal and state utilities, most are small organisations that purchase electricity and distribute and supply it to their communities. Being publicly owned, these last two groups are subject to limited independent regulation, that is, they are self-regulating, and varying tax regimes. The fourth type of economic entity is privately owned independent power producers ("non-utility generators" or NUGs). These now account for about nine per cent of generating capacity and are expected to be responsible for more than 40 per cent of capacity increases over the period 1999 to 2001. The fifth type of economic actors are power marketers and brokers, who act as middlemen in the markets for power. These five types of entities have different degrees of vertical integration, owners, objectives, and subjection to independent regulation and other laws.

In addition to the economic actors, there are two other major types of actors in the electricity sector of the United States. Independent regulatory bodies were created by federal and state governments to ensure that economic and public policy objectives are met by the privately owned utilities. Voluntary organisations of private and public utilities provide co-ordination and reliability of the electric system. The pinnacle of this system is the North American Electric Reliability Council and its successor organisation, the North American Electric Reliability Organization, which establish voluntary policies and standards, monitor their compliance by members, and assess the future reliability of the system over the United States, Canada, and a small part of northern Mexico (NERC, 1997b).

The mix of type of generation varies greatly from one area of the country to another. The Pacific Northwest has overwhelmingly hydropower, the Midwest overwhelmingly coal, the mid-Atlantic coal and nuclear, and the Northeast a mix of coal, oil, and nuclear. This heterogeneity results in a range of average state prices,[2] hence of stranded costs, and the pattern of public ownership (since, in the United States, large water control projects are, by tradition, publicly owned).

Traditional economic regulation of private utilities in the United States, takes the form of guaranteeing, *ex ante*, that expected total revenues exceed expected total cost by an amount sufficient to compensate for risk and attract sufficient capital. Public rate hearings, which are essentially adversarial in nature, reflecting the wider regulatory culture (see Chapter 2), are used to oversee the prudence of investment decisions and to allocate costs to be covered by the various classes of end-users. Estimates of quantity sold to each of the classes then determine the price for each class. This system was modified to allow more frequent adjustments for fuel costs after they became more volatile. The practical application of this system changed during the recession of the early 1980s when several large investments were found not to be prudent after they were made, so were not allowed to be recovered through regulated prices. Further, during periods of high inflation, the "fair" rate of return did not equal rates of return for alternative similar investments. Thus, in practice, the *ex post* equality of total revenues and total cost[3] did not always hold, although that was the principle.

Box 1. Major federal electricity industry participants

US Army Corps of Engineers: owns and operates 75 hydro-power/irrigation projects, totalling 20 720 MW (about 24 per cent of total hydropower capacity in the country), and transmission in the western United States.

Bureau of Reclamation of the US Department of Interior:* owns and operates 59 hydro-power/irrigation projects, totalling 14 640 MW capacity (about 17 per cent of the country's hydropower capacity), and transmission in the western United States.

US Department of Energy: includes Bonneville Power Administration (17 080 MW capacity, of which 90 per cent is hydropower, representing half of all the electric power of the Northwest region – states of Washington, Oregon, Idaho and portions of others; owns three-quarters of transmission in its region as well as links to other regions), Western Area Power Administration (10 600 MW capacity, of which almost all hydropower, and substantial transmission, including links to other regions, in the Southwest and Rocky Mountains), and three other power marketing agencies that generate and sell predominantly hydropower, operating under various legislative requirements; formerly included United States Enrichment Corporation, which makes fuel for nuclear power plants.

Tennessee Valley Authority: federal corporation with 28 000 MW generating capacity (73 per cent coal-fired) and substantial transmission in south-eastern United States.

---

*   The US Department of Interior has responsibility for natural resources, hence is not comparable to ministries with similar names in other countries.

Table 1. Geographic distribution of generation by energy source

Census division*	Terawatt-hours	1997 net generation by energy source (percentage)					
		Coal	Petroleum	Gas	Hydro	Nuclear	Other
New England	73.0	26.2	30.8	14.1	6.4	22.5	
Middle Atlantic	308.4	43.4	3.5	7.6	9.4	36.0	
East North Central	520.0	79.9	0.4	1.2	0.8	17.7	
West North Central	253.4	74.9	0.5	1.5	6.7	16.4	
South Atlantic	633.4	60.3	4.7	6.0	2.0	27.0	
East South Central	331.5	70.1	0.9	2.0	7.3	19.7	
West South Central	429.9	49.4	0.2	33.4	1.9	15.1	
Mountain	282.1	69.0	0.1	3.9	16.6	10.4	
Pacific Contiguous	273.7	3.1	0.1	13.9	69.3	13.6	
Pacific Noncontiguous	12.7	1.9	66.1	23.8	8.2	0	
US Total	3 125.5	57.2	2.5	9.1	10.8	20.1	0.2

* New England is Connecticut, Maine, Massachusetts, New Hampshire, Rhode Island, and Vermont; Middle Atlantic is New Jersey, New York, and Pennsylvania; East North Central is Illinois, Indiana, Michigan, Ohio, and Wisconsin; West North Central is Iowa, Kansas, Minnesota, Missouri, Nebraska, North Dakota, and South Dakota; South Atlantic is Delaware, District of Columbia, Florida, Georgia, Maryland, North Carolina, South Carolina, Virginia, and West Virginia; East South Central is Alabama, Kentucky, Mississippi, and Tennessee; West South Central is Arkansas, Louisiana, Oklahoma, and Texas; Mountain is Arizona, Colorado, Idaho, Montana, Nevada, New Mexico, Utah, and Wyoming; Pacific Contiguous is California, Oregon, and Washington; Pacific Noncontiguous is Alaska and Hawaii

Source: US Department of Energy, Energy Information Administration 1998*d*, Tables 7 to 13.

Box 2. Overview of the US electricity industry

Primary fuels (all energy usage): coal 31 per cent, natural gas 27 per cent, oil 22 per cent, nuclear ten per cent, hydroelectric five per cent, other five per cent (DOE 1998*b*, Fig. 4). One-fifth of the total is imported. Energy consumption per capita and per unit GDP is among the highest in the world (IEA, 1998).

Fuels used for electricity generation (1997): coal 57 per cent, nuclear 20 per cent, gas nine per cent, hydropower eleven per cent, oil two per cent, non-hydro renewable fuels 2×10^{-3} (about 7 500 mWh) (EIA, 1998*b*).

Electricity end-users (1996): 35 per cent residential customers, 29 per cent commercial sector, 33 per cent industrial sector and 3 per cent other end-users such as governments (EIA, 1998*a*).

Book value of electricity sector assets (1994): US$700 billion (10 per cent of the US total book value).

Sales of electricity (1997): US$214 billion (EIA, 1998*d*).

Average revenue (1997): US$0.0687/kWh (EIA, 1998*d*).

International trade (1996), in billion kWh: Imports 46.5 (45.3 Canada, 1.26 Mexico); Exports 9.02 (7.7 Canada, 1.32 Mexico), that is, less than one per cent of total generation.

Cost structure (1996): generation 74 per cent, transmission seven per cent, distribution 19 per cent.

Generation total: 3 652 teraWatthours; by ownership: 73 per cent investor owned utilities (about 350), of which about 11 per cent by non-utility power producers; 15 per cent publicly owned utilities (about 2 000), 10 per cent rural co-operatives (about 1 000); by size: the 34 largest utilities generate more than half the total (IEA, 1998).

Physical structure: there are five interconnections in North America, within which frequency is synchronised and between which are limited direct current links. Of these, three – East, West, and Texas – are predominantly in the United States. 157 control areas balance electric flows in their area and with adjacent areas, and some co-ordinate planning. There are nine reliability councils.

Emissions: the electricity industry accounts for about 65 per cent of SO_2 emissions and about 30 per cent of NO_X emissions in the country.

More recently, economic regulation of private utilities has begun to move toward "performance based regulation" of monopoly activities, a variant of price caps and the "RPI minus x" type of regulation in the United Kingdom. The independent regulator sets maximum prices for various goods and services, defines a price index, and sets a factor "x" that reflects, say, expected efficiency gains. Maximum prices in the next period are automatically set at the current period prices, adjusted by the change in the price index and the "x" factor. Additional adjustments can be made only at predetermined review periods. However, unlike pure price caps, the regulator also sets non-price performance standards, such as for reliability, in addition to the price standards.

There is substantial trade among utilities. The non-integrated utilities have always bought electric power, primarily under long-term contracts, and the federal utilities have always sold electric power, but earlier reforms (*e.g.*, the 1978 Public Utility Regulatory Policy Act) induced entry by non-utility generators. A significant amount of short term "economy" transactions also takes place. The introduction of NUGs as well as, perhaps, an increased risk that investments might not be allowed to be recovered under the regulatory regime, expanded an already developed market for both short-term (spot) and long-term power transactions amongst utilities. Presently, about 55 per cent of total electricity consumed is not generated by the utility that sells it to the end-user (EIA, 1998*g*).

An unusual feature of the current American reforms in the sector is the high level of public participation in the debates. The federal and various state reforms have been preceded and accompanied by discussions by utilities, academics, regulators and other parts of government, consumer, environmental and other special interests at conferences and public meetings, as well as in the newspapers, trade press and academic literature.[4] Much of the discussion and information is available on the Internet, so

271

participation has likely been broader than it would have been had it taken place only a few years earlier. The public discussion has stimulated sophisticated arguments over the design of mechanisms and institutions, which has diminished the threat of "capture" by special interests and in principle resulted in a superior final design of the overall reform.

Another feature that distinguishes the American electricity reform from those of many other OECD countries is that it takes place against a backdrop of an already deregulated gas sector. Open, non-discriminatory access to the pipeline infrastructure is established, and large users are free to choose their supplier, which results in about 50 per cent of gas being sold by a non-traditional supplier. Some states are moving toward allowing small users and residential end-users to choose their gas supplier (IEA, 1998). Given that the remaining liberalisation in gas is limited to small end-users who, because of their load characteristics, are not particularly attractive to entrants, there is not expected to be significant interactions between the continuing liberalisation of electricity and, residually, of gas. However, changes in pipeline tariff setting could affect interactions between gas and electricity during periods of peak energy demand.

1.2. Policy objectives

Policy objectives of the United States, as set out in the Comprehensive Electricity Competition Plan (DOE, 1998a), include both economic goals and social goals. The economic goals are lower prices, reduced government outlays, greater innovation and new services, and increased reliability of the grid. The social goals include environmental goals – cleaner generation, increased energy efficiency, and reduced greenhouse gas emissions – and protection of consumers and adequate service to the poor. To comply with the Kyoto Protocol to the United Nations Framework Convention on Climate, which the United States has not yet ratified, greenhouse gas emissions would have to be much lower than current projections.[5]

States' policy objectives often differ from those at the federal level. In the high-priced states, reducing the price of electricity is a key, indeed driving, objective (White). In the low-priced states, maintaining low prices despite liberalisation in adjacent states is a key objective. (After high-priced states liberalise, utilities prefer selling into high-priced states to selling into low-priced states.) There is a positive correlation between price and reform (industrial and residential users apply greater pressure for reform in the higher-priced states). Arguments for granting end-user access all at once focus on fairness rather than on cost-benefit analyses of such access. The states also differ in their environmental priorities, from reducing SO_2, NO_X, greenhouse gas and other emissions in fossil-fuel based states to maintaining wild salmon, other migrating fish, and migrating bird populations in hydropower-based states. The heterogeneity of the fifty states' objectives presents a challenge for reform.

2. REGULATION AND ITS REFORM

2.1. Main lines of reform

The United States is in the process of shaping one of the most liberalised electricity sectors in the world. Electricity reforms in the United States are distinct from those in most other OECD countries. First, they vary significantly from state to state. The state-to-state variation is greater than in, e.g., Australia, another federal country, but is comparable to that among Member States of the European Union. The variety of state reforms enables them to act as "test beds" for federal reforms, while at the same time providing flexibility to better match reforms to the individual states' starting points. However, this flexibility is constrained by the federal reforms, which form a framework within which the state reforms must fit. Second, where end-users get direct access to the electricity market, they typically all get access simultaneously (or over a very short period), unlike in Australia, New Zealand, and the European Union Member States, where access is phased in over several years, and not always to all end-users. Third, the reforms do not start from a unified, publicly owned system as they do in, e.g., France, New Zealand, and England and Wales. Having private rather than public initial ownership

---

Box 3.   Conditions for competition in the electricity industry

Competition requires a number of linked conditions along the whole supply chain:
- Non-discriminatory access to the transmission grid and provision of ancillary services.
- Sufficient grid capacity to support trade.
- Ownership or control of generators that is sufficiently deconcentrated to give rise to competitive rivalry.
- Competition law and policy that effectively prevent anticompetitive conduct or mergers.

Competition is enhanced by:
- Efficient access, including economically rational pricing, to the grid.
- Control of the grid fully independent from that of generators.
- Low barriers to entry into generation.
- A non-discriminatory, efficient market mechanism for electricity trade.
- A stranded cost recovery scheme that is non-distortionary and fair.
- Greater elasticity of demand, that is, that the buying side of the market be exposed to, and have the technology to react to, price changes, such as through time-of-use meters.
- End-user choice, with competition in retail supply to end-users.

---

implies a much greater concern in the United States about stranded costs.[6] On the other hand, like in many other countries, the reforms in the United States have not included privatisation of publicly owned utilities.

The United States places increasing reliance on markets to attain its policy objectives. The electricity reforms are fully consistent with this broad theme. As set out in its Comprehensive Electricity Competition Act, a proposed law introduced into Congress, the Administration intends *inter alia* to establish the necessary conditions – structural and regulatory – for competitive markets in generation ("wholesale competition" in American parlance) and encourage states to do the same for competition in retail supply ("retail competition").[7] Another main element of the reform is the mitigation, measurement, and recovery of stranded costs, which is a pre-condition for establishing competition in supply.

A major part of the over-all reform effort is reforms to intensify competition between generators to supply electricity, that is, "competition in generation". Among the requirements for such competition is non-discriminatory access to the transmission grid and provision of ancillary services. Complete divestiture of generation from transmission would accomplish this, but divestiture to establish competition in generation is limited in the United States by pervasive private property in the sector: Many regulators cannot order divestiture of private property outright. Some states such as California, however, are providing powerful financial incentives to partially divest generation to owners from outside the present market. Indeed, significant fossil-fuel generating capacity in California and New England has already been divested to owners from outside of the respective areas. As an alternative to divestiture of all generation, a new structure has been devised to reduce the ability to discriminate in grid access. "Independent system operators" have been established in California, as well as in the Northeast and the mid-Atlantic seaboard (the PJM Interconnection). The ISOs operate and control the transmission grid, while the grid remains owned by the vertically integrated utilities. The ISOs are managerially and operationally independent of the vertically integrated utilities. While the Federal Energy Regulatory Commission (FERC) presently requires only "functional separation", a weak form of separation, of transmission from generation marketing activities, and encourages the formation of regional independent system operators (ISOs), the Administration proposes giving FERC authority to order the establishment of ISOs. FERC further limits discrimination by transmission owners by requiring third parties to be offered transmission service comparably flexible to that enjoyed by the owners themselves, and to be provided information about transmission systems in real-time.

Efficient access to the grid also enhances competition in generation. "Efficient access" involves access prices and conditions that are transparent, cost-reflective, and maximise economic welfare. Efficient access is to be ensured by FERC, the primary regulator of transmission access prices and conditions. FERC requires cost- or congestion-based open access tariffs. The PJM Interconnection (in the mid-Atlantic States) has adopted nodal pricing of electricity, a pricing scheme which aims to provide incentives for more efficient transmission use at each time period. Now, FERC has jurisdiction only over privately owned transmission; the Administration proposes extending FERC jurisdiction to all transmission in order to ensure a consistent non-discriminatory access regime.

Competition in generation also requires sufficiently unconcentrated ownership of generating plants. In California, the divestiture of generating capacity, mentioned above, was to multiple owners, in order to deconcentrate generation. Market concentration can also be reduced by increasing transmission capacity.

Spot markets, independently run, have also been established in the more liberalised jurisdictions. Spot markets, by providing price transparency, liquidity, and otherwise reducing transactions costs, facilitate competition by letting buyers more easily compare and switch among competing generators.

Current reforms also target other potential barriers to competition in generation, such as barriers to entry into generation. Regulatory barriers to entry into generation were significantly reduced in the Energy Policy Act of 1992 through the establishment of a new class of generators that are exempt from costly cogeneration or renewable fuels requirements under earlier laws. However, siting of both generation and transmission is often problematic because states and localities retain authority to approve siting.

The second major reform element in the United States is the promotion of competition to supply all end-users ("retail competition" or "full end-user choice"). It is allowed but not required under the Energy Policy Act of 1992, thus is, presently, a matter of state regulatory policies (FERC, 1996b). As of July 1998, Massachusetts, California, and Rhode Island (partially) had introduced supply competition, nine other states had enacted legislation that provided for competition to supply all end-users (by dates ranging from 2000 to 2004), and several others were working on legislation (DOE, 1998i). The Administration proposes that each utility be required to permit all end-users to choose their own electric power supplier by 1 January 2003, except where States or non-regulated utilities find, on the basis of a public proceeding, that an alternative policy would better serve consumers.

The third major element of the United States reform is the mitigation, measurement, and compensation for stranded costs. Stranded costs are unamortised costs, prudently incurred[8] under the prior regulatory regime, that will not be recovered under the new, more market-based regulatory regime. Compensation for stranded costs is a necessary condition for gaining support for the intensification of competition in the electricity sector.[9] Stranded costs are measured and recovered according to the rules of their corresponding regulators, federal or state. Mechanisms used to recover stranded costs include lump-sum exit fees and non-bypassable charges on end-users. The design of the recovery mechanism can distort competition.

Stranded costs are mostly attributed to investments in nuclear generation and in long-term power purchase agreements under the Public Utility Regulatory Policies Act of 1978. The range of stranded cost estimates is US$70 billion to US$500 billion; an often-quoted likely mid-range is US$135bn to US$200 billion (IEA, 1998). Estimates are sensitive to assumptions about future market prices for electric power and the date on which end-users have direct access to the market.[10] As sales of fossil fuel generating assets have taken place, prices received have exceeded earlier estimates (IEA, 1998); this suggests that estimates of total stranded cost will decrease somewhat. Stranded costs will also diminish as book values diminish, in line with accounting depreciation. As more generating assets are sold, the prices received provide better information about the market value of other, unsold, generating assets; this means that estimates of total stranded costs should become more precise. Compared with the book value and annual sales in the sector, estimated stranded costs are sufficiently large that the design of the recovery system will have important effects on the subsequent evolution of the sector.

While the more reformist states are moving at different rates along similar albeit not identical reform paths, other states are engaging in only limited reforms. Two examples of less reformist states are Idaho and Michigan. Idaho, having preferential access to federally owned hydropower that results in almost the lowest electricity prices in the country, is not liberalising and is working to retain its preferential access. Michigan, with a local duopoly and constrained import transmission, also controlled by the duopolists, allows a limited fraction of end-users to pay to switch electricity supplier, but has made few other changes.[11] By contrast, while the situation in the state of Virginia is similar to that of Michigan, with monopoly control over transmission raising concern that competition from "outside" generators may be blocked, full retail competition in Virginia is nevertheless set to begin in 2004 (EIA 1998h). Figures 1 and 2 illustrate the current pattern of how states have selected themselves to undertake more or less reform.

Other policy goals in the United States are pursued by a combination of markets and direct government intervention. Environmental goals, for example, are pursued through subsidies – cash, tax advantages, or, newly, explicit surcharges on end-users – to support research, development, and adoption of emerging technologies for, *e.g.*, energy efficiency and cleaner generation; market-based regulation, such as the SO_2 emissions permits trading programme; and more traditional command and control regulation. The Administration proposes a requirement that a pre-determined percentage of electricity be generated from non-hydropower renewable energy sources, subject to a price ceiling. (Similar requirements have been adopted in some states.) Efficiency in the generation of "green" electricity would be encouraged by using market mechanisms to determine the technology, the generator, and the price received.

Policy goals with respect to reliability[12] of the electricity system would be assured, under the Administration's proposal, by moving from a set of voluntary agreements basis under the North

Figure 1. **Average revenue from electricity sales to all retail customers**
(1996, cents/kWh, by state)

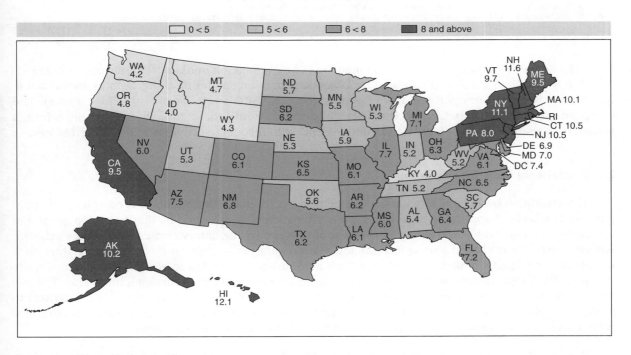

Note: US average = 6.9 cents per kWh.
Source: US Department of Energy.

Figure 2. **Status of state electric utility deregulation activity**
As of September 1, 1998

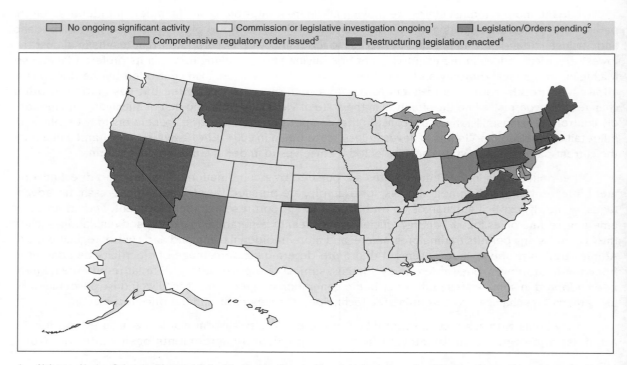

1. Alabama, Alaska, Colorado, District of Columbia, Florida, Georgia, Hawaii, Idaho, Indiana, Iowa, Kansas, Kentucky, Louisiana, Minnesota, Mississippi, Nebraska, North Carolina, North Dakota, South Dakota, Tennessee, Utah, Washington, West Virginia, Wisconsin, and Wyoming.
2. Missouri, Ohio, Oregon, and South Carolina.
3. Michigan, New York, and Vermont.
4. Arizona, Arkansas, California, Connecticut, Delaware, Illinois, Maine, Maryland, Massachusetts, Montana, Nevada, New Hampshire, New Jersey, New Mexico, Oklahoma, Pennsylvania, Rhode Island, Texas, and Virginia.
Source: US Department of Energy, Energy Information Administration, Electric Industry Restructuring, monthly update.

American Reliability Council to a system of mandatory self-regulation under a NERC successor organisation, the North American Electric Reliability Organisation, overseen for its United States-based activities by the Federal Energy Regulatory Commission.[13] NAERO awaits approval (NERC 1997*b*). The comprehensive Electricity Competition Act, if adopted, would make this change in status from a voluntary to a self regulatory organisation under FERC, with respect to activities in the United States.

2.2. Institutional basis for regulation

The institution basis for regulation of the electricity sector in the United States is complex and rather opaque. The body of applicable regulations is a combination of laws passed by the federal Congress and relevant state legislatures, decisions and regulations issued by regulatory bodies, and court decisions. Power to regulate is shared among federal and state regulators, and some municipal regulators, with sometimes ambiguous boundaries between their authorities. In addition to economic regulators, there are specialised regulators for nuclear power, financial instruments, and environmental protection. There is also a boundary between those activities that are subject to economic regulation and those subject to market discipline. A significant portion of economic entities in the sector are publicly owned or otherwise have unusual legal statuses, thus are subject to only limited independent regulation.

Private firms in the sector have been subject to independent economic regulation since early in the twentieth century. Regulatory authorities are independent – in personnel, operations and funding –

of the companies regulated. Typically, the authorities hold public hearings to collect relevant information and to hear opposing points of view. Decisions must be made in public and are accompanied by reasoned, public explanations. Decisions can be appealed to the judiciary.

The main federal economic regulator for the electricity sector is the Federal Energy Regulatory Commission (FERC). FERC is an independent commission, governed by five commissioners appointed by the President and confirmed by the Senate, for five-year terms. FERC has jurisdiction over all privately owned lines used in interstate transmission (that is, authority over rates, terms and conditions); in practice, this gives FERC jurisdiction over all privately owned transmission. Since the boundary between transmission and distribution is somewhat arbitrary, so also is the limit of FERC jurisdiction until specific lines are labelled as one or the other. FERC also has jurisdiction over sales of electric power for resale. FERC has only limited jurisdiction over entities owned by the public sector, which own about one-third of the grid and about a quarter of generation.[14] FERC does not have authority to order electric transmission siting (which contrasts with its authority to order gas pipeline siting).

State public utility commissions have jurisdiction over generation (excluding federally-owned), distribution, transmission siting and environmental concerns, residual revenue necessary to pay for the costs of transmission lines, and service and prices to end-users. They often do not have jurisdiction over municipal utilities: *e.g.*, municipal utilities may be able to opt-out of the reforms in their respective states. Thus, for example, Los Angeles Department of Water and Power decides whether Los Angeles end-users may choose their own electricity suppliers and the Massachusetts law requires municipal utilities to allow retail competition only if they seek to compete outside of their service areas.

Box 4. **Regulatory institutions at a glance**

Federal Energy Regulatory Commission (FERC): regulates interstate transmission, sale of electricity for resale, and mergers (concurrent jurisdiction with Antitrust Division and Federal Trade Commission).

State public utility commissions: regulate generation, distribution, service and prices to end-users, transmission siting, and environmental concerns.

US Department of Energy (DOE): develops energy policy, sponsors energy research, and approves construction of international electric transmission lines.

Environmental Protection Agency (EPA): enforces federal environmental protection legislation, usually works in conjunction with state environmental departments; is an independent federal agency.

Nuclear Regulatory Commission (NRC): is responsible for ensuring safe operation of commercial nuclear power plants and that there are sufficient funds for their decommissioning; specifies maintenance rules, inspects, and issues public inspection reports; is an independent federal agency.

North American Electric Reliability Council (NERC): a non-profit corporation that oversees voluntary agreements to protect reliability across the United States, Canada and part of Mexico; is a non-profit corporation. In 1998 its successor organisation, the North American Electric Reliability Organisation (NAERO) was created.

Antitrust Division of the US Department of Justice: has concurrent jurisdiction with FERC and Federal Trade Commission for mergers, concurrent jurisdiction with FTC for anticompetitive behaviour.

Federal Trade Commission (FTC): has jurisdiction for consumer protection concerning marketing and advertising, concurrent jurisdiction with FERC and Antitrust Division for mergers, concurrent jurisdiction with Antitrust Division for anticompetitive behaviour; is an independent federal agency.

Commodity Futures Trading Commission (CFTC): regulates markets for futures and options based on electric power.

Securities and Exchange Commission (SEC): has jurisdiction over some mergers under the Public Utility Holding Company Act of 1935, regulates markets for utility stocks.

277

Entities such as federal corporations, power marketing agencies, municipal utilities, irrigation districts, and co-operatives are subject to different regulations. Often their economic behaviour is controlled by their founding legislation or regulations. For example, they may be required to have revenues cover certain costs, or to sell power preferentially to publicly owned utilities.

In addition to the boundaries between various regulators' jurisdictions, there is also a boundary between that which is subject to economic regulation and that which is subject to antitrust law enforcement. This is defined, in part, by the antitrust laws' "state action doctrine". This doctrine removes, from the sphere of antitrust prosecution, behaviour that suppresses competition but that is an action of a state, or a political subdivision (such as a city) to which the state has delegated authority to regulate, or an action by a firm or individual actively supervised by a state, and taken pursuant to a clearly articulated state policy to displace competition. (See Chapter 3.) The Antitrust Division of the US Department of Justice and the Federal Trade Commission are the federal institutions that enforce the antitrust laws. State attorneys general enforce antitrust laws, and have an interest in competition in the electricity sector.

Two important non-economic regulators are the North American Electric Reliability Council (NERC) and the federal Environmental Protection Agency (EPA). NERC is a voluntary organisation of utilities covering much of the continent. It promulgates voluntary policies and standards to promote reliability of the electric supply in North America. (It is being succeeded by NAERO, see above.) The EPA and the state environment departments share a complex layering of authority over environmental protection. Key federal laws are the National Environmental Policy Act of 1969 that requires federal agencies to prepare environmental impact statements on major federal actions, the Clean Air Act[15] – which deal with the SO_2 emissions trading programme and NO_x reduction programme – and the Clean Water Act, which covers wastewater discharges.

2.3. Regulations and related policy instruments in the electricity sector

2.3.1. Regulation of entry

Entry into electricity generation promotes competition by increasing the number of generators with independent incentives taking independent decisions. Entry into electricity generation is unregulated *per se*, and the regulation-induced cost of entry has fallen in the past decade. The Energy Policy Act of 1992 (EPAct) substantially reduced regulatory entry costs by relieving entrants of cogeneration and renewable fuels obligations.[16] Indeed, as noted above, non-utility generators now account for a large fraction of new capacity. However, some regulations continue to affect significantly the cost of entry. These include those for connection charges, siting rules, and emissions permits. Siting of generation and transmission assets is heavily influenced by zoning and other local use regulation, as well as by pressure from local citizens that the facilities be located "not in my backyard". Reducing the time required to get siting approval would reduce the time required for entry, hence reduce its cost. The asymmetric treatment of existing and new generators in the SO_2 emissions permit trading system (the former are given permits, the latter must buy them) is a regulation-created entry barrier. In practice, however, operating economics in many parts of the US favor gas-fired generating plants, which are relatively easy to site and require few SO_2 permits. Finally, entry into generation in one geographic area by an existing generator located in another area is facilitated or blocked by the terms and conditions of access to transmission, as well as the availability of sufficient transmission capacity. (This is discussed later in Section 3 on markets.)

Restrictions on foreign entry into nuclear generation are contained in the Atomic Energy Act, which provides that a license to operate nuclear generating plants cannot be issued to anyone owned, controlled by or dominated by an alien, foreign corporation or a foreign government (42 USC Sec. 2133 (Sec. 103)). "Control" and "domination" are defined on a case-by-case basis. These restrictions may in the event be flexible, as indicated by announcements by British Energy to acquire and operate, through a joint venture, nuclear power plants in the United States.

Entry into retail supply is regulated at the state level through licensing requirements that do not restrict the number of entrants, but do, in order to provide some consumer protection, require a certain level of financial stability. One regulatory entry barrier into retail supply, one which also reduces incentives to enter generation, is created by introducing an asymmetry in consumers' switching cost: Massachusetts does so, by combining a low regulated price, the "standard offer", with a rule that end-users who switch to an entrant cannot later switch back to qualify for the "standard offer".

Further reducing regulatory entry costs would facilitate the development of competition in generation and, paradoxically, could decrease stranded costs. In particular, if foreign managers of nuclear plants are more efficient than domestic managers, then reducing barriers to the purchase of nuclear plants by foreign owners would increase their market value, thus diminishing stranded costs. In addition, eliminating regulation-caused switching cost asymmetries, such as that in Massachusetts, would facilitate competition in retail supply.

2.3.2. *Grid access and transmission pricing regulation*

The terms and conditions of access to the transmission grid influence competition in generation, and whether the grid is used and augmented in a cost-minimising way. The Federal Energy Regulatory Commission (FERC), the regulator for privately owned transmission,[17] regulates transmission tariffs, requiring grid owners to file open access non-discriminatory transmission tariffs. FERC also requires non-discrimination with respect to flexibility of service and information about the transmission grid. Transmission tariffs are cost- or congestion based. Whereas FERC formerly allowed only postage-stamp or contract-path pricing (see definitions in the box below), it has subsequently allowed incremental cost pricing for grid expansion or upgrades that relieve a grid constraint, and opportunity cost pricing for a change in operations that relieves a grid constraint. Distance-sensitive and flow-based pricing have been allowed more recently.

Two schemes for transmission pricing that have recently been introduced in parts of the United States are nodal pricing and zonal pricing. Under nodal pricing, there is a distinct price for electric power at each location in a grid that is used by the system operator in its model of the system. These prices equate demand and supply at each node. Under zonal pricing, there is a distinct price for electricity in each zone, which incorporates several nodes. California, for example, uses about 25 zones, whereas the somewhat larger PJM Interconnection (Pennsylvania, New Jersey, Maryland and Delaware and the District of Columbia) uses about 2 000 nodes, of which some are near-duplicates. Electricity prices change frequently, hourly in California and more frequently in PJM Interconnection.

The transmission tariffs are derived from the electricity prices in a way that reflects congestion. The tariffs have two parts, a fixed part and a variable part. The variable part of the transmission tariff is the difference between the price of electricity at the origin (a node or a zone) and the price of electricity at the destination. This difference is the congestion cost. When transmission is congested, transmission tariffs are high. Nodal and zonal pricing schemes are usually accompanied by fixed transmission rights. These rights are equivalent to perfectly tradable firm transmission rights (Hogan, 1998). They can be used to hedge, partially, against variations in transmission tariffs. They also ensure that using transmission rights to block access is costly.

Zonal pricing was adopted in California in 1998 and was tried in 1997 in the PJM Interconnection (Pennsylvania, New Jersey, Maryland and Delaware and the District of Columbia). Under the California system, zonal prices are found only when there is congestion: otherwise, there is a single spot price, in the day-ahead market of the Power Exchange, everywhere in the state. Market participants submit bids to the day-ahead market that may include how they would want the quantity they supply or demand to change as price changes. If the independent system operator (ISO) finds that there is congestion (*i.e.*, the state-wide market clearing price in the day-ahead market would imply physically impossible flows of power), the ISO uses the supply and demand bids to find the least-cost way of relieving the congestion. The congestion charges for each congested transmission path are calculated on the basis of the cost of relieving the congestion, *i.e.*, the bids and, if necessary, a default price. In addition, the schedule that comes out of the ISO's congestion-relieving process gives the incremental cost of power in each zone.

The zonal market-clearing price in each zone must meet three conditions:

- It must cover the zonal incremental cost (the incremental cost of generating or delivering more power in that zone).

- The difference in zonal market-clearing prices in two zones must be equal to the congestion charges determined by the ISO for the same two zones.

- It is no higher than necessary to satisfy the two conditions above.

The zonal pricing scheme in California has built-in adjustment mechanisms. For example, conditions under which new zones are hived off from old zones were specified from the beginning. Thus, in the first year of operation, the number of zones increased from two to 25 to reflect congestion. Over time, the California zonal pricing scheme may become more like a nodal pricing scheme.

In the PJM Interconnection, the zonal pricing scheme did not work well: Congestion was underpriced, so market participants scheduled more bilateral transactions than could be accommodated by the grid, hence the independent system operator had to intervene administratively, constraining choice in the market, to preserve reliability. This experiment in zonal pricing in PJM was followed by the adoption of nodal pricing in April 1998.[18]

Under the nodal pricing scheme adopted by PJM Interconnection, prices are discovered in a spot market for about 2 000 locations. Under conditions of effective competition, the price at each node equals the system marginal cost at that node. Given these prices, each generator produces at its short-run profit maximising output. Therefore, the market equilibrium supports the necessary dispatch given transmission constraints. During the first five months of nodal pricing, PJM Interconnection has often experienced congestion, that is, times when prices varied significantly from one node to another.[19] At times, some nodal prices of electricity are negative, reflecting the value of "counterflow" in the system. This experience with nodal pricing shows that the constraints of a zonal pricing scheme (that nodal prices be identical within zones) would indeed be binding over significant periods of time. This experience has demonstrated that the independent system operator can indeed calculate and report nodal prices at five-minute intervals, sufficiently frequently for market participants to react (Hogan, 1998). One criticism has been that the individual markets are too thin to support the development of hedging instruments. However, trade in financial instruments for a few locations in the PJM Interconnection does occur. As trade concentrates at a few nodes, markets become sufficiently deep for hedging to take place.

FERC tries to reduce the scope for discrimination by vertically integrated utilities by requiring transmission owners to offer flexibility of service to third parties that is comparable to that the owners enjoy (FERC, 1996a, pp. 29-39), and to provide, in real-time, the same information the utility itself uses about its transmission systems (according to FERC Order 888). The information is posted on Internet bulletin boards, and is supposed to facilitate the arrangement of sales of electric power across transmission lines owned by others. However, the present rules do not prevent transmission owners from understating transmission capacity or availability.

Transmission access pricing, as traditionally practised in the United States, is not fully consistent with liberalised electricity markets. The adoption of a nodal pricing by the PJM Interconnection and zonal pricing by California, by demonstrating that such schemes are, in fact, workable over a period of time, provide impetus for more widespread adoption of pricing schemes that better reflect transmission costs. It is too early to tell, however, whether nodal pricing, even when a fixed part is added to the transmission tariff, will indeed provide sufficient incentives for grid augmentation and for locating new generating capacity where it minimises system cost. The difficulty of inducing optimal transmission investment is discussed below in the section on independent system operators.

Box 5. Grid pricing in the United States

The operation of the grid and dispatch of generation is always done in the United States in a way that maintains engineering system stability; investment is done so as to provide sufficient physical assets. Under the traditional system of regulation of the sector, the grid pricing scheme, if there were one, had only to ensure sufficient total revenues; operating decisions were made according to engineering reliability criteria and the marginal cost of generating plant. However, when American regulatory reform provides utilities with incentives to change their behaviour, the economic incentives of a grid pricing scheme become relevant. Grid pricing schemes that better align economic incentives with engineering requirements for stability reduce the scope over which system operators need to take administrative rather than market based decisions in order to maintain stability. Grid pricing schemes that better align economic incentives with requirements for investment reduce the scope over which command and control for investment is needed. A key characteristic of a transmission pricing scheme that aligns economic incentives with engineering requirements is that prices reflect transmission congestion, that is, that prices take into account externalities of transmission.

Any transmission pricing scheme must be complemented by a moment-to-moment control mechanism, which uses these prices as inputs along with the engineering reliability constraints. (In some places, such as in the New England region, system operators have long operated with the objective of reliability-constrained, economic dispatch, so this is not a large innovation.)

Transmission tariffs can be multi-part so that, for example, one part of the tariff varies with usage and another, usage-insensitive part, can be used to equate revenues to a regulated target.

Among the several grid pricing schemes in use in the United States are:

- *Postage-stamp pricing*: one price regardless of the locations of the buyer and seller.
- *Contract-path pricing*: summing prices of segments of transmission line between buyer and seller.
- *Grid pricing implied by zonal pricing of power*: Two-part transmission tariff, where the variable part of the tariff for transmission between two zones equals the difference in electricity prices in those two zones. Zones are defined so that their boundaries are where transmission congestion occurs. The price of electricity at any one moment in time is equal within each zone.
- *Grid pricing implied by nodal pricing of power*: Two-part transmission tariff, where the variable part of the tariff for transmission between two nodes equals the difference in electricity prices in those two nodes. Nodes are the nodes used by the system operator for system operation. The price of electricity at each node equates supply and demand at that node. In the absence of market power, the price at a location would equal the marginal cost of supplying load at that location, where the marginal cost is the sum of marginal generating cost and transmission.

Neither postage-stamp nor contract-path pricing is related to the actual flow – hence cost – of delivered electricity, nor do they reflect the economic value of a part of the grid under a particular pattern of use. Thus, these pricing schemes do not provide incentives for efficient grid use or augmentation. Nodal pricing, combined with effective competition, appears to induce efficient grid operation and dispatch. Different forms of grid pricing have different costs of setting up and operation, notably for information technology, so there may be a trade-off between these costs and the efficiency of the pricing scheme.

2.3.3. *End-user tariff regulation*

Tariffs charged end-users are traditionally regulated because utilities were, traditionally, monopolies with substantial protection from competitive entry. Where there is not direct access by end-users to electricity market (*i.e.*, not retail supply competition), the regulated tariff scheme may, or may not, reflect the marginal cost of delivered electricity, hence may, or may not, provide economic incentives for the efficient use of electricity. In general in the United States, regulated tariffs do not reflect the marginal cost of delivered electricity. Tariffs are, mostly, regulated by the state public utility commissions. Under the traditional system, generally each end-user was assigned to a category of user (*e.g.*, residential, commercial, small industrial, or industrial) and paid the regulated price for its category. The state public utility commissions regulated tariffs to provide for sufficient investment, a fair rate of return, and for "social" purposes (see Section 2.4.5). However, as technological change allowed larger users to threaten credibly to leave the system by generating power themselves (or moving to another region), they were able to negotiate individual tariffs. To the extent that utilities' revenues are constant, these tariff concessions were at the expense of other customers.

The states that are granting all end-users direct access to the power market are, in essence, expanding the ability to negotiate price to all users. However, there is usually a transitional arrangement whereby residential end-users have access to a regulated maximum price for several years into the future. In both California and Massachusetts, for example, the apparent maximum residential price is 10 per cent below the former regulated price. States may define categories to favour certain types of customers; *e.g.*, Massachusetts has a special "farm tariff". State public utility commissions also regulate for "social" purposes, which is being changed as end-users gain direct access to electricity markets (see Section 2.4.5).

To the extent that there is not market power in electricity markets, market prices should reflect the marginal cost of electricity. Hence, if these market prices are reflected in prices charged end-users then they should, in general, provide incentives to end-users to use electricity efficiently, and in particular to shift their usage of electricity away from periods of peak demand. (This is discussed in greater detail in Section 3.1.) Of course, this change in behaviour requires time-of-use metering as well as time-of-use pricing, and the fixed costs of such meters may be sufficient to deter small end-users from buying such meters.

2.3.4. Nuclear safety regulation

Electricity sector reform changes the economic incentives of owners of commercial nuclear power plants. Concern has been expressed that owners have reduced incentives for safe operation. However, the NRC has found that "safety concerns exist, in many cases, independently of economic deregulation" and that there is no correlation between a licensee's financial health and general indicators of safety (NRC, 1997). Hence, electricity sector reform is unlikely to decrease the level of safety at nuclear power plants. Indeed, the experience of the United Kingdom nuclear power plants suggests that economic efficiency and safety increase together.

2.4. Regulation for restructuring

2.4.1. Vertical integration

The ubiquitous vertically integrated utilities are increasingly required to vertically separate, in one form or another, generation from transmission and distribution. In *Order* 888, adopted in 1996, FERC required functional separation, maintaining as safeguards procedures whereby any person can file a complaint at FERC about misbehaviour and FERC monitoring of markets (FERC 1996*a*, pp. 57-59). The competition authorities had recommended operational separation over functional separation, and had noted the advantage of completely separating ownership and control (FTC, 1995, DOJ, 1995). The FTC argued that functional separation would leave in place both the incentive and the opportunity for utilities to discriminate against competitors, and that regulatory oversight to detect, *e.g.*, subtle reduction in quality of service to competitors, such as delays, would be very difficult, as would provision of timely remedies. More recently, the Administration has noted clear benefits from operational separation and, under the proposed Comprehensive Electricity Competition Act, would grant FERC the power to require the establishment of independent system operators.

Some state regulators are providing strong financial incentives for vertically integrated utilities to divest generation. For example, California is doing so for fossil-fuel generation.[20] In response, the three IOUs in California are divesting much of their fossil fuel generating plants, largely to IOUs that do not have generating facilities in the region.[21] In the Northeast, US$1.6 billion of fossil fuel and hydropower facilities were divested in 1998. In Arizona, utilities must divest all of their generation assets if they want complete recovery of stranded costs. In Connecticut, all non-nuclear generation must be sold by 2000, and all nuclear generation by 2004 (EIA, 1998*h*).

Box 6. Types of vertical separation between generation and transmission
in the United States

Generation is vertically separated from transmission in order to ensure non-discriminatory access to the transmission grid and to reduce the scope for evasion of regulation. In order to ensure non-discrimination, both the vertically integrated utility's ability and its incentive to discriminate against a rival generator must be eliminated. Discrimination can be subtle, including for example delays, complications, and informational disadvantages. Discrimination hampers competition, thus resulting in inefficiency in the short-run and discouragement of efficient entry in the long run. Evasion of regulation, in which utilities shift costs from competitive to regulated activities, decreases efficiency in the competitive activities by disadvantaging lower-cost competitors. Regulatory evasion also attenuates the distributional effects of the regulatory regime. Types of vertical separation between generation and transmission include (ordered from stronger to weaker types):

Divestiture or ownership separation: Generation and transmission are separated into distinct legal entities without significant common ownership, management, control, or operations.

Operational separation: Operation of and decisions about investment in the transmission grid are the responsibility of an entity that is fully independent of the owner(s) of generation; ownership of the transmission grid remains with the owner(s) of generation.

Functional separation: Accounting separation, plus 1) relying on the same information about its transmission system as its customers when buying and selling power and 2) separating employees involved in transmission from those involved in power sales.

Accounting separation: Keeping separate accounts of the generation from the transmission activities within the same vertically integrated entity. This includes a vertically integrated entity charging itself the same prices for transmission services, including ancillary services, as it does others, and stating separate prices for generation, transmission, and ancillary services.

Of the four degrees of separation listed here, divestiture is the only one that eliminates incentives to discriminate. Divestiture also fully eliminates the ability to discriminate. Operational separation removes the ability to operate the grid or to make grid investments in a discriminatory manner, because all these decisions are made by an entity that is distinct from the owner of generation. Functional separation only somewhat reduces the ability to discriminate: common management and a common pool of staff can co-ordinate efforts across the functional divide. It thus requires an effective back-up system of regulation. Accounting separation affects neither the ability nor the incentive to discriminate; while effective oversight would force regulatory evasion, cross subsidies, and discriminatory pricing into the open, discriminatory behaviour and information access would remain undetected, and the allocation of joint costs and benefits would necessarily be arbitrary.

Where generation and transmission are not separated operationally or by divestiture, and an independent regulator is expected to enforce non-discrimination under accounting or functional separation, a variety of failures can occur. Detecting and proving anticompetitive behaviour can be difficult, since monitoring subtle and short-lived anticompetitive behaviour, as might be profitable in a complex environment such as electric systems operations, is complex and costly. Second, incentives to exploit market power will remain. Third, rules designed to reduce the use of market power can misidentify anticompetitive behaviour, thus "chilling" competition and increasing administrative and litigation costs (FTC, 1998b).

Divestiture, so that the transmission owner no longer also owns generation, implies that the transmission owner cannot increase its profits by favouring a subsidiary generator over other generators. In all the other types of separation, ownership of both transmission and generation remains with a single entity, so the incentive and ability to discriminate remains. If there is not divestiture, then non-discrimination requires the vertically-integrated utility to ignore its own economic interest. Not divesting also leaves in place incentives to find ways to evade regulatory constraints.

"Operational separation" is implemented, in the United States, with the establishment of Independent System Operators (ISOs). The effectiveness of this form of separation relative to functional

---

Box 7. Vertical separation of ancillary services from electric power

Ancillary services provide the critical real-time balance of the system.* In effect, many ancillary services are the backup that allow the system to deliver consistent power to all customers, even as demand fluctuates or particular pieces of equipment unexpected fail. Traditionally, they were provided by vertically integrated utilities as part of their bundled energy product, but some reforms include the separate pricing and provision of some ancillary services from that of electric power, even though the actual decisions about how much of each service is needed at each hour, and where, remain primarily under the authority of the system operator. (It is the only institution with the real-time information to know what services are required, and it can arrange the provision of these services for the aggregate load rather than, at higher cost, for individual loads [DOE, 1998c].) Ancillary services operate over various time scales, from seconds to hours, and, because they can be transmitted only over certain distances, are differentiated as to place as well as time.

---

* There are many different ancillary services. Some are, essentially, a co-ordination function, ranging from real-time to longer periods beforehand. Others maintain the balance between generation and load, over periods ranging from seconds to minutes to hours, through the centralised control (for those with quick reaction times) and use of generating units at various levels of readiness. Other ancillary services inject or absorb reactive power to maintain voltages. There are also services for metering and communications. Another service enables a network to restart operations after a blackout. Some ancillary services are provided by generators, others by the transmission grid, and others by a control centre (DOE, 1998c).

---

or accounting separation depends on the degree of independence of the ISO from the vertically integrated utilities. Where the ISO is not truly independent, the problems of discrimination and regulatory evasion remain. Hence, the governance of the ISO is critical. This is discussed below in Section 3.2. Divestiture, by contrast, does not require the creation of a governance structure that ensures independent yet efficiency-enhancing and efficient decision-making.

The split of ancillary services from power is also addressed in *Order* 888. FERC defined ancillary services and ruled that six are to be offered with, but priced separately from, transmission services and that others may be self-provided or provided by the transmitter or by third parties.[22] (FERC, 1996a, pp. 198-225, 246). The FERC imposes cost-based price caps for those ancillary services for which a utility has not demonstrated a lack of market power. The utility can offer discounts to reflect cost variations or to match rates available from third parties (FERC, 1996a, pp. 250-251). The difficulty for FERC is to set the price-caps so that a utility cannot prevent efficient entry through dropping prices charged those customers who are the most attractive customers for new entrants while subsidising from revenues gained from other customers.

The vertical separation between generation and retail supply promotes competition in generation.[23] While in principle the retail supply part of a vertically integrated entity can be required, by regulation, to purchase the "most economic" energy, in practice it is difficult to price the insurance that is implicit in electric supply contracts, especially requirements contracts, so it is difficult for independent regulators to oversee that, indeed, the most economic energy is purchased. Structural separation of retail supply from generation, with the imposition of a hard budget constraint, provides incentives to purchase the most economic energy, thus increase demand elasticity for electric power, thus competition in generation. The separation and reform of economic regulation of retail supply increases economic efficiency by reducing cross-subsidies to expensive-to-serve end-users, since entrants into retail supply would otherwise creme-skim the cheap-to-serve users. Retail supply separation permits other-than-geographic aggregation of end-users; *i.e.*, geographically diverse end-users may form joint buying groups.

The separation of retail supply from distribution raises issues that are similar to but not identical with those raised with respect to the separation of generation from transmission. The potential for regulatory evasion (the cross-subsidisation of the "competitive" activity-retail supply – by the "regulated" activity – distribution) is present here as well, and can take the form of using the trademark and established reputation from a long existence as a regulated monopolist in order to compete in the retail supply markets. The problem of subtle discrimination, such as delays in providing information or services to non-affiliated retail suppliers, exists in this vertical relationship as well. However, if all suppliers have equal access to information about extensions of the distribution grid, such as to new buildings or houses, then scope for discrimination is smaller than it is between generation and transmission. (This information flow from distribution to supply should not be confused with the informational advantage of the incumbent supplier over entrants into supply, which constitutes an entry barrier.)

In the more reformist states, entry by independent retail suppliers is unregulated, save for regulations to provide consumer protection. Traditionally, municipal utilities in the United States purchased the great majority of the electric energy they re-sold to end-users; the municipal utilities were free to choose their energy supplier. With effective oversight by end-users/voters, they should have had the incentives to procure least-cost energy. Hence, the extent of any entry by competitive suppliers and any resulting price decrease may be a measure of the effectiveness of this oversight.

2.4.2. *Competition law and policy*

There are three major strands to the competition law in the United States: monopolisation (akin to abuse of dominance in other countries),[24] agreements and mergers. (See Chapter 3 for more detail.) Each of these is relevant to the electricity sector, which is subject to shared jurisdiction by the FERC and the antitrust laws. In addition to enforcement by the federal competition authorities, any person, including individuals and corporations, who is injured by anticompetitive behaviour, including mergers, can sue directly under the antitrust laws, as civil actions, as can state attorneys general. Indeed, private lawsuits account for the vast majority of lawsuits under the American antitrust laws.

American antitrust law treats severely agreements among competitors on price, quantities or who will serve which customers; these agreements are prohibited and are subject to criminal prosecution. Where the same parties engage in repeated bidding against one another, under similar circumstances, they might be expected to learn about each other's bidding strategies. It is an unsettled area of law precisely where increased understanding of the other parties' strategies, and optimal responses putting that understanding to use, leads to a meeting of minds, which would constitute an illegal agreement. Such repeated interactions might occur in electric power pools.

Mergers in the electricity sector are reviewed both by the antitrust authorities and FERC. They apply different formal standards,[25] have available different sets of remedies,[26] but use a common framework, albeit differently interpreted, for evaluating the effect of a proposed merger on competition. The staffs exchange views about how to evaluate mergers in principle but, given the experience in other industries with dual oversight of mergers, such as airlines and railroads, these do not guarantee a common view on any given merger.

To evaluate the likely effect of a proposed merger on competition, both the antitrust authorities and FERC use the DOJ/FTC Horizontal Merger Guidelines, which set out both an analytical framework and specific standards. The five parts of the evaluation are: market definition, measurement and concentration; the potential for adverse competitive effects of the transaction; entry; efficiencies; and failure and exiting assets. This framework is applied on a case-by-case basis in a forward-looking manner, so that mergers in the sector would be subject to an evaluation under the new regulatory regime rather than under assumptions of the continuation of past patterns of *inter alia* inter-utility trade. The evaluation of mergers during the sector's regulatory transition is difficult because predictions about the future effects of a merger are more uncertain.[27] FERC has defined a "safe harbour" for mergers so that transactions that fall within its definition will not be subject to a full FERC hearing on the competition aspects of the merger (FERC, 1996c).

The antitrust laws provide an important safeguard in the liberalisation of the electricity sector. However, they are costly to employ and not omnipotent. One result is limited post-liberalisation

---

Box 8. Merger evaluation in the electricity sector in the United States

Markets usually have two dimensions, product and geographic. While there are potentially many different relevant product markets, it may be sufficient to consider only a few scenarios, such as peak, intermediate, and base, that present distinct competitive conditions and occur with sufficient frequency to be of concern. Product markets might also be delineated by duration and the date on which the energy is delivered, which could be several years hence. For each product market, a geographic market is defined. Geographic markets for energy and some ancillary services are limited by transmission congestion, line losses, and charges for transmission. Since these may vary from hour to hour, the scope of geographic markets may vary hour to hour. A refined analysis of a particular merger would likely require a sophisticated transmission model.

After defining markets, sellers into those markets are identified and their market shares are measured. Sellers are determined by the physical location of the generating units, except in the market(s) for reactive supply, which can be provided both from generation and transmission facilities. Market shares reflect generating units' marginal operating costs (*i.e.*, whether they are units that operate at baseload, intermediate, or peakload) and contractual or other commitments of that capacity. Market shares are calculated on the basis of capacity with marginal operating cost below or equal to the price in the market under consideration; *e.g.*, market shares in the intermediate load market would reflect capacity used at baseload and intermediate load. The market shares are used to calculate a measure of market concentration, the "Herfindahl-Hirschmann Index", which is used to form refutable presumptions about the likely effect of the merger. This presumption can be and often is overcome by other factors in the analysis.* (Under the DOJ/FTC Horizontal Merger Guidelines, an HHI above 1 800, which corresponds to fewer than five equal-sized firms, is considered "highly concentrated".) Entry is evaluated on the basis of timing (within two years), likelihood, and sufficiency (size).

In addition to mergers between electric utilities, three other kinds of mergers can potentially raise competition issues: between an electric generator and its fuel supplier ("convergence" mergers), between an unregulated and a regulated entity, and between an electric utility and a natural gas utility serving the same geographic area. Convergence mergers raise two sorts of competition issues, the potential to raise rivals' costs and the potential for price increases resulting from unfair access to rivals' confidential information. The first might arise if the generator acquires the only or one of the few suppliers to its rivals, there are no other choices for the rivals or for the downstream customers, and the costs of the generator and its rivals are similar. The second issue might arise if access to rivals' cost information could be used to raise and sustain, *e.g.*, bids into a pool. The second sort of merger might facilitate regulatory evasion, whereby the utility subsidises its unregulated activities from its regulated activities, raising the costs to the latter customers and inducing inefficiencies in both markets. The third sort of merger might reduce competition if the two sources of energy were considered substitutes for, *e.g.*, residential cooking, water heating, or space heating or cooling.

---

* Among the factors are the responsiveness to competitors to increases in market prices, the incentives of the merged firm to raise prices, the existence of contracts that undermine the ability to detect or punish defections from a price cartel or that enhance buyers' bargaining position *vis-à-vis* sellers, and factors related to the repeated nature of the interactions of sellers, under a pool system, which may make collusion easier to arrive at and to sustain.

---

remedies to insufficient competition in power markets, which has caused some states to encouraged or require divestiture of some generating assets as a part of the overall reform. Indeed, the proposed Comprehensive Electricity Competition Act would grant FERC the authority to order such divestiture. This seems to be a reasonable safeguard.

2.4.3. Reliability

Reliability[28] is provided through the North American Electric Reliability Council. NERC is a voluntary association whose membership constitutes virtually all investor-owned utilities and increasing numbers of independent generators in the United States, Canada, and part of northern Mexico. NERC establishes voluntary policies and standards that increase the reliability of the grid, monitors compliance, and assess the future reliability of the system. Much of the work is done by volunteers, with the large utilities providing the bulk of the expertise and money and wielding much of the power. NERC has an established reputation for technically sound judgement.

Under the old regulatory regime, utilities were content to comply with NERC guidelines. Under rate-of-return regulation, utilities did not have incentives to shirk in their reliability operations because regulators tended to allow all prudently incurred capital and operating costs to be recovered by regulated revenues. When the allowed rate of return was greater than their cost of capital, utilities had incentives to make reliability-promoting investments. Under the new regulatory regime, utilities can take actions that affect their profits but that may incidentally affect reliability. Also, utilities may seek to influence independent system operators in profit-increasing but reliability-decreasing directions. Further, deregulation has increased the number and heterogeneity of economic actors in the sector, thus the number of interests that have to be satisfied to reach a consensus. As a result of all these factors, voluntary compliance with reliability standards is expected to decline (NERC, 1997*b*).

In response to these changes, NERC created a new organisation, North American Electric Reliability Organisation, in mid-1998. NAERO is expected to continue the work of NERC, but with an intention to broaden participation and sources of funding, and to be prepared to be overseen by the appropriate regulatory authorities in the three countries. The latter change would enable mandatory reliability standards to be enforced and is intended to reduce antitrust liability in the United States for co-ordination by erstwhile competitors in order to comply with these standards. The Comprehensive Electricity Competition Act, if adopted, would make this change in status from a voluntary to a self-regulatory organisation under FERC, with respect to activities in the United States.

During the transition to competitive markets, reliability may decline from its current level, though to what extent is unclear. It might decline for two reasons. First, the pattern of use of the transmission grid under competition may be different from its pattern of use under the former regulatory regime, for which the grid was designed. In particular, there may be more long distance transmission. This different pattern of use may place the system under stress more frequently until the appropriate investments can be made. This effect can be reduced if independent system operators (ISOs) are regional, thus able better to take into account transmission congestion over larger regions. In addition, appropriate pricing of transmission, as discussed above, would discourage patterns of use that give rise to reliability concerns, and encourage congestion-relieving investment in the long-run. Explicitly pricing reliability would provide a spur to these investments, but there may nevertheless be a transitional period during which not all transactions desired by market participants can be made and there are financial incentives to operate closer to the limits of the system. (Explicitly pricing of reliability enables larger end-users who highly value reliability to pay for it, while allowing those with a low willingness-to-pay to buy lower-priced interruptible supply contracts. Whereas under the old regime, all customers had to be convinced to support investments for reliability, now those who highly value reliability can compensate utilities for their reliability-promoting investments and operating procedures. Of course, explicit pricing of reliability requires the ability to assign liability in the event of failure.)

The second potential cause of a decline in reliability is that the transition from the existing integrated planning process to a market-driven process of investment in generation and transmission may take some time. Decreased co-ordination of investment during the regime change can reduce reliability. At present, there appears to be a lack of effective mechanisms for paying for transmission extensions that benefit utilities or end-users who are in different states. Both the EIA and NERC have expressed concern that no one is taking responsibility for building new lines and supplying equipment to serve customers in other states.[29] However, if reliability were priced explicitly, or if ISOs were sufficiently large, then such a payment mechanism would likely exist. The Department of Energy has formed a special task-force to assess the impact of competition on reliability, and to recommend measures to help prevent reliability from declining to an uneconomic degree.

For smaller end-users, for whom the installation of equipment for shedding load may be too costly, "reliability" is associated more with weather-related outages, such as trees falling on power lines. For these end-users, reliability is a public good: investment to increase one neighbour's reliability cannot exclude the next door neighbour from benefiting. Regulation of distribution is needed to ensure sufficient provision of such public good reliability.[30]

The reliability regime, which has worked well over the past three decades, will necessarily change as economic regulation of the electricity sector changes. The regime will likely change toward mandatory self-regulation, overseen by the independent regulators of the three North American countries. It is not clear whether efficient long distance transmission investments can indeed be made under a system of state-by-state as well as federal regulation. Finally, it is not clear how the introduction of independent system operators will transform the reliability regime, still based primarily on utilities.

2.4.4. *Environmental regulation and subsidies*

There are three main points of intersection between environmental and electricity sector regulation. First, some emissions from generating plants are regulated. Second, "renewable portfolio standards", according to which a minimum fraction of electricity would be generated using non-hydropower renewable fuels, have been established in several states and has been proposed nation-wide by the Administration. Third, research, development, and demonstration for the adoption of new technologies to increase energy efficiency and to decrease emissions from generation, is subsidised both at state and federal levels. In addition, there are consumer protection concerns about potentially false claims about the "green-ness" of power.

A nation-wide sulphur dioxide emissions permit trading programme significantly reduced SO_2 emissions from generating plants at costs much lower than expected. (See Chapter 2.) The programme combines fully tradable permits for the emission of SO_2 and requirements for monitoring equipment with a safeguard that, permits notwithstanding, no utility may emit SO_2 above certain limits. Power plants are given permits, the quantity of which is based on historic fuel consumption and a specific emissions rate; new sources, *i.e.*, those joining the programme after January 2000, must buy permits from other participants. Permits can be traded, sold or "banked" (not used until a future year). The first phase, implemented January 1995, applied to 263 units at 110 power plants, mostly coal-burning and located in the east and Midwest. The second phase, beginning January 2000, applies to all utilities generating at least 25 MW. Continuous emissions monitoring systems must be installed in all fossil-fuel generating units over 25 MW and in new units under 25 MW that use fuel containing more than a specified percentage of sulphur (EPA, 1997).

The cost of reducing SO_2 emissions has been considerably lower than forecast: the price of a permit in early 1998 was about US$100/ton, versus expected prices of US$250 to US$400/ton. The average cost of reducing SO_2 emissions using retrofitted smokestack scrubbers was about US$270/ton in 1995, versus expected prices of US$450 to US$500/ton. Part of the reason prices are lower than anticipated is that unexpectedly low rail freight rates (due to changes in regulation of that sector) made switching to burning low sulphur Wyoming coal an unexpectedly cheap alternative to the installation of scrubbers. Also, 1998 prices are considered to be below the long-run average compliance cost because utilities are believed to have over-invested in scrubbers on the basis of pessimistic projections of permit prices (CEA, 1998).

As compared with SO_2, control of NO_x is more difficult because utilities, which are easy to monitor, are not the primary emissions sources: Transportation accounts for about 49 per cent of emissions and non-utility combustion for 18 per cent. Utilities are subject to performance standards on NO_x emissions that apply to some types of coal-fired boilers since January 1996, and will apply to the remaining coal-fired boilers after 2000. Together, two phases will result in reductions of annual NO_x emissions from utilities of 2.4 million tons (EPA, 1998). The development of regional NO_x emissions reductions trading is being encouraged by the Administration.

Reduction in the emission of CO_2, as set forth in the Kyoto Protocol on Climate Change, is the object of a number of initiatives. (The United States emits about one-quarter of the world total of CO_2.) Of those initiatives with domestic effect, the Administration estimates that its electricity sector restructuring proposal will reduce greenhouse gases by about 25 to 40 million tonnes per year, despite increased demand due to lower prices. This reduction is expected, by the Administration, both from changes in incentives for utilities to be efficient and from a number of associated initiatives. Much of the decrease in CO_2 emissions is anticipated to come from an accelerated shift from coal-fired to gas-fired power plants due to a more competitive marketplace. Important initiatives include the "renewables portfolio standards" detailed below, cross-subsidies to renewable energy and energy efficiency, "green" labelling to enable voluntary consumer switching to "green" electricity, and "net metering" to encourage small scale renewable fuel-based systems. The Administration proposes spending $6.3 billion for R&D and tax initiatives to promote energy efficiency and renewable energy. If these measures are found to be insufficient as the Kyoto implementation timeframe approaches, the Administration proposes a domestic greenhouse gas emissions allowance trading programme, to be integrated with various international flexibility mechanisms such as international emissions allowances trading, "joint implementation" within Annex I countries, and the Clean Development Mechanism (under which "clean development" investments in developing countries "earn" allowances) (Administration 1998).

"Renewables portfolio standards" is a market-based regulatory mechanism to promote the generation of electricity by, usually, non-hydropower renewable fuels. Under such a programme, a specified per centage of electricity must be generated by renewable fuels. No restriction is placed on the technology or the generator.[31] In practice, the programme creates two separate markets, one for electricity generated by renewable fuels and another for all other electricity. Typically, the per centage required is reduced if the cost of renewable fuelled generation exceeds the price of other generation plus an adjustment factor. The "green" electricity is then traded in the competitive market, at whatever price can be received. The mechanism is used in some states, and the Administration has proposed its extension nation-wide. The state of Maine has imposed the largest share of "green" generation of any state, requiring that 30 per cent be produced by hydro-power or renewable fuels (EIA, 1998h). In Massachusetts, the minimum share of non-hydro renewable fuelled generation increases according to a schedule that depends on the difference between the average cost of renewable technology and average spot market price. If the cost constraint does not bind, then 1 per cent of electricity sold in Massachusetts is to be generated from non-hydro renewable fuels by 2003.[32] The Administration's proposal would slowly increase the nation-wide share to 5.5 per cent in 2010-2015, but with a cost cap of US$0.015/kWh. By contrast, almost all (97.8 per cent) of the net generation of electricity by renewable sources in the United States was by hydropower (in 1996 and 1997) (EIA 1998d).

Other environmental programmes take the form of direct subsidies to research, development, and demonstration projects for energy efficiency, cleaner generation, and renewable fuels. With respect to energy efficiency, some US Department of Energy programmes are aimed at buildings and industry, such as changing building codes to admit more efficient techniques, while others are aimed at increasing efficiency of conversion of fuels into electricity. Programmes for cleaner generation focus on coal. There are wind, solar, biomass, and photovoltaic system programmes. E.g., the use of biomass for electricity generation is promoted by subsidies to research and development, studies and demonstration projects through partnerships with private entities, as well as a US$0.015/kWh tax credit for closed-loop biomass projects (those using dedicated energy crops) (DOE, 1996).

Some environmental programmes are funded through non-bypassable wires charges. For example, California and Massachusetts use this means to fund energy efficiency activities, including weatherisation of houses for poor families, and the development and promotion of renewable energy projects. The Administration has proposed that non-bypassable wires charges be used nation-wide for such environmental programmes. In California, consumers who choose a qualified "green" electric power provider will get credits (up to US$0.015/kWh), and the renewable power industry is directly subsidised.

Box 9. Environmental effects of electricity sector reform

The environmental objectives for the electricity sector include reduced emissions of and SO_2, NO_x, various other noxious gases, CO_2 and other greenhouse gases, and secure storage of spent nuclear fuel. The control of some of these gases, notably of greenhouse gases but also NO_x and SO_2, goes well beyond the electricity sector as the gases have significant sources (and for greenhouse gases, sinks) that are not part of the sector. The reform of the sector indirectly affects the level of emissions through possible changes in marginal input fuels, price-induced changes in quantity of electricity generated, and competition- and regulation-induced changes in efficiency. In particular, the introduction of competition in generation can induce changes in patterns of investment for generation that have implications for the mix of fuels used. For example, earlier retirement of coal-fired generation plants and replacement with gas-fired plants implies a reduction in emissions of several gases. Earlier retirement of nuclear power plants and replacement with fossil-fuel plants implies an increase in emissions of several gases. At the same time, if competition induces greater economic efficiency than the traditional form of regulation, then there would be greater incentives to reduce fuel costs, hence for greater technical efficiency of conversion of fuel into electricity, and thus a reduction in associated emission. Further, increased use of time-of-use pricing will discourage demand at peak periods, thus the use of less efficient older plants.

Table 2. **Estimated 1995 emissions from fossil fuel steam electric generating units at electric utilities by fuel type**

Thousand short tons

Fuel	Net generation (TWh)	SO_2	NO_x	CO_2
Coal	1 653	11 248	6 508	1 752 527
Gas	307	1	533	161 969
Petroleum	61	321	92	50 878

Source: Electric Power Annual 1995, Volume 2. Energy Information Administration, US Department of Energy, DOE/EIA-0348(98)/2, December 1996; cited in EPA 1997.

The movement away from pervasive rate-of-return regulation toward greater competition can have effects on the environment directly, as well as indirectly through changing incentives under environmental regulations. The shift toward markets is expected to accelerate the shift toward gas-fired plants and away from coal and oil, which would reduce SO_2 and CO_2 emissions, but could also change the relative usage of baseload and peakload generators. The table below shows the relatively low levels of emissions from gas as compared to coal and oil.

The reform of pricing to end-users changes incentives to subsidise energy efficiency-enhancing investments of the type made under "demand side management" programmes. Under the old regulatory regime, all consumers bore the cost of adding new generating capacity; if a subsidy to another consumer to reduce his demand, especially his peak load demand, was cheaper than the capacity addition, the subsidy reduced total cost to the subsidising consumers so was rational for them to pay. Under the new system, consumers who buy power at peaks will themselves pay substantially higher prices,[33] thus internalising the cost of capacity additions. Consumers' reactions may be to invest in time-of-use meters and "smart" appliances that can shift their use of electric power to off-peak periods. The overall reform of the sector can have other effects on incentives to make efficiency-enhancing investments: If the reforms do deliver lower electricity prices, or reduce the cost of new generating capacity, then these investments become less attractive.

Liberalised electricity markets and state-level environmental rules may have complex interactions. Electricity markets are generally larger than states, so generators competing in the same market generally are subject to different state environmental rules. In general, different rules create different costs of compliance. Liberalisation implies that there are limits to sustainable differences in compliance cost between states in the same electricity markets, because if a state imposes rules that increase generating costs significantly above those in an adjacent state, more power might be generated and exported by units in the other state. To prevent this, Massachusetts requires all electric energy sold within its boundaries to meet its own environmental rules, whether the electricity is generated in the state or not.[34] Effective brokerage of state environmental policies at the federal level, or the formation of regional pacts, may be a more efficient way of ensuring that environmental externalities, whether cross-border or not, are fully internalised.

2.4.5. *Social legislation*

Social legislation for the electricity sector is primarily under state, rather than federal control. Reforms of the sector are designed not to endanger existing social protections. For example, in both California and Massachusetts subsidies to low-income consumers will continue to be paid out of a fee assessed on all end-users. Most systems incorporating retail supply competition provide for a "retail supplier of last resort", so that consumers are not cut-off from electricity supply (Brockway). One example of social legislation changing in response to electricity market liberalisation is that, in California, special provision is made for an information system so that end-users with life support equipment (and thus needing special protection from being cut-off) are centrally identified even after they switch suppliers.

2.4.6. *Consumer protection*

In states where small end-users have direct access to electricity markets, there are consumer protection issues specific to the transition as well as traditional concerns. In some of the reforming states, utilities that have sent explanations of the reform and its implications for consumers with their monthly bills. California has spent $89 million, mandated by the public utility commission, to inform consumers about their new right to switch electric energy suppliers.[35]

In the United States, "slamming" has occurred in the telecommunications industry and commentators have drawn consumer protection analogies between the two industries. Provisions in, for example, the California law, for third party verification that the consumer really wants to switch supplier, and a three day period in which a small consumer can costlessly cancel a supplier change, should reduce this problem. The registration of all sellers, marketers and aggregators provides some protection that consumers will not be cheated by "fly-by-night" suppliers. In California, all electric service providers offering services to residential or small commercial customers must provide "proof of financial viability" and "proof of technical and operational ability" in order to register.

Box 10. **Consumer protection in a liberalised electricity sector**

Consumer protection for this sector includes both variations on consumer protection provided in other sectors and, where end-users have direct access to markets, transitional issues that arise because consumers are newly empowered to take additional decisions. With expanded choice, consumers need expanded truthful information.

The more traditional consumer protection issues involve "slamming", "fly-by-night" sellers, false advertising, "red-lining", and the truthful disclosure of electricity supply contract terms and conditions. "Slamming" means switching consumers from one supplier to another without their knowledge. False advertising may take many forms, but a concern in this sector is that suppliers might falsely label the source of the generated electricity as "green", thereby falsely leading consumers to believe they are self-taxing toward a social goal when they buy a supplier's premium-priced energy. Suppliers might, also, falsely claim that switching suppliers would save consumers large amounts on their electricity bill, when in fact switching suppliers can only reduce charges for energy and not, for example, charges for wires and for stranded costs. "Red-lining" is discrimination on the basis of geographic location of the consumer.

With respect to false advertising regarding "green" generation, the Federal Trade Commission has Guides for the Use of Environmental Marketing Claims that explain the application of the general requirement that such claims be truthful and adequately substantiated. "Red-lining" is being countered in California with the requirement that the utilities supply areas they were assigned before 31 March 1998. Finally, requiring the uniform disclosure to consumers of the separate charges (*e.g.*, for energy, wires, public goods and stranded costs), other terms and conditions, and other characteristics (*e.g.*, fuel mix and emissions) will help consumers to compare prices and to evaluate claims about the benefits of switching suppliers (which cannot regulated charges).[36] Consumer protection in this sector is, therefore, not different from that required for other goods and services save that, like other newly liberalised sectors, there is a particular transition role for consumer education.

2.4.7. *Competitive neutrality*

Where privately owned and publicly owned entities, involved in the same activities, receive different treatment, resulting in different costs, because of the difference in ownership, total cost is higher than it would be under equal treatment. The diverse types of economic entities are subject to diverse rules on taxation, regulatory oversight, access to federal hydropower, and other laws. In addition, publicly owned entities operate under accounting and budget rules that do not necessarily require the same accounting procedures for valuing assets or market-like rates of return on equity or market-like debt repayments. Together, these differences result in *inter alia* different costs of purchased electricity and different costs of capital, thus imply that there is not competitive neutrality.[37]

There are substantial differences in the cost of purchased power that result from preferential treatment under laws and regulations. Specifically, some utilities have preferential access to electricity generated by federal hydropower schemes. Electricity thus generated is not sold at market prices; rather, it is rationed, giving publicly owned utilities first call, with privately owned utilities allowed to buy any excess. The price at which this electric power is sold is determined by its marginal accounting cost, charges for irrigation water (a joint product), government accounting rules, and by budget rules that specify net budget flows, interest rates, and repayment terms for the cost of dams and associated infrastructure. These projects have very low marginal costs: Bonneville Power Administration (BPA) and Western Area Power Administration (WAPA), have short-run marginal costs of about US$0.016/kWh and US$0.011/kWh respectively. In 1997, BPA's "preference rate"[38] was US$0.0239/kWh and WAPA's average revenues were US$0.016/kWh, respectively. These figures compare with 1995 industry average revenues of US$0.060/kWh (BPA, 1997, BPA, 1998, WAPA, 1997). Thus, being a preferred customer of the federal hydropower schemes is a valuable status; in essence, it is a subsidy. In addition, the rationing process does not ensure, as a free market would, that electricity goes to those buyers who value it the highest. Hence, replacement by a market would result in a more efficient allocation of electricity generated by federal hydro-power schemes, and overall savings on the generation of electricity.

Differences in the cost of capital are also large. Debt is subject to different tax rules; for example, local publicly-owned utilities may issue bonds that are exempt from federal taxation, subject to some restriction. The cost of capital is lower for some public entities not only because of different tax treatment, but also because of markets perceiving their debt to be less risky because it is backed by a taxing authority and, for some, because they may not be required to return a market rate of return on investments to their owners or to make market-like debt repayments.

There are a variety of other unequal treatments. For example, the federal corporation Tennessee Valley Authority and federal power marketing administrations such as BPA and WAPA, are exempt from federal and state corporate income taxes. Publicly owned utilities may not be subject to regulatory oversight, notably with respect to their charges for transmission (although this would change under the Administration's proposed Comprehensive Electricity Competition Act), and may be exempt from various laws that affect their costs, ranging from environmental to labour standards laws. Further, as provided in the Energy Policy Act, certain companies have preferential access to research and development funding.[39] On the other hand, privately owned utilities, or their ratepayers, bear the costs of complying with regulation, *e.g.*, the cost of credibly conveying information to the independent regulator, a cost which is not borne by publicly owned utilities.

The Tennessee Valley Authority provides an example, albeit perhaps an unusual one, of the effect of the special treatment. While the TVA is required to be self-financing with respect to electric power, its prices do not reflect US$14 billion of non-producing nuclear assets. The implicit federal government guarantee has enabled TVA to borrow US$26 billion (as of September 1994) at low interest rates.[40] It pays no federal income tax. TVA is protected from competition by the EPAct, which does not require TVA to comply with the new grid access requirements, and by provisions in TVA's contracts with distribution companies that severely limit distributors' abilities to buy from other sources. (The contracts provide that TVA supplies all their electric power and, if a distributor wishes to cancel the contract, it must provide ten years notice.) However, TVA can be and has been ordered to provide transmission access to specific requestors. Despite these advantages, the Government Accounting Office writes that, "TVA would likely be unable to compete with its neighbouring utilities in the long term" (GAO, 1995).

Publicly owned utilities sell their power on average about one-sixth to one-fifth cheaper than do investor owned utilities. The American Public Power Association (an organisation of publicly owned utilities) estimates that tax-exempt financing accounts for four to five per centage points, and preferential access to federal hydroelectric power accounts for another 1.5 to 2 percentage points of this difference; the Edison Electric Institute (an organisation of IOUs) estimates that the entire gap is explained by tax, legal and regulatory advantages (IEA, 1998). However, if publicly owned utilities are not 11 to 13 per cent (of revenue) more efficient than IOUs (that is, if the remaining price difference is not explained by differences in efficiency), then the large difference in average price of power sold suggests that, even by conservative estimates, there is significant competitive non-neutrality.

2.5. Stranded costs

The third main part of the United States electricity reform is the measurement and recovery of stranded costs. This part is primarily about the redistribution of rents: the assets are already sunk in the sector, but the revenues that they will generate under the new regulatory regime are expected to be lower than the revenues they would have generated had the former regime continued. At the same time, a poorly designed recovery system can inflict real costs on the economy through distorting prices of electricity or distorting entry decisions.

Roughly two-thirds of the total stranded costs in the United States are estimated to stem from nuclear investment and the remaining one-third from high-priced power purchase requirements of cogeneration and renewable energies mandated by the Public Utility Regulatory Policies Act of 1978 (PURPA). Direct access to power markets by all end-users is estimated to cause 80 per cent to 90 per cent of the total (IEA, 1998). Owners of nuclear power plants are required, by independent regulators, to be prepared to bear the cost of decommissioning.[41] This regulation has not changed in the reforms. If electricity reform results in earlier than planned shutdown of nuclear plants, then this would be provided for as via the same mechanisms as other stranded costs.

Given that United States has radically reformed the regulation of numerous sectors, often in ways that changed the value of private assets, it is reasonable to ask, what is different about this sector that stranded costs are recovered? During the reform of natural gas regulation, a sector also under the responsibility of the FERC, the reform was challenged in court. That court told FERC that it must take into account the transition costs borne by regulated utilities when the Commission changes the regulatory "rules of the game". Hence, while much of the public discussion has focused on the fairness, or not, of requiring shareholders or captive customers to bear the costs of transition because of a regulatory change beyond their control, the FERC states that, "We learned from our experience with natural gas that, as both a legal and a policy matter, we cannot ignore these costs" (FERC, 1996a, p. 453).[42]

The FERC defines "wholesale stranded costs" as "any legitimate, prudent and verifiable cost incurred by a public utility or a transmitting utility to provide service to: 1) a wholesale requirements

---

Box 11. **Stranded costs**

"Stranded costs" are those unamortised costs of prior investments or ongoing costs because of contractual obligations, prudently incurred under the prior regulatory regime, that will not be recovered under the new, more market-based regulatory regime. At the same time, some assets or rights are made more valuable by the reform. Stranded costs are associated with, and defined by, each regulatory authority that changes the regulatory "rules of the game".

The key reform elements are to provide incentives for incumbents to mitigate (reduce) stranded costs, to measure them accurately, and to assign their recovery in a way that is "fair" and that does not impede efficient entry or pricing of energy. Putting stranded cost charges in a usage-insensitive part of a multi-part tariff reduces their distortionary effects on future market behaviour. Making payments for stranded costs non-bypassable by users will not impede efficient entry decisions. The distribution of stranded costs and benefits has important wealth effects, so their assignment can influence whether efficiency-enhancing regulatory reform has sufficient support to be adopted.

---

customer that subsequently becomes, in whole or in part, an unbundled wholesale transmission services customer of such public utility or transmitting utility, or 2) a retail customer, or a newly created wholesale power sales customer, that subsequently becomes, in whole or in part, an unbundled wholesale transmission services customer of such public utility or transmitting utility" (FERC, 1996a, p. 618). The idea is for the utility to recover costs incurred to serve a customer who now chooses to buy energy from another utility. The costs can only be recovered where the utility has shown that it had a "reasonable expectation" that the customer would remain in the generation system. Stranded costs must be directly assigned to the customer for whom those costs were incurred, and that customer must pay for all the costs assigned to it. Payment is either as a lump-sum or a surcharge on transmission.

According to FERC *Order* 888, the amount of stranded cost is calculated as the revenues that the customer would have paid had it remained a customer, for so long as the seller could reasonably have expected such purchases to continue, less the market value of the power the customer would have bought[43] (FERC, 1996a, pp. 492, 501, 573). There is no stranded cost unless the market price of electricity (when the customer leaves) is lower than the utility's cost. The stranded cost for a customer is finally determined only if that customer actually leaves the utility (FERC, 1996a, p. 479). (Customers who stay with their original utility continue to pay for past investments as part of the tariff for their bundled electricity service.) Divestiture of generating assets by utilities increases the information about the market value of generating assets, so that the market value of those assets that are not sold can be more precisely estimated.

In California, for example, the definition of stranded costs (called "transition costs") reflects the assets and activities over which the California Public Utility Commission (CPUC) has jurisdiction.[44] The CPUC determines the amount of transition costs,[45] and cannot adjust these costs after 2015. The transition costs for generation-related assets net out above-market and below-market transition costs of all utility-owned generation-related assets (CPUC 1997c). (In other words, if some generation-related assets have a market value above net book value, then these must be used to offset those that do not have a market value above net book value.) Transition costs are allocated to the various customer classes in substantially the same proportion as similar costs were recovered on 10 June 1996. Transition costs are non-bypassable and a "firewall" ensures that residential and small business customers do not pay more than their allocated transition costs. Transition costs are based on each customer's purchase of electricity. Departing load customers must pay a lump-sum fee that is equal to the net present value of the customer's remaining transition cost obligation (CPUC, 1997b). While most transition costs are intended to be paid off by end 2001, the transition costs for residential customers and the January 1998 rate reduction will not be. Instead, through 2002, residential and small commercial customers will pay "fixed transition amounts", a surcharge, to a financing entity. These revenues will pay off "rate reduction bonds", the proceeds of which pay the transition costs and financing costs thereof. These transition charges account for about one-third of residential monthly bills (EIA, 1998*h*).

3. MARKET STRUCTURE

3.1. Market definition and market power

Liberalisation of the electricity sector in the United States has substantially increased the number and scope of markets. The United States is sufficiently large, and the transmission grid insufficiently dense, that there is not a single geographic market.

Power markets have been examined in a few regions in the United States. Borenstein *et al.* looked at California and PJM Interconnection (in the mid-Atlantic region). They found that there was almost no market power at low levels of demand but that, at high levels of demand when transmission becomes congested, there is market power in sub-regions in both parts of the country. They state that, "In almost every electricity market that we, or others, have examined there is little potential for market power in off-peak, low demand hours. In many markets, however, there is significant potential for market power during peak hours" (Borenstein *et al.*, 1998).

Notwithstanding the general limits on the predictive value of generation capacity measures, where concentration is high and transmission is sometimes congested there is likely to be market power during periods of congestion. The IEA 1998 review of the United States noted several examples of regional market power in the following:

- Southwest Power Pool, within which Entergy owns 68 per cent of total generating capacity and 80 per cent of peak generating capacity, and which imports only five per cent of total sales (FT Energy World, 1998).

- Michigan, in which Detroit Edison and Consumers' Power own virtually all the generating capacity and transmission assets, and which has severely constrained transmission lines.

- The area served by Virginia Power, in which the company controls virtually all generation and the maximum transmission import capacity is only three GW to four GW to serve a peak load of about 15 GW (Virginia SCC, 1997).

There are two principal forms of entry into electric generation markets: new or expanded generating capacity within the existing product and geographic market, which may also serve to reduce transmission constraints thus expanding the geographic scope of markets, and enhanced access to existing generating capacity because of new or expanded transmission capacity (FTC, 1998*b*). Significant entry into generation is occurring: While only about 10 per cent of current generation is owned by "non-utilities", it is estimated that 50 per cent of all incremental generating capacity projected to come online within the next decade belongs to independent generating companies (NYMEX).

Increasing the elasticity of demand is another part of the development of markets for electricity in the United States. This is accomplished by the introduction of time-of-use metering and time-of-use pricing. When these are introduced, end-users have incentives and ability to react to changes in price. So long as consumers do not have a choice of supplier, so that they must pay the average price of electricity, and time-of-use meters are sufficiently costly, suppliers do not have incentive to separate consumers with price-sensitive demand from consumers with less price-sensitive demand. However, where there is competition in supply, suppliers have incentives to introduce time-of-use pricing and meters to separate consumers with price-sensitive demand, since these consumers can be supplied at lower cost that average consumers, when they are faced with time-of-use pricing. Granting direct access to electricity markets by all end-users in the more reformist states should increase elasticity of demand, as should innovations in pricing to better transmit to end-users the marginal cost of their choices.

Box 12. **Market issues in the electricity industry**

The more fundamental reforms establish markets for electric power, some ancillary services, and financial instruments based on electricity. Markets for transmission rights could also be established. While electric energy *per se* is homogeneous, it is differentiated in time, duration, location, and reliability.[1] For example, the delivery date may be several years in the future, or within the next hour. Markets are defined by regulations (what is permitted to be bought and sold, who is permitted to participate). If regulations are not binding, the geographic extent of a market for electricity is determined primarily by transmission congestion and charges for transmission, as well as, secondarily, line losses.[2] These in turn greatly affect the degree of market power. The geographic scope of electricity markets may vary greatly over the short term: As more electricity is generated, transmission congestion increases, the geographic scope of markets shrinks (regions become isolated), the number of potential suppliers of electricity falls (changing the market structure), and their market power increases.

Market concentration

If power markets are to operate competitively, then the ownership or control of generators must not be unduly concentrated. Deconcentration can be promoted by augmenting transmission links between areas, thus expanding the geographic scope of markets, and by promoting divestiture of generating capacity or of long-term capacity contracts in a market to multiple owners.

Concentration of generating capacity does not always accurately predict the degree of competition in an electricity market because some underlying assumptions of the economic models that motivate the use of concentration measures may be violated, and because these measures do not account for the effects on competition of entry and vertical integration. First, a number of would-be competitors, the publicly owned entities, do not try to maximise profit. Second, many consumers are not price-sensitive; indeed, many are charged only an average of the market price. Third, an institution at the heart of the market, the system operator, makes commercially sensitive decisions on engineering rather than commercial bases. Each of these facts is a significant deviation from the usual assumptions in market models; this implies that the relationship between market power and measures of capacity concentration is more tenuous than usual.[3]

In addition to these shortcomings, market concentration measures ignore entry conditions and the degree of vertical integration. Entry, in the short-run, depends on transmission constraints and the opportunity cost of competitive generation capacity (that is, the profit that is given up if electricity is not sold into another market but rather into the market under discussion). Where transmission is constrained, generators near a load centre might profitably sell to the less than most efficient purchaser increasing constraints on transmission into its area, and thereby "separating" or "isolating" its area from a larger market. Where generation and transmission have common owners and the available capacity of or terms of access to transmission can be influenced by the owner, such variables may be used to affect competition in the generation markets. Most models underlying concentration measures implicitly assume no entry and competitive input markets. Therefore, market power is better measured using more sophisticated models that explicitly take into account the specific characteristics of the electricity supply industry, including transmission constraints.

Entry

Actual entry into generation markets reduces market power by reducing the concentration of generators. Given the significant sunk costs of entry and the likelihood that the "best" locations are occupied by incumbents, potential entry is relevant only for markets for electricity a few years in the future, or where entry could be effected over existing, uncongested transmission lines or sufficiently near load (a concentration of electricity users).

Demand-side effects

Demand influences market power in electricity markets. In particular, where demand is more inelastic (*i.e.*, less responsive to price changes), generators can receive higher prices. Where end-users have direct access to the market for electricity, the elasticity of demand can be increased by better price signals to end-users and increasing the ability of end-users to respond to price signals (*e.g.*, by more time-of-use pricing and interruptible contracts). Where end-uses do not have direct access to a market for electricity, the elasticity of demand can be increased by altering the regulation of franchise suppliers to increase their incentives to ensure lowest cost procurement in the wholesale electricity market(s), and by, for example, making the end-user tariff scheme more reflective of cost.

Box 12. Market issues in the electricity industry (*cont.*)

Markets for ancillary services

Some ancillary services can have rather unusual substitutes: reactive power produced by generators might be partially substituted by capacitors or other reactive compensation devices located at load centres (Borenstein, 1995); and demand for supplemental reserves can be reduced by increased use of interruptible supply contracts and time-of-use meters. Because the same infrastructure (generators) can supply either power or some ancillary services, where both are provided in markets there will be substantial interactions. Most generator-provided ancillary services can be transmitted over some distance so competitive markets could develop. However, other services provided by generators can be transmitted only over short distances, hence are likely to have very small geographic markets, which implies that competitive markets are less likely to develop[4] (DOE, 1998c).

---

1. There are also, potentially, markets for various ancillary services, similarly differentiated in time, duration and location. Also, there can be other markets in which end-users are provided, bundled or un-bundled, a variety of metering, billing, energy management, and other services.
2. The existing pattern of flows cannot be taken as an indicator of the extent of geographic markets for electric power because lines that are not, or rarely, used can make credible the threat of generating and transmitting energy from the "other end of the line", thus providing competition to generators (Borenstein *et al.*, 1997).
3. Market concentration measures can take account of the differing marginal costs of various capacity so that, *e.g.*, market concentration for capacity with marginal cost below $USx/kwh can be calculated.
4. In particular, the energy services associated with regulation, load following, spinning reserve, supplemental reserve, backup supply, energy imbalance and loss replacement can be transmitted some distance, but voltage control, blackstart capability and network stability cannot.

3.1.1. *Market transparency*

Market transparency can refer to both markets for power and markets for transmission. Market transparency for the former is increased when there is greater publicly available information about prices of traded electricity. These prices might be spot market prices or prices for bilateral contracts. While prices for bilateral contracts are usually not public information, one of the advantages of an established spot market, such as the Power Exchange in California, is that the market clearing prices are immediately publicly known. The price spikes experienced in the Midwest in Summer 1998 (up to US$7.50/kWh – perhaps 200 times higher than average – for one hourly contract) are partially attributed to a lack of a centralised, deep, spot market, and one of the recommendations made to reduce the likelihood and magnitude of such a future event is the establishment of such a market (FERC, 1998b). It has been suggested that, given the relative lack of knowledge about how markets will work in the United

---

Box 13. Market transparency

Where trade occurs primarily as non-public bilateral transactions, there is little price transparency. This makes it difficult for regulators to detect excessively high prices, and for economic entities to make rational decisions about entry or expansion. The introduction of anonymous, public trade in electricity-based financial instruments with immediate disclosure of prices provides price references and price transparency, and a liquid market for better handling of risk by generators, users and intermediaries.* Examples of risks that can be hedged are changes in the relative price of electricity and gas and changes in relative prices of electricity at different locations.

---

* Liquid markets require *inter alia* a sufficient number of participants.

States electricity sector, there be stringent market information reporting rules that might allow regulators to detect the exercise of market power. Such information should not be made available in a way to promote parallel pricing, that is, co-ordinated (but not agreed) pricing by utilities.

Market transparency in the United States with respect to transmission is increased by FERC *Order* 889, combined with other FERC rules, that ensure that open access tariffs and real-time information about the availability of transmission are publicly available. In other areas, notably the PJM Interconnection, fixed transmission rights are traded in a market.

Table 3.   **Electricity imports 1990-1996, in terawatthours**

	1990	1991	1992	1993	1994	1995	1996
Imports							
United States	22.6	30.8	37.2	39.1	52.2	46.8	46.5
Mexico	0.6	0.6	1.0	0.8	1.1	1.2	1.3
Canada	19.4	7.9	7.9	9.8	6.5	8.0	7.7
Exports							
United States	20.5	8.5	8.9	10.7	7.6	9.1	9.0
Mexico	2.0	2.1	2.0	2.0	2.0	2.3	1.3
Canada	20.1	28.7	35.2	37.1	50.2	44.5	45.3

Source: Energy Information Agency, US Department of Energy, International Electricity Data, at http://www.eia.doe.gov/emeu/international/contents.

3.1.2. *International trade*

There is some international trade in electricity both with Canada and Mexico, although the Canadian-United States trade is much more substantial. Canada exports locally significant amount of electricity to particular parts of the United States, notably by Hydro-Quebec from Quebec to the major cities in the Northeast. As compared with total generation in the United States of more than 3 500 TWh, imports are small, albeit exports are significant in Canadian terms. However, since the United States is not a single market for electricity, a comparison of nation-wide statistics has limited importance. The following table provides the summary data.

The reciprocity requirement in FERC *Order* 888 has come to the attention of trade officials in Canada. Essentially, it requires that a utility that wishes to use another's transmission, offer transmission access to that utility. While the requirement might have been aimed at utilities in the United States, it has had an effect on Canadian utilities. In particular, it has been applied by FERC so as to require Canadian utilities that wish to sell into the United States at market-based rates to offer open access transmission tariffs.

Implementation of the *Order* 888 reciprocity test has impacted Canadian utilities in different ways. For provincial utilities in Manitoba, Quebec, and British Colombia, where energy exports represent a core business, domestically-generated power is highly competitive, and wholesale loads are negligible (so that providing open access to transmission lines was not viewed as exerting much, if any, competitive pressure on existing market share), compliance with the FERC reciprocity requirement proved the chosen course for accessing the US wholesale market.

For another provincial utility, however – Ontario Hydro – the reciprocity issue has played out very differently. Due to fundamental differences in the Ontario industry structure, the province was not in a position to comply with the reciprocity requirement,[46] resulting in denial of its bid for open access to the US wholesale market. Ontario Hydro has subsequently challenged FERC's authority to order open access as a condition of Canadian participation in the US market, an issue which is before US courts. In the meantime, Ontario Hydro has claimed that US border utilities have been able to exert market power over it by refusing to sell transmission services.

These types of sector-specific restrictions may be based on legitimate public policy objectives. Whether or not such legitimate domestic objectives can be met through less restrictive means, however, seems a fair question.[47]

3.1.3. *Financial markets*

Financial contracts based on electricity are traded on the New York Mercantile Exchange, which is also the exchange for contracts based on crude oil, refined petroleum products, and gas, as well as a handful of other exchanges. Since 1997, electricity futures have been traded. Initially based on two nominal locations in the West (at the California-Oregon Intertie and the Palo Verde, Arizona switchyard) there are now futures with nominal locations elsewhere in the country. Other locations are being added. Options contracts have also been introduced. While the contracts allow physical delivery, only about one per cent is delivered (NYMEX).

Financial contracts can be used to reduce market price risk. As there is greater use of spot markets, utilities and end-users may wish to reduce their exposure to the riskiness of the spot market. A utility, for example, can buy a financial instrument that establishes a position that is opposite to its position in the "cash market", thus insuring itself regarding the price it will obtain for electricity. Financial instruments can even be used to shift risk onto entities that are neither utilities nor significant electricity end-users.

Box 14.   Financial markets

Financial contracts greatly expand the possibilities for generators, users and intermediaries to manage market risk. The exchange of these financial contracts in an anonymous, public market with immediate disclosure of prices provides price references and price transparency, and a liquid market for better handling of risk. Examples of risks that can be hedged are changes in the relative price of electricity and gas and changes in relative prices of electricity at different locations.

3.2. Independent system operators: A new institution

A number of ways to organise regional transmission are under consideration or implemented. These include independent system operators (ISOs) and transmission companies (transcos). ISOs are newly developed institutions, designed to ensure non-discriminatory access to the transmission grid even while it is owned by vertically integrated utilities, and to ensure continued reliability of the power system. Four independent system operators (ISOs) have been approved, some conditionally, as of July 1998, in New England, the PJM Interconnection (in the mid-Atlantic states), California, and New York. A number of other ISOs are under discussion. It is important to note that the ISOs are heterogeneous, differing in important respects. Interestingly, there has been speculation that concerns about reliability and competition might lead to the consolidation of ISOs into as few as three ISOs to cover all forty-eight contiguous states (FTC, 1998*b*). A transco combines the ownership of the grid with the responsibilities of an ISO.

The governance structure of ISOs treads a fine line between maintaining independence from generators and transmission owners and users on the one hand, and having sufficient technical competence to ensure safe and reliable operation on the other hand. (Much of the technical competence rests within the vertically integrated utilities.) The ISOs must be, and be perceived to be, independent from the vertically integrated utilities; if they are not, then not only will independent generators will be hesitant to make investments in the territory of the ISO, but also grid expansion and grid access may be discriminatory, further discouraging entry.

The governance issue has been addressed in New England, PJM and California. In the former two, there is a two-tiered system, in which an independent non-stakeholder governing board, members of which are not affiliated with market participants, is advised by committees of stakeholders (FERC,

1998). For New England, this represented a broadening of governance from that of NEPOOL, the predecessor organisation. Oversight of both the ISO and the operator of the spot market in California is provided by a board of political appointees; ISO-NE is monitored by the state regulator.

The responsibilities of ISOs can vary from one ISO to another. For example, PJM is responsible for centralised dispatch, system stability and reliability, managing the open access transmission tariff, facilitating the spot market and accounting for energy and ancillary services (PJM). ISO-New England, in the northeastern states, has similar responsibilities, save the accounting functions. By contrast, in California, Cal-ISO controls the transmission grid, but does not centrally dispatch. However, the cost-minimising merit order that is established in the PX (the spot market) is subsequently revised by Cal-ISO to take into account feasible and cost-minimising operation of the transmission grid.

While FERC has not mandated the establishment of ISOs, it has encouraged their development and provides principles for ISOs as a way to provide guidance for their approval. In essence, an ISO should have a governance structure that is fair and non-discriminatory, should provide open access to the transmission grid and services under its control, should have transmission and ancillary services pricing policies that promote efficient use of and investment in transmission, generation, and consumption, and should have responsibility for short-term reliability over its area (FERC, 1996a, pp. 280-286). An ISO does not necessarily have responsibility for transmission system augmentation.

One aspect of governance that has not been effectively addressed is how to provide an ISO with incentives to operate efficiently and to make economically appropriate investment decisions regarding expansion of the transmission grid. If it is difficult for an independent regulator to detect subtle discrimination, then it would also seem to be difficult for an ISO governing board to monitor and control the same activities. A transco, where the ownership of the transmission grid and the ISO are in the same hands, might reduce some of these incentive problems. No one has yet designed, however, regulations to ensure that a transco will discover the optimal investments and make them. The difficulties of devising operating rules for ISOs would remain even in a transco, since their objectives will continue to deviate from the socially optimal objective: The transco would seek profits while the desired operating rules would seek to minimise system cost.

The geographic scope of an ISO can affect its effectiveness. An ISO with limited geographic scope may suffer from two problems: insufficiently deconcentrated generation (hence problems of market dominance in generation) and insufficient diversity in generation (number and type) for adequate system reliability. Divestiture of generation to several different owners can eliminate market power or dominance in the area of an ISO. (Divestiture may have the additional benefit of improving the governance structure.) Further, a larger ISO, having greater incentives to strengthen transmission links in its area in order to avoid transmission bottlenecks, can increase overall reliability. As noted above, there have been suggestions that the 48 contiguous states may, in the end, have perhaps as few as three ISOs.

The institutional structure of ISOs is still evolving in response to actual experience in the United States markets. While some of the limits of the possible institutional structure have been identified on the basis of analysis of incentives of participants, no ISO has yet operated for a sufficiently long time that it is clear that this new institution will deliver on its promise, in practice. Hence, even where a reform does not require divestiture of generation from transmission, it is important that reforms contain the option to require divestiture in the event that an ISO does not, in practice, deliver the appropriate operational and investment outcomes.

4. PERFORMANCE

4.1. Prices, costs and productivity

Electricity prices in the United States are low by comparison with other OECD countries. In 1996, average revenues per kWh (for sales to final consumers) were 7.12 cents for investor-owned utilities (about 75 per cent of the total quantity sold), 6.01 cents for publicly owned utilities, 6.74 cents for co-operatives, and 2.52 cents for the very limited sales to end-users by federally owned utilities. According to the IEA, average revenue (or expenditure) per kilowatt-hour for industrial customers was US$0.046 in the United States, but US$0.056 (at purchasing power parities) in the OECD as a whole, in 1996. For households, the corresponding figures were US$0.084 cents and US$0.104 cents, respectively (IEA, 1998b). (Given that the United States has a large weight in OECD averages, and its prices are significantly lower than average, the comparison here understates the price differences with other countries.) Given that utilities have been regulated so that revenues covered costs (including a "fair" return to capital) and that utilities operating in the liberalised markets are privately owned (thus over time revenues must exceed costs), low electricity prices imply low costs of generating and delivering electricity.

These average prices, however, mask sizeable variances in production costs and efficiency among producers. Within the United States there are significant differences in the cost of building comparable generating facilities, both nuclear and fossil fuel. There are also significant differences in the speed with which utilities adopt new technologies (Joskow, 1997). These imply that there is scope for increased productive economic efficiency in the sector over the medium to long-term.

The statistics on average revenue per kilowatt-hour do not give information about the structure of prices. As described earlier, price structure can significantly affect economic efficiency by encouraging or discouraging purchases when the marginal value of additional energy to end-users is higher than its marginal cost. At present, multi-part time-of-use pricing systems are not in widespread use; the traditional "average total embedded cost" pricing system is still dominant. Hence, there may be substantial allocative efficiency losses. One estimate that prices would be six to 13 per cent lower with marginal rather than average cost pricing, (EIA, 1997f) implies that large allocative efficiency gains would be possible.

Economic efficiency gains over the past two decades have been substantial, as the amount of inter-utility trading and the number of independent power producers have increased. Non-fuel operations and maintenance (labour, rent, lubricants, coolants, limestone and other services needed to run a plant) have declined 22 per cent from 1981 to 1995. The number of employees per megawatt of capacity fell 20 per cent over this period (EIA 1998g). Labour cost per kilowatt-hour decreased from about 0.7 cent per kWh in 1986 to about 0.5 cent per kWh in 1995 (EIA, 1997e, Figure 17). Average availability rates for coal plants increased from 76 per cent to 81 per cent from 1984 to 1993 (EIA, 1997f).

4.2. Environmental performance

Another measure of performance, in terms of the United States' policy goals, is environmental performance. Emissions from utility-operated fossil fuel plants plus non-utility plants larger than one MW totalled about 6.2 tonnes of SO_2, 4.0 tonnes of NO_X, and 1 198 tonnes of CO_2. With respect to CO_2 emissions, in 1995 the US emitted 0.86 kg per dollar of Gross Domestic Product, which compares with an OECD average of 0.60 kg/US$ (using 1990 prices and exchange rates). (The comparable figures for OECD Members in Europe and in the Pacific are, respectively, 0.46 kg/US$ and 0.41 kg/US$) (IEA, 1997).

With respect to emissions, the value of the environmental externalities from SO_2 and NO_X would be expected to vary from location to location; hence, it is difficult to interpret a simple sum of emissions.

4.3. Reliability and security

The United States (and Canadian) performance as regards reliability, as evaluated by the North American Electric Reliability Council, is good. (The NERC standard is that no customer should lose power more than once in ten years.) Reliability is expected to be adequate over the next three to five years, with some short-term concern in regions where nuclear generation unavailability could cause capacity shortages during peak conditions. However, little investment has gone into strengthening the bulk transmission system over the past ten years. Further, the time required to plan, site, gain the necessary approvals and construct major transmission system projects is increasing (NERC, 1997c). National capacity margins were 18.9 per cent for the summer peak and 28.7 per cent for the winter peak (EIA 1998f).

The United States has a diverse fuel mix, as shown in Table 1. In addition, mechanisms are in place that encourage appropriate diversity: The choice of fuel inputs is not restricted in the United States, fuels can be and are purchased through liquid markets, markets for financial instruments derived from some fuels and electricity are developing, there is significant trade in electricity among utilities, and there is increasingly competition for sales of electricity directly to end-users. The first four conditions imply that utilities have the ability, and the last that they have the incentives, to provide an appropriate level of fuel diversity.

4.4. Other aspects of performance

The above measures of performance have been rather static. Another aspect of performance of a sector is its ability to deal with unexpected events. The evolving market and regulatory system demonstrated its robustness, although with a less than optimal performance, during price spikes in summer 1998. In June 1998, a combination of factors – weather, generation outages, and transmission constraints – resulted in dramatic price spikes in the Midwest. At its peak, there were significant hourly purchases in the US\$3 000 to US\$6 000 range, and one hourly price reached US\$7 500/MWh. Some aspects of the market did not perform adequately. Nevertheless, there was adequate electricity delivered. In response, changes in tariffs and institutions have been proposed.[48]

Overall, the electricity sector in the United States performs well,[49] both relative to other OECD countries and in terms of the Administration's stated policy objectives. Prices are low, compared with those in other countries; given that revenues must equal costs for the regulated privately owned utilities, and they are the dominant form of enterprise, this suggests that the United States electricity sector is relatively efficient. In terms of environmental goals, much has been done toward reducing SO_2, NO_x, and other noxious emissions. However, little has been done in the United States toward reducing emissions of CO_2. Further, performance as measured by energy efficiency *per capita* and per unit GDP is low by the standards of IEA countries. Reliability is currently good, but ensuring adequate transmission investment may become a concern in the longer term.

5. CONCLUSIONS AND POLICY OPTIONS FOR REFORM

5.1. General assessment of current strengths and weaknesses

The United States has made substantial progress toward reforming its regulatory regime for the electricity sector, and is en route to attaining many of its policy objectives, but has not yet completed the journey. The reforms presently envisaged, if adopted, will likely achieve many economic objectives for the sector, but meeting the environmental objectives may require additional efforts. Social protections, *e.g.*, subsidies to poor consumers and consumer protection, are secured. The wide participation of interested parties, the public nature of the discussion, decision-making, and explanations of decisions, has protected the legitimacy of the reform and may well cause a superior outcome. There remain, however, unfinished aspects to the reforms, primarily with respect to the operation of and investment in the transmission grid, system operation, stranded cost recovery, and competition to supply end-users ("retail competition"), that have implications for economic efficiency and reliability.

The United States electricity sector seems to be well on the way to increasing economic efficiency. Electricity trading among utilities has already resulted in efficiency gains over the past several years. Nevertheless, the federal reforms to provide for non-discriminatory, efficient access to transmission and further grid investment, to support this trading, could be further strengthened.[50] The movement away from a cost-plus system of economic regulation toward greater competition in generation and retail supply and performance-based regulation of transmission and distribution should increase incentives for efficient entry of new competitors using new technologies, to reduce internal economic inefficiencies, to price more efficiently (*i.e.*, reflect cost and value to the buyer), and to provide new products that better meet the needs of end-users.

However, the extension of access to the electricity markets to end-users ("retail competition") is not yet complete. Indeed, it is in the dimension of retail competition that the heterogeneity of the American reforms has the greatest visibility and effect, not only directly, but also through its implications for other regulatory changes. The differences among states arise, in part, because the states are at different stages along similar reform paths, but also because there is not agreement that retail competition is, indeed, the path that every state wishes to take. While federal institutions are influential, state legislatures ultimately are responsible for the decision whether to allow retail competition. The federal-state split in responsibilities makes reaching a nation-wide decision difficult.

The heterogeneity of the United States electricity sector reforms creates opportunities and costs. The opportunities include faster innovation in regulatory regimes from learning from parallel yet different state reforms, as well as being able better to design reform appropriate to the starting point. Costs include building interfaces between different regulatory regimes, lost efficiencies from regional markets having to operate under multiple regulatory regimes, and increased compliance costs from utilities operating in multiple regimes. Regional pacts regarding the regulation of the sector, where the regions are coincident with electricity markets, could reduce some of these costs, while retaining the flexibility and heterogeneity to allow regulatory innovation. Indeed, FERC is moving to implement this type of solution with its announced generic Notice of Proposed Rulemaking on regional independent transmission entities. Conveying to FERC, DOE's authority to organise regions of the country for reliability purposes may further this process.

The measurement of stranded costs seems to be converging toward a mechanism that also enables the post-transition structure to be conducive to competition, that is, by measuring the market value of assets by the price they receive when they are actually sold. As more assets are sold, their prices provide information that can be used to estimate more accurately the market value of assets that are not, in the end, sold. However, the recovery of stranded costs is not always designed in the US to minimise distortions. There are two potential types of distortions: too much (too little) electricity purchased, and too much (too little) entry. If stranded costs are recovered through a usage-sensitive fee (*i.e.*, on a per kilowatt-hour basis), then the fee acts like a tax, thus implies that too little electricity is purchased. If stranded costs are bypassable, then there may be too much entry because entrants would be able to sell to those users who can bypass, even if the entrants had higher costs than incumbents. If switching costs for users are high, then there may be too little entry. If stranded costs depend on prices actually realised in the market, then incumbents have an incentive to lower prices, excluding entrants, and receive their payments through higher stranded cost recovery. Beyond these concerns, the recovery of stranded costs is largely a political question, that can only be resolved through negotiation.

The structure of transmission pricing has undergone only partial reform. The structure of transmission pricing must complement the structure for dispatch (whether and how each generating unit is used) and transmission investment decisions. Nodal pricing has been adopted in only part of the country, and experimented with elsewhere, but the remainder of the country remains under zonal pricing or other types of pricing that depart further from pricing that would induce efficient short-term behaviour. While nodal pricing can be expected in theory to provide the signals for efficient operation and investment in transmission, implementation issues remain, as for any transmission pricing system. In addition, it is not clear that any pricing scheme, alone, will overcome regulatory difficulties of siting new transmission lines.

Similarly, the structure of prices offered to end-users is only at the beginning of reform. Pricing structure reform could induce more efficient use of electric power. Allocative economic efficiency[51] is highest when price equals marginal *social* cost,[52] which is the total of the value of environmental and other externalities and the marginal cost of delivered electric power. Leaving aside the difficulty of calculating the value of the externalities, the marginal cost of delivered electricity is independent of stranded costs, and varies by time of use (low when demand is low, high when demand is high). Thus, moving stranded cost recovery from a usage-sensitive charge to a usage-insensitive charge (a "fixed" part of a multi-part tariff) would allow prices to move toward the level of marginal cost. Similarly, the introduction of time-of-use pricing would provide incentives to build more peak load capacity where it is needed and for consumers to shift demand away from peak periods. Clearly, there are fixed costs to switching pricing schemes: In choosing among the menu of pricing schemes, end-users would compare the benefits they would receive from time-of-use pricing with the fixed costs of time-of-use meters[53] plus, *e.g.*, the incremental cost of "smart" rather than "not-smart" appliances. Hence, the introduction of time-of-use pricing into the menu of pricing schemes will likely not immediately greatly increase the elasticity of demand, but may do so over time.

Competition has already resulted in new products being offered to end-users. For example, large end-users are offered interruptible contracts, according to which end-users lose electric power under conditions of the utility's choosing in exchange for lower prices. (In other words, reliability is explicitly priced.) In some states, end-users are offered "green" electricity, according to which a specified percentage of electric power is generated from specified (renewable) fuels. A greater degree of freedom in the structure of pricing can give rise to additional products that incorporate investments in energy efficiency and financial instruments (which has the effect of separately pricing electricity price risk).

If reliability is not explicitly priced, the effect of increased competition combined with the reduction in cost-plus regulation may reduce reliability over the medium and longer term. The Administration's proposal would address much of this concern by promoting mandatory self-regulation through the North American Electric Reliability Organisation with oversight, for its activities in the United States, by FERC.

The reforms are likely to help meet environmental objectives, though precisely to what extent remains unclear. The main positive environmental effects of the reforms act through their effect on incentives to generate from gas rather than coal, where gas has lower emissions per kilowatt-hour (FERC, 1996*a*). New generation is dominated by gas-fired units, which account for about three-quarters of new capacity announced for the next several years (Table 17, EIA, 1998*e*). This pattern results from past increases in competition in generation, so would be expected to continue with increasingly intense competition, provided the price of gas relative to the price of other fuels does not change significantly. Other, likely smaller environmental effects of the increase in competition will be incremental emissions if prices fall (since more electricity will be used), or if coal-fired plants are run more (due to increased electricity trade); or, on the other hand, reduced emissions caused by competition- and regulation-spurred increases in energy efficiency of conversion of primary fuel into electric power delivered to the end-user. (Compared to traditional cost-based regulation, competition provides greater incentives to reduce cost, thus may provide greater incentives to more energy efficient generation and transmission.) Competition also provides incentives for more widespread time-of-use pricing,[54] which encourages shifts from peak to off-peak usage, which means that the typically less efficient plants that are run at peak periods will be run less, and baseload plants may be run more. Finally, a competitive electricity industry is compatible with tradable emissions permits for greenhouse gases, such as those already in use for SO_2, as well as user surcharges and taxpayer-financed subsidies to support energy efficiency research, development and demonstration, and taxes such as carbon taxes. The programmes for tradable permits and direct subsidies to RD&D may need to be expanded in order to meet the environmental goals for this sector, so as not to diminish unnecessarily the economic efficiency gains from the reforms.

The reforms to date demonstrate certain weaknesses. For example, in some regions, such as Virginia and Michigan and other so-called load pockets, the ownership structure is just not conducive to competition: There is no spare transmission capacity and ownership of generation is highly concentrated. How to develop competition in these regions has not been adequately addressed. The concept of independent system operators is not satisfactorily developed: How can ISOs induce transmission expansion that might increase competition, if transmission assets remain in the hands of firms with substantial generation that would be harmed by an increase in competition? How can ISOs, which after all will have an expertise limited to the electricity sector, effectively deduce whether there is anticompetitive behaviour in a market? The reform has not adequately addressed how to promote transmission investments for inter-regional trading (*i.e.*, beyond the borders of a single ISO), including how to induce state regulators to take sufficient account of the interests of out-of-state, out-of-ISO utilities and consumers when considering transmission extensions. Finally, in an increasingly competitive environment, the absence of competitive neutrality, such as between investor-owned utilities, US Government utilities, and co-operatives and municipal systems, will result not only in transfers of rents, as they do today, but also in real inefficiencies.

The direct cost of the regulatory reform is relatively high. The cost of the California transition is perhaps the easiest to calculate. There, the sum of the costs of setting up the spot market (PX), the independent system operator, and restructuring to enable direct access to the electricity markets likely captures almost all of the direct costs. (While indeed utilities' shareholders have experienced losses and some end-users have gained or lost, these are transfers, not net costs to the economy.) These "restructuring implementation costs", totalled US$98 million in 1997, and were estimated to total US$980 million through 2001 for the three private utilities in filings submitted to the California Public Utilities Commission (CPUC, 1998*b*). In addition to these costs, the ISO and the PX may themselves incur costs. The ISO has been authorised by FERC to issue up to US$310million in long term debt (*ibid.*). Hence, one estimate of the cost of setting up the Californian regime is US$1.29 billion, or about US$42 per person. The California system may be extendable to other states at less than proportional cost due to experience already gained. An estimate for the cost of setting up the PJM system is much lower, well below US$100 million.

The high level of public participation in the reform, by which all interests are provided access to the public forums, the adversarial nature of the regulatory system, and public decision-making by regulators and legislators, together ensure that implications of policy changes are noted. Because there are practical limits on the ability to research and consider each of these policy linkages given time constraints, the thorough consideration of some policy linkages is deferred until after reform is partially implemented. For example, providing for investment in transmission to facilitate inter-regional trading is not yet resolved, despite the fact that reforms in some states have already been implemented. If these complex issues had had to be resolved before embarking on reform, then reform might have been blocked. While this approach runs certain risks, the regulatory regime seems sufficiently flexible to resolve issues sequentially, if the reforms provide sufficient efficiency gains to compensate, at each stage, rents lost, at each stage, by the sequential resolution of issues.

5.2. Potential benefits and costs of further regulatory reform

Electricity sector reform in the United States should continue until a suitable long-term solution is reached. In particular the elements for establishing competition in power are only partly established: conditions to prevent discriminatory access to the transmission grid are not yet fully in place, incentives for efficient grid and reliability investment and extension are not complete, and concentration in some markets at some times remains high. Further, the relationships between more liberalised and less liberalised states have not been properly addressed. Hence, there remain significant benefits to further regulatory reform.

These benefits may come from multiple sources. Some observers of the United States reforms do not expect them to come from improvements in productive efficiency in the short-run, because utilities had already developed co-operative pools and economic dispatch arrangements, which provide for dispatch on the basis of short-run marginal cost.[55] However, as the structure of pricing to end-users improves, benefits may flow from increases in allocative efficiency, and increased productive efficiency as demand is shifted away from peak periods where less efficient plants normally operate. Substantial benefits from the United States reforms are expected to flow from long-run productive efficiency gains from market-based investment decisions in generation and transmission capacity.

The Administration claims that its proposed legislation, the Comprehensive Electricity Competition Act, will result in US$20 billion in annual consumer benefits, which is about ten per cent of annual sales in the sector. These estimated savings arise from a variety of sources. Estimated cost reductions are: US$6.7 billion from improved fuel acquisition, US$0.9 billion from improved heat rates on generating equipment, US$11.0 billion on non-fuel operation and management, US$6.0 billion on administrative and general expenses. Other savings are estimated to be US$0.6 billion from improved dispatch efficiency, US$0.8 to 2.6 billion from improved capital utilisation, and US$0.3 to 3.8 billion from reduced capital additions. This totals US$26.3 to 31.6 billion. The basic methodology is to assume that reform will raise the average utility's performance to the level of the top quartile, today. The magnitude of estimated cost savings does not seem to be excessive.

Potential costs of further reform, also, have multiple sources. One source is the potential for mis-design of the stranded cost recovery scheme: whereas much of the discussion centres around the real-location of rents, which creates neither cost nor benefit to the economy, as mentioned above the design can be costly either in terms of providing incorrect incentives for entry or for electricity usage. A second source of potential costs are the social costs of reduced employment in the sector. Given that the rate of unemployment in the United States at present is very low, these social costs would be limited to those directly associated with changing employers and sectors. A third source of potential costs are those of designing and implementing the institutional structures to support the new regulatory regime, *i.e.*, those costs analogous to the US$1.29 billion spent in California. In principle, learning should reduce the costs of implementing a similar system elsewhere.

5.3. Policy options for consideration

The following policy options are based on the Recommendations accepted by Member countries in the OECD *Report on Regulatory Reform* (June 1997).

1. *Adopt at the political level broad programmes of regulatory reform that establish clear objectives and frameworks for implementation.*

Ministers have recommended that overlapping or duplicative responsibilities among regulatory authorities and levels of government be avoided, and that regulations be clear, simple, and practical for users. Regulatory reform in the United States electricity sector has been hampered by the complexities of the relationships among federal and state authorities. In addition, the developing electricity markets extend across regions that comprise several states. Also, utilities experience higher compliance costs where states have heterogeneous regulatory systems. **In order to reduce overlapping or duplicative regulatory responsibilities, and to promote clearer, simpler and more practical regulation, a framework for the establishment of regional pacts among states for electricity regulation should be established, and the delineation of the respective roles of federal and state regulators should be clarified.**

Ministers have noted that regulation should serve clearly identified policy goals, be effective in achieving those goals, and minimise costs and market distortions. The United States has articulated economic efficiency as a policy goal in this sector. Allocative economic efficiency can be increased by changing the structure of end-users electricity tariffs so that the marginal price reflects marginal social cost (*i.e.*, marginal cost including environmental costs and other externalities). Marginal cost changes substantially as the quantity of electricity generated changes, that is, by the time of use. Given the cost structure of generation, marginal cost pricing may not alone provide sufficient revenue to cover total cost; multi-part tariffs can enable sufficient revenues to be recovered. (The simplest multi-part tariff would be a two-part tariff, with a fixed charge and a charge for energy; the latter might vary by time-of-use.) Where end-user tariffs are not regulated, time-of-use multi-part tariffs imply that marginal price will be no less than marginal cost (taking account of operating requirements) at any given time. The shift from average cost to time-of-use tariffs shifts some price risk onto end-users; others may be better able to bear that risk. **In order to achieve the stated goal of promoting economic efficiency, the use of time-of-use multi-part tariffs for end-users, with separate fixed and marginal cost-based elements, should be expanded; the development of financial instruments and markets for risk shifting should also be promoted.**

Ministers have said that regulation should produce benefits that justify costs (considering the distribution of effects across society), minimise cost and market distortions, promote innovation through market incentives and goal-based approaches, be clear, simple, and practical for users, and be compatible as far as possible with competition, trade and investment-facilitating principles at domestic and international levels. The regulation of transmission prices can substantially affect the achievement of these goals in the electricity sector. Electricity transactions, by causing transmission congestion, affect the costs of other transactions on the grid. Transmission pricing schemes that more closely reflect these effects would reduce the need for system operators to make reliability-constrained administrative decisions regarding use of the grid, thus would reduce market distortions and facilitate entry and competition in generation. Nodal marginal pricing of electricity, reflecting congestion costs, should theoretically provide appropriate market signals for efficient dispatch. Multi-part transmission tariffs, where the variable part is nodal, can provide appropriate incentives for expansion of generating and transmission facilities where they are most needed. However, since experience with nodal pricing is limited, practical issues remain for its wider implementation. Regulatory difficulties with siting may also inhibit optimal investment in transmisssion facilities regardless of the transmission pricing regime. *In order to achieve the goals of good regulation, further experimentation in locational pricing of electric power should be undertaken, with a view to its wider implementation. Consideration should also be given to multi-part transmission tariffs to provide appropriate incentives for grid investment.*

The achievement of policy goals is helped by the availability of high-quality information, because it makes easier the monitoring of the effects of regulation. *The United States should continue to collect and analyse key information about the electricity sector, notably including investment.*

2. *Ensure that regulations and regulatory processes are transparent, non-discriminatory and efficiently applied.*

A key part of the regulations to ensure non-discriminatory access to the transmission grid is the requirement of transmission owners to use OASIS, which is intended to provide real-time information about the availability of transmission. If OASIS works as planned, it should provide potential sellers and buyers of electricity with accurate and timely information about transmission available, augmenting efficient trade, and enhancing competition in general. *The regulators should evaluate the effectiveness of the OASIS system and improve upon it as appropriate to ensure accurate and timely reporting.*

3. *Review and strengthen where necessary the scope, effectiveness and enforcement of competition policy.*

Ministers have recommended that sectoral gaps in coverage of competition law be eliminated, unless evidence suggests that compelling public interests cannot be served in better ways. They have further recommended that competition law be enforced vigorously where collusive behaviour, abuse of dominant position, or anticompetitive merger risk frustrating reform. They recommend that competition authorities be provided with the authority and capacity to advocate reform. In the United States, surveillance of the spot market for anticompetitive indications is sometimes under the responsibility of the independent system operator. Review of mergers is under the joint jurisdiction of the antitrust authorities and the Federal Energy Regulatory Commission. *The antitrust authorities should continue their advocacy of competition in this sector at both federal and state levels. In order to ensure adequate enforcement of the competition law, the competition authorities should refine the methodology for reviewing mergers in this sector, should closely oversee the spot market surveillance by the independent system operators, and be responsible for investigating and remedying anticompetitive behaviour detected through this surveillance.*

4. *Reform economic regulations in all sectors to stimulate competition, and eliminate them except where clear evidence demonstrates that they are the best way to serve broad public interests.*

Ministers recommended that those aspects of regulation that restrict entry, exit, pricing, output, normal commercial practices and forms of business organisation be reviewed as a high priority. A significant barrier to entry for generation, hence to the development of competition, is the cost of receiving approval for the siting of facilities, most importantly those for transmission that would expand transfer capacity. The value of additional transmission capacity may accrue significantly outside any particular state because markets extend beyond individual states. *Consideration should be given to granting to the Federal Energy Regulatory Commission siting authority for transmission.*

In order to promote efficiency and the transition to effective competition, where economic regulation continues to be needed because of the potential for abuse of market power, Ministers recommended that: 1) potentially competitive activities be separated from regulated utility networks, and

307

that other restructuring be done as needed to reduce the market power of incumbents; 2) access to essential network facilities be guaranteed to all market participants on a transparent and non-discriminatory basis; 3) price caps and other mechanisms be used to encourage efficiency gains when price controls are needed during the transition to competition. Generation and retail supply are competitive or potentially competitive, but distribution and transmission are regulated networks because of their natural monopoly characteristics. The Federal Energy Regulatory Commission requires only "functional separation" of generation and transmission, and non-discriminatory transmission tariffs and access to information about transmission availability. Vertically-integrated albeit functionally-separated firms retain the incentives and perhaps the means to discriminate, overtly or subtly, against their competitors in granting access to the network. *In order to achieve effective competition in generation and transparent, non-discriminatory access to the transmission grid and system operation, divestiture of generation from transmission should be required in the United States; where there is market power, divestiture should be to multiple owners; where mandatory divestiture is not feasible, "operational separation" should be required and divestiture encouraged. Transmission augmentation should also be used, where feasible, to reduce market power. Connections for new generation to the existing transmission grid should be provided on non-discriminatory terms. In order to achieve effective competition in supply, entry into supply should not be economically restricted and non-discriminatory access to distribution should be ensured. In order to provide greater incentives for efficiency in the sector, direct access by all end-users to electricity markets ("retail competition") should be granted as soon as possible as far as technically feasible. The governance of entities such as independent system operators, power exchanges and reliability councils should be structured in such a way as to avoid discrimination.*

5. *Eliminate unnecessary regulatory barriers to trade and investment by enhancing implementation of international agreements and strengthening international principles.*

Ministers recommended that countries implement, and work with other countries to strengthen, international rules and principles to liberalise trade and investment (such as transparency, non-discrimination, avoidance of unnecessary trade restrictiveness, and attention to competition principles), as contained in WTO agreements, OECD recommendations and policy guidelines, and other agreements. Federal Energy Regulatory Commission Order No. 888 provides that utilities that do not provide access to their transmission lines, on specified terms, may not sell electric power into the service areas of utilities that do provide such access. The effect is to limit the growth of competition in more reformist states that are adjacent to less reformist states or Canadian provinces, while holding out, as an inducement to reform, the promise of profitable trade to those utilities located in less reformist jurisdictions. **The United States should consider whether the objectives of the reciprocity requirement in Order No. 888 could be met in a less trade restrictive manner.**

The Atomic Energy Act provides that nuclear-powered electricity generation plants may not be owned or operated by foreign entities. However, given the incidence of nuclear power plants around the world, foreign entities may be better able to manage nuclear power plants in a safe and efficient manner than some current owners or operators. If so, then the value of those assets would be higher under foreign management. Further, opening the ownership of nuclear power plants to foreign entities would increase the number of potential buyers. Both of these would reduce the quantity of stranded costs. **The United States should, consistent with maintaining national security, health and safety, consider loosening the restrictions on foreign ownership and operation of nuclear power plants.**

6. *Identify important linkages with other policy objectives and develop policies to achieve those objectives in ways that support reform.*

Ministers recommended that prudential and other public policies in areas such as safety, health, consumer protection, and energy security should be adapted as necessary. Electricity reliability is a function both of activities on the supply side (investment, operating procedures) as well as activities the demand side (time-of-use pricing, interruptible supply contracts, insurance contracts). Increasing the size of independent system operators enables them to provide reliability at lower cost. **In order to reduce the cost of reliability, larger independent system operators should be promoted; where independent** *system operators are sufficiently large, they should be given some responsibility for reliability.* Reliability councils increase the level of reliability, thus reduce total cost of the electricity system. Because reliability councils are voluntary organisations, utilities can opt-out of co-operation during crises, thus increasing costs. Further, because they do not appear to benefit from the State Action Doctrine, co-operative actions may expose them to antitrust liability. *In order to adapt the reliability regime to the development of markets for electricity, the Federal Energy Regulatory Commission should be given oversight of reliability councils, such as NAERO, and their recommendations should become mandatory.*

Traditionally, incumbent electric utilities subsidised activities to support other public policies, such as subsidies to R&D, electricity generated from "green" sources, and to support poor, rural or other consumers, were funded through revenues generated from other customers. Internal cross-subsidisation to meet other public policies is unsustainable under free competition. *Subsidies for public purposes should be supported by non-bypassable and transparent fees. The regulatory system to promote "green" generation should provide incentives for such generation to be provided at least-cost. Provision should be made for consumers to be allowed voluntarily to buy "green" generated electricity beyond that required.*

Ministers recommended that non-regulatory policies, including subsidies, taxes, and other support policies, be reviewed and reformed when they unnecessarily distort competition. Publicly owned utilities, which are subject to advantageous tax treatment and have access to cheap, federally-provided hydropower, supply electricity at lower prices than would be indicated by their productive efficiency. Competition is distorted. *Distortions of competition should be reduced by making appropriate changes in the tax and subsidy systems, the jurisdiction of FERC and the antitrust authorities, and any other different treatment of public and private utilities. Consideration should be given to privatisation of the electricity-generating businesses of publicly-owned utilities, or at least corporatisation with market-like returns to debt and equityholders for each of their commercial activities. Distortions of energy choices through subsidies, taxes, and other support policies should not unnecessarily distort competition.*

Ministers recommended that programmes designed to ease the potential costs of regulatory reform be focused, transitional and facilitate, rather than delay, reform. The measurement and recovery of stranded costs are a key part of ensuring support for reform in the United States. *The recovery of stranded costs should not distort market prices, should not be bypassable, and should not affect the relative competitive positions of incumbents and entrants. The treatment of stranded costs should not imperil future changes in regulatory regime, nor unduly delay the onset of competition.*

NOTES

1. A "requirements contract" is one under which all or a portion of the requirements for electricity will be supplied on a firm basis. Hence, planning and timely investment for such requirements load are the responsibility of the supplier.

2. Average state prices for industrial users varied from 2.7 cents per kilowatt-hour to 10.0 cents per kilowatt-hour in 1996 (EIA, 1998a). In California, the price of electric power was 30 to 50 per cent higher than the United States average. Much of the five-fold difference in average cost among 136 vertically integrated IOUs is attributed to the degree of participation in nuclear power. Smaller factors are the degree of exposure to independent power purchase agreements under the 1978 Public Utilities Regulatory Policy Act, and exposure to exogenous regional differences in factor prices and resource endowments (White, p. 218).

3. "Total cost" includes *inter alia* capital costs, fuel, and operating costs.

4. The open consultation process might be partly explained by the existence of an earlier court decision. FERC's consultation and decision-making process was designed to be consistent with that decision in that it explained fully FERC's decision, provided ample opportunity for all concerned to present arguments, and it ensured mitigation of market power in transmission (FERC, 1996a, pp. 453, 465, 470).

5. The Kyoto Protocol calls for the United States to reduce its average annual emissions of greenhouse gases to seven per cent below 1990 levels over the period 2008-2012. This reduction is net of adjustments for hydrofluorocarbons, per fluorocarbons, sulfur hexafluoride, and carbon sequestration.

6. Only if government budgets measured changes in the market value of their assets would "public stranded costs" be an issue; by contrast, private stranded costs are easily detected.

7. There can be confusion in terminology, as "wholesale" and "retail" have varying definitions, depending on the context and the author. IEA 1998 has an extensive discussion.

8. "Prudently incurred" means that the relevant economic regulator, *e.g.*, a state public utility commission, had examined a cost or investment and agreed to its recovery through regulated tariffs.

9. Clearly, utilities prefer higher compensation for stranded costs to lower.

10. The later end-user choice is introduced, the greater the fraction of book value that has been depreciated and recovered under the old regulatory regime, hence the smaller the stranded costs. Also, discounting further into the future reduces present value.

11. In particular, end-users bid (a "transition charge") to be in the 2.5 per cent (increasing to 12 per cent by 2002) of load that is free to choose electricity supplier. Hence, those end-users with the greatest incentive to switch will do so.

12. Reliability is the constant delivery of electric power within the standards specified with respect to frequency, voltage, and other dimensions. This is sometimes called "security of supply". There are other dimensions of "security" which relate to the wider energy market. Indeed, these other dimensions of energy security are being met through other government interventions such as the Strategic Petroleum Reserve and direct protection of energy infrastructure from physical and cyber threats.

13. Other parts of the Administration's proposed reforms for ensuring against disruption of primary fuel supply are beyond the scope of this study on reform in the electricity sector.

14. FERC's jurisdiction is limited but not absent; in 1997 it ordered the federally-owned Tennessee Valley Authority to provide access to its transmission grid.

15. These Acts have been amended since originally enacted.

16. The EPAct established a new class of generators, "exempt wholesale generators" (EWGs). These are exempt from the Public Utilities Holding Company Act (PUHCA) (FERC, 1996a, p. 42), which implies that EWGs do not need to meet PURPA's cogeneration or renewable fuels limitations, and utilities are not required to purchase

their power. The Public Utilities Regulatory Policies Act (PURPA) of 1978 required utilities to purchase power from qualifying facilities (QFs) at a price not to exceed the utility's avoided costs, and to provide backup power to QFs. QFs were subject to technological and size limitations, as well as restrictions on utility ownership (FERC, 1996a, pp. 21-25, 42).

17. Access issues also fall under the jurisdiction of the antitrust authorities, although the extent of that jurisdiction is limited by the State Action Doctrine. Under the Administration's proposed Comprehensive Electricity Competition Act, FERC jurisdiction would be extended to transmission services provided by the Tennessee Valley Authority, the federal power marketing administrations, municipal utilities, other publicly owned utilities, and co-operatives. However, under this proposal, FERC could modify or suspend its open access rules if it found that these entities did not have available adequate stranded cost recovery mechanisms.

18. The independent system operator operates a spot market, accepting bilateral schedules and voluntary bids. It finds an economic, secure dispatch and calculates the associated nodal prices. Spot market sales are made at those nodal prices. Bilateral trades are charged the difference between the price at origin and at destination for transmission. Financial hedges for nodal price differences are also traded under an associated system of "fixed transmission rights".

19. The contemporaneous differences between lowest and highest price (per megawatt-hour) in PJM Interconnection during constrained periods in the first five months of operation are: April (average = US$49, median = $33), May (average = $75, median = $66), June (average = $64, median = $57), July (average = $46, median = $39), August (average = $47, median = $11). The contemporaneous price range exceeded US$1/MWh for 17 per cent of the time in April, 25 per cent in May, 13 per cent in June, 20 per cent in July, and 7 per cent in August.

20. The California Public Utilities Commission reduced the rate of return on equity to ten per cent below the long-term cost of debt. (Several reasons were provided for the reduced return on equity: there is reduced business risk from accelerated depreciation, it is equitable that ratepayers benefit somewhat and shareholders receive lower returns during the transition, it provides utilities incentives to mitigate transition costs, and it does not provide incentives to utilities to bid lower in the power exchange, thus increasing transition costs.) At the same time, the CPUC would eliminate this 10 per cent reduction if the utility would divest itself of at least 50 per cent of its fossil-fuel generation, and indeed the CPUC would provide for a 10 basis point increase in return on equity for each ten per cent of fossil-fuel generation divested (CPUC 1997c, pp. 172-175). The stranded cost implications of this process are discussed below.

21. They are retaining ownership of transmission and distribution, which are regulated by the CPUC. Pacific Gas & Electric will sell 7 400 MW, or 98 per cent of its fossil and all of its geothermal and hydro capacity. Southern California Edison will divest 10 300 MW or two-thirds of its total generating capacity to various buyers, keeping only its nuclear, coal and hydro plants (FT Energy World, 5/1998). San Diego Gas & Electric will divest its entire generating capacity – fossil, nuclear, and long-term purchased power contracts – but a related subsidiary will build a large gas-fired plant in Nevada (Enova 1998, pp. 36-7).

22. FERC required system control, and reactive supply and voltage control from generation sources, to be bundled with transmission; regulation, energy imbalance, and both spinning and supplemental operating reserve to be offered with transmission but customers be allowed to buy from third parties or self provide; and did not require transmission providers to offer load following, real power loss replacement, dynamic scheduling, backup supply, system blackstart capability or network stability services.

23. The separation of supply from distribution is less important for the development of competition in supply because the threat of discrimination against non-integrated supply competitors is relatively small. If all suppliers have equal access to information about extensions of the distribution grid, such as to new buildings or houses, then scope for discrimination is virtually foreclosed. (This information flow from distribution to supply should not be confused with the informational advantage of the incumbent supplier over entrants into supply, which constitutes an entry barrier.)

24. Monopolisation entails both the possession of monopoly power in the relevant market and the wilful acquisition or maintenance of that power. Hence, unlike abuse of dominance, charging "high" prices is not monopolisation. Market share is the most important factor in determining the existence of monopoly power, so market definition is crucial; the second important factor is barriers to entry. One of the more famous monopolisation cases is *United States v. Otter Tail Power Co.*, 410 US 366 (1973), in which the Supreme Court found that Otter Tail, an investor-owned utility, had engaged in monopolisation by *inter alia* refusing to sell electric power at wholesale to municipal distribution companies, as well as refusing to allow them access to its transmission grid in order to buy electric power from other generators, despite Otter Tail's ability to provide such access.

311

25. The FERC reviews mergers under the Federal Power Act standard that mergers must be consistent with the public interest, although a positive benefit is not necessary, whereas the antitrust agencies review mergers under the Clayton Act standard that prohibits mergers or acquisitions where "the effect of such acquisition may be substantially to lessen competition, or to tend to create a monopoly". The FERC considers three factors: the effect on competition, the effect on rates, and the effect on regulation (FERC, 1996c).

26. The Antitrust Division and the FTC would not usually require divestiture if electric power markets turn out to be too concentrated after liberalisation. By contrast, remedies available to FERC include a variety of structural and behavioural remedies: requiring transmission expansion, requiring the merging parties not to use a constrained path for its own off-system trade when other transmission service requests are pending, divestiture of generating plants or of ownership rights to energy and capacity, deferring to an independent system operator, or, with other remedies, introducing time-of-use pricing.

27. When evaluating a proposed merger, the antitrust authorities will normally examine the present and past operation of the market(s). However, because the economic environment of the electricity sector is changing radically, the past is not a good indication of the future. Given the limited information about how competitive electric markets in the United States operate, and the inability to order *ex post* divestitures, the head of the Antitrust Division has suggested the consideration of changing the burden of proof for some electricity sector mergers during the period of transition to competitive markets (Klein, 1998).

28. "Reliability" as used here means short-term, operational stability and investment in assets.

29. "No group in the electric power industry has stepped forward to take responsibility for building new lines and supplying equipment to support out-of-state electrical system usage. Unbundled electric utilities will not consider projects outside their service territories or competitive markets. However, how system reliability will function in a period of downsizing and cost cutting remains to be seen" (EIA, 1998g, Chapter 7). NERC, responsible for reliability, "expect[s] states to show reluctance in allowing the construction of transmission enhancements that serve customers in other states. We cannot depend on market forces to provide incentives to enhancement while transmission is regulated as it is. Quality of the transmission system could deteriorate in the future. That would not only hamper the development of an open and competitive electricity market, but it would also lead to a deterioration of reliability. The future of the transmission grid requires far more attention than it has gotten, to date, in the discussions of deregulation" (NERC, 1997b, p. 35).

30. In other countries that may be taking a different approach from that taken by the United States, specific instruments have been devised to counter potential failures in the regulatory-market system, *e.g.*, so-called capacity payments to generators in England and Wales – which are now being abandoned.

31. Precisely what sources of primary energy qualify for the "portfolio standard" varies from jurisdiction to jurisdiction. E.g., the state of Maine includes hydro-power in its "portfolio standard", but many other jurisdictions exclude it. Within sources of primary energy, the "portfolio standards" are often technology-neutral, *i.e.*, they do not specify how that primary energy gets transformed into electrical energy, nor do they specify the identity of the owner of the generator. A key element in incorporating non-hydro renewables fueled generation into an electric system is the provision of ancillary services, *e.g.*, backup power, to those generators.

32. Precisely, the schedule is: one per cent by end 2003 or one year after the average cost of any renewable technology is within ten per cent of the average spot-market price, whichever is soonest; 0.5 per cent for each year thereafter until end 2009; one per cent for each year thereafter until a date yet undetermined (Section 50 of Massachusetts Act).

33. The EIA estimates that in the United States, generation prices could fluctuate from less than two cents to as much as 15 cents per kilowatt-hour, increasing to as much as 50 cents per kWh during times of capacity shortage (EIA 1997c).

34. If a regional emissions pact among the north-eastern states is agreed before a given date, then this unilateral emissions rule does not come into force.

35. Only 9 000 had switched as of the end of February 1998. The small number is likely the result of the 10 per cent mandated consumer rate reduction, that reduced the scope for suppliers' offers to induce switching.

36. In California, consumers' monthly electric bills will separately itemise the amounts paid for electric energy, transmission, the competitive transition charge, and the public goods charge.

37. Competitive neutrality means that economic entities are treated symmetrically without regard for their type of owner or legal form.

38. The "preference rate" is the rate BPA charges public or people's utility districts, municipal utilities, co-operatives, and federal agencies in the Pacific Northwest.

39. The EPAct authorised federal programs and industry-government joint ventures to provide financial assistance for a number of energy-related purposes, including for research and development in fuel efficiency, renewable energy and advanced manufacturing in the energy sector. To receive funds under this Act, firms must make investments in the United States in research, development and manufacturing. Further, the recipient must be a US-owned company or a US-incorporated company whose parent is incorporated in a country which affords adequate and effective protection of intellectual property rights of US-owned firms and provides to US-owned companies access to such joint ventures and local investment opportunities comparable to that afforded to any other company (OECD 1995).

40. Financing costs of the debt in 1994 were 35 per cent of its power revenues, as compared with an average of 16 per cent for neighbouring utilities.

41. Proof of an ability to pay for decommissioning funds is made in two ways: electric utilities must set aside funds during the operation of the plant, and non-utilities must make up-front assurances of having adequate funds. Licensees who formerly qualified as "electric utilities" might, under rate deregulation, be transformed into non-utilities subject to the tougher decommissioning funding requirements applied to non-utilities.

42. The arguments advanced regarding electricity reforms may or may not be parallel to those advanced regarding natural gas reforms.

43. This is the rule for contracts executed before 11 July 1994. 11 July 1994 is the date the initial Stranded Cost Notice of Proposed Rule-Making was published. For contracts executed after 11 July 1994, the amount of stranded cost that can be recovered is that amount that is specified in the contract; if there is none it is zero, unless there is language like "as the FERC determines" in which case there is a default calculation.

44. "Transition costs" are defined as "the costs, and categories of costs, of an electrical corporation for generation-related assets and obligations, consisting of generating facilities, generation-related regulatory assets, nuclear settlements, and power purchase contracts, including, but not limited to, voluntary restructurings, renegotiations, or terminations thereof approved by the commission, that were being collected in commission-approved rates on 20 December 1995, and that may become uneconomic as a result of a competitive generation market in that those costs may not be recoverable in market prices in a competitive market [...] Transition costs shall also include the costs of refinancing or retiring debt or equity capital of the electrical corporation, and associated federal and state tax liabilities" (California, 1996, Section 11 adding Section 840 of the Public Utilities Code). "Uneconomic assets" are those assets whose net book value (original cost recorded in the company's books, less depreciation) exceeds their market value (CPUC, 1997c, pp. 2, 187). This determination is to be made on an asset-specific basis.

45. On 3 September 1997, the CPUC authorised, respectively, $3.5 billion to Pacific Gas & Electric, $3.0 billion to Southern California Edison and $0.8 billion to San Diego Gas & Electric, the three privately owned utilities active in California (CPUC, 1998a).

46. In contrast to most US utilities that have less than 10 per cent wholesale load (and FERC-guaranteed recovery of stranded assets in the move to greater competition), Ontario Hydro has a 70 per cent wholesale load and no analogous mechanism for stranded asset recovery. Ontario Hydro maintains that it cannot offer open access until provincial industry restructuring is complete – expected in the year 2000.

47. Further, the effect of such reciprocity provisions would be expected to vary, depending on the incentives (including regulatory regime) and cultures of the utilities involved.

48. In particular, there were dramatic price increases in the wholesale electricity markets in the Midwest. Unseasonably hot weather increased demand; above-average planned and unplanned outages (notably of large quantity of baseload nuclear plant) reduced generating capacity available in the region, and transmission constraints reduced the ability to move power to where it was needed. Prices, for some hourly transactions, rose from around US$25/MWh to as much as US$2 600/MWh, with significant hourly purchases in the US$3 000 to US$6 000 range, and one hourly price reached US$7 500/MWh. At the same time, weighted average price for the week was about US$60/MWh. (The difference is due to the relatively small quantity of electricity transacted on hourly markets.) In addition to the "physical" factors cited above, other contributing supply-side factors to the price spikes included a lack of timely, objective price information and fear of default by trading counterparties. On the demand-side, since small end-users do not have incentives to adjust their demand based on price, utilities made public appeals for voluntary usage reduction, which did result in some reductions. The market response has demonstrated the robustness of the system. Some utilities are proposing new tariffs that allow certain industrial users to sell their firm power entitlements back to their local utility under peakload conditions. Utilities have said that they changed their trading strategies. There is recognition of the need for timely, more complete provision of information about market prices. Planned expansions of generating capacity is proceeding. Despite

suggestions for the imposition of price caps, the FERC staff were offered no compelling arguments for such a movement away from competition. This experience, of extraordinary high spot market prices, and the responses of the market participants and the regulator, demonstrate the robustness of a market system, while also suggesting that further market refinements would be in order (FERC, 1998*b*).

49. One observer has noted, "In particular, it supplies electricity with a high level of reliability; investment in new capacity has been readily financed to keep up with (or often exceed) demand growth; system losses (both physical and those from theft of service) are low; and electricity is available virtually universally" (Joskow, 1997).

50. FERC estimated the potential cost savings from non-discriminatory transmission access to be about US$3.8 to US$5.4 billion per year, plus better use of existing assets and institutions, new market mechanisms, technical innovation, and less rate distortion (FERC Order No. 888-A (Order on Rehearing) 4 March 1997).

51. Allocative economic efficiency is highest when there is no other allocation of resources that would make someone better off without making someone else worse off.

52. Marginal cost means the cost of an additional unit.

53. In the United States, customers typically buy their own meters.

54. If end-users may choose whether to have time-of-use pricing, then those with less costly to serve load profiles will opt for it, leaving behind end-users with costlier load profiles, thus raising their average prices. Absent competition, the cross-subsidies could be maintained.

55. Baumol, Joskow and Kahn state that, "In our opinion, the opportunities for improvements in *productive* efficiency flowing from a fuller opening of electric generation to competition are very limited in the *short-run*" (emphasis theirs, Baumol, 1995, p. 23).

REFERENCES

Antitrust Division, US Department of Justice (1996),
   "Application of the Horizontal Merger Guidelines to Mergers of Electric Utilities: Appendix to Comments of the US Department of Justice in FERC Docket No. RM96-6-000, Merger Policy under the Federal Power Act".

Baumol, William J., Joskow, Paul L., and Kahn, Alfred E. (1995),
   "The Challenge for Federal and State Regulators: Transition from Regulation to Efficient Competition in Electric Power", Edison Electric Institute, Industry Structure Monograph Series No. 1.

Beamon, J. Alan (1998),
   Competitive Electricity Pricing: An Update. <http://www.eia.doe.gov/>.

Bonneville Power Administration (1997),
   1997 BPA Fast Facts. <http://www.bpa.gov>.

Bonneville Power Administration (1998),
   Bonneville Cost Review Background Materials, FCRPS Cost Review: FCRPS Financial Indicators.
   < http://www.nwppc.org/fcrpsfin.pdf>.

Borenstein, Severin, Bushnell James, Kahn Edward and Stoft Steven (1995),
   "Market Power in California Electricity Markets", University of California Energy Institute, Power Working Paper Series PWP-036, mimeo, December.

Borenstein, Severin, Bushnell James, and Stoft Steven (1997),
   "The Competitive Effects of Transmission Capacity in a Deregulated Electricity Industry". mimeo, June.

Borenstein, Severin, Bushnell James and Knittel Christopher R. (1998),
   "Market Power in Electricity Markets: Beyond Concentration Measures", University of California Energy Institute, Power Working Paper Series PWP-059, April.

Brockway, Nancy (1997),
   "Electricity Deregulation May Leave Poor in the Dark", Forum for Applied Research and Public Policy, Fall.

Burns, Robert E. and Eifert Mark (1994),
   "A Cooperative Approach Toward Resolving Electric Transmission Jurisdictional Disputes", NRRI 94-06, the National Regulatory Research Institute, Ohio State University, March.

California Public Utilities Commission (1997a),
   Opinion Regarding the Retail Settlements and Information Flow Workshop and Related Filings. Decision 97-12-090 16 December 1997. Order Instituting Rulemaking on the Commission's Proposed Policies Governing Restructuring California's Electric Services Industry and Reforming Regulation, Rulemaking 94-04-031 (filed 20 April 1994); Order Instituting Investigation on the Commission's Proposed Policies Governing Restructuring California's Electric Services Industry and Reforming Regulation, Rulemaking 94-04-0312 (filed 20 April 1994), <http://www.cpuc.ca.gov/electric_restructuring/decisions.shtml>.

California Public Utilities Commission (1997b),
   Final Opinion: Transition Cost Tariff Issues, Decision 97-12-039 on 3 December 1997.
   <http://www.cpuc.ca.gov/electric_restructuring/decisions/d9712039/d9712039.htm>.

California Public Utilities Commission (1997c),
   Interim Opinion: Transition Cost Eligibility, Decision 97-11-074 on 19 November.
   <http://www.cpuc.ca.gov/electric_restructuring/decisions/d9711074/d9711074.htm>.

California Public Utilities Commission (1997d),
   Electricity Restructuring in California: An Informational Report (March).
   <http://www.cpuc.ca.gov/divisions/energy/environmental/restruct/open.htm>.

California Public Utilities Commission (1998a),
   Electric Restructuring Status Report, 19 February.
   <http://www.cpuc.ca.gov/electric_restructuring/status/980219_status.html>.

California Public Utilities Commission (1998*b*),
Electric Restructuring Status Report, 2 July.
<http://www.cpuc.ca.gov/electric_restructuring/status/980702_status.html>.

California (1996),
AB 1890 *Public Utilities: Restructuring*, 31 August.

California Energy Commission (1998),
A Quick Look at Electricity Deregulation in California.
<http://www.energy.ca.gov/restructuring/quick_look.html>.

Council of Economic Advisers (1998),
Economic Report of the President.

DELGADO, Jose (1998),
"Reliability and Inter-Regional Transfers", presentation at Harvard Electricity Policy Group Sixteenth Plenary Session, 21 May. <http://ksgwww.harvard.edu/hepg/Delgado052198.sld0001.htm>.

Department of Energy (1996),
DOE Biomass Power Program, Strategic Plan 1996-2015. DOE/GO-10096-345. December 1996.
< http://www.eren.doe.gov/biopower/biomaspp.pdf>.

Department of Energy (1998*a*),
Comprehensive Electricity Competition Plan. <http://www.hr.doe.gov/electric/cecp.htm>.

Department of Energy (1998*b*),
Comprehensive National Energy Strategy: National Energy Policy Plan Pursuant to Section 801 of the Department of Energy Organization Act, April. <http://www.doe.gov>.

Department of Energy (1998*c*),
Ancillary Services and Bulk-Power Reliability, a Position Paper of the Electric-System Reliability Task Force, Secretary of Energy Advisory Board. 12 May. <http://www.hr.doe.gov/seab/elec_rep.html>.

Department of Energy, Wind Energy Program.
<http://www.eren.doe.gov/wind/program.html>.

Environmental Protection Agency (1997),
EPA Office of Compliance Sector Notebook Project: Profile of the Fossil Fuel Electric Power Generation Industry. EPA/310-R-97-007, September.

Energy Information Administration, US Department of Energy (1997*a*),
Electric Power Monthly (March). <http://www.inel.gov/national/hydropower/facts/generate.htm>.

Energy Information Administration, US Department of Energy (1997*b*),
Nuclear Power Generation and Fuel Cycle Report 1997, "Nuclear Fuel Cycle: Recent Developments; Supply and Demand Projections". <http://www.eia.doe.gov/cneaf/nuclear/n_pwr_fc/ch2.html>.

Energy Information Administration, US Department of Energy (1997*c*),
US Electric Utility Demand-Side Management: Trends and Analysis.
<http://www.eia.doe.gov/cneaf/pubs_html/feat_dsm/contents.html>.

Energy Information Administration, US Department of Energy (1997*d*),
US Electric Utility Demand-Side Management 1996, DOE/EIA-0589(96), December.
<http://www.eia.doe.gov/cneaf/electricity/page/at_a_glance/plt_tabs.html>.

Energy Information Administration, US Department of Energy (1997*e*),
Electric Utility Restructuring. <http://www.eia.doe.gov/cneaf/electricity/page/at_a_glance/restruct.html>.

Energy Information Administration, US Department of Energy (1997*f*),
Electricity Prices in a Competitive Environment: Marginal Cost Pricing of Generation Services and Financial Status of Electric Utilities: A Preliminary Analysis Through 2015. <http://www.eia.doe.gov/oiaf/elepri97/comp.html>.

Energy Information Administration, US Department of Energy (EIA 1997*g*),
Financial Statistics of Major US Investor-Owned Electric Utilities 1996 Data Tables.
<http://www.eia.doe.gov/cneaf/electricity/invest/t33.txt>.

Energy Information Administration, US Department of Energy (EIA 1997*h*),
Electric Sales and Revenue 1996. <http://www.eia.doe.gov/cneaf/esr/esr_sum.htm>.

Energy Information Administration, US Department of Energy, (1998*a*),
The Restructuring of the Electric Power Industry.
<http://www.eia.doe.gov/cneaf/electricity/chg_str/brochure/retail.htm>.

Energy Information Administration, US Department of Energy (1998*b*),
    US Electric Power Summary Statistics. < http://www.eia.doe.gov/cneaf/electricity/epm/epmt2.dat>.

Energy Information Administration, US Department of Energy (1998*c*),
    Electric Power Monthly (May) DOE/EIA-0226(98/05). < http://www.eia.doe.gov/cneaf/electricity/epm/ind_dev.htm>.

Energy Information Administration, US Department of Energy (1998*d*),
    Electric Power Monthly (March) DOE/EIA-0226(98/03). <02269803.pdf at ftp://ftp.eia.doe.gov/pub/pdf/electricity>.

Energy Information Administration, US Department of Energy (1998*e*),
    Inventory of Power Plants in the United States-As of 1 January 1997.
    <http://www.eia.doe.gov/cneaf/electricity/ipp/ipp_sum.html>.

Energy Information Administration, US Department of Energy (1998*f*),
    Electric Power Annual 1996, Vol. II. <http://www.eia.doe.gov/cneaf/electricity/epa/epav2/epa2_sum.html>.

Energy Information Administration, US Department of Energy (1998*g*),
    The Changing Structure of the Electric Power Industry: Selected Issues, 1998.
    <http://www.eia.doe.gov/cneaf/electricity/chg_str_issu/summary/chg_str_issu_sum.html>.

Energy Information Administration, US Department of Energy (EIA 1998*h*),
    Status of State Electric Utility Deregulation Activity, Monthly Update.
    <http://www.eia.doe.gov/cneaf/electricity/chg_str/tab5rev.html>.

Enova Corporation (1997),
    SEC filing 10-K/A, *Annual Report* for fiscal year ended 31 December 1997.

Environmental Protection Agency (1998),
    Nitrogen Oxide (NO_X) Reduction Program. <http://www.epa.gov/acidrain/noxpg.html>.

Federal Energy Regulatory Commission (1996*a*),
    Order No. 888 Final Rule (issued 24 April 1996). 75 FERC 61 080. Promoting Wholesale Competition through Open
    Access Non-discriminatory Transmission Services by Public Utilities, Docket No. RM95-8-000; Recovery of
    Stranded Costs by Public Utilities and Transmitting Utilities, Docket No. RM94-7-001.

Federal Energy Regulatory Commission (1996*b*),
    Order No. 889 Final Rule (issued 24 April 1996). 75 FERC 61 078. Open Access Same-Time Information System
    (formerly Real-Time Information Networks) and Standards of Conduct, Docket No. RM95-9-000.

Federal Energy Regulatory Commission (1996),
    18 CRF Part 2 (Docket No. RM96-6-000), Inquiry Concerning the Commission's Merger Policy Under the Federal
    Power Act: Policy Statement, Order No. 592, issued 18 December.

Federal Energy Regulatory Commission (1998),
    Inquiry Concerning the Commission's Policy on Independent System Operators, Docket No. PL98-5-000, Notice
    of Conference, 13 March.

Federal Energy Regulatory Commission (1998*b*),
    Staff Report to the Federal Energy Regulatory Commission on the Causes of Wholesale Electric Pricing
    Abnormalities in the Midwest During June 1998, 22 September.

Federal Trade Commission (1995),
    Comments of the Staff of the Bureau of Economics of the Federal Trade Commission, In the Matter of Promoting
    Wholesale Competition Through Open Access Non-discriminatory Transmission Services by Public Utilities and
    Transmitting Utilities; Proposed Rulemaking and Supplemental Notice of Proposed Rulemaking, Docket
    Nos. RM95-8-000 and RM94-7-001, 7 August. <http://www.ftc.gov/be/v950008.htm >.

Federal Trade Commission (1998*a*),
    Comments of the Staff of the Bureau of Economics of the Federal Trade Commission Before The Federal Energy
    Regulatory Commission, Department of Energy. Inquiry Concerning the Commission's Policy on Independent
    System Operators, Docket No. PL98-5-000, 1 May. <http://www.ftc.gov/be/isodraf3.htm>.

Federal Trade Commission (1998*b*),
    Comments of the Staff of the Bureau of Economics of the Federal Trade Commission Before the Louisiana Public
    Service Commission Regarding "Market Structure, Market Power, Reliability, and ISOs"Docket Number U-21453,
    15 May. <http://www.ftc.gov/ev980010.htm>.

Financial Times Energy World (1998),
    No. 5, Winter.

General Accounting Office (1995),
    Tennessee Valley Authority: Financial Problems Raise Questions About Long-Term Viability. GAO/AIMD/RCED-95-134. August.

317

Hogan, William W. (1998),
"Getting the Prices Right in PJM: Analysis and Summary: April through August" (September 7). <http://www.ksg.harvard.edu/people/whogan/>.

ISO New England (1998),
About the ISO. <http://www.iso-ne.com>.

International Energy Agency (1997),
CO_2 Emissions from Fuel Combustion: A New Basis for Comparing Emissions of a Major Greenhouse Gas 1972-1995. OECD/IEA, Paris.

International Energy Agency (1998),
Energy Policies of the United States 1998 Review. OECD/IEA, Paris.

Joskow, Paul l. (1997),
"Restructuring, Competition and Regulatory Reform in the US Electricity Sector", Journal of Economic Perspectives, Vol. 11, No. 3, summer, pp. 119-138.

Klein, Joel (1998),
"Making the Transition from Regulation to Competition: Thinking about Merger Policy During the Process Electric Power Restructuring". Speech before the Federal Energy Regulatory Commission, 21 January.

New York Mercantile Exchange (1998),
Electricity Futures and Options. <http://www.nymex.com/contract/electric.html on 21 May 1998>.

North American Reliability Council (1997a),
Maintaining Bulk-Power Reliability through Use of a Self-Regulating Organisation: Position Paper. 6 November. <http://www.nerc.com/download/doe_sro.html>.

North American Reliability Council (1997b),
Reliable Power: Renewing the North American Electric Reliability Oversight System, NERC Electric Reliability Panel, 22 December. <http://www.nerc.com/pub/sys/all_updl/docs/misc/erp-bot.pdf>.

North American Reliability Council (1997c),
Reliability Assessment 1997-2006, October. <http://www.nerc.com/~ec/syscond.html>.

Nuclear Regulatory Commission,
Nuclear Reactors. <http://www.nrc.gov/NRC/reactors.htm>.

Nuclear Regulatory Commission, 1997,
Final Policy Statement on the Restructuring and Economic Deregulation of the Electric Utility Industry. 10 CFR Part 50. 20 October 1997. <http://www.nrc.gov/OPA/reports/drgstmt.htm>.

Organisation for Economic Co-operation and Development (1995),
OECD Reviews of Foreign Direct Investment: United States, Paris.

PJM Interconnection (1998),
Who We Are – What We Do. <http://www.pjm.com/about/general.htm>.

Tennessee Valley Authority (1997),
Government Performance and Results Act, Strategic Plan, FY 1997-2002. Submitted to Congress and the Office of Management and Budget 30 September.

Tennessee Valley Authority (1998),
TVA's Fossil Fuel Operations. <http://www.tva.gov/orgs/fossil/fsslfax.htm>.

United States Enrichment Corporation (1998),
< http://www.usec.com>.

United States Government (1998),
"The Kyoto Protocol and the President's Policies to Address Climate Change: Administration Economic Analysis", June. <http://www.epa.gov/globalwarming/reports/pubs/wh_econ/index.html>.

Virginia State Corporation Commission Staff (1997),
"Draft Working Model for Restructuring the Electric Utility Industry in Virginia". <http://dit1.state.va.us/scc/news/streprt3.htm>.

Western Area Power Administration (1997),
Annual Report. <http://www.wapa.gov/western/annrpts.htm>.

White, Matthew W. (1996),
"Power Struggles: Explaining Deregulatory Reforms in Electricity Markets", Brookings Papers on Economic Activity: Microeconomics, pp. 201-250.

BACKGROUND REPORT
ON REGULATORY REFORM
IN THE TELECOMMUNICATIONS INDUSTRY[*]

* This report was principally prepared by **Darryl Biggar** and **Patrick Hughes**, Administrators of the Directorate for Financial, Fiscal, and Enterprise Affairs, with the participation of **Bernard J. Phillips**, Division Head, of the Directorate for Financial, Fiscal, and Enterprise Affairs, and **Dimitri Ypsilanti** of the Directorate on Science, Technology, and Industry. It has benefited from extensive comments provided by colleagues throughout the OECD Secretariat, by the Government of the United States, and by Member countries as part of the peer review process. This report was peer reviewed in September 1998 by the OECD's Working Party on Telecommunication and Information Services Policies and by the Competition Law and Policy Committee.

TABLE OF CONTENTS

OECD 1999

Executive Summary

Background Report on Regulatory Reform in the Telecommunications Industry

The telecommunications industry has seen significant regulatory reform in OECD countries in recent years. Twenty-three OECD countries now have unrestricted market access to all forms of telecommunications, including voice telephony, infrastructure investment and investment by foreign enterprises, compared to only a handful only a few years ago. The success of the liberalisation process depends on the presence of a transparent and effective regulatory regime that enables the development of full competition, while effectively protecting other public interests. There is a need to promote entry in markets where formerly regulated monopolists remain dominant and to consider elimination of traditionally separate regulatory frameworks applicable to telecommunications infrastructures and services, and to broadcasting infrastructures and services.

The United States has led the world in the reform of telecommunications regulation. The 1984 divestiture was, at the time, a bold step that led to lower prices and more consumer choice in markets for long-distance and international services. It also opened network equipment markets thus contributing to the dramatic fall in telecommunication switching and transmission costs. The recent WTO Agreement builds on these successes in the international context.

The 1996 Telecommunications Act prohibited state and local governments from retaining legal barriers to local entry into local telecommunication markets. The Act was concerned to let competitors choose the mode of entry that makes the most technical and economic sense to them. Accordingly the Telecommunications Act maintained three entry routes for new competitors – resale, unbundling and separate facilities. To date, all three methods have been used in efforts to enter the local market.

While the Act was, in principle, a salutary measure in pro-competitive regulatory reform, many legal, technical and economic issues have had to be addressed and competition has not developed quickly in local and short-distance toll markets under state jurisdiction.

1. THE TELECOMMUNICATIONS SECTOR IN THE UNITED STATES

1.1. The national context for telecommunications policies

By any measure, the telecommunications market in the United States is large. Although NTT (the incumbent telecommunications company in Japan) is the world's single largest telecommunications company, nine of the world's twenty largest carriers are American. The total revenue of the US market at a little over $250 billion is equivalent to forty per cent of the OECD total.

It is also a dynamic industry that has adopted innovations quickly. In part, this is due to the leading role the United States has taken among OECD countries in pro-competitive telecommunications regulatory reform. Over fifteen years ago, with the intent of promoting competition, the 1984 divestiture split the incumbent telecommunications operator into a long-distance company and seven regional local operating companies. At the time, the divestiture was a bold step that led to lower prices and more consumer choice in markets for long-distance and international telecommunications services. It also helped to indirectly open network equipment markets and thus contributed, as one of many factors, to the dramatic decline in telecommunications switching and transmission costs. Today, the US has one of the most competitive domestic long-distance market in the world.

To date, the benefits of regulatory reform in the United States by way of price falls have been concentrated in long-distance, international and mobile communications markets. As FCC data presented in Box 1 indicates, price reductions of some 30 per cent and higher have caused the overall costs to subscribers of long distance toll and international services (as well as mobile) to fall significantly[1] for business and residential subscribers.

Box 1. Indicators of the benefits of regulatory reform

	Price (nominal)	Incumbent Market Share	
	'84-'92	'92-'96	'84-'96
Local Residential:	Up 45%	Up 5%	Still near 100%
Intra-state Toll:	Down 10%[1]	Up 3%[1]	Around 75%[2]
Inter-state Toll:	Down 50%[3]	Down 17%	85% down to 55%
International:	N/A.	Down 33%	100% down to 55%
Mobile:	N/A.	Down 37%	Competitive

1. Based on Bureau of Labor Statistics data that does not include discount plans. Thus the data may understate price reductions.
2. Incumbent market share in individual states varies considerably.
3. Includes both long-distance and international and composed only of AT&T information.

Source: FCC (1998), *Trends in Telephone Service*, CCB, July. Local price is the average monthly rate including taxes and the subscriber line charge, long-distance (interstate) and international is average revenue per minute. Mobile is average monthly bill and includes both cellular and broadband Personal Communications Service. Incumbent market share is according to total revenue.

The distribution of consumer benefits due to price reductions has, however, been unevenly distributed across users of telecommunications services. Large business customers have experienced the most substantial gains while the savings experienced by individual residential subscribers varies depending on their calling patterns. In particular, as Box 1 indicates, customers who mainly consume local services have not benefited from the significant price reductions that have occurred in long distance and international services.

Disadvantaged groups have received special attention. Indeed, the promotion of "universal service" has been a central objective of US telecommunications policy.[2]

Reductions in the price of telecommunications services benefit US consumers also indirectly since reductions in the telecommunications costs of doing business permit lower prices for goods and services throughout the economy. Moreover there are other benefits that are difficult to fully quantify[3] partly because some of them will manifest only in the longer term and because these benefits include dynamic changes such as the introduction of new products and increased consumer choice. Indeed, perhaps the most important observation concerning the impact of regulatory reform in the US is the extraordinary level of innovation that has flourished and transformed the telecommunications industry with significant positive effects throughout the economy. Regulatory decisions such as the *Computer* I, II *and* III inquiries played an important role in facilitating the development of markets for competitive value added network services (*i.e.*, enhanced services) and for the rapid diffusion of the Internet in an unregulated environment. Available estimates suggest that over thirty million people in the US use the Internet. Further diffusion of innovation is likely in future years as new initiatives, such as Internet II,[4] are considered.

1.2. General features of the regulatory regime and market participants

Decisions of the Federal Communications Commission (the "FCC") over many years have shaped the general features of the regulatory regime as well as the identity of market participants. The *Hush-A-Phone* and *Carterfone* decisions, for example, facilitated the development of competition in customer premise equipment. Decisions in the early 1980s also provided a basis for vigorous resale competition while, as noted above, the *Computer* II and *Computer* III decisions played an important role in facilitating the development of markets for competitive value added network services (*i.e.*, enhanced services). These decisions were emulated in other OECD countries where, in many cases, incumbents tried to extend their dominant positions to value added network services.

Over the 1960s and early 1970s, the FCC started to allow the private use of the radio frequency spectrum giving rise to several competitors entering long-distance markets. To this point, there were no established provisions to mandate access to the incumbent's public switched telephone network, and the regulatory regime did not establish effective controls to restrict cross-subsidisation (whereby the incumbent is able to support low prices for some *e.g.*, competitive services, through high prices charged to captive subscribers of its monopoly supplied services). The FCC responded to the changing market conditions of the 1970s by beginning to develop competitive safeguards including interconnection requirements and accounting mechanisms to prevent cross-subsidies from monopoly activities, but these were not effective.[5]

The root cause of the problem was that the incumbent was participating in both regulated monopoly and competitive markets. The scope this presented for anticompetitive conduct was magnified by the control of a bottleneck facility – the local exchange – possessed by the regulated monopolist. Such an incumbent can and has an incentive to protect its market power in newly competitive markets by denying new entrants equal access to its network.

The 1984 antitrust decree, was essentially a response to this problem.[6] It established a market structure in the United States unique in OECD countries. Under the terms of the decree, AT&T was required to divest its local operating subsidiaries, creating seven Regional Bell Operating companies (the "RBOCs") which, subject to several waivers and exceptions, were not allowed to provide "long-distance" service. These restraints on providing long-distance was designed to ensure that regulated monopolists of local loops would not participate in competitive long distance markets, thus eliminating the incentive to discriminate.[7] The divestiture was also premised on the view that local exchanges had natural monopoly properties but technological developments since 1984 have eroded such properties.

The divestiture established a distinction between long-distance (or inter-exchange) services and local exchange services. It defined 164 different Local Access and Transport Areas ("LATAs"), generally smaller than states, and stipulated that RBOCs were not allowed to provide any services that crossed these lines.[8] It also stipulated that RBOCs were not allowed to provide information services. The basic idea behind the divestiture was address natural monopoly concerns by ensuring that RBOCs provided only basic telecommunications services subject to regulation.

Following the 1984 divestiture, vigorous competition in long-distance markets between AT&T and new inter-exchange carriers developed in the market for inter-LATA/inter-state telecommunications services under federal jurisdiction as well as the market for inter-LATA/intra-state services under state jurisdiction.[9] These markets account for roughly half of the US telecommunication market by revenue. The divestiture did not, however, facilitate the introduction of competition into intra-state/intra-LATA or local exchange services. In fact, most states maintained legal entry restrictions into intra-state/intra-LATA and local exchange markets throughout the 1980s and early 1990s. In revenue terms, intra-state/intra-LATA is a relatively small but not unimportant segment of the market that constitutes a little under ten per cent of total industry revenue.[10] At the end of 1997, there were approximately 1 300 licensed Competitive Local Exchange Carriers ("CLECs"). The top ten CLECs have switches in 132 cities spanning 33 states and the District of Columbia. Over the past two years, $14 billion has been invested in CLECs, and their combined market capitalisation is over $20 billion. Since the 1996 Act, the RBOCs and GTE have lost more than 1.5 million access lines. As a result of this loss in access lines by local exchange carriers, the total market share of CLECs is about 2 per cent.[11]

Changes in the regulatory framework, as well as changes in the competitive strategies used by telecommunication operators, have given rise to significant changes in market structure. Most significantly, the number of important carriers in the market has increased as competition has been introduced. Box 2 notes some selected aspects of the evolution of the market structure in the US telecommunications industry.

There has been mounting pressure for change in the structure of the US telecommunications market. Beginning in the mid-1990s, US long-distance carriers entered into international alliances with carriers from other countries. As part of a policy to promote open international competition, the alliances were permitted on the condition that safeguards be put in place to assure that other US carriers were not discriminated against in regard to the terms of access to foreign local exchanges. In an important recent development, British Telecom announced that it plans to enter into an international agreement with AT&T.

Another notable development is the recent increase in concentration at the level of local exchange carriers. Two mergers approved in 1997 (Nynex/Bell Atlantic and SBC/Pacific Telesis) have reduced the number of major local exchange carriers from eight to six. There are two additional merger proposals pending (Ameritech/SBC and Bell Atlantic/GTE) which would reduce the number of local exchange carriers still further to four.

An important recent development in the US domestic long distance market is the recent merger between MCI and WorldCom that has reduced the number of major long-distance carriers to three. Not surprisingly MCI and WorldCom were the second and fourth largest providers of domestic long-distance services in the US. Moreover, MCI and WorldCom also had a significant presence in the market for international and Internet backbone services. Not surprisingly, the merger proposal was subject to review by the FCC as well as the US Department of Justice, Antitrust Division (the "DOJ") and antitrust authorities in the European Union. In its analysis of the market for domestic long distance services, the FCC stated that: "In light of the significant new transmission capacity that we believe will become available by the end of 1999, we conclude that existing market participants as well as potential market entrants will likely be capable of using the newly available capacity to constrain any attempted exercise of market power".[12] Also, market share information shows that there is a relatively large competitive fringe – *i.e.*, the market share held by inter-exchange carriers other than AT&T, Sprint and the merged MCI/WorldCom carrier is comparable to MCI's pre-merger market share. Thus, the FCC held that the merger was in the public interest subject to the condition that MCI sold its Internet business to a competitor.[13]

Box 2. The evolving market structure in US telecommunications

1960s and '70s Rivals such as MCI and Sprint entered the long-distance market. Inadequate competitive safeguards limited the competitive significance of these entrants. Competition was also allowed in customer premise equipment.

Early 1980s Numerous competitors entered as resellers.

Early 1980s The Bell system was broken into AT&T (which competed with rivals such as MCI in long-distance and international) and seven RBOCs with geographically separate local monopolies: Bell Atlantic, NYNEX, SBC Communications (formerly South-western Bell), US West, Pacific Telesis, Ameritech and Bell South. Line-of-business restrictions enforced a vertical separation.

Mid-1980s Cellular licences originally issued in 1981 were put into commercial use and a new product market emerged. The initial market structure was a duopoly in each of separate license regions. Market penetration of cellular services expanded markedly, though somewhat slower than some other OECD countries.*

1980s and '90s Long-distance competitors became firmly established as the divestiture provided an effective safeguard against the incentive for local exchange carriers to discriminate against rival carriers on access terms. The market share levels attained by new entrants in long-distance increased significantly beyond levels experienced in other OECD countries.

1994 Acquisition of the leading cellular provider, McCaw by AT&T.

Jan. 1998 The February 1997 WTO Agreement on basic telecommunications services was signed by sixty-nine countries. By 1998, twenty-two of the OECD countries had unrestricted market access to all forms of telecommunications, including voice telephony, infrastructure investment and investment by foreign enterprises.

Mid-1990s British Telecom/MCI and Sprint/Deutsche Telekom/France Telecom entered into alliances.

1997 Local operating companies: SBC/Pacific Telesis and NYNEX/Bell Atlantic merged.

1997-98 Four applications by RBOCs to provide long-distance service were denied by the FCC.

1998 The number two and number four long-distance providers, MCI and WorldCom merge.

July 1998 AT&T acquires a leading Competitive Access Provider, Teleport.

---

*   OECD (1997), *The OECD Report on Regulatory Reform: Volume I: Sectoral Studies*, Figure 3.1, Paris, p. 44.

As in several other OECD countries, mobile telecommunications services provides an example of where market liberalisation has had a significant impact. In the US, the FCC introduced cellular competition through a duopoly licensing process. Throughout the 1990s, mobile service penetration grew strongly in the US, but has nevertheless lagged behind the growth in other countries.[14] The US mobile market has recently been opened further through the use of auctions to allocate licenses for the use of spectrum to provide PCS (Personal Communications Services). Some highlights relating to the development of mobile competition are provided in Box 3.

1.3. The promotion of local competition

In the years since the 1984 divestiture, the promotion of local competition has been a central policy focus. Conditions of entry into local markets varied, and still vary, significantly across states. In the early 1990s, some state regulators developed initiatives to extend the beneficial effects of regulatory reform into their local markets. By 1995, at least twenty-three states had certified one or more local competitors. Competitive Access Providers were the first carriers to break into local monopolies. Starting with Teleport's entry in New York,[15] cable companies and new fiber carriers began providing dedicated access for large business customers to the increasingly competitive inter-exchange market. This entry was a form of by-pass of the incumbent's local exchange network. Competitive Access Providers

---

Box 3. **Developments in the emergence of competition in mobile communications**

- In the early 1980s, two cellular licenses were granted in each of numerous separate geographic areas across the United States. One license was reserved for the in-region local exchange carrier, a second license was granted to an independent player.

- Throughout the 1980s and early 1990s, cellular communications constituted a fairly small segment of the telecommunications industry, appealing largely to a narrow sub-set of subscribers with quite specialised needs. As of December 1993, national subscribership was about 16 million and the penetration rate was about 6 per cent. The average monthly bill was just over $60.

- As part of the 1993 Budget Act, Congress authorised the FCC to use competitive bidding to award certain licenses for the right to use the electromagnetic spectrum. Over 1995 and 1996, four blocks of spectrum used for broadband Personal Communications Services were auctioned.

- By December 1997, mobile communications (*i.e.*, both cellular and PCS) had become a large and growing segment of the telecommunications market. National subscribership was about 55 million and the penetration rate was just over 20 per cent with the average monthly bill had falling to just over $40.*

- In its Third Annual CMRS Competition Report published in June 1998, the FCC concluded: "... this past year has seen the beginnings of a shift in the relationship between wireless and wireline services. A number of wireless technologies have begun to take aim at services long thought of as the sole province of wireline operators".

---

* Where the average "bill" is revenue per unit. The FCC notes that actual price per minute, and thus a subscriber's actual bill, varies significantly depending on an individual customer's service plan. According to one study (published in January 1998), the average price for service in the most expensive plans is over $0.50 per minute while the least expensive plans average in the mid-$0.20 range.

offered little, if any, switched local exchange services. Entry into local switched services was also allowed in Connecticut, the state of Washington, Maryland, Massachusetts, Michigan and New York.

In the early 1990s there were high expectations surrounding the prospects for cable companies and Competitive Access Providers as possible entrants into local telecommunications. Providers of cable services were seen to possess the potential for offering alternative access since they "pass-by" more than 95 per cent of residences in the United States.[16] Cable companies themselves announced optimistic investment plans, and alliances between cable providers and out-of-region RBOCs were explored. Several Competitive Access Providers applied for permission to provide switched local services, and as noted above, by 1995 several states had authorised entry. Some commentators were quick to conclude that entry into local markets was imminent. Potential new entrants into local have not yet been a significant competitive influence. Despite disappointments in regard to the extent of successful entry so far, cable companies remain strong potential competitors in the coming years, particularly as they develop the ability to provide broadband Internet access on a widespread commercial basis.

In addition to permitting entry, initiatives were taken by some states, in co-operation with the FCC, to actively promote local competition. In November 1993, Ameritech submitted its "Customers First" plan to the DOJ under which Ameritech offered to "unbundle" its service offerings in Illinois so as to facilitate entry.[17] In January 1995, the New York Public Utility Commission approved Rochester Telephone's "Open Market Plan".[18] In exchange for relief from regulatory rules, Rochester Telephone voluntarily separated itself into a network operator and a retail company. The network operator intended not to engage in any direct sales to individual subscribers to instead act as a carriers' carrier, providing service on a wholesale basis to its own retail company as well as any entrants at a rate 5 per cent below the regulated retail price. Time Warner entered the market on a trial basis, providing access through its cable plant and relying on the Rochester Tel network company for other elements of local service.

The approach taken to promoting local competition differed from that taken in regard to promoting competition in long-distance markets in 1984. Rather than implementing a structural divestiture,

US policy makers attempted to promote entry by relying on co-operation from incumbent local exchange carriers. The basic theory behind the Ameritech and Rochester initiatives was that even if natural monopoly characteristics made full-scale facilities-based entry into local markets uneconomic, it may be possible for competitors to engage in some aspects of local competition.

In the Rochester Telephone case, the intention was that cable companies might be able to use their cable access to individual subscribers and rely on Rochester Telephone's network for switching, aggregation and termination. In the Ameritech example, the idea was that entrants could self-supply some services and rely on Ameritech's network for the services that were the most difficult or expensive to self-supply. Thus, for example, inter-exchange carriers or Competitive Access Providers might be able to supply their own bulk transport and switching, but rely on Ameritech for access to individual subscribers (*i.e.*, Ameritech's local loops). Neither of these strategies to open local markets has, as yet, proven to be effective.

The next significant development in the policy to promote local competition was the *Telecommunications Act of* 1996, which represents a renewed attempt to facilitate the development of competition in all telecommunications markets, including local. The *Act* was implemented by three major FCC orders known as the "Competition Trilogy" – local competition; universal service reform; and access charge reform – designed to reform the regulatory regime. The interconnection, unbundling and resale provisions of the 1996 *Act* are closely related to earlier attempts to facilitate local entry. In fact, specific aspects of the implementation of these provisions are modelled after pre-existing initiatives of state Public Utility Commissions (the "PUCs"). The *Act* attempts to strengthen these initiatives by making approval to enter in-region inter-LATA toll markets contingent on a demonstration that local markets are open to competition. Key provisions of the 1996 *Act* are summarised in Box 4 below.

Box 4.   Key features of the 1996 Telecommunications Act

Interconnection: incumbent local exchange carriers (the incumbent "LECs") are required to provide interconnection to any requesting carrier at any technically feasible point. The FCC concluded that prices should be based on Total Element Long-Run Incremental Cost (TELRIC) plus a reasonable share of forward-looking joint and common costs.

Unbundling: incumbent LECs are required to provide requesting telecommunications carriers non-discriminatory access to network elements on an unbundled basis at any technically feasible point. The FCC concludes that prices should be based on TELRIC plus a reasonable share of forward looking joint and common costs.

Resale: incumbent LECs are required to offer for resale, any telecommunications service that the carrier provides at retail to subscribers. The FCC concludes that the price of resale services should be set at a discount off retail based on the costs that the incumbent LEC can avoid by selling at wholesale rather than retail.

Universal Service: an explicit mechanism to maintain local rates at affordable rates is mandated.

Access Charge Reform: to facilitate the development of an explicit mechanism for universal service, the FCC reformed the access charge rate structure.

Entry into long-distance: RBOCs are allowed to provide out-of-region inter-LATA service. A procedure is provided for under which the RBOCs are permitted to enter in-region inter-LATA when their local markets are found to be sufficiently open to competition. In assessing whether the local markets are open, the FCC is directed to give "substantial weight" to the DOJ's assessment of a "competitive checklist". Once an RBOC gains approval to offer inter-LATA service, they are required to do so subject to an accounting separation for a three year period.

Forbearance: the FCC is directed to forbear from aspects of regulation that are deemed to be unnecessary.

Removal of State Barriers to Entry: state regulation that raises barriers to entry into local markets is pre-empted.

**Box 5.   Questions regarding the failure of local competition
to develop as quickly as anticipated**

Local Rate Distortions? Are continuing subsidies that hold down the price of local service maintaining disincentives to entry?

Technical Impediments? Many states do not provide intra-LATA equal access and number portability will not be fully implemented until 1999. Unlike traditional telecommunications carriers, cable networks' voice telephony service cannot operate in the case of a power outage. Have these technical barriers made entry unattractive?

Restraints on Competition? RBOCs have been prevented from providing one-stop-shopping – *i.e.*, providing local and long-distance service on a single bill. Prior to the 1996, AT&T and other inter-exchange carriers were faced with legal barriers to intra-LATA entry in some states. Are these barriers to the provision of one-stop-shopping inhibiting competition?

Judicial Uncertainty? Central aspects of regulatory policy are currently the subject of judicial challenge. Has uncertainty surrounding regulatory rules created a disincentive for investments by new entrants?

No Clear Strategy to Promote Facilities-Based Competition? Local competition initiatives in the US has encouraged resale entry as well as some facilities-based entry. Would a focused effort to promote local interconnection at a small number of points of the network, and selected unbundling of elements (if any are necessary) be more successful?

Technical Problems Faced by Cable Operators? Efforts to provide telephony on cable networks have experienced technical problems. Were claims in the early 1990s that cable systems are capable of providing two-way communications excessively optimistic?

Incumbent LEC Anticompetitive Conduct? An objective of the 1996 Act was to give incumbent LECs an incentive to co-operate in facilitating competition. Was the promise of inter-LATA toll entry a sufficient incentive?

In public statements, the FCC and DOJ have acknowledged that local competition has not developed as quickly as hoped.[19] The current share of nation-wide local service revenues of new entrants is about 1.4 per cent.[20] In response to Section 271 applications in Michigan, Louisiana, Oklahoma and South Carolina, the DOJ concluded that the local markets in question were not sufficiently open to competition and the FCC rejected the RBOC applications to provide inter-LATA service. The FCC established recently a Local Competition Task Force to "identify trouble spots" and "initiate enforcement actions" to ensure open entry into local markets, and undertook a survey to better understand local competition.

There remains considerable promise that local competition will develop. Technological advances such as digitalisation, compression, and fiber optics are expected to pave the way for a variety of alternative delivery systems. Information stemming from technological trials and small scale new entry[21] suggest that alternative networks can provide local access that is superior to traditional networks in terms of bandwidth and speed. These technological advantages indicate that new networks will emerge to provide both traditional voice telephony and new services such as interactive broadband video services, tele-medicine or electronic commerce. Exactly what networks or standards will emerge, and which new information services will be demanded on a widespread basis is unpredictable. There is, however, strong evidence that relative costs are changing in a manner that will create new markets and new infrastructures capable of offering new as well as existing information services.[22]

Potential alternative technologies to provide telephone service include cable systems, mobile services and wireless local loop. A primary advantage of cable systems is their access link to a large number of homes. Cable systems "pass by" over 95 per cent of homes with a broadband access. In coming years, this broadband access link will is likely to allow cable companies to provide not only traditional voice telephony, but also Internet service on a widespread commercial basis. The current technological challenge for cable systems is to "upgrade" their networks to allow for interactive communications.

Existing networks providing mobile services (including cellular and PCS) provide a second potential substitute for the provision of traditional local telecommunications. When they were initially introduced, price and reliability considerations meant that mobile services were used almost exclusively as a complement to primary wireline. Increasingly, however, cellular and now digital PCS are gaining acceptance as a substitute as well as a complement to traditional wireline telephony.

The scope for mobile telecommunications services to provide competition for wireline telephony could be increased if the option of "calling party pays" is made more widely available. It is common in the US that mobile carriers cannot offer billing arrangements under which subscribers pay only for the calls they originate and not those they receive. One important reason is that local exchange providers often do not provide the identity of the originating party to the mobile carriers. The availability of "calling party pays" would enhance the ability of subscribers to control their monthly bills for mobile telecommunications service. This issue has attracted the attention of the FCC which has initiated a hearing on this matter.

New technologies employing wireless local loop access provide a third potential entrant to local markets. Networks using these technologies are currently less developed than cable or mobile telecommunications networks. However, such alternative networks are likely to have a considerable comparative advantage in providing access services to rural or remote subscribers. An added advantage is that the investments necessary for entry are less likely to involve irreversible (i.e., "sunk") investments.[23]

The speed with which these alternative delivery systems are likely to develop depends in part on regulatory developments such as local rate rebalancing. Current geographic rate averaging requirements mean that some high-cost (e.g., rural) subscribers are served at prices below economic cost. These are the customers for which wireless technologies are likely to be best suited. The speed with which these alternative delivery systems are likely to develop also depends on how quickly new information services are introduced. There is an increased incentive for entry if a new network can expect to earn revenue from both voice telephony and other new information services.

It is notable, however, that Section 706 of the Telecommunications Act directs the FCC to examine whether advanced telecommunications services are being made available to all Americans on a reasonable and timely basis.

2. REGULATORY STRUCTURES AND THEIR REFORM

2.1. Regulatory institutions

The regulatory structure in the United States is a complex web that involves the interface of jurisdiction over sector-specific regulation between the states and the federal government, the relationship between sector-specific regulation and antitrust law, as well as between these agencies and the courts. In other OECD countries such as Canada and Australia, the regulatory structure is somewhat simpler because there is exclusive federal jurisdiction. The dual federal-state role can give rise to both costs and benefits. While the scope for states to pursue different policy initiatives can sometimes promote the development of innovative schemes to forward regulatory reform, the jurisdictional overlap also generates costs and uncertainties in policy development. The dual federal-state role in the US telecommunications industry has been the source of numerous jurisdictional battles in the Court of Appeals.[24] Box 6 describes institutions relevant to the regulatory regime.

2.2. Telecommunications regulation and related policy instruments

Regulation of entry and service provision

Historically, regulation of entry and service provision have varied depending on whether the market was under state or federal jurisdiction. Entry conditions have been significantly liberalised in markets under federal jurisdiction many years before comparable reforms were undertaken in other OECD countries. The liberalisation of entry conditions in markets under state jurisdiction has proceeded more slowly.

At the federal level, the FCC liberalised entry conditions through a number of decisions dating back as early as the 1950s and continuing over many years. For example, FCC decisions liberalised the conditions of entry into customer premise equipment, value-added and resale markets. In regard to facilities-based entry into long-distance, entry conditions were liberalised gradually. In 1959, in the Above 890 decision, the FCC permitted private use of the spectrum, in effect allowing rivals to enter into the provision of long distance services.[25] In the late 1960s, the FCC took additional steps to lower barriers to entry in the *Carterphone* decision as well as decisions to grant microwave licenses in 1969 and 1971.[26]

Important barriers to entry into inter-LATA markets remain. Section 271 of the Act requires RBOCs to show that the local market in a particular state is sufficiently open to competitors before it is permitted to enter into the provision of inter-LATA service within that state. Under this section, the FCC "shall not approve" a RBOC application to enter long distance markets unless it finds that the RBOC has concluded agreements with one or more facilities-based competitors to provide access or interconnection (which satisfies the "competitive checklist") as well as a public interest test. Alternatively, if a RBOC has not received a qualifying interconnection request within a designated period of time, the 271 test can be satisfied by providing a statement of generally available terms and conditions that complies with the competitive checklist and that "has been approved or permitted to take effect by the [relevant] state commission". Importantly, in the assessment of a Section 271 application, the FCC must give "substantial weight" to the DOJ's evaluation.

Box 6. **Regulatory institutions for the telecommunications industry**

- The US regulatory regime provides for joint Federal and State jurisdiction:
- Federal Communications Commission (the "FCC"): The FCC is an independent agency consisting of five Commissioners. Commissioners are nominated by the President subject to confirmation by the Senate. Once confirmed, they cannot usually be removed from office during their five year term. One of the Commissioners is appointed Chair by the President. Decisions are made by simple majority rule of the Commissioners. The Federal Communications Commission has exclusive jurisdiction over inter-state matters, as well as intra-state matters where legislation pre-empts State authority.
- State Public Utility Commissions (the "PUCs"): Each of the fifty states and the District of Columbia have public utility commissions. The legal authority of PUCs derives from the relevant State legislature. The State PUCs, in general, have jurisdiction over intra-state matters such as prices and entry conditions into local markets as well as intra-LATA long-distance.
- In addition, a number of other federal level institutions play a role:
- The Department of Justice, Antitrust Division (the "DOJ"): For historical reasons, the DOJ rather than the Federal Trade Commission takes the lead role in antitrust enforcement in telecommunications.
- The Courts: Regulatory or antitrust decisions in telecommunications can in general be appealed to the Courts. Prior to the 1996 Telecommunications Act, the divestiture consent decree (*i.e.*, Modification of Final Judgement) was administered by the US District Court for the District of Columbia.
- The National Telecommunications & Information Administration: an agency of the US Department of Commerce, is the Executive Branch's principal voice on domestic and international telecommunications and information technology issues. The NTIA focuses on telecommunications infrastructure and the US government's legislative initiatives in telecommunications.
- The Office of the US Trade Representative: is responsible for developing and co-ordinating US international trade, commodity, and direct investment policy, and leading or directing negotiations with other countries on such matters (including telecommunications issues). The US Trade Representative is a Cabinet member who acts as the principle trade advisor, negotiator, and spokesperson for the President on trade and related matters.

331

Section 271 of the Communications Act, as amended by the Telecommunications Act of 1996, maintains the pre-1996 Act prohibition against a RBOC providing inter-LATA long-distance service originating in a state within its local service region until the FCC approves an application demonstrating that the RBOCs local telephone market is open to competition. Section 271 contemplates that to permit the RBOCs immediate entry into the long-distance market would allow the RBOCs to leverage their bottleneck control in the local market into the long-distance market, thus both threatening competition in the long-distance market and entrenching the RBOCs monopoly in the local market. Apparently, the US Congress believed that unless the RBOCs had some incentive to open their markets to competition, it was highly unlikely that competition would develop quickly in the local market. Congress thus decided to use the promise of long distance entry to entice the RBOCs to open their markets to competition.

The rationale underlying Section 271 of the Act, which is to offer entry into long-distance (a highly competitive relatively low profit margin market), as an incentive for RBOCs to open their high margin, monopolistic local markets, has been open to question.

The analysis of local competition by the DOJ and FCC in recent Section 271 applications makes a strong case that, based on the available facts, the specific markets considered were not "irreversibly" open to competition. Thus, this analysis shows that a potentially important role remains for the restraints on RBOC entry. The DOJ analysis follows the framework provided by the so-called "competitive check-list". The approach relies on the proposition that, by denying inter-LATA authority, the prospects for local competition are advanced because the relevant RBOC would have an incentive to co-operate with new entrants.

The RBOCs argue that as a result of the Section 271 restraints they, as well as consumers, forego the benefits of potentially important economies of scope in the joint provision of local and long-distance service. Because of the RBOCs bottleneck control of the local market and the early stage in the opening of local markets, the Section 271 restraints will likely remain in place under the existing regime for the foreseeable future.

The FCC has promoted flexibility in spectrum licensing in order to reduce barriers to entry that spectrum scarcity would otherwise impose on communications markets. In recent proceedings to license personal communications services and general wireless services, the FCC permitted extensive flexibility in licenses. Such flexibility can help assure that spectrum use adjusts to accommodate new technologies that might become available in the future. Also, allowing flexibility to transfer authorisations to use the spectrum causes licensees to bear the opportunity costs of allowing spectrum to remain idle. This reduces barriers to entry and reduces the incentive that might otherwise exist for license holders to withhold spectrum from the market for anticompetitive purposes.[27]

An additional example of the role the FCC can play in promoting competition is provided by the policy framework in mobile telecommunications. In 1993, Congress amended the Communications Act to provide for an expanded federal role to lower entry barriers by authorising competitive bidding to allocate spectrum to the private sector (e.g., spectrum currently being used to provide PCS services) and to broadly prohibit state regulation of mobile services.[28] The successful development of competition in mobile services may be indicative of the benefits of an expansive federal role in telecommunications regulations.[29]

State PUCs have been slower to promote entry into inter-state toll and local markets. Thus, the 1996 Telecommunications Act attempted to address this barrier by pre-empting state legislation and imposing expanded obligations on incumbent local exchange carriers with a view to promoting local entry. Notably the Act maintains three main paths of entry: i) through resale of the incumbent's network services; ii) through purchase of unbundled network elements; and iii) through largely facilities-based entry.

Regulation of interconnection

The need for mandated interconnection to an incumbent's networks as a competitive safeguard is well established. As a result of network externalities inherent in communications networks, the value of service provided to a subscriber is a function of the number of other subscribers that can be reached on a given network. Absent interconnection to the public switched local telephone networks of local exchange carriers, entry by competitors to an incumbent provider with a nearly one hundred per cent installed base, would not be feasible. It is necessary for regulation to mandate the terms of interconnection since incumbents typically have a incentive to foreclose competition.[30]

Progress toward a procompetitive interconnection regime has been considerably faster in inter-state (*i.e.*, inter-LATA) markets. This progress has been seen both in the quality and pricing of access. The regulation of interconnection has been an important factor underlying the relative success of regulatory reform in inter-state markets.

In regard to the price of interconnection, inter-state access charges have fallen toward forward-looking cost much faster than intra-state access charges. In 1985, the inter-state common carrier line charge for switched access service (termination only) was about 10 per cent higher than the median of the corresponding intra-state rate. Between 1985 and 1990, the inter-state rate for termination fell much faster than the intra-state rate, and by 1990, the inter-state rate was about 50 per cent below the median of intra-state rates.[31] The inter-state rate continued to fall over the 1990s. In terms of the total charge per conversation minute (*i.e.*, including charges both at origin and termination), the interstate charge has fallen dramatically, from over 17 cents on 1984 to less than 4 cents in 1998.[32]

In regard to quality of interconnection, a primary issue has been "equal access" (sometimes referred to as "dialling parity"). Equal access was implemented much more quickly in regard to inter-state services. FCC information shows that equal access for subscribers was implemented rapidly after the 1984 divestiture in regard to inter-LATA toll.[33] Equal access in regard to intra-LATA markets has been implemented much more slowly. The result is that, in many states, a subscriber who chooses to switch to a rival intra-LATA toll carrier must dial extra digits every time he or she makes a call. The Telecommunications Act imposed a three-year moratorium on states introducing intra-LATA dialling parity. This moratorium expires in February 1999.

The 1996 Act builds on policies to reduce interstate access fees. First, as discussed above, the FCC concluded in the *Local Competition* decision that interconnection prices should be based on Total Service Long Run Incremental Cost plus a "reasonable share" of forward-looking joint and common costs. Second, it provides for an explicit mechanism to fund universal service. This has allowed the elimination of the implicit subsidy that excessive interstate access fees formerly provided while allowing other policy objectives to be met. The observable result has been effective competition in inter-LATA long-distance markets.

The 1996 Telecommunications Act, provides for the concept of interconnection to be extended into local markets.[34] The *Local Competition* decision provides that, at a minimum, incumbent local exchange carriers must provide interconnection at four points: the line-side of a local switch, the trunk-side of a local switch, the trunk interconnection points for a tandem switch, and central office cross-connect points. The idea behind interconnection at these points on the local network is to lower barriers to entry and increase the incentive for new entrants to make investments in their own local networks. In this regard, if incumbent local exchange carriers could deny interconnection within the local network, it could raise rivals costs by forcing the new entrant to interconnect at the same point as inter-exchange carriers. By mandating four minimum points of interconnection, the FCC sought to avoid favouring the entry of one technology over others.

Some state PUCs have "mirrored" federal initiatives relating to the price of interconnection. However, access charges remain considerably above comparable federal levels in many states. The continuation of above cost access charges in these states restricts the ability of rivals of local exchange companies (both domestic and foreign) to compete.

An emerging issue for US telecommunications policy in the area of interconnection charges is the treatment of Internet traffic. Internet service providers generally pay incumbent local exchange companies a flat monthly rate for their connections regardless of the amount of usage they generate.[35] This

333

pricing arrangement, designed for circuit-switched basic telephony, may not be well suited for packet-switched uses and could give rise to concerns about switch congestion.[36] Pricing of access to the Internet using local exchange networks is becoming a particularly pressing issue as convergence increasingly allows traditional telecommunications services to be provided over the Internet (*e.g.*, Internet telephony).

Unbundling and resale competition

As discussed above, beginning with the FCC's Open Network Architecture initiative as well as the Rochester Tel and Ameritech experiments, the FCC and some state PUCs have been attempting to promote local entry through making unbundled elements of the local exchange network available to entrants. The 1996 Act takes these initiatives one step further by requiring an incumbent local exchange carrier to base prices of a specific network element on Total Long Run Incremental cost plus a reasonable share of forward-looking joint and common costs.[37] The 1996 Act also requires that incumbent local exchange carriers sell wholesale service for resale by competitors at prices that equal the retail price minus the cost that the local exchange carrier avoids by not having to retail the service itself.

The main procompetitive rationale for resale and unbundling is that it may accelerate the development of competition. Resale can play a role in accelerating and sustaining competition in telecommunications services. Both resale and unbundling may be effective entry vehicles for new entrants that may initially lack the necessary capital to build their own networks, in whole or in part. Resale may also allow small competitors that do not intend to become facilities-based players to offer service. Indeed, such resellers may stimulate the usage of the incumbent's network, and thus may benefit the incumbent facilities-based provider and further the growth of an information economy. Restricting methods of entry can result in investment distortions and higher prices.

It is important to note that resale can also impede facilities competition if, in practice, the price is set too low. Specifically, if elements are made available at low prices relative to economic cost, entrants will use the incumbent's facilities even if, on a stand-alone basis, the investment would have been an economic proposition for the entrant. That is, there is a danger that regulatory prescriptions for unbundling at prices that are excessively low may act against the consumer's longer run interests through the reduction of incentives for companies to install their own wired (or wireless) networks. In general, the obligation on an incumbent to permit resale should be used as a temporary measure since the method of determining the price (a discount relative to retail that reflects avoided cost) incorporates any distortions embodied in the retail price.

Regulation of pricing

Historically, the goal of promoting universal service has given rise to prices that do not reflect relative costs.[38] Prices charged to business users and for long-distance services were set at higher than competitive levels to allow low rates (sometimes below cost) for local service to be maintained. At the same time, local rates in rural and remote areas were held at low levels relative to rates in urban areas. The maintenance of low rates for local telecommunications service in rural and remote areas can be particularly distorting since these are generally serviced at higher cost.

The adoption of policies to rebalance these rates have been an important feature of telecommunications regulatory reform in the United States. Three main types of rate rebalancing are long-distance/local, urban/rural and business/residential.

The increase in competition in inter-LATA markets since the 1984 divestiture has given rise to significant long-distance/local rate rebalancing. Information on changes in prices of local service, intra-state toll (including some inter-LATA and some intra-LATA) and inter-state toll (*i.e.*, inter-LATA) service since 1984 are provided in Box 7. As the box illustrates, while there has been considerable rebalancing of inter-state rates, there has been less rebalancing of intra-state prices.[39]

This data suggests that reductions in toll prices have been concentrated in inter-state markets.[40] This is consistent with the FCC's analysis of AT&T's market power which led to the finding that AT&T was

Box 7. Changes in prices in intra-state and inter-state markets

The Bureau of Labor Statistics provides information on the percentage change in real (1984 = 100) prices of: flat-rate local monthly calling (for residential users), inter-state (inter-LATA) toll and intra-state toll (which includes intra-LATA and inter-LATA). The FCC also provides information on revenue per minute in interstate toll markets. This information is provided graphically below to illustrate the degree to which long-distance toll rates have fallen relative to local monthly rates.

The FCC reports that in 1992, inter-exchange carriers began to increase the basic rate while at the same time, greatly expanding their range of discount plans available to subscribers. It is for this reason that reported interstate revenue per minute is significantly below the interstate price index reported by the Bureau of Labor Statistics.

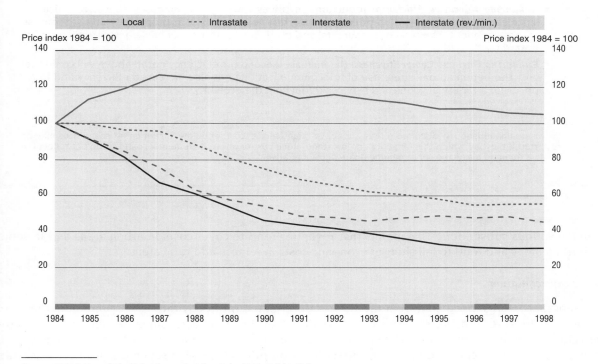

Source: FCC, Trends in Telephone Service, July 1998, Table 13.2.

non-dominant. At the same time, it appears that RBOCs remain as dominant incumbents in intra-LATA markets. Commentators such as Vogelsang and Mitchell (1997) conclude that competition in these markets is currently comparable to that which existed in inter-LATA prior to divestiture.[41] Progress toward rate rebalancing in inter-state markets (particularly intra-LATA) has been slower. The lack of viable intra-LATA competition is probably due to a lack of presubscription for intra-LATA service Box 8 discusses economic arguments for such rate rebalancing.

The ability to maintain intra-LATA prices above competitive levels limits the pressure on state PUCs to rate rebalance because it provides continued scope for some prices to remain below true economic cost. The degree to which individual local rates are below cost varies significantly depending on the specific fact situation in a state or municipality. It is less expensive to provide local loops in densely populated urban areas and central business districts than in suburban and rural areas. In most cases, geographic tariff averaging limits the extent to which carriers can tailor prices depending on the costs of

---

Box 8. Economic arguments for rate rebalancing

There are three main economic benefits of rate rebalancing:

- **Enhancing Productive Efficiency**: the maintenance of rates either above or below their true economic cost distorts entry decisions and thus constricts productive efficiency.* For example, the maintenance of prices above costs for long-distance calls may lead subscribers to choose less efficient arrangements or networks that "by pass" the national network. Alternatively, the maintenance of below cost rural rates may impede substitution toward more efficient technologies for providing access such as wireless. Rate rebalancing that raises rates for local service to economic cost, particularly in high cost rural areas but also less dense suburban areas, promotes local entry because it removes an artificial incentive for subscribers to remain with the wireline incumbent network rather than switch to carriers with the most efficient technology.

- **Enhancing Allocative Efficiency**: reductions in prices toward cost increases allocative efficiency since consumers, faced with a price reflecting true relative costs, appropriately adjust their use of these services. The total of consumers' and producers' surplus is enhanced where prices move toward cost.

- **Enhancing Business Competitiveness**: the increased economic efficiency noted above will confer not only the benefits from direct use of telecommunications but also increased efficiency and lower prices for a variety of goods and services throughout the economy.

---

* Prices are unambiguously distorted if they are above "stand alone" cost, or below "incremental" cost. Prices may be distorted if they are within this range (*i.e.*, below stand-alone cost or above incremental cost) but do not reflect the relative demand elasticities or remaining differences in relative costs.

---

serving various subscribers. This means that revenues tend to cover costs in urban areas and in some suburban areas and tend to fall short of economic costs in remote and rural areas.

Price cap regulation

For many years, price control in the US was determined indirectly through regulation of the level of profit – the so-called "Rate-of-Return" regulation. As it became increasingly recognised that "rate-of-return" regulation generated strong incentives for inefficient expansion and use of capacity, the concern over profits changed to a more direct focus on prices through a scheme known as "price cap regulation". In essence, under such a scheme, price increases would be permitted so long as, on average, prices do not exceed the level of inflation minus some agreed productivity improvement expectation. The "Inflation-X" price cap scheme (now in use in an increasing number of countries) was first applied to AT&T in 1989 and subsequently to a growing number of Local Exchange Carriers.[42] Access charges are regulated by a price cap scheme, with an "X" factor of 6.5% (raised from 5.3% in May 1997 at which time the profit sharing provision that had required carriers to return profit above 10.5% to customers was abandoned).

The fact that interstate switched access and trunking prices have remained close to the FCC prescribed price cap maximum suggests that regulation has played an important part in containing ILEC price increases. It is noteworthy that price caps on AT&T's competitive services were withdrawn in 1994 when the FCC found the company to be no longer dominant. It is noteworthy also that in the UK, price cap coverage of BT's services have been significantly reduced[43] (from about 63% of revenue to some 23%) for the current price cap regime (which is expected to be the last). Special note has been made of this withdrawal of price control since – as an increasing number of countries apply price caps – it is important to reiterate the advice that price caps are meant to be temporary. As competition increases, price caps should be streamlined then removed since price regulation is undoubtedly distorting, particularly when maintained for long periods.[44] The example of the US (and the UK) in doing so is therefore to be commended and followed by other countries. The US itself should bear this in mind in regard to its regulation of LEC prices.

This withdrawal of price regulation and the constricting effect it can have over the level and structure of prices for telecommunications becomes even more important with convergence. Innovative pricing packages must be allowed to play a key role in promoting new convergent services in the Information Age, including the stimulation of a wide take-up and use of on-line and other services.

Social regulation, including universal service obligations

As noted above, the promotion of "universal service", has been a central policy goal of the United States.[45] For many years, state regulators have maintained low prices for telecommunications services to meet a variety of other policy objectives.

Policies aimed at promoting universal service through distorting prices impede regulatory reform efforts to rebalance rates and thus giving rise to reductions in economic efficiency.[46] Furthermore, the introduction of competition erodes the ability to maintain price distortions thus causing proponents of other policy goals to oppose regulatory reform initiatives so as to protect implicit subsidies.[47] Cross-subsidies, which have traditionally been the mechanism used to support universal service programmes, are coming under increased pressure as competition develops . As a result, a growing number of countries are establishing alternative competitively neutral mechanisms such as general tax revenues (Chile), contributions from carriers (United States, Dominican Republic) or contributions from spectrum auctions (Guatemala).

There are three principal universal service programs in the US. First, the traditional programs to subsidise service to high cost areas are continued with operators delivering universal service[48] being able to draw compensating support from a Universal Service Fund. Second, the "Lifeline Assistance" and "Link Up" programs are designed to subsidise hook-up cost and the cost of monthly phone bills to qualifying low income customers provided by all eligible telecommunications carriers. Third, discounts to assist schools, libraries and rural health care centres to connect to the "Information Superhighway" have been initiated. These discounts became colloquially known as the "E-rate" and were designed to cut between 20 and 90 per cent off the monthly charges of connecting to the network, and in some cases, some of the internal wiring costs. The discounts attracted applications from more than 40 000 schools and libraries. Box 9 provides highlights of recent reforms to universal service.[49]

Box 9. Reforms to universal service

1. Introduction of transparent and explicit support for universal service. All carriers satisfying specific conditions can obtain support from the federal Universal Service Fund regardless of the technology used. All carriers, including wireless carriers, are required to make contributions to the universal service fund based on end-user revenues. To qualify for access to the fund, a carrier must be able to offer (and advertise) service throughout a geographic region known as a "service area". The size of these service areas is left to the discretion of state regulators.

2. Revision and extension of support for low-income customers (Lifeline and Link-Up America).

3. Introduction of a specific fund for the needs of schools, libraries and rural health care centres.

4. Restructuring of the Subscriber Line Charge and the Common Carrier Line Charge, to partially transfer Universal Service Fund support costs to subscribers and inter-exchange carriers; increased subscriber line charges for second residential lines and multiline business customers; gradual phasing out of the existing traffic sensitive Common Carrier Line charge with a flat-rate Presubscribed Inter-exchange Carrier charge.

A central economic principle for the development of a universal service fund is that it should achieve other policy goals in the manner that distorts competition as little as possible. That is, any subsidies to carriers should be portable and available to all competitors. In principle the fund should be financed to the extent possible from general tax revenues.[50] In practice, however, few countries (Chile is one exception) fund universal service through general tax revenues. Competitively neutral contributions from all carriers can contain the economic distortions that could otherwise result from universal service funding.

An additional principle is that the fund should be targeted so that, for a fund of a particular size, maximum positive impact toward the relevant policy goals is achieved. To the extent that high telephone penetration is a policy goal, funding should be focused on marginal subscribers that are most likely to fall off the network as a response to a price increase. Similarly, to the extent that income redistribution is a policy goal, funding should be targeted on low income subscribers. In this regard, it is noteworthy that the US Link-up and Lifeline programs are targeted to those with the most need.

It should be noted that rate rebalancing and other entry promoting reforms need not threaten but on the contrary can promote the achievement of universal service goals. Increasing competition may expand the availability of low-cost telephone services. In some countries (*e.g.*, the United Kingdom) niche market operators have begun operating payphones profitably even though, due to their previously unprofitable provision by the incumbent carrier, payphones had to be mandated as an aspect of universal service obligations (*e.g.*, in the UK and Australia). It should be recognised that low priced subsidised services delivered as part of universal service programs can generate disincentives for commercial provision.

Important aspects of the initiative to reform universal service funding in the US have not yet been fully implemented. The FCC is currently examining models to establish revenue benchmarks that will allow universal service funding to be targeted at high cost subscribers. This initiative appears to hold considerable promise as a means of promoting the policy goals related to universal service without distorting competition. On the other hand, initiatives to reform universal service funding do not currently apply to rural telephone companies that service many of the areas where local prices do not cover costs by a large margin.[51]

International aspects

As discussed in the background report on Enhancing Market Openness through Regulatory Reform, progressive liberalisation of the US market for telecommunications services over time has meant that the sector has a strong historical record of international market openness. Certain US service sectors such as domestic long distance, international value added network services, and the IMTS switched resale (basic telephony) market have been open to foreign participation for years. More recently, important policy developments at national and international levels have dramatically altered the competitive landscape for telecommunications services and further improved prospects for enhanced market openness in the sector. At the national level, the *Foreign Carrier Entry Order* issued by the FCC in November 1995 ushered in a new regulatory philosophy on foreign participation in the US telecommunications market. But the defining event in shaping the current US regulatory regime for foreign participation in the telecommunications services market was the successful conclusion in February 1997 of the WTO agreement on basic telecommunications.[52]

Recent substantive regulation and market openness in the sector are thus best understood from pre and post-WTO agreement perspectives. Pre-WTO, foreign participation in the market was regulated on the basis of the *Foreign Carrier Entry Order* and through application of a reciprocity-based "effective competitive opportunities" (ECO) test as part of an overall public interest analysis for authorisations relating to the provision of international telecommunications services. The ECO policy ordinarily required several months to process each application by a foreign carrier seeking to provide service in the US market. For example, applications by Japanese carriers to enter the US were delayed over a year before they were ultimately approved.

New FCC rules introduced in anticipation of the entry into force of the WTO agreement took effect on 9 February 1998. The *Foreign Participation Order* significantly liberalised treatment of foreign telecommunications carriers and investors from countries that are signatories to the WTO agreement. A key outcome of this process was the removal of the ECO test in favour of an open entry standard for carriers from WTO Member countries. To explain briefly, open entry standard means that these carriers benefit from a rebuttable presumption that applications do not introduce concerns that would justify denial on competitive grounds.

The revised rules retain certain safeguards designed to prevent foreign carriers with market power from distorting competition in the US market and by maintaining the Commission's authority to deny or condition such entry if required by the public interest. The FCC therefore retains discretionary power to decline licenses for reasons which may be unrelated to anticompetitive conduct in the international telecommunications services market. Some foreign carriers interviewed for this project expressed concern that this leveraging of licenses in support of US objectives in other policy areas may inhibit license applications by other prospective competitors, thereby eroding prospects for enhanced foreign participation in the sector.

Improvements in processing procedures concerning the FCC's undertaking to act on Section 214 license applications should contribute to market openness. With its adoption of the new foreign participation rules, the FCC committed to act within 90 days on all Section 214 applications except those that raise issues of "extraordinary complexity". In addition, the Commission expanded its streamlined processing rules under which, absent any objections, a license may be presumed granted after 35 days. Foreign and domestic carriers alike have benefited from streamlined treatment: recent examples of foreign beneficiaries include an application by Japan's NTTA Communications to operate as facilities-based and resale carrier to Japan and an application by Canada's Teleglobe Inc. for the transfer of control of Excel Communications to Teleglobe. However, processing of applications by carriers affiliated with foreign carriers that possess market power in non-WTO markets are not eligible for streamlined processing. On a broader level, potential new market entrants, whether they are domestic or foreign, may encounter licensing and approval delays when incumbent competitors introduce opposing arguments to pending applications. The degree to which such applications (and those which raise issues of extraordinary complexity) may experience such delays in processing remains of considerable concern to affected carriers.

More specific concerns sometimes arise regarding regulatory treatment of foreign-affiliated carriers. Licenses granted under Section 214 enable a foreign carrier to use its own facilities (*e.g.*, its own cable circuits) or engage in resale of existing US carrier facilities in order to provide a service. Applications for global switched resale service by carriers from WTO countries are eligible for streamlined processing without restriction. Applicants for facilities-based and switched resale service with affiliates with market power in non-WTO countries will receive authorisation to provide service on the affiliated route only to the extent that the foreign market satisfies the FCC's ECO test. In the experience of one foreign-affiliated carrier with geographically far-flung operations around the world (many of which are located in non-WTO countries where "monopoly" models prevail), such licensing criteria have proven particularly onerous. In one illustrative case, the same carrier processing a Section 214 application for a global calling card service based in the United Kingdom dropped a number of desired destination countries from its application in order to meet licensing criteria, with attendant consequences *vis-à-vis* competing calling card schemes.

The US led initiatives to reform the existing international settlement system. However, in the continuing absence of a global solution to the issue, international settlement rates (per-minute rates paid by US and foreign carriers to terminate international traffic at its domestic destination) continue to generate tension with foreign competitors. Much of the issue turns on the FCC *Benchmark Order*, which would require US carriers to reduce the settlement rates they pay to foreign carriers and impose certain conditions on participation in the US market aimed at "reducing the incentives and ability of a foreign carrier to act anticompetitively to the detriment of US consumers". Thus, facilities-based licenses to serve markets in which a licensee's affiliate possesses market power would not be activated until the affiliated foreign carrier agrees with US carriers to *benchmark settlement rates* linked to the level of economic development in a terminating country. Under the proposed matrix, target benchmark rates of 15, 19 and 23 cents per minute would apply to high, medium and low-income countries respectively.[53]

An additional issue from an international perspective relates to intra-state interconnection charges. As noted above, some states have not "mirrored" reductions in federal charges and have continued to maintain above cost rates. Such rates impede competition from both domestic and foreign carriers.

Number portability

Number portability is defined by the 1996 Telecommunications Act as the ability of users of telecommunications services to retain, at the same location, existing telecommunications numbers without impairment of quality, reliability, or convenience when switching from one telecommunications carrier to another. As noted in the *Local Competition* decision, vigorous competition would be impeded by technical disadvantages and other handicaps that prevent a new entrant from offering services that consumers perceive to be of equal quality to the offerings of incumbent LECs. Thus, the FCC undertook to eliminate the "operational" barrier to competition that an absence of number portability would generate. The *Local Competition* decision required that long-term number portability be completely deployed by 31 December, 1998.

In August 1997, the FCC took action to address various long-term number portability implementation issues by adopting, with minor modifications, the recommendations of the North America Numbering Council.[54] The various working groups are currently implementing number portability.

Streamlining regulation

As an independent commission the FCC is, in general, not covered by presidential orders on regulatory quality. This is rooted in the historical relations between the independent commissions and the President. In some circumstances, systematic initiatives to promote regulatory quality are applied (the *Paperwork Reduction Act* and the *Regulatory Flexibility Act*).[55] Until recently, however, initiatives to assure that regulations are only used when benefits exceed costs have been undertaken through an *ad hoc* approach in the case of telecommunications. Section 11 of the Communications Act as amended by the 1996 Telecommunications Act requires the FCC to review all its regulations applicable to providers of telecommunications service in every even numbered year beginning in 1998, to determine whether the regulations are no longer in the public interest due to the development of effective competition and whether such regulations should be appealed or modified. Beginning in January 1998, the FCC initiated a series of rulemaking proceedings as part of its 1998 Biennial Regulatory Review.

The FCC has long recognised that economic regulation imposes costs on market participants and thus articulated the view in the 1995 AT&T non-dominance proceeding that: "when the economic costs of regulation exceed the public interest benefits, the Commission should reconsider the validity of continuing to impose such regulation on the market". Thus in its administration of rate regulation requirements, in the early 1980s, the FCC significantly relaxed the degree of price regulation non-dominant inter-exchange carriers such as MCI and Sprint were subjected to. The non-dominance test assessed: whether the carrier possessed market power, and whether the carrier controlled "bottleneck facilities".

In 1995, AT&T was reclassified as non-dominant and, as a result, the degree of price regulation imposed on it were similarly relaxed. In declaring AT&T non-dominant, the FCC recognised that the degree of market power possessed by AT&T had declined to the point where the benefits of regulation (*i.e.*, constraining AT&T's ability to increase price) were exceeded by the costs. According to this approach, market forces were deemed to be a more efficient way of constraining any residual market power that AT&T possessed.

The 1996 Act provides two mechanisms for systematic review of FCC regulations. First, as noted, the Act requires a so-called "Biennial Regulatory Review". This formal requirement to conduct a biennial review of whether a specific regulation continues to be necessary is a commendable measure of emulation by other countries.

Second, the 1996 Act provides explicit "forbearance" procedures whereby the concept of eliminating regulations that are no longer necessary given current market conditions is codified.[56] The forbearance procedures are of central importance because there is scope for carriers to request the initiation of the procedure in cases where regulations are a commercially important restraint on business conduct. While the enactment of these provisions is an important step, it is important to note that they do not include an explicit recognition of the costs that regulation imposes, and important provisions of the 1996 Act are exempted.[57]

Application of competition principles

The United States telecommunications industry provides a striking example of the central role for competition policy in regulatory reform. As discussed above, the 1984 divestiture was a pivotal step that promoted complementary regulatory safeguards such as interconnection and equal access. By directly addressing underlying anticompetitive incentives, the antitrust action provided a sound foundation for procompetitive regulatory reform. Today, the market share of the incumbent, AT&T, in long-distance is below 50 per cent and there is no longer any regulation of inter-LATA long-distance prices.

Important aspects of the consent order implementation process have correctly been criticised by some observers. First, even at the time the LATAs were established they may have been larger than they needed to be today. Second, the remedy embodied in the consent order may have been conceptually sound, the lack of a sunset or significant adjustment to the terms of the decree failed to keep it focused on any "natural" monopoly elements of the network.

It was foreseen at the time that the distinctions created by the divestiture would have to be adjusted over time. For example, for any new services, a decision would have to be made as to which carriers would be permitted to provide it under the terms of the decree. Similarly, it was envisioned that dynamic technological developments would require the distinction between "enhanced" and "basic" services to be subject to ongoing review.[58] In theory, such a regulatory distinction can delay new product introduction and (especially given the complexity of distinctions that may need to be drawn in a dynamic industry such as telecommunications) can impose costs on market participants.

Developments since 1984 eroded the basis for the distinctions the consent order created. First, in 1986, the FCC abandoned the distinction between monopoly and competitive services drawn in *Computer* II. It replaced structural separation (*i.e.*, the requirement that AT&T could engage in competitive services, such as enhanced services, only by forming a separate corporate affiliate) with non-structural (*i.e.*, accounting and pricing) safeguards that would ensure that neither AT&T nor the RBOCs could use revenues from their basic services operations to cross subsidise their provision of competitive services. Second, over time, the distinction between the switching, transport and aggregation functions that had been drawn before divestiture on the basis of whether they were used to provide local or long-distance services has largely disappeared Finally, in a related point, information services are now often provided by both local and long-distance networks. At the same time, functions and services that were likely "monopoly" services in 1984 (*e.g.*, local exchange and intra-LATA toll services) are potentially competitive. There are possible substitutes for most, if not all, parts of RBOC networks – including even the local loop. This suggests that the pre-divestiture notion that some aspects of the RBOC networks are a "natural" monopoly is no longer applicable. Yet, it is unclear whether the limited entry by new competitors into many RBOC local exchange areas suggests that some elements of the RBOC networks remain as natural monopolies. Until the 1996 Telecommunications Act, the decision to allow competition in the local exchange area was under the authority of the states and many states did not allow such competition. With implementation of the 1996 Act, legal barriers to local entry have been removed and it is believed that, over time, local competition will develop.

On balance, however, it would appear that over the 12 years the decree remained in force, the benefits resulting from the market structure created by the divestiture decree outweighed any detriments that resulted from implementation of that decree. The order allowed the creation of a competitive market structure with three major and many smaller inter-exchange carriers. The decree also allowed the emergence of several major local exchange companies. The regime mandated by the divestiture decree that required interconnection between inter-exchange carriers and local exchange companies is well established. With these effective regulatory safeguards firmly in place, the need for the antitrust divestiture is not as strong as in 1984.

In the transition to a relaxation of restraints on competition between local and inter-exchange carriers, there will be a need for vigilant enforcement of competition law. The scope to provide inter-LATA services will increase the incentive for local exchange carriers to discriminate against competitors in inter-exchange markets. In addition, the prospect of impending competition in local markets increases the incentive of RBOCs to merge with potential entrants, including other RBOCs and long distance firms such as AT&T. Given the inherent difficulties in assessing mergers involving parties that are, or were recently, "precluded" from competing with each other, a transitional merger ban may be necessary by FCC regulation (subject to sunset provisions). As an alternative, DOJ antitrust review of particular cases must be rigorous. In this regard, the volume of proposed mergers (in some cases involving firms becoming significantly less regulated) is unusually large in historical terms.

2.3. The dynamic view: convergence in communications markets

While traditional telecommunications and broadcasting are both regulated by the FCC at the federal level, there are significant differences between the regulatory regime applied to these sectors. As technology develops, the possibility of entry into broadcasting by telecommunications carriers is quickly becoming more realistic. In fact, many users of the Internet are currently making use of telecommunications networks to download video images. As a result, traditional distinctions between broadcasting and telecommunications are quickly breaking down.

With the convergence of communications media, it is becoming increasingly difficult to designate individual operators and even services as falling into one category or another. Such fragmented regulation not only restricts companies from taking full advantage of technological innovation and business opportunities but also prevents users from enjoying better possible services. Problems raised by relatively burdensome broadcasting regulation can be crucial since it may determine the extent to which convergence is effectively reflected in laws, policy initiatives and regulations.[59]

3. MARKET STRUCTURE AND PERFORMANCE

3.1. The structure of the market

The telecommunications industry is a relatively large part of the US economy which encompasses traditional common carrier service as well as other activities such as network equipment manufacturing, customer premise equipment, and private line services, and accounts for about $600 billion in economic activity.[60] Looking specifically at total revenue from traditional common carrier services, the most comprehensive data is available for 1996. In 1996, total revenue from traditional common carrier services was about $222 billion. Local exchange carriers accounted for about $96.5 billion and inter-exchange carriers accounted for about $93.2 billion. Cellular and PCS providers accounted for about $26 billion and resellers of various services accounted for about $6.5 billion. Box 10 sets out this data.

As in most countries, telecommunications services in the US are differentiated on the basis of whether they are local or long distance communications. However, in the United States, long-distance communications are divided into intra-LATA and inter-LATA regions and carriers charge differently depending on service areas. Local service is generally billed on a flat, per month basis and in 1996 accounted for about $96 billion. Long distance toll is generally billed per minute and accounted for about $93.2 billion during the same time period, $74.8 billion for domestic toll and $18.5 billion for international toll.[61]

Box 10. 1996 total revenue of US carriers (in millions)

	Local service	Long distance	International
CAPs and CLECs	$1 328.1 (1.4%)	0	0
Local Exchange Carriers	$95 188 (98.6%)	12.0%	0
AT&T	0	42.1% ($39 300)	$8 900
MCI	0	17.6% ($16 400)	$3 800
Sprint	0	8.5% ($7 900)	$1 700
World Com	0	4.8% ($4 500)	$600
Other IXCs	0	15.0 %	

Source: FCC Trends in Telephone Service, July 1998.

The revenue figures in Box 10 demonstrate the dichotomy in the structure of the US market. Local exchange carriers continue to dominate local service, neither inter-exchange carriers or cable service providers have established a significant market presence. Similarly, local exchange carriers are restricted in their ability to compete in long distance and international markets. Most of the LECs twelve per cent market share consists of intra-LATA long distance, though as noted above, the 1996 Act allowed them to provide out-or-region inter-LATA services. In February 1997, the FCC extended this authority to include international services originating from "out-of-region" points in the US and terminating at various international points.[62]

3.2. Market performance

The rationale for regulatory reform is the desired effects it is expected to deliver. Thus in assessing the performance of regulatory reform, the primary criterion is how well it has delivered these desired effects. The perspective adopted here is primarily that of the customer. This is appropriate since government policy makers, as well as telecommunication regulators (including those in the US) have repeatedly declared that it is the impact on the customer (both residential and business) which should and does drive regulatory policy. The main elements of market performance are:

– Lower prices.
– Increased range of product choice.
– Improved quality of service.
– Services based on leading edge technology and infrastructure.

These effects are among those promised by effective competition. Indeed, it is this promise of such desirable effects that has been the primary driver of competition-enhancing regulatory reform that is now widespread. The remainder of this Section considers available indicators of these main elements of performance. SubSection 1 considers recent price trends and indicators of profit levels. SubSection 2 discusses available information on customer choice. SubSection 3 comments on indicators of product quality. SubSection 4 provides information on technological developments.

Price and quantity trends

The price effect of regulatory reform on individual subscribers depends crucially on how much long distance service they demand. The average total monthly local telephone rate paid by residential customers has increased in nominal terms from $13.35 in 1984 to $19.07 in 1994 (or 3.4 per cent per year).[63] Thus a subscriber who consumes no long distance services has not been made significantly better off, and depending on the consumer price index used to account for inflation over the period, may have been made marginally worse off. As discussed below, subscribers who consume long-distance or international services have been made considerably better off.

A full assessment of the effects of cuts in long-distance and international price levels is difficult because much price competition has taken the form of price discounts for off-peak use. As competition developed, a wide range of price discounts have been introduced, with varying discounts and eligibility conditions, including up front fees for some schemes.[64] Apart from price discounts, various promotional offerings have included free months of calling, airline frequent flyer points, and coupons toward merchandise at national buying clubs.[65] Information on average revenue per minute for long-distance and international services is available, as is information on average monthly bills for cellular service. This information was noted earlier in Box 1.

Customer choice and prescribed lines

A telephone line is said to be "prescribed" to the long distance carrier that receives the ordinary long distance calls placed on that line. Monitoring changes in prescribed lines is important because it indicates the potential for customers to choose between suppliers of a service. In this context it is notable that AT&T's share of prescribed lines has decreased in favour of other carriers. By the end of 1996, about 63% of lines were prescribed to AT&T, 15% to MCI, 7% to Sprint, and 3% to WorldCom. Over 600 smaller carriers serving 19.2 million lines accounted for the remaining 12% of the industry.[66] This trend of a diminishing share of prescribed lines for AT&T indicates that customers were in fact given an effective choice of long distance which an increasing number exercised in favour of AT&T's competitors. Indeed, according to MCI, in 1993, an estimated 20 million people switched long-distance companies, with the number growing to 27 million in 1994, to 42 million in 1995 and to 50 million in 1996.[67]

Quality

The quality of telecommunications service in the US has improved, particularly for large business customers, because of technological improvements and also because service quality is a major feature of competitive strategy for major telecommunication operators. The FCC's published data on quality of service is extensive and includes the number and nature of customer complaints. During 1996, the FCC processed 35 095 written complaints and inquiries. Of these, 36% involved slamming issues (becoming the customers' telephone service provider without their knowledge or consent), 13% involved pay-per-call services, and 12% involved operator service provider rates and services.[68] The remaining complaints covered a range of issues including international telephone rates, unsolicited calls or faxes and telemarketing.

The number of households with telephones increased over the period. In 1988, the fraction of households with telephone service was 85.4 per cent and the fraction of additional lines for households with telephones was 2.7 per cent. By 1992, the respective fractions had risen to 91 per cent and 9.1 per cent. By 1996, the respective fractions were 95.1 per cent and 16.5 per cent.

Productivity and technological development

FCC statistics provide information on labour productivity index for the telecommunications industry which relates output to the employee hours expended in producing that output. The growth in average labour productivity is higher than in other US industries. This higher-than-average annual growth rate is likely the result of telephone companies installing more efficient, advanced technology as well as increases in human capital. Information on labor productivity is shown in Box 11.

There are signs that even the limited amount of competition in local service markets has stimulated network modernisation. The new local service competitors (CLECs) doubled the total amount of fiber optic transmission systems they had in place from approximately 0.6 million fiber miles at the end of 1995 to about 1.3 million fiber miles at the end of 1996. By contrast, the incumbent local telephone companies, which still have an estimated 90% of their facilities linking customers to the first point of

---

Box 11. Labour productivity

Investments in new technologies, particularly by inter-exchange carriers, have increased the quality of capital available. Information published by the FCC from the US Bureau of Labour Statistics relates output per employee hours expended. Over the period 1951-1995, the index rose an average 5.8 per cent. The FCC reports that this labour productivity factor is higher than the average in other industries (typically between three and four per cent):

Labour Productivity Index (1987 = 100) for the Telephone Communications Industry
Measured in Output per Hour

Year	Index	Year	Index	Year	Index	Year	Index
1965	28.9	1980	67.6	1991	119.8	1994	141.6
1970	35.6	1985	88.9	1992	127.7	1995	144.6
1975	49.3	1990	113.3	1993	135.2		

Source: FCC (Common Carrier Bureau), *Trends in Telephone Service*, February 1998, Table 5.2.

---

switching in copper-based facilities, increased their fiber miles by 15% in 1966 over 1995. Nevertheless, these modernisation programs mean that fiber technology is being deployed closer to customers.

Newer signalling systems have been developed that permit calls to be set up more quickly and efficiently. From 1990 to 1996, the proportion of fiber used for transmission paths or carrier links that connect switching offices increased from 60% to over 90% and ISDN penetration has spread. The Bell companies, computer companies and cable operators have announced standards for a ground-breaking digital modem and phone service that promises to bring mass market, high-speed Internet access to every US home and business. The agreement between the Bells, Microsoft, Intel and others involves digital subscriber line technology that allows copper phone lines to transport multiple channels of data. Originally developed for video transmission, the new technology will move data at speeds between 0.6-1.5 Mbps compared to today's modems which operate at a top speed of 56 kbps.

Qwest, IXC, Williams Communications and Level 3 Communications Inc. are expected to build new fiber networks which will result in six national long-distance networks in operation. Moreover, several firms, including GTE and Frontier, are purchasing fiber from these firms to use in their networks. The challenge from these new entrants is pressurising the major long distance carriers to further modernise their networks. For instance, MCI has announced plans to quadruple transmission speeds, thereby significantly increasing the capacity of its fiber network.

In regard to international service, AT&T has disclosed that during 1992-1995, it had added more transatlantic telecommunications circuits than in all prior years combined. For instance, the TAT-12/TAT-13 system doubled capacity. These cables, using fiber optic technology, are capable of carrying 5 gigabits (billion bits) per second. In October 1996, the FCC granted MFS Communications Company a license to construct a $500 million, 10 gigabits per second, non-common carrier optic fiber system between the United States and the United Kingdom. In the Atlantic region, the amount of capacity has increased dramatically as is projected to increase. In March 1997, AT&T, MCI, Sprint, SBS Communications and six Asian carriers signed an agreement to build the first undersea fiber optic cable to directly link the United States and China at a cost of $1.4 billion.

Another gauge of the degree of competition and efficiency is the level of profits, with high and increasing profits taken to suggest low levels of effective competition or increasing efficiency. This profit indicator is less applicable where price controls prevail. In the US, despite the price cap regulation some carriers became subject to in 1991, and despite falls in access charges, the RBOCs return on equity has grown each year from about 13% in 1991 to some 20% in 1995.[69] The return on equity achieved by the RBOCs have exceeded the return for the Standard & Poors (S&P) 500. This improved financial performance resulted in part from an improved productivity performance and strong growth in ILEC access minutes.

In a discussion of technological development, it is also informative to consider employment levels. Despite considerable "downsizing" by telecommunications carriers, since 1990 employment in the tele- phone communications industry as a whole has in fact grown modestly. Most of the growth in employ- ment over this period is the result of substantial increases in the radiotelephone (cellular, beepers, paging) industry, which grew at an annual average growth rate of approximately 20%.

4. CONCLUSIONS AND RECOMMENDATIONS

The United States has been the world leader in terms of regulatory reform of telecommunications and has had a long history in efforts to promote competition. Notably regulatory reform has contributed to the dynamism of the US telecommunications industry that now leads the world in such areas as in the development of the Internet and electronic commerce. The benefits experienced by the US indicate the nature and extent of benefits that are attainable by other OECD countries through pro-competitive regulatory reform.

4.1. General assessment of current strengths and weaknesses

For other OECD countries, the US example provides an important example from which to draw insights. Many policy ideas and initiatives have been experimented with by US policy makers and thus other OECD countries can use the experience, both positive and negative aspects, to fine-tune their own policy initiatives. A list of selected strengths and weaknesses of the US regulatory reform experience is presented below to highlight lessons learned.

Box 12.   **Strengths**

- Economically efficient interstate interconnection pricing based on forward-looking costs.
- Effective role of competition policy.
- Domestic market structure with several carriers with facilities and a customer base (as well as resellers and competitive access providers) which, if the conditions were right, could compete in all markets including local.
- Modern telecommunications infrastructure, particularly in regard to long distance and international.
- Quickly converging markets.
- Flexible spectrum licensing regime.

The establishment of effective competitive safeguards that facilitated long-distance competition is an important strength of US telecommunications reform. The regime establishing interconnection between inter-exchange carriers and local exchange carriers is well developed and rates have been reduced significantly toward levels dictated by economic efficiency. The FCC and individual carriers have many years of experience with the regime and technical specifications are clearly established and understood. This success demonstrates the potential effectiveness of structural divestiture remedies in markets where competition is not well developed.

The United States telecommunications industry provides an example of the central role for competition policy in regulatory reform. As discussed above, the 1984 divestiture was a pivotal step that promoted complementary regulatory safeguards such as interconnection and equal access. Today, the market share of the incumbent, AT&T, in long-distance is below 50 per cent and there is no longer any regulation of inter-LATA long-distance prices.

As a result of the divestiture in the early 1980s, domestic US market structure is characterised by numerous carriers with facilities and a customer base (as well as resellers and competitive access providers) which, if the conditions were right, could compete in all telecommunications markets, including local. There are three major inter-exchange carriers with extensive national fiber networks and brand names that enjoy considerable customer recognition. Also, there are five remaining RBOCs with existing customer relationships and local networks. These local networks have been modernised in terms of digital switching, but local loops use much the same technology as they have for decades. Investments in ISDN technology has upgraded the access link, but only to a limited degree.

The Internet has a strong presence in the US and telecommunications networks provide packet-switching and other functions that are necessary to promote further Internet growth. The Internet, which originated in the US, as a strong presence. There are alternative infrastructures such as cable systems and digital broadcast satellites that can provide telecommunications services. Cellular and wireless providers are also present. As a result, there are a number of potential competitors to telecommunications carriers that have the potential, in the future, to significantly erode incumbent market power. The availability of these alternative infrastructures also provides the opportunity for efficient networks, including hybrids, to evolve to efficiently provide communications services.

The modern telecommunications infrastructure provides a sound basis for rapid convergence between communications services. Even today, technology is being used that allows traditional broadcasting services to be carried on telecommunications networks and that allows voice telephony to be carried using packet-switching rather than circuit-switched means. At the same time, ISDN has already been widely introduced as a faster access technology, and even faster broadband access technologies are on the horizon.

As in most OECD countries, the US has recently taken steps to significantly increase spectrum available to new entrants into services such as mobile communications. The US has led other countries in adopting flexible licensing frameworks that allow spectrum to be allocated to carriers that can use it most effectively.

Box 13. **Weaknesses**

- *Increasing economic costs of maintaining inter-LATA and information restraints on RBOCs.*
- *Limited competitive entry into the local market.*
- *Overlap in jurisdiction between state and federal regulators.*

As discussed above, local markets are largely monopolies (although not in law). Rather than implementing a structural divestiture to directly address anticompetitive safeguards, policy has attempted to promote co-operation by incumbents with remaining dominant positions. Local prices have not fallen and the technology to provide subscriber access – the twisted copper pair – has remained static for decades. The US experience in local markets demonstrates the difficulties that can arise when policy makers depend on co-operation from incumbents to facilitate entry into markets where competition is at an early stage.

The restrictions on RBOCs arising from the divestiture are become increasingly burdensome and costly to the economy (e.g., loss of scope economies). These restrictions have had beneficial effects as a competitive safeguard and as an incentive to open local markets. However, as technological developments increase the importance of being able to provide "one-stop-shopping", the burden imposed by these restraints will become greater over time.

Relative to other OECD countries, the regulatory structure in the US is a complex web that involves overlapping jurisdiction over sector-specific regulation between the states and the federal government. While the scope for states to pursue different policy initiatives can sometimes promote the development of innovative schemes to promote regulatory reform, the jurisdictional overlap can also generate costs and uncertainties in policy development. Further, the preceding analysis shows that advances in reducing barriers to entry, promoting cost-based interconnection, rate rebalancing and equal access have been most pronounced at the federal level. It may have also limited the scope of procompetitive federal initiatives to promote competition.

Regulations adopted by the FCC are subject to systematic review through biennial review and forbearance procedures. While the enactment of these processes is a significant step, it is important to note that the forbearance provisions do not include an explicit recognition of the costs that regulation imposes, and important provisions of the 1996 Act are exempted. There are likely additional benefits that can be achieved if the overall streamlining process is made more systematic.

4.2. Potential benefits and costs of further regulatory reform

Regulatory reform has already provided significant benefits to the US economy. The most concrete benefit has been the dramatic reduction in the overall costs to subscribers of inter-LATA long distance and international telecommunications services. Further reductions in prices during 1995 to present, as well as reductions in the price of mobile telecommunications have provided additional concrete benefits.

These benefits are likely the product of two main factors. First, market power of firms in international and long distance markets has been significantly reduced, thus eroding the distortions of pricing above competitive levels. Second, due to a number of factors including technological change and increased competition in both service and equipment markets, the costs of switching and transmission have fallen dramatically. The degree of the adoption of technological change is reflected in the level of investments in fiber optics and digital switching discussed above.

From a longer-term perspective, the most important impact of regulatory reform is its contribution to facilitating dynamic growth and innovation. Despite the lack of local competition, technological change will continue to improve the prospects for entry in the next few years. A potential task of further reform is to put in place the conditions that allow competition to evolve in the local exchange network. Revenues from local exchanges are considerably larger than inter-LATA long distance and international markets combined. Competition could speed the adoption of new technologies in local exchanges and facilitate the introduction of new services. Competition in local markets could allow a rapid deregulation of many aspects of telecommunications. Eliminating local market power is the most effective way of dealing with competitive concerns of vertical integration.

The development of a broadband subscriber access to national fiber networks would eliminate a technical bottleneck and allow enormous increases in speed and capacity of networks. The new products and services that consumers might demand from such a network are difficult, if not impossible to predict. But the possibilities and potential benefits are substantial.

4.3. Policy options for consideration

There is an extensive analysis of regulatory reform in the US telecommunications industry. Drawing on this analysis, this Section builds on international consensus regarding steps to promote good regulatory practices applied to the market realities in the US telecommunications industry. The following recommendations are also based on the "Policy Recommendations for Regulatory Reform" set out in the OECD *Report on Regulatory Reform* (OECD, June 1997).

> – *Promote streamlining of regulation of the* **US** *telecommunications industry by extending mandatory regulatory quality controls in executive orders to the regulatory activities of the* **Federal Communications Commission.**

Ministers have recommended that proposals for new regulations, as well as existing regulations, be reviewed. In general, as effective competitive safeguards are implemented in telecommunications industries and market forces introduced, the need for sector-specific economic regulation declines. As dominant positions of formerly regulated monopolists erode, reliance on market forces subject to economy-wide competition policy rules becomes a more effective means of promoting economic efficiency in the industry. There is a need to continually review and streamline economic regulation as underlying market conditions change.

The US has been effective in implementing effective competitive safeguards to promote competition in markets under federal jurisdiction and in many markets competition is advanced well beyond that in other OECD countries. However, the Federal Communications Commission is not subject to the mandatory regulatory quality controls required by executive orders for most regulatory activities. Regulations adopted by the FCC are subject to systematic review through biennial review and forbearance procedures. While the enactment of these processes is a significant step, it is important to note that the forbearance provisions do not include an explicit recognition of the costs that regulation imposes, and important provisions of the 1996 Act are exempted. There are likely additional benefits that can be achieved if the overall streamlining process is made more systematic.

> – *Competition in intra-LATA markets should be promoted by federal initiative as a necessary step to promote rebalancing of rates to reflect economic costs and thus to promote entry into local markets. If current initiatives fail to eliminate state actions that have the effect of raising barriers to entry, consideration should be given to vesting exclusive authority in the federal government as is done in Australia and Canada.*

Ministers have recommended that those aspects of economic regulation that restrict entry, exit, pricing, output, normal commercial practices and forms of business organisation be reviewed as a high priority. An important challenge relates to barriers to entry and competition in intra-LATA markets. Some state regulators have continued the policy of encouraging intra-LATA prices above competitive levels to limit local rate rebalancing. By allowing intra-LATA toll prices to exceed competitive levels, there is increased scope to maintain artificially low prices for the local services of some subscribers, particularly in rural areas. Historically, states have been able to resist pressures for local rate rebalancing due to the overlap of federal and state jurisdiction.

Regulatory reform initiatives have clearly been more successful in markets under federal jurisdiction. In 1984, limits to federal regulatory reform initiatives reflected market realities in that intra-LATA markets may have had natural monopoly characteristics. Today, however, remaining natural monopolies are much smaller, and therefore the introduction of competition into local and intra-LATA markets is now feasible.

The 1996 Telecommunications Act provides for the pre-emption of state legislation that raises barriers to entry. While it is too early to assess the implementation of this provision, it is a positive step in the right direction. Most, if not all, states have eliminated limits on intra-LATA competition. Promoting entry and competition in these markets will reduce intra-LATA prices toward competitive levels and will promote efficient entry into local markets by significantly reducing the scope to charge local rates to some customers that are below true economic cost. However, additional institutional steps may be necessary. In other OECD countries such as Australia and Canada, the nation-wide impact of regulatory reform initiatives have been enhanced by exclusive federal jurisdiction.

  – *Promote economic efficiency by establishing a level playing field between Internet-based services and other communications services by harmonising and, in the longer term, phasing out sector-specific obligations.*

Ministers have recommended that governments ensure that procedures for applying regulations are transparent, non-discriminatory, contain an appeals process, and do not unduly delay business decisions. Current policy treats traditional voice telephony and voice telecommunications over the Internet differently in regard to the important issue of interconnection pricing. As Internet telephony becomes a more significant medium for subscribers, it will become increasingly important to assure symmetric regulatory treatment so that usage is not distorted by differential usage fees.

  – *Reduce barriers to entry by alternative communications networks by eliminating asymmetries in the treatment of communications services. In particular, the regulatory regime for broadcasting should be reviewed, in the light of convergence, as soon as possible.*

As noted above, Ministers have recommended that governments ensure that procedures for applying regulations are transparent and non-discriminatory. Future local competition will depend importantly on the ability of alternative infrastructures to offer both voice telephony services and newly developing information services. However, as convergence brings the telecommunications and broadcasting industries closed together, fragmented regulation in these areas restricts companies and users from taking advantage of the benefits of convergence. In the United States, one significant asymmetry in regulatory treatment is existing broadcasting licensing procedures designed to promote other public interests. Thus, to promote entry of new alternative networks that could provide voice telephony, non-discriminatory and transparent regulation of entry into other communications services should be advanced.

NOTES

1. The benefit to consumers through price reductions reflects both income transfers from producers to consumers, as well as net increases in overall economic welfare.

2. For example, the *Communications Act of* 1934 specifies as a policy objective in communications to: "Make available, so far as possible, to all people of the United States a rapid, efficient, nation-wide, and world-wide wire and radio communication service with adequate facilities at reasonable charges".

3. Crandall and Waverman (1995) provide an estimate of between $4 and $30 billion.

4. For discussion see, for example, President William J. Clinton and Vice-President Albert Gore Jr., "A Framework for Global Electronic Commerce", posted July, 1997 at <www.iift.nist.gov/telecom/ecomm.htm#background>.

5. One reason for the inadequacy of these competitive safeguards was a technical one – *i.e.*, the absence of so-called "equal access". That is, in the 1970s, subscribers choosing to use alternative long-distance carriers had to dial extra digits because the incumbent carrier was the only carrier available as the "default" carrier.

6. The divestiture was very much a "last resort". By 1980, MCI had turned to the legislature, the regulator and private antitrust action but had been unsuccessful in securing a remedy providing effective competitive safeguards.

7. For a more detailed explanation of the theory, see: Timothy J. Brennan, "Is the Theory behind US *v.* AT&T Applicable Today?" *Antitrust Bulletin*, Vol. 40, No. 3, pp. 455-482.

8. Soon after the divestiture, the FCC mandated equal access in regard to inter-LATA long-distance, allowing subscribers to choose among long-distance carrier as the default carrier on an equal basis.

9. By the late 1980s, the share of switched minutes held by new entrants was well in excess of 30 per cent – a level that exceeds comparable new entrant market share figures in other OECD countries such as Australia, Canada, New Zealand, Japan and the United Kingdom even today. See OECD (1997), *The OECD Report on Regulatory Reform: Volume I: Sectoral Studies*, Paris.

10. In January 1998, for example, the FCC reported that inter-state toll accounted for $58 billion, intra-state/inter-LATA toll accounts for $19 billion, intra-state/intra-LATA toll accounted for $11 billion and local exchange (flat-rate monthly unlimited local calling) accounted for $55 billion in total revenue. Five jurisdictions had no inter-LATA revenue (the District of Columbia, Hawaii, Maine, New Hampshire, Rhode Island and Vermont), presumably because they are one-LATA states. See James Eisner (1998), "Distribution of Intrastate and Interstate telephone by Revenue", *Mimeo*, January.

11. The market share of CLECs based on 1996 market share is 1.4 per cent. Recently, the figure 2.6 per cent was quoted in: Joel Klein (1997), "The Race For Local Competition: A Long Distance Run, Not a Sprint", Speech before the American Enterprise Institute, 5 November.

12. FCC (1998), CC Docket No. 97-211, 14 September, p. 32.

13. FCC (1998), CC Docket No. 97-211, 14 September.

14. FCC 98-91, June 1998. Growth of mobile penetration has been faster in OECD countries with competitive market structures than those with duopoly or monopoly markets.

15. Application of Teleport Communications NY 7 FCCR 5986, 5988 (1992).

16. See FCC, In the Matter of the Annual Assessment of the Status of CS Docket No. 97-141 Competition in Markets for Video Programming. In June 1997, the number of homes capable of receiving cable programming was 94.2 million, which accounts for 97.1 per cent of television homes.

17. Under the plan, Ameritech acted to argue for the elimination of state barriers to entry, to provide equal access to intra-LATA toll and to provide access to its network for new entrants into the local exchange. For discussion, see DOJ (1995), "Memorandum of the United States in Support of its Motion for a Modification of the Decree to Permit a Limited Trial of Inter-exchange Service by Ameritech", *Mimeo*, 1 May.

18. Hearing Order, "Petition of Rochester Telephone Company for Approval of Proposed Restructuring Plan; Petition of Rochester Telephone Corporation for Approval of a Multi Year Rate Stability Agreement", New York Public Service Commission, Case 93-C0133, Opinion No. 94-25, 10 November, 1994.

19. See Joel Klein (1997), "The Race For Local Competition: A Long Distance Run, Not a Sprint", Speech before the American Enterprise Institute, Nov. 5, and William E. Kennard (1998), "Section 271 of the Telecommunications Act of 1996", Statement before the Subcommittee on Communications of the Committee on Commerce, Science, and Transportation, United States Senate, March 25. In particular, Chairman Kennard stated: "I do not come here, however, to announce my satisfaction with the pace of competition. We can and must do better".

20. FCC, "Local Competition Factsheet", *supra*, note 1.

21. For detailed discussion of the impact of these technological advances see, for example, the FCC's *En Banc* hearing dated July 9, 1998 posted at: <www.fcc.gov/enbanc/070998/tr070998.txt> and the FCC's *Bandwidth Forum* dated 23 January, 1997 posted at <www.fcc.gov/Reports/970123.txt>. The UK provides an additional example of the capacity of cable to provide telephony service. See, for example, Affidavit of Oliver E. Williamson, at p. 14 (31 May 1994), submitted on behalf of Motion by Bell Atlantic Corporation, Bell South Corporation, Nynex Corporation and South-western Bell Corporation to vacate the Decree, United States *v.* Western Electric Co., No. 82-0192 (DDC filed 6 July 1994) cited in Robert W. Crandall and J. Gregory Sidak (1995), "Competition and Regulatory Policies for interactive Broadband Networks", *Southern California Law Review*, July.

22. See, for example, Robert W. Crandall and J. Gregory Sidak (1995), "Competition and Regulatory Policies for interactive Broadband Networks", *Southern California Law Review*, July.

23. In theory, satellite systems provide a fourth possible entrant into local telecommunications markets. However, the prospects for satellite entry on a widespread commercial basis in the coming years is limited. Importantly, satellite communications involve a delay of about one-third of a second that can impede convenient voice communications.

24. See Jonathan Jacob Nadler (1995), "Give Peace a Chance: FCC-State Relations After *California* III" *Federal Communications Law Journal*, Vol. 47; 3 April.

25. 27 FCC 359, Docket 11866 (1959).

26. 13 FCC 2d 420, 18 FCC 953 (1969) and 29 FCC 2d 870 (the *Specialised Common Carrier* decision).

27. For discussion, particularly of the notion of "flexibility" in licenses, see: Gregory L. Rosston and Jeffrey S. Steinberg (1997), "Using Market-Based Spectrum Policy to Promote the Public Interest", FCC Discussion Paper, January.

28. Subject to limited exceptions, see FCC PR Docket No. 94-107, Released 19 May, 1995.

29. See for example, Leonard J. Kennedy and Heather A. Percell (1998), Section 332 of the Communications Act of 1934: A Federal Regulatory Framework That Is "Hog Tight, Horse High, and Bull Strong", *Federal Communications Law Journal*, 50; 3.

30. For a discussion of foreclosure effects in network industries see, for example, Jeffrey Church and Neil Gandal (1992), "Network Effects, Software Provision, and Standardisation", *Journal of Industrial Economics*, Vol. 40, March; or Stanley M. Besen and Joseph Farrell (1994), "Choosing How to Compete: Strategies and Tactics in Standardisation", *Journal of Economic Perspectives*, Vol. 8, Spring.

31. These comparisons using median rates are suggestive of general trends, but hide some of the variation between states. In 1990, Texas, Wyoming, Minnesota, North Carolina, South Carolina and Louisiana had access fees well in excess of triple the comparable interstate rate. States such as Illinois and Virginia that even in 1990 had made significant progress toward regulatory reform in intra-state markets had no common carrier access fee whatsoever. In general, states with high common carrier access fees are predominantly rural. Ingo Volgosang and Bridger M. Mitchell (1997), *Telecommunications Competition: The Last Ten Miles*, Washington DC, AEI, p. 133.

32. The specific numbers are 17.26 cents in 1984 and 3.82 cents in 1998, see FCC (1998), Trends in Telephone Service, July, Table 1.2. Figures reported here from Table 1.2 do not include Primary Inter-exchange Carrier Charges (PICCs). If these charges are included, as the FCC had done in its January 1998 "Trends in Telephone Service" report, the per conversation minute total charge would be about one cent per minute higher.

33. RBOCs, which serve about 75 per cent of all customers, converted almost half their lines to equal access between December 1984 and December 1985, and an additional 40 per cent in the next three years. See FCC (1998), "Trends in Telephone Service", February, p. 22. More than a decade after equal access was widely introduced in inter-LATA toll markets, in February 1996, Minnesota was one of the first states to introduce intra-LATA dialling parity.

34. The 1996 Act requires incumbent local exchange carriers to provide interconnection to any requesting carrier at any technically feasible point. The FCC has concluded that prices should be based in Total Element Long Run Incremental Cost plus a reasonable share of forward-looking joint and common costs.

35. CC Docket 96-262, paras 283-290, <www.fcc.gov/Bureaus/Common_Carrier/Notices/fcc96488.txt>. The reason is that Internet service providers typically pay business line rates (that typically do not include usage sensitive prices for incoming calls) and the appropriate subscriber line charge rather than the corresponding per-minute interstate access charges.

36. Barbra Esbin, (1998), "Internet Over Cable: Defining the Future in Terms of the Past", FCC, OPP Working Paper Series: No. 30, August, p. 68.

37. The 1996 Act requires incumbent local exchange carriers to provide interconnection to any requesting carrier at any technically feasible point. In its *Local* Competition decision, the FCC has concluded that prices should be based on Total Element Long Run Incremental Cost. Under this costing methodology, an incumbent LEC must base prices of a specific network element on TELRIC plus a reasonable share of forward-looking joint and common costs.

38. The FCC has characterised the historic structure of telecommunications prices a "patchwork quilt of implicit and explicit subsidies". See, for example, FCC CC Docket No. 96-45 [the Joint Federal-State Report to Congress on Universal Service].

39. There are a number of underlying factors that have contributed to the ability of incumbents to maintain higher intra-LATA prices. First, these markets were not divested from the incumbent local exchange carriers in the 1984 divestiture. Second, as noted above, state regulators have been slow to promote entry into these markets, and in instances where entry has been allowed, interconnection on equal quality terms has not been available. These two factors provide a significant incumbency advantage that has contributed to the maintenance of pre-divestiture market power in regard to intra-LATA services.

40. More inclusive and reliable data in Box 1 on revenue per minute reinforce this conclusion since it shows that interstate prices fell about 50 per cent over the 1984 to 1992 period, and fell about 17 per cent between 1992 and 1996.

41. Ingo Volgelsang and Bridger M. Mitchell (1997), *Telecommunications Competition: The Last Ten Miles*, AEI, Washington DC. The conclusion that competition remains weak in intra-LATA can also be found in Marius Schwartz (1997), "Competitive Implications of Bell Operating Company Entry Into Long-Distance Telecommunications Services: Affidavit of Marius Schwartz", *Mimeo.*, 14 May.

42. For full details on price cap regulation see FCC (1997), "In the matter of Price Cap Performance Review", Fourth Report and Order in CC Docket No. 94-1, 7 May.

43. OFTEL (1996), *Telecoms Price Control: the Final Phase*, June, London.

44. For a detailed analysis, see OECD (1995), *Price Cap Regulation: Policies and Experiences*, Paris.

45. It has sometimes been argued that low local rates are a subsidy to promote high penetration of telephone service that is made necessary to correct for network externalities. As Farrell notes, however, there is little or no evidence to support the notion that that the universal service system or its goals are based on this See Joseph Farrell (1996), "Creating Local Competition", *Federal Communications Law Journal*, Vol. 49; 1, November. Furthermore, as Hausman shows, econometric evidence on demand elasticities does not indicate that low prices are necessary to maintain high penetration rates. For discussion see, Michael Riordan (1998), "Conundrums for Telecommunications Policy", *Mimeo.*, 28 May.

46. As former FCC Chief Economist Michael Riordan commented: "The tension between universal service and competition is the great drama in the Telecom Act. These are like two horseshoe magnets, that, when held face-to-face, repel each other. Yet there is an abiding belief that, if one could just turn one of the magnets upside down, and look at it differently, everything would be all right". Michael Riordan (1998), "Conundrums for Telecommunications Policy", *Mimeo.*, May 28.

47. As Lawrence White put it, "cross-subsidies are the enemy of competition *because* competition is the enemy of cross-subsidies". See Joseph Farrell (1996), "Creating Local Competition", *Federal Communications Law Journal*, Vol. 49; 1, November.

48. The FCC has adopted the following definition of universal service: voice grade access (500-4000 Hz); dual tone multifrequency signalling or digital equipment; single party service; access to 911, directory services, operator services and inter-exchange services In addition, call blocking service is supported for low income consumers.

49. Until the end of 1997, universal service programs were financed by per line monthly charges imposed on long distance carriers. Under the new rules which took effect in January 1998, the per-line charges previously paid

by large long distance carriers have been discontinued. Instead, all providers of interstate telecommunications, including local exchange carriers, long-distance providers and wireless carriers, now contribute to the provision of universal service based on the amount of their telecommunications revenues.

50. Collecting funds through general tax revenues is generally less distortionary because it is collected from a broader base and thus there is less distortion of relative prices.

51. Local rates are likely below economic cost by the largest margin in rural and remote areas. Moreover, information reported by the FCC indicates that monthly charges in rural areas are about 20 per cent *lower* than in urban areas. FCC (1998), Industry Analysis Division, "Reference Book on Rates, Price Indices and Expenditures for Telephone Service", M*imeo.*, July. The average rate reported in a survey of 89 cities by the Bureau of Labour Statistics indicates that the flat-rate local rate (not including subscriber line charge, 911 charges or taxes) was $13.71 while the corresponding average rate reported by rural carriers was $11.17 in 1996. The Rural Utilities Service of the US Department of Agriculture's National Information Infrastructure initiative provides nearly $11 billion in approved loans to rural telephone companies.

52. With its entry into force on 5 February 1998, the agreement set telecommunications services on the path of progressive liberalisation and pro-competitive regulatory reform in 72 signatory countries, including the United States and most of the world's major trading nations. The United States made significant market-opening commitments in the agreement and joined 64 other WTO Members in subscribing to a Reference Paper on Pro-Competitive Regulatory Principles.

53. Moreover, foreign-affiliated carriers with Section 214 authorisations granted prior to 1 January 1998 are effectively exempted from the benchmark settlement rate condition insofar as the Order applies only to *new* market entrants. A later adjustment to the Order requiring US carriers to adopt the benchmark rates by a date certain has been extended indefinitely. Thus, depending on their particular circumstances, foreign-affiliated carriers seeking to launch new facilities-based services may find themselves at a competitive disadvantage *vis-à-vis* established foreign and domestic entities. As discussed above, however, all carriers from WTO countries are eligible for streamlined global authorisation to provide switched resale service.

54. This council is a federal authority committee created by the FCC. Its purpose is to advise the FCC and to make recommendations, reached through industry consensus, that foster efficient and impartial number administration.

55. Pursuant to the former, the Office of Management and Budget (the "OMB") approved all FCC information requirements on 1 April 1997 [*Notice of Office Management and Budget* Action, OMB No. 3060-0760].

56. Sections 401 and 402 of the 1996 Telecommunications Act provide procedures to forbear from regulation in response to specific petitions and to review its own regulations to check if they are no longer in the public interest. Importantly, these streamlining provisions do not include an explicit recognition of the costs imposed by continued regulation

57. Section 401(d) exempts sections 251(c), (*i.e.*, interconnection and unbundling requirements) and 271 (the in-region inter-LATA restraints on BOCs) from consideration under a forbearance petition.

58. The administrative and enforcement burden imposed by line-of-business restrictions has been an ongoing concern. The line-of-business restrictions in the divestiture decree created a complicated system of contested and uncontested "waivers" that essentially allowed RBOCs to offer new services or otherwise amend the restrictions (*e.g.*, update LATA boundaries to reflect network developments). It has been argued that the process has been slow, delaying new product innovations and impeding competition. [See, for example, the affidavit of Paul H. Rubin, June 14, 1994, submitted on behalf of Motion of Bell Atlantic Corporation, BellSouth Corporation, Nynex Corporation, and South-western Bell Corporation to Vacate the Decree, *United States* v. *Western Electric Co.* No. 82-0192 (DDC filed July 6, 1994]. These concerns do not appear to have been eliminated by the transfer of authority to the FCC. In its scrutiny of FCC regulatory practices under the *Paperwork Reduction Act* the Office of Management and Budget made only one recommendation, that it should: "minimise the number of new filings that firms must create [...] in order to demonstrate that they meet the *Telecommunications Act of* 1996 requirements for provision of inter-LATA services within their operating regions".

59. Thus there is a need to lower barriers to entry through the elimination of licensing requirements (or replacing them with notification procedures) and achieving other policy goals through direct subsidies. For more discussion see, for example, OECD (1998), "Regulation and Competition Issues in the Light of Convergence", OECD Background Paper, October, Paris.

60. See Statement of Ambassador Charlene Barshefsky, WTO Agreement, Testimony before the House Commerce Committee – Subcommittee on Telecommunications, Trade & Consumer Protection, 19 March, 1997.

61. The remaining revenue accrues to CAPs, CLECs as well as paging and other mobile carriers. Also, resellers of various services accounted for $6.5 billion. FCC, *Telecommunications Industry Revenue: TRS Fund Worksheet Data*, Industry Analysis Division.

62. In August 1997, the FCC removed the interim separation conditions it had imposed on RBOCs and independent LECs as a condition for non-dominant treatment of their international telecommunications services originating from points outside their local exchange areas. This action is consistent with the policy recently adopted by the FCC governing the RBOCs' and independent LECs' provision of interstate, domestic inter-exchange services originating in out-of-region areas.

63. However, since 1991, the monthly rate has increased only slightly from $18.66 to $19.58 in 1996. These monthly charges include unlimited local calling. The minimum connection charge has increased from $36.76 in 1983 to $43.42 in 1996. As discussed earlier in Section 2.3, interstate switched access and trunking prices have remained close to the FCC prescribed price cap maximum suggesting that it is regulation (rather than competition) that has contained ILEC prices. For business customers, the average total monthly local telephone rates was $36.76 in 1983 and $43.33 in 1996 – an increase of 18 per cent over the 13 year period. The average charge for a five-minute (same zone) daytime business call increased by about seven per cent between 1983 and 1996.

64. This means that detailed information on customer subscribership to schemes and usage profiles, are necessary to make a full assessment of the effects on the prices paid by subscribers. For a detailed discussion see P. Xavier (1998), "Price discount schemes and international price comparisons", *Telecommunications Policy*, June.

65. Several innovative pricing schemes have emerged. With Complete Access, customers can obtain Qwest long distance for just seven cents a minute during evenings and weekends, while businesses can obtain long distance for 9.5 cents a minute all day.

66. Zolnierek, J and Rangos, K. (1998), *Long Distance Market Shares, Fourth Quarter 1997*, Industry Analysis Division, Common carrier Bureau, March.

67. MCI (1997), *True Competition in the Long-Distance Market*, January.

68. FCC (1998), *Trends in Telephone Service*, Industry Analysis Division, Common Carrier Bureau, February.

69. FCC (1997), *Rate of Return Report* 1997.

OECD PUBLICATIONS, 2, rue André-Pascal, 75775 PARIS CEDEX 16
PRINTED IN FRANCE
(42 1999 03 1 P) ISBN 92-64-17075-8 – No. 50815 1999